The Works of John Owen

VOLUME XIII

The Works of JOHN OWEN

EDITED BY

William H. Goold

VOLUME XIII

The Banner of Truth Trust

This Edition of
THE WORKS OF JOHN OWEN
first published by Johnstone & Hunter, 1850–53

Reprinted by
THE BANNER OF TRUTH TRUST
3 Murrayfield Road, Edinburgh EH12 6EL
PO Box 621, Carlisle, Pennsylvania 17013, USA

VOLUME XIII

1967
Second printing 1976
Third printing 1983
ISBN 0 85151 063 9

Fletcher & Son Ltd, Norwich

CONTENTS OF VOLUME XIII.

THE DUTY OF PASTORS AND PEOPLE DISTINGUISHED.

ESHCOL;
A CLUSTER OF THE FRUIT OF CANAAN.

OF SCHISM.

A REVIEW OF THE TRUE NATURE OF SCHISM.

AN ANSWER TO A LATE TREATISE ABOUT THE NATURE OF SCHISM.

A BRIEF VINDICATION OF THE NONCONFORMISTS FROM THE CHARGE OF SCHISM.

TRUTH AND INNOCENCE VINDICATED.

TWO QUESTIONS CONCERNING THE POWER OF THE SUPREME MAGISTRATE, ETC.

INDULGENCE AND TOLERATION CONSIDERED.

A PEACE-OFFERING.

GROUNDS AND REASONS ON WHICH PROTESTANT DISSENTERS DESIRE THEIR LIBERTY.

THE CASE OF PRESENT DISTRESSES ON NONCONFORMISTS EXAMINED.

POSTHUMOUS.

STATE OF THE KINGDOM WITH RESPECT TO THE PRESENT BILL AGAINST CONVENTICLES.

A WORD OF ADVICE TO THE CITIZENS OF LONDON.

THE

DUTY OF PASTORS AND PEOPLE DISTINGUISHED:

OR,

A BRIEF DISCOURSE TOUCHING THE ADMINISTRATION OF THINGS COMMANDED IN RELIGION;

ESPECIALLY CONCERNING THE MEANS TO BE USED BY THE PEOPLE OF GOD (DISTINCT
FROM CHURCH OFFICERS) FOR THE INCREASING OF DIVINE KNOWLEDGE
IN THEMSELVES AND OTHERS:

WHEREIN BOUNDS ARE PRESCRIBED TO THEIR PERFORMANCES; THEIR LIBERTY IS ENLARGED
TO THE UTMOST EXTENT OF THE DICTATES OF NATURE AND RULES OF CHARITY;
THEIR DUTY LAID DOWN IN DIRECTIONS DRAWN FROM SCRIPTURE
PRECEPTS AND THE PRACTICE OF GOD'S PEOPLE IN ALL AGES.

TOGETHER WITH

THE SEVERAL WAYS OF EXTRAORDINARY CALLING TO THE OFFICE OF PUBLIC TEACHING,

WITH WHAT ASSURANCE SUCH TEACHERS MAY HAVE OF THEIR CALLING, AND
WHAT EVIDENCE THEY CAN GIVE OF IT UNTO OTHERS.

By JOHN OWEN, M.A., of Q. Col. O.

———

M.DC.XLIV.

PREFATORY NOTE.

THE title-page of the following treatise indicates that it was published in the year 1644; but in the second chapter of " The Review of the True Nature of Schism," in this volume, it is stated that the date is a misprint for 1643. The work is dedicated to Sir Edward Scot, in whose family, it would appear, the author had for some time resided, and who had offered him some " ecclesiastical preferment" when it was vacant. Owen here declares himself to be in sentiment a Presbyterian, in opposition to Prelacy and Independency. He afterwards changed his views on church-government; but in the work on schism, to which we have just referred, he declares that, on the subjects under discussion in this treatise, his principles had undergone no essential change: " When I compare what I then wrote with my present judgment, I am scarce able to find the least difference between the one and the other."

Two chapters of the work are occupied with a statement of the provision made for conducting religious instruction and worship under the patriarchal and Mosaic dispensations. An interesting chapter follows on the spiritual priesthood of all believers, as destructive of the superstitious tenet which invests the office of the ministry with esoteric virtue and sanctity. The several ways under which men may be constrained, under an extraordinary call, to impart religious instruction publicly to others, are next considered. The treatise closes with an assertion of the right and obligation of private Christians to conduct certain kinds of divine worship, without interfering with the official functions of the Christian ministry.

The tractate to which he alludes, " De Sacerdotio Christi, contra Armin. Socin. et Papistas," is described as not yet published, and seems never to have been published. It may have supplied part of the long and valuable exercitations on the priesthood of Christ prefixed to the Exposition of the Epistle to the Hebrews, as, from the slight allusion to it in this treatise, the same topics appear to have been handled in it. He refers, also, in the close of this treatise, to an answer, drawn up for the satisfaction of some private friends, to the arguments of the Remonstrants for liberty of prophesying. Mr Orme supposes this unpublished document to be identical with the " Tractatus de Christi Sacerdotio." We are not aware of any grounds for supposing such an identity. The subjects which these unpublished tracts seem to have discussed are obviously different.—ED.

I HAVE perused this Discourse touching " The Administration of Things Commanded in Religion," and conceive it written with much clearness of judgment and moderation of spirit ; and therefore do approve of it to be published in print.

JOSEPH CARYL.

May 11, 1644.

TO THE TRULY NOBLE AND MY EVER HONOURED FRIEND,

SIR EDWARD SCOT,

OF SCOT'S HALL IN KENT,
KNIGHT OF THE HONOURABLE ORDER OF THE BATH.

SIR,

HAVING of late been deprived of the happiness to see you, I make bold to send to visit you; and because that the times are troublesome, I have made choice of this messenger, who, having obtained a licence to pass, fears no searching. He brings no news, at least to you, but that which was from the beginning, and must continue unto the end, which you have heard, and which (for some part thereof) you have practised out of the word of God. He hath no secret messages prejudicial to the state of church or commonwealth; neither, I hope, will he entertain any such comments by the way, considering from whom he comes and to whom he goes; of whom the one would disclaim him and the other punish him. Ambitious I am not of any entertainment for these few sheets, neither care much what success they find in their travel, setting them out merely in my own defence, to be freed from the continued solicitations of some honest, judicious men, who were acquainted with their contents, being nothing but an hour's country discourse, resolved from the ordinary pulpit method into its own principles. When I first thought of sending it to you, I made full account to use the benefit of the advantage in recounting of and returning thanks for some of those many undeserved favours which I have received from you; but addressing myself to the performance, I fainted in the very entrance, finding their score so large that I know not where to begin, neither should I know how to end. Only one I cannot suffer to lie hid in the crowd, though other engagements hindered me from embracing it,—namely, your free proffer of an ecclesiastical preferment, then vacant and in your donation. Yet, truly, all received courtesies have no power to oblige me unto you in comparison of that abundant worth which, by experience, I have found to be dwelling in you. Twice, by God's providence, have I been with you when your county hath been in great danger to be ruined,—once by the horrid insurrection of a rude, godless multitude, and again by the invasion of a potent enemy prevailing in the neighbour county; at both which times, besides the general calamity justly feared, particular threatenings were daily brought unto you: under which sad dispensations, I must crave leave to say (only to put you in mind of yourself, if it should please God again to reduce you to the like straits), that I never saw more resolved constancy, more cheerful, unmoved Christian courage in any man. Such a valiant heart in a weak body, such a directing head where the hand was but feeble. such unwearied endeavours under the pressures of a painful infirmity, so well advised resolves in the midst of imminent danger, did I then behold, as I know not where to parallel. Neither can I say less, in her kind, of your virtuous lady, whose known goodness to all, and particular indulgences to me, make her, as she is in herself, very precious in my thoughts and remembrance: whom having named, I desire to take the advantage thankfully to mention her worthy son, my noble and very dear friend C. Westrow; whose judgment to discern the differences of these times, and his valour in prosecuting what he is resolved to be just and lawful, place him among the number of those very few to whom it is given to know aright the causes of things, and vigorously to execute holy and laudable designs. But farther of him I choose to say nothing, because if I would, I cannot but say too little. Neither will I longer detain you from the ensuing discourse, which I desire to commend to your favourable acceptance, and with my hearty prayers that the Lord would meet you and yours in all those ways of mercy and grace which are necessary to carry you along through all your engagements, until you arrive at the haven of everlasting glory, where you would be. I rest your most obliged servant in Jesus Christ, our common Master,

JOHN OWEN.

PREFACE.

THE glass of our lives seems to run and keep pace with the extremity of time. The end of those "ends of the world"[1] which began with the gospel is doubtless coming upon us. He that was instructed what should be till time should be no more,[2] said it was ἰσχάτη ὥρα,[3] the last hour, in his time. Much sand cannot be behind, and Christ shakes the glass; many minutes of that hour cannot remain; the next measure we are to expect is but "a moment, the twinkling of an eye, wherein we shall all be changed."[4] Now, as if the horoscope of the decaying age had some secret influence into the wills of men to comply with the decrepit world, they generally delight to run into extremes. Not that I would have the fate of the times to bear the faults of men,[5] like him who cried, Οὐκ ἐγὼ αἴτιός εἰμι ἀλλὰ Ζεὺς καὶ μοῖρα, to free himself, entitling God and fate to his sins; but only to show how the all-disposing providence of the Most High works such a compliance of times and persons as may jointly drive at his glorious aims, causing men to set out in such seasons as are fittest for their travel. This epidemical disease of the aged world is the cause why, in that great diversity of contrary opinions wherewith men's heads and hearts are now replenished, the truth pretended to be sought with so much earnestness may be often gathered up quite neglected between the parties litigant. "Medio tutissimus" is a sure rule, but that fiery spirits,—

> " Pyroeis, Eous, et Æthon,
> —— Quartusque Phlegon,"—

will be mounting. In the matter concerning which I propose my weak essay, some would have all Christians to be *almost ministers*; others, *none but ministers* to be God's *clergy*. Those would give the people the keys, these use them to lock them out of the church; the one ascribing to them primarily all ecclesiastical power for the ruling of the congregation, the other abridging them of the performance of spiritual duties for the building of their own souls: as though there were no habitable earth between the valley (I had almost said the pit) of *democratical confusion* and the precipitous rock of *hierarchical tyranny*. When unskilful archers shoot, the safest place to avoid the arrow is the *white*. Going as near as God shall direct me to the truth of this matter, I hope to avoid the strokes of the combatants on every side; and therefore will not handle it ἐριστικῶς, with opposition to any man or opinion, but δογματικῶς, briefly proposing mine own required judgment: the summary result whereof is, that the sacred calling may retain its ancient dignity, though the people of God be not deprived of their Christian liberty. To clear which proposal some things I shall briefly premise.

[1] 1 Cor. x. 11, Τὰ τέλη τῶν αἰώνων.　　　　[2] Rev. x. 6.
[3] 1 John ii. 18; Matt. xxiv. 33.
[4] 1 Cor. xv. 52; Zanch. de fine sec. Mol. acc. Proph.　　　[5] Rom. ix. 19.

THE

DUTY OF PASTORS AND PEOPLE DISTINGUISHED.

CHAPTER I.

Of the administration of holy things among the patriarchs before the law.

CONCERNING the ancient patriarchs: From these, some, who would have Judaism to be but an intercision of Christianity,[1] derive the pedigree of Christians, affirming the difference between us and them to be solely in the name, and not the thing itself. Of this, thus much at least is true, that "the law of commandments contained in ordinances"[2] did much more diversify the administration of the covenant before and after Christ than those plain moralities wherewith in their days it was clothed. Where the assertion is deficient, antiquity hath given its authors sanctuary from farther pursuit. Their practice, then, were it clear, can be no precedent for Christians. All light brought to the gospel, in comparison of those full and glorious beams that shine in itself, is but a candle set up in the sun; yet for their sakes who found out the former unity, I will (not following the conceit of any, nor the comments of many) give you such a bare narration, as the Scripture will supply me withal, of their administration of the holy things and practice of their religion (as it seems Christianity, though not so called). And doubt you not of divine approbation and institution; for all prelacy, at least until Nimrod hunted for preferment, was "de jure divino."

I find, then, that before the giving of the law, the chief men among the servants of the true God did, every one in their own families, with their neighbours adjoining of the same persuasion, perform those things which they knew to be required, by the *law of nature, tradition,* or *special revelation* (the unwritten word of those times), in the service of God; instructing their children and servants in the knowledge of their creed concerning the nature and goodness of God, the fall and sin of man, the use of sacrifices, and the promised seed (the sum of their religion); and, moreover, performing τὰ πρὸς τὸν Θεόν, things appertaining unto God. This we have delivered con-

---

[1] Euseb. Eccles. Hist. lib. i. cap. 4; Ambr. de Sacra. lib. iv.   [2] Eph. ii. 15.

cerning Seth, Enoch, Noah, Abraham, Lot, Isaac, Jacob, Jethro, Job, and others.[1] Now, whether they did this as any way peculiarly designed unto it as an office, or rather in obedient duty to the prime law of nature, in which and to whose performance many of them were instructed and encouraged by divine revelation (as seems most probable), is not necessary to be insisted on. To me, truly, it seems evident that there were no determinate ministers of divine worship before the law; for where find we any such office instituted? where the duties of those officers prescribed? or were they of human invention?[2] God would never allow that in any regard the will of the creature should be the measure of his honour and worship. "But the right and exercise of the priesthood," say some, "was in the first-born;" but a proof of this will be for ever wanting. Abel was not Adam's eldest son, yet, if any thing were peculiar to such an office, it was by him performed. That both the brothers carried their sacrifices to their father is a vain surmise.[3] Who was priest, then, when Adam died? Neither can any order of descent be handsomely contrived. Noah had three sons: grant the eldest only a priest; were the eldest sons of his other sons priests, or no? If not, how many men fearing God were scattered over the face of the earth utterly deprived of the means of right worship ! if so, there must be a new rule produced beyond the prescript of nature, whereby a man may be enabled by generation to convey that to others which he hath not in himself. I speak not of Melchizedek and his extraordinary priesthood; why should any speak where the Holy Ghost is silent? If we pretend to know him, we overthrow the whole mystery, and run cross to the apostle, affirming him to be ἀπάτορα ἀμήτορα, without father, mother, or genealogy. For so long time, then, as the greatest combination of men was in distinct families (which sometimes were very great[4]), politics and economics being of the same extent, all the way of instruction in the service and knowledge of God was by the way of *paternal admonition,*—for the discharge of which duty Abraham is commended, Gen. xviii. 19; whereunto the instructors had no particular engagement, but only the general obligation of the law of nature. What rule they had for their performances towards God doth not appear. All positive law, in every kind, is ordained for the good of community. That *then* being not, no such rule was assigned until God gathered a people, and lifted up the standard of circumcision for his subjects to repair unto. The world in the days of Abraham beginning generally to incline to idolatry and polytheism,[5] the

---

[1] Gen. iv. 26, v. 22, vi. 8, 9, etc., viii. 20, ix. 25-27, xviii. 19, xix. 9, xxviii. 1, 2, xxxv. 3-5; Exod. xviii. 12; Job i. 5, xlii. 8-10.

[2] Tho. 22, æ. q. 87, ad 3.

[3] Jacob. Armin. de Sacerd. Ch. Orat.

[4] Gen. xiv. 14.

[5] "Eccles. malignantium."—Aug. con. Faust. lib. xix. cap. 11.

first evident irreconcilable division was made between his people and the malignants, which before lay hid in his decree. Visible signs and prescript rules were necessary for such a gathered church. This before I conceive to have been supplied by special revelation.

The *law of nature* a long time prevailed for the worship of the one true God. The manner of this worship, the generality had at first (as may be conceived) from the vocal instruction of Adam, full of the knowledge of divine things; this afterward their children had from them by *tradition,* helped forward by such who received *particular revelations* in their generation, such as Noah, thence called "A preacher of righteousness." So knowledge of God's will increased,[1] until sin quite prevailed, and " all flesh had corrupted his way." All apostasy for the most part begins in the will, which is more bruised by the fall than the understanding. Nature is more corrupted in respect of the desire of good than the knowledge of truth. The knowledge of God would have flourished longer in men's minds had not sin banished the love of God out of their hearts.

The sum is, that before the giving of the law, every one in his own person served God according to that knowledge he had of his will. Public performances were assigned to none, farther than the obligation of the law of nature to their duty in their own families. I have purposely omitted to speak of Melchizedek, as I said before, having spoken all that I can or dare concerning him on another occasion. Only this I will add: they who so confidently affirm him to be Shem, the son of Noah, and to have his priesthood in an ordinary way, by virtue of his primogeniture, might have done well to ask leave of the Holy Ghost for the revealing of that which he purposely concealed to set forth no small mystery, by them quite overthrown. And he who of late makes him look upon Abraham and the four kings, all of his posterity, fighting for the inheritance of Canaan (of which cause of their quarrel the Scripture is silent), robs him at least of one of his titles, a "king of peace," making him neither king nor peaceable, but a bloody grandsire, that either could not or would not part his fighting children, contending for that whose right was in him to bestow on whom he would.

And thus was it with them in the administration of sacred things: There was no divine determination of the priestly office on any order of men. When things appertaining unto God were to be performed in the name of a whole family (as afterward, 1 Sam. xx. 6), perhaps the honour of the performance was by consent given to the first-born. Farther; the way of teaching others was by paternal admonition (so Gen. xviii. 19); motives thereunto, and rules of their

---

[1] "Per incrementa temporum crevit divinæ cognitiones incrementum."—Greg. Hom. xvi. in Ezek. a med.

proceeding therein, being the law of nature and special revelation. Prescription of positive law, ordained for the good of community, could have no place when all society was domestical. To instruct others (upon occasion) wanting instruction, for their good, is an undeniable dictate of the first principles of nature, obedience to which was all the ordinary warrant they had for preaching to any beyond their own families; observed by Lot, Gen. xix. 7, though his sermon contained a little false doctrine, verse 8. Again; as special revelation leaves a great impression on the mind of him to whom it is made, so an effectual obligation for the performance of what it directeth unto: "The lion hath roared, who will not fear? the Lord GOD hath spoken, who can but prophesy?" Amos iii. 8. And this was Noah's warrant for those performances from whence he was called "A preacher of righteousness," 2 Pet. ii. 5. Thus, although I do not find any determinate order of priesthood by divine institution, yet do I not thence conclude, with Aquin. 12. æ. quest. 3. a. 1. (if I noted right at the reading of it), that all the worship of God (I mean for the manner of it) was of human invention, yea, sacrifices themselves; for this will-worship, as I showed before, God always rejected. No doubt but sacrifices and the manner of them were of divine institution, albeit their particular original in regard of precept, though not of practice, be to us unknown. For what in all this concerns us, we may observe that a superinstitution of a new ordinance doth not overthrow any thing that went before in the same kind, universally moral or extraordinary, nor at all change it, unless by express exception; as, by the introduction of the ceremonial law, the offering of sacrifices, which before was common to all, was restrained to the posterity of Levi. Look, then, what performances in the service of God that primitive household of faith was in the general directed unto by the law of nature, the same, regulated by gospel light (not particularly excepted), ought the generality of Christians to perform; which what they were may be collected from what was fore-spoken.

CHAPTER II.

Of the same among the Jews, and of the duty of that people distinct from their church officers.

CONCERNING the Jews after the giving of Moses' law: The people of God were then gathered in one, and a standard was set up for all his to repair unto, and the church of God became like a city upon a hill, conspicuous to all, and a certain rule set down for every one to observe that would approach unto him. As, then, before the law, we sought for the manner of God's worship from the *practice of men,* so now, since the change of the external administration of the covenant, from the *prescription of God.* Then we guessed at what was *commanded* by what was *done;* now, at what was *done* by what was *commanded.* And this is all the certainty we can have in either kind, though the consequence from the precept to the performance, and on the contrary, in this corrupted state of nature, be not of absolute necessity; only, the difference is, where things are obscured, it is a safer way to prove the practice of men by God's precept, charitably supposing them to have been obedient, than to wrest the divine rule to their observation, knowing how prone men are to deify themselves by mixing their inventions with the worship of God. The administration of God's providence towards his church hath been various, and the communication of himself unto it, at "sundry times," hath been in "divers manners;" especially, it pleased him not to bring it to perfection but by degrees, as the earth bringeth forth fruit; "first the blade, then the ear, after that the full corn in the ear."[1] Thus, the church, before the giving of Moses' law, seems to have had two main *defects,* which the Lord at that time supplied;—one in *discipline* or government, in that every family exercised the public worship of God within itself or apart (though some do otherwise conclude from Gen. iv. 26), which was first removed by establishing a consistory of elders; the other in the *doctrine,* wanting the rule of the written word, being directed by tradition, the manifold defects whereof were made up by a special revelation. To neither of these defects was the church since exposed. Whether there was any thing written before the giving of the law is not worth contending about. Austin thought Enoch's prophecy was written by him;[2] and Josephus affirms that there were two pillars erected, one of stone, the other of brick, before the flood, wherein divers things were engraven;[3] and Sixtus Senensis, that the book of the wars of the Lord was a volume ancienter than the books of Moses;[4]—but the contrary opinion is most received: so Chrysost. Hom. 1. in Mali.[5] After its giving, none ever doubted of the perfection of the written word for the end to which it was ordained, until the Jews had broached their Talmud to oppose Christ, and the Papists their traditions to advance Antichrist; doubtless the sole aim of the work, whatever were the intentions of the workmen.

The lights which God maketh are sufficient to rule the seasons for which they are ordained. As, in creating of the world, God " made

---

[1] Mark iv. 28. [2] Aug. de Civit. Dei, lib. xv. cap. 23.
[3] Joseph. Antiq. lib. i. cap. 3. [4] Sixt. Senens. Bib. lib. ii.
[5] The only place in the works of Chrysostom in which we can find this opinion, is in "Ad. Pop. Antioch., Homil. ix." It is upon Ps. xix. 1, and "in Mali" seems a misprint for " in ' Cœli, etc.,' "—" Cœli enarrant gloriam Dei."—ED.

two great lights, the greater light to rule the day, and the lesser light to rule the night;" so, in the erection of the new world of his church, he set up two great lights,—the lesser light of the Old Testament to guide the night, the dark space of time under the law, and the greater light of the New Testament to rule the glorious day of the gospel. And these two lights do sufficiently enlighten every man that cometh into this new world. There is no need of the false fire of tradition where God sets up such glorious lights. This be premised for the proneness of men to deflect from the golden rule and heavenly pole-star in the investigation of the truth, especially in things of this nature concerning which we treat, wherein ordinary endeavours are far greater in searching after what men have done than what they ought to have done; and when the fact is once evidenced from the pen of a rabbi or a father, presently to conclude the right. Amongst many, we may take a late treatise, for instance, entitled, " Of Religious Assemblies and the Public Service of God,"[1] whose author would prescribe the manner of God's worship among Christians from the custom of the Jews; and their observations he would prove from the rabbis, not at all taking notice that from such observances they were long ago recalled to the "law and to the testimony," and afterward for them sharply rebuked by Truth itself.[2] Doubtless it is a worthy knowledge to be able, and a commendable diligence, to search into those coiners of curiosities ; but to embrace the fancies of those wild heads, which have nothing but novelty to commend them, and to seek their imposition on others, is but an abusing of their own leisure and others' industry. The issue of such a temper seems to be the greatest part of that treatise; which because I wait only for some spare hours to demonstrate in a particular tract, I shall for the present omit the handling of divers things there spoken of, though otherwise they might very opportunely here be mentioned,—as the office and duty of prophets, the manner of God's worship in their synagogues, the original and institution of their later teachers, scribes and Pharisees, etc.,—and briefly only observe those things which are most immediately conducing to my proposed subject.

The worship of God among them was either moral or ceremonial and typical. The performances belonging unto the latter, with all things thereunto conducing, were appropriated to them whom God had peculiarly set apart for that purpose. By *ceremonial* worship I understand all sacrifices and offerings, the whole service of the tabernacle, and afterward of the temple; all which were typical, and established merely for the present dispensation, not without purpose of their abrogation, when that which was to be more perfect should

---

[1] Herbert Thorndike, a learned divine, and one of Walton's assistants in the preparation of his Polyglott, published a treatise under this title in 1642. It is clear that it is to this treatise Owen alludes.—ED.

[2] Isa. viii. 20; Matt. v., vi.

appear. Now, the several officers, with their distinct employments in and about this service, were so punctually prescribed and limited by Almighty God, that as none of them might ἀλλοτριοεπισκοπεῖν, without presumptuous impiety, intrude into the function of others not allotted to them, as Num. xvi. 1–10; so none of their brethren might presume to intrude into the least part of their office without manifest sacrilege, Josh. xxii. 11–20. True it is, that there is mention of divers in the Scripture that offered sacrifices, or vowed so to do, who were strangers from the priest's office, yea, from the tribe of Levi: as Jephthah, Judges xi.; Manoah, chap. xiii.; David, 2 Sam. vi., and again, 2 Sam. xxiv.; Solomon, 1 Kings iii., and again, chap. ix. But following our former rule of interpreting the practice by the precept, we may find, and that truly, that all the expressions of their offerings signify no more but they brought those things to be offered, and caused the priests to do what in their own persons they ought not to perform. Now, hence, by the way, we may observe that the people of God under the New Testament, contradistinct from their teachers, have a greater interest in the performance of spiritual duties belonging to the worship of God, and more in that regard is granted unto them and required of them than was of the ancient people of the Jews, considered as distinguished from their priests, because their duty is prescribed unto them under the notion of those things which then were appropriate only to the priests, as of offering incense, sacrifice, oblations, and the like; which, in their original institution, were never permitted to the people of the Jews, but yet tralatitiously and by analogy are enjoined to all Christians. But of these afterward.

The main question is about the duty of the people of God in performances for their own edification, and the extent of their lawful undertakings for others' instruction. For the first, which is of nearest concernment unto themselves, the sum of their duty in this kind may be reduced to these two heads:—*First*, To *hear the word and law of God read attentively*, especially when it was expounded; *secondly*, To *meditate* therein themselves, to study it by day and night, and to get their senses exercised in that rule of their duty: concerning each of which we have both the precept and the practice, God's command and their performance. The one in that injunction given unto the priest, Deut. xxxi. 11–13, "When all Israel is come to appear before the LORD thy God, in the place which he shall choose, thou shalt read this law before all Israel in their hearing. Gather the people together, men, and women, and children, and thy stranger that is within thy gates, that they may hear, and that they may learn, and fear the LORD your God, and observe to do all the words of this law; and that their children, which have not known, may hear and learn." All which we find punctually performed on both sides, Neh. viii. 1–8.

Ezra the priest, standing on a pulpit of wood, read the law and gave the meaning of it; and the " ears of all the people were attentive to the book of the law." Which course continued until there was an end put to the observances of that law; as Acts xv. 21, "Moses of old time hath in every city them that preach him, being read in the synagogues every sabbath-day." On which ground, not receding from their ancient observations, the people assembled to hear our Saviour teaching with authority, Luke xxi. 38; and St Paul divers times took advantage of their ordinary assemblies to preach the gospel unto them. For the other, which concerns their own searching into the law and studying of the word, we have a strict command, Deut. vi. 6–9, " And these words, which I command thee this day, shall be in thine heart: and thou shalt teach them diligently unto thy children, and shalt talk of them when thou sittest in thine house, and when thou walkest by the way, and when thou liest down, and when thou risest up. And thou shalt bind them for a sign upon thine hand, and they shall be as frontlets between thine eyes. And thou shalt write them upon the posts of thy house, and on thy gates." Which strict charge is again repeated, chap. xi. 18, summarily comprehending all ways whereby they might become exercised in the law. Now, because this charge is in particular given to the king, chap. xvii. 18–20, the performance of a king in obedience thereunto will give us light enough into the practice of the people. And this we have in that most excellent psalm of David, namely, cxix.; which for the most part is spent in petitions for light, direction, and assistance in that study, in expressions of the performance of this duty, and in spiritual glorying of his success in his divine meditations; especially, verse 99, he ascribeth his proficiency in heavenly wisdom and understanding above his teachers, not to any special revelation, not to that prophetical light wherewith he was endued (which, indeed, consisting in a transient irradiation of the mind, being a supernatural impulsion, commensurate to such things as are connatural only unto God, doth of itself give neither wisdom nor understanding), but unto his study in the testimonies of God. The blessings pronounced upon and promises annexed to the performance of this duty concern not the matter in hand; only, from the words wherein the former command is delivered, two things may be observed:—1. That the paternal teaching and instruction of families in things which appertain to God being a duty of the law of nature, remained in its full vigour, and was not at all impaired by the institution of a new order of teachers for assemblies beyond domestical, then established. Neither, without doubt, ought it to cease amongst Christians, there being no other reason why now it should but that which then was not effectual.

Secondly, That the people of God were not only permitted, but enjoined also, to read the Scriptures, and upon all occasions, in their own houses and elsewhere, to talk of them, or communicate their knowledge in them, unto others. There had been then no council at Trent to forbid the one; nor, perhaps, was there any strict canon to bring the other within the compass of a "conventicle." But now, for the solemn public teaching and instructing of others, it was otherwise ordained; for this was committed to them, in regard of ordinary performance, who were set apart by God; as for others before named, so also for that purpose. The author of the treatise I before mentioned concludeth that the people were not taught at the public assemblies by priests as such,—that is, teaching the people was no part of their office or duty; but, on the contrary, that seems to be a man's duty in the service or worship of God which God requires of him, and that appertains to his office, whose performance is expressly enjoined unto him as such, and for whose neglect he is rebuked or punished. Now, all this we find concerning the priests' public teaching of the people; for the proof of which the recital of a few pertinent places shall suffice. Lev. x. 11, we have an injunction laid upon Aaron and his sons to "teach the children of Israel all the statutes which the LORD had spoken unto them by the hand of Moses." And of the Levites it is affirmed, Deut. xxxiii. 10, "They shall teach Jacob thy statutes, and Israel thy law." Now, though some restrain these places to the discerning of leprosies, and between holy and unholy, with their determination of difficulty emergent out of the law, yet this no way impairs the truth of that I intend to prove by them; for even those things belonged to that kind of public teaching which was necessary under that administration of the covenant. But instead of many, I will name one not liable to exception: Mal. ii. 7, "The priest's lips should keep knowledge, and they should seek the law at his mouth; for he is the messenger of the LORD of hosts;"—where both a recital of his own duty, that he should be full of knowledge to instruct; the intimation to the people, that they should seek unto him, or give heed to his teaching; with the reason of them both, "For he is the LORD'S messenger" (one of the highest titles of the ministers of the gospel, performing the same office),—do abundantly confirm that instructing of the people in the moral worship of God was a duty of the priestly office, or of the priests as such, especially considering the effect of this teaching, mentioned verse 6, the "turning of many away from iniquity," the proper end of teaching in assemblies: all which we find exactly performed by an excellent priest, preaching to the people on a pulpit of wood, Neh. viii. 1–8. Farther; for a neglect of this, the priests are threatened with the rejection from their office, Hosea iv. 6. Now, it doth not seem justice that a man should be put out of his office for a neglect of that whose performance doth not belong unto it. The fault of every neglect ariseth from the description of a duty. Until something, then, of more force than any thing as yet I have seen be objected to the contrary, we may take it for granted that the teaching of the people under the law in public assemblies was performed ordinarily by the priests, as belonging to their duty and office. Men endued with gifts supernatural, extraordinarily called, and immediately sent by God himself for the instruction of his people, the reformation of his church, and foretelling things to come, —such as were the prophets, who, whenever they met with opposition, stayed themselves upon their extraordinary calling,—come not within the compass of my disquisition. The institution, also, of the schools of the prophets, the employment of the sons of the prophets, the original of the scribes, and those other possessors of Moses' chair in our Saviour's time, wherein he conversed here below, being necessarily to be handled in my observations on the fore-named treatise, I shall omit until more leisure and an enjoyment of the small remainder of my poor library shall better enable me. For the present, because treating " in causâ facili," although writing without books, I hope I am not beside the truth. The book of truth, praised be God, is easy to be obtained; and God is not tied to means in discovering the truth of that book.

Come we, then, to the consideration of what duty in the service of God, beyond those belonging unto several families, were permitted to any of the people not peculiarly set apart for such a purpose. The ceremonial part of God's worship, as we saw before, was so appropriated to the priests that God usually revenged the transgression of that ordinance very severely. The examples of Uzzah and Uzziah[1] are dreadful testimonies of his wrath in that kind. It was an unalterable law by virtue whereof the priests excommunicated[2] that presumptuous king. For that which we chiefly intend, the public teaching of others, as to some it was enjoined as an act of their duty, so it might at first seem that it was permitted to all who, having ability thereunto, were called by charity or necessity. So the princes of Jehoshaphat taught the people out of the law of God, as well as the priests and Levites, 2 Chron. xvii. 7-9. So also Nehemiah and others of the chiefs of the people are reckoned among them who taught the people, Neh. viii. 9. And afterward, when St Paul at any time entered into their synagogues, they never questioned any thing but his abilities; if he had "any word of exhortation for the people," he might "say on."[3] And the scribes, questioning the authority of our

---

[1] 2 Sam. vi. 6, 7; 2 Chron. xxvi. 18, 19.   [2] " Cast him out," John ix. 34.
[3] Acts xiii. 15.

Saviour for his teaching, were moved to it, not because he *taught*, but because he taught *so* and *such* things,—with authority and against their traditions; otherwise, they rather troubled *themselves* to think how he should become *able* to teach, Mark vi. 2, 3, than *him* because he *did*. There are, indeed, many sharp reproofs in the Old Testament of those who undertook to be God's messengers without his warrant; as Jer. xxii. 21, 22, " I have not sent these prophets, yet they ran; I have not spoken to them, yet they prophesied. But if they had stood in my counsel," etc.;—to which, and the like places, it may satisfactorily be answered, that howsoever, by the way of analogy, they may be drawn into rule for these times of the gospel, yet they were spoken only in reference to them who falsely pretended to extraordinary revelations and a power of foretelling things to come, whom the Lord forewarned his people of, and appointed punishments for them, Deut. xiii. 1–6; with which sort of pretenders that nation was ever replenished, for which the very heathen often derided them. He who makes it his employment to counterfeit God's dispensations had then no more glorious work to imitate than that of prophecy; wherein he was not idle. Yet, notwithstanding all this, I do not conceive the former discourse to be punctually true in the latitude thereof, as though it were permitted to all men, or any men, besides the priests and prophets, to teach publicly at all times, and in all estates of that church. Only, I conceive that the usual answers given to the fore-cited places, when objected, are not sufficient. Take an instance in one, 2 Chron. xvii. 7–9, of the princes of Jehoshaphat teaching with the priests. The author of the book before intimated conceives that neither priests nor princes taught at all in that way we now treat of, but only that the priests rode circuit to administer judgment, and had the princes with them to do execution. But this interpretation he borroweth only to confirm his πρῶτον ψεῦδος, that priests did not teach *as such*. The very circumstance of the place enforces a contrary sense. And in chap. xix. 5–7, there is express mention of appointing judges for the determination of civil causes in every city; which evidently was a distinct work, distinguished from that mentioned in this place. And, upon the like ground, I conceive it to be no intimation of a movable sanhedrim; which, although of such a mixed constitution, yet was not itinerant, and is mentioned in that other place. Neither is that other ordinary gloss more probable, " They were sent to teach, that is, to countenance the teaching of the law,"—a duty which seldom implores the assistance of human countenance; and if for the present it did, the king's authority commanding it was of more value than the presence of the princes. Besides, there is nothing in the text, nor the circumstances thereof, which should hold out this sense unto us; neither do we find any other rule, precept, or practice, whose analogy might lead us to such an interpretation. That which to me seems to come nearest the truth is, that they taught also, not in a ministerial way, like the priests and Levites, but imperially and judicially, declaring the sense of the law, the offences against it, and the punishments due to such offences, especially inasmuch as they had reference to the peace of the commonwealth; which differs not much from that which I rest upon,—to wit, that in a collapsed and corrupted state of the church, when the ordinary teachers are either utterly ignorant and cannot, or negligent and will not, perform their duty, gifts in any one to be a teacher, and consent in others by him to be taught, are a sufficient warrant for the performance of it; and than this the places cited out of the Old Testament prove no more. For the proceedings of St Paul in the synagogues, their great want of teaching (being a people before forsaken of the Spirit, and then withering) might be a warrant for them to desire it, and his apostolical mission for him to do it. It doth not, then, at all from hence appear that there was then any liberty of teaching in public assemblies granted unto or assumed by any, in such an estate of the church as wherein it ought to be. When, indeed, it is ruinously declining, every one of God's servants hath a sufficient warrant to help or prevent the fall; this latter being but a common duty of zeal and charity, the former an authoritative act of the keys, the minister whereof is only an instrumental agent, that from whence it hath its efficacy residing in another, in whose stead, and under whose person it is done, 2 Cor. v. 19, 20. Now, whoever doth any thing in another's stead, not by express patent from him, is a plain impostor; and a grant of this nature made unto all in general doth not appear. I am bold to speak of these things under the notion of the "keys," though in the time of the law; for I cannot assent to those schoolmen[1] who will not allow that the keys in any sense were granted to the legal priests. Their power of teaching, discerning, judging, receiving in and casting out, import the thing, though the name (no more than that of "regnum cœlorum," as Jerome and Augustine observe) be not to be found in the Old Testament; and, doubtless, God ratified the execution of his own ordinances in heaven then as well as now. What the immediate effect of their services was, how far by their own force they reached, and what they typified, how in signification only, and not immediately, they extended to an admission into and exclusion from the heavenly tabernacle, and wherein lies the secret power of gospel commissions beyond theirs to attain the ultimate end, I have declared elsewhere.[2]

Thus much of what the ancient people of God, distinguished from

---

[1] Aquin., Durand. Socin. et Papistas, nondum edito.   [2] Tractatu de Sacerdotio Christi, contra Armin. [See Prefatory Note.]

their priests, might not do; now briefly of what they might, or rather of what they ought, and what their obedience and profession declared that they thought themselves obliged unto. Private exhortations, re-bukings, and such dictates of the law of nature, being pre-supposed, we find them farther " speaking often one to another" of those things which concerned the fear and worship of the Lord, Mal. iii. 16; by their " lips feeding many with wisdom," Prov. x. 21; discoursing of God's laws upon all occasions, Deut. vi. 6, 7; by multitudes en-couraging each other to the service of God, Zech. viii. 20, 21, Isa. ii. 2, 3; jointly praising God with cheerful hearts, Ps. xlii. 4; giving and receiving mutual consolation, Ps. lv. 14; and all this, with much more of the same nature, at their meetings, either occasional or for that purpose indicted;—always provided that they abstained from fingering the ark, or meddling with those things which were appro-priated to the office of the priests, and concerning them hitherto.

CHAPTER III.

Containing a digression concerning the name of "priests," the right of Christians thereunto by their interest in the priesthood of Christ, with the presumption of any particularly appropriating it to themselves.

AND now the transaction of these things in the Christian church presents itself to our consideration; in handling whereof I shall not at all discourse concerning the several church-officers instituted by Christ and his apostles for the edification of his body, nor concern-ing the difference between them who were partakers at first of an extraordinary vocation and those who since have been called to the same work in an ordinary manner, divinely appointed for the direc-tion of the church. Neither yet doth that diversity of the adminis-tration of government in the churches, *then* when they were under the plenitude of apostolical power, and *now* when they follow rules prescribed for their reiglement, come in my way.

Farther; who are the subject of the keys, in whom all that second-ary ecclesiastical power which is committed to men doth reside, after the determinations of so many learned men by clear Scripture light, shall not by me be called in question. All these, though conducing to the business in hand, would require a large discussion, and such a scholastical handling as would make it an inconsutilous[1] piece of this popular discourse; my intent being only to show,—*seeing there are, as all acknowledge, some under the New Testament, as well as the Old, peculiarly set apart by God's own appointment for the admi-nistration of Christ's ordinances, especially teaching of others by preaching of the gospel, in the way of office and duty,—what re-*

[1] Improperly sewn together, not suited to the rest of the discourse.—ED.

*maineth for the rest of God's people to do, for their own and others'
edification.*

1. But here, before I enter directly upon the matter, I must remove
one stone of offence, concerning the common appellation of those who
are set apart for the preaching of the gospel. That which is most
frequently used for them in the New Testament is διάκονοι, so 1 Cor.
iii. 5; 2 Cor. iii. 6, vi. 4, xi. 15, 23; 1 Tim. iv. 6, and in divers other
places; to which add ὑπηρέται, 1 Cor. iv. 1, a word though of another
original, yet of the same signification with the former, and both rightly
translated "ministers." The names of "ambassadors," "stewards,"
and the like, wherewith they are often honoured, are figurative, and
given unto them by allusion only. That the former belonged unto
them, and were proper for them, none ever denied but some Rab-
shakehs of antichrist. Another name there is, which some have assumed unto themselves as an honour, and others have imposed the
same upon them for a reproach, namely, that of " priest;" which, to
the takers, seemed to import a more mysterious employment, a greater
advancement above the rest of their brethren, a nearer approach
unto God, in the performances of their office, than that of "ministers;"
wherefore they embraced it either voluntarily, alluding to the service
of God and the administration thereof amongst his ancient people
the Jews, or thought that they ought necessarily to undergo it, as belonging properly to them who are to celebrate those mysteries and
offer those sacrifices which they imagined were to them prescribed.
The imposers, on the contrary, pretend divers reasons why now that
name can signify none but men rejected from God's work, and given
up to superstitious vanities; attending, in their minds, the old priests
of Baal, and the now shavelings of Antichrist. It was a new etymo-
logy of this name which that learned man cleaved unto, who, unhappily, was engaged into the defence of such errors as he could not
but see and did often confess,[1]—to which, also, he had an entrance
made by an archbishop,[2]—to wit, that it was but an abbreviation of
"presbyters;" knowing full well, not only that the signification of these
words is diverse amongst them to whom belong "jus et norma lo-
quendi," but also that they are widely different in holy writ: yea,
farther, that those who first dignified themselves with this title
never called themselves presbyters by way of distinction from the
people, but only to have a note of distance among themselves, there
being more than one sort of them that were sacrificers, and which,
" eo nomine," accounted themselves priests. Setting aside, then, all
such evasions and distinctions as the people of God are not bound
to take notice of, and taking the word in its ordinary acceptation, I
shall briefly declare what I conceive of the use thereof, in respect of

[1] Hooker's Eccles. Polit. lib. v.   [2] Whitgift, Ans. to the Admon.

them who are ministers of the gospel; which I shall labour to clear by these following observations:—

(1.) All faithful ministers of the gospel, inasmuch as they are in-grafted into Christ and are true believers, *may*, as all other true Christians, *be called priests;* but this inasmuch as they are members of Christ, not ministers of the gospel. It respecteth their persons, not their function, or not them as such. Now, I conceive it may give some light to this discourse if we consider the grounds and reasons of this metaphorical appellation, in divers places of the gospel ascribed to the worshippers of Christ,[1] and how the analogy which the present dis-pensation holds with what was established under the administration of the Old Testament may take place; for there we find the Lord thus be-speaking his people, "Ye shall be unto me a kingdom of priests, and an holy nation," Exod. xix. 6: so that it should seem that there was then a twofold priesthood;—a *ritual* priesthood, conferred upon the tribe of Levi; and a *royal* priesthood, belonging to the whole people. The first is quite abrogated and swallowed up in the priesthood of Christ; the other is put over unto us under the gospel, being ascribed to them and us, and every one in covenant with God, not *directly* and pro-perly, as denoting the function peculiarly so called, but *comparatively*, with reference had to them that are without: for as those who were properly called priests had a nearer access unto God than the rest of the people, especially in his solemn worship, so all the people that are in covenant with God have such an approximation unto him by virtue thereof, in comparison of them that are without, that in respect thereof they are said to be priests. Now, the outward covenant, made with them who were the children of Abraham after the flesh, was repre-sentative of the covenant of grace made with the children of promise, and that whole people typified the hidden elect people of God; so that of both there is the same reason. Thus, as "the priests the sons of Levi" are said to "come near unto God," Deut. xxi. 5, and God tells them that "him whom he hath chosen, he will cause to come near unto him," Num. xvi. 5,—chosen by a particular calling "ad munus," to the office of the ritual priesthood; so in regard of that other kind, comparatively so called, it is said of the whole people, "What nation is there so great, who hath God so nigh unto them, as the LORD our God is in all things that we call upon him for?" Deut. iv. 7. Their approaching nigh unto God made them all a nation of priests, in comparison of those "dogs" and unclean Gentiles that were out of the covenant. Now, this prerogative is often ap-propriated to the faithful in the New Testament: for "through Christ we have access by one Spirit unto the Father," Eph. ii. 18; and chap. iii. 12, "We have boldness and access with confidence;" so

---

[1] Rev. i. 6, v. 10, xx. 6; 1 Pet. ii. 5, 9, etc.

James iv. 8, "Draw nigh to God, and he will draw nigh to you;" —which access and approximation unto God seemed, as before was spoken, to be uttered in allusion to the priests of the old law, who had this privilege above others in the public worship, in which respect only things then were typical; since, because we enjoy that prerogative in the truth of the thing itself, which they had only in type, we also are called priests. And as they were said to "draw nigh" in reference to the rest of the people, so we in respect of them who are "strangers from the covenants," that now are said to be "afar off," Eph. ii. 17, and hereafter shall be "without;" for "without are dogs," etc., Rev. xxii. 15. Thus, this metaphorical appellation of priests is, in the first place an intimation of that transcendent privilege of grace and favour which Jesus Christ hath purchased for every one that is sanctified with the blood of the covenant.

(2.) We have an interest in this appellation of priests *by virtue of our union with Christ.* Being one with our high priest, we also are priests. There is a twofold union between Christ and us;—the one, by his taking upon him our nature; the other, by bestowing on us his Spirit: for as in his incarnation he took upon him our flesh and blood by the work of the Spirit, so in our regeneration he bestoweth on us his flesh and blood by the operation of the same Spirit. Yea, so strict is this latter union which we have with Christ, that as the former is truly said to be a union of two natures into one person, so this of many persons into one nature; for by it we are "made partakers of the divine nature," 2 Pet. i. 4, becoming "members of his body, of his flesh, and of his bones," Eph. v. 30. We are so parts of him, of his mystical body, that we and he become thereby, as it were, one Christ: "For as the body is one, and hath many members, and all the members of that one body, being many, are one body: so also is Christ," 1 Cor. xii. 12. And the ground of this is, because the same Spirit is in him and us. In him, indeed, dwelleth the *fulness* of it, when it is bestowed upon us only by *measure;* but yet it is still the *same* Spirit, and so makes us, according to his own prayer, one with him, as the soul of man, being one, makes the whole body with it to be but one man. Two men cannot be one, because they have two souls; no more could we be one with Christ were it not the same Spirit in him and us. Now, let a man be never so big or tall, so that his feet rest upon the earth and his head reach to heaven, yet, having but one soul, he is still but one man. Now, though Christ for the present, in respect of our nature assumed, be never so far remote and distant from us in heaven, yet, by the effectual energy and inhabitation of the same Spirit, he is still the head of that one body whereof we are members, still but one with us. Hence ariseth to us a twofold right to the title of priests:—

[1.] Because being in him, and members of him, *we* are accounted to have done, *in him* and *with him*, whatsoever *he* hath done *for us:* We are " dead with him," Rom. vi. 8; "buried with him," verse 4; "quickened together with him," Eph. ii. 5; "risen with him," Col. iii. 1; being "raised up," we "sit together with him in heavenly places," Eph. ii. 6. Now, all these in Christ were in some sense sacerdotal; wherefore we, having an interest in their performance, by reason of that heavenly participation derived from them unto us, and being united unto him that in them was so properly, are therefore called priests.

[2.] By virtue of this union there is such an analogy between that which Christ *hath done for us* as a priest and *what he worketh in us* by his Holy Spirit, that those acts of ours come to be called by the same name with his, and we for them to be termed priests. Thus, because Christ's death and shedding of his blood, so offering up himself by the eternal Spirit, was a true, proper sacrifice for sin, even our spiritual death unto sin is described to be such, both in the nature of it, to be an offering or sacrifice (for, " I beseech you, brethren," saith St Paul, " by the mercies of God, that ye present your bodies a living sacrifice," etc., Rom. xii. 1), and for the manner of it; our " old man is crucified with him, that the body of sin might be destroyed," Rom. vi. 6.

(3.) We are priests as we are Christians, or *partakers of a holy unction*, whereby we are anointed to the participation of all Christ's glorious offices. We are not called Christians for nothing. If truly we are so, then have we an "unction from the Holy One," whereby we "know all things," 1 John. ii. 20. And thus also were all God's people under the old covenant, when God gave that caution concerning them, " Touch not my CHRISTIANS,[1] and do my prophets no harm," Ps. cv. 15. The unction, then, of the Holy Spirit implies a participation of all those endowments which were typified by the anointing with oil in the Old Testament, and invests us with the privileges, in a spiritual acceptation, of all the sorts of men which then were so anointed,—to wit, of kings, priests, and prophets: so that by being made Christians (every one is not so that bears that name), we are ingrafted into Christ, and do attain to a kind of holy and intimate communion with him in all his glorious offices; and in that regard are called priests.

(4.) The *sacrifices* we are enjoined to offer give ground to this appellation. Now, they are of divers sorts, though all in general *eucharistical;*—as, first, Of *prayers and thanksgivings:* Ps. cxvi. 17, " I will offer unto thee the sacrifice of thanksgiving, and will call upon the name of the LORD;" and again, " Let my prayer be set forth

---

[1] Owen here alludes to the meaning of the name, as derived from Christ—" the anointed."—ED.

before thee as incense, and the lifting up of my hands as the evening sacrifice," Ps. cxli. 2: so Heb. xiii. 15, " Let us offer the sacrifice of praise to God,"—that is, the " fruit of our lips." Secondly, Of *good works:* Heb. xiii. 16, " To do good and to communicate forget not; for with such sacrifices God is well pleased." Thirdly, Αὐτοθυσίας, or *self-slaughter*, crucifying the old man, killing sin, and offering up our souls and bodies an acceptable sacrifice unto God, Rom. xii. 1. Fourthly, The sweet incense of martyrdom: " Yea, and if I be offered upon the sacrifice and service of your faith," etc., Phil. ii. 17. Now, these and sundry other services acceptable to God, receiving this appellation in the Scripture, denominate the performers of them priests. Now, here it must be observed, that these aforenamed holy duties are called " sacrifices," not properly, but metaphorically only,—not in regard of the external acts, as were those under the law, but in regard of the internal purity of heart from whence they proceed. And because pure sacrifices, by his own appointment, were heretofore the most acceptable service of Almighty God, therefore now, when he would declare himself to be very much delighted with the spiritual acts of our duty, he calls them "oblations," "incense," "sacrifices," "offerings," etc.; to intimate, also, a participation with Him in his offices who properly and directly is the only priest of his church, and by the communication of the virtue of whose sacrifice we are made priests, not having authority in our own names to go unto God for *others*, but having liberty, through him, and in his name, to go unto GOD for *ourselves*.

Not to lose myself and reader in this digression, the sum is,—The unspeakable blessings which the priesthood of Christ hath obtained for us are a strong obligation for the duty of praise and thanksgiving; of which that in some measure we may discharge ourselves, he hath furnished us with sacrifices of that kind to be offered unto God. For our own parts, we are poor, and blind, and lame, and naked; neither in the field nor in the fold, in our hearts nor among our actions, can we find any thing worth the presenting unto him: wherefore, he himself provides them for us; especially for that purpose sanctifying and consecrating our souls and bodies with the sprinkling of his blood and the unction of the Holy Spirit. Farther; he hath erected an altar (to sanctify our gifts) in heaven, before the throne of grace, which, being spread over with his blood, is consecrated unto God, that the sacrifices of his servants may for ever appear thereon. Add to this, what he also hath added, the eternal and never-expiring fire of the favour of God, which kindleth and consumes the sacrifices laid on that altar. And to the end that all this may be rightly accomplished, he hath consecrated us with his blood to be kings and priests to God for evermore. So that the close of this discourse will

be, that all true believers, by virtue of their interest in Jesus Christ,
are in the holy Scripture, by reason of divers allusions, called priests;
which name, in the sense before related, belonging unto them as
such, cannot, on this ground, be ascribed to any part of them distinguished any ways from the rest by virtue of such distinction.

2. The second thing I observe concerning the business in hand is,
that the offering up unto God of some metaphorical sacrifices, in a
peculiar manner, *is appropriate unto men set apart for the work of
the ministry;* as the slaying of men's lusts, and the offering up of
them, being converted by the preaching of the gospel, unto God.   So
St Paul of his ministry, Rom. xv. 16, " That I should be the
minister of Jesus Christ unto the Gentiles, ministering the gospel of
God, that the offering up of the Gentiles might be acceptable," etc.
Ministers preaching the gospel to the conversion of souls are said to
kill men's lusts, and offer them up unto God as the fruit of their
calling, as Abel brought unto him an acceptable sacrifice of the fruit
of his flock; and so also in respect of divers other acts of their duty,
which they perform in the name of their congregations.   Now, these
sacrifices are appropriated to the ministers of the gospel, not in regard
of the matter,—for others also may convert souls unto God, and offer up
prayers and praises in the name of their companions,—but in respect
of the manner: they do it publicly and ordinarily; others, privately
or in extraordinary cases.   Now, if the ministers, who are thus God's
instruments for the conversion of souls, be themselves ingrafted into
Christ, all the acts they perform in that great work are but parts of
their own duty, of the same nature in that regard with the rest of
our spiritual sacrifices; so that they have not by them any farther,
peculiar interest in the office of the priesthood more than others.
But if these preachers themselves do not belong unto the covenant
of grace, as God oftentimes, out of his care for his flock, bestows gifts
upon some for the good of others, on whom he will bestow no graces
for the benefit of their own souls, men may administer that consolation out of the word unto their flock which themselves never tasted,—
preach to others, and be themselves cast-aways.   St Paul tells us that
some preach Christ out of envy and contention, not sincerely, but on
purpose to add to his affliction; and yet, saith he, " whether in pretence, or in truth, Christ is preached; and I therein do rejoice, yea,
and will rejoice," Phil. i. 16–18.   Surely, had there been no good
effected by such preaching, St Paul would not have rejoiced in it;
and yet, doubtless, it was no evidence of sanctification to preach
Christ merely out of contention, and on purpose to add to the affliction of his servants.   But, I say, if the Lord shall be pleased at any
time to make use of such as instruments in his glorious work of
converting souls, shall we think that it is looked upon as their sacri-

fice unto God? No, surely. The soul of the Lord is delighted with the repentance of sinners; but all the sacrifices of these wicked men are an abomination unto him, and therefore they have no interest in it. Neither can they from hence be said to be priests of God, seeing they continue "dogs" and "unclean beasts," etc. So that all the right unto this priestly office seems to be resolved into, and to be the same with, the common interest of all believers in Christ, whereby they have a participation of his office. Whence I affirm,—

3. That the name of priests is nowhere in the Scripture attributed *peculiarly and distinctively to the ministers of the gospel as such.* Let any produce an instance to the contrary, and this controversy is at an end. Yea, that which puts a difference between them and the rest of the people of God's holiness seems to be a more immediate participation of Christ's prophetical office, to teach, instruct, and declare the will of God unto men; and not of his sacerdotal, to offer sacrifices for men unto God. Now, I could never observe that any of those who were so forward of late to style themselves priests were at all greedy of the appellation of prophets. No; this they were content to let go, name and thing. And yet, when Christ ascended on high, he gave some to be prophets, for the edification of his body, Eph. iv. 11; none, as we find, to be priests. Priests, then (like prelates), are a sort of church-officers whom Christ never appointed. Whence I conclude,—

4. That whosoever maintaineth any priests of the New Testament as properly so called, in relation to any altar or sacrifice by them to be offered, doth as much as in him lieth *disannul the covenant of grace,* and is blasphemously injurious to the priesthood of Christ. The priest and the sacrifice under the New Testament are one and the same; and therefore, they who make themselves priests must also make themselves Christs, or get another sacrifice of their own. As there is but "one God," so there is but "one mediator between God and men, the man Christ Jesus," 1 Tim. ii. 5. Now, he became the mediator of the New Testament chiefly by his priesthood, because "through the eternal Spirit he offered himself to God," Heb. ix. 14, 15. Neither is any now called of God to be a priest, as was Aaron; and without such divine vocation to this office none ought to undertake it, as the apostle argues, Heb. v. 4. Now, the end of any such vocation and office is quite ceased, being nothing but to "offer gifts and sacrifices" unto God, Heb. viii. 3: for Christ hath offered one sacrifice for sins for ever, and is "set down at the right hand of God," chap. x. 12; yea, "by one offering he hath perfected for ever them that are sanctified," verse 14; and if that did procure remission of sins, there must be "no more offering for sin," verse 18; and the surrogation of another makes the blood of Christ to be no better than that of bulls

and goats.   Now, one of these they must do who make themselves
priests (in that sense concerning which we now treat),—either get them
a *new sacrifice* of their own, or pretend *to offer Christ again*.[1]   The
first seems to have been the fault of those of ours who made a *sacrifice of the sacrament*, yet pretended not to believe the real presence
of Christ in or under the outward elements or species of them; the
other of the Romanists, whose priests in their mass blasphemously
make themselves mediators between God and his Son, and offering
up Christ Jesus for a sacrifice, desire God to accept him,—so charging
that sacrifice with imperfection which he offered on the altar of the
cross, and making it necessary not only that he should annually, but
daily, yea hourly, suffer afresh, so recrucifying unto themselves the
Lord of glory.   Farther; themselves confessing that, to be a true sacrifice, it is required that that which is offered unto God be destroyed,
and cease to be what it was, they do confess by what lies in them to
destroy the Son of God; and by their mass have transubstantiated
their altars into crosses, their temples into Golgothas, their prelates
into Pilates, their priests into hangmen, tormentors of Jesus Christ!
Concerning them and ours, we may shut up this discourse with what
the apostle intimates to the Hebrews,—namely, that all priests are
ceased who were mortal.   Now, small cause have we to believe them
to be immaterial spirits, among whom we find the works of the flesh
to have been so frequent.

And this may give us some light into the iniquity of those times
whereinto we were lately fallen; in which lord bishops and priests
had almost quite oppressed the bishops of the Lord and ministers of
the gospel.   How unthankful men were we for the light of the gospel!
—men that loved darkness rather than light.   "A wonderful and
horrible thing was committed in the land; the prophets prophesied
falsely, the priests bare rule by their means;" almost the whole
"people loved to have it so: and what will we now do in the end
thereof?" Jer. v. 30, 31.   Such a hasty apostasy was growing on us
as we might justly wonder at, because unparalleled in any church, of
any age.   But our revolters were profound hasty men, and eager in
their master's service.   So, what a height of impiety and opposition
to Christ the Roman apostasy in a thousand years attained unto!
and yet I dare aver that never so many errors and suspicions in a
hundred years crept into that church as did into ours of England in
sixteen.   And yet I cannot herein give the commendation of so much
as industry to our innovators (I accuse not the whole church, but
particulars in it, and that had seized themselves of its authority),

---

[1] For offering the host, or their Christ, they pray: " Supra quæ, propitio ac sereno
vultu respicere digneris, et accepta habere sicut dignatus es munera pueri tui justi Abel,
et sacrificium patriarchæ nostri Abrahæ;" with many more to that purpose.

because they had a platform before them, and materials provided to their hand, and therefore it was an easy thing for them to erect a Babel of antichristian confusion, when the workmen in the Roman apostasy were forced to build in the plain of Christianity without any pre-existent materials, but were fain to use brick and slime of their own provision. Besides, they were unacquainted with the main design of Satan, who set them on work, and therefore it is no wonder if those Nimrods ofttimes hunted counter, and disturbed each other in their progress. Yea, the first mover in church apostasy knows that now his time is but short, and therefore it behoves him to make speedy work in seducing, lest he be prevented by the coming of Christ.

Then, having himself a long tract of time granted unto him, he allowed his agents to take leisure also; but what he doth *now* must be done quickly, or his whole design will be quashed: and this made him inspire the present business with so much life and vigour. Moreover, he was compelled then to sow his tares in the dark, "while men slept,"—taking advantage of the ignorance and embroilment of the times. If any man had leisure enough to search, and learning enough to see and find him at it, he commonly filled the world with clamours against him, and scarce any but his avowed champions durst be his advocates. In our time he was grown bold and impudent, working at noonday; yea, he openly accused and condemned all that durst accuse him for sowing any thing but good wheat, that durst say that the tares of his Arminianism and Popery were any thing but true doctrine. Let us give so much way to indignation. We know Satan's trade what it is,—to accuse the brethren: as men are called after their professions, one a lawyer, another a physician, so is he "The accuser of the brethren." Now, surely, if ever he set up a shop on earth to practise his trade in, it was our High Commission Court, as of late employed; but ἀπέχεσθε.

CHAPTER IV.

Of the duty of God's people in cases extraordinary concerning his worship.

THIS being thus determined, I return again to the main ζητούμενον, concerning the duty and privilege of the common people of Christianity in sacred things; and, first, in cases extraordinary, in which, perhaps, it may be affirmed that every one (of those, I mean, before named) is so far a minister of the gospel as to teach and declare the faith to others, although he have no outward calling thereunto. And yet, in this case, every one for such an undertaking must have a warrant by an immediate call from God. And when God calls there must be no opposition; the thing itself he sends us upon becomes lawful by his mission: "What God hath cleansed, that call not thou common," Acts x. 15. Never fear the equity of what God sets thee upon. No excuses of disability or any other impediment ought to take place; the Lord can and will supply all such defects. This was Moses' case, Exod. iv. 10, 11: "O my Lord," saith he, " I am not eloquent, neither heretofore, nor since thou hast spoken unto thy servant: but I am slow of speech, and of a slow tongue. And the LORD said unto him, Who hath made man's mouth ? have not I the LORD ?" So also was it with the prophet Jeremiah. When God told him that he had ordained him a prophet unto the nations, he replies, " Ah, Lord GOD! behold, I cannot speak: for I am a child. But the LORD," saith he, " said unto me, Say not, I am a child: for thou shalt go to all that I shall send thee, and whatsoever I command thee thou shalt speak," Jer. i. 6, 7. Nothing can excuse any from going on His message who can perfect his praise out of the mouths of babes and sucklings. This the prophet Amos rested upon when he was questioned, although he were unfit for that heavenly employment either by education or course of life: " I was no prophet, neither was I a prophet's son; but I was an herdman, and a gatherer of sycomore fruit: and the LORD took me as I followed the flock, and said unto me, Go, prophesy unto my people Israel," Amos vii. 14, 15. So, on the contrary, St Paul, a man of strong parts, great learning, and endowments, of indefatigable industry and large abilities, yet affirms of himself that when God called him to preach his word, he " conferred not with flesh and blood," but went on presently with his work, Gal. i. 15–17.

CHAPTER V.

Of the several ways of extraordinary calling to the teaching of others—
The first way.

NOW, three ways may a man receive, and be assured that he hath received, this divine mission, or know that he is called of God to the preaching of the word; I mean not that persuasion of divine concurrence which is necessary also for them that are partakers of an ordinary vocation, but that which is required in extraordinary cases to them in whom all outward calling is wanting:—1. By immediate *revelation;* 2. By a *concurrence of Scripture rules* directory for such occasions; 3. By some *outward acts of Providence,* necessitating him thereunto.

For the FIRST,—not to speak of light prophetical, whether it consists in a habit, or rather in a transient irradiating motion, nor to discourse of the species whereby supernatural things are conveyed to the natural faculty, with the several ways of divine revelation (for St Paul affirmeth it to have been πολυτρόπως as well as πολυμερῶς), with the sundry appellations it received from the manner whereby it came,—I shall only show what assurance such a one as is thus called may have in himself that he is so called, and how he may manifest it unto others. That men receiving any revelation from God had always an assurance that such it was, to me seems most certain: neither could I ever approve the note of Gregory on Ezek. i.,— namely, "That prophets, being accustomed to prophesying, did oftentimes speak of their own spirit, supposing that it proceeded from the Spirit of prophecy."[1] What is this but to question the truth of all prophetical revelations, and to shake the faith that is built upon it? Surely the prophet Jeremiah had an infallible assurance of the author of his message, when he pleaded for himself before the princes, "Of a truth the LORD hath sent me unto you to speak all these words in your ears," chap. xxvi. 15. And Abraham certainly had need of a good assurance whence that motion did proceed which made him address himself to the sacrificing the son of promise. And that all other prophets had the like evidence of knowledge concerning the divine verity of their revelations is unquestionable. Hence are those allusions in the Scripture, whereby it is compared unto things whereof we may be most certain by the assurance of sense. So Amos iii. 8, "The lion hath roared, who will not fear? the Lord GOD hath spoken, who can but prophesy?" and Jer. xx. 9, "His word was in mine heart as a burning fire shut up in my bones;"—things sensible enough. Haply Satan may so far delude false prophets as to make them suppose their lying vanities are from above; whence they are said to be "prophets of the deceit of their own heart," Jer. xxiii. 26, being deceived as well as deceivers, thinking in themselves as well as speaking unto others, "He saith," verse 31. But that any true prophets should not know a true revelation from a motion of their own hearts wants not much of blasphemy. The Lord surely supposes that assurance of discerning when he gives that command, "The prophet that hath a dream, let him tell a dream; and he that hath my word, let him speak my word faithfully. What is the chaff to the wheat?" Jer. xxiii. 28. He must be both blind and mad that shall mistake wheat for chaff, and on the contrary. What some men speak of a hidden instinct from God moving the minds of men, yet so as they know not whether it be from him or no, may better serve

---

[1] "Sciendum est quod aliquando prophetæ sancti dum consuluntur, ex magno usu prophetandi quædam ex suo spiritu proferunt, et se hoc ex prophetiæ spiritu dicere suspicantur."—Greg. Hom. i. in Ezek.

to illustrate Plutarch's discourse of Socrates' demon than any passage in holy writ. St Austin says his mother would affirm, that though she could not express it, yet she could discern the difference between God's revelation and her own dreams;[1] in which relation I doubt not but the learned father took advantage, from the good old woman's words of what *she* could do, to declare what might be done of every one that had such immediate revelations. Briefly, then; the Spirit of God never so extraordinarily moveth the mind of man to apprehend any thing of this kind whereof we speak, but it also illustrateth it with a knowledge and assurance that it is divinely moved to this apprehension. Now, because it is agreed on all sides that light prophetical is no permanent habit in the minds of the prophets, but a transient impression, of itself not apt to give any such assurance, it may be questioned from what other principle it doth proceed. But, not to pry into things perhaps not fully revealed, and seeing St Paul shows us that, in such heavenly raptures, there are some things unutterable of them and incomprehensible of us, we may let this rest amongst those ἄῤῥητα. It appeareth, then, from the preceding discourse, that a man pretending to extraordinary vocation by immediate revelation, in respect of self-persuasion of the truth of his call, must be as ascertained of it as he could be of a burning fire in his bones, if there shut up.

CHAPTER VI.

What assurance men extraordinarily called can give to others that they are so called in the former way.

THE next thing to be considered is, what assurance he can give to others, and by what means, that he is so called. Now, the matter or subject of their employment may give us some light to this consideration; and this is, either the *inchoation* of some divine work to be established amongst men, by virtue of a new and never-before-heard-of revelation of God's will, or a *restoration* of the same, when collapsed and corrupted by the sin of men. To the first of these: God never sendeth any but whom he doth so extraordinarily and immediately call and ordain for that purpose; and that this may be manifested unto others, he always accompanieth them with his own almighty power, in the working of such miracles as may make them be believed, for the very works' sake which God by them doth effect. This we may see in Moses and (after Jesus Christ, anointed with the

---

[1] "Dicebat se discernere (nescio quo sapore quem verbis explicare non poterat) quid interesset inter Deum revelantem et animam suam somniantem."—Aug. Conf.

oil of gladness above his fellows to preach the gospel) the apostles. But this may pass, for nothing in such a way shall ever again take place, God having ultimately revealed his mind concerning his worship and our salvation, a curse being denounced to man or angel that shall pretend to revelation for the altering or changing one jot or tittle of the gospel. For the other, the work of reformation, there being, ever since the writing of his word, an infallible rule for the performance of it, making it fall within the duty and ability of men partaking of an ordinary vocation, and instructed with ordinary gifts, God doth not always immediately call men unto it; but yet, because oftentimes he hath so done, we may inquire what assurance they could give of this their calling to that employment. Our Saviour Christ informs us that a prophet is often without honour in his own country. The honour of a prophet is to have credence given to his message (of which, it should seem, Jonah was above measure zealous); yet such is the cursed infidelity and hardness of men's hearts, that though they cried, "Thus saith the LORD," yet they would reply, "The LORD hath not spoken." Hence are those pleadings betwixt the prophet Jeremiah and his enemies; the prophet averring, "Of a truth the LORD hath sent me unto you," and they contesting that the LORD had not sent him, but that he lied in the name of the LORD. Now, to leave them inexcusable, and, whether they would hear or whether they would forbear, to convince them that there hath been a prophet amongst them, as also to give the greater credibility to their extraordinary message to them that were to believe their report, it is necessary that "the arm of the LORD should be revealed," working in and by them in some extraordinary manner. It is certain enough that God never sent any one extraordinarily, instructed only with ordinary gifts and for an ordinary end. The aim of their employment I showed before was extraordinary, even the reparation of something instituted by God and collapsed by the sin of man. That it may be credible, or appear of a truth that God had sent them for this purpose, they were always furnished with such gifts and abilities as the utmost reach of human endeavours, with the assistance of common grace, cannot possibly attain. The general opinion is, that God always supplies such with the gift of miracles. Take the word in a large sense, for every supernatural product, beyond the ordinary activity of that secondary cause whereby it is effected, and I easily grant it; but in the usual restrained acceptation of it, for outward wonderful works, the power of whose production consists in operation, I something doubt the universal truth of the assertion. We do not read of any such miracles wrought by the prophet Amos, and yet he stands upon his extraordinary immediate vocation, " I was no prophet, neither was I a prophet's son, but the LORD took me," etc.   It sufficeth, then, that they be furnished with a supernatural power, either in,—1. *Discerning;* 2. *Speaking;* or 3. *Working.* First, The power of *discerning*, according to the things by it discernible, may be said to be of two sorts: for it is either of things present, beyond the power of human investigation, as to know the thoughts of other men's hearts, or their words not ordinarily to be known,—as Elisha discovered the bed-chamber discourse of the king of Syria (not that by virtue of their calling they come to be καρδιογνώσται, " knowers of the heart," which is God's property alone, but that God doth sometimes reveal such things unto them; for otherwise no such power is included in the nature of the gift, which is perfective of their knowledge, not by the way of habit, but actual motion in respect of some particulars; and when this was absent, the same Elisha affirmeth that he knew not why the Shunammitish woman was troubled); or, secondly, of things future and contingent in respect of their secondary causes, not precisely necessitated by their own internal principle of operation for the effecting of the things so foreknown; and, therefore, the truth of the foreknowledge consists in a commensuration to God's purpose. Now, effects of this power are all those predictions of such things which we find in the Old and New Testament, and divers also since. Secondly, The supernatural gift *in speaking* I intimate is that of tongues, proper to the times of the gospel, when the worship of God was no longer to be confined to the people of one nation. The third, *working*, is that which strictly and properly is called the gift of miracles, which are hard, rare, and strange effects, exceeding the whole order of created nature, for whose production God sometimes useth his servants instrumentally, moving and enabling them thereunto by a transient impression of his powerful grace; of which sort the holy Scripture hath innumerable relations. Now, with one of those extraordinary gifts at least, sometimes with all, doth the Lord furnish those his messengers of whom we treat; which makes their message a sufficient revelation of God's will, and gives it credibility enough to stir up faith in some, and leave others inexcusable. All the difficulty is, that there have been Simon Maguses, and there are Antichrists, falsely pretending to have in themselves this mighty power of God, in one or other of the forenamed kinds. Hence were those many false prophets, dreamers, and wizards mentioned in the Old Testament, which the Lord himself forewarns us of; as also those agents of that man of sin, "whose coming is after the working of Satan, with all power and signs and lying wonders," 2 Thess. ii. 9. I mean the juggling priests and Jesuits, pretending falsely by their impostures to the power of miracle-working, though their employment be not to reform, but professedly to corrupt the worship of God. Now, in such a case as this, we have,—1. The *mercy of God* to rely upon, whereby he will guide his into the way of truth; and the purpose or decree of God, making it impossible that his elect should be deceived by them. 2. *Human diligence*, accompanied with God's blessing, may help us wonderfully in a discovery whether the pretended miracles be of God or no, for there is nothing more certain than that a true and real miracle is beyond the activity of all created power (for if it be not, it is not a miracle); so that the devil and all his emissaries are not able to effect any one act truly miraculous, but in all their pretences there is a defect discernible, either in respect of the thing itself pretended to be done, or of the manner of its doing, not truly exceeding the power of art or nature, though the apprehension of it, by reason of some hell-conceived circumstances, be above our capacity.   Briefly: either the thing is a lie, and so it is easy to feign miracles; or the performance of it is pure juggling, and so it is easy to delude poor mortals.   Innumerable of this sort, at the beginning of the Reformation, were discovered among the agents of that wonder-working "man of sin," by the blessing of God upon human endeavours.   Now, from such discoveries a good conclusion may be drawn against the doctrine they desire by such means to confirm; for as God never worketh true miracles but for the confirmation of the truth, so will not men pretend such as are false, but to persuade that to others for a truth which themselves have just reason to be persuaded is a lie.   Now, if this means fail,—3. God himself hath set down *a rule of direction* for us in the time of such difficulty : Deut. xiii. 1–5, "If there arise among you a prophet, or a dreamer of dreams, and giveth thee a sign or a wonder, and the sign or the wonder come to pass, whereof he spake unto thee, saying, Let us go after other gods, which thou hast not known, and let us serve them; thou shalt not hearken unto the words of that prophet, or that dreamer of dreams: for the LORD your God proveth you, to know whether ye love the LORD your God with all your heart and with all your soul.   Ye shall walk after the LORD your God, and fear him, and keep his commandments, and obey his voice, and ye shall serve him, and cleave unto him.   And that prophet, or that dreamer of dreams, shall be put to death."   The sum is, that seeing such men pretend that their revelations and miracles are from heaven, let us search whether the doctrine they seek to confirm by them be from heaven or no.   If it be not, let them be stoned or accursed, for they seek to draw us from our God; if it be, let not the curse of a stony heart, to refuse them, be upon us.   Where the miracles are true, the doctrine cannot be false; and if the doctrine be true, in all probability the miracles confirming it are not false.   And so much of them who are immediately called of God from heaven, [as to] what assurance they may have in themselves of such a call, and what assurance they can make of it to others. Now, such are not to expect any ordinary vocation from men below, God calling them aside to his work from the midst of their brethren. The Lord of the harvest may send labourers into his field without asking his steward's consent, and they shall speak whatever he saith unto them.

CHAPTER VII.

The second way whereby a man may be called extraordinarily.

SECONDLY, A man may be extraordinarily called to the preaching and publishing of God's word *by a concurrence of Scripture rules*, directory for such occasions, occurrences, and opportunities of time, place, and persons, as he liveth in and under. Rules in this kind may be drawn either from express precept or approved practice. Some of these I shall intimate, and leave it to the indifferent reader to judge whether or no they hold in the application; and all that in this kind I shall propose, I do with submission to better judgments.

1. Consider, then, that of our Saviour to St Peter, Luke xxii. 32, "When thou art converted, strengthen thy brethren;" which containing nothing but an application of one of the prime dictates of the law of nature, cannot, ought not, to be restrained unto men of any peculiar calling as such. Not to multiply many of this kind (whereof in the Scripture is plenty), add only that of St James, chap. v. 19, 20, "Brethren, if any of you do err from the truth, and one convert him, let him know, that he which converteth the sinner from the error of his way shall save a soul from death," etc. From these and the like places it appears to me, that,—

There is a general obligation on all Christians to promote the conversion and instruction of sinners, and men erring from the right way.

2. Again, consider that of our Saviour, Matt. v. 15, "Men do not light a candle and put it under a bushel, but on a candlestick, and it giveth light unto all that are in the house;" to which add that of the apostle, "If any thing be revealed to another that sitteth by, let the first hold his peace," 1 Cor. xiv. 30: which words, although primarily they intend extraordinary immediate revelations, yet I see no reason why in their equity and extent they may not be directory for the use of things revealed unto us by Scripture light. At least, we may deduce from them, by the way of analogy, that,—

Whatsoever necessary truth is revealed to any out of the word of God, not before known, he ought to have an uncontradicted liberty of declaring that truth, provided that he use such regulated ways for that his declaration as the church wherein he liveth (if a right church) doth allow.

3. Farther, see Amos iii. 8, "The lion hath roared, who will not fear? the Lord GOD hath spoken, who can but prophesy?" and Jer. xx. 9, "Then I said, I will not make mention of him, nor speak any more in his name. But his word was in mine heart as a burning fire shut up in my bones; and I was weary with forbearing, and I could not stay;" with the answer of Peter and John to the rulers of the Jews, Acts iv. 19, 20, "Whether it be right in the sight of God to hearken unto you more than unto God, judge ye; for we cannot but speak the things which we have seen and heard." Whence it appears, that,—

Truth revealed unto any carries along with it an unmovable persuasion of conscience (which is powerfully obligatory) that it ought to be published and spoken to others.

That none may take advantage of this to introduce confusion into our congregations, I gave a sufficient caution in the second rule.

Many other observations giving light to the business in hand might be taken from the common dictates of nature, concurring with many general precepts we have in the Scripture, but, omitting them, the next thing I propose is the practice, etc.,—

1. Of our Saviour Christ himself, who did not only pose the doctors when he was but twelve years old, Luke ii. 46, but also afterward preached in the synagogue of Nazareth, chap. iv. 16–22, being neither doctor, nor scribe, nor Levite, but of the tribe of Judah (concerning which tribe it is evident that Moses spake nothing concerning the priesthood).

2. Again, in the eighth of the Acts, great persecution arising against the church after the death of Stephen, "they were all scattered abroad from Jerusalem," verse 1,—that is, all the faithful members of the church,—who being thus dispersed, "went everywhere preaching the word," verse 4; and to this their publishing of the gospel (having no warrant but the general engagement of all Christians to further the propagation of Christ's kingdom), occasioned by their own persecution, the Lord gave such a blessing, that they were thereby the first planters of a settled congregation among the Gentiles, they and their converts being the first that were honoured by the name of Christians, Acts xi. 21, 26.

3. Neither is the example of St Paul altogether impertinent, who with his companions repaired unto the synagogues of the Jews,

and taught them publicly, yea, upon their own request, Acts xiii. 15. Apollos also spake boldly and preached fervently when he knew only the baptism of John, and needed himself farther instruction. Acts xviii. 24–26. It should seem, then, in that juncture of time, he that was instructed in any truth not ordinarily known might publicly acquaint others with it, though he himself were ignorant in other points of high concernment; yet, perhaps, now it is not possible that any occurrences should require a precise imitation of what was not only lawful but also expedient in that dawning towards the clear day of the last unchangeable revelation of God's will. Now, in these and the like there is so much variety, such several grounds and circumstances, that no direct rule can from them be drawn; only, they may give strength to what from the former shall be concluded.

For a farther light to this discourse, consider what desolate estate the church of God hath been, may be, and at this present in divers places is, reduced to. Her silver may become dross, and her wine be mixed with water, the faithful city becoming a harlot; her shepherds may be turned into dumb, sleeping dogs, and devouring wolves; the watchmen may be turned smiters, her prophets to prophesy falsely, and her priests to bear rule by lies; the commandments of God being made void by the traditions of men, superstition, human inventions, will-worship, may defile and contaminate the service of God; yea, and greater abominations may men possessing Moses' chair by succession do.[1] Now, that the temple of God hath been thus made a den of thieves, that the abomination of desolation hath been set up in the holy place, is evident from the Jewish and Christian church; for in the one it was clearly so when the government of it was devolved to the scribes and Pharisees, and in the other when the man of sin had exalted himself in the midst thereof. Now, suppose a man living in the midst and height of such a sad apostasy, when a universal darkness had spread itself over the face of the church; if the Lord be pleased to reveal unto him out of his word some points of faith, then either not at all known or generally disbelieved, yet a right belief whereof is necessary to salvation; and, farther, out of the same word shall discover unto him the wickedness of that apostasy, and the means to remove it,—I demand whether that man, without expecting any call from the fomenters and maintainers of those errors with which the church at that time is only not destroyed, may not preach, publish, and publicly declare the said truths to others (the knowledge of them being so necessary for the good of their souls), and conclude himself thereunto called of God, by virtue of the fore-named and other the like rules? Truly,

[1] Ezek. xxii. 27, 28, viii. 13.

for my part (under correction), I conceive he may, nay, he ought; neither is any other outward call requisite to constitute him a preacher of the gospel than the consent of God's people to be instructed by him. For instance: suppose that God should reveal the truth of the gospel to "a mere layman" (as they say) in Italy, so that he be fully convinced thereof, what shall he now do? abstain from publishing it, though he be persuaded in conscience that a great door of utterance might be granted unto him, only because some heretical, simoniacal, wicked, antichristian prelate hath not ordained him minister, who yet would not do it unless he will subscribe to those errors and heresies which he is persuaded to be such? Truly, I think by so abstaining he should sin against *the law of charity*, in seeing, not the ox or ass of his brother falling into the pit, but their precious souls sinking to everlasting damnation, and not preventing it when he might; and were he indeed truly angry with his whole nation, he might have the advantage of an Italian revenge.

Moreover, he should sin against the *precept* of Christ, by hiding his light under a bushel, and napkening up his talent, an increase whereof will be required of him at the last day. Now, with this I was always so well satisfied, that I ever deemed all curious disquisition after the outward vocation of our first reformers, Luther, Calvin, etc., altogether needless, the case in their days being exactly that which I have laid down.

Come we now to the THIRD and last way whereby men, not partakers of any outward ordinary vocation, may yet receive a sufficient warrant for the preaching and publishing of the gospel, and that by some outward act of Providence guiding them thereunto. For example: put case a Christian man should, by any chance of providence, be cast, by shipwreck, or otherwise upon the country of some barbarous people that never heard of the name of Christ, and there, by His goodness that brought him thither, be received amongst them into civil human society, may he not, nay, ought he not, to preach Christ unto them? and if God give a blessing to his endeavours, may he not become a pastor to the converted souls? None, I hope, makes any doubt of it; and in the primitive times nothing was more frequent than such examples. Thus were the Indians and the Moors turned to the faith, as you may see in Eusebius; yea, great was the liberty which in the first church was used in this kind, presently after the supernatural gift of tongues ceased amongst men.

CHAPTER VIII.

Of the liberty and duty of gifted uncalled Christians in the exercise of divers acts of God's worship.

AND thus have I declared what I conceive concerning extraordinary calling to the public teaching of the word, in what cases only it useth to take place; whence I conclude, that whosoever pretends unto it, not warranted by an evidence of one of those three ways that God taketh in such proceedings, is but a pretender, an impostor, and ought, accordingly, to be rejected of all God's people. In other cases, not to disuse what outward ordinary occasion, from them who are intrusted by commission from God with that power, doth confer upon persons so called, we must needs grant it a negative voice in the admission of any to the public preaching of the gospel. If they come not in at that door, they do climb over the wall, if they make any entrance at all. It remains, then, to shut up all, that it be declared what private Christians, living in a pure, orthodox, well-ordered church, may do, and how far they may interest themselves in holy, soul-concerning affairs, both in respect of their own particular and of their brethren in the midst of whom they live; in which determination, because it concerneth men of low degree, and those that comparatively may be said to be unlearned, I shall labour to express the conceivings of my mind in as familiar, plain observations as I can. Only, thus much I desire may be premised, that the principles and rules of that church government from which, in the following assertions, I desire not to wander are of that kind (to which I do, and always, in my poor judgment, have adhered, since, by God's assistance, I had engaged myself to the study of his word) which commonly are called presbyterial or synodical, in opposition to prelatical or diocesan on the one side, and that which is commonly called independent or congregational on the other.

First, then, a *diligent searching* of the Scriptures, with fervent prayers to Almighty God for the taking away that veil of ignorance which by nature is before their eyes, that they may come to a saving knowledge in and a right understanding of them, is not only *lawful* and *convenient* for all men professing the name of Christ, but also absolutely *necessary;* because *commanded,* yea indeed commanded, because the end so to be attained is absolutely necessary to salvation. To confirm this I need not multiply precepts out of the Old or New Testament, (such as that of Isa. viii. 20, " To the law and to the testimony;" and that of John v. 39, "Search the Scriptures,") which are innumerable; nor yet heap up motives unto it, such as are the description of the heavenly country whither we are going, in them contained, John xiv. 2; 2 Cor. v. 1; Rev. xxii. 1, etc.; the way by which we are to travel, laid down John v. 39, xiv. 5, 6; Jesus Christ, whom we must labour to be like, painted out, Gal. iii. 1; and the back parts of God discovered, Deut. xxix. 29. By them only true spiritual wisdom is conveyed to our souls, Jer. viii. 9, whereby we may become even wiser than our teachers, Ps. cxix. 99; in them all comfort and consolation is to be had in the time of danger and trouble, Ps. cxix. 54, 71, 72; in brief, the knowledge of Christ, which is "life eternal," John xvii. 3; yea, all that can be said in this kind comes infinitely short of those treasures of wisdom, riches, and goodness which are contained in them: "The law of the LORD is perfect, converting the soul; the testimony of the LORD is sure, making wise the simple," Ps. xix. 7. But this duty of the people is clear and confessed, the objections of the Papists against it being, for the most part, so many blasphemies against the holy word of God. They accuse it of difficulty, which God affirms to "make wise the simple;" of obscurity, which "openeth the eyes of the blind;" to be a dead letter, a nose of wax, which is "quick and powerful, piercing to the dividing asunder of the soul and spirit;" to be weak and insufficient, which "is able to make the man of God perfect," and "wise unto salvation." Yea, that word which the apostle affirmeth to be "profitable for reproof" is not in any thing more full than in reproving of this blasphemy.

Secondly, They may not only (as before) search the Scriptures, but also examine and *try by them the doctrine that publicly is taught unto them.* The people of God must not be like "children, tossed to and fro, and carried about with every wind of doctrine, by the sleight of men, and cunning craftiness, whereby they lie in wait to deceive," Eph. iv. 14. All is not presently gospel that is spoken in the pulpit; it is not long since that altar-worship, Arminianism, Popery, superstition, etc., were freely preached in this kingdom. Now, what shall the people of God do in such a case? Yield to every breath, to every puff of false doctrine? or rather try it by the word of God, and if it be not agreeable thereunto, cast it out like salt that hath lost its savour? Must not the people take care that they be not seduced? Must they not "beware of false prophets, which come unto them in sheep's clothing, but inwardly are ravening wolves?" And how shall they do this? what way remains but a trying their doctrine by the rule? In these evil days wherein we live, I hear many daily complaining that there is such difference and contrariety among preachers, they know not what to do nor scarce what to believe. My answer is, Do but your own duty, and this trouble is at an end. Is there any contrariety in the book of God? Pin not your faith upon men's opinions; the Bible is the touchstone.   That there is such diversity amongst teachers is their fault, who should think all the same thing; but that this is so troublesome to you is your own fault, for neglecting your duty of trying all things by the word. Alas! you are in a miserable condition, if you have all this while relied on the authority of men in heavenly things.   He that builds his faith upon preachers, though they preach nothing but truth, and he pretend to believe it, hath indeed no faith at all, but a wavering opinion, built upon a rotten foundation.   Whatever, then, is taught you, you must go with it "to the law and to the testimony: if they speak not according to this word, it is because there is no light in them," Isa. viii. 20.   Yea, the Bereans are highly extolled for searching whether the doctrine concerning our Saviour preached by St Paul were so or no, Acts xvii. 11; agreeably to the precept of the same preacher, 1 Thess. v. 21, " Prove all things, hold fast that which is good;" as also to that of St John, 1 Epist. iv. 1, " Beloved, believe not every spirit, but try the spirits whether they be of God; because many false prophets are gone out into the world."   Prophets, then, must be tried before they be trusted.   Now, the reason of this holds still.   There are many false teachers abroad in the world; wherefore try every one, try his spirit, his spiritual gift of teaching, and that by the word of God.   And here you have a clear rule laid down how you may extricate yourselves from the former perplexity. Nay, St Paul himself, speaking to understanding Christians, requires them to judge of it: 1 Cor. x. 15, " I speak as to wise men; judge ye what I say."   Hence are those cautions that the people should look that none do seduce them, Matt. xxiv. 4; to which end they must have their souls "exercised" in the word of God, "to discern both good and evil," Heb. v. 14.   Thus, also, in one place Christ biddeth his followers hear the Pharisees, and do what they should command, because they sat in Moses' chair, Matt. xxiii. 2, 3; and yet in another place gives them a caution to beware of the doctrine of the Pharisees, Matt. xvi. 12. It remaineth, then, that the people are bound to hear those who possess the place of teaching in the church, but withal they must beware that it contain nothing of the old leaven; to which end they must try it by the word of God; when, as St Paul prayeth for the Philippians, " their love may abound yet more and more in knowledge, and all judgment, that they may approve things that are excellent," Phil. i. 9, 10.   Unless ministers will answer for all those souls they shall mislead, and excuse them before God at the day of trial, they ought not to debar them from trying their doctrine. Now this they cannot do; for " if the blind lead the blind, both shall fall into the pit" of destruction.   And here I might have just occasion of complaint:—1. Of the superstitious pride of the late clergy of this land, who could not endure to have their doctrine tried by their auditors, crying to poor men, with the Pharisees, John ix. 34, "'Ye were altogether born in sins, and do ye teach us?' A pretty world it is like to be, when the sheep will needs teach their pastors!" Nothing would serve them but a blind submission to the loose dictates of their cobweb homilies. He saw farther, sure, in the darkness of Popery, who contended that a whole general council ought to give place to a simple layman urging Scripture or speaking reason. Now, surely this is very far from that gentleness, meekness, and aptness to teach, which St Paul requireth in a man of God, a minister of the gospel. 2. The negligence of the people, also, might here come under a just reproof, who have not laboured to discern the voice of the hireling from that of the true shepherd, but have promiscuously followed the new-fangledness and heretical errors of every time-serving starver of souls. Whence proceedeth all that misery the land now groaneth under, but that we have had a people willing to be led by a corrupted clergy, freely drinking in the poison wherewith they are tainted? "The prophets prophesied falsely, the priests bare rule by their means, the people loved to have it so; but what shall we now do in the end thereof?" Who could ever have thought that the people of England would have yielded a willing ear to so many popish errors, and an obedient shoulder to such a heavy burden of superstitions, as in a few years were instilled into them, and laid upon them voluntarily, by their own sinful neglect, ensnaring their consciences by the omission of this duty we insist upon, of examining by the word what is taught unto them?[1] But this is no place for complaints. And this is a second thing which the people, distinct from their pastors, may do for their own edification. Now, whether they do this privately, every one apart, or by assembling more together, is altogether indifferent. And that this was observed by private Christians in the primitive times is very apparent.

Come we, in the third place, to what either their duty ·binds them to, or otherwise by the word they are allowed to do, in sacred performances having reference to others. Look, then, in general upon those things we find them tied unto by virtue of special precept, such as are, to warn the unruly, comfort the feeble-minded, support the weak, 1 Thess. v. 14; to admonish and reprove offending brethren, Matt. xviii. 15; to instruct the ignorant, John iv. 29, Acts xviii. 26; to exhort the negligent, Heb. iii. 13, x. 24, 25; to comfort the afflicted, 1 Thess. v. 11; to restore him that falleth, Gal. vi. 1; to visit the sick, Matt. xxv. 36, 40; to reconcile those that are at variance, Matt. v. 9; to contend for the faith, Jude 3, 1 Pet.

---

[1] "Vos facite quod scriptum est, ut uno dicente, omnes examinent, me ergo dicente quod sentio, vos discernite et examinate."—Orig. in Josh. Hom. xxi.

iii. 15; to pray for the sinner not unto death, 1 John v. 16; to edify one another in their most holy faith, Jude 20; to speak to themselves in psalms, and hymns, and spiritual songs, Eph. v. 19; to be ready to answer every man in giving account of their faith, Col. iv. 6; to mark them that make divisions, Rom. xvi. 17; with innumerable others to the like purpose. It remaineth for them to consider, secondly, in particular, what course they may take, beyond private conference between man and man, by indiction of time or place for the fulfilling of what, by these precepts and the like, is of them required. To which I answer,—

First, Lawful things must be done *lawfully.* If any unlawful circumstance attend the performance of a lawful action, it vitiates the whole work; for " bonum oritur ex integris." For instance, to reprove an offender is a Christian duty, but for a private man to do it in the public congregation whilst the minister is preaching, were, instead of a good act, a foul crime, being a notorious disturbance of church decency and order.

Secondly, That for a *public, formal, ministerial teaching,* two things are required in the teacher:—*first, Gifts from God; secondly, Authority* from the church (I speak now of ordinary cases). He that wants either is no true pastor. For the first, God sends none upon an employment but whom he fits with gifts for it. 1. Not one command in the Scripture made to teachers; 2. Not one rule for their direction; 3. Not one promise to their endeavours; 4. Not any end of their employment; 5. Not one encouragement to their duty; 6. Not one reproof for their negligence; 7. Not the least intimation of their reward,—but cuts off ungifted, idle pastors from any true interest in the calling. And for the others, that want authority from the church, neither ought they to undertake any formal act properly belonging to the ministry, such as is solemn teaching of the word; for,—1. They are none of Christ's officers, Eph. iv. 11. 2. They are expressly forbidden it, Jer. xxiii. 21; Heb. v. 4. 3. The blessing on the word is promised only to sent teachers, Rom. x. 14, 15. 4. If to be gifted be to be called, then,—(1.) Every one might undertake so much in sacred duties as he fancies himself to be able to perform; (2.) Children (as they report of Athanasius[1]) might baptize; (3.) Every common Christian might administer the communion. But endless are the arguments that might be multiplied against this fancy. In a word, if our Saviour Christ be the God of order, he hath left his church to no such confusion.

Thirdly, That to appoint *time* and *place* for the doing of that which God hath appointed indefinitely to be done in time and place, rather commends than vitiates the duty. So did Job's friends in the duty of

[1] Eusebius, Ruf.

comforting the afflicted; they made an appointment together to come and comfort him, Job ii. 11; and so did they, Zech. viii. 21; and so did David, Ps. cxix. 62.

Fourthly, There is much difference between *opening* or interpreting the word, and *applying* the word upon the advantage of such an approved interpretation; as also between an authoritative act, or doing a thing by virtue of special office, and a charitable act, or doing a thing out of a motion of Christian love.

Fifthly, It may be observed concerning gifts,—

1. That the gifts and graces of God's Spirit are of two sorts, some being bestowed for the sanctification of God's people, some for the edification of his church; some of a private allay, looking primarily inwards to the saving of his soul on whom they are bestowed (though in their fruits also they have a relation and habitude to others), other some aiming at the commonwealth or profit of the whole church as such. Of the first sort are those mentioned Gal. v. 22, 23, " The fruit of the Spirit is love, joy, peace," etc., with all other graces that are necessary to make the man of God perfect in all holiness and the fear of the Lord; the other are those χαρίσματα πνευματικά, spiritual gifts of teaching, praying, prophesying, mentioned 1 Cor. xiv., and in other places.

2. That all these gifts, coming down from the Father of lights, are given by the same Spirit, " dividing to every man severally as he will," 1 Cor. xii. 11. He is not tied, in the bestowing of his gifts, to any sort, estate, calling, or condition of men; but worketh them freely, as it pleaseth him, in whom he will. The Spirit there mentioned is that God which " worketh all things after the counsel of his own will," Eph. i. 11; they are neither deserved by our goodness nor obtained by our endeavours.

3. That the end why God bestoweth these gifts on any is merely that, within the bounds of their own calling (in which they are circumscribed, 1 Cor. i. 26), they should use them to his glory and the edification of his church; for " the manifestation of the Spirit is given to every man to profit withal," 1 Cor. xii. 7. Christ gives none of his talents to be bound up in napkins, but expects his own with increase.[1]

And from these considerations it is easily discernible both what the people of God, distinct from their pastors, in a well-ordered church, may do in this kind whereof we treat, and how. In general, then, I assert,—

That, for the improving of knowledge, the increasing of Christian charity, for the furtherance of a strict and holy communion of that spiritual love and amity which ought to be amongst the brethren, they may of their own accord assemble together, to consider one

[1] Eccles. xii. 9.

another, to provoke unto love and good works, to stir up the gifts that are in them, yielding and receiving mutual consolation by the fruits of their most holy faith.

Now, because there be many Uzzahs amongst us, who have an itching desire to be fingering of the ark, thinking more highly of themselves than they ought to think, and, like the ambitious sons of Levi, taking too much upon them, it will not be amiss to give two cautions, deducted from the former rules:—

First, That they do not, under a pretence of Christian liberty and freedom of conscience, cast away all brotherly amity, and cut themselves off from the communion of the church.   Christ hath not purchased a liberty for any to rend his body.   They will prove at length to be no duties of piety which break the sacred bonds of charity.

Men ought not, under a pretence of congregating themselves to serve their God, separate from their brethren, neglecting the public assemblies; as was the manner of some rebuked by the apostle, Heb. x. 25.   There be peculiar blessings and transcendent privileges an-nexed to public assemblies, which accompany not private men to their recesses.   The sharp-edged sword becomes more keen when set on by a skilful master of the assemblies; and when the water of the word flows there, the Spirit of God moves upon the face thereof, to make it effectual in our hearts.   " What! despise ye the church of God?" 1 Cor. xi. 22.

Secondly, As the ministry, so also ought the ministers to have that regard, respect, and obedience, which is due to their labours in that sacred calling.   Would we could not too frequently see more puffed up with the conceit of their own gifts, into a contempt of the most learned and pious pastors!—these are "spots in your feasts of charity, clouds without water, carried about of winds."   It must, doubtless, be an evil root that bringeth forth such bitter fruit.   Wherefore, let not our brethren fall into this condemnation, lest there be an evil report raised by them that are without; but "remember them which have the rule over you, who have spoken unto you the word of God," Heb. xiii. 7.   There is no greater evidence of the heavenly improvement you make by your recesses than that you obey them that are guides unto you, and submit yourselves: for "they watch for your souls, as they that must give an account, that they may do it with joy, and not with grief: for that is unprofitable for you," verse 17.   Let not them who despise a faithful, painful minister in public, flatter themselves with hope of a blessing on their endeavours in private.   Let them pretend what they will, they have not an equal respect unto all God's ordinances.   Wherefore, that the coming together in this sort may be for the better, and not for the worse, observe these things:—

Now, for what gifts (that are, as before, freely bestowed) whose exercise is permitted unto such men so assembled; I mean in a private family, or two or three met ὁμοθυμαδόν, in one.

And first we may name the gift of *prayer*, whose exercise must not be exempted from such assemblies, if any be granted. These are the times wherein the Spirit of grace and of supplications is promised to be poured out upon the Jerusalem of God, Zech. xii. 10. Now, God having bestowed the gift, and requiring the duty, his people ought not to be hindered in the performance of it. Are all those precepts to pray, in the Scriptures, only for our closets? When the church was in distress for the imprisonment of Peter, there was a meeting at the house of Mary, the mother of John, Acts xii. 12. "Many were gathered together praying," saith the text;—a sufficient warrant for the people of God in like cases. The churches are in no less distress now than at that time; and in some congregations the ministers are so oppressed that publicly they dare not, in others so corrupted that they will not, pray for the prosperity of Jerusalem. Now, truly, it were a disconsolate thing for any one of God's servants to say, "During all these straits, I never joined with any of God's children in the pouring out of my prayer in the behalf of his church:" neither can I see how this can possibly be prevented but by the former means; to which add the counsel of St Paul, "Speaking to themselves in psalms and hymns and spiritual songs, singing and making melody in their hearts unto the Lord," Eph. v. 19.

Secondly, They may exercise the gifts of *wisdom, knowledge,* and *understanding* in the ways of the Lord; comforting, strengthening, and encouraging each other with the same consolations and promises which, by the benefit of the public ministry, they have received from the word. Thus, in time of distress, the prophet Malachi tells us that " they that feared the LORD spake often one to another, and the LORD hearkened, and heard," etc., chap. iii. 16;—comforting, as it appears, one another in the promises of God made unto his church, against the flourishing of the wicked and overflowing of ungodliness, the persecution of tyrants and impurity of transgressors.

Thirdly, They may make *use of " the tongue of the learned"* (if given unto them) to "speak a word in season to him that is weary," Isa. l. 4; for being commanded to "confess their faults one to another," James v. 16, they have power also to apply to them that are penitent the promises of mercy. We should never be commanded to open our wounds to them who have no balm to pour into them; he shall have cold comfort who seeks for counsel from a dumb man. So that in this, and the like cases, they may apply unto and instruct one another in the word of God; doing it as a charitable duty, and not as out of necessary function, even as Aquila and Priscilla expounded unto Apollos the word of God more perfectly than he knew it before, Acts xviii. 24–26. In sum, and not to enlarge this discourse with any more particulars, the people of God are allowed all quiet and peaceable means, whereby they may help each other forward in the knowledge of godliness and the way towards heaven.

Now, for the close of this discourse, I will remove some objections that I have heard godly men, and men not unlearned, lay against it, out of a zeal (not unlike that of Joshua for Moses' sake) [for] the constitute pastor's sake; to whom, though I might briefly answer, with Moses, "'Would God all the LORD's people were prophets!'—I heartily wish that every one of them had such a plentiful measure of spiritual endowments that they might become wise unto salvation, above many of their teachers;" in which vote I make no doubt but every one will concur with me who has the least experimental knowledge what a burden upon the shoulders, what a grief unto the soul of a minister knowing and desiring to discharge his duty, is an ignorant congregation (of which, thanks to our prelates, pluralists, non-residents, homilies, service-book, and ceremonies, we have too many in this kingdom; the many, also, of our ministers in this church taking for their directory the laws and penalties of men, informing what they should not do if they would avoid their punishment, and not the precepts of God, what they should as their duty do if they meant to please him, and knowing there was no statute whereon they might be sued for (pardon the expression) the dilapidation of souls: so their own houses were ceiled, they cared not at all though the church of God lay waste);—I say, though I might thus answer, with opening my desire for the increasing of knowledge among the people, of which I take this to be an effectual means, yet I will give brief answers to the several objections:—

Objection 1. "Then this seems to favour all allowance of licentious *conventicles*, which in all places the laws have condemned, and learned men in all ages have abhorred, as the seminaries of faction and schism in the church of God."

Ans. That (under correction) I conceive the law layeth hold of none, as peccant in such a kind, but only those who have pre-declared themselves to be opposers of the worship of God in the public assemblies of that church wherein they live. Now, the patronage of any such I before rejected. Neither do I conceive that they ought at all to be allowed the benefit of private meetings who wilfully abstain from the public congregations, so long as the true worship of God is held forth in them. Yea, how averse I have ever been from that kind of confused licentiousness in any church, I have some while since declared, in an answer (drawn up for my own and private friends' satisfaction) to the arguments of the Remonstrants in their Apology, and replies to Vedelius, with other treatises, for such a "liberty of prophesying," as they term it. If, then, the law account only such assemblies to be conventicles wherein the assemblers contemn and despise the service of God in public, I have not spoken one word in favour of them. And for that canon which was mounted against them, whether intentionally, in the first institution of it, it was moulded and framed against Anabaptists or no, I cannot tell; but this I am sure, that in the discharge of it, it did execution oftentimes upon such as had Christ's precept and promise to warrant their assembling, Matt. xviii. 19, 20. Not to contend about words, would to God that which is good might not be persecuted under odious appellations, and called evil when it is otherwise; so to expose it to the tyrannical oppression of the enemies of the gospel! The thing itself, rightly understood, can scarce be condemned of any who envies not the salvation of souls. They that would banish the gospel from our *houses* would not much care if it were gone from our *hearts;* from our houses, I say, for it is all one whether these duties be performed in one family or a collection of more. Some one is bigger than ten others; shall their assembling to perform what is lawful for that one be condemned for a conventicle? Where is the law for that? or what is there in all this more than God required of his ancient people, as I showed before? Or must a master of a family cease praying in his family, and instructing his children and servants in the ways of the Lord, for fear of being counted a preacher in a tub? Things were scarcely carried with an equal hand for the kingdom of Christ, when orders came forth on the one side to give liberty to the profane multitude to assemble themselves at heathenish sports, with bestial exclamations, on the Lord's own day; and on the other, to punish them who durst gather themselves together for prayer or the singing of psalms. But I hope, through God's blessing, we shall be for ever quit of all such ecclesiastical discipline as must be exercised according to the interest of idle drones, whom it concerneth to see that there be none to try or examine their doctrine, or of superstitious innovators, who desire to obtrude their fancies upon the unwary people. Whence comes it that we have such an innumerable multitude of ignorant, stupid souls, unacquainted with the very *principles* of religion, but from the discountenancing of these means of increasing knowledge by men who would not labour to do it themselves? O that we could see the many swearers, and drunkards, and Sabbath-breakers, etc., in this nation, guilty only of this crime! Would the kingdom were so happy, the church so holy!

Obj. 2. "Men are *apt to pride themselves in their gifts,* and flatter themselves in their performances, so that let them approach as nigh as the tabernacle, and you shall quickly have them encroaching upon the priest's office also, and, by an overweening of their own endeavours, create themselves pastors in separate congregations.

Ans. It cannot be but offences will come, so long as there is malice in Satan and corruption in men. There is no doubt but there is danger of some such thing; but hereof the liberty mentioned is not the cause, but an accidental occasion only, no way blamable. Gifts must not be condemned because they may be abused. God-fearing men will remember Korah, knowing, as one says well, that "Uzzah had better ventured the falling than the fingering of the ark." They that truly love their souls will not suffer themselves to be carried away by false conceit, so far as to help to overthrow the very constitution of any church by confusion, or the flourishing of it by ignorance; both which would certainly follow such courses. Knowledge if alone puffeth up, but joined to charity it edifieth.

Obj. 3. "But may not this be a means for men to *vent and broach their own private fancies unto others?* to foment and cherish errors in one another? to give false interpretations of the word, there being no way to prevent it?"

Ans. For interpreting of the word I speak not, but applying of it, being rightly interpreted. And for the rest, would to God the complaints were not true of those things that have for divers years in this church been done publicly and outwardly according to order! But, that no inconvenience arise from hence, the care rests on them to whom the dispensation of the word is committed, whose sedulous endeavour to reprove and convince all unsound doctrine, not agreeing to the form of wholesome words, is the sovereign and only remedy to cure, or means to prevent, this evil. For the close of all, we may observe that those who are most offended and afraid lest others should encroach upon their callings are, for the most part, such as have almost deserted it themselves, neglecting their own employment, when they are the busiest of mortals in things of this world. To conclude, then, for what I have delivered in this particular, I conceive that I have the judgment and practice of the whole church of Scotland, agreeable to the word of God, for my warrant. Witness the act of their assembly at Edinburgh, anno 1641, wherewith the learned Rutherford concludes his defence of their discipline, with whose words I will shut up this discourse: "Our assembly, also, commandeth godly conference at all occasional meetings, or as God's providence shall dispose, as the word of God commandeth, providing none invade the pastor's office, to preach the word, who are not called thereunto by God and his church."

Τῷ Θεῷ ἀριστομεγίστῳ δόξα.

ESHCOL;

A CLUSTER OF THE FRUIT OF CANAAN,

BROUGHT TO THE BORDERS FOR THE ENCOURAGEMENT OF THE SAINTS TRAVELLING
THITHERWARD, WITH THEIR FACES TOWARDS ZION:

OR,

RULES OF DIRECTION FOR THE WALKING OF THE SAINTS IN FELLOWSHIP,
ACCORDING TO THE ORDER OF THE GOSPEL.

———

For so is the will of God, that with well-doing ye may put to silence the ignorance of foolish
men.—1 PET. ii. 15.

PREFATORY NOTE.

THIS little book was published in 1647, soon after Owen had formed a church on the principles of Independency at Coggeshall, in Essex. It is designed to exhibit scriptural rules on the subject of ecclesiastical fellowship and discipline; the first part containing seven rules, on the duties of members of a church to their pastor; and the second fifteen, on their duties to one another. It was prepared by our author after he had adopted Congregational views, but is of such a nature as to be applicable and useful under any form of ecclesiastical polity. Each rule is established by a body of evidence from Scripture, and is followed by a general explanation. Several editions of this treatise have appeared; and we cannot wonder at its favourable reception with the religious public, for it is as remarkable as any work of our author, for deep piety, sound judgment, lucid arrangement, and a comprehensive knowledge of Scripture, and forms a manual on church-fellowship which is to this day unsurpassed. One feature of it can hardly escape the reader's attention,—Owen is here, for once, a master in the art of condensation.—ED.

TO THE READER.

THERE are, Christian reader, certain principles in church affairs generally consented unto by all men aiming at reformation and the furtherance of the power of godliness therein, however diversified among themselves by singular persuasions, or distinguished by imposed and assumed names and titles. Some of these, though not here mentioned, are the bottom and foundation of this following collection of rules for our walking in the fellowship of the gospel; amongst which these four are the principal:—

First, That particular congregations or assemblies of believers, gathered into one body for a participation of the ordinances of Jesus Christ, under officers of their own, are of divine institution.

Secondly, That every faithful believer is bound, by virtue of positive precepts, to join himself to some such single congregation, having the notes and marks whereby a true church may be known and discerned.

Thirdly, That every man's own voluntary consent and submission to the ordinances of Christ, in that church whereunto he is joined, is required for his union therewith and fellowship therein.

Fourthly, That it is convenient that all believers of one place should join themselves in one congregation, unless, through their being too numerous, they are by common consent distinguished into more; which order cannot be disturbed without danger, strife, emulation, and breach of love.

These principles, evident in the word, clear in themselves, and owned in the main by all pretending to regular church reformation, not liable to any colourable exception from the Scripture or pure antiquity, were supposed and taken for granted at the collection of these ensuing rules.

The apostolical direction and precept in such cases is, that "whereunto we have attained, we should walk according to the same rule;" unto whose performance the promise annexed is, that "if any one be otherwise minded, God will also reveal that unto him." The remaining differences about church order and discipline are for continuance so ancient, and by the disputes of men made so involved and intricate, the parties at variance so prejudiced and engaged, that although all things of concernment appear to me, as to others both consenting with me and dissenting from me, clear in the Scriptures, yet I have little hopes of the accomplishment of the promise in revelation, of the truth as yet contested about, in men differently minded, until the obedience of walking suitably and answerably to the same rules agreed on be more sincerely accomplished.

This persuasion is the more firmly fixed on me every day, because I see men, for the most part, to spend their strength and time more in the opposing of those things wherein others differ from them than in the practice of those which by themselves and others are owned as of the most necessary concernment. To recall the minds of men,—at least of those who, having not much light to judge of things under debate (especially considering their way of handling in this disputing age), may have yet much heat and love towards the ways of gospel obedience,— from the entanglements of controversies about church affairs, and to engage them into a serious, humble performance of those duties which are, by the express command of Jesus Christ, incumbent on them in what way of order they walk, are these leaves designed.   I shall only add, that though the ensuing rules or directions may be observed, and the duties prescribed performed with much beauty and many advantages by those who are engaged in some reformed church society; yet they are, if not all of them, yet for the most part, such as are to be the constant practice of all Christians in their daily conversation, though they are not persuaded of the necessity of any such reformation as is pleaded for.   And herein I am fully resolved that the practice of any one duty here mentioned, by any one soul before neglected, shall be an abundant recompense for the publishing my name with these papers, savouring so little of those ornaments of art or learning which in things that come to public view men desire to hold out.

ESHCOL;

A CLUSTER OF THE FRUIT OF CANAAN.

Rules of walking in fellowship, with reference to the pastor or minister that watcheth for our souls.

RULE I. THE word and all ordinances dispensed in the administration to him committed, by virtue of ministerial authority, are to be diligently attended and submitted unto, with ready obedience in the Lord.

1 Cor. iv. 1, " Let a man so account of us, as of the ministers of Christ, and stewards of the mysteries of God."

2 Cor. v. 18, 20, " God hath given to us the ministry of reconciliation. Now then we are ambassadors for Christ, as though God did beseech you by us." Chap. iv. 7, " We have this treasure in earthen vessels, that the excellency of the power may be of God, and not of us." See chap. vi. 1.

Gal. iv. 14, " Ye received me as an angel of God, even as Christ Jesus."

2 Thess. iii. 14, " If any man obey not our word, note that man, and have no company with him."

Heb. xiii. 7, 17, " Remember them which have the rule over you, who have spoken unto you the word of God. Obey them that have the rule over you, and submit yourselves: for they watch for your souls, as they that must give account, that they may do it with joy, and not with grief: for that is unprofitable for you."

EXPLICATION I. There is a twofold power for the dispensing of the word:—1. Δύναμις, or ability; 2. ᾿Εξουσία, or authority. The first, with the attending qualifications, mentioned and recounted 1 Tim. iii. 2–7, Tit. i. 6–9, and many other places, is required to be previously in those, as bestowed on them, who are to be called to office of ministration: and may be, in several degrees and measures, in such as are never set apart thereunto, who thereby are warranted to declare the gospel, when called by the providence of God thereunto,

Rom. x. 14, 15; for the work of preaching unto the conversion of souls being a moral duty, comprised under that general precept of doing good unto all, the appointment of some to the performance of that work, by the way of office, doth not enclose it.

The second, or authority, proper to them who orderly are set apart thereunto, ariseth from,—

1. Christ's institution of the office, Eph. iv. 11.

2. God's providential designation of the persons, Matt. ix. 38.

3. The church's call, election, appointment, acceptation, submission, Gal. iv. 14; Acts xiv. 23; 1 Thess. v. 12, 13; Acts vi. 3; 2 Cor. viii. 5: which do not give them dominion over the faith of believers, 2 Cor. i. 24, nor make them lords over God's heritage, 1 Pet. v. 3; but intrust them with a stewardly power in the house of God, 1 Cor. iv. 1, 2,—that is, the peculiar flock over which, in particular, they are made overseers, Acts xx. 28. Of whom the word is to be received,—

(1.) As the truth of God; as also from all others speaking according to gospel order in his name.

(2.) As the truth held out with ministerial authority to them in particular, according to the institution of Christ.

Want of a due consideration of these things lies at the bottom of all that negligence, carelessness, sloth, and wantonness in hearing, which have possessed many professors in these days. There is nothing but a respect to the truth and authority of God in the administration of the word that will establish the minds of men in a sober and profitable attending unto it. Neither are men weary of hearing until they are weary of practising.

Motives to the observance of this rule are:—

1. The name wherein they speak and administer, 2 Cor. v. 20.

2. The work which they do, 1 Cor. iii. 9; 2 Cor. vi. 1; 1 Tim. iv. 16.

3. The return that they make, Heb. xiii. 17.

4. The regard that the Lord hath of them in his employment, Matt. x. 40, 41; Luke x. 16.

5. The account that hearers must make of the word dispensed by them, 2 Chron. xxxvi. 15, 16; Prov. i. 22–29, xiii. 13; Luke x. 16; Mark iv. 24; Heb. ii. 1–3, iv. 2.

RULE II. His conversation is to be observed and diligently followed, so far as he walks in the steps of Jesus Christ.

1 Cor. iv. 16, "I beseech you, be ye followers of me." Chap. xi. 1, "Be ye followers of me, even as I also am of Christ."

Heb. xiii. 7, "Remember them which have the rule over you, who have spoken unto you the word of God: whose faith follow, considering the end of their conversation."

2 Thess. iii. 7, "Yourselves know how ye ought to follow us: for we behaved not ourselves disorderly among you."

Phil. iii. 17, "Brethren, be followers together of me, and mark them which walk so as ye have us for an ensample."

1 Tim. iv. 12, "Be thou an example of the believers, in word, in conversation, in charity, in spirit, in faith, in purity."

1 Pet. v. 3, "Be ensamples to the flock."

EXPLICATION II. That an exemplary conversation was ever required in the dispensers of holy things, both under the Old Testament and New, is apparent. The glorious vestments of the old ministering priests, the soundness and integrity of their person, without maim, imperfection, or blemish, Urim and Thummim, with many other ornaments, though primitively typical of Jesus Christ, yet did not obscurely set out the purity and holiness required in the administrators themselves, Zech. iii. 4. In the New, the shining of their light in all good works, Matt. v. 16, is eminently exacted; and this not only that no offence be taken at the ways of God, and his worship by them administered (as hath fallen out in the Old Testament, 1 Sam. ii. 17; and in the New, Phil. iii. 18, 19), but also that those who are without may be convinced, 1 Tim. iii. 7, and the churches directed in the practice of all the will and mind of God by them revealed, as in the places cited A pastor's life should be vocal; sermons must be practised as well as preached. Though Noah's workmen built the ark, yet themselves were drowned. God will not accept of the tongue where the devil hath the soul. Jesus did "do and teach," Acts i. 1. If a man teach uprightly and walk crookedly, more will fall down in the night of his life than he built in the day of his doctrine.

Now, as to the completing of the exemplary life of a minister, it is required that the principle of it be that of the life of Christ in him, Gal. ii. 20, that when he hath taught others he be not himself "a cast-away," 1 Cor. ix. 27; with which he hath a spiritual understanding, and light given him into the counsel of God, which he is to communicate, 1 John v. 20; 1 Cor. ii. 12, 16; 2 Cor. iv. 6, 7;—and that the course of it be singular, Matt. v. 46, Luke vi. 32; whereunto so many eminent qualifications of the person and duties of conversation are required, 1 Tim. ii. 2–7, etc., Titus i. 6–9;—and his aim to be exemplar to the glory of God, 1 Tim. iv. 12. So is their general course and the end of their faith to be eyed, Heb. xiii. 7. And their infirmities, whilst really such, and appearing through the manifold temptations whereunto they are in these days exposed, or imposed on them through the zeal of their adversaries that contend against them, [are] to be covered with love, Gal. iv. 13, 14. And this men will do when they conscientiously consider that even the lives of their teachers are an ordinance of God, for their relief under temptations, and provocation unto holiness, zeal, meekness, and self-denial.

RULE III. Prayer and supplications are continually to be made on his behalf for assistance and success in the work committed to him. Eph. vi. 18–20, "Praying always with all prayer and supplication in the Spirit for me, that utterance may be given unto me, that I may open my mouth boldly, to make known the mystery of the gospel, for which I am an ambassador." 2 Thess. iii. 1, 2, "Brethren, pray for us, that the word of the Lord may have free course and be glorified; and that we may be delivered from unreasonable and wicked men ;" 1 Thess. v. 25. Col. iv. 3, "Pray also for us, that God would open unto us a door of utterance, to speak the mystery of Christ;" Heb. xiii. 18.

Acts xii. 5, " Prayer was made without ceasing of the church unto God for him;" Heb. xiii. 7.

EXPLICATION III. The greatness of the work (for which who is sufficient? 2 Cor. ii. 16);—the strength of the opposition which lies against it, 1 Cor. xvi. 9; Rev. xii. 12; 2 Tim. iv. 3–5;—the concernment of men's souls therein, Acts xx. 26–28; Heb. xiii. 7; 1 Tim. iv. 16;—the conviction which is to be brought upon the world thereby, Ezek. ii. 5; 1 Cor. i. 23, 24; 2 Cor. iii. 15, 16;—its aim and tendency to the glory of God in Christ,—call aloud for the most effectual daily concurrence of the saints in their supplications for their supportment. That these are to be for assistance, encouragement, abilities, success, deliverance, and protection, is proved in the rule. As their temptations are multiplied, so ought prayers in their behalf. They have many curses of men against them, Jer. xv. 10;—it is hoped that God hears some prayers for them. When many are not ashamed to revile them in public, some ought to be ashamed not to remember them in private. Motives:—

1. The word will doubtless be effectual, when ability for its administration is a return of prayers, Acts x. 1–6.

2. The minister's failing is the people's punishment, Amos viii. 11, 12; Isa. xxx. 20.

3. His prayers are continually for the church, Isa. lxii. 6, 7; Rom. i. 9, etc.

4. That for which he stands in so much need of prayers is the saints' good, and not peculiarly his own. Help him who carries the burden, Eph. vi. 18–20; Phil ii. 17; Col. i. 24.

RULE IV. Reverential estimation of him, with submission unto him for his work's sake.

1 Cor. iv. 1, "Let a man so account of us, as of the ministers of Christ, and stewards of the mysteries of God."

1 Thess. v. 12, 13, "We beseech you, brethren, to know them which labour among you, and are over you in the Lord, and admonish you; and to esteem them very highly in love for their work's sake."

1 Tim. v. 17, "Let the elders that rule well be counted worthy of double honour, especially they who labour in the word and doctrine."

1 Pet. v. 5, "Submit yourselves unto the elders."

Heb. xiii. 17, "Obey them that have the rule over you, and submit yourselves."

EXPLICATION IV. The respect and estimation here required is civil, the motive sacred ; whence the honour of the minister is the grace of the church, and the regard to him a gospel duty acceptable to God in Christ, 1 Tim. v. 17. Honour and reverence is due only to eminency in some kind or other. This is given to pastors by their employment; proved by their titles. They are called "angels," Rev. i. 20; Heb. xii. 22;—"bishops," or overseers, Ezek. iii. 17; Acts xx. 28 ; Titus i. 7;—"ambassadors," 2 Cor. v. 20;—"stewards," 1 Cor. iv. 1; —"men of God," 1 Sam. ii. 27; 1 Tim. vi. 11;—"rulers," Heb. xiii. 7, 17;—"lights," Matt. v. 14;—"salt," Matt. v. 13;—"fathers," 1 Cor. iv. 15. And by many more such-like terms are they described. If under these notions they honour God as they ought, God will also honour them as he hath promised; and his people are in conscience to esteem them highly for their work's sake. But if any of them be fallen angels, thrown-down stars, negligent bishops, treacherous ambassadors, lordly revelling stewards, tyrannical or foolish rulers, blind guides, unsavoury salt, insatiate dogs, the Lord and his people shall abhor them and cut them off in a month, Zech. xi. 8.

RULE V. Maintenance for them and their families, by the administration of earthly things suitable to the state and condition of the churches, is required from their flocks.

1 Tim. v. 17, 18, "Let the elders that rule well be counted worthy of double honour, especially they who labour in the word and doctrine. For the Scripture saith, Thou shalt not muzzle the ox that treadeth out the corn. And, The labourer is worthy of his reward."

Gal. vi. 6, 7, "Let him that is taught in the word communicate unto him that teacheth in all good things. Be not deceived; God is not mocked: for whatsoever a man soweth, that shall he also reap."

1 Cor. ix. 7, 9–11, 13, 14, "Who goeth a warfare any time at his own charges? who planteth a vineyard, and eateth not of the fruit thereof? who feedeth a flock, and eateth not of the milk of the flock? It is written in the law of Moses, Thou shalt not muzzle the mouth of the ox that treadeth out the corn. Doth God take care for oxen? or saith he it altogether for our sakes? For our sakes, no

doubt, this is written: that he that ploweth should plow in hope; and that he that thresheth in hope should be partaker of his hope. If we have sown unto you spiritual things, is it a great thing if we shall reap your carnal things? Do ye not know that they which minister about holy things live of the things of the temple? and they which wait at the altar are partakers with the altar? Even so hath the Lord ordained that they which preach the gospel should live of the gospel." Matt. x. 9, 10, "Provide neither gold, nor silver, nor brass in your purses, nor scrip for your journey, neither two coats, neither shoes, nor yet staves: for the workman is worthy of his meat."

Add to these and the like places the analogy of the primitive allowance in the church of the Jews.

EXPLICATION V. It is a promise to the church under the gospel, that "kings should be her nursing fathers, and queens her nursing mothers," Isa. xlix. 23. To such it belongs principally to provide food and protection for those committed to them. The fruit of this promise the churches in many ages have enjoyed; laws by supreme and kingly power have been enacted, giving portions and granting privileges to churches and their pastors. It is so in many places in the days wherein we live. On this ground, where equitable and righteous laws have allowed a supportment in earthly things to the pastors of churches, arising from such as may receive spiritual benefit by their labour in the gospel, it is thankfully to be accepted and embraced, as an issue of God's providence for the good of his. Besides, our Saviour warranteth his disciples to take and eat of their things, by their consent, to whomsoever the word is preached, Luke x. 8. But it is not always thus; these things may sometimes fail: wherefore, the continual care, and frequently the burden, or rather labour of love, in providing for the pastors, lies, as in the rule, upon the churches themselves; which they are to do in such a manner as is suitable to the condition wherein they are, and the increase given them of God. This the whole in general, and each member in particular, is obliged unto; for which they have as motives,—

1. God's *appointment*, as in the texts cited.

2. The *necessity* of it. How shall he go on warfare if he be troubled about the necessities of this life? They are to give themselves wholly to the work of the ministry, 1 Tim. iv. 15.

Other works had need to be done for them.

3. The *equity* of the duty. Our Saviour and the apostles plead it out from grounds of equity and justice, and all kinds of laws and rules of righteousness, among all sorts of men, Matt. x. 9, 10, 1 Cor. ix. 10; allowing proportionable rectitude in the way of recompense to it with the wages of the labourer, which to detain is a crying sin,

James v. 4, 5,—the wretched endeavours of men of corrupt minds to rob and spoil them of all that, by the providence of God, on any other account, they are righteously possessed of.

RULE VI. Adhering to him and abiding by him in all trials and persecutions for the word.

2 Tim. iv. 16, "At my first answer no man stood with me, but all men forsook me: I pray God that it may not be laid to their charge." 2 Tim. i. 16–18, "The Lord give mercy unto the house of Onesiphorus; for he oft refreshed me, and was not ashamed of my chain: but, when he was in Rome, he sought me out very diligently, and found me. The Lord grant unto him that he may find mercy of the Lord in that day: and in how many things he ministered unto me at Ephesus, thou knowest very well."

EXPLICATION VI. A common cause should be carried on by common assistance. That which concerneth all should be supported by all. When persecution ariseth for the word's sake, generally it begins with the leaders, 1 Pet. iv. 17, 18. The common way to scatter the sheep is by smiting the shepherds, Zech. xiii. 7, 8. It is for the church's sake he is reviled and persecuted, 2 Tim. ii. 10, Col. i. 24; and, therefore, it is the church's duty to share with him and help to bear his burden. All the fault in scattering congregations hath not been in ministers; the people stood not by them in their trial. The Lord lay it not to their charge! The captain is betrayed, and forced to mean conditions with his enemy, who going on, with the assurance of being followed by his soldiers, looking back in the entrance of danger, he finds them all run away. In England, usually, no sooner had persecution laid hold of a minister, but the people willingly received another, perhaps a wolf, instead of a shepherd. Should a wife forsake her husband because he is come into trouble for her sake? When a known duty in such a relation is incumbent upon a man, is the crime of a backslider in spiritual things less? Whilst a pastor lives, if he suffer for the truth, the church cannot desert him, nor cease the performance of all required duties, without horrid contempt of the ordinances of Jesus Christ. This is a burden that is commonly laid on the shoulders of ministers, that for no cause whatsoever they must remove from their charge, when those that lay it on will oftentimes freely leave them and their ministry without any cause at all.

RULE VII. Gathering together in the assembly upon his appointment, with theirs joined with him.

Acts xiv. 27, "When they were come, and had gathered the church together."

These are some of the heads wherein the church's duty consisteth towards him or them that are set over it in the Lord, by all means giving them encouragement to the work; saying also unto them, "Take heed to the ministry ye have received in the Lord, that ye fulfil it," Col. iv. 17. For what concerneth other officers may easily be deduced hence by analogy and proportion.

Rules to be observed by those who walk in fellowship, and considered, to stir up their remembrance in things of mutual duty one towards another, which consisteth in,—

RULE I. Affectionate, sincere love in all things, without dissimulation towards one another, like that which Christ bare to his church.

John xv. 12, "This is my commandment, That ye love one another, as I have loved you."

John xiii. 34, 35, "A new commandment I give unto you, That ye love one another; as I have loved you, that ye also love one another. By this shall all men know that ye are my disciples, if ye have love one to another."

Rom. xiii. 8, "Owe no man any thing, but to love one another: for he that loveth another hath fulfilled the law."

Eph. v. 2, "Walk in love, as Christ also hath loved us."

1 Thess. iii. 12, "The Lord make you to increase and abound in love one toward another."

1 Thess. iv. 9, "Yourselves are taught of God to love one another."

1 Pet. i. 22, "Seeing ye have purified your souls in obeying the truth through the Spirit unto unfeigned love of the brethren, see that ye love one another with a pure heart fervently."

1 John iv. 21, "This commandment have we from him, That he who loveth God love his brother also."

Rom. xii. 10, "Be kindly affectioned one to another with brotherly love."

EXPLICATION I. Love is the fountain of all duties towards God and man, Matt. xxii. 37, the substance of all rules that concerneth the saints, the bond of communion, "the fulfilling of the law," Rom. xiii. 8–10, the advancement of the honour of the Lord Jesus, and the glory of the gospel. The primitive Christians had a proverbial speech, received, as they said, from Christ, "Never rejoice but when thou seest thy brother in love;" and it was common among the heathens concerning them, "See how they love one another!" from their readiness for the accomplishment of that royal precept of laying down their lives for their brethren. It is the fountain, rule, scope, aim, and fruit of gospel communion. And of no one thing of present performance is the doctrine of the Lord Jesus more eximious and eminent above all other directions than in this of mutual, intense, affectionate love amongst his followers; for which he gives them innumerable precepts, exhortations, and motives, but, above all, his own heavenly example. To treat of love, in its causes, nature, subject, fruits, effects, tendency, eminency, and exaltation, or but to repeat the places of Scripture wherein these things are mentioned, would not suit with our present intention; only, it may be plainly affirmed, that if there were no cause besides of reformation and walking in fellowship but this one,—that thereby the power and practice of this grace, shamefully, to the dishonour of Christ and his gospel, lost amongst those who call themselves Christians, might be recovered,—it were abundantly enough to give encouragement for the undertaking of it, notwithstanding any oppositions. Now, this love is a spiritual grace, wrought by the Holy Ghost, Gal. v. 22, in the hearts of believers, 1 Pet. i. 22, whereby their souls are carried out, 1 Thess. ii. 8, to seek the good of the children of God as such, Philem. 5, Eph. i. 15, Heb. xiii. 1, uniting the heart unto the object so beloved, attended with joy, delight, and complacency in their good. The motives unto love, and the grounds of its enforcement from,—

1. The *command of God*, and nature of the whole law, whereof love is the accomplishment, Lev. xix. 34; Matt. xix. 19; Rom. xiii. 9, 10:

2. The eternal, peculiar, distinguishing, *faithful love of God* towards believers, and the end aimed at therein by him, Ezek. xvi. 8; Deut. vii. 8, xxxiii. 3; Zeph. iii. 17; Rom. v. 8; Eph. i. 4:

3. The intense, *inexpressible love of Jesus Christ*, in his whole humiliation and laying down his life for us, expressly proposed as an example unto us, Cant. iii. 10; John xv. 13; Eph. v. 2:

4. The eminent *renewal of the old command of love*, with such new enforcements that it is called "A new commandment," and is peculiarly the law of Christ, John xiii. 34, xv. 12; 1 Thess. iv. 9; 2 John 5:

5. The state and condition of the persons between whom this duty is naturally to be exercised, as,—(1.) Children of one Father, Mal. ii. 10; (2.) Members of one body, 1 Cor. xii. 12, 13; (3.) Partakers of the same hope, Eph. iv. 4; (4.) Objects of the same hate of the world, 1 John iii. 13:

6. The eminency of this grace,—(1.) In itself, and divine nature, Col. ii. 2; 1 John iv. 7; 1 Cor. xiii.; (2.) In its usefulness, Prov. x. 12, xv. 17; Gal. v. 13; Heb. xiii. 1; (3.) In its acceptance with the saints, Eph. i. 15, 16; Ps. v. 11; 1 Cor. xiii.:

7. The impossibility of performing any other duty without it, Gal. v. 6; 1 Thess. i. 3; 1 John iv. 20:

8. The great sin of want of love, with all its aggravations, Matt. xxiv. 12; 1 John iii. 14, 15, and the like;—are so many, and of such various consideration, as not now to be insisted on.

Love, which is the bond of communion, maketh out itself and is peculiarly exercised in these things following:—

Rule II. Continual prayer for the prosperous state of the church, in God's protection towards it.

Ps. cxxii. 6, " Pray for the peace of Jerusalem: they shall prosper that love thee."

Phil. i. 4, 5, " Always in every prayer of mine for you all making request with joy, for your fellowship in the gospel from the first day until now."

Rom. i. 9, "Without ceasing I make mention of you always in my prayers."

Acts xii. 5, " Peter was kept in prison: but prayer was made without ceasing of the church unto God for him."

Isa. lxii. 6, 7, " Ye that make mention of the LORD, keep not silence; and give him no rest, till he establish, and till he make Jerusalem a praise in the earth."

Eph. vi. 18, " Praying always with all prayer and supplication in the Spirit, and watching thereunto with all perseverance and supplication for all saints."

Col. iv. 12, " Epaphras, who is one of you, a servant of Christ, saluteth you, always labouring fervently for you in prayers, that ye may stand perfect and complete in all the will of God."

Explication II. Prayer, as it is the great engine whereby to prevail with the Almighty, Isa. xlv. 11, so it is the sure refuge of the saints at all times, both in their own behalf, Ps. lxi. 2, and also of others, Acts xii. 5. It is a benefit which the poorest believer may bestow, and the greatest potentate hath no power to refuse. This is the beaten way of the soul's communion with God, for which the saints have many gracious promises of assistance, Zech. xii. 10, Rom. viii. 26; innumerable precepts for performance, Matt. vii. 7, 1 Thess. v. 17, 1 Tim. ii. 8; with encouragements thereunto, James i. 5, Luke xi. 9; with precious promises of acceptance, Matt. xxi. 22, John xvi. 24, Ps. l. 15;—by all which, and divers other ways, the Lord hath abundantly testified his delight in this sacrifice of his people. Now, as the saints are bound to pray for all men, of what sort soever, 1 Tim. ii. 1, 2, unless they are such as sin unto death, 1 John v. 16, yea, for their persecutors, Matt. v. 44, and them that hold them in bondage, Jer. xxix. 7, so most especially for all saints, Phil. i. 4, and peculiarly for those with whom they are in fellowship, Col. iv. 12. The Lord having promised that " upon every dwelling-place of mount Zion, and upon her assemblies" there shall be "a cloud and smoke by day, and the shining of a flaming fire by night," Isa. iv. 5, it is every one's duty to pray for its accomplishment. He is not worthy of the privileges of the church who continues not in prayer for a defence upon that glory. Prayer, then, for the good, prosperity, flourishing, peace, increase, edification, and protection of the church is a duty every day required of all the members thereof.

1. Estimation of the ordinances; 2. Concernment for God's glory; 3. The honour of Jesus Christ; 4. Our own benefit and spiritual interest; with, 5. The expressness of the command, are sufficient motives hereunto.

RULE III. Earnest striving and contending, in all lawful ways, by doing and suffering, for the purity of the ordinances, honour, liberty, and privileges of the congregation, being jointly assistant against opposers and common adversaries.

Jude 3, "And exhort you that ye should earnestly contend for the faith which was once delivered unto the saints."

Heb. xii. 3, 4, "Consider him that endured such contradiction of sinners against himself, lest ye be wearied and faint in your minds. Ye have not yet resisted unto blood, striving against sin."

1 John iii. 16, "Hereby perceive we the love of God, because he laid down his life for us: and we ought to lay down our lives for the brethren."

Gal. v. 1, 13, "Stand fast therefore in the liberty wherewith Christ hath made us free, and be not entangled again with the yoke of bondage. For, brethren, ye have been called unto liberty."

1 Cor. vii. 23, "Ye are bought with a price; be not ye the servants of men."

Cant. vi. 4, "Thou art beautiful, O my love; . . . . terrible as an army with banners."

1 Pet. iii. 15, "Be ready always to give an answer to every man that asketh you a reason of the hope that is in you with meekness and fear."

EXPLICATION III. The former rule concerned our dealing with God in the behalf of the church; this, our dealing with men. To the right performance hereof many things are required; as,—

1. Diligent labouring in the word, with fervent prayer, to acquaint ourselves with the mind and will of God concerning the way of worship which we profess, and the rules of walking which we desire to practise, that so we may be able to give an account to humble inquirers, and stop the mouths of stubborn opposers. According to our knowledge, such will be our valuation of the ordinances we enjoy. A man will not contend unless he know his title.

2. An estimation of all the aspersions cast on and injuries done

to the church to be Christ's, and also our own,—Christ wounded through the sides of his servants, and his ways. And if we are of his, though the blow light not immediately on us, we are not without pain; all such reproaches and rebukes fall on us.

3. Just vindication of the church against calumnies and false imputations. Who can endure to hear his parents in the flesh falsely traduced? and shall we be senseless of her reproaches who bears us unto Christ?

4. Joint refusal of subjection, with all gospel opposition, to any persons or things which, contrary to or beside the word, under what name soever, do labour for power over the church, to the abridging of it of any of those liberties and privileges which it claimeth as part of the purchase of Christ. To them that would inthral us we are not to give place, no not for an hour.

RULE IV. Sedulous care and endeavouring for the preservation of unity, both in particular and in general.

Phil. ii. 1–3, "If there be therefore any consolation in Christ, if any comfort of love, if any fellowship of the Spirit, if any bowels and mercies, fulfil ye my joy, that ye be like-minded, having the same love, being of one accord, of one mind. Let nothing be done through strife or vain-glory; but in lowliness of mind let each esteem other better than themselves."

Eph. iv. 3, 4, "Endeavouring to keep the unity of the Spirit in the bond of peace. There is one body, and one Spirit," etc.

1 Cor. i. 10, "Now I beseech you, brethren, by the name of our Lord Jesus Christ, that ye all speak the same thing, and that there be no divisions among you; but that ye be perfectly joined together in the same mind and in the same judgment."

2 Cor. xiii. 11, "Be perfect, be of good comfort, be of one mind, live in peace; and the God of love and peace shall be with you."

Rom. xiv. 19, "Let us therefore follow after the things which make for peace, and things wherewith one may edify another."

Rom. xv. 5, "Now the God of patience and consolation grant you to be like-minded one toward another," etc.

1 Cor. vi. 5–7, "Is it so, that there is not a wise man among you? no, not one that shall be able to judge between his brethren? but brother goeth to law with brother. Now therefore there is utterly a fault among you."

Acts iv. 32, "The multitude of them that believed were of one heart and of one soul."

EXPLICATION IV. Union is the main aim and most proper fruit of love; neither is there any thing or duty of the saints in the gospel pressed with more earnestness and vehemency of exhortation than this. Now, unity is threefold: First, Purely *spiritual*, by the participation of the same Spirit of grace; communication in the same Christ,—one head to all. This we have with all the saints in the world, in what condition soever they be; yea, with those that are departed, sitting down in the kingdom of heaven with Abraham, Isaac, and Jacob. Secondly, *Ecclesiastical*, or church communion in the participation of ordinances, according to the order of the gospel. This is a fruit and branch of the former; opposed to schism, divisions, rents, evil-surmisings, self-practices, causeless differences in judgment in spiritual things concerning the kingdom of Christ, with whatsoever else goeth off from closeness of affection, oneness of mind, consent in judgment to the form of wholesome words, conformity of practice to the rule. And this is that which in the churches, and among them, is so earnestly pressed, commanded, desired, as the glory of Christ, the honour of the gospel, the joy and crown of the saints. Thirdly, *Civil unity*, or an agreement in things of this life, not contending with [for?] them nor about them, every one seeking the welfare of each other. Striving is unseemly for brethren. Why should they contend about the world who shall jointly judge the world?

Motives to the preservation of both these are,—

1. The remarkable earnestness of Christ and his apostles in their prayers for, and precepts of, this duty.

2. The certain dishonour of the Lord Jesus, scandal to the gospel, ruin to the churches, shame and sorrow to the saints, that the neglect of it is accompanied withal, Gal. v. 15.

3. The gracious issues and sweet heavenly consolation which attendeth a right observance of them.

4. The many fearful aggravations wherewith the sin of rending the body of Christ is attended.

5. The sad contempt and profanation of ordinances which want of this hath brought upon many churches.

For a right performance of this duty, we must,—

1. Labour, by prayer and faith, to have our hearts and spirits throughly seasoned with that affectionate love which our first rule requireth.

2. Carefully observe, in ourselves or others, the first beginnings of strife; which are as the letting out of water, and, if not prevented, will make a breach like the sea.

3. Sedulously apply ourselves to the removal of the first appearance of divisions; and in case of not prevailing, to consult the church.

4. Daily to strike at the root of all dissension, by labouring for universal conformity to Jesus Christ.

RULE V. Separation and sequestration from the world and men

of the world, with all ways of false worship, until we be apparently
a people dwelling alone, not reckoned among the nations.

Numb. xxiii. 9, "Lo, the people shall dwell alone, and shall not
be reckoned among the nations."

John xv. 19, "Ye are not of the world, but I have chosen you
out of the world, therefore the world hateth you."

2 Cor. vi. 14–18, "Be ye not unequally yoked together with un-
believers: for what fellowship hath righteousness with unrighteousness? and what communion hath light with darkness? and what
concord hath Christ with Belial? or what part hath he that believeth
with an infidel? and what agreement hath the temple of God with
idols? for ye are the temple of the living God. Wherefore come
out from among them, and be ye separate, saith the Lord, and touch
not the unclean thing; and I will receive you, and will be a Father
unto you, and ye shall be my sons and daughters, saith the Lord
Almighty."

Eph. v. 8, 11, "Walk as children of light. And have no fellowship with the unfruitful works of darkness."

2 Tim. iii. 5, "Having a form of godliness, but denying the power
thereof; from such turn away."

Hosea iv. 15, "Though thou, Israel, play the harlot, yet let not
Judah offend; and come not ye unto Gilgal, neither go ye up to
Beth-aven."

Rev. xviii. 4, "Come out of her, my people, that ye be not partakers of her sins, and that ye receive not of her plagues."

Prov. xiv. 7, "Go from the presence of a foolish man, when thou
perceivest not in him the lips of knowledge."

EXPLICATION V. Separation generally hears ill in the world, and
yet there is a separation suitable to the mind of God. He that will
not separate from the world and false worship is *a separate* from
Christ.

Now, the separation here commanded from any persons is not in
respect of natural affections, nor spiritual care for the good of their
souls, Rom. ix. 3; nor yet in respect of duties of relation, 1 Cor. vii.
13; nor yet in offices of love and civil converse, 1 Cor. v. 10; 1 Thess.
iv. 12; much less in not seeking their good and prosperity, 1 Tim. ii.
1, 2, or not communicating good things unto them, Gal. vi. 10, or
not living profitably and peaceably with them, Rom. xii. 18: but in,—
1. Manner of walking and conversation, Rom. xii. 2; Eph. iv. 17–19;
2. Delightful converse and familiarity where enmity and opposition
appear, Eph. v. 3, 4, 6–8, 10, 11 ; 3. In ways of worship and ordinances of fellowship, Rev. xviii. 4, not running out into the same compass of excess and riot with them in any thing: for these three, and
the like commands and discoveries of the will of God, are most ex-

press, as in the places annexed to the rule; necessity abundantly urgent, spiritual profit, and edification, no less requiring it. Causeless separation from established churches, walking according to the order of the gospel (though perhaps failing in the practice of some things of small concernment), is no small sin; but separation from the sinful practices, and disorderly walkings, and false unwarranted ways of worship in any, is to fulfil the precept of not partaking in other men's sins. To delight in the company, fellowship, society, and converse of unsavoury, disorderly persons, proclaims a spirit not endeared to Christ.

Let motives hereunto be,—

1. God's command.

2. Our own preservation from sin and protection from punishment, that with others we be not infected and plagued.

3. Christ's delight in the purity of his ordinances.

4. His distinguishing love to his saints; provided that, in the practice of this rule, abundance of meekness, patience, gentleness, wisdom, and tenderness be exercised. Let no offence be given justly to any.

RULE VI. Frequent spiritual communication for edification, according to gifts received.

Mal. iii. 16, "Then they that feared the LORD spake often one to another; and the LORD hearkened, and heard it, and a book of remembrance was written before him for them that feared the LORD, and that thought upon his name."

Job ii. 11, "Now when Job's three friends heard of all this evil that was come upon him, they came every one from his own place; for they had made an appointment together to come to mourn with him and to comfort him."

Eph. iv. 29, "Let no corrupt communication proceed out of your mouth, but that which is good to the use of edifying, that it may minister grace unto the hearers."

Col. iv. 6, "Let your speech be alway with grace, seasoned with salt, that ye may know how ye ought to answer every man."

Eph. v. 4, "Neither filthiness, nor foolish talking, nor jesting, which are not convenient: but rather giving of thanks."

1 Thess. v. 11, "Wherefore comfort yourselves together, and edify one another, even as also ye do."

Heb. iii. 13, "Exhort one another daily, while it is called To-day; lest any of you be hardened through the deceitfulness of sin."

Jude 20, "Building up yourselves on your most holy faith, praying in the Holy Ghost."

Heb. x. 24, 25, "Let us consider one another to provoke unto

love and good works : not forsaking the assembling of ourselves together, as the manner of some is; but exhorting one another: and
so much the more, as ye see the day approaching."

Acts xviii. 26, " Whom when Aquila and Priscilla had heard, they
took him unto them, and expounded unto him the way of God more
perfectly."

1 Cor. xii. 7, "The manifestation of the Spirit is given to every
man to profit withal."

EXPLICATION VI. That men not solemnly called and set apart to
the office of public teaching may yet be endued with useful gifts for
edification was before declared. The not using of such gifts, in an
orderly way, according to the rule and custom of the churches, is to
napkin up the talent given to trade and profit withal. That every
man ought to labour that he may walk and dwell in knowledge in
his family, none doubts. That we should also labour to do so in the
church or family of God is no less apparent.

This the Scriptures annexed to the rule declare; which in an
especial manner hold out prayer, exhortation, instruction from the
word, and consolation. Now, the performance of this duty of mutual
edification is incumbent on the saints,—

1. *Ordinarily*, Eph. iv. 29, v. 3, 4; Heb. iii. 13. Believers, in their
ordinary daily converse, ought to be continually making mention of
the Lord, with savoury discourses tending to edification, and not
waste their opportunities with foolish, light, frothy speeches that are
not convenient.

2. *Occasionally*, Luke xxiv. 14; Mal. iii. 16. If any thing of
weight and concernment to the church be brought forth by Providence, a spiritual improvement of it, by a due consideration amongst
believers, is required.

3. *By assembling of more together, by appointment*, for prayer
and instruction from the word, Acts x. 24, xii. 12; Job ii. 11;
Eph. v. 19; James v. 16; Jude 20; 1 Thess. v. 14 ; this being a
special ordinance and appointment of God, for the increasing of
knowledge, love, charity, experience, and the improving of gifts received, every one contributing to the building of the tabernacle. Let
then, all vain communication be far away. The time is short, and
the days are evil. Let it suffice us that we have neglected so many
precious opportunities of growing in the knowledge of our Lord Jesus
Christ, and doing good to one another; let the remainder of our
few and evil days be spent in living to him who died for us. Be not
conformed to this world, nor the men thereof.

RULE VII. Mutually to bear with each other's infirmities, weakness,
tenderness, failings, in meekness, patience, pity, and with assistance.

Eph. iv. 32, " Be ye kind one to another, tender-hearted, forgiving one another, even as God for Christ's sake hath forgiven you."

Matt. xviii. 21, 22, " Then came Peter to him, and said, Lord, how oft shall my brother sin against me, and I forgive him? till seven times? Jesus saith unto him, I say not unto thee, Until seven times: but, Until seventy times seven."

Mark xi. 25, 26, " When ye stand praying, forgive, if ye have ought against any: that your Father also which is in heaven may forgive you your trespasses. But if ye do not forgive, neither will your Father which is in heaven forgive your trespasses."

Rom. xiv. 13, " Let us not therefore judge one another any more: but judge this rather, that no man put a stumbling-block or an occasion to fall in his brother's way." See verses 3, 4.

Rom. xv. 1, 2, " We then that are strong ought to bear the infirmities of the weak, and not to please ourselves. Let every one of us please his neighbour for his good to edification."

1 Cor. xiii. 4–7, " Charity suffereth long, and is kind; charity envieth not; charity is not rash, is not puffed up, doth not behave itself unseemly, seeketh not her own, is not easily provoked, thinketh no evil; rejoiceth not in iniquity, but rejoiceth in the truth; beareth all things, believeth all things, hopeth all things, endureth all things."

Gal. vi. 1, " Brethren, if a man be overtaken in a fault, ye which are spiritual restore such an one in the spirit of meekness; considering thyself, lest thou also be tempted."

Col. iii. 12–14, " Put on therefore, as the elect of God, holy and beloved, bowels of mercies, kindness, humbleness of mind, meekness, long-suffering; forbearing one another, and forgiving one another, if any man have a quarrel against any: even as Christ forgave you, so also do ye. And above all these things put on charity, which is the bond of perfection."

EXPLICATION VII. "It is the glory of God to conceal a thing," Prov. xxv. 2. Free pardon is the substance of the gospel, the work of God in perfection, Isa. lv.; proposed to us for imitation, Matt. xviii. 23–35. Whilst we are clothed with flesh we do all things imperfectly. Freedom from failings is a fruit of glory. We see here darkly, as in a glass,—know but in part. In many things we offend all; who knoweth how often? Mutual failings to be borne with, offences to be pardoned, weakness to be supported, may mind us in these pence of the talents forgiven us. Let him that is without fault throw stones at others. Some men rejoice in others' failings; they are malicious, and fail more in that sinful joy than their brethren in that which they rejoice at. Some are angry at weaknesses and infirmities; they are proud and conceited, not considering that they themselves also are in the flesh. Some delight to dwell always upon a frailty; they deserve to find no charity in the like kind. For injuries, who almost can bear until seven times? Peter thought it much. Some more study revenge than pardon. Some pretend to forgive, but yet every slight offence makes a continued alienation of the affections and separation of converse. Some will carry a smooth face over a rough heart. Christ is in none of these ways. They have no savour of the gospel. Meekness, patience, forbearance, and forgiveness, hiding, covering, removing of offences, are the footsteps of Christ. Seest thou thy brother fail? pity him. Doth he continue in it? earnestly pray for him, admonish him. Cannot another sin but you must sin too? If you be angry, vexed, rejoiced, alienated from, you are partner with him in evil, instead of helping him. Suppose thy God should be angry every time thou givest cause, and strike every time thou provokest him. When thy brother offendeth thee, do but stay thy heart until thou takest a faithful view of the patience and forbearance of God towards thee, and then consider his command to thee to go and do likewise. Let, then, all tenderness of affection and bowels of compassion towards one another be put on amongst us, as becometh saints. Let pity, not envy; mercy, not malice; patience, not passion; Christ, not flesh; grace, not nature; pardon, not spite or revenge,—be our guides and companions in our conversations.

Motives hereunto are,—

1. God's infinite mercy, patience, forbearance, long-suffering, and free grace towards us, sparing, pardoning, pitying, bearing with us, in innumerable daily, hourly failings and provocations; especially all this being proposed for our imitation in our measure, Matt. xviii. 23–35.

2. The goodness, unwearied and unchangeable love of the Lord Jesus Christ putting in every day for us, not ceasing to plead in our behalf, notwithstanding our continual backsliding, 1 John ii. 1, 2.

3. The experience which our own hearts have of the need wherein we stand of others' patience, forbearance, and pardon, Eccles. vii. 20–22.

4. The strictness of the command, with the threatenings attending its non-performance.

5. The great glory of the gospel, which is in the walking of the brethren with a right foot as to this rule.

RULE VIII. Tender and affectionate participation with one another in their several states and conditions,—bearing each other's burdens.

Gal. vi. 2, "Bear ye one another's burdens, and so fulfil the law of Christ."

Heb. xiii. 3, "Remember them that are in bonds, as bound with them; and them which suffer adversity, as being yourselves also in the body."

1 Cor. xii. 25, 26, " That there should be no schism in the body; but that the members should have the same care one for another. And whether one member suffer, all the members suffer with it; or one member be honoured, all the members rejoice with it."

2 Cor. xi. 29, " Who is weak, and I am not weak? who is offended, and I burn not?"

James i. 27, " Pure religion and undefiled before God and the Father is this, To visit the fatherless and widows in their affliction," etc.

Matt. xxv. 35, 36, 40, " I was an hungered, and ye gave me meat: I was thirsty, and ye gave me drink: I was a stranger, and ye took me in: naked, and ye clothed me: I was sick, and ye visited me: I was in prison, and ye came unto me. Verily I say unto you, Inasmuch as ye have done it unto one of the least of these my brethren, ye have done it unto me."

2 Tim. i. 16, 17, " The Lord give mercy unto the house of Onesiphorus; for he oft refreshed me, and was not ashamed of my chain: but, when he was in Rome, he sought me out very diligently, and found me."

Acts xx. 35, " I have showed you all things, how that so labouring ye ought to support the weak," etc.

EXPLICATION VIII. The former rule concerned the carriage and frame of spirit towards our brethren in their failings; this is in their miseries and afflictions. In this, also, conformity to Christ is required, who in all the afflictions of his people is afflicted, Isa. lxiii. 9, and persecuted in their distresses, Acts ix. 4. Could we bring up our spiritual union to hold any proportion with the mutual union of many members in one body, to which it is frequently compared, this duty would be excellently performed. No man ever yet hated his own flesh. If one member be in pain, the rest have little comfort or ease. It is a rotten member which is not affected with the anguish of its companions. They are marked particularly for destruction who, in the midst of plentiful enjoyments, forget the miseries of their brethren, Amos vi. 6. If we will not feel the weight of our brethren's afflictions, burdens, and sorrow, it is a righteous thing that our own should be doubled. The desolations of the church make Nehemiah grow pale in the court of a great king, Neh. ii. 1–3. They who are not concerned in the troubles, sorrows, visitations, wants, poverties, persecutions of the saints, not so far as to pity their woundings, to feel their strokes, to refresh their spirits, help bear their burdens upon their own shoulders, can never assure themselves that they are united to the Head of those saints. Now, to a right performance of this duty, and in the discharge of it, are required,—

1. A due valuation, strong desire, and high esteem of the church's prosperity, in every member of it, Ps. cxxii. 6.

2. Bowels of compassion as a fruit of love; to be sensible of, and intimately moved for, the several burdens of the saints, Col. iii. 12.

3. Courage and boldness to own them without shame in all conditions, 2 Tim. i. 16, 17.

4. Personal visitations in sicknesses, troubles, and restraints, to advise, comfort, and refresh them, Matt. xxv. 36.

5. Suitable supportment, by administration of spiritual or temporal assistances, to the condition wherein they are. The motives are the same as to the former rule.

RULE IX. Free contribution and communication of temporal things to them that are poor indeed, suitable to their necessities, wants, and afflictions.

1 John iii. 17, 18, " Whoso hath this world's good, and seeth his brother have need, and shutteth up his bowels of compassion from him, how dwelleth the love of God in him? My little children, let us not love in word, neither in tongue; but in deed and in truth."

1 Cor. xvi. 1, 2, " Now concerning the collection for the saints, as I have given order to the churches of Galatia, even so do ye. Upon the first day of the week let every one of you lay by him in store, as God hath prospered him."

2 Cor. ix. 5–7, " Let your gift be ready as a matter of bounty, and not as of covetousness. He which soweth sparingly shall reap also sparingly, and he which soweth bountifully, shall reap also bountifully. Every man according as he purposeth in his heart, so let him give; not grudgingly, or of necessity: for God loveth a cheerful giver." So the whole eighth and ninth chapters of this epistle.

Rom. xii. 13, " Distributing to the necessity of saints; given to hospitality."

Gal. vi. 10, " As we have therefore opportunity, let us do good unto all men, especially unto them who are of the household of faith."

1 Tim. vi. 17–19, " Charge them that are rich in this world, that they be not high-minded, nor trust in uncertain riches, but in the living God, who giveth us richly all things to enjoy; that they do good, that they be rich in good works, ready to distribute, willing to communicate; laying up in store for themselves a good foundation against the time to come."

Heb. xiii. 16, " To do good and to communicate forget not: for with such sacrifices God is well pleased."

Lev. xxv. 35, " If thy brother be waxen poor, and fallen in decay with thee, then thou shalt relieve him."

Matt. xxv. 34–36, 40, " Come, ye blessed of my Father, inherit the kingdom prepared for you from the foundation of the world: for I was an hungered, and ye gave me meat: I was thirsty, and ye gave me drink: I was a stranger, and ye took me in: naked, and ye clothed me: I was sick, and ye visited me: I was in prison, and ye came unto me. Verily I say unto you, Inasmuch as ye have done it unto one of the least of these my brethren, ye have done it unto me."

EXPLICATION IX. The having of poor always amongst us and of us, according to our Saviour's prediction, Matt. xxvi. 11, and the promise of God, Deut. xv. 11, serves for the trial of themselves and others: of their own content with Christ alone, with submission to the all-disposing sovereignty of God; of others, how freely they can part, for Christ's sake, with those things wherewith their hand is filled. When God gave manna for food unto his people, every one had an equal share: Exod. xvi. 18, "He that gathered much had nothing over, and he that gathered little had no lack;" 2 Cor. viii. 15. This distribution in equality was again, for the necessity of the church, reduced into practice in the days of the apostles, Acts iv. 35. Of the total sum of the possessions of believers, distribution was made to every man according to his need.

That every man, by the ordinance and appointment of God, hath a peculiar right to the use and disposal of the earthly things wherewith he is in particular intrusted, is unquestionable. The very precepts for free distribution and communication are enough to prove it. But that these things are altogether given to men for themselves and their own use is denied; friends are to be made of mammon. Christ needs in some what he bestows on others. If he hath given thee thine own and thy brother's portion also to keep, wilt thou be false to thy trust, and defraud thy brother? Christ being rich, became poor for our sakes; if he make us rich, it is that we may feed the poor for his sake. Neither doth this duty lie only (though chiefly) on those who are greatly increased; those who have nothing but their labour should spare out of that for those who cannot work, Eph. iv. 28. The two mites are required as well as accepted. Now, the relief of the poor brethren in the church hath a twofold rule:—

First, Their necessity; Secondly, Others' abilities.

Unto these two must assistance be proportioned, provided that those which are poor walk suitably to their condition, 2 Thess. iii. 10, 11. And as we ought to relieve men in their poverty, so we ought by all lawful means to prevent their being poor. To keep a man from falling is an equal mercy to the helping of him up when he is down.

Motives to this duty are:—

1. The love of God unto us, 1 John iii. 16.

2. The glory of the gospel, exceedingly exalted thereby, Titus iii. 8, 14; Matt. v. 7.

3. The union whereinto we are brought in Christ, with the common inheritance promised to us all.

4. The testimony of the Lord Jesus, witnessing what is done in this kind to be done unto himself, Matt. xxv. 35, 36, 40.

5. The promise annexed to it, Eccles. xi. 1; Prov. xix. 17; Deut. xv. 10; Matt. x. 42.

The way whereby it is to be done is by appointing some, Acts vi. 1–6, to take what is voluntarily contributed by the brethren, according as God hath blessed them, on the first day of the week, 1 Cor. xvi. 2, and to distribute to the necessity of the saints, according to the advice of the church; besides private distributions, wherein we ought to abound, Matt. vi. 3; Heb. xiii. 16.

RULE X. To mark diligently and avoid carefully all causes and causers of divisions; especially to shun seducers, false teachers, and broachers of heresies and errors, contrary to the form of wholesome words.

Rom. xvi. 17, 18, "Now I beseech you, brethren, mark them which cause divisions and offences contrary to the doctrine which ye have learned; and avoid them. For they that are such serve not our Lord Jesus Christ, but their own belly; and by good words and fair speeches deceive the hearts of the simple."

Matt. xxiv. 4, 5, 23–25, "Jesus said unto them, Take heed that no man deceive you. For many shall come in my name, saying, I am Christ; and shall deceive many. Then if any man shall say unto you, Lo, here is Christ, or there; believe it not. For there shall arise false Christs, and false prophets, and shall show great signs and wonders; insomuch that, if it were possible, they shall deceive the very elect. Behold, I have told you before."

1 Tim. vi. 3–5, "If any man teach otherwise, and consent not to wholesome words, even the words of our Lord Jesus Christ, and to the doctrine which is according to godliness; he is proud, knowing nothing, but doting about questions and strifes of words, whereof cometh envy, strife, railings, evil surmisings, perverse disputings of men of corrupt minds, and destitute of the truth, supposing that gain is godliness: from such withdraw thyself."

2 Tim. ii. 16, 17, "Shun profane and vain babblings: for they will increase unto more ungodliness. And their word will eat as doth a canker."

Tit. iii. 9–11, "Avoid foolish questions, and genealogies, and contentions, and strivings about the law; for they are unprofitable and vain. A man that is an heretic after the first and second admonition reject; knowing that he that is such is subverted, and sinneth, being condemned of himself."

1 John ii. 18, 19, " Little children, it is the last time: and as ye have heard that antichrist shall come, even now are there many antichrists; whereby we know that it is the last time. They went out from us, but they were not of us; for if they had been of us, they would no doubt have continued with us: but they went out, that they might be made manifest that they were not all of us."

1 John iv. 1, " Beloved, believe not every spirit, but try the spirits whether they are of God: because many false prophets are gone out into the world."

2 John 10, 11, " If there come any unto you, and bring not this doctrine, receive him not into your house, neither bid him God-speed: for he that biddeth him God-speed is partaker of his evil deeds."

Acts xx. 29–31, "I know this, that after my departing shall grievous wolves enter in among you, not sparing the flock. Also of your own selves shall men arise, speaking perverse things, to draw away disciples after them. Therefore watch."

Rev. ii. 14–16, " I have a few things against thee, because thou hast there them that hold the doctrine of Balaam. So hast thou also them that hold the doctrine of the Nicolaitanes, which thing I hate. Repent; or else I will come unto thee quickly, and will fight against them with the sword of my mouth."

EXPLICATION X. The former part of this rule was something spoken to, Rule iv. If the preservation of unity ought to be our aim, then certainly the causes and causers of division ought to be avoided. " From such turn away." There is a generation of men whose tongues seem to be acted by the devil; James calls it, " Set on fire of hell," chap. iii. 6. As though they were the mere offspring of serpents, they delight in nothing but in the fire of contention; disputing, quarrelling, backbiting, endless strivings, are that they live upon. " Note such men, and avoid them." Generally they are men of private interests, fleshly ends, high conceits, and proud spirits. " From such turn away." For the latter part of the rule in particular, concerning seducers, that a judgment of discerning by the Spirit rests in the church and the several members thereof is apparent, 1 John ii. 27; 1 Cor. ii. 15; Isa. viii. 20. To the exercise of this duty they are commanded, 1 John iv. 1; 1 Cor. xiv. 29: so it is commended, Acts xvii. 11; and hereunto are they encouraged, Phil. i. 9, 10; Heb. v. 14. "If the blind lead the blind, both will fall into the ditch." That gold may be suspected which would not be tried. Christians must choose the good, and refuse the evil. If their teachers could excuse them if they lead them aside, they might well require blind submission from them. Now, that the brethren may exercise this duty aright, and perform obedience to this rule, it is required,—

1. That they get their senses exercised in the word, "to discern

good and evil," Heb. v. 14; especially, that they get from the Scripture a "form of sound words," 2 Tim. i. 13, of the main truths of the gospel and fundamental articles of religion; so that, upon the first apprehension of the contrary, they may turn away from him that brings it, and not bid him "God-speed," 2 John 10.

2. That they attend and hearken to nothing but what comes to them in the way of God. Some men, yea, very many in our days, have such itching ears after novelty, that they run greedily after every one that lies in wait to deceive with cunning enticing words, to make out some new pretended revelations; and this from a pretended liberty, yea, duty of trying all things, little considering that God will have his own work done only in his own way. How they come it matters not, so they may be heard. Most of the seducers and false prophets of our days are men apparently out of God's way, leaving their own callings to wander without a call, ordinary or extraordinary,—without providence or promise. For a man to put himself voluntarily, uncalled, upon the hearing of them, is to tempt God; with whom it is just and righteous to deliver them up to the efficacy of error, that they may believe the lies they hear. Attend only, then, to, and try only that which comes in the way of, God. To others bid not God-speed.

3. To be always ready furnished with and to bear in mind the characters which the Holy Ghost hath given us in the word of seducers, which are indeed the very same, whereby poor unstable souls are seduced by them; as,—First, That they should come in "sheep's clothing," Matt. vii. 15,—goodly pretences of innocency and holiness. Secondly, With "good words and fair speeches," Rom. xvi. 17, 18, smooth as butter and oil. Thirdly, Answering men's lusts in their doctrine, 2 Tim. iv. 3,—bringing doctrines suitable to some beloved lusts of men, especially a broad and easy way of salvation. Fourthly, Pretences of glorious discoveries and revelations, Matt. xxiv. 24; 2 Thess. ii. 2.

4. Utterly reject and separate from such as have had means of conviction and admonition, Tit. iii. 10.

5. Not to receive any without testimony from some of the brethren of known integrity in the churches. Such is the misery of our days, that men will run to hear those that they know not from whence they come, nor what they are. The laudable practice of the first churches, to give testimonials to them that were to pass from one place to another, 1 Cor. xvi. 3, and not to receive any without them, Acts ix. 26, is quite laid aside.

6. To walk orderly, not attending to the doctrine of any not known to and approved by the churches.

7. To remove far away all delight in novelties, disputes, janglings,

contentions about words not tending to godliness; which usually
are beginnings of fearful apostasies, Tit. iii. 9; 2 Tim. iv. 3; 1 Tim.
ii. 3–5.

RULE XI. Cheerfully to undergo the lot and portion of the whole
church, in prosperity and affliction, and not to draw back upon any
occasion whatever.

Matt. xiii. 20, 21, "He that received the seed into stony places,
the same is he that heareth the word, and anon with joy receiveth
it; yet hath he not root in himself, but dureth for a while: for when
tribulation or persecution ariseth because of the word, by and by he
is offended."

Heb. x. 23–25, 32–39, "Let us hold fast the profession of our
faith without wavering; (for he is faithful that promised;) and
let us consider one another to provoke unto love and to good
works: not forsaking the assembling of ourselves together, as the
manner of some is; but exhorting one another: and so much the
more, as ye see the day approaching.   But call to remembrance the
former days, in which, after ye were illuminated, ye endured a great
fight of afflictions; partly, whilst ye were made a gazing-stock
both by reproaches and afflictions; and partly, whilst ye became
companions of them that were so used.   For ye had compassion of
me in my bonds, and took joyfully the spoiling of your goods, knowing
in yourselves that ye have in heaven a better and an enduring substance.   Cast not away therefore your confidence, which hath great
recompense of reward.   For ye have need of patience, that, after ye
have done the will of God, ye might receive the promise.   For yet
a little while, and he that shall come will come, and will not tarry.
Now the just shall live by faith: but if any man draw back, my soul
shall have no pleasure in him.   But we are not of them who draw
back unto perdition; but of them that believe to the saving of the
soul."

2 Tim. iv. 10, 16, "Demas hath forsaken me, having loved this
present world. . . . . At my first answer no man stood with me, but
all men forsook me: I pray God that it may not be laid to their
charge."

EXPLICATION XI. Backsliding from the practice of any way of
Christ or use of any ordinances, taken up upon conviction of his
institution, is in no small degree an apostasy from Christ himself.

Apostasy, in what degree soever, is attended with all that aggravation which a renunciation of a tasted sweetness and goodness from
God for transitory things can lay upon it.   Seldom it is that back-
sliders are without pretences.   Commonly of what they forsake, in
respect of what they pretend to retain, they say, as Lot of Zoar, " Is

it not a little one?" But yet we see, without exception, that such things universally tend to more ungodliness. Every unrecovered step backward from any way of Christ maketh a discovery of falseness in the heart, whatever former pretences have been.

They who, from motives of any sort, for things that are seen, which are but temporal, will seek for, or embrace, being presented, colours or pretences for declining from any gospel duty, will not want them for the residue, if they should be tempted thereunto.

The beginnings of great evils are to be resisted. That the neglect of the duty whereof we treat,—which is always accompanied with contempt of the communion of saints,—hath been a main cause of the great dishonour and confusion whereinto most churches in the world are fallen, was in part touched before; it being a righteous thing with God to suffer the sons of men to wax vain in their imaginations, in whom neither the love of Christ nor terror of the Lord can prevail against the fear of men.

Let this, then, with the danger and abomination of backsliding, make such an impression on the hearts of the saints, that with full "purpose of heart they might cleave unto the Lord," and "follow hard after him," in all his ordinances; so that if persecution arise, they may cheerfully "follow the Lamb whithersoever he goeth;" and, by their close adhering one to another, receive such mutual assistance and supportment, as that their joint prayers may prevail with the goodness of God, and their joint sufferings overcome the wickedness of men.

Now, to a close adhering to the church wherein we walk in fellowship, in all conditions whatsoever, without dismission attained upon just and equitable grounds, for the embracing of communion in some other churches. Motives are,—

1. The eminency and excellency of the ordinances enjoyed.

2. The danger of backsliding, and evidence of unsoundness in every degree thereof.

3. The scandal, confusion, and disorder of the churches, by neglect thereof.

RULE XII. In church affairs to make no difference of persons, but to condescend to the meanest persons and services for the use of the brethren.

James ii. 1–6, " My brethren, have not the faith of our Lord Jesus Christ, the Lord of glory, with respect of persons. For if there come unto your assembly a man with a gold ring, in goodly apparel, and there come in also a poor man in vile raiment; and ye have respect to him that weareth the gay clothing, and say unto him, Sit thou here in a good place; and say to the poor, Stand thou there, or sit here under my footstool: are ye not then partial in yourselves, and are become judges of evil thoughts? Hearken, my beloved brethren, Hath not God chosen the poor of this world rich in faith, and heirs of the kingdom which he hath promised to them that love him? But ye have despised the poor," etc.

Matt. xx. 26, 27, " It shall not be so among you: but whosoever will be great among you, let him be your minister; and whosoever will be chief among you, let him be your servant."

Rom. xii. 16, " Be of the same mind one toward another. Mind not high things, but condescend to men of low estate. Be not wise in your own conceits."

John xiii. 12–16, " So after he had washed their feet, and had taken his garments, and was set down again, he said unto them, Know ye what I have done to you? Ye call me Master and Lord: and ye say well; for so I am. If I then, your Lord and Master, have washed your feet; ye ought also to wash one another's feet. For I have given you an example, that ye should do as I have done to you. Verily, verily, I say unto you, The servant is not greater than his lord; neither he that is sent greater than he that sent him."

EXPLICATION XII. Where the Lord hath not distinguished, neither ought we. In Jesus Christ there is neither rich nor poor, high nor low, but a new creature. Generally, " God hath chosen the poor of this world to confound the mighty."

Experience shows us that not many great, not many wise, not many mighty after the flesh, are partakers of the heavenly calling; —not that the gospel of Christ doth any way oppose or take away those many differences and distinctions among the sons of men, caused by power, authority, relation, enjoyment of earthly blessings, gifts, age, or any other eminency whatsoever, according to the institution and appointment of God, with all that respect, reverence, duty, obedience, and subjection due unto persons in those distinctions, much less pull up the ancient bounds of propriety and interest in earthly things; but only declares, that in things purely spiritual, these outward things, which for the most part happen alike unto all, are of no value or esteem. Men in the church are considered as saints, and not as great or rich. All are equal, all are naked, before God.

Free grace is the only distinguisher,—all being brethren in the same family, servants of the same Master, employed about the same work, acted by the same precious faith, enjoying the same purchased privileges, expecting the same recompense of reward and eternal abode. Whence should any difference arise? Let, then, the greatest account it their greatest honour to perform the meanest necessary service to the meanest of the saints. A community in all spiritual advantages should give equality in spiritual affairs. Not he that is richest, not he that is poorest, but he that is humblest, is accepted before the Lord.

Motives hereunto are,—1. Christ's example; 2. Scripture precepts; 3. God's not accepting persons; 4. Joint participation of the same common faith, hope, etc.; 5. The unprofitableness of all causes of outward differences in the things of God.

RULE XIII. If any be in distress, persecution, or affliction, the whole church is to be humbled, and to be earnest in prayer in their behalf.

Acts xii. 5, 7, 12, " Peter therefore was kept in prison: but prayer was made without ceasing of the church unto God for him. And, behold, the angel of the Lord came upon him, and a light shined in the prison: and he smote Peter on the side, and raised him up, saying, Arise up quickly. And his chains fell off from his hands. And when he had considered the thing, he came to the house of Mary the mother of John, whose surname was Mark; where many were gathered together praying."

Rom. xii. 15, " Rejoice with them that do rejoice, and weep with them that weep."

1 Ccr. xii. 26, 27, " Whether one member suffer, all the members suffer with it; or one member be honoured, all the members rejoice with it. Now ye are the body of Christ, and members in particular."

2 Thess. iii. 1, 2, " Brethren, pray for us, that we may be delivered from unreasonable and wicked men."

EXPLICATION XIII. This duty being in general made out from, and included in, other former rules, we shall need to speak the less unto it, especially seeing that, upon consideration and supposition of our fellow-membership, it is no more than very nature requireth and calleth for. God delighteth as in the thankful praises, so in the fervent prayers of his churches; therefore, he variously calleth them, by several dispensations, to the performance of these duties. Now, this ofttimes, to spare the whole church, he doth by the afflictions of some one or other of the members thereof; knowing that that near relation which, by his institution and Spirit, is between them will make their distress common and their prayers closely combined. Spiritual union is more noble and excellent than natural; and yet in this it were monstrous that either any member in particular, or the whole in general, should not both suffer with and care for the distress of every part and member. That member is rotten and to be cut off, for fear of infecting the body, which feels not the pains of its associates. If, then, any members of the church do lie under the immediate afflicting hand of God or the persecuting rage of man, it is the duty of every fellow-member, and of the church in general, to be sensible of it, and account themselves so sharers therein as to be instant with God by earnest supplication, and helpful to them by suitable assistance, that their spiritual concernment in that affliction may be apparent; and that because,—First, The will of God is thereby fulfilled. Secondly, The glory of the gospel is thereby exalted. Thirdly, Preservation and deliverance to the whole church procured. Fourthly, Conformity with Christ's sufferings in his saints attained. Fifthly, An inestimable benefit of church-fellowship enjoyed, etc.

RULE XIV. Vigilant watchfulness over each other's conversation, attended with mutual admonition in case of disorderly walking, with rendering an account to the church if the party offending be not prevailed with.

Matt. xviii. 15–17, " If thy brother shall trespass against thee, go and tell him his fault between thee and him alone: if he shall hear thee, thou hast gained thy brother. But if he will not hear thee, then take with thee one or two more, that in the mouth of two or three witnesses every word may be established. And if he shall neglect to hear them, tell it unto the church."

1 Thess. v. 14, " Now we exhort you, brethren, warn them that are unruly."

Heb. iii. 12, 13, " Take heed, brethren, lest there be in any of you an evil heart of unbelief, in departing from the living God. But exhort one another daily, while it is called To-day; lest any of you be hardened through the deceitfulness of sin."

Heb. x. 24, 25, " Let us consider one another to provoke unto love and to good works: exhorting one another; and so much the more, as ye see the day approaching."

Heb. xii. 13, 15, 16, " Make straight paths for your feet, lest that which is lame be turned out of the way; but let it rather be healed. Looking diligently lest any man fail of the grace of God; lest any root of bitterness springing up trouble you, and thereby many be defiled ; lest there be any fornicator, or profane person, as Esau, who for one morsel of meat sold his birthright."

Lev. xix. 17, " Thou shalt not hate thy brother in thine heart : thou shalt in any wise rebuke thy neighbour, and not suffer sin upon him."

2 Thess. iii. 15, " Count him not as an enemy, but admonish him as a brother."

Rom. xv. 14, " I myself also am persuaded of you, my brethren, that ye also are full of goodness, filled with all knowledge, able also to admonish one another."

James v. 19, 20, "Brethren, if any of you do err from the truth, and one convert him; let him know, that he which converteth the sinner from the error of his way shall save a soul from death, and shall hide a multitude of sins."

Prov. xxix. 1, "He that, being often reproved, hardeneth his neck, shall suddenly be destroyed, and that without remedy."

EXPLICATION XIV. There is a threefold duty included in this rule, the main whereof, and here chiefly intended, is that of admonition; whereunto the first is previous and conducing; the latter in some cases consequent, and attending Christians' conversation. Whether you consider the glory of God and the gospel therein concerned, or the bonds of relation, with those mutual endearments wherein they stand engaged, and obligations that are upon them for the general good and spiritual edification one of another, this duty is of eminent necessity and usefulness. Not that we should curiously pry into one another's failings, much less maliciously search into doubtful unknown things, for the trouble or disparagement of our brethren, both which are contrary to that love which "thinketh no evil," but "hideth a multitude of sins;" but only, out of a sense of the glory of God, the honour of the gospel, and care of each other's souls, we are to observe their walking, that what is exemplary therein may be followed, what faileth may be directed, what is amiss may be reproved, that in all things God may be glorified and Christ exalted.

Now, admonition is twofold :—1. Authoritative, by the way of power; 2. Fraternal, by the way of love. The first, again, is twofold :—(1.) Doctrinal, by the way of teaching ; (2.) Disciplinary, which belongeth to the whole church. Of these we do not treat. The latter, also, is twofold :—*hortatory*, to encourage unto good ; and *monitory*, to reprove that which is amiss. It is this last which is peculiarly aimed at and intended in the rule. This, then, we assert as the duty of every church member towards them with whom he walks in fellowship, to admonish any from the word whom he perceives not walking in any thing with a right foot, as becometh the gospel; thereby to recover his soul to the right way. That much caution and wisdom, tenderness and moderation, is required in the persons performing this duty, for want whereof it often degenerates from a peaceable remedy of evil into fuel for strife and debate, is granted. Let them, then, who are called to perform this duty diligently consider these things: 1. That in the whole action he transgress not that rule of charity which we have, 1 Cor. xiii. 7, Gal. vi. 2. Let him have peace at home, by an assurance of constant labouring to cast out all beams and motes from his own eye, Matt. vii. 5. 3. Let him so perform it that it may evidently appear that he hath no other aim but the glory of God and the good of his brother reproved, all envy and rejoicing in evil being far away.   4. Let him be sure to draw his admonitions from the word, that the authority of God may appear therein, and without the word let him not presume to speak.   5. Let all circumstances attending time, place, persons, and the like, be duly weighed, that all provocation in the least manner may be fully avoided.   6. Let it be considered as an ordinance whereunto Christ hath an especial regard.   7. Let him carefully distinguish between personal injuries unto himself,—whose mention must have far more of forgiveness than reproof,—and other offences tending to public scandal.   Lastly, Let self-examination concerning the same or the like miscarriage always accompany the brotherly admonition.

These and the like things being duly weighed, let every brother, with Christian courage, admonish from the word every one whom he judgeth to walk disorderly in any particular whatsoever, not to suffer sin upon him, being ready to receive content and satisfaction upon just defence, or promised amendment; and without this, in case of just offence, a man cannot be freed from the guilt of other men's sins.   Let also the person admonished, with all Christian patience, accept of the admonition, without any more regret of spirit than he would have against him who should break the weapon wherewith he was in danger to be slain; considering,—

1. The authority of Him who hath appointed it;

2. The privilege and mercy he enjoyeth by such a spiritual prevention of such a danger or out of such an evil, which perhaps himself did not discern;

3. The dreadful judgments which are everywhere threatened to despisers of reproofs, Prov. xxix. 1; and so thankfully accept just admonition from the meanest in the congregation.

For the last, or repairing unto the church in case of not prevailing by private admonition, our Saviour hath so plainly laid down both the manner and end of proceeding in Matt. xviii. 15-17, that it needeth no explanation.   Only I shall observe, that by "church" there, verse 17, cannot be understood the elders of the church alone, but rather the whole congregation; for if the offended brother should take with him two or three of the elders unto the offender, as he may, then were they the church, and the church should be told of the offence before the reproof hath been managed by two or three; which is contrary to the rule.

RULE XV. Exemplary walking in all holiness and godliness of conversation, to the glory of the gospel, edification of the church, and conviction of them which are without.

Ps. xxiv. 3, 4, " Who shall ascend into the hill of the LORD? or who shall stand in his holy place? He that hath clean hands, and a pure heart; who hath not lifted up his soul unto vanity, nor sworn deceitfully."

Matt. v. 16, 20, "Let your light so shine before men, that they may see your good works, and glorify your Father which is in heaven. For I say unto you, That except your righteousness shall exceed the righteousness of the scribes and Pharisees, ye shall in no case enter into the kingdom of heaven."

Matt. xxi. 19, "When he saw a fig-tree in the way, he came to it, and found nothing thereon, but leaves only, and said unto it, Let no fruit grow on thee henceforward for ever," etc.

2 Cor. vii. 1, "Having therefore these promises, dearly beloved, let us cleanse ourselves from all filthiness of the flesh and spirit, perfecting holiness in the fear of God."

2 Tim. ii. 19, "Let every one that nameth the name of Christ depart from iniquity." Tit. ii. 11, 12, 14, "The grace of God that bringeth salvation hath appeared to all men, teaching us that, denying ungodliness and worldly lusts, we should live soberly, righteously, and godly, in this present world. . . . . . Who gave himself for us, that he might redeem us from all iniquity, and purify unto himself a peculiar people, zealous of good works." Eph. iv. 21–23, "If so be that ye have heard him, and have been taught by him, as the truth is in Jesus: that ye put off concerning the former conversation the old man, which is corrupt according to the deceitful lusts; and be renewed in the spirit of your mind." 1 Pet. iii. 1, 2, "Likewise, ye wives, be in subjection to your own husbands; that, if any obey not the word, they also may without the word be won by the conversation of the wives; while they behold your chaste conversation coupled with fear." Heb. xii. 14, "Follow peace with all men, and holiness, without which no man shall see the Lord." Eph. v. 15, 16, "See then that ye walk circumspectly, not as fools, but as wise, redeeming the time, because the days are evil." 2 Sam. xii. 14, "Howbeit, because by this deed thou hast given great occasion to the enemies of the LORD to blaspheme, the child also that is born unto thee shall surely die."

EXPLICATION XV. Holiness becometh the house of the Lord for ever; without it none shall see God. Christ died to wash his church, to present it before his Father without spot or blemish; to purchase unto himself a peculiar people, zealous of good works. It is the kingdom of God within us, and by which it appeareth unto all that we are the children of the kingdom. Let this, then, be the great discriminating character of the church from the world, that they are a holy, humble, self-denying people. Our Master is holy; his doctrine and worship are holy: let us strive that our hearts may also be holy.

This is our wisdom towards them that are without, whereby they may be guided or convinced; this is the means whereby we build up one another most effectually. Examples are a sharper way of instruction than precepts. Loose walking, causing the name of God to be blasphemed, the little ones of Christ to be offended, and his enemies to rejoice, is attended with most dreadful woes. O that all who are called to a holy profession, and do enjoy holy ordinances, did shine also in holiness of conversation, that those who accuse them as evil-doers might have their mouths stopped and their hearts filled with shame, to the glory of the gospel! To this general head belongeth wise walking, in all patience, meekness, and long-suffering towards those that are without, until they evidently appear to be fighters against God, when they are to be prayed for. Hither, also, might be referred the patience of the saints in all tribulations, sufferings, and persecutions for the name of Christ.

Motives for the exercise of universal holiness, in acts internal and external, private and public, personal and of all relations, are,—

1. The utter insufficiency of the most precious ordinances for any communion with God without it.

2. The miserable issue of deceived souls, with their barren, empty, fruitless faith.

3. The glory of the gospel, when the power thereof hath an evident impression on the hearts, thoughts, words, actions, and lives of professors.

4. Scandal of the gospel, the advantage of its adversaries, the shame of the church, and fierce wrath of God, following the unsuitable walking of professors.

5. The sweet reward which the practice of holiness bringeth along with it even in this life, with that eternal weight of glory whereunto it leadeth hereafter;—unto which the holy Son of God bring us all, through the sprinkling of his most holy blood !

And these are some of those rules whose practice is required from the persons, and adorneth the profession, of those who have obtained this grace, to walk together in fellowship, according to the rule of the gospel; towards others also ought they, with several limitations, and in the full latitude towards the brethren of the congregations in communion with them, to be observed.

OF SCHISM:

THE TRUE NATURE OF IT DISCOVERED AND CONSIDERED

WITH REFERENCE TO THE PRESENT DIFFERENCES IN RELIGION.

BY JOHN OWEN, D.D.,

OXFORD.

———

ANNO DOM. M.DC.LVII.

UNLIKE most of Owen's works, the following treatise on schism has neither dedication, nor preface, nor note to the reader, from which we might have inferred his reasons for undertaking the preparation of it. There is no reference to any authors of the day by whose writings he might have been stimulated to defend his position as an Independent. Perhaps the design of Owen was more effectually promoted by the care with which he abstains from all personal controversies. The charge of schism was frequently resorted to by the different ecclesiastical parties of that age; and so long as the term was shrouded in a certain vague mystery of import, it told on some minds with peculiar effect. Romanists were fond of it as a weapon of no mean power in their dispute with the Church of England, and several treatises might be named, written about this period, in which the latter is earnestly defended from the charge. The members of that church, on the other hand, used the same plea against the Presbyterians and Independents; while Presbyterians, fresh from the task of replying to the charge of schism preferred against themselves, delighted in urging it against their brethren of Congregational views.

As the nature of the sin itself was left undefined, and the term, as borrowed from Scripture, was employed with much laxity of application, the religious party to which Owen belonged stood especially obnoxious to the reproach of following a divisive and schismatic course. If not a new denomination, they had only of late risen to such strength as to exert an influence on the national movements; and their first appearance in public affairs had traversed the designs of the Presbyterians, by first thwarting and latterly superseding them in the enjoyment of political supremacy. The latter were thus tempted to resort to the accusation of schism against the Independents, while the acrimony with which the accusation was made could not fail to be enhanced by the circumstance that Independency, as new to its opponents, would be in some measure misunderstood. Its theory of particular churches, united under no bond of common jurisdiction, seemed to involve the essence of schism and a palpable breach of Christian unity; and its practice of "gathering churches out of churches" wore an aspect too aggressive to meet with silent connivance on the part of other Christian bodies. Our author, in defence of his party, refrains from all recrimination, and, instead of bandying with their opponents the charge of schismatic views and tendencies, in one of those broad, masterly, and comprehensive statements which shed such light upon a complex question as effectually redeems it from a world of error and confusion, examines the scriptural import of the term "schism," and proves that it denotes, not a rupture in ecclesiastical communion, but causeless divisions within the pale of a church. This argument was obviously not the less effective that it was of equal avail to the Anglican church against the Romanist, and to the Presbyterian against the former, while it was of peculiar service to the Independent against them all. The questions on which they differed came to be adjusted on their proper merits, and not under the perverting influence of the magic and mystery of an ambiguous word.

Thus far the discussion has been brought in the course of the first three chapters. The task, however, was but half done, if, whatever might be the scriptural usage of the term "schism," a breach of Christian unity were still a sin, and Independents, from their views of the nature of a church, were involved in it. That they were not justly open to this charge, he proves in reference to the different meanings of the word "church." If it be taken to denote *the body of the elect,* Independents, though separate from other religious bodies, and contending for a certain isolation among their churches, so far as jurisdiction was concerned, might still be saints of God, and in the church of the elect, chap. iv. If by the "church" is meant *the universal body of Christian professors,* the bond that connects them is not subjection to the authority of rulers or to the decrees of councils, but the maintenance of the common faith, so that deviation from it, not merely a separate fellowship, must constitute the evidence and measure of the guilt of schism, chap. v.; and our author links in connection with this argument a reply to the Romish charge of schism, which is met on the principle just stated, chap. vi. Finally, he makes reference to *particular churches,* and after showing in what their unity consists,—submission to the authority of Christ, and the exercise of Christian love among the brethren,—he claims it for his own denomination, and falls back on his original argument, as to the meaning of schism in Scripture, affirming it to be inapplicable "to the secession of any man or men from any *particular church,*" or to the refusal of one church to hold communion with another, or, lastly, to the departure of any man quietly, and under the dictates of conscience, from the communion of *any church whatever,* chap. vii. In the last chapter he meets the charge of schism as urged by the church of England against all Christians who cannot acquiesce in an episcopal polity.

Much of all this discussion may now be superseded and out of date by the prevalence of sounder views and a spirit more benign and charitable among evangelical churches, since the time when a vague charge of schism helped a limping argument and heightened the zeal of partisanship; this treatise of Owen, however, is a model, for the Christian temper with which the reasoning is prosecuted, and a master-piece of controversial tact, even though we may demur to some of his most important conclusions. It should be added, that he guards himself against any disparagement of the obligation to unity, and deplores in strong terms the divisions that rend the church of Christ.—ED.

OF SCHISM.

CHAPTER I.

Aggravations of the evil of schism, from the authority of the ancients—Their incompetency to determine in this case, instanced in the sayings of Austin and Jerome—The saying of Aristides—Judgment of the ancients subjected to disquisition—Some men's advantage in charging others with schism—The actors' part privileged—The Romanists' interest herein—The charge of schism not to be despised—The iniquity of accusers justifies not the accused—Several persons charged with schism on several accounts—The design of this discourse in reference to them—Justification of differences unpleasant—Attempts for peace and reconciliation considered—Several persuasions hereabout, and endeavours of men to that end—Their issues.

It is the manner of men of all persuasions who undertake to treat of schism, to make their entrance with invectives against the evils thereof, with aggravations of its heinousness. All men, whether intending the charge of others or their own acquitment, esteem themselves concerned so to do. Sentences out of the fathers, and determinations of schoolmen, making it the greatest sin imaginable, are usually produced to this purpose. A course this is which men's apprehensions have rendered useful, and the state of things in former days easy. Indeed, whole volumes of the ancients, written when they were actors in this cause, charging others with the guilt of it, and, consequently, with the vehemency of men contending for that wherein their own interest lay, might (if it were to our purpose) be transcribed to this end. But as they had the happiness to deal with men evidently guilty of many miscarriages, and, for the most part, absurd and foolish, so many of them having fallen upon such a notion of the catholic church and schism as hath given occasion to many woful mistakes and much darkness in the following ages, I cannot so easily give up the nature of this evil to their determination and judgment. About the aggravations of its sinfulness I shall not contend.

The evidence which remains of an indulgence in the best of them τῇ ἀμετρίᾳ τῆς ἀνθολκῆς, in this business especially, deters from that procedure. From what other principle were these words of Augustine: "Obscurius dixerunt prophetæ de Christo quam de ecclesia:

puto propterea quia videbant in spiritu contra ecclesiam homines facturos esse particulas; et de Christo non tantam litem habituros, de ecclesia magnas contentiones excitaturos?" Conc. ii. ad Ps. xxx. Neither the affirmation itself nor the reason assigned can have any better root. Is any thing more clearly and fully prophesied of than Christ? or was it possible that good men should forget with what contests the whole church of God, all the world over, had been exercised from its infancy about the person of Christ? Shall the tumultuating of a few in a corner of Africa blot out the remembrance of the late diffusion of Arianism over the world? But Jerome hath given a rule for the interpretation of what they delivered in their polemical engagements, telling us plainly, in his Apology for himself to Pammachius, that he had not so much regarded what was exactly to be spoken in the controversy he had in hand, as what was fit to lay load upon Jovinian. And if we may believe him, this was the manner of all men in those days. If they were engaged, they did not what the truth only, but what the defence of their cause also required! Though I believe him not as to all he mentions, yet, doubtless, we may say to many of them, as the apostle in another case, "Ολως ἥττημα ἐν ὑμῖν ἐστιν. Though Aristides obtained the name of Just for his uprightness in the management of his own private affairs, yet being engaged in the administration of those of the commonwealth, he did many things professedly unjust, giving this reason, he did them πρὸς τὴν ὑπόθεσιν τῆς πατρίδος συχνῆς ἀδικίας δεομένης.

Besides, the age wherein we live having, by virtue of that precept of our Saviour, "Call no man master," in a good measure freed itself from the bondage of subjection to the dictates of men (and the innumerable evils, with endless entanglements, thence ensuing), because they lived so many hundreds of years before us, that course of procedure, though retaining its facility, hath lost its usefulness, and is confessedly impertinent. What the Scripture expressly saith of this sin, and what from that it saith may regularly and rationally be deduced (whereunto we stand and fall), shall be afterward declared; and what is spoken sensibly thereunto by any, of old or of late, shall be cheerfully also received. But it may not be expected that I should build upon their authority whose principles I shall be necessitated to examine; and I am therefore contented to lie low as to any expectation of success in my present undertaking, because I have the prejudice of many ages, the interest of most Christians, and the mutual consent of parties at variance (which commonly is taken for an unquestionable evidence of truth), to contend withal. But my endeavours being to go "non quà itur, sed quà eundum est," I am not solicitous about the event.

In dealing about this business among Christians, the advantage hath been extremely hitherto on their part who found it their interest to begin the charge; for whereas, perhaps, themselves were and are of all men most guilty of the crime, yet by their clamorous accusation, putting others upon the defence of themselves, they have in a manner clearly escaped from the trial of their own guilt, and cast the issue of the question purely on them whom they have accused. The actors' or complainants' part was so privileged by some laws and customs, that he who had desperately wounded another chose rather to enter against him the frivolous plea that he received not his whole sword into his body, than to stand to his best defence, on the complaint of the wounded man. An accusation managed with the craft of men guilty, and a confidence becoming men wronged and innocent, is not every one's work to slight and waive; and he is, in ordinary judgments, immediately acquitted who avers that his charge is but recrimination. What advantage the Romanists have had on this account, how they have expatiated in the aggravation of the sin of schism, whilst they have kept others on the defence, and would fain make the only thing in question to be whether they are guilty of it or no, is known to all; and, therefore, ever since they have been convinced of their disability to debate the things in difference between them and us unto any advantage from the Scripture, they have almost wholly insisted on this one business; wherein they would have it wisely thought that our concernment only comes to the trial, knowing that in these things their defence is weak who have nothing else. Nor do they need any other advantage; for if any party of men can estate themselves at large in all the privileges granted and promises made to the church in general, they need not be solicitous about dealing with them that oppose them, having at once rendered them no better than Jews and Mohammedans,[1] heathens or publicans, by appropriating the privileges mentioned unto themselves. And whereas the parties litigant, by all rules of law and equity, ought to stand under an equal regard until the severals of their differences have been heard and stated, one party is hereby utterly condemned before it is heard, and it is all one unto them whether they are in the right or wrong. But we may possibly, in the issue, state it upon another foot of account.

In the meantime, it cannot be denied but that their vigorous adhering to the advantage which they have made to themselves (a thing to be expected from men wise in their generation), hath exposed some of them whom they have wrongfully accused to a con-

---

[1] " Solis nosse Deos et Cœli numina vobis ——
—— aut solis nescire datum."

trary evil, whilst, in a sense of their own innocency, they have insensibly slipped (as is the manner of men) into slight and contemptible thoughts of the thing itself whereof they are accused. Where the thing in question is but a name or *term of reproach*, invented amongst men, this is incomparably the best way of defence. But this contains a *crime*, and no man is to set light by it. To live in *schism* is to live in *sin;* which, unrepented of, will ruin a man's eternal condition. Every one charged with it must either desert his station, which gives foundation to this charge, or acquit himself of the crime in that station. This latter is that which, in reference to myself and others, I do propose, assenting in the gross to all the aggravations of this sin that, with any pretence from Scripture or reason, are heaped on it.

And I would beg of men fearing God that they would not think that the iniquity of their accusers doth in the least extenuate the crime whereof they are accused. Schism is schism still, though they may be unjustly charged with it; and he that will defend and satisfy himself by prejudices against them with whom he hath to do, though he may be no schismatic, yet, if he were so, it is certain he would justify himself in his state and condition. Seeing men, on false grounds and self-interest, may yet sometimes manage a good cause, which perhaps they have embraced upon better principles, a conscientious tenderness and fear of being mistaken will drive this business to another issue. "Blessed is he who feareth alway."

It is well known how things stand with us in this world. As we are *Protestants*, we are accused by the *Papists* to be schismatics; and all other pleas and disputes are neglected. This is that which at present (as is evident from their many late treatises on this subject, full of their wonted confidence, contempt, reviling, and scurrility) is chiefly insisted on by them.

Farther; among Protestants, as being *Reformatists*, or as they call us, *Calvinists*, we are condemned for schismatics by the *Lutherans*, and for sacramentarian sectaries, for no other crime in the world but because we submit not to all they teach, for in no instituted church relation would they ever admit us to stand with them; which is as considerable an instance of the power of prejudice as this age can give. We are condemned for separation by them who refuse to admit us into union! But what hath not an irrational attempt of enthroning opinions put men upon?

The differences nearer home about episcopal government, with the matter of fact in the rejecting of it, and somewhat of the external way of the worship of God formerly used amongst us, hath given occasion to a new charge of the guilt of the same crime on some; as it is not to be supposed that wise and able men, suffering to a great extremity, will oversee or omit any thing from whence they may hope to prevail themselves against those by whose means they think they suffer. It cannot be helped (the engagement being past), but this account must be carried on one step farther. Amongst them who in these late days have engaged, as they profess, unto *Reformation* (and not to believe that to have been their intention is fit only for them who are concerned that it should be thought to be otherwise, whose prejudice may furnish them with a contrary persuasion), not walking all in the same light as to some few particulars, whilst each party, as the manner is, gathered together what they thought conduced to the furtherance and improvement of the way wherein they differed one from another, some, unhappily, to the heightening of the differences, took up this charge of schism against their brethren; which yet, in a small process of time, being almost sunk of itself, will ask the less pains utterly to remove and take off. In the meantime, it is, amongst other things (which is to be confessed), an evidence that we are not yet arrived at that inward frame of spirit which was aimed at, Phil. iii. 15, 16, whatever we have attained as to the outward administration of ordinances.

This being the state of things, the concernment of some of us lying in all the particulars mentioned, of all Protestants in some, it may be worth while to consider whether there be not general principles, of irrefragable evidence, whereon both all and some may be acquitted from their several concernments in this charge, and the whole guilt of this crime put into the ephah, and carried to build it a house in the land of Shinar, to establish it upon its own base.

I confess I would rather, much rather, spend all my time and days in making up and healing the breaches and schisms that are amongst Christians than one hour in justifying our divisions, even therein wherein, on the one side, they are capable of a fair defence. But who is sufficient for such an attempt? The closing of differences amongst Christians is like opening the book in the Revelation,—there is none able or worthy to do it, in heaven or in earth, but the Lamb: when he will put forth the greatness of his power for it, it shall be accomplished, and not before. In the meantime, a reconciliation amongst all Protestants is our *duty*, and *practicable*, and had perhaps ere this been in some forwardness of accomplishment had men rightly understood wherein such a reconciliation, according to the mind of God, doth consist. When men have laboured as much in the improvement of the principle of forbearance as they have done to subdue other men to their opinions, religion will have another appearance in the world.

I have considered and endeavoured to search into the bottom of the two general ways fixed on respectively by sundry persons for the compassing of peace and union among Christians, but in one nation, with the issue and success of them in several places;—namely, that of *enforcing uniformity* by a secular power on the one side, as was the case in this nation not many years ago (and is yet liked by the most, being a suitable judgment for the most); and that of *toleration* on the other, which is our present condition. Concerning them both, I dare say that though men of a good zeal and small experience, or otherwise on any account full of their own apprehensions, may promise to themselves much of peace, union, and love, from the one or the other (as they may be severally favoured by men of different interests in this world, in respect of their conducingness to their ends), yet a little observation of events, if they are not able to consider the causes of things, with the light and posture of the minds of men in this generation, will unburden them of the trouble of their expectations. It is something else that must give peace unto Christians than what is a product of the prudential considerations of men.

This I shall only add as to the former of these,—of enforcing uniformity: As it hath lost its reputation of giving temporal tranquillity to states, kingdoms, and commonwealths (which with some is only valuable, whatever became of the souls of men, forced to the profession of that which they did not believe), [and is] the readiest means in the world to root out all religion from the hearts of men,—the letters of which plea are, in most nations in Europe, washed out with rivers of blood (and the residue wait their season for the same issue); so it continues in the possession of this advantage against the other, that it sees and openly complains of the evil and dangerous consequences of it, when against its own, where it prevails, it suffers no complaints to lie. As it is ludicrously said of physicians, the effects of their skill lie in the sun, but their mistakes are covered in the churchyard; so is it with this persuasion: what it doth well, whilst it prevails, is evident; the anxiety of conscience in some, hypocrisy, formality, no better than atheism, in others, wherewith it is attended, are buried out of sight.

But as I have some while since ceased to be moved by the clamours of men concerning "bloody *persecution*" on the one hand, and " cursed, intolerable *toleration*" on the other, by finding, all the world over, that events and executions follow not the conscientious embracing of the one or other of these decried principles and persuasions, but are suited to the providence of God, stating the civil interests of the nations: so I am persuaded that a general alteration of the state of the churches of Christ in this world must determine that controversy; which when the light of it appears, we shall easily see the vanity of those reasonings wherewith men are entangled, and [which] are perfectly suited to the present condition of religion. But hereof I have spoken elsewhere.

Farther; let any man consider the proposals and attempts that have been made for ecclesiastical peace in the world, both of old and in these latter days; let him consult the rescripts of princes, the edicts of nations, advices of politicians, that would have the world in quietness on any terms, consultations, conferences, debates, assemblies, councils of the clergy, who are commonly zealots in their several ways, and are by many thought to be willing rather to hurl the whole world into confusion than to abate any thing of the rigour of their opinions,—and he will quickly assume the liberty of affirming concerning them all, that as wise men might easily see flaws in all of them, and an unsuitableness to the end proposed; and as good men might see so much of carnal interest, self, and hypocrisy in them, as might discourage them from any great expectations; so, upon many other accounts, a better issue was not to be looked for from them than hath been actually obtained: which hath, for the most part, been this, that those that could dissemble most deeply have been thought to have the greatest advantage. In *disputations*, indeed, the truth, for the most part, hath been a gainer; but in attempts for *reconciliation*, those who have come with the least candour, most fraud, hypocrisy, secular baits for the subverting of others, have, in appearance, for a season seemed to obtain success. And in this spirit of craft and contention are things yet carried on in the world.

Yea, I suppose the parties at variance are so well acquainted at length with each other's principles, arguments, interests, prejudices, and real distance of their causes, that none of them expect any reconciliation, but merely by one party keeping its station and the other coming over wholly thereunto. And therefore a Romanist, in his preface to a late pamphlet about schism, to the two universities, tells us plainly, "That if we will have any peace, we must, without limitation, submit to and receive those κυρίας δόξας, those commanding oracles which God by his holy spouse propoundeth to our obedience:" the sense of which expressions we are full well acquainted with. And in pursuit of that principle, he tells us again, p. 238, " That suppose the church should in necessary points teach error, yet even in that case every child of the church must exteriorly carry himself quiet, and not make commotions" (that is, declare against her); "for that were to seek a cure worse than the disease." Now, if it seem reasonable to these gentlemen that we should renounce our sense and reason, with all that understanding which we have, or at least are fully convinced that we have, of the mind of God in the Scripture, and submit blindly to the commands and guidance of their church, that we may have peace and union with them, because of their huge

interest and advantage, which lies in our so doing, we profess ourselves to be invincibly concluded under the power of a contrary persuasion, and consequently an impossibility of reconciliation.

As to attempts, then, for reconciliation between parties at variance
about the things of God, and the removal of schism by that means,
they are come to this issue among them by whom they have been
usually managed,—namely, *politicians* and *divines*,—that the former,
perceiving the tenaciousness in all things of the latter, their prompt-
ness and readiness to dispute, and to continue in so doing with confidence of success (a frame of spirit that indeed will never praise
God, nor be useful to bring forth truth in the world), do judge them
at length not to have that prudence which is requisite to advise in
matters diffused into such variety of concernments as these are, or
not able to break through their unspeakable prejudices and interests
to the due improvement of that wisdom they seem to have; and the
latter, observing the facile condescension of the former in all things
that may have a consistency with that peace and secular advantage
they aim at, do conclude that, notwithstanding all their pretences,
they have indeed in such consultations little or no regard to the
truth.   Whereupon, having a mutual diffidence in each other, they
grow weary of all endeavours to be carried on jointly in this kind;—
the one betaking themselves wholly to keep things in as good state
in the world as they can, let what will become of religion; the other,
to labour for success against their adversaries, let what will become
of the world or the peace thereof.   And this is like to be the state
of things until another spirit be poured out on the professors of
Christianity than that wherewith at present they seem mostly to be
acted.

The only course, then, remaining to be fixed on, whilst our divisions continue, is to inquire wherein the guilt of them doth consist,
and who is justly charged therewith; in especial, what is and who is
guilty of the sin of schism.   And this shall we do, if God permit.

It may, I confess, seem superfluous to add any thing more on this
subject, which hath been so fully already handled by others.   But, as I
said, the present concernment of some fearing God lying beyond what
they have undertaken, and their endeavours, for the most part, having tended rather to convince their adversaries of the insufficiency
of their charge and accusation than rightly and clearly to state the
thing or matter contended about, something may be farther added
as to the satisfaction of the consciences of men unjustly accused of
this crime; which is my aim, and which I shall now fall upon.

CHAPTER II.

The nature of schism to be determined from Scripture only—This principle by some opposed—Necessity of abiding in it—Parity of reason allowed—Of the name of schism—Its constant use in Scripture—In things civil and religious—The whole doctrine of schism in the epistles to the Corinthians—The case of that church proposed to consideration—Schism entirely in one church; not in the separation of any from a church; nor in subtraction of obedience from governors—Of the second schism in the church of Corinth—Of Clement's epistle—The state of the church of Corinth in those days: Ἐκκλησία παροικοῦσα Κόρινθον—Πάροικος, who; παροικία, what—Πάροχος, " parœcia"—To whom the epistle of Clement was precisely written—Corinth not a metropolitical church—Allowance of what by parity of reason may be deduced from what is of schism affirmed—Things required to make a man guilty of schism—Arbitrary definitions of schism rejected—That of Austin considered; as also that of Basil—The common use and acceptation of it in these days—Separation from any church in its own nature not schism—Aggravations of the evil of schism ungrounded—The evil of it from its proper nature and consequences evinced—Inferences from the whole of this discourse—The church of Rome, if a church, the most schismatical church in the world—The church of Rome no church of Christ; a complete image of the empire—Final acquitment of Protestants from schism on the principle evinced, peculiarly of them of the late reformation in England—False notions of schism the ground of sin and disorder.

THE thing whereof we treat being a disorder in the instituted worship of God, and that which is of pure revelation, I suppose it a modest request, to desire that we may abide solely by that discovery and description which is made of it in Scripture,—that that alone shall be esteemed schism which is there so called, or which hath the entire nature of that which is there so called. Other things may be other crimes; schism they are not, if in the Scripture they have neither the name nor nature of it attributed to them.

He that shall consider the irreconcilable differences that are among Christians all the world over about this matter, as also what hath passed concerning it in former ages, and shall weigh what prejudices the several parties at variance are entangled with in reference hereunto, will be ready to think that this naked appeal to the only common principle amongst us all is so just, necessary, and reasonable, that it will be readily on all hands condescended unto. But as this is openly opposed by the Papists, as a most destructive way of procedure, so I fear that when the tendency of it is discovered, it will meet with reluctancy from others. But let the reader know that as I have determined προτιμᾷν τὴν ἀλήθειαν, so to take the measure of it from the Scripture only. " Consuetudo sine veritate est vetustas erroris," Cyp. Ep. ad Pomp.; and the sole measure of evangelical truth is His word of whom it was said, Ὁ λόγος ὁ σὸς ἀλήθειά ἐστι. " Id verius quod prius, id prius quod ab initio, id ab initio quod ab apostolis," says Tertullian. It is to me a sufficient answer to that fond question, " Where was your religion before Luther? where was your religion in the days of Christ and his apostles?" My thoughts as to this particular are the same with Chrysostom's on the general account of truth, Ἔρχεται Ἕλλην καὶ λέγει, ὅτι βούλομαι γενέσθαι Χριστιανὸς ἀλλὰ οὐκ οἶδα τίνι προσθῶμαι· μάχη παρ' ὑμῖν πολλὴ καὶ στάσις, πολὺς θόρυβος, ποῖον ἔλομαι δόγμα; τί αἱρήσομαι; ἕκαστος λέγει ὅτι ἐγὼ ἀληθεύω, τίνι πειθῶ μηδὲν ὅλως εἰδὼς ἐν ταῖς γραφαῖς; κἀκεῖνοι τὸ αὐτὸ προβάλλονται πάνυ γε τοῦτο ὑπὲρ ἡμῶν, εἰ μὲν γὰρ λογισμοῖς ἐλέγομεν πείθεσθαι εἰκότως ἐθορύβου, εἰ δὲ ταῖς γραφαῖς λέγομεν πιστεύειν, αὐταὶ δὲ ἁπλαῖ καὶ ἀληθεῖς, εὔκολόν σοι τὸ κρινό-μενον, εἴτις ἐκείναις συμφωνεῖ οὗτος Χριστιανός· εἴτις μάχεται οὗτος πόρρω τοῦ κανόνος τούτου. Homil. iii. in Acta.[1]

But yet, lest this should seem too strait, as being, at first view, exclusive of the learned debates and disputes which we have had about this matter, I shall, after the consideration of the precise Scripture notion of the name and thing,—wherein the conscience of a believer is alone concerned,—propose and argue also what by a parity of reason may thence be deduced as to the ecclesiastical common use of them, and our concernment in the one and the other.

The word, which is metaphorical, as to the business we have in hand, is used in the Scripture both in its primitive native sense, in reference to things natural, as also in the tralatitious use of it, about things politic and spiritual, or moral. In its first sense we have the noun, Matt. ix. 16, Καὶ χεῖρον σχίσμα γίνεται, " And the rent" (in the cloth) " is made worse;"—and the verb, Matt. xxvii. 51, Καταπέτασμα τοῦ ναοῦ ἐσχίσθη, " The vail of the temple was rent;" Καὶ αἱ πέτραι ἐσχίσθησαν, " And the rocks were rent:" both denoting an interruption of continuity by an external power in things merely passive. And this is the first sense of the word,—a scissure or division of parts before continued, by force or violent dissolution. The use of the word in a political sense is also frequent: John vii. 43, Σχίσμα οὖν ἐν τῷ ὄχλῳ, " There was a division among the people," some being of one mind, some of another; John ix. 16, Καὶ σχίσμα ἦν ἐν αὐτοῖς, " There was a division among them ;" and chap x. 19 likewise. So Acts xiv. 4, Ἐσχίσθη δὲ τὸ πλῆθος τῆς πόλεως, " The multitude of the city was divided;" and chap. xxiii. 7, " There arose a dissension between the Pharisees and the Sadducees," καὶ ἐσχίσθη τὸ πλῆθος, " and the multitude was divided," some following one, some another of their leaders in that dissension. The same thing is expressed by a word answering unto it in Latin:—"Scinditur incertum studia in contraria vulgus." And in this sense, relating to civil things, it is often used.[2]

---

[1] We have not been able to discover the passage quoted in the homily referred to. We have ventured on some slight corrections from conjecture.—ED.

[2] Οἱ τὴν Ῥώμην οἰκοῦντες διεμερίσθησαν εἰς τὰ μέρη, καὶ οὐκέτι ὡμονόησαν πρὸς ἀλλήλους· καὶ ἐγένετο μέγα σχίσμα.—Chronic. Antioch. Joh. Male. p. 98, A. MS. Bib. Bod.

This being the next posture of that word, from whence it immediately slips into its ecclesiastical use, expressing a thing moral or spiritual, there may some light be given into its importance when so appropriated, from its constant use in this state and condition to denote *differences of mind and judgment, with troubles ensuing thereon, amongst men met in some one assembly, about the compassing of a common end and design.*

In the sense contended about it is used only by Paul in his First Epistle to the Corinthians, and therein frequently: Chap. i. 10, " I exhort you, μὴ ᾖ ἐν ὑμῖν σχίσματα,"—" that there be no schisms among you." Chap. xi. 18, " When ye come together in the church, ἀκούω σχίσματα ἐν ὑμῖν ὑπάρχειν,"—" I hear that there be schisms among you." Chap. xii. 25, the word is used in reference to the natural body, but with an application to the ecclesiastical. Other words there are of the same importance, which shall also be considered, as Rom. xvi. 17, 18. Of schism in any other place, or in reference to any other persons, but only to this church of Corinth, we hear nothing.

Here, then, being the principal foundation, if it hath any, of that great fabric about schism which in latter ages hath been set up, it must be duly considered, that, if it be possible, we may discover by what secret engines or artifices the discourses about it, which fill the world, have been hence deduced,—being, for the most part, universally unlike the thing here mentioned,—or find out that they are built on certain prejudices and presumptions nothing relating thereto. The church of Corinth was founded by Paul, Acts xviii. 8–11; with him there were Aquila and Priscilla, verses 2, 18. After his departure, Apollos came thither, and effectually watered what he had planted, 1 Cor. iii. 6. It is probable that either Peter had been there also, or at least that sundry persons converted by him were come thither, for he still mentions Cephas and Apollos with himself, chap. i. 12, iii. 22. This church, thus watered and planted, came together for the worship of God, ἐπὶ τὸ αὐτό, chap. xi. 20, and for the administration of discipline in particular, chap. v. 4, 5. After a while, through the craft of Satan, various evils, in doctrine, conversation, and church-order crept in amongst them. As for *doctrine*, besides their mistake about eating things offered to idols, chap. viii. 4, some of them denied the resurrection of the dead, chap. xv. 12. In *conversation* they had not only the eruption of a scandalous particular sin amongst them, chap. v. 1, but grievous sinful miscarriages when they "came together" about holy administrations, chap. xi. 20, 21. These the apostle distinctly reproves in them. Their *church-order*, as to that love, peace, and union of heart and mind wherein they ought to have walked, was wofully disturbed with divisions and sidings about their teachers, chap. i. 12. And not content to make this difference the matter of their debates and disputes from house to house, even when they met for public worship, or that which they all met in and for, they were divided on that account, chap. xi. 18. This was the schism the apostle dehorts them from, charges them with, and shows them the evil thereof. They had differences amongst themselves about unnecessary things. On these they engaged in disputes and sidings even in their solemn assemblies, when they came all together for the same worship, about which they differed not. Probably, much vain jangling, alienation of affections, exasperation of spirit, with a neglect of due offices of love, ensued hereupon. All this appears from the entrance the apostle gives to his discourse on this subject: 1 Cor. i. 10, Παρακαλῶ ὑμᾶς, ἵνα τὸ αὐτὸ λέγητε πάντες,—" I beseech you that ye all speak the same thing." They were of various minds and opinions about their church affairs; which was attended with the confusion of disputings. " Let it not be so," saith the apostle; καὶ μὴ ᾖ ἐν ὑμῖν σχίσματα, " and let there be no schisms among you," which consist in such differences and janglings. He adds, ῏Ητε δὲ κατηρτισμένοι ἐν τῷ αὐτῷ νοΐ καὶ ἐν τῇ αὐτῇ γνώμῃ,—" But that ye be perfectly joined together in the same mind and in the same judgment." They were joined together in the same church-order and fellowship, but he would have them so also in oneness of mind and judgment; which if they were not, though they continued together in their church-order, yet schisms would be amongst them. This was the state of that church, this the frame and carriage of the members of it, this the fault and evil whereon the apostle charges them with schism and the guilt thereof. The grounds whereon he manageth his reproof are their common interest in Christ, chap. i. 13; the nothingness of the instruments of preaching the gospel, about whom they contended, chap. i. 27, iii. 4, 5; their church-order instituted by God, chap. xii. 13: of which afterward.

This being, as I said, the principal seat of all that is taught in the Scripture about schism, we are here, or hardly at all, to learn what it is and wherein it doth consist. The arbitrary definitions of men, with their superstructions and inferences upon them, we are not concerned in: at least, I hope I shall have leave from hence to state the true nature of the thing, before it be judged necessary to take into consideration what, by parity of reason, may be deduced from it. In things purely moral and of natural equity, the most general notion of them is to be the rule, whereby all particulars claiming an interest in their nature are to be measured and regulated. In things of institution, the particular instituted is first and principally to be regarded ; how far the general reason of it may be extended is of after-consideration. And as is the case in respect of duty, so it is in respect of the evils that are contrary thereto.

True and false are indicated and tried by the same rule. Here, then, our foot is to be fixed; what compass may be taken to fetch in things of a like kin will in its proper place follow. Observe, then,—

1. That the thing mentioned is entirely in *one church*, amongst the members of *one particular* society. No mention is there in the least of one church divided against another, or separated from another or others,—whether all true or some true, some false or but pretended. Whatever the crime be, it lies wholly within the verge of one church, that met together for the worship of God and administration of the ordinances of the gospel; and unless men will condescend so to state it upon the evidence tendered, I shall not hope to prevail much in the process of this discourse.

2. Here is no mention of any *particular man's*, or any *number* of men's, separation from the holy assemblies of the whole church, or of subduction of themselves from its power: nor doth the apostle lay any such thing to their charge, but plainly declares that they continued all in the joint celebration of that worship and performance together of those duties which were required of them in their assemblies; only, they had groundless, causeless differences amongst themselves, as I shall show afterward. All the divisions of one church from another, or others, the separation of any one or more persons from any church or churches, are things of another nature, made good or evil by their circumstances, and not that at all which the Scripture knows and calls by the name of schism; and therefore there was no such thing or name as schism, in such a sense, known in the Judaical church, though in the former it abounded. All the different sects to the last still communicated in the same carnal ordinances; and those who utterly deserted them were apostates, not schismatics. So were the body of the Samaritans; they worshipped they knew not what, nor was salvation among them, John iv. 22.

3. Here is no mention of any *subtraction of obedience* from bishops or rulers, in what degree soever, no exhortation to regular submission unto them,—much less from the pope or church of Rome. Nor doth the apostle thunder out against them, "You are departed from the unity of the catholic church, have rent Christ's seamless coat, set up 'altare contra altare,' have forsaken the visible head of the church, the fountain of all unity; you refuse due subjection to the prince of the apostles;" nor, "You are schismatics from the national church of Achaia, or have cast off the rule of your governors;" with the like language of after days;—but, "When ye come together, ye have divisions amongst you." "Behold how great a matter a little fire kindleth!"

A condition not unlike to this befalling this very church of Corinth, sundry years after the strifes now mentioned were allayed by the epistle of the apostle, doth again exhibit to us the case and evil treated on. Some few unquiet persons among them drew the whole society (upon the matter) into division and an opposition to their elders. They who were the causes, μιαρᾶς καὶ ἀνοσίου στάσεως, as Clement tells them in the name of the church at Rome, were ὀλίγα πρόσωπα, a few men acted by pride and madness; yet such power had those persons in the congregation, that they prevailed with the multitude to depose the elders and cast them out of office. So the same Clement tells them, Ὁρῶμεν ὅτι ἐνίους ὑμεῖς μετηγάγετε καλῶς πολιτευομένους ἐκ τῆς ἀμέμπτως αὐτοῖς τετιμημένης λειτουργίας. What he intends by his μετηγάγετε, etc., he declares in the words foregoing, where he calls the elders that were departed this life happy and blessed, as not being subject or liable to expulsion out of their offices: Οὐ γὰρ εὐλα-βοῦνται μή τις αὐτοὺς μεταστήσῃ ἀπὸ τοῦ ἱδρυμένου αὐτοῖς τόπου. Whether these men who caused the differences and sedition against those elders that were deposed were themselves by the church substituted into their room and place, I know not. This difference in that church the church of Rome, in that epistle of Clement, calls everywhere schism, as it also expresses the same thing, or the evil frame of their minds and their actings, by many other words. Ζῆλος, ἔρις, στάσις, διωγμός, ἀκαταστασία, ἀλαζονεία, τύφος, πόλεμος, are laid to their charge. That there was any separation from the church, that the deposed elders, or any for their sakes, withdrew themselves from the communion of it, or ceased to assemble with it for the celebration of the ordinances of the gospel, there is not any mention; only the difference in the church is the schism whereof they are accused. Nor are they accused of schism for the deposition of the elders, but for their differences amongst themselves, which was the ground of their so doing.

It is alleged, indeed, that it is not the single church of Corinth that is here intended, but all the churches of Achaia, whereof that was the metropolis; which though, as to the nature of schism, it be not at all prejudicial to what· hath been asserted, supposing such a church to be, yet, because it sets up in opposition to some principles of truth that must afterward be improved, I shall briefly review the arguments whereby it is attempted to be made good.

The title of the epistle, in the first place, is pretended to this purpose. It is: Ἡ ἐκκλησία Θεοῦ ἡ παροικοῦσα Ῥώμην τῇ ἐκκλησίᾳ τοῦ Θεοῦ παροικούσῃ Κόρινθον "wherein" (as it is said) " on each part the παροικία, or whole province, as of Rome, so of Corinth, the region and territory that belonged to those metropolises is intended." But, as I have formerly elsewhere said, we are beholden to the frame and fabric of church affairs in after ages for such interpretations as these. The simplicity of the first knew them not. They who talked of the church of God that did παροικεῖν at Rome little then thought of province or region. Ἐκκλησία παροικοῦσα Ῥώμην is as much as ἐκκλησία ἐν Ἱεροσολύμοις, Acts viii. 1. Πάροικος is a man that dwells at such a place, properly one that dwells in another's house or soil, or that hath removed from one place and settled in another; whence it is often used in the same sense with μέτοικος. He is such an inhabitant as hath yet some such consideration attending him as makes him a kind of a foreigner to the place where he is. So, Eph. ii. 19, πάροικοι and συμπολῖται are opposed. Hence is παροικία, which, as Budæus says, differs from κατοικία in that it denotes a temporary habitation, this a stable and abiding one. Παροικέω is so to "inhabit," to dwell in a place, where yet something makes a man a kind of a stranger. So it is said of Abraham, Πίστει παρώκησεν εἰς τὴν γῆν τῆς ἐπαγγελίας ὡς ἀλλοτρίαν, Heb. xi. 9; joined with παρεπίδημος, 1 Pet. ii. 11 (hence this word by the learned publisher of this epistle is rendered "peregrinatur, diversatur"); and more clearly Luke xxiv. 18, Σὺ μόνος παροικεῖς ἐν Ἱερουσαλήμ; which we have rendered, "Art thou only a stranger in Jerusalem?" Whether παροικία and "parœcia" is from hence or no by some is doubted. Πάροχος is "convivator," and παροχή, "præbitio," Gloss. vetus; so that "parochiæ" may be called so from them who met together to break bread and to eat. Allow "parochia" to be barbarous, and our only word to be "parœcia," from παροικία, then it is as much as the voisinage, men living near together for any end whatever. So says Budæus, πάροικοι are πρόσοικοι· thence churches were called παροικίαι, consisting of a number of them, who were πάροικοι or πρόσοικοι. The saints of God, expressing the place which they inhabited, and the manner, as strangers, said of the churches whereof they were, Ἐκκλησία παροικοῦσα Ῥώμην, and Ἐκκλησία παροικοῦσα Κόρινθον. This is now made to denote a region, a territory, the adjacent region to a metropolis, and such-like things as the poor primitive pilgrims little thought of. This will scarcely, as I suppose, evince the assertion we are dealing about. There may be a church of God dwelling at Rome or Corinth, without any adjacent region annexed to it, I think. Besides, those who first used the word in the sense now supposed did not understand a province by παροικία, which was with them (as originally) the charge of him that was a bishop, and no more. Επαρχία was with them a province that belonged to a metropolitan, such as the bishop of Corinth is supposed to be. I do not remember where a metropolitan's province is called his παροικία, there being many of these in every one of them. But at present I will not herein concern myself.

But it is said that this epistle of Clement was written to them to whom Paul's epistles were written; which appears, as from the common title, so also from hence, that Clement advises them to whom he writes to take and consider that epistle which Paul had formerly wrote to them. Now, Paul's epistle was written to all the churches of Achaia, as it is said expressly in the second, " Unto the church of God which is at Corinth, with all the saints, which are in all Achaia," chap. i. 1. And for the former, that also is directed πᾶσι ἐπικαλουμένοις τὸ ὄνομα τοῦ Χριστοῦ ἐν παντὶ τόπῳ. And the same form is used at the close of this [Clement's]: Καὶ μετὰ πάντων πανταχῇ κεκλημένων ὑπὸ τοῦ Θεοῦ, wherein all places in Achaia (and everywhere therein) not absolutely are intended; for if they should, then this epistle would be a catholic epistle, and would conclude the things mentioned in it of the letter received by the apostle, etc., to relate to the catholic church.

Ans. It is confessed that the epistles of Paul and Clement have one common title; so that Τῇ ἐκκλησίᾳ παροικούσῃ Κόρινθον, which is Clement's expression, is the same with Τῇ ἐκκλησίᾳ τῇ οὔσῃ ἐν Κορίνθῳ, which is Paul's in both his epistles; which adds little strength to the former argument from the word παροικοῦσα, οὔσῃ ἐν Κορίνθῳ, as I suppose, confining it thither. It is true, Paul's second epistle, after its inscription, Τῇ ἐκκλησίᾳ τῇ οὔσῃ ἐν Κορίνθῳ, adds, σὺν τοῖς ἁγίοις πᾶσι τοῖς οὖσιν ἐν ὅλῃ τῇ Ἀχαΐα. He mentions not anywhere any more churches in Achaia than that of Corinth and that at Cenchrea, nor doth he speak of any churches here in this salutation, but only of the saints; and he plainly makes Achaia and Corinth to be all one, 2 Cor. ix. 2: so that to me it appears that there were not as yet, any more churches brought into order in Achaia but that mentioned, with that other at Cenchrea, which, I suppose, comes under the same name with that of Corinth. Nor am I persuaded that it was a completed congregation in those days. Saints in Achaia that lived not at Corinth there were perhaps many, but, being scattered up and down, they were not formed into societies, but belonged to the church of Corinth, and assembled therewith, as they could, for the participation of ordinances. So that there is not the least evidence that this epistle of Paul was directed to any other church but that of Corinth. For the first, it can scarce be questioned. Paul writing an epistle for the instruction of the saints of God and disciples of Christ in all ages, by the inspiration of the Holy Ghost, salutes in its beginning and ending all them that on that general account are concerned in it. In this sense all his epistles were catholic, even those he wrote to single persons. The occasion of writing this epistle was, indeed, from a particular church, and the chief subject-matter of it was concerning the affairs of that church; hence it is in the first place particularly directed to them. And our present inquiry is not after all that by any means were or might be concerned in that which was then written, as to their present or future direction, but after them who administered the occasion to what was so written, and whose particular condition was spoken to. This, I say, was the single church of Corinth. That πάντες οἱ ἐπικαλούμενοι τὸ ὄνομα τοῦ Χριστοῦ ἐν παντὶ τόπῳ, "all in every place," should be all only in Achaia, or that Clement's μετὰ πάντων πανταχῇ τῶν κεκλημένων ὑπὸ τοῦ Θεοῦ, should be, "with them that are called in Achaia," I can yet see no ground to conjecture. Paul writes an epistle to the church of Ephesus, and concludes it, Ἡ χάρις μετὰ πάντων τῶν ἀγαπώντων τὸν Κύριον ἡμῶν Ἰησοῦν Χριστόν ἐν ἀφθαρσίᾳ,—the extent of which prayer is supposed to reach farther than Ephesus and the region adjacent. It doth not, then, as yet appear that Paul wrote his epistles particularly to any other but the particular church at Corinth. If concerning the latter, because of that expression, "with all the saints which are in all Achaia," it be granted there were more churches than that of Corinth, with its neighbour Cenchrea (which whether it were a stated distinct church or no I know not), yet it will not at all follow, as was said before, that Clement, attending the particular occasion only about which he and the church of Rome were consulted, did so direct his epistle, seeing he makes no mention in the least that so he did. But yet, by the way, there is one thing more that I would be willingly resolved about in this discourse, and that is this: seeing that it is evident that the apostle by his πάντες ἐν παντὶ τόπῳ, and Clement by his πάντων πανταχῇ κεκλημένων, intend an enlargement beyond the first and immediate direction to the church of Corinth, if by the church of Corinth, as it is pleaded, they intend to express that whole region of Achaia, what does either the apostle or Clement obtain by that enlargement, if restrained to that same place?

It is, indeed, said that at this time *there were many other episcopal sees* in Achaia; which, until it is attempted to be put upon some kind of proof, may be passed by. It is granted that Paul speaks of that which was done at Corinth to be done in Achaia, Rom. xv. 26, as what is done in London is without doubt done in England ; but that which lies in expectation of some light or evidence to be given unto it. is, that there was a metropolitical see at Corinth at this time, whereunto many episcopal sees in Achaia were in subordination, being all the παροικία of Corinth, all which are called the church of Corinth, by virtue of their subjection thereunto. When this is proved, I shall confess some principles I afterward insist on will be impaired thereby.

This, then, is added by the same author, "That the ecclesiastical estate was then conformed to the civil. Wherever there was a metropolis in a civil-political sense, there was seated also a metropolitical church. Now, that Corinth was a metropolis, the proconsul of Achaia keeping his residence there, in the first sense is confessed." And besides what follows from thence, by virtue of the principle now laid down, Chrysostom calls it a metropolis, relating to the time where-in Paul wrote his epistle to the church there, in the latter sense also.

The plea about metropolitical churches, I suppose, will be thought very impertinent to what I have now in hand, so it shall not at present be insisted on. That the state of churches in after ages was moulded and framed after the pattern of the civil government of the Roman empire is granted; and that conformity (without offence to any be it spoken) we take to be a fruit of the working of "the mystery of iniquity." But that there was any such order instituted in the churches of Christ by the apostles, or any intrusted with authority from their Lord and Ruler, is utterly denied; nor is any thing but very uncertain conjectures from the sayings of men of after ages produced to attest any such order or constitution. When the order, spirituality, beauty, and glory of the church of Christ shall return, and men obtain a light whereby they are able to discern a beauty and excellency in the inward, more noble, spiritual part, indeed life and soul, of the worship of God, these disputes will have an issue. Chrysostom says, indeed, that Corinth was the metropolis of Achaia; but in what sense he says not. The political is granted; the ecclesiastical not proved. Nor are we inquiring what was the state of the churches of Christ in the days of Chrysostom, but of Paul. But to return.

If any one now shall say, "Will you conclude, because this evil mentioned by the apostle is *schism*, therefore nothing else is so?"

I answer, that having before asserted this to be the chief and only seat of the doctrine of schism, I am inclinable so to do. And this I am resolved of, that unless any man can prove that something else is termed schism by some divine writer, or blamed on that head of account by the Holy Ghost elsewhere, and is not expressly reproved as another crime, I will be at liberty from admitting it so to be.

But yet for what may hence by a parity of reason be deduced, I shall close with and debate at large, as I have professed.

The schism, then, here described by the apostle, and blamed by him, consists in *causeless differences and contentions amongst the members of a particular church, contrary to that [exercise] of love, prudence, and forbearance, which are required of them to be exercised amongst themselves, and towards one another;* which is also termed στάσις, Acts xv. 2, and διχοστασία, Rom. xvi. 17. And he is a schismatic that is guilty of this sin of schism,—that is, who raiseth, or entertaineth, or persisteth in such differences. Nor are these terms used by the divine writers in any other sense.

That any men may fall under this guilt, it is required,—

1. That they be *members* of or belong to some *one church*, which is so by the institution and appointment of Jesus Christ. And we

shall see that there is more required hereunto than the bare being a believer or a Christian.

2. That they either *raise or entertain*, and persist in, causeless differences with others of that church, more or less, to the interruption of that exercise of love, in all the fruits of it, which ought to be amongst them, and the disturbance of the due performance of the duties required of the church in the worship of God; as Clement in the fore-mentioned epistle, Φιλόνεικοί ἐστε ἀδελφοὶ καὶ ζηλωταὶ περὶ μὴ ἀνηκόντων εἰς σωτηρίαν.

3. That these differences be *occasioned* by and do belong to some things, in a remoter or nearer distance, *appertaining to the worship of God*. Their differences on a civil account are elsewhere mentioned and reproved, 1 Epist., chap. vi.; for therein, also, there was, from the then state of things, an ἥττημα, verse 7.

This is that crime which the apostle rebukes, blames, condemns, under the name of schism, and tells them that were guilty of it that they showed themselves to be carnal, or to have indulged to the flesh, and the corrupt principle of self, and their own wills, which should have been subdued to the obedience of the gospel. Men's definitions of things are for the most part arbitrary and loose, fitted and suited to their several apprehensions of principles and conclusions, so that nothing clear or fixed is generally to be expected from them; from the Romanists' description of schism, who violently, without the least colour or pretence, thrust in the pope and his headship into all that they affirm in church matters, least of all. I can allow men that they may extend their definitions of things unto what they apprehend of an alike nature to that which gives rise to the whole disquisition, and is the first thing defined; but at this I must profess myself to be somewhat entangled, that I could never yet meet with a definition of schism that did comprise, that was not exclusive of, that which alone in the Scripture is affirmed so to be.

Austin's definition contains the sum of what hath since been insisted on. Saith he, " Schisma ni fallor est eadem opinantem, et eodem ritu utentem solo congregationis delectari dissidio," Con. Faust. lib. xx. cap. 3. By " dissidium congregationis" he intends separation from the church into a peculiar congregation; a definition directly suited to the cause he had in hand and was pleading against the Donatists. Basil, in Epist. ad Amphiloch. Con. xliv., distinguisheth between αἵρεσις, σχίσμα, and παρασυναγωγή. And as he makes schism to be a division arising from some church controversies, suitable to what those days experienced, and in the substance true, so he tells us that παρασυναγωγή is when either presbyters, or bishops, or laics hold unlawful meetings, assemblies, or conventicles; which was not long since with us the only schism.

Since those days, schism in general hath passed for a *causeless separation from the communion and worship of any true church of Christ* ("The Catholic church," saith the Papist), with a relinquishment of its society, as to a joint celebration of the ordinances of the gospel. How far this may pass for schism, and what may be granted in this description of it, the process of our discourse will declare. In the meantime, I am most certain that a separation from some churches, true or pretended so to be, is commanded in the Scriptures; so that the withdrawing from or relinquishment of any church or society whatever, upon the plea of its corruption, be it true or false, with a mind and resolution to serve God in the due observation of church institutions, according to that light which men have received, is nowhere called schism, nor condemned as a thing of that nature, but is a matter that must be tried out, whether it be good or evil, by virtue of such general rules and directions as are given us in the Scriptures for our orderly and blameless walking with God in all his ways.

As for them who suppose all church power to be invested in some certain church officers originally (I mean that which they call of jurisdiction), who on that account are "eminenter" the church, the union of the whole consisting in a subjection to those officers, according to rules, orders, and canons of their appointment, whereby they are necessitated to state the business of schism on the rejection of their power and authority, I shall speak to them afterward at large. For the present, I must take leave to say, that I look upon the whole of such a fabric as a product of prudence and necessity.

I cannot but fear lest some men's surmisings may prompt them to say that the evil of schism is thus stated in a compliance with that and them which before we blamed, and seems to serve to raise slight and contemptible thoughts of it, so that men need not be shaken though justly charged with it. But besides that sufficient testimony which I have to the contrary, that will abundantly shelter me from this accusation, by an assurance that I have not the least aim δουλεύειν ὑποθέσει, I shall farther add my apprehension of the greatness of the evil of this sin, if I may first be borne with a little in declaring what usual aggravations of it I do either not understand or else cannot assent unto.

Those who say it is a *rending of the seamless coat of Christ* (in which metaphorical expression men have wonderfully pleased themselves) seem to have mistaken their aim, and, instead of an aggravation of its evil, by that figure of speech, to have extenuated it. A rent of the body well compacted is not heightened to any one's apprehension in its being called the rending of a seamless coat. But men may be indulged the use of the most improper and groundless expressions, so they place no power of argument in them, whilst they find them moving their own, and suppose them to have an alike efficacy upon the affections of others. I can scarce think that any ever supposed that the coat of Christ was a type of his church, his church being clothed with him, not he with it. And, therefore, with commendation of his success who first invented that illusion, I leave it in the possession of them who want better arguments to evince the evil of this sin.

It is most usually said to be *a sin against charity*, as heresy is against faith. Heresy is a sin against faith, if I may so speak, both as it is taken for the doctrine of faith which is to be believed, and the assent of the mind whereby we do believe. He that is a heretic (I speak of him in the usual acceptation of the word, and the sense of them who make this comparison, in neither of which I am satisfied) rejects the doctrine of faith, and denies all assent unto it. Indeed, he doth the former by doing the latter. But is schism so a sin against charity? Doth it supplant and root love out of the heart? Is it an affection of the mind attended with an inconsistency therewith? I much question it.

The apostle tells us that "love is the bond of perfectness," Col. iii. 14, because, in the several and various ways whereby it exerts itself, it maintains and preserves, notwithstanding all hinderances and oppositions, that perfect and beautiful order which Christ hath appointed amongst his saints. When men by schism are kept off and withheld from the performance of any of those offices and duties of love which are useful or necessary for the preservation of the bond of perfection, then is it, or may in some sense be said to be, a sin against love.

Those who have seemed to aim nearest the apprehension of the nature of it in these days have described it to be an *open breach of love*, or charity. That that expression is warily to be understood is evident in the light of this single consideration : It is possible for a man to be all and do all that those were and did whom the apostle judges for schismatics, under the power of some violent temptation, and yet have his heart full of love to the saints of the communion disturbed by him. It is thus far, then, in its own nature a breach of love, in that in such men love cannot exert itself in its utmost tendency in wisdom and forbearance for the preservation of the perfect order instituted by Christ in his church. However, I shall freely say that the schoolmen's notion of it, who insist on this as its nature, that it is a sin against charity, as heresy is against faith, is fond and becoming them; and so will others also that shall be pleased to consider what they intend by charity.

Some say it is *a rebellion against the church,*—that is, the rulers and officers of the church. I doubt not but that there must be either a neglect in the church in the performance of its duty, or of the authority of it in so doing, wherever there is any schism, though the discovery of this also have innumerable entanglements attending it. But that to refuse the authority of the church is to rebel against the rulers or guides of it will receive farther light than what it hath done, when once a pregnant instance is produced, not where the church signifies the officers of it, but where it doth not signify the body of the congregation in contradistinction from them, or comprising them therein.

Add unto these those who dispute whether schismatics do belong to the church or no, and conclude in the negative, seeing, according to the discovery already made, it is impossible a man should be a schismatic unless he be a church member. Other crimes a man may be guilty of on other accounts; of schism, only in a church. What is the formal reason of any man's relation to a church, in what sense soever that word is used, must be afterward at large discussed.

But now this foundation being laid, that schism is a causeless difference or division amongst the members of any particular church that meet together, or ought so to do, for the worship of God and celebration of the same numerical ordinances, to the disturbance of the order appointed by Jesus Christ, and contrary to that exercise of love in wisdom and mutual forbearance which is required of them, it will be easy to see wherein the iniquity of it doth consist, and upon what considerations its aggravations do arise.

It is evidently a *despising of the authority of Jesus Christ,* the great sovereign Lord and Head of the church. How often hath he commanded us to forbear one another, to forgive one another, to have peace among ourselves, that we may be known to be his disciples, to bear with them that are in any thing contrary-minded to ourselves! To give light to this consideration, let that which at any time is the cause of such hateful divisions, rendered as considerable as the prejudices and most importune affections of men can represent it to be, be brought to the rule of love and forbearance in the latitude of it, as prescribed to us by Christ, and it will evidently bear no proportion thereunto ; so that such differences, though arising on real miscarriages and faults of some, because they might otherwise be handled and healed, and ought to be so, cannot be persisted in without the contempt of the immediate authority of Jesus Christ. If it were considered that he " standeth in the congregation of the mighty," Ps. lxxxii. 1; that he dwells in the church in glory, " as in Sinai, in the holy place," Ps. lxviii. 17, 18, walking " in the midst of the candlesticks," Rev. i. 13, with his eyes upon us as a "flame of fire," verse 14, his presence and authority would, perhaps, be more prevalent with some than they seem to be.

Again; *His wisdom,* whereby he hath ordered all things in his church on set purpose that schism and divisions may be prevented, *is no less despised.* Christ, who is the wisdom of the Father, 1 Cor. i. 24, the stone on which are seven eyes, Zech. iii. 9, upon whose shoulder the government is laid, Isa. ix. 6, 7, hath, in his infinite wisdom, so ordered all the officers, orders, gifts, administrations of and in his church, as that this evil might take no place. To manifest this is the design of the Holy Ghost, Rom. xii. 3–9; 1 Cor. xii.; Eph. iv. 8–13. The consideration, in particular, of this wisdom of Christ,—suiting the officers of his church, in respect of the places they hold, the authority wherewith from him they are invested, the way whereby they are entered into their functions; distributing the gifts of his Spirit in marvellous variety unto several kinds of usefulness, and with such distance and dissimilitude in the particular members, as, in a due correspondency and proportion, give comeliness and beauty to the whole; disposing of the order of his worship, and sundry ordinances in especial, to be expressive of the highest love and union; pointing all of them against such causeless divisions;—might be of use, were that my present intendment.

The grace and goodness of Christ, whence he hath promised to give us one heart and one way, to leave us peace such as the world cannot give, with innumerable other promises of the like importance, are disregarded thereby. So also is his prayer for us. With what affection and zeal did he pour out his soul to his Father for our union in love! That seems to be the thing his heart was chiefly fixed on when he was leaving this world, John xvii. What weight he laid thereon, how thereby we may be known to be his disciples, and the world be convinced that he was sent of God, is there also manifested.

How far the exercise of love and charity is obstructed by it hath been declared. The consideration of the *nature, excellency, property, effects, usefulness* of this grace in all the saints in all their ways, its especial *designation* by our Lord and Master to be the bond of union and perfection, in the way and order instituted for the comely celebration of the ordinances of the gospel, will add weight to this aggravation.

Its constant growing to farther evil, in some to apostasy itself,—its usual and certain ending in strife, variance, debate, evil surmisings, wrath, confusion, disturbances public and private,—are also to be laid all at its door. What farther of this nature and kind may be added (as much may be added) to evince the heinousness of this sin of schism, I shall willingly subscribe unto; so that I shall

not trouble the reader in abounding in what on all hands is confessed.

It is incumbent upon him who would have me to go farther in
the description of this evil than as formerly stated, to evince from
Scripture another notion of the name or thing than that given;
which when he hath done, he shall not find me refractory. In the
meantime, I shall both consider what may be objected against that
which hath been delivered, and also discuss the present state of our
divisions on the usual principles and common acceptation of schism,
if, first, I may have leave to make some few inferences or deductions from what hath already been spoken, and, as I hope, evinced.

On supposition that the church of Rome is a church of Christ, it
will appear to be the most schismatical church in the world. I say
on supposition that it is a church, and that there is such a thing as
a schismatical church (as perhaps a church may from its intestine
differences be not unfitly so denominated), that is the state and
condition thereof. The pope is the head of their church; several
nations of Europe are members of it. Have we not seen that head
taking his flesh in his teeth,—tearing his body and his limbs to pieces?
Have some of them thought on any thing else but, "Arise, Peter,
kill and eat," all their days? Have we not seen this goodly head, in
disputes about Peter's patrimony and his own jurisdiction, wage
war, fight, and shed blood,—the blood of his own members? Must
we believe armies raised, and battles fought, towns fired, all in pure
love and perfect church order? not to mention their old "altare
contra altare," anti-popes, anti-councils. Look all over their church,
on their potentates, bishops, friars,—there is no end of their vari-
ances. What do the chiefest, choicest pillars, eldest sons, and I
know not what, of their church at this day? Do they not kill, destroy, and ruin each other, as they are able? Let them not say these
are the divisions of the nations that are in their church, not of the
church; for all these nations, on their hypothesis, are members of
that one church. And that church which hath no means to prevent its members from designed, resolved on, and continued mur-
dering one of another, nor can remove them from its society, shall
never have me in its communion, as being bloodily schismatical.
Nor is there any necessity that men should forego their respective
civil interests by being members of one church. Prejudicate apprehensions of the nature of a church and its authority lie at the bottom of that difficulty. Christ hath ordained no church that inwraps
such interests as on the account whereof the members of it may
murder one another. Whatever, then, they pretend of unity, and
however they make it a note of the true church (as it is a property
of it), that which is like it amongst them is made up of these two

ingredients,—*subjection to the pope, either for fear of their lives or advantage to their livelihood, and a conspiracy for the destruction and suppression of them that oppose their interests;* wherein they agree like those who maintained Jerusalem in its last siege by Titus,—they all consented to oppose the Romans, and yet fought out all other things among themselves. That they are not so openly clamorous about the differences at present as in former ages is merely from the pressure of Protestants round about them. However, let them at this day silence the Jesuits and Dominicans, especially the Baijans and the Jansenians on the one part, and the Molinists on the other;—take off the Gallican church from its schismatical refusal of the council of Trent;—cause the king of Spain to quit his claim to Sicily, that they need not excommunicate him every year;—compel the commonwealth of Venice to receive the Jesuits; stop the mouths of the Sorbonnists about the authority of a general council above the pope, and of all those whom, opposing the papal omnipotency, they call politicians;—quiet the contest of the Franciscans and Dominicans about the blessed Virgin;—burn Bellarmine's books, who almost on every controversy of Christian religion gives an account of their intestine divisions; branding some of their opinions as heretical, as that of Medina about bishops and presbyters; some as idolatrical, as that of Thomas about the worship of the cross with " latria," etc.;—and they may give a better colour to their pretences than any as yet they wear.

But what need I insist upon this supposition, when I am not more certain that there is any instituted church in the world, owned by Christ as such, than I am that the church of Rome is none, properly so called? Nor shall I be thought singular in this persuasion, if it be duly considered what this amounts unto. Some learned men of latter days in this nation, pleading in the justification of the church of England as to her departure from Rome, did grant that the church of Rome doth not err in fundamentals, or maintained no errors remedilessly pernicious and destructive of salvation. How far they entangled themselves by this concession I argue not. The foundation of it lies in this clear truth, that no church whatever, universal or particular, can possibly err in fundamentals; for by so doing it would cease to be a church. My denying, then, the synagogue of Rome to be a church, according to their principles, amounts to no more than this,—the Papists maintain, in their public confessions, fundamental errors; in which assertion it is known I am not alone.

But this is not the principle, at least not the sole or main principle, whereon I ground my judgment in this case; but this, that there was never any such thing, in any tolerable likeness or similitude, as that which is called the church of Rome, allowing the most skilful of its rabbis to give in the characters and delineations of it, instituted in reference to the worship of God by Jesus Christ. The truth is, the whole of it is but an imitation and exemplar of the old imperial government. One is set up in chief, and made ἀνυπεύθυνος in spirituals, as the emperors were in several things; from him all power flows to others. And as there was a communication of power by the emperors, in the civil state to prefects, proconsuls, vicars, presidents, governors of the lesser and greater nations, with those under them, in various civil subordinations, according to the dignity of the places where they did bear rule and preside; and in the military to generals, legates, tribunes, and the inferior officers;—so is there by the pope to patriarchs, archbishops, bishops, in their several subordinations, which are as his civil state; and to generals of religious orders, provincials, and their dependants, which are as his military. And it is by some (not in all things agreeing with them) confessed that the government pleaded for by them in the church was brought in and established in correspondency and accommodation to the civil government of the empire; which is undeniably evident and certain. Now, this being not thoroughly done till the empire had received an incurable wound, it seems to me to be the making of an image to the beast, giving life to it, and causing it to speak. So that the present Roman church is nothing else but an image or similitude of the Roman empire, set up, in its declining, among and over the same persons in succession, by the craft of Satan, through principles of deceit, subtlety, and spiritual wickedness, as the other was by force and violence, for the same ends of power, dominion, fleshliness, and persecution with the former.

The exactness of this correspondency in all things, both in respect of those who claim to be the stated body of his ecclesiastical commonwealth, and those who are merely dependent on his will, bound unto him professedly by a military sacrament, exempted from the ordinary rules and government of his fixed rulers in their several subordinations, under officers of their own, immediately commissionated by him, with his management of both these parties to balance and keep them mutually in quiet and in order for his service (especially confiding in his men of war, like the emperors of old), may elsewhere be farther manifested.

I suppose it will not be needful to add any thing to evince the vanity of the pretensions of the Romanists or others against all or any of us on the account of schism, upon a grant of the principles laid down, it lies so clear in them without need of farther deduction; and I speak with some confidence that I am not in expectation of any hasty confutation of them,—I mean, that which is so indeed. [As for] the earnestness of their clamours, importuning us to take notice of them, by the way, before I enter upon a direct debate of the cause, as it stands stated in reference to them, I shall only tell them, that, seeking to repose our consciences on the mind of God revealed in the Scriptures, we are not at all concerned in the noise they make in the world. For what have we done? Wherein doth our guilt consist? Wherein lies the peculiar concernment of these ἀλλοτριοεπίσ- κοποι? Let them go to the churches with whom we walk, of whom we are, and ask of them concerning our ways, our love, and the duties of it. Do we live in strife and variance? Do we not bear with each other? Do we not worship God without disputes and divisions? Have we differences and contentions in our assemblies? Do we break any bond of union wherein we are bound by the express institutions of Jesus Christ? If we have, let the righteous reprove us; we will own our guilt, confess we have been carnal, and endea- vour reformation. If not, what have the Romanists, Italians, to do to judge us? Knew we not your design, your interest, your lives, your doctrines, your worship, we might possibly think that you might intermeddle out of love and mistaken zeal; but " ad populum pha- leras,"—you would be making shrines, and thence is this stir and uproar. " But we are schismatics, in that we have departed from the catholic church; and for our own conventicles, they are no churches, but sties of beasts." But this is most false. We abide in the ca- tholic church, under all the bonds wherein, by the will of Christ, we stand related unto it; which if we prove not with as much evidence as the nature of such things will bear, though you are not at all concerned in it, yet we will give you leave to triumph over us. And if our own congregations be not churches, whatsoever we are, we are not schismatics; for schism is an evil amongst the members of a church, if St Paul may be believed. " But we have forsaken the church of Rome." But, gentlemen, show first how we were ever of it. No man hath lost that which he never had, nor hath left the place or station wherein he never was. Tell me when or how we were members of your church? We know not your language; you are barbarians to us. It is impossible we should assemble with you. " But your forefathers left that church, and you persist in their evil." Prove that our forefathers were ever of your church in any com- munion instituted by Christ, and you say somewhat. To desert a man's station and relation, which he had on any other account, good or bad, is not schism, as shall farther be manifested.

Upon the same principle, a plea for freedom from the charge of any church, real or pretended, as *national*, may be founded and confirmed. Either we are of the national church of England (to give that instance) or we are not;—if we are not, and are exempted by our protestation as before, whatever we are, we are not schismatics;

if we are fatally bound unto it, and must be members of it whether we will or no, being made so we know not how, and continuing so we know not why, show us, then, what duty or office of love is incumbent on us that we do not perform. Do we not join in external acts of worship in peace with the whole church? Call the whole church together, and try what we will do. Do we not join in every congregation in the nation? This is not charged on us, nor will any say that we have right so to do without a relation to some particular church in the nation. I know where the sore lies. A national officer or officers, with others acting under them in several subordinations, with various distributions of power, are the church intended. A non-submission to their rules and constitutions is the schism we are guilty of.

"Quem das finem, rex magne, laborum!"

But this pretence shall afterward be sifted to the utmost. In the meantime, let any one inform me what duty I ought to perform towards a national church, on supposition there is any such thing by virtue of an institution of Jesus Christ, that is possible for me to perform, and I shall, σὺν Θεῷ, address myself unto it.

To close these considerations with things of more immediate concernment: Of the divisions that have fallen out amongst us in things of religion since the last revolutions of this nation, there is no one thing hath been so effectual a promotion (such is the power of tradition and prejudice, which even bear all before them in human affairs) as the mutual charging one another with the guilt of schism. That the notion of schism whereon this charge is built by the most, if not all, was invented by some of the ancients, to promote their plea and advantage with them with whom they had to do, without due regard to the simplicity of the gospel, at least in a suitableness to the present state of the church in those days, is too evident; for on very small foundations have mighty fabrics and μορμωλυκεῖα in religion been raised. As an ability to judge of the present posture and condition of affairs, with counsel to give direction for their order and management towards any end proposed,—not an ability to contrive for events, and to knit on one thing upon another, according to a probability of success, for continuance, which is almost constantly disturbed by unexpected providential interveniences, leaving the contrivers at a perplexing loss,—will be found to be the sum of human wisdom; so it will be our wisdom, in the things of God, not to judge according to what by any means is made present to us, and its principles on that account rendered ready to exert themselves, but ever to recoil to the original and first institution. When a man first falls into some current, he finds it strong and almost impassable; trace it to its fountain, and it is but a dribbling gutter. Paul tells the members of the church of Corinth that there were divisions amongst them, breaches of that love and order that ought to be observed in religious assemblies. Hence there is a sin of schism raised; which, when considered as now stated, doth no more relate to that treated on by the apostle than "Simon, son of Jonas, lovest thou me?" doth to the pope's supremacy; or Christ saying to Peter of John, "If I will that he tarry till I come, what is that to thee?" did to the report that afterward went abroad, "that that disciple should not die." When God shall have reduced his churches to their primitive purity and institution, when they are risen and have shaken themselves out of the dust, and things of religion return to their native simplicity, it is scarce possible to imagine what vizards will fall off, and what a contrary appearance many things will have to what they now walk up and down in.

I wish that those who are indeed really concerned in this business, —namely, the members of particular churches who have voluntarily given up themselves to walk in them according to the appointment of Christ,—would seriously consider what evil lies at the door if they give place to causeless differences and divisions amongst themselves. Had this sin of schism been rightly stated, as it ought, and the guilt of it charged in its proper place, perhaps some would have been more careful in their deportment, in their relations. At present the dispute in the world relating hereunto is about *subjection to the pope* and the church of Rome, as it is called; and this managed on the principles of edicts and of councils, with the practices of princes and nations, in the days long ago past, with the like considerations, wherein the concernment of Christians is doubtless very small; or of obedience and conformity to metropolitan and diocesan bishops in their constitutions and ways of worship, jointly or severally prescribed by them. In more ancient times, that which was agitated under the same name was about persons or churches renouncing the communion and society of saints with all other churches in the world, yet consenting with them in the same confession of faith, for the substance of it. And these differences respectively are handled in reference to what the state of things was and is grown unto in the days wherein they are managed. When Paul wrote his epistle, there was no occasion given to any such controversies, nor foundation laid making them possible. That the disciples of Christ ought everywhere to abound in love and forbearance towards one another, especially to carry all things in union and peace in those societies wherein they were joined for the worship of God, were his endeavours and exhortations: of these things he is utterly silent. Let them who aim to recover themselves into the like state and condition consider his commands, exhortations, and reproofs. Things are now generally otherwise stated, which furnisheth men with objections against what hath been spoken; to whose removal, and farther clearing of the whole matter, I shall now address myself.

CHAPTER III.

Objections against the former discourse proposed to consideration—Separation from any church in the Scripture not called schism—Grounds of such separation; apostasy, irregular walking, sensuality—Of separation on the account of reformation—Of commands for separation—No example of churches departing from the communion of one another—Of the common notion of schism, and the use made of it—Schism a breach of union—The union instituted by Christ.

" THAT which lies obvious to every man against what hath been delivered, and which is comprehensive of what particular objections it seems liable and obnoxious to, is, that according to this description of schism, separation of any man or men from a true church, or of one church from others, is not schism, seeing that is an evil only amongst the members of one church, whilst they continue so to be; which is so contrary to the judgment of the generality of Christians in this business that it ought to be rejected as fond and absurd."

Of what hath been the judgment of most men in former ages, what it is in this, what strength there is in an argument deduced from the consent pretended, I am not as yet arrived to the consideration. Nor have I yet manifested what I grant of the general notion of schism, as it may be drawn, by way of analogy or proportion of reason, from what is delivered in the Scriptures concerning it.

I am upon the precise signification of the word and description of the thing, as used and given by the Holy Ghost. In this sense I deny that there is any relinquishment, departure, or separation from any church or churches mentioned or intimated in the Scriptures, which is or is called schism, or agreeth with the description by them given us of that term. Let them that are contrary minded attempt the proof of what they affirm. As far as a negative proposition is capable of evidence from any thing but the weakness of the opposition made unto it, that laid down will receive it by the ensuing considerations:—

All blamable departure from any church or churches, or relinquishment of them mentioned in the gospel, may be reduced to one of these three heads or causes:—1. *Apostasy;* 2. *Irregularity of walking;* 3. *Professed sensuality.*

1. Apostasy, or falling away from the faith of the gospel, and

thereupon forsaking the congregations or assemblies for the worship of God in Jesus Christ, is mentioned, Heb. x. 25, Μὴ ἐγκαταλείποντες τὴν ἐπισυναγωγὴν ἑαυτῶν,—"Not wholly deserting the assembling ourselves, as is the manner of some." A separation from and relinquishment of the communion of that church or those churches with whom men have assembled for the worship of God is the guilt here charged on some by the apostle. Upon what account they so separated themselves is declared, verse 26, They "sinned wilfully, after they had received the knowledge of the truth;" thereby slipping out their necks from the yoke of Christ, verse 38, and "drawing back unto perdition," verse 39 ;—that is, they departed off to Judaism. I much question whether any one would think fit to call these men schismatics, or whether we should so judge or so speak of any that in these days should forsake our churches and turn Mohammedans; such departure makes men apostates, not schismatics. Of this sort many are mentioned in the Scriptures. Nor are they not at all accounted schismatics because the lesser crime is swallowed up and drowned in the greater, but because their sin is wholly of another nature.

Of some who withdraw themselves from church communion, at least for a season, by their disorderly and irregular walking, we have also mention. The apostle calls them ἄτακτοι, 1 Thess v. 14, "unruly," or "disorderly" persons, not abiding in obedience to the order prescribed by Christ in and unto his churches, and says they walked ἀτάκτως, 2 Thess. iii. 6, out of all church order; whom he would have warned and avoided : so also, ἀτόπους, verse 2, persons that abide quietly in no place or station, but wander up and down; whom, whatever their profession be, he denies to have faith. That there were many of this sort in the primitive times, who, through a vain and slight spirit, neglected and fell off from church assemblies, when yet they would not openly renounce the faith of Christ, is known. Of such disorderly persons we have many in our days wherein we live, whom we charge not with schism, but vanity, folly, disobedience to the precepts of Christ in general.

Men also separated themselves from the churches of Christ upon the account of sensuality, that they might freely indulge to their lusts, and live in all manner of pleasure all their days: Jude 19, "These be they who separate themselves, sensual, having not the Spirit." Who are these? They that "turn the grace of our God into lasciviousness," and that "deny the only Lord God, and our Saviour Jesus Christ," verse 4; that "defile the flesh," after the manner of Sodom and Gomorrah, verses 7, 8; that "speak evil of things they know not," and in "things they know naturally, as brute beasts, they corrupt themselves," verses 10,—sinning openly, like beasts, against the light of nature: so verses 12, 13, 16. "These," saith the apostle, "be they who separate themselves," men given over to work all uncleanness with delight and greediness in the face of the sun, abusing themselves, and justifying their abominations with a pretence of the grace of God.

That there is any blamable separation from or relinquishment of any church or churches of Christ mentioned in the Scripture, but what may be referred to one of those heads, I am yet to learn. Now, whether the men of these abominations are to be accounted schismatics, or their crime in separating themselves to be esteemed schism, it is not hard to judge. If, on any of these accounts, any persons have withdrawn themselves from the communion of any church of Christ; if they have on any motives of fear or love apostatized from the faith of the gospel; if they do it by walking disorderly and loosely in their conversations; if they give themselves up to sensuality and uncleanness, and so be no more able to bear the society of them whom God hath called to holiness and purity of life and worship,—they shall assuredly bear their own burden.

But none of these instances are comprehensive of the case inquired after; so that, for a close of them, I say, for a man to withdraw or withhold himself from the communion external and visible of any church or churches, on the pretension and plea, be it true or otherwise, that the worship, doctrine, or discipline, instituted by Christ is corrupted among them, with which corruption he dares not defile himself, it is nowhere in the Scripture called schism. Nor is that case particularly exemplified or expressly supposed whereby a judgment may be made of the fact at large; but we are left upon the whole matter to the guidance of such general principles and rules as are given us for that end and purpose.

What may regularly, on the other hand, be deduced from the commands given to "turn away from them who have only a form of godliness," 2 Tim. iii. 5; to "withdraw from them that walk disorderly," 2 Thess. iii. 6; not to bear nor endure in communion men of corrupt principles and wicked lives, Rev. ii. 14; but positively to separate from an apostate church, chap. xviii. 4, that in all things we may worship Christ according to his mind and appointment; what is the force of these commands Ἀποτρέπεσθαι, μὴ συναναμίγνυσθαι, παραπίπτεσθαι, ἐκκλίνειν, μὴ κοινωνεῖν, μὴ λέγειν χαίρειν, φεύγειν, and the like,—is without the compass of what I am now treating about.

Of one particular church departing from that communion with another or others, be it what it will, which it ought to hold, unless in the departing of some of them in some things from the common faith, which is supposed not to relate to schism, in the Scripture we have no example. Diotrephes, assuming an authority over that church wherein he was placed, 3 John 9, 10, and for a season hindering the brethren from the performance of the duty incumbent upon them toward the great apostle and others, makes the nearest approach to such a division, but yet in such a distance that it is not at all to our purpose in hand. When I come to consider that communion that churches have, or ought to have, among themselves, this will be more fully discussed. Neither is this my sense alone, that there is no instance of any such separation as that which is the matter of our debate to be found in the Scripture; it is confessed by others differing from me in and about church affairs. To "leave all ordinary communion in any church with dislike, where opposition or offence offers itself, is to separate from such a church in the Scripture sense; such separation was not in being in the apostles' time," say they, Pap. Accom. p. 55. But how they came to know exactly the sense of the Scriptures in and about things not mentioned in them, I know not. As I said before, were I unwilling, I do not as yet understand how I may be compelled to carry on the notion of schism any farther. Nor is there need of adding any thing to demonstrate how little the conscience of a godly man, walking peaceably in any particular church-society, is concerned in all the clamorous disputes of this age about it, these being built on false hypotheses, presumptions, and notions, no other way considerable but as received by tradition from our fathers.

But I shall, for the sake of some, carry on this discourse to a fuller issue. There is another common notion of schism, which pleads for an original from that spoken expressly of it by a parity of reason; which, tolerable in itself, hath been, and is, injuriously applied and used, according as it hath fallen into the hands of men who needed it as an engine to fix or improve them in the station wherein they are or were, and wherewith they are pleased. Indeed, being invented for several purposes, there is nothing more frequent than for men who are scarce able to keep off the force of it from their own heads, whilst managed against them by them above, at the same time vigorously to apply it for the oppression of all under them. What is on all hands consented unto as its general nature I shall freely grant, that I might have liberty and advantage thence to debate the restriction and application of it to the several purposes of men prevailing themselves thereon.

Let, then, the general demand be granted, that schism is διαίρεσις τῆς ἑνότητος, "the breach of union," which I shall attend with one reasonable postulatum,—namely, that this union be a union of the appointment of Jesus Christ. The consideration, then of what or what sort of union in reference to the worship of God, according to the gospel, is instituted and appointed by Jesus Christ, is the proper foundation of what I have farther to offer in this business. Let the breach of this, if you please, be accounted schism; for being an evil,

I shall not contend by what name or title it be distinguished. It is
not pleaded that any kind of relinquishment or desertion of any
church or churches is presently schism, but only such a separation
as breaks the bond of union instituted by Christ.

Now, this union being instituted in the church, according to the
various acceptations of that word, so is it distinguished. Therefore,
for a discovery of the nature of that which is particularly to be
spoken to, and also its contrary, I must show,—

1. The several *considerations of the church* wherein and with
which union is to be preserved.

2. What that *union* is, and wherein it doth consist, which, according to the mind of Christ, we are to keep and observe with the
church, under the several notions of it respectively.

3. And *how that union is broken*, and what is that sin whereby
it is done.

In handling this triple proposal, I desire that it may not be expected that I should much insist on any thing that falls in my way,
though never so useful to my end and purpose, which hath been
already proved and confirmed by others beyond all possibility of
control; and such will many, if not most, of the principles that I
proceed upon appear to be.

CHAPTER IV.

Several acceptations in the Scripture of the name "church"—Of the church catholic,
properly so called—Of the church visible—Perpetuity of particular churches—
A mistake rectified—The nature of the church catholic evinced—Bellarmine's
description of the church catholic—Union of the church catholic, wherein it
consists—Union by way of consequence—Unity of faith, of love—The communion of the catholic church in and with itself—The breach of the union of
the church catholic, wherein it consisteth—Not morally possible—Protestants
not guilty of it—The papal world out of interest in the church catholic—As
partly profane—Miracles no evidence of holiness—Partly ignorant—Self-justiciaries—Idolatrous—Worshippers of the beast.

To begin with the first thing proposed: The church of Christ living
in this world, as to our present concernment, is taken in Scripture
three ways:—

1. For the *mystical body* of Christ, his elect, redeemed, justified,
and sanctified ones throughout the world; commonly called *the
church catholic militant*.

2. For the *universality* of men throughout the world *called* by
the preaching of the word, visibly professing and yielding obedience
to the gospel; called by some *the church catholic visible*.

3. For a *particular church* of some place, wherein the instituted worship of God in Christ is celebrated according to his mind.

From the rise and nature of the things themselves doth this distinction of the signification of the word " church" arise: for whereas the church is a society of men called out of the world, it is evident there is mention of a twofold call in Scripture;—one *effectual*, according to the purpose of God, Rom. viii. 28; the other only *external.* The church must be distinguished according to its answer and obedience to these calls, which gives us the first two states and considerations of it. And this is confessed by the ordinary gloss, ad Rom. viii. " Vocatio exterior fit per prædicatores, et est communis bonorum et malorum, interior vero tantum est electorum." And whereas there are laws and external rules for joint communion given to them that are called, which is confessed, the necessity of churches in the last acceptation, wherein obedience can alone be yielded to those laws, is hereby established.

In the first sense the church hath, as such, the properties of *perpetuity, invisibility, infallibility,* as to all necessary means of salvation, attending of it; not as notes whereby it may be known, either in the whole or any considerable part of it, but as certain adjuncts of its nature and existence. Neither are there any signs of less or more certainty whereby the whole may be discerned or known as such, though there are of the individuals whereof it doth consist.

In the second, the church hath *perpetuity, visibility,* and *infallibility,* as qualified above, in a secondary sense,—namely, not as such, not as visible and confessing, but as comprising the individuals whereof the catholic church doth consist; for all that truly believe profess, though all that profess do not truly believe.

Whether Christ hath had always a church, in the last sense and acceptation of the word, in the world, is a most needless inquiry; nor are we concerned in it any farther than in other matters of fact that are recorded in story: though I am apt to believe that although very many, in all ages, kept up their station in and relation to the church in the two former acceptations, yet there was in some of them scarce any visible society of worshippers, so far answering the institution of Christ as to render them fit to be owned and joined withal as a visible particular church of Christ. But yet, though the notions of men were generally corrupt, the practice of all professors throughout the world, whereof so little is recorded, and least of them that did best, is not rashly to be determined of. Nor can our judgment be censured in this by them who think that when Christ lay in the grave there was no believer left but his mother, and that the church was preserved in that one person. So was Bernard minded, Tractat. de Pass. Dom. " Ego sum vitis," cap. ii., " [B. Virgo] sola per illud

triste sabbathum stetit in fide, et salvata fuit ecclesia in ipsâ solâ."
Of the same mind is Marsilius in Sent., quæst. 20, art. 3; as are also
others of that sort of men: see Bannes, in 2, 2; Thom., quæst. 1,
art. 10. I no way doubt of the perpetual existence of innumerable
believers in every age, and such as made the profession that is absolutely necessary to salvation, one way or other, though I question a
regular association of men for the celebration of instituted worship,
according to the mind of Christ. The seven thousand in Israel, in
the days of Elijah, were members of the church of God, and yet did
not constitute a church-state among the ten tribes. But these things
must be farther spoken to.

I cannot but by the way remind a learned person,[1] with whom I
have formerly occasionally had some debate in print about episcopacy and the state of the first churches, of a mistake of his, which
he might have prevented with a little inquiry into the judgment of
them whom he undertook to confute at a venture. I have said that
"there was not any ordinary church-officer instituted in the first
times, relating to more churches in his office, or to any other church,
than a single particular congregation." He replies, that "this is the
very same which his memory suggested to him out of the 'Saints'
Belief,' printed twelve or fourteen years since, where, instead of that
article of the apostolic symbol, 'The holy catholic church,' this very
hypothesis was substituted." If he really believed that, in professing
I owned no instituted church with officers of one denomination in
Scripture beyond a single congregation, I renounced the catholic
church, or was any way necessitated so to do, I suppose he may, by
what hath now been expressed, be rectified in his apprehension. If
he was willing only to make use of the advantage, wherewith he
supposed himself accommodated by that expression, to press the persuasion owned on the minds of ignorant men, who could not but
startle at the noise of denying the catholic church, it may pass at
the same rate that most of the repartees in such discourses are to be
allowed at. But to proceed:—

I. In the first sense the word is used Matt. xvi. 18, "Upon this rock
I will build my church, and the gates of hell shall not prevail against
it." This is the *church of the elect,* redeemed, justified, sanctified
ones, that are so built on Christ, and these only; and all these are
interested in the promise made to the church. There is no promise
made to the church, as such in any sense, but is peculiarly made
therein to every one that is truly and properly a part and member

---

[1] Dr Hammond, with whom Owen had some controversy in regard to the sentiments
of Grotius, and the divine authority of episcopal government. See Owen's preface to
his work on "The Perseverance of the Saints," his "Vindiciæ Evangelicæ," and "Review
of the Annotations of Grotius."—ED.

of that church. Who, and who only, are interested in that promise Christ himself declares, John vi. 40, x. 27–29, xvii. 20, 24. They that will apply this to the church in any other sense must know that it is incumbent on them to establish the promise made to it unto every one that is a true member of the church in that sense; which, whatever be the sense of the promise, I suppose they will find difficult work of. Eph. v. 25–27, "Christ loved the church, and gave himself for it, that he might sanctify and cleanse it with the washing of water by the word, that he might present it to himself a glorious church, not having spot, or wrinkle, or any such thing." He speaks only of those whom Christ loved antecedently to his dying for them, whereof his love to them was the cause : who they are is manifest, John x. 15, xvii. 17, even those on whom, by his death, he accomplished the effects mentioned, by washing, cleansing, and sanctifying, bringing them into the condition promised to the "bride, the Lamb's wife," Rev. xix. 8, which is the "new Jerusalem," xxi. 2, of elected and saved ones, verse 27. Col. i. 18 contains an expression of the same light and evidence, "Christ is the head of the body, the church;" not only a governing head, to give it rules and laws, but, as it were, a natural head unto the body, which is influenced by him with a new spiritual life;—which Bellarmine protesteth against as any requisite condition to the members of the catholic church, which he pleaded for. In that same sense, verse 24, saith the apostle, "I fill up that which is behind of the afflictions of Christ in my flesh, for his body's sake, which is the church;" which assertion is exactly parallel to that of 2 Tim. ii. 10, "Therefore I endure all things for the elect's sakes, that they may obtain salvation." So that the *elect* and the *church* are the same persons under several considerations. And therefore even a particular church, on the account of its participation of the nature of the catholic, is called "elect," 1 Pet. v. 13; and so the church, Matt. xvi. 18, is expounded by our Saviour himself, chap. xxiv. 24. But to prove at large, by a multiplication of arguments and testimonies, that the catholic church, or mystical body of Christ, consists of the whole number of the elect, as redeemed, justified, sanctified, called, believing, and yielding obedience to Christ throughout the world (I speak of it as militant in any age), and of them only, were as needlessly "actum agere" as a man can well devise. It is done already, and that to the purpose uncontrollably, "terque quaterque." And the substance of the doctrine is delivered by Aquinas himself, p. 3, q. 8, a. 3. In brief, the sum of the inquiry upon this head is concerning the matter of that church concerning which such glorious things are spoken in Scripture,—namely, that it is "the spouse, the wife, the bride, the sister, the only one of Christ, his dove, his undefiled, his temple, elect, redeemed, his Zion, his body, his new Jerusalem;" concerning which inquiry the reader knows where he may abundantly find satisfaction.

That the asserting the catholic church in this sense is no new apprehension is known to them who have at all looked backward to what was past before us. " Omnibus consideratis," saith Austin, " puto me non temere dicere, alios ita esse in domo Dei, ut ipsi etiam sint eadem domus Dei, quæ dicitur ædificari supra petram, quæ unica columba appellatur, quæ sponsa pulchra sine macula, et ruga, et hortus conclusus, fons signatus, puteus aquæ vivæ, paradisus cum fructu pomorum, alios autem ita constat esse in domo, ut non pertineant ad compagem domûs, sed sicut esse palea dicitur in frumentis," De Bapt., lib. i. cap. 51; who is herein followed by not a few of the Papists. Hence saith Biel., " Accipitur etiam ecclesia pro tota multitudine prædestinatorum," in Canon. Miss. Lec. 22. In what sense this church is visible was before declared. Men elected, redeemed, justified, as such, are not visible, for that which makes them so is not; but this hinders not but they may be so upon the other consideration, sometimes to more, sometimes to fewer, yea, they are so always to some. Those that are may be seen; and when we say they are visible, we do not intend that they are actually seen by any that we know, but that they may be so.

Bellarmine gives us a description of this catholic church (as the name hath of late been used at the pleasure of men, and wrested to serve every design that was needful to be carried on) to the interest which he was to contend for, but in itself perfectly ridiculous. He tells us, out of Austin, that the church is *a living body*, wherein is a body and a soul. Thence, saith he, the *soul* is the *internal graces* of the Spirit, faith, hope, and love; the *body* is the *external profession* of faith. Some are of the soul and body, perfectly united to Christ by faith and the profession of it; some are of the soul that are not of the body, as the catechumeni, which are not as yet admitted to be members of the visible church, but yet are true believers; some, saith he, are of the body that are not of the soul, who having no true grace, yet, out of hope or temporal fear, do make profession of the faith, and these are like the hair, nails, and ill humours in a human body. Now, saith Bellarmine, our definition of a church compriseth only the last sort, whilst they are under the head the pope;—which is all one as if he had defined a man to be a dead creature, composed of hair, nails, and ill humours, under a hat. But of the church in this sense so far.

It remaineth, then, that we inquire what is the union which the church in this sense hath from the wisdom of its head, Jesus Christ. That it is one, that it hath a union with its head and in itself, is not questioned. It is one sheepfold, one body, one spouse of Christ, his

" only one" as unto him; and that it might have oneness in itself, with all the fruits of it, our Saviour prays, John xvii. 19–23. The whole of it is described, Eph. iv. 15, 16, " May grow up into him in all things, which is the head, even Christ: from whom the whole body fitly joined together and compacted by that which every joint supplieth, according to the effectual working in the measure of every part, maketh increase of the body unto the edifying itself in love." And of the same importance is that of the same apostle, Col. ii. 19, " Not holding the Head, from which all the body by joints and bands having nourishment ministered, and knit together, increaseth with the increase of God."

Now, in the union of the church, in every sense, there is considerable both the " formalis ratio" of it, whence it is, what it is, and the way and means whereby it exerts itself and is useful and active in communion. The first, in the church as now stated, consists in its joint holding the Head, and growing up into him by virtue of the communication of supplies unto it therefrom for that end and purpose. That which is the formal reason and cause of the union of the members with the head is the formal reason and cause of the union of the members with themselves. The original union of the members is in and with the head; and by the same have they union with themselves as one body. Now, the inhabitation of the same Spirit in him and them is that which makes Christ personal and his church to be one Christ mystical, 1 Cor. xii. 12, 13. Peter tells us that we are by the promises " made partakers of the divine nature," 2 Epist. i. 4. We are θείας κοινωνοὶ φύσεως,—we have communion with it. That θεία φύσις is no more but καινὴ κτίσις, I cannot easily consent. Now, it is in the person of the Spirit, whereof we are by the promise made partakers. He is the " Spirit of promise," Eph. i. 13; promised by God to Christ, Acts ii. 33, 'Επαγγελίαν τοῦ ἁγίου Πνεύματος λαβὼν παρὰ τοῦ Πατρός, and by him to us, John xiv. 16, 17; being of old the great promise of the covenant, Isa. lix. 21; Ezek. xi. 19, xxxvi. 26, 27. Now, in the participation of the divine nature consists the union of the saints with Christ. John vi. 56, our Saviour tells us that it arises from eating his flesh and drinking his blood: " He that eateth my flesh, and drinketh my blood, dwelleth in me, and I in him." This he expounds, verse 63: "It is the Spirit that quickeneth; the flesh profiteth nothing." By the quickening Spirit, inhabitation in Christ, and Christ in it, is intended. And the same he manifests in his prayer, that his church may be one in the Father and the Son, as the Father is in him and he in the Father, John xvii. 21: for the Spirit being the love of the Father and of the Son, is " vinculum Trinitatis;" and so here of our union in some resemblance.

The unity of members in the body natural with one head is often

chosen to set forth the union of the church, 1 Cor. xii. 12, xi. 3; Eph.
v. 23; Col. i. 18. Now, every man can tell that union of the head
and members whereby they become all one body, that and not another, is oneness of soul, whereby the whole is animated; which makes
the body, be it less or greater, to be one body. That which answers
hereunto in the mystical body of Christ is the animation of the whole
by his Spirit, as the apostle fully [states], 1 Cor. xv. 45. The union
between husband and wife is also chosen by the Holy Ghost to illustrate the union between Christ and his church: "For this cause shall
a man leave his father and mother, and shall be joined unto his wife,
and they two shall be one flesh. This is a great mystery: but I speak
concerning Christ and the church," Eph. v. 31, 32. The union between man and wife we have, Gen. ii. 24; "They are no more twain,
but one flesh," Matt. xix. 6;—of Christ and his church, that they are
one spirit, "He that is joined unto the Lord is one spirit," 1 Cor.
vi. 17. See also another similitude of the same importance, John
xv. 5; Rom. xi. 16, 17. This, I say, is the *fountain-radical* union of
the church catholic in itself, with its head and formal reason of it.

Hence flows a double consequential union that it hath also:—

1. Of *faith*. All men united to Christ by the inhabitation of the
same Spirit in him and them, are by it, from and according to the
word, "taught of God," Isa. liv. 13; John vi. 45: so taught, every one
of them, as to come to Christ, verse 47; that is, by believing, by faith.
They are so taught of God as that they shall certainly have that
measure of knowledge and faith which is needful to bring them to
Christ, and to God by him. And this they have by the unction or
Spirit which they have received, 1 John ii. 20, 27, accompanying the
word, by virtue of God's covenant with them, Isa. lix. 21. And
hereby are all the members of the church catholic, however divided
in their visible profession by any differences among themselves, or
differenced by the several measures of gifts and graces they have received, brought to the perfection aimed at, to the "unity of the faith,
and to the acknowledgment of the Son of God, unto a perfect man,
unto the measure of the stature of the fulness of Christ," Eph. iv. 13.

Nor was this hidden from some of the Papists themselves: "Ecclesia sancta corpus est Christi uno Spiritu vivificata, unita fide unâ,
et sanctificata," saith Hugo de Victore, de Sacram., lib. ii., as he had
said before in the former chapter: "Sicut scriptum est, qui non habet
Spiritum Christi, hic non est ejus; qui non habet Spiritum Christi,
non est membrum Christi. In corpore uno Spiritus unus, nihil in
corpore mortuum, nihil extra corpus vivum." See to the same purpose, Enchirid. Concil. Colon. in Symbol.

2. With peculiar reference to the members themselves, there is
another necessary consequence of the union mentioned, and that is

the *mutual love* of all those united in the head, as before, towards one another, and of every one towards the whole, as so united in the head, Christ Jesus. There is an "increase made of the body to the edifying itself in love," Eph. iv. 16; and so it becomes the bond of perfectness to this body of Christ. I cannot say that the members or parts of this church have their union in themselves by love, because they have that with and in Christ whereby they are one in themselves, John xvii. 21, 23; they are one in God, even in Christ, where their life is hid, Col. iii. 3;—but it is the next and immediate principle of that communion which they severally have one with another, and the whole body in and with itself. I say, then, that the communion which the catholic church, the mystical body of Christ, hath with and in itself, springing from the union which it hath in and with Christ, and in itself thereby, consists in love exerting itself in inexpressible variety, according to the present state of the whole, its relation to Christ, to saints and angels, with the conditions and occasions of the members of it respectively, 1 Cor. xii. 26, 27.

What hath been spoken concerning the union and communion of this church will not, I suppose, meet with any contradiction. Granting that there is such a church as that we speak of, " cœtus prædestinatorum credentium," the Papists themselves will grant that Christ alone is its head, and that its union ariseth from its subjection to him and dependence on him. Their modesty makes them contented with constituting the pope in the room of Christ, as he is, as it were, a political head for government. They have not as yet directly put in their claim to his office as a mystical head, influencing the body with life and motion; though by their figment of the sacraments communicating grace, "ex opere operato," and investing the original power of dispensing them in the pope only, they have contended fair for it. But if any one can inform me of any other union or communion of the church, described as above, than these laid down, I shall willingly attend unto his instructions. In the meantime, to carry on the present discourse unto that which is aimed at, it is manifest that the breach of this union must consist in these two things:—

1. *The casting out, expelling, and losing that Spirit which, abiding in us, gives us this union.*

2. *The loss of that love* which thence flows into the body of Christ, and believers as parts and members thereof.

This being the state of the church under the first consideration of it, certainly it would be an extravagancy scarcely to be paralleled for any one to affirm a breach of this union, as such, to be schism, under that notion of it which we are inquiring after. But because there is very little security to be enjoyed in an expectation of the sobriety of men in things wherein they are, or suppose they may be, concerned, that they may know beforehand what is farther incumbent on them if, in reference to us, they would prevail themselves of any such notion, I here inform them that our persuasion is, that this union was never utterly broken by any man taken into it, nor ever shall be to the end of the world; and I suppose they esteem it vain to dispute about the adjuncts of that which is denied to be.

But yet this persuasion being not common to us with them with whom we have to do in this matter, I shall not farther make use of it as to our present defence. That any other union of the catholic church, as such, can possibly be fancied or imagined by any (as to the substance of what hath been pleaded), leaving him a plea for the ordinary soundness of his intellectuals, is denied.

Let us see now, then, what is our concernment in this discourse: Unless men can prove that we have not the Spirit of God, that we do not savingly believe in Jesus Christ, that we do not sincerely love all the saints, his whole body, and every member of it, they cannot disprove our interest in the catholic church. It is true, indeed, men that have so great a confidence of their own abilities, and such a contempt of the world, as to undertake to dispute men out of conclusions from their natural senses about their proper objects, in what they see, feel, and handle, and will not be satisfied that they have not proved there is no motion, whilst a man walks for a conviction under their eye, may probably venture to disprove us in our spiritual sense and experience also, and to give us arguments to persuade us that we have not that communion with Christ which we know we have every day. Although I have a very mean persuasion of my own abilities, yet I must needs say I cannot think that any man in the world can convince me that I do not love Jesus Christ in sincerity, because I do not love the pope, as he is so. Spiritual experience is a security against a more cunning sophister than any Jesuit in the world, with whom the saints of God have to deal all their lives, Eph. vi. 12. And, doubtless, through the rich grace of our God, help will arise to us, that we shall never make a covenant with these men for peace, upon conditions far worse than those that Nahash would have exacted on the men of Jabesh-gilead; which were but the loss of one eye, with an abiding reproach; they requiring of us the deprivation of whatsoever we have to see by, whether as men or Christians, and that with a reproach never to be blotted out.

But as we daily put our consciences upon trial as to this thing, 2 Cor. xiii. 5, and are put unto it by Satan, so are we ready at all times to give an account to our adversaries of the hope that is in us. Let them sift us to the utmost, it will be to our advantage. Only let them not bring frivolous objections, and such as they know are of no weight with us, speaking (as is their constant manner) about the pope and their church,—things utterly foreign to what we are presently about, miserably begging the thing in question. Let them weigh, if they are able, the true nature of union with Christ, of faith in him, of love to the saints; consider them in their proper causes, adjuncts, and effects, with a spiritual eye, laying aside their prejudices and intolerable impositions;—if we are found wanting as to the truth and sincerity of these things, if we cannot give some account of our translation from death to life, of our implantation into Christ, and our participation of the Spirit, we must bear our own burden. If otherwise, we stand fast on the most noble and best account of church-union whatever; and whilst this shield is safe, we are less anxious about the issue of the ensuing contest. Whatever may be the apprehensions of other men, I am not in this thing solicitous. (I speak not of myself, but assuming for the present the person of one concerning whom these things may be spoken). Whilst the efficacy of the gospel accomplisheth in my heart all those divine and mighty effects which are ascribed unto it as peculiarly its work towards them that believe; whilst I know this one thing, that whereas I was blind, now I see,—whereas I was a servant of sin, I am now free to righteousness, and at liberty from bondage unto death, and instead of the fruits of the flesh, I find all the fruits of the Spirit brought forth in me, to the praise of God's glorious grace; whilst I have an experience of that powerful work of conversion and being born again, which I am able to manage against all the accusations of Satan, having peace with God upon justification by faith, with the love of God shed abroad in my heart by the Holy Ghost, investing me in the privileges of adoption,—I shall not certainly be moved with the disputes of men that would persuade me I do not belong to the catholic church, because I do not follow this, or that, or any party of men in the world.

" But you will say, this you will allow to them also with whom you have to do, that they may be members of the catholic church?" I leave other men to stand or fall to their own master. Only, as to the papal multitude, on the account of several inconsistencies between them and the members of this church, I shall place some swords in the way, which will reduce their number to an invisible scantling. I might content myself by affirming at once, that, upon what hath been spoken, I must exclude from the catholic church all and every one whom Bellarmine intends to include in it as such,—namely, those who belong to the church as hairs and ill humours to the body of a man. But I add in particular,—

1. All *wicked and profane persons*, of whom the Scripture speaks expressly that they shall not enter into the kingdom of God, are in-

disputably cut off. Whatever they pretend in show at any time, in the outward duties of devotion, they have neither faith in Christ nor love to the saints; and so have part and fellowship neither in the union nor communion of the catholic church.

How great a proportion of that synagogue whereof we are speaking will be taken off by this sword,—of their popes, princes, prelates, clergy, votaries, and people,—and that not by a rule of private surmises, but upon the visible issue of their being servants to sin, haters of God and good men, is obvious to all. Persons of really so much as reformed lives amongst them are like the berries after the shaking of an olive tree, 1 Cor. vi. 7–10; Rev. xxii. 15.

I find some persons of late appropriating holiness and regeneration[1] to the Roman party on this account, that among them only miracles are wrought; "which is," say they, "the only proof of true holiness." But these men err as their predecessors, "not knowing the Scriptures, nor the power of God." Amongst all the evidences that are given in Scripture of regeneration, I suppose they will scarcely find this to be one. And they who have no other assurance that they are themselves born of God, but that some of their church work miracles, had need maintain also that no man can be assured thereof in this life. They will find that a broken reed,[2] if they lean upon it. Will it evince all the members of their church to be regenerate, or only some? If they say all, I ask then what becomes of Bellarmine's church, which is made up of them who are not regenerate? If some only, I desire to know on what account the miracles of one man may be an evidence to some in his society that they are regenerate, and not to others? or whether the foundation of that distinction must not lie in themselves? But the truth is, the miracles now pretended are an evidence of a contrary condition to what these men are willing to own, 2 Thess. ii. 8–12.

2. All *ignorant* persons, into whose hearts God hath not shined, "to give them the knowledge of his glory in the face of Jesus Christ," are to be added to the former account. There is a measure of knowledge of absolute and indispensable necessity to salvation, whereof how short the most of them are is evident. Among the open abominations of the papal combination, for which they ought to be an abhorrency to mankind, their professed design of keeping the people in ignorance is not the least, Hos. iv. 6. That it was devotion to themselves, and not to God, which they aimed to advance thereby, is by experience sufficiently evinced; but that whose

---

[1] "Ille cœtus Christianorum qui solus in orbe claret regeneratis est ecclesia; solus cœtus Christianorum papæ subditorum claret regeneratis; apud illos solos sunt qui miracula faciunt. ergo."—Val. Mag.

[2] Deut. xiii. 1–3; Matt. vii. 22, 23; Exod. viii. 7.

reverence is to be preserved by its being hid is in itself contemptible. What other thoughts wise men could have of Christian religion, in their management of it, I know not. Woe to you, Romish clergy! " for ye have taken away the key of knowledge; ye entered not in yourselves, and them that were entering in ye hindered." The people have perished under your hands, for want of knowledge: Zech. xi. 15–17. The figment of an implicit faith, as managed by these men, to charm the spirits and consciences of poor perishing creatures with security in this life, will be found as pernicious to them in the issue as their purgatory, invented on the same account, will be useless.

3. Add to these all *hypocritical self-justiciaries*, who seek for a righteousness as it were by the works of the law, which they never attain to, Rom. ix. 31, 32, though they take pains about it, chap. x. 2; Eph. ii. 8–10. By this sword will fall the fattest cattle of their herd. How the hand of the Lord on this account sweeps away their devotionists, and therein takes down the pride of their glory, the day will discover. Yet, besides these, there are two other things that will cut them down as the grass falls before the scythe of the mower.

4. The first of these is *idolatry:* " Be not deceived; no idolaters shall inherit the kingdom of God," 1 Cor. vi. 9, 10; "Without are idolaters," Rev. xxii. 15. This added to their lives hath made Christian religion, where known only as by them professed, to be an abomination to Jews and Gentiles. Some will one day, besides himself, answer for Averroës thus determining of the case as to his soul : " Quoniam Christiani adorant quod comedunt, anima mea sit cum philosophis." Whether they are idolaters or no, whether they yield the worship due to the Creator to the creature, hath been sifted to the utmost, and the charge of its evil, which the jealous God doth of all things most abhor, so fastened on them, beyond all possibility of escape, that one of the wisest of them hath at length fixed on that most desperate and profligate refuge, that some kind of idolatry is lawful, because Peter mentions " abominable idolatries," 1 Pet. iv. 3; who is therein so far from distinguishing of several sorts and kinds of it to any such purpose, as that he aggravates all sorts and kinds of it with the epithet of " nefarious" or " abominable."

A man may say, What is there almost that they have not committed lewdness in this kind withal? On every hill, and under every green tree, is the filth of their abomination found. Saints and angels in heaven, images of some that never were, of others that had been better they never had been, bread and wine, cross and nails, altars, wood, and iron, and the pope on earth, are by them adored. The truth is, if we have any assurance left us of any thing in the world, that we either see or hear, feel or taste, and so, consequently, that we are alive, and not other men, the poor Indians who worship a piece of red cloth are not more gross idolaters than they are.

5. *All that worship the beast set up by the dragon*, all that receive his mark in their hand or forehead, are said not to have their names written in the book of life of the Lamb, Rev. xiii. 8, 16; which what aspect it bears towards the visible Roman church, time will manifest.

All these sorts of persons we except against, as those that have no interest in the union of the catholic church,—all profane, ignorant, self-justiciaries, all idolaters, worshippers, or adorers of the papal power. If any remain among them, not one way or other visibly separated from them, who fall not under some one or more of these exceptions, as we grant they may be members of the catholic church, so we deny that they are of that which is called the Roman. And I must needs inform others by the way, that whilst the course of their conversation, ignorance of the mystery of the gospel, hatred of good men, contempt of the Spirit of God, his gifts and graces, do testify to the consciences of them that fear the Lord that they belong not to the church catholic, it renders their rebuking of others for separating from any instituted church, national (as is pretended), or more restrained, very weak and contemptible. All discourses about motes have a worm at the root, whilst there is a beam lies in the eye. Do men suppose that a man who hath tasted how gracious the Lord is, and hath by grace obtained communion with the Father and his Son Jesus Christ, walking at peace with God, and in a sense of his love all his days, filled with the Holy Ghost, and by him with joy unspeakable and glorious in believing, is not strengthened against the rebukes and disputes of men whom he sees and knows by their fruits to be destitute of the Spirit of God, uninterested in the fellowship of the gospel and communion thereof?

CHAPTER V.

Of the catholic church visible—Of the nature thereof—In what sense the universality of professors is called a church—Amyraldus' judgment in this business—The union of the church in this sense, wherein it consists—Not the same with the union of the church catholic, nor that of a particular instituted church—Not in relation to any one officer, or more, in subordination to one another—Such a subordination not provable—Τὰ ἀρχαῖα of the Nicene synod—Of general councils—Union of the church visible not in a general council—The true unity of the universality of professors asserted—Things necessary to this union—Story of a martyr at Bagdad—The apostasy of churches from the unity of the faith—Testimony of Hegesippus vindicated—Papal apostasy—Protestants not guilty of the breach of this unity—The catholic church, in the sense insisted on, granted by the ancients—Not a political body.

II. THE second general notion of the church, as it is usually taken, signifies the *universality of men professing the doctrine of the gospel* and obedience to God in Christ, according to it, throughout the world. This is that which is commonly called the visible catholic church, which now, together with the union which it hath in itself, and how that unity is broken, falls under consideration.

That all professors of the gospel throughout the world, called to the knowledge of Christ by the word, do make up and constitute his visible kingdom, by their professed subjection to him, and so may be called his church, I grant. That they are precisely so called in Scripture is not unquestionable. What relation it stands in to all particular churches, whether as a genus to its species, or as a *totum* to its parts, hath lately by many been discussed. I must crave leave to deny that it is capable of filling up or of being included in any of these denominations and relations. The universal church we are speaking of is not a thing that hath, as such, a specificative form, from which it should be called a universal church, as a particular hath for its ground of being so called. It is but a collection of all that are duly called Christians in respect of their profession. Nor are the several particular churches of Christ in the world so parts and members of any catholic church as that it should be constituted or made up by them and of them for the order and purpose of an instituted church,—that is, the celebration of the worship of God and institutions of Jesus Christ according to the gospel; which to assert were to overthrow a remarkable difference between the economy of the Old Testament and the New. Nor do I think that particular congregations do stand unto it in the relation of species unto a genus, in which the whole nature of it should be preserved and comprised; which would deprive every one of membership in this universal church which is not joined actually to some particular church or congregation, than which nothing can be more devoid of truth. To debate the thing in particular is not my present intention, nor is needful to the purpose in hand.

The sum is, The *universal church* is not so called upon the same account that a *particular church* is so called. The formal reason constituting a particular church to be a particular church is, that those of whom it doth consist do join together, according to the mind of Christ, in the exercise of the same numerical ordinances for his worship. And in this sense the universal church cannot be said to be a church, as though it had such a particular form of its own; which that it hath, or should have, is not only false but impossible. But it is so called because all Christians throughout the world (excepting some individual persons, providentially excluded) do, upon the enjoyment of the same preaching of the word, the same sacraments administered in *specie, profess one common faith and hope.*

But, to the joint performance of any exercise of religion, that they should hear one sermon together, or partake of one sacrament, or have one officer for their rule and government, is ridiculous to imagine; nor do any profess to think so, as to any of the particulars mentioned, but those only who have profit by the fable. As to the description of this church, I shall acquiesce in that lately given of it by a very learned man. Saith he, "Ecclesia universalis, est communio, seu societas omnium coetuum" (I had rather he had said, and he had done it more agreeably to principles by himself laid down, "Omnium fidem Christianam profitentium sive illi ad ecclesias aliquas particulares pertineant, sive non pertineant"), "qui religionem Christianam profitentur, consistens in eo, quod tametsi neque exercitia pietatis uno numero frequentent, neque sacramenta eadem numero participent, neque uno eodemque omnino ordine regantur et gubernentur, unum tamen corpus in eo constituunt, quod eundem Christum servatorem habere se profitentur, uno in evangelio propositum, iisdem promissionibus comprehensum, quas obsignant et confirmant sacramenta, ex eadem institutione pendentia," Amyrald. Thes. de Eccles. Nom. et. Defin. Thes. 29.

There being, then, in the world a great multitude, which no man can number, of all nations, kindreds, people, and languages, professing the doctrine of the gospel, not tied to mountains or hills, John iv. 21, 23, but worshipping ἐν παντὶ τόπῳ, 1 Cor. i. 2, 1 Tim. ii. 8, let us consider what union there is amongst them as such, wrapping them all in the bond thereof by the will and appointment of Jesus Christ, and wherein the breach of that union doth consist, and how any man is or may be guilty thereof:

1. I suppose this will be granted, that only elect believers belong to the church, in this sense considered, is a chimera feigned in the brains of the Romanists, and fastened on the reformed divines. I wholly assent to Austin's dispute on this head against the Donatists. And the whole entanglement that hath been about this matter hath arisen from obstinacy in the Papists in not receiving the catholic church in the sense mentioned before; which to do they know would be injurious to their interest.

This church being visible and professing, and being now considered under that constituting difference, that the union of it cannot be the same with that of the catholic church before mentioned, it is clear from hence that multitudes of men belong unto it who have not the relation mentioned before to Christ and his body, which is required in all comprehended in that union, seeing "many are called, but few are chosen."

2. Nor can it consist in a joint assembly, either ordinary or extraordinary, for the celebration of the ordinances of the gospel, or any one of them, as was the case of the church of the Jews, which met

at set times in one place for the performance of that worship which was then required, nor could otherwise be accomplished: for as it is not at all possible that any such thing should ever be done, considering what is and shall be the estate of Christ's visible kingdom to the end of the world, so it is not (that I know of) pleaded that Christ hath made any such appointment; yea, it is on all hands confessed, at least cannot reasonably be denied, that there is a *supersedeas* granted to all supposals of any such duty incumbent on the whole visible church, by the institution of particular churches, wherein all the ordinances of Christ are duly to be administered.

I shall only add, that if there be not an institution for the joining in the same numerical ordinances, the union of this church is not really a church-union,—I mean of an instituted church, which consists therein,—but something of another nature. Neither can that have the formal reason of an instituted church as such, which as such can join in no one act of the worship of God instituted to be performed in such societies. So that he that shall take into his thoughts the condition of all the Christians in the world, their present state, what it hath been for fifteen hundred years, and what it is like to be ἕως τῆς συντελείας τοῦ αἰῶνος, will easily understand what church-state they stand in and relate unto.

3. It cannot possibly have its union by a *relation to any one officer* given to the whole, such a one as the Papists pretend the pope to be; for though it be possible that one officer may have relation to all the churches in the world, as the apostles severally had (when Paul said the care of all the churches lay on him), who, by virtue of their apostolical commission, were to be received and submitted to in all the churches in the world, being antecedent in office to them, yet this neither did nor could make all the churches one church, no more than if one man were an officer or magistrate in every corporation in England, this would make all those corporations to be one corporation. I do not suppose the pope to be an officer to the whole church visible as such, which I deny to have a union or order capable of any such thing. But suppose him an officer to every particular church, no union of the whole would thence ensue. That which is one church must join at least in some one church act, numerically one. So that though it should be granted that the pope were a general officer unto all and every church in the world, yet this would not prove that they all made one church, and had their church-union in subjection to him who was so an officer to them all; because to the constitution of such a union, as hath been showed, there is that required which, in reference to the universal society of Christians, is utterly and absolutely impossible. But the non-institution of any such officer ordinarily to bear rule in and over

all the churches of God hath been so abundantly proved by the divines of the reformed churches, and he who alone puts in his claim to that prerogative so clearly manifested to be quite another thing, that I will not needlessly go over that work again. Something, however, shall afterward be remarked as to his pretensions, from the principles whereon I proceed in the whole business.

There is, indeed, by some pleaded a subordination of officers in this church, tending towards a union on that account; as that ordinary ministers should be subjected to diocesan bishops, they to archbishops or metropolitans, they again to patriarchs, where some would bound the process, though a parity of reason would call for a pope: nor will the arguments pleaded for such a subordination rest until they come to be centred in some such thing.

But, first, before this plea be admitted, it must be proved that all these officers are appointed by Jesus Christ, or it will not concern us, who are inquiring solely after his will, and the settling of conscience therein. To do this with such an evidence [as] that the consciences of all those who are bound to yield obedience to Jesus Christ may appear to be therein concerned, will be a difficult task, as I suppose. And, to settle this once for all, I am not dealing with the men of that lazy persuasion, that church affairs are to be ordered by the prudence of our civil superiors and governors; and so seeking to justify a non-submission to any of their constitutions in the things of this nature, or to evidence that the so doing is not schism. Nor do I concern myself in the order and appointment of ancient times, by men assembled in synods and councils; wherein, whatever was the force of their determinations in their own seasons, we are not at all concerned, knowing of nothing that is obligatory to us, not pleading from sovereign authority or our own consent: but it is after things of pure institution that I am inquiring. With them who say there is no such thing in these matters, we must proceed to other principles than any yet laid down.

Also, it must be proved that all these officers are given and do belong to the catholic church as such, and not to the particular churches of several measures and dimensions to which they relate; which is not as yet, that I know of, so much as pretended by them that plead for this order. They tell us, indeed, of various arbitrary distributions of the world, or rather of the Roman empire, into patriarchates, with the dependent jurisdictions mentioned, and that all within the precincts of those patriarchates must fall within the lines of the subordination, subjection, and communication before described; but as there is no subordination between the officers of one denomination in the inferior parts, no more is there any between the superior themselves, but they are independent of each other. Now, it is easily discernible that these patriarchates, how many or how few soever they are, are particular churches, not any one of them the catholic, nor altogether comprising all that are comprehended in the precincts of it (which none will say that ever they did); and, therefore, this may speak something as to a combination of those churches, nothing as to the union of the catholic as such, which they are not.

Supposing this assertion to the purpose in hand, which it is not at all, it would prove only a combination of all the officers of several churches, consisting in the subordination and dependence mentioned, not of the whole church itself, though all the members of it should be at once imagined or fancied (as what shall hinder men from fancying what they please?) to be comprised within the limits of those distributions, unless it be also proved that Christ hath instituted several sorts of particular churches, parochial, diocesan, metropolitical, patriarchal (I use the words in the present vulgar acceptation, their signification having been somewhat otherwise formerly; "parœcia" being the care of a private bishop, "provincia" of a metropolitan, and "diœcesis" of a patriarch), in the order mentioned, and hath pointed out which of his churches shall be of those several kinds throughout the world; which that it will not be done to the disturbance of my principles whilst I live, I have some present good security.

And because I take the men of this persuasion to be charitable men, that will not think much of taking a little pains for the reducing any person whatever from the error of his way, I would entreat them that they would inform me what patriarchate, according to the institution of Christ, I (who by the providence of God live here at Oxon) do "de jure" belong unto; that so I may know how to preserve the union of that church, and to behave myself therein. And this I shall promise them, that if I were singly, or in conjunction with any others, so considerable, that those great officers should contend about whose subjects we should be (as was done heretofore about the Bulgarians), that it should not at all startle me about the truth and excellency of Christian religion, as it did those poor creatures; who, being newly converted to the faith, knew nothing of it but what they received from men of such principles.

But that this constitution is human, and the distributions of Christians, in subjection unto church-officers, into such and such divisions of nations and countries, prudential and arbitrary, I suppose will not be denied. The τὰ ἀρχαῖα of the Nicene synod intend no more; nor is in any thing of institution, nor so much as of apostolical tradition, pleaded therein. The following ages were of the same persuasion. Hence in the council of Chalcedon, the archiepiscopacy of Constantinople was advanced into a patriarchate, and many provinces cast in subjection thereunto; wherein the primates of Ephesus and Thrace were cut short of what they might plead τὰ ἀρχαῖα for, and sundry other alterations were likewise made in the same kind, Socrat. lib. v. cap. 8: the ground and reason of which procedure the fathers assembled sufficiently manifest in the reason assigned for the advancement of the bishops of Constantinople; which was for the city's sake: Διὰ τὸ εἶναι αὐτὴν νέαν Ρώμην, Can. iii., Con. Constan. And what was the judgment of the council of Chalcedon upon this matter may be seen in the composition and determination of the strife between Maximus bishop of Antioch and Juvenalis of Jerusalem, Ac. vii. Con. Cal., with translation of provinces from the jurisdiction of one to another. And he that shall suppose that such assemblies as these were instituted by the will and appointment of Christ in the gospel, with church-authority for such dispositions and determinations, so as to make them of concernment to the unity of the church, will, if I mistake not, be hardly bestead in giving the ground of that his supposal.

4. I would know of them who desire to be under this law, whether the power with which Jesus Christ hath furnished the officers of his church come forth from the supreme mentioned patriarchs and archbishops, and is by them communicated to the inferiors, or "vice versa;" or whether all have their power in an equal immediation from Christ? If the latter be granted, there will be a greater independency established than most men are aware of (though the Papalins[1] understood it in the council of Trent), and a wound given to successive episcopal ordination not easily to be healed. That power is communicated from the inferiors to the superiors will not be pleaded. And seeing the first must be insisted on, I beseech them not to be too hasty with men not so sharp-sighted as themselves, if, finding the names they speak of barbarous and foreign as to the Scriptures, and the things themselves not at all delineated therein, ἐπέχουσι.

5. The truth is, the whole subordination of this kind, which "de facto" hath been in the world, was so clearly a human invention or a prudential constitution, as hath been showed (which being done by men professing authority in the church, gave it, as it was called "vim ecclesiasticam"), that nothing else, in the issue, is pleaded for it. And now, though I shall, if called thereunto, manifest both the unreasonableness and unsuitableness to the design of Christ for his worship under the gospel, and the comparative novelty and mischievous issue, of that constitution, yet, at the present, being no farther concerned but only to evince that the union of the general visible church doth

---

[1] See Paul Sarpi's History of the Council of Trent, book vii., sect. xi, xii. In the course of a dispute respecting the superiority of bishops over priests, the Spanish bishops held the institution and superiority of bishops to be "de jure divino," and not merely "de jure pontificio." The legates and their party,—since this implied that the bishops were independent of the pope,—maintained that the pope only was a bishop of divine institution, and the other bishops were merely his delegates and vicars. The latter party bear the name of Papalins in Sarpi's History.—Ed.

not therein consist, I shall not need to add any thing to what hath been spoken.

The Nicene council, which first made towards the confirmation of something like somewhat of what was afterward introduced in some places, pleaded only, as I said before, the τὰ ἀρχαῖα, old usage for it; which it would not have done could it have given a better original thereunto. And whatever the antiquities then pretended might be, we know that ἀπ᾽ ἀρχῆς οὐ γέγονεν οὕτω. And I do not fear to say, what others have done before me, concerning the canons of that first and best general council, as it is called, they are all hay and stubble. Nor yet doth the laying this custom on τὰ ἀρχαῖα, in my apprehension, evince their judgment of any long prescription. Peter, speaking of a thing that was done a few years before, says that it was done ἀφ᾽ ἡμερῶν ἀρχαίων, Acts xv. 7. Somewhat a greater antiquity than that by him intended, I can freely grant to the custom by the fathers pretended.

But a general council is pleaded with the best colour and pretence for a bond of union to this general and visible church. In consideration hereof I shall not divert to the handling of the rise, right use, authority, necessity, of such councils; about all which somewhat in due time towards satisfaction may be offered to those who are not in bondage to names and traditions;—nor shall I remark what hath been the management of the things of God in all ages in those assemblies; many of which have been the stains and ulcers of Christian religion;—nor yet shall I say with what little disadvantage to the religion of Jesus Christ I suppose a loss of all the canons of all councils that ever were in the world since the apostles' days, with their acts and contests (considering what use is made of them), might be undergone;—nor yet shall I digress to the usefulness of the assemblies of several churches in their representatives, to consider and determine about things of common concernment to them, with their tendency to the preservation of that communion which ought to be amongst them;—but as to the present instance only offer,—

1. That such general councils, being things purely extraordinary and occasional, as is confessed, cannot be *an ordinary standing bond of union* to the catholic church. And if any one shall reply, that though in themselves and in their own continuance they cannot be so, yet in their authority, laws, and canons they may; I must say, that besides the very many reasons I have to call into question the power of law-making for the whole society of Christians in the world, in all the general councils that have been or possibly can be on the earth, the disputes about the title of those assemblies which pretend to this honour, which are to be admitted, which excluded, are so endless; the rules of judging them so dark, lubricous, and uncertain,

framed to the interest of contenders on all hands; the laws of them, which "de facto" have gone under that title and name, so innumerable, burdensome, uncertain, and frivolous, in a great part so grossly contradictory to one another,—that I cannot suppose that any man upon second thoughts can abide in such an assertion. If any shall, I must be bold to declare my affection to the doctrine of the gospel maintained in some of those assemblies for some hundreds of years, and then to desire him to prove that any general council, since the apostles fell asleep, hath been so convened and managed as to be enabled to claim that authority to itself which is or would be due to such an assembly instituted according to the mind of Christ.

That it hath been of advantage to the truth of the gospel, that godly learned men, bishops of churches, have convened and witnessed a good confession in reference to the doctrine thereof, and declared their abhorrence of the errors that are contrary thereunto, is confessed. That any man or men is, are, or ever were, intrusted by Christ with authority so to convene them, as that thereupon and by virtue thereof they should be invested with a new authority, power, and jurisdiction, at such a convention, and thence should take upon them to make laws and canons that should be ecclesiastically binding to any persons or churches, as theirs, is not as yet, to me, attended with any convincing evidence of truth. And seeing at length it must be spoken, I shall do it with submission to the thoughts of good men that are any way acquainted with these things, and in sincerity therein commend my conscience to God, that I do not know any thing that is extant bearing clearer witness to the sad degeneracy of Christian religion in the profession thereof, nor more evidently discovering the efficacy of another spirit than what was poured out by Christ at his ascension, nor containing more hay and stubble, that is to be burned and consumed, than the stories of the acts and laws of the councils and synods that have been in the world.

2. But, to take them as they are, as to that alone wherein the first councils had any evidence of the presence of the Holy Ghost with them,—namely, in the declaring the doctrine of the gospel,— it falls in with that which I shall give in for the bond of union unto the church in the sense pleaded about.

3. Such an assembly arising cumulative out of particular churches, as it is evident that it doth, it cannot first and properly belong to the church generally as such; but it is only a means of communion between those particular churches as such, of whose representatives (I mean virtually, for formally the persons convening for many years ceased to be so) it doth consist.

4. There is nothing more ridiculous than to imagine a general council that should represent the whole catholic church, or so much as all the particular churches that are in the world. And let him that

is otherwise minded, that there hath been such a one, or that it is possible there should be such a one, prove by instance that such there hath been since the apostles' times, or by reason that such may be in the present age, or be justly expected in those that are to succeed, and we will, as we are able, crown him for his discovery.

5. Indeed, I know not how any council, that hath been in the world these thirteen hundred years and somewhat upwards, could be said to represent the church in any sense, or any churches whatever. Their convention, as is known, hath been always by imperial or papal authority, the persons convened such, and only they who, as was pretended and pleaded, had right of suffrage, with all necessary authority, in such conventions, from the order, degree, and office which personally they held in their several churches. Indeed, a pope or bishop sent his legate or proxy to represent, or rather personate, him and his authority. But that any of them were sent or delegated by the church wherein they did preside is not so evident.

I desire, then, that some man more skilled in laws and common usages than myself would inform me on what account such a convention could come to be a church-representative, or the persons of it to be representatives of any churches. General grounds of reason and equity, I am persuaded, cannot be pleaded for it. The lords in parliament in this nation, who, being summoned by regal authority, sat there in their own personal right, were never esteemed to represent the body of the people. Supposing, indeed, all church power in any particular church, of whatever extract or composition, to be solely vested in one single person, a collection of those persons, if instituted, would bring together the authority of the whole; but yet this would not make that assembly to be a church-representative, if you will allow the name of the church to any but that single person. But for men who have but a partial power and authority in the church, and perhaps, separated from it, none at all, without any delegation from the churches, to convene, and in their own authority to take upon them to represent those churches, is absolute presumption.

These several pretensions being excluded, let us see wherein the unity of this church,—namely, of the great society of men professing the gospel, and obedience to Christ according to it, throughout the world,—doth consist. This is summed up by the apostle, Eph. iv. 5, " One Lord, one faith, one baptism." It is the unity of the doctrine of faith which men profess, in subjection to one Lord, Jesus Christ, being initiated into that profession by baptism. I say, the saving doctrine of the gospel of salvation by Jesus Christ, and obedience through him to God, as professed by them, is the bond of that union whereby they are made one body, are distinguished from all other societies, have one head, Christ Jesus, which as to profession they hold; and whilst they do so they are of this body, in one professed hope of their calling.

1. Now, that this union be preserved, it is required that all those *grand and necessary truths of the gospel,* without the knowledge whereof no man can be saved by Jesus Christ, be so far believed as to be outwardly and visibly professed, in that variety of ways wherein they are or may be called out thereunto. There is a "proportion of faith," Rom. xii. 6; a "unity of faith, and of the knowledge of the Son of God," Eph. iv. 13; a measure of saving truths, the explicit knowledge whereof in men, enjoying the use of reason within and the means of grace without, is of indispensable necessity to salvation, —without which it is impossible that any soul, in an ordinary way, should have communion with God in Christ, having not light sufficient for converse with him, according to the tenor of the covenant of grace. These are commonly called fundamentals, or first principles; which are justly argued by many to be clear, perspicuous, few, lying in an evident tendency to obedience. Now, look what truths are savingly to be believed to render a man a member of the church catholic invisible,—that is, whatever is required in any one, unto such a receiving of Jesus Christ as that thereby he may have power given to him to become the son of God,—the profession of those truths is required to instate a man in the unity of the church visible.

2. That *no other internal principle of the mind,* that hath an utter inconsistency with the real belief of the truths necessary to be professed, be manifested by professors. Paul tells us of some who, though they would be called Christians, yet they so walked as that they manifested themselves to be "enemies of the cross of Christ," Phil. iii. 18. Certainly those who on one account are open and manifest enemies of the cross of Christ, are not on any members of his church. There is "one Lord" and "one faith" required, as well as "one baptism;" and a protestation contrary to evidence of fact is in all law null. Let a man profess ten thousand times that he believes all the saving truths of the gospel, and, by the course of a wicked and profane conversation, evidence to all that he believes no one of them, shall his protestation be admitted? Shall he be accounted a servant in and of my family who will call me master, and come into my house only to do me and mine a mischief, not doing any thing I require of him, but openly and professedly the contrary? Paul says of such, Tit. i. 16, "They profess that they know God, but in works they deny him, being abominable, and disobedient, and unto every good work reprobate;" which, though peculiarly spoken of the Jews, yet contains a general rule, that men's profession of the

knowledge of God, contradicted by a course of wickedness, is not to be admitted as a thing giving any privilege whatever.

3. That no *thing, opinion, error, or false doctrine, everting* or overthrowing any of the necessary saving truths professed as above, be added in and with that profession, or deliberately be professed also. This principle the apostle lays down and proves, Gal. v. 3, 4. Notwithstanding the profession of the gospel, he tells the Galatians that if they were bewitched to profess also the necessity of circumcision and keeping of the law for justification, Christ or the profession of him would not profit them. On this account the ancients excluded many heretics from the name of Christians: so Justin Martyr of the Marcionites, and others, ῏Ων οὐδενὶ κοινωνοῦμεν οἱ γνωρί-ζοντες ἀθέους καὶ ἀσεβεῖς, καὶ ἀδίκους, καὶ ἀνόμους αὐτοὺς ὑπάρχοντας, καὶ ἀντὶ τοῦ τὸν Ἰησοῦν σέβειν, ὀνόματι μόνον ὁμολογεῖν, καὶ Χριστιανοὺς ἑαυτοὺς λέγουσιν, ὃν τρόπον οἱ ἐν τοῖς ἔθνεσι τὸ ὄνομα τοῦ Θεοῦ ἐπιγράφουσι τοῖς χειρο-ποιήτοις.

We are at length, then, arrived at this issue: The belief and profession of all the necessary saving truths of the gospel, without the manifestation of an internal principle of the mind inconsistent with the belief of them, or adding of other things in profession that are destructive to the truths so professed, is the bond of the unity of the visible professing church of Christ. Where this is found in any man, or number of men, though otherwise accompanied with many failings, sins, and errors, the unity of the faith is by him or them so far preserved as that they are thereby rendered members of the visible church of Christ, and are by him so esteemed.

Let us suppose a man, by a bare reading of the Scriptures, brought to him by some providence of God (as finding the Bible on the highway), and evidencing their authority by their own light, instructed in the knowledge of the truths of the gospel, who shall thereupon make profession of them amongst them with whom he lives, although he be thousands of miles distant from any particular church wherein the ordinances of Christ are administered, nor perhaps knows there is any such church in the world, much less hath ever heard of the pope of Rome (which is utterly impossible he should, supposing him instructed only by reading of the Scriptures);—I ask whether this man, making open profession of Christ according to the gospel, shall be esteemed a member of the visible church in the sense insisted on, or no?

That this may not seem to be such a fiction of a case as may involve in it any impossible supposition, which, being granted, will hold a door open for other absurdities, I shall exemplify it, in its most material "postulata," by a story of unquestionable truth.

Elmacinus, who wrote the story of the Saracens, being secretary to one of the caliphs of Bagdad, informs us that in the year 309 of their hegira (about the year 921 of our account), Muctadinus the caliph of Bagdad, by the counsel of his wise men, commanded one Huseinus, the son of Mansor, to be crucified for certain poems, whereof some verses are recited by the historian, and are thus rendered by Erpenius:—

"Laus ei qui manifestavit humilitatem suam, celavit inter nos divinitatem suam permeantem donec cœpit in creatura sua apparere sub specie edentis et bibentis.

"Jamque aspexit eum creatura ejus, sicuti supercilium obliquum respiciat spercilium."

From which remnant of his work it is easy to perceive that the crime whereof he was accused, and for which he was condemned and crucified, was the confession of Jesus Christ, the Son of God. As he went to the cross he added, says the same author, these that follow:

"Compotor meus nihil plane habet in se iniquitatis, bibendum mihi dedit simile ejus quod bibit, fecit hospitem in hospite."

And so he died constantly (as it appears) in the profession of the Lord Jesus.

Bagdad was a city built not long before by the Saracens, wherein, it is probable, there were not at that time any Christians abiding. Add now to this story what our Saviour speaks, Luke xii. 8, "I say unto you, Whosoever shall confess me before men, him shall the Son of man also confess before the angels of God;" and consider the unlimitedness of the expression as to any outward consideration, and tell me whether this man, or any other in the like condition, be not to be reckoned as a subject of Christ's visible kingdom, a member of his church in the world?

Let us now recall to mind what we have in design. Granting, for our process' sake, that schism is the breach of any unity instituted and appointed by Christ, in what sense soever it is spoken of, our inquiry is, whether we are guilty in any kind of such a breach, or the breach of such a unity. This, then, now insisted on being the union of the church of Christ, as visibly professing the Word, according to his own mind, when I have laid down some general foundations of what is to ensue, I shall consider whether we are guilty of the breach of this union, and argue the several pretensions of men against us, especially of the Romanists, on this account.

1. I confess that this union of the general visible church was once comprehensive of all the churches in the world, the faith once delivered to the saints being received amongst them. From this unity it is taken also for granted that a separation is made, and it continues not as it was at the first institution of the churches of Christ, though some small breaches were made upon it immediately after their

first planting. The Papists say, as to the European churches (wherein their and our concernment principally lies), this breach was made in the days of our forefathers, by their departure from the common faith in those ages, though begun by a few some ages before. We are otherwise minded, and affirm that this secession was made by them and their predecessors in apostasy, in several generations, by several degrees; which we manifest by comparing the present profession and worship with that in each kind which we know was at first embraced, because we find it instituted. At once, then, we say this schism lies at their doors, who not only have deviated from the common faith themselves, but do also actually cause and attempt to destroy temporally and eternally all that will not join with them therein ; for as the "mystery of iniquity" began to work in the apostles' days, so we have a testimony beyond exception in the complaint of those that lived in them, that not long after, the operation of it became more effectual, and the infection of it to be more diffused in the church. This is that of Hegesippus in Eusebius, Eccles. Hist. lib. iv. cap. 22; who affirms that the church remained a virgin (whilst the apostles lived),—pure and uncorrupted; but when that sacred society had ended its pilgrimage, and the generation that heard and received the word from them were fallen asleep, many false doctrines were preached and divulged therein.

I know who hath endeavoured to elude the sense of this complaint, as though it concerned not any thing in the church, but *the despisers and persecutors of it, the Gnostics:* but yet I know, also, that no man would so do but such a one as hath a just confidence of his own ability to make passable at least any thing that he shall venture to say or utter ; for why should that be referred by Hegesippus to the ages after the apostles and their hearers were dead, with an exception against its being so in their days, when, if the person thus expounding this testimony may be credited, the Gnostics were never more busy nor prevalent than in that time which alone is excepted from the evil here spoken of ? Nor can I understand how the opposition and persecution of the church should be insinuated to be the deflouring and violating of its chastity, which is commonly a great purifying of it. So that, speaking of that broaching and preaching of errors, which was not in the apostles' times, nor in the time of their hearers, —the chiefest time of the rage and madness of the Gnostics,—such as spotted the pure and uncorrupted virginity of the church, which nothing can attain unto that is foreign unto it, and that which gave original unto sedition in the church, I am of the mind, and so I conceive was Eusebius that recited those words, that the good man intended corruptions in the church, not out of it, nor oppositions to it.

The process made in after ages in a deviation from the unity of the faith, till it arrived to that height wherein it is now stated in the papal apostasy, hath been the work of others to declare. Therein, then, I state the rise and progress of the present schism (if it may be so called) of the visible church.

2. As to our concernment in this business, they that will make good a charge against us, that we are departed from the unity of the church catholic, it is incumbent on them to evidence,—(1.) That we either do not believe and make profession of all the truths of the gospel indispensably necessary to be known, that a man may have a communion with God in Christ and be saved; or,—

(2.) That doing so, in the course of our lives we manifest and declare a principle that is utterly inconsistent with the belief of those truths which outwardly we profess; or,—

(3.) That we add unto them, in opinion or worship, that or those things which are in very deed destructive of them, or do any way render them insufficient to be saving unto us.

If neither of these three can be proved against a man, he may justly claim the privilege of being a member of the visible church of Christ in the world, though he never in all his life be a member of a particular church; which yet, if he have fitting opportunity and advantage for it, is his duty to be.

And thus much be spoken as to the state and condition of the visible catholic church, and in this sense we grant it to be, and the unity thereof. In the late practice of men, that expression of the "catholic church" hath been an "individuum vagum," few knowing what to make of it; a "cothurnus," that every one accommodated at pleasure to his own principles and pretensions. I have no otherwise described it than did Irenæus of old. Said he, "Judicabit omnes eos, qui sunt extra veritatem, id est, extra ecclesiam," lib. iv. cap. 62. And on the same account is a particular church sometimes called by some the catholic: "Quandoque ego Remigius episcopus de hac luce transiero, tu mihi hæres esto, sancta et venerabilis ecclesia catholica urbis Remorum," Flodoardus, lib. i.

In the sense insisted on was it so frequently described by the ancients.

So again Irenæus: "Etsi in mundo loquelæ dissimiles sunt, sed tamen virtus traditionis una et eadem est, et neque hæ quæ in Germania sunt fundatæ ecclesiæ aliter credunt, aut aliter tradunt; neque hæ quæ in Hiberis sunt, neque hæ quæ in Celtis, neque hæ quæ in Oriente, neque hæ quæ in Ægypto, neque hæ quæ in Libya, neque hæ quæ in medio mundi constitutæ. Sed sicut sol, creatura Dei, in universo mundo unus et idem est, sic et lumen, prædicatio veritatis ubique lucet," lib. i. cap. 10. To the same purpose Justin Martyr:

Οὐδὲ ἕν γὰρ ὅλως ἐστὶ τὸ γένος ἀνθρώπων εἴτε βαρβάρων, εἴτε Ἑλλήνων, εἴτε ἁπλῶς ὡτινιοῦν ὀνόματι προσαγορευομένων, ἢ ἀμαξοβίων, ἢ ἀοίκων καλουμένων, ἢ ἐν σκηναῖς κτηνοτρόφων οἰκούντων, ἐν οἷς μὴ διὰ τοῦ ὀνόματος τοῦ σταυρωθέντος Ἰησοῦ εὐχαὶ καὶ εὐχαριστίαι τῷ πατρὶ καὶ ποιητῇ τῶν ὅλων γίνωνται. Dialog. cum Tryphone.

The generality of all sorts of men worshipping God in Jesus Christ is the church we speak of, whose extent in his days Tertullian thus related: " In quem alium crediderunt gentes universæ, nisi in ipsum, qui jam venit? Cui enim aliæ gentes crediderunt, Parthi, Medi, et Elamitæ, et qui habitant Mesopotamiam, Armeniam, Phrygiam, et incolentes Ægyptum et regionem Africæ quæ est trans Cyrenem, Romani et incolæ; tunc et in Hierusalem Judæi, et gentes cæteræ, ut jam Gætulorum varietates, et Maurorum multi fines, Hispaniarum omnes termini, et Galliarum diversæ nationes, et Brittanorum inaccessa Romanis loca, Christo vero subdita; et Sarmatarum et Dacorum et Germanorum et Scytharum et abditarum multarum gentium et provinciarum et insularum multarum nobis ignotarum, et quæ enumerare non possumus? In quibus omnibus locis Christi nomen, qui jam venit, regnat ad Judæos." [Adver. Jud., cap. vii.]

Some have said, and do yet say, that the church in this sense is a *visible, organical, political* body. That it is visible is confessed; both its matter and form bespeak visibility, as an inseparable adjunct of its subsisting. That it is a body also in the general sense wherein that word is used, or a society of men embodied by the profession of the same faith, is also granted. Organical in this business is an ambiguous term; the use of it is plainly metaphorical, taken from the members, instruments, and organs of a natural body. Because Paul hath said that in "one body there are many members, as eyes, feet, hands, yet the body is but one, so is the church," it hath been usually said that the church is an organical body. What church Paul speaks of in that place is not evident, but what he alludes unto is. The difference he speaks of in the individual persons of the church is not in respect of office, power, and authority, but gifts or graces, and usefulness on that account. Such an organical body we confess the church catholic visible to be. In it are persons endued with variety of gifts and graces for the benefit and ornament of the whole.

An organical political body is a thing of another nature. A politic body or commonwealth is a society of a certain portion of mankind, united under some form of rule or government, whose supreme and subordinate administration is committed to several persons, according to the tenor of such laws and customs as that society hath or doth consent unto. This also is said to be organical on a metaphorical account,—because the officers and members that are in it and over it hold proportion to the more noble parts of the body. Kings are said to be heads; counsellors, ὀφθαλμοὶ βασιλέων. To the constitution of such a commonwealth distinctly, as such, it is required that the whole hath the same laws, but not that only. Two nations most distinct and different, on account of other ends and interests, may yet have the same individual laws and customs for the distribution of justice and preservation of peace among themselves. An entire form of regimen and government peculiar thereunto is required for the constitution of a distinct political body. In this sense we deny the church whereof we speak to be an organical, political body, as not having indeed any of the requisites thereunto, not one law of order. The same individual moral law, or law of moral duties, it hath; but a law given to the whole as such, for order, polity, rule, it hath not. All the members of it are obliged to the same law of order and polity in their several societies; but the whole, as such, hath no such law. It hath no such head or governor, as such. Nor will it suffice to say that Christ is its head; for if, as a visible political body, it hath a political head, that head also must be visible. The commonwealth of the Jews was a political body; of this God was the head and king; hence their historian saith their government was Θεοκρατία. And when they would choose a king, God said they rejected him who was their political head, to whom a shekel was paid yearly as tribute, called the "shekel of the sanctuary." Now, they rejected him, not by asking a king simply, but a king after the manner of the nations. Yet, that it might be a visible political body, it required a visible supreme magistrate to the whole; which when there was none, all polity was dissolved amongst them, Judges xxi. 25. Christ is the head of every particular church, its lawgiver and ruler; but yet, to make a church a visible, organical, political body, it is required that it hath visible governors and rulers, and of the whole. Nor can it be said that it is a political body that hath a supreme government and order in it, as it is made up and constituted of particular churches, and that in the representatives convened doth the supreme visible power of it consist; for such a convention in the judgment of all ought to be extraordinary only, in ours is utterly impossible, and "de facto" was not among the churches for three hundred years,—yea, never. Besides, the visible catholic church is not made up of particular churches, as such; for if so, then no man can be member of it but by virtue of his being a member of some visible church, which is false. Profession of the truth, as before stated, is the formal reason and cause of any person's relation to the church visible; which he hath thereby, whether he belong to any particular church or no.

Let it be evidenced that the universal church whereof we speak hath any law or rule of order and government, as such, given unto it; or that it is in possibility, as such, to put any such law or rule

into execution; that it hath any homogeneous ruler or rulers, that
have the care of the administration of the rule and government of
the whole, as such, committed to him or them by Jesus Christ; that
as it hath the same common spiritual and known orders and interest, and the same specifical ecclesiastical rule given to all its members, so it hath the same political interest, order, and conversation,
as such; or that it hath any one cause constitutive of a political
body, whereby it is such, or hath at all the form of an instituted
church, or is capable of any such form,—and they that do so shall be
farther attended to.

CHAPTER VI.

Romanists' charge of schism on the account of separation from the church catholic
    proposed to consideration—The importance of this plea on both sides—The sum
    of their charge—The church of Rome not the church catholic; not a church
    in any sense—Of antichrist in the temple—The catholic church, how intrusted
    with interpretation of Scripture—Of interpretation of Scripture by tradition
    —The interest of the Roman church herein discharged—All necessary truths
    believed by Protestants—No contrary principle by them manifested—Pro-
    fane persons no members of the church catholic—Of the late Roman prose-
    lytes—Of the Donatists—Their business reported and case stated—The pre-
    sent state of things unsuited to that of old—Apostasy from the unity of the
    church catholic charged on the Romanists—Their claim to be that church
    sanguinary, false—Their plea to this purpose considered—The blasphemous
    management of their plea by some of late—The whole dissolved—Their in-
    ferences on their plea practically prodigious—Their apostasy proved by in-
    stances—Their grand argument in this cause proposed; answered—Conse-
    quences of denying the Roman church to be a church of Christ weighed.

LET us see now what as to conscience can be charged on us, Protestants I mean, who are all concerned herein as to the breach of
this union. The Papists are the persons that undertake to manage
this charge against us. To lay aside the whole plea "subesse Ro-
mano pontifici," and all those fears wherewith they juggled when
the whole world sat in darkness, which they do now use at the entrance of their charge, the sum of what they insist upon, firstly,
is: The catholic church is intrusted with the interpretation of the
Scripture, and declaration of the truths therein contained; which
being by it so declared, the not receiving of them implicitly or ex-
plicitly,—that is, the disbelieving of them as so proposed and declared,
—cuts off any man from being a member of the church, Christ himself having said that he that hears not the church is to be as a
heathen man and a publican; which church they are, that is certain.
It is all one, then, what we believe or do not believe, seeing that we
believe not all that the catholic church proposeth to be believed, and
what we do believe we believe not on that account.

Ans. Their insisting on this plea so much as they do is sufficient
to evince their despair of making good by instance our failure, in respect of the way and principles by which the unity of the visible
church may be lost or broken. Fail they in this, they are gone; and
if they carry this plea, we are all at their disposal. The sum of it is,
The catholic church is intrusted with the sole power of delivering what
is truth, and what is necessary to be believed: this catholic church
is the church of Rome,—that is, the pope, or what else may in any
juncture of time serve their interest. But, as it is known,—

1. *We deny their church, as it is styled, to be the catholic church,*
or as such any part of it, as particular churches are called or
esteemed; so that, of all men in the world, they are least concerned
in this assertion. Nay, I shall go farther. Suppose all the members
of the Roman church to be sound in the faith as to all necessary
truths, and no way to prejudice the advantages and privileges which
accrue to them by the profession thereof, whereby the several individuals of it would be true members of the catholic church, yet I
should not only deny it to be the catholic church, but also,—abiding
in its present order and constitution, being that which by themselves
it is supposed to be,—to be any particular church of Christ at all, as
wanting many things necessary to constitute them so, and having
many things destructive utterly to the very essence and being of that
order that Christ hath appointed in his churches.

The best plea that I know for their church-state is, that Antichrist
sits in the temple of God. Now, although we might justly omit the
examination of this pretence until those who are concerned in it will
professedly own it as their plea, yet as it lies in our way in the
thoughts of some, I say to it that I am not so certain that καθίσαι εἰς
τὸν ναὸν τοῦ Θεοῦ, signifies " to sit in the temple of God;" seeing a
learned man long ago thought it rather to be a "setting up against
the temple of God," Aug. de Civitate Dei, lib. x. cap. 59. But
grant the sense of the expression to be as it is usually received, it
imports no more but that the man of sin shall set up his power
against God in the midst of them who, by their outward visible profession, have right to be called his temple; which entitles him and
his copartners in apostasy to the name of the church as much as
changing of money and selling of cattle were ordinances of God
under the old temple, when, by some men's practising of them in it,
it was made a den of thieves.

2. Though as to the plea of them and their interest with whom
we have to do, we have nothing requiring our judgments in the case,
yet, "ex abundanti," we add, that *we deny that, by the will and appointment of Jesus Christ, the catholic church visible is in any
sense intrusted with such an interpretation of Scripture* as that

her declaration of truth should be the measure of what should be believed; or that, as such, it is intrusted with any power of that nature at all, or is enabled to propose a rule of faith to be received, as so proposed, to the most contemptible individual in the world; or that it is possible that any voice of it should be heard or understood, but only this, "I believe the necessary saving truths contained in the Scripture;" or that it can be consulted withal, or is, as such, intrusted with any power, authority, or jurisdiction; nor shall we ever consent that the office and authority of the Scriptures be actually taken from it on any pretence. As to that of our Saviour, of telling the church, it is so evidently spoken of a particular church, that may immediately be consulted in case of difference between brethren, and does so no way relate to the business in hand, that I shall not trouble the reader with a debate of it. But do we not receive the Scripture itself upon the authority of the church? I say, if we did so, yet this concerns not Rome, which we account no church at all. That we have received the Scriptures from the church of Rome at first,—that is, so much as the book itself,—is an intolerable figment. But it is worse to say that we receive and own their authority from the authority of any church, or all the churches in the world. It is the expression of our learned Whitaker, "Qui Scripturam non credit esse divinam, nisi propter ecclesiæ vocem, Christianus non est." To deny that the Scripture hath immediate force and efficacy to evince its own authority is plainly to deny it. On that account, being brought unto us by the providence of God (wherein I comprise all subservient helps of human testimony), we receive them, and on no other.

But is not the Scripture to be interpreted according to the tradition of the catholic church? and are not those interpretations so made to be received?

I say, among all the figments that these latter ages have invented,—I shall add, amongst the true stories of Lucian,—there is not one more remote from truth than this assertion, that any one text of Scripture may be interpreted according to the universal tradition of the catholic church, and be made appear so to be; any farther than that, in general, the catholic church hath not believed any such sense to be in any portion of Scripture, which to receive were destructive of salvation. And, therefore, the Romanists tell us that the present church (that is, theirs) is the keeper and interpreter of these traditions; or rather, that its power, authority and infallibility, being the same that it hath been in former ages, what it determines is to be received to be the tradition of the catholic church. For the trial whereof, whether it be so or no, there is no rule but its own determination; which if they can persuade us to acquiesce in, I shall grant that they have acquired such an absolute dominion over us and our faith, that it is fit that we should be, soul and body, at their disposal.

It being, then, the work of the Scripture to propose the saving truths of Christ (the belief and profession whereof are necessary to make a man a member of the church) so as to make them of indispensable necessity to be received, if they can from them convince us that we do not believe and profess all and every one of the truths or articles of faith so necessary as expressed, we shall fall down under the authority of such conviction; if not, we profess our consciences to be no more concerned in the authority of their church than we judge their church to be in the privileges of the church catholic.

But, secondly, it may be we are chargeable with manifesting some *principles of profaneness*, wherewith the belief of the truth we profess hath an absolute inconsistency. For those who are liable and obnoxious to this charge, I say, let them plead for themselves; for let them profess what they will, and cry out ten thousand times that they are Christians, I shall never acknowledge them for other than visible enemies of the cross, kingdom, and church of Christ. Traitors and rebels are not, "de facto," subjects of that king or ruler in reference to whom they are so. Of some, who said they were Jews, Christ said they lied, and were not, but "the synagogue of Satan," Rev. ii. 9. Though such as these say they are Christians, I will be bold to say they lie, "they are not, but slaves of Satan." Though they live within the pale, as they call it, of the church (the catholic church being an enclosure as to profession, not place), yet they are not within it nor of it any more than a Jew or Mohammedan within the same precinct. Suppose they have been baptized, yet if their belly be their god, and their lives dedicated to Satan, all the advantage they have thereby is, that they are apostates and renegadoes.

That we have added any thing of our own, making profession of any thing in religion absolutely destructive to the fundamentals we profess, I know not that we are accused, seeing our crime is asserted to consist in detracting, not adding. Now, unless we are convinced of failing on one of these three accounts, we shall not at all question but that we abide in the unity of the visible catholic church.

It is the common cry of the Romanists that we are *schismatics*. Why so? Because we have separated ourselves from the communion of the catholic church. What this catholic church is, and how little they are concerned in it, hath been declared. How much they have prevailed themselves with ignorant souls by this plea, we know. Nor was any other success to be expected in respect of many whom they have won over to themselves; who, being persons ignorant of the righteousness of God and the power of the faith they have professed, not having had experience of communion with the Lord Jesus under the conduct of them, have been, upon every provocation and temptation, a ready prey to deceivers.

Take a little view of their late proselytes, and it will quickly appear what little cause they have to boast in them. With some, by the craft and folly of some relations, they are admitted to treat, when they are drawing to their dissolution. These, for the most part, having been persons of dissolute and profligate lives, never having tasted the power of any religion, whatever they have professed, in their weakness and disturbed dying thoughts, may be apt to receive any impression that with confidence and violence is imposed upon them. Besides, it is a far easier proposal to be reconciled to the church of Rome, and so by purgatory to get to heaven, than to be told of regeneration, repentance, faith, and the covenant of grace, things of difficulty to such poor creatures. Others that have been cast down from their hopes and expectations, or out from their enjoyments, by the late revolution in these nations, have by their discontent or necessity made themselves an easy prey to their zeal. What hath been the residue of their proselytes? What one who hath ever manifested himself to share in the power of our religion, or was not prepared by principles of superstition almost as deep as their own, have they prevailed on? But I shall not farther insist on these things. To return:—

Our communion with the visible catholic church is in the unity of the faith only. The breach of this union, and therein a relinquishment of the communion of the church, lies in a relinquishment of, or some opposition to, some or all of the saving, necessary truths of the gospel; now, this is not schism, but heresy or apostasy;—or it is done by an open profligateness of life: so that, indeed, this charge is nothing at all to the purpose in hand; though, through grace, in a confidence of our own innocency, we are willing to debate the guilt of the crime under any name or title whatever.

Unto what hath been spoken, I shall only add the removal of some common objections, with a recharge on them with whom principally we have as yet had to do, and come to the last thing proposed. The case of some of old, who were charged with schism for separating from the catholic church on an account wholly and clearly distinct from that of a departure from the faith, is an instance of the judgment of antiquity lying in an opposition to the notion of departure from the church now delivered. "Doth not Augustine, do not the rest of his orthodox contemporaries, charge the Donatists with schism because they departed from the catholic

church? and doth not the charge rise up with equal efficacy against
you as them? at least, doth it not give you the nature of schism in
another sense than is by you granted?"

The reader knows sufficiently, if he hath at all taken notice of
these things, where to find this cloud scattered, without the least
annoyance or detriment to the Protestant cause, or of any concerned
in that name, however by lesser differences diversified among themselves. I shall not repeat what by others hath been at large insisted
on. In brief, put the whole church of God into that condition of
liberty and soundness of doctrine which it was in when the great
uproar was made by the Donatists, and we shall be concerned to
give in our judgments concerning them.

To press an example of former days, as binding unto duty or convincing of evil, in respect of any now, without stating the whole
"substratum" of the business and complete cause, as it was in the
days and seasons wherein the example was given, we judge it not
equal. Yet, although none can with ingenuity press me with the
crime they were guilty of, unless they can prove themselves to be
instated in the very same condition as they were against whom that
crime was committed,—which I am fully assured none in the world
can, the communion of the catholic church then pleaded for being, in the judgment of all, an effect of men's free liberty and
choice, now pressed as an issue of the tyranny of some few,—I shall
freely deliver my thoughts concerning the Donatists; which will be
comprehensive also of those others that suffer with them in former
and after ages under the same imputation.

1. Then, I am persuaded that in the matter of fact the Donatists[1]
were some of them *deceived*, and others of them did *deceive*, in
charging Cæcilianus to be ordained by "traditores;" which they
made the main ground of their separation, however they took in
other things (as is usual) into their defence afterward. Whether
any of themselves were ordained by such persons, as they are re-
charged, I know not.

2. On supposition that he was so, and they that ordained him
were known to him to have been so, yet he being not guilty of the
crime, renouncing communion with them therein, and themselves
repenting of their sin, as did Peter, whose sin exceeded theirs, this
was no just cause of casting him out of communion, he walking and
acting in all other things suitably to principles by themselves acknowledged.

3. That on supposition they had just cause hereupon to renounce

[1] Owen had occasion afterwards to consider more fully the case of the Donatists, so
far as it bears on the charge of schism brought against the Nonconformists. See his
"Inquiry concerning Evangelical Churches," vol. xv. p. 369.—Ed.

the communion of Cæcilianus,—which, according to the principles of those days, retained by themselves, was most false,—yet they had no ground of separating from the church of Carthage, where were many elders not obnoxious to that charge. Indeed, to raise a jealousy of a fault in any man, which is denied by him, which we are not able to prove, which if it were proved were of little or no importance, and on pretence thereof to separate from all who will not believe what we surmise, is a wild and unchristian course of proceeding.

4. Yet grant, farther, that men of tender consciences, regulated by the principle then generally received, might be startled at the communion of that church wherein Cæcilianus did preside, yet nothing but the height of madness, pride, and corrupt fleshly interest, could make men declare hostility against all the churches of Christ in the world who would communicate with or did not condemn that church; which were to regulate all the churches in the world by their own fancy and imagination.

5. Though men, out of such pride and folly, might judge all the residue of Christians to be faulty and guilty in this particular, of not condemning and separating from the church of Carthage, yet to proceed to cast them out from the very name of Christians, and so disannul their privileges and ordinances that they had been made partakers of, as manifestly they did, by rebaptizing all that entered into their communion, was such unparalleled Pharisaism and tyranny as was wholly to be condemned and intolerable.

6. The divisions, outrages, and enthusiastical furies and riots that befell them, or they fell into, in their way, were, in my judgment, tokens of the hand of God against them; so that, upon the whole matter, their undertaking and enterprise was utterly undue and unlawful.

I shall farther add, as to the management of the cause by their adversaries, that there is in their writings, especially those of Austin, for the most part, a sweet and gracious spirit breathing, full of zeal for the glory of God, peace, love, union among Christians: and as to the issue of the cause under debate, it is evident that they did sufficiently foil their adversaries on principles then generally confessed and acknowledged on all hands, though some of them seem to have been considering, learned, and dexterous men.

How little we are at this day, in any contests that are managed amongst us about the things of God, concerned in those differences of theirs, these few considerations will evince; yet, notwithstanding all this, I must take liberty to profess, that although the fathers justly charged the Donatists with disclaiming of all the churches of Christ as a thing wicked and unjust, yet many of the principles whereon they did it were such as I cannot assent to. Yea, I shall say, that though Austin was sufficiently clear on the nature of the invisible church catholic, yet his frequent confounding it with a mistaken notion of the visible general church hath given no small occasion of stumbling and sundry unhappy entanglements to divers in after ages. His own book, "De Unitate Ecclesiæ," which contains the sum and substance of what he had written elsewhere, or disputed against the Donatists, would afford me instances enough to make good my assertion, were it now under consideration or proof.

Being, then, thus come off from this part of our charge and accusation of schism, for the relinquishment of the catholic visible church,—which as we have not done, so to do is not schism, but a sin of another nature and importance,—according to the method proposed, a recharge on the Romanists in reference to their present condition, and its unsuitableness to the unity of the church evinced, must briefly ensue.

Their claim is known to be no less than that they are this catholic church, out of whose communion there is no salvation (as the Donatists' was of old); also, that the union of this church consists in its subjection to its head, the pope, and worshipping of God according to his appointment, in and with his several qualifications and attendancies. Now, this claim of theirs, to our apprehension and consciences, is,—

1. *Cruel* and *sanguinary*, condemning millions to hell that invocate and call on the name of the Lord Jesus Christ, believing all things that are written in the Old and New Testaments; for no other cause in the world but because they are not convinced that it is their duty to give up reason, faith, soul, and all, to him and his disposal whom they have not only unconquerable presumptions against as an evil and wicked person, but are also resolved and fully persuaded in their consciences that he is an enemy to their dear Lord Jesus Christ, out of love to whom they cannot bear him. Especially will this appear to be so if we consider their farther improvement of this principle to the killing, hanging, torturing to death, burning of all that they are able, who are in the condition before mentioned. This, upon the matter, is the great principle of their religion. All persons that will not be subject (at least in spiritual things) to the pope are to be hanged or burned in this world, or by other means destroyed, and damned for ever hereafter. This is the substance of the gospel they preach, the centre wherein all the lines of their writings do meet; and to this must the holy, pure word of God be wrested to give countenance. Blessed be the God of our salvation! who as he never gave merciless men power over the souls and eternal condition of his saints, so he hath begun to work a deliverance of the outward condition of his people from their rage and

cruelty, which, in his good time, he will perfect in their irrecoverable ruin. In the meantime, I say, the guilt of the blood of millions of innocent persons, yea, saints of God, lies at their door. And although things are so stated in this age that in some nations they have left none to kill, in others are restrained, that they can kill no more, yet retaining the same principles with their forefathers, and justifying them in their paths of blood, I look upon them all as guilty of murder, and so not to have " eternal life abiding in them;" being of that wicked one, as Cain, who slew his brother. I speak not of individuals, but of those in general that constitute their governing church.

2. *Most false*, and such as nothing but either judiciary hardness from God, sending men strong delusions that they might believe a lie, or the dominion of cursed lusts, pride, ambition, covetousness, desire of rule, can lie at the bottom of; for,—

(1.) It is false that the union of the catholic church, in the notion now under consideration, *consists in subjection to any officer* or officers; or that it hath any peculiar form, constituting one church in relation to them, or in joint participation of the same individual ordinances whatever, by all the members of it; or that any such oneness is at all possible, or any unity whatever, but that of the faith which by it is believed, and of the truth professed.

(2.) It is most ridiculous that they are *this catholic church*, or that their communion is comprehensive of it in its latitude. He must be blind, uncharitable, a judge of what he cannot see or know, who can once entertain a thought of any such thing. Let us run a little over the foundations of this assertion.

First, "*Peter was the prince of the apostles.*" It is denied; arguments lie clear against it. The Gospel, the Acts of the Apostles, all confute it. The express testimony of Paul lies against it; our Saviour denies that it was so, gives order that it should not be so. The name and thing are foreign to the times of the apostles. It was a ministry, not a principality, they had committed to them; therein they were all equal. It is from that spirit whence they inquired after a kingdom and dominion, before they had received the Spirit of the gospel, as it was dispensed after Christ's ascension, that such assertions are now insisted on. But let that be supposed, what is next? "*He had a universal monarchical jurisdiction committed to him over all Christians;* for Christ said, 'Tu es Petrus, tibi dabo claves, et pasce oves meas.'" But these terms are barbarous to the Scripture. Monarchy is not the English of, "Vos autem non sic." Jurisdiction is a name of a right, for the exercise of *civil* power. Christ hath left no such thing as jurisdiction, in the sense wherein it is now used, to Peter or his church. Men do but make sport, and expose themselves to the contempt of considering persons, who talk of the institutions of our Lord in the language of the last ages, or expressions suitable to what was in practice in them. He that shall compare the fraternal church admonition and censures of the primitive institution, with the courts, powers, and jurisdictions set up in pretence and colour of them in after ages, will admire at the likeness and correspondency of the one with the other. The administration of ecclesiastical jurisdiction in the Papacy, and under the Prelacy here in England, had no more relation to any institution of Christ (unless it be that it effectually excluded the exercise of his institutions) than other civil courts of justice among Christians have. Peter had the power and authority of an apostle in and over the churches of Christ, to teach, to instruct them, to ordain elders in them by their consent, wherever he came; so had the rest of the apostles. But as to this monarchy of Peter over the rest of the apostles, let them show what authority he ever exercised over them while he and they lived together. We read that he was once reproved by one of them, not that he ever reproved the meanest of them. If Christ made the grant of pre-eminency to him when he said, " Tu es Petrus," why did the apostles inquire afterward who among them should be greatest? And why did not our Saviour, on that dispute, plainly satisfy them that Peter was to be chief, but chose rather to so determine the question as to evince them of the vanity of any such inquiry? And yet the determination of it is that that lies at the bottom of the papal monarchy. And why doth Paul say that he was in nothing inferior to any of the apostles, when (if these gentlemen say true) he was in many things inferior to Peter? What special place hath the name of Peter in the foundation of the new Jerusalem? Rev. xxi. 14. What exaltation hath his throne among the twelve, whereon the apostles judge the world and house of Israel? Matt. xix. 28. What eminency of commission had he for teaching all nations or forgiving sins? What had his keys more than those of the rest of the apostles? What was peculiar in that triple command of feeding the sheep of Christ, but his triple denial that preceded? John xxi. 15–17. Is an injunction for the performance of duty a grant of new authority? But that we may make some progress, suppose this also, " *Why, this power, privilege, and jurisdiction of Peter, was to be transferred to his successors, when the power of all the other apostles, as such, died with them.*" But what pretence or colour of it is there for this assertion? What one tittle or *ιῶτα* is there in the whole book of God giving the least countenance to this imagination? What distinction between Peter and the rest of the apostles on this account is once made, or in any kind insinuated? Certainly, this was a thing of great importance to the churches to have been acquainted with it. When Paul so sadly tells

the church, that after his departure grievous wolves would spoil the
flock, and many among themselves would arise, speaking perverse
things, to draw disciples after them, why did he not give them the
least direction to make their address to him that should succeed
Peter in his power and office, for relief and redress? Strange, that
it should be of necessity to salvation to be subject to him in whom
this power of Peter was to be continued; that he was to be one in
whom the saints were to be consummated; that in relation to him
the unity of the catholic church, to be preserved under pain of damnation, should consist;—and yet not a word spoken of him in the whole
word of God!

But they say, "*Peter had not only an apostolical power with the
rest of the apostles, but also an ordinary power, that was to be continued in the church.*" But the Scripture being confessedly silent
of any such thing, let us hear what proof is tendered for the establishment of this uncouth assertion. Herein, then, thus they proceed:
"It will be confessed that Jesus Christ ordained his church wisely,
according to his infinite wisdom, which he exercised about his body.
Now, to this wisdom of his, for the prevention of innumerable evils,
it is agreeable that he should appoint some one person with that
power of declaring truth, and of jurisdiction to enforce the receiving
of it, which we plead for; for this was in Peter, as is proved from
the texts of Scripture before mentioned: therefore, it is continued in
them that succeed him." And here lies the great stress of their
cause,—that, to prevent evils and inconveniencies, it became the
wisdom of Jesus Christ to appoint a person with all that authority,
power, and infallibility, to continue in his church to the end of the
world. And this plea they manage variously, with much sophistry,
rhetoric, and testimonies of antiquity. But suppose all this should
be granted, yet I am full well assured that they can never bring it
home to their concernment by any argument, but only the actual
claim of the pope, wherein he stands singly now in the world; which
that it is satisfactory, to make it good "de fide" that he is so, will
not easily be granted. The truth is, of all the attempts they make
against the Lord Jesus Christ, this is one of the greatest, wherein
they will assert that it became his wisdom to do that which by no
means they can prove that he hath done; which is plainly to tell us
what in their judgment he ought to have done, though he hath not,
and that, therefore, it is incumbent on them to supply what he hath
been defective in. Had he taken the care he should of them and
their master, that he and they might have ruled and revelled over
and in the house of God, he would have appointed things as now
they are; which they affirm to have become his wisdom. He was a
king that once cried, "Si Deo in creatione adfuissem, mundum me-

lius ordinassem." But every friar or monk can say of Jesus Christ, had they been present at his framing the world to come (whereof we speak), they would have told him what had become his wisdom to do. Our blessed Lord hath left sufficient provision against all future emergencies and inconveniencies in his word and Spirit, given and promised to his saints. And the one remedy which these men have found out, with the contempt and blasphemy of him and them, hath proved worse than all the other evils and diseases for whose prevention he made provision; which he hath done also for that remedy of theirs, but that some are hardened through the righteous judgment of God and deceitfulness of sin.

The management of this plea by some of late is very considerable. Say they, " Quia non de verbis solum Scripturæ, sed etiam de sensu plurima controversia est, si ecclesiæ interpretatio non est certa intelligendi norma, ecquis erit istiusmodi controversiæ judex? Sensum enim suum pro sua virili quisque defendet; quod si in explorandâ verbi Dei intelligentiâ nullus est certus judex, audemus dicere nullam rempublicam fuisse stultius constitutam. Sin autem apostoli tradiderunt ecclesiis verbum Dei sine intelligentia verbi Dei, quomodo prædicârunt evangelium omni creaturæ? quomodo docuerunt omnes gentes servare quæcunque illis fuerunt a Christo commendata. Non est puerorum aut psittacorum prædicatio, qui sine mente dant, accipiuntque sonum," Walemburg, Con. 4, Num. 26.

It is well that at length these men speak out plainly. If the pope be not a visible supreme judge in and over the church, Christ hath, in the constitution of his church, dealt more foolishly than ever any did in the constitution of a commonwealth! If he have not an infallible power of determining the sense of the Scripture, the Scripture is but an empty, insignificant word, like the speech of parrots or popinjays! Though Christ hath, by his apostles, given the Scripture to make the man of God wise unto salvation, and promised his Spirit unto them that believe, by whose assistance the Scripture gives out its own sense to them, yet all is folly if the pope be not supreme and infallible! The Lord rebuke them who thus boldly blaspheme his word and wisdom! But let us proceed.

" This Peter, thus invested in power that was to be traduced to others, went to Rome, and preached the gospel there." It is most certain, nor will themselves deny it, that if this be not so, and believed, their whole fabric will fall to the ground. But can this be necessary for all sorts of Christians, and every individual of men among them, to believe, when there is not the least insinuation of any such thing in the Scripture? Certainly, though it be only a matter of fact, yet being of such huge importance and consequence, and such a doctrine of absolute and indispensable necessity to be believed, as is

pretended, depending upon it, if it were true, and true in reference
to such an end and purpose as is pleaded, it would not have been
passed over in silence there, where so many things of inconceivably
less concernment to the church of God (though all in their respective
degrees tending to edification) are recorded. As to what is recorded
in story, the order and series of things, with the discovery afforded
us of Peter's course and place of abode in Scripture, do prevail with
me to think steadfastly that he was never there, against the self-
contradicting testimonies of some few, who took up vulgar reports
then when the mystery of iniquity had so far operated, at least, that
it was judged meet that the chief of the apostles should have lived
in the chief city of the world.

But that we may proceed, grant this also, that Peter was at Rome,
which they shall never be able to prove, and that he did preach the
gospel there,—yet so he did, by their own confession, at other
places, making his residence at Antioch for some years,—what will
this avail towards the settling of the matter under consideration?
"There Christ appointed him to fix his chair, and make that church
the place of his residence,"—λῆροι!

Of his meeting Simon Magus at Rome, who in all probability
was never there (for Semo Sangus was not Simon Magus, nor Sanc-
tus, nor Deus Magnus), of the conquest made of him and his devils,
of his being instructed of Christ not to go from Rome, but tarry there
and suffer, something may be said from old legends; but of his
chair, and fixing of it at Rome, of his confinement, as it were, to that
place, in direct opposition to the tenor of his apostolical commission,
who first told the story I know not. But this I know, they will one
day be ashamed of their chair, thrones, and sees, and jurisdictions,
wherein they now so please themselves.

But what is next to this? "*The bishop of Rome succeeds Peter in
all that power, jurisdiction, infallibility, with whatsoever else was
fancied before in him, as the ordinary lord of the church; and therefore the Roman church is the catholic,*" "quod erat demonstrandum."
Now, though this inference will no way follow upon these principles,
though they should all be supposed to be true, whereof not one is so
much as probable, and though this last assertion be vain and ridiculous,
nothing at all being pleaded to ground this succession, no institution
of Christ, no act of any council of the church, no will or testament
of Peter, but only it is so fallen out, as the world was composed of
a casual concurrence of atoms; yet seeing they will have it so, I
desire a little farther information in one thing that yet remains, and
that is this: The charter, patents, and grant of all this power, and
right of succession unto Peter, in all the advantages, privileges, and
jurisdiction before mentioned, being wholly in their own keeping,

whereof I never saw letter or tittle, nor ever conversed with any one, no not of themselves, that did, I would be gladly informed whether this grant be made to him absolutely, without any manner of condition whatever, so that whoever comes to be pope of Rome, and possessed of Peter's chair there, by what means soever he is possessed of it, whether he believe the gospel or no, or any of the saving truths therein contained, and so their church must be the catholic church, though it follow him in all abominations; or whether it be made on any condition to him, especially that of cleaving to the doctrine of Christ revealed in the gospel? If they say the first, that it is an absolute grant that is made to him, without any condition expressed or necessarily to be understood, I am at an issue, and have nothing to add but my desire that the grant may be produced; for whilst we are at this variance, it is against all law and equity that the parties litigant should be admitted to plead bare allegations without proof. If the latter, though we should grant all the former monstrous suppositions, yet we are perfectly secure against all their pretensions, knowing nothing more clearly and evidently than that he and they have broken all conditions that can possibly be imagined, by corrupting and perverting almost the whole doctrine of the gospel.

And whereas it may be supposed that the great condition of such a grant would consist in his diligent attendance to the Scriptures, the word of God, herein doth the filth of their abominations appear above all other things. The guilt that is in that society or combination of men in locking up the Scripture in an unknown tongue; forbidding the people to read it; burning some men to death for the studying of it, and no more; disputing against its power to make good its own authority; charging it with obscurity, imperfection, insufficiency; frightening men from the perusal of it, with the danger of being seduced and made heretics by so doing; setting up their own traditions in an equality with it, if not exalting them above it; studying by all means to decry it as useless and contemptible, at least comparatively with themselves; will not be purged from them for ever.

But you will say, "This is a simple question, for the pope of Rome hath a promise that he shall still be such a one as is fit to be trusted with the power mentioned, and not one that shall defend Mohammed to be the prophet of God sent into the world, or the like abominations; at least, that be he what he will, placed in the chair, he shall not err nor mistake in what he delivereth for truth." Now, seeing themselves, as was said, are the sole keepers of this promise and grant also, which they have not as yet showed to the world, I am necessitated to ask, once more, whether it be made to him merely upon condition of mounting into his chair, or also upon this condition, that he use the means appointed by God to come to the knowledge of the truth? If they say the former, I must needs say, that it is so remote from my apprehension that God, who will be worshipped in spirit and in truth only, should now, under the gospel, promise to any persons, that be they never so wicked and abominable, never so openly and evidently sworn enemies of him and his Anointed, whether they use any means or not by him appointed, they shall always in all things speak the truth, which they hate, in love, which they have not, with that authority which all his saints must bow unto, especially not having intimated any one word of any such promise in the Scripture, that I know not whatever I heard of in my life that I cannot as soon believe. If they say the latter, we close then as we did our former inquiry.

Upon the credit and strength of these sandy foundations and principles, which neither severally nor jointly will bear the weight of a feather, in a long-continued course of apostasy, have men conquered all policy, religion, and honesty, and built up that stupendous fabric, coupled together with subtle and scarce discernible joints and ligaments, which they call the catholic church.

(1.) In despite of policy, they have not only enslaved kings, kingdoms, commonwealths, nations, and people to be their vassals and at their disposal; but also, contrary to all rules of government, beyond the thoughts and conjectures of all or any that ever wrote of or instituted a government in the world, they have in most nations of Europe set up a *government*, authority, and jurisdiction, within another government and authority, settled on other accounts, the one independent of the other, and have brought these things to some kind of consistency: which that it might be accomplished never entered into the heart of any wise man once to imagine, nor had ever been by them effected without such advantages as none in the world ever had in such a continuance but themselves, unless the Druids of old in some nations obtained some such thing.[1]

(2.) In despite of religion itself, they have made a *new creed*, invented new ways of worship, given a whole sum and system of their own, altogether alien from the word of God, without an open disclaiming of that word, which in innumerable places bears testimony to its own perfection and fulness.

(3.) Contrary to common honesty, the first principles of reason, with

[1] " Si quis, aut privatus aut publicus, eorum decreto non stetit, sacrificiis interdicunt. Hæc pœna apud eos est gravissima. Quibus ita est interdictum, ii numero impiorum et sceleratorum habentur: iis omnes decedunt, aditum eorum sermonemque defugiunt, ne quid ex contagione incommodi accipiant; neque iis petentibus jus redditur, neque honos ullus communicatur. His autem omnibus Druidibus præest unus, qui summam inter eos habet authoritatem. Hoc mortuo, si quis ex reliquis excellit dignitate, succedit: at si sunt plures pares, suffragio Druidum allegitur, nonnunquam etiam armis de principatu contendunt."—Cæs. lib. vi. 13, de Bell. Gall.

violence to the evident dictates of the law of nature, they will, in confidence of these principles, have the word and sentence of a pope, though a beast, a witch, a conjuror (as by their own confession many of them have been), to be implicitly submitted to in and about things which he neither knoweth, nor loveth, nor careth for, being yet such in themselves as immediately and directly concern the everlasting condition of the souls of men. And this is our second return to their pretence of being the catholic church; to which I add,—

3. That their plea is so far from truth, that they are, and they only, the catholic church, that indeed they belong not to it, because they keep not the *unity of the faith*, which is required to constitute any person whatever a member of that church, but fail in all the conditions of it; for,—

(1.) To proceed, by way of instance, they do not profess nor believe a *justification distinct from sanctification*, and acceptance thereof; the doctrine whereof is of absolute and indispensable necessity to the preservation of the unity of the faith; and so fail in the first condition of professing all necessary truths. I know what they say of justification, what they have determined concerning it in the council of Trent, what they dispute about it in their books of controversies ; but I deny that which they contend for to be a justification. So that they do not deny only justification by faith, but positively, over and above, the infusion of grace, and the acceptance of the obedience thence arising;—that there is any justification at all, consisting in the free and full absolution of a sinner, on the account of Christ.

(2.) *They discover principles corrupt and depraved*, utterly inconsistent with those truths and the receiving of them which in general, by owning the Scriptures, they do profess. Herein, to pass by the principles of atheism, wickedness, and profaneness, that effectually work and manifest themselves in the generality of their priests and people, that of self-righteousness, that is in the best of their devotionists, is utterly inconsistent with the whole doctrine of the gospel, and all saving truths concerning the mediation of Jesus Christ therein contained.

(3.) That in their doctrine of the *pope's supremacy, of merits, satisfaction, the mass, the worshipping of images*, they add such things to their profession as enervate the efficacy of all the saving truths they do profess, and so fail in the third condition. This hath so abundantly been manifested by others, that I shall not need to add any thing to give the charge of it upon them any farther evidence or demonstration.

Thus it is unhappily fallen out with these men, that what of all men they most pretend unto, that of all men they have the least interest in. Athenæus tells us of one Thrasilaus an Athenian, who being frenetically distempered, whatever ships came into the Piræus he looked on them and thought them his own, and rejoiced as the master of so great wealth, when he was not the owner of so much as a boat. Such a distemper of pride and folly hath in the like manner seized on these persons with whom we have to do, that wherever in Scripture they meet with the name *church*, presently, as though they were intended by it, they rejoice in the privileges of it, when their concernment lies not at all therein.

To close this whole discourse, I shall bring the grand argument of the Romanists (with whom I shall now, in this treatise, have little more to do), wherewith they make such a noise in the world, to an issue. Of the many forms and shapes whereinto by them it is cast, this seems to be the most perspicuously expressive of their intention:—

" Voluntarily to forsake the communion of the church of Christ is schism, and they that do so are guilty of it;

" You have voluntarily forsaken the communion of the church of Christ:

"Therefore, you are guilty of the sin of schism."

I have purposely omitted the interposing of the term *catholic*, that the reason of the argument might run to its length: for upon the taking in of that term we have nothing to do but only to deny the minor proposition, seeing the Roman church, be it what it will, is not the church catholic; but as it is without that limitation called the church of Christ indefinitely, it leaves place for a farther and fuller answer.

To this, by way of inference, they add, "That schism, as it is declared by St Austin and St Thomas of Aquin, being so great and dam- nable a sin, and whereas it is plain that out of the church, which, as Peter says, is as Noah's ark, 1 Pet. iii. 20, 21, there is no salvation, it is clear you will be damned." This is the sum of their plea.

Now, as for the fore-mentioned argument, some of our divines answer to the minor proposition, and that both as to the terms of " voluntary forsaking," and that also of the " communion of the church." For the first, they say they did not *voluntarily* forsake the communion of the church that then was, but being necessitated by the command of God to reform themselves in sundry things, they were driven out by bell, book, and candle, cursed out, killed out, driven out by all manner of violence, ecclesiastical and civil; which is a strange way of men's becoming schismatic.

Secondly, That they forsook not the *communion* of the church, but the *corruptions* of it, or the communion of it in its corruption, not in other things wherein it was lawful to continue communion with it.

To give strength to this answer they farther add, that though they grant the church of Rome to have been at the time of the first separa- tion a true church of Christ, yet they deny it to be the catholic church, or only visible church then in the world, the churches in the east claiming that title by as good a right as she. So they. Others principally answer to the major proposition, and tell you that separation is either causeless, or upon just ground and cause; that it is a causeless separation only from the church of Christ that is schism; that there can be no cause of schism, for if there be a cause of schism materially, it ceaseth to be schism formally. And so, to strengthen their answer "in hypothesi," they fall upon the idolatries, heresies, tyranny, and apostasy of the church of Rome as just causes of separation from her. Nor will their plea be shaken to eternity; so that being true and popular, understood by the meanest, though it contain not the whole truth, I shall not in the least impair it.

For them who have found out new ways of justifying our separation from Rome, on principles of limiting the jurisdiction of the bishop of Rome to a peculiar patriarchate, and granting a power to kings or nations to erect patriarchs or metropolitans within their own territories, and the like, the protestant cause is not concerned in their plea; the whole of it on both hands being foreign to the Scripture, relating mostly to human constitutions, wherein they may have liberty to exercise their wits and abilities.

Not receding from what hath by others solidly been pleaded on the answers above mentioned, in answer to the principles I have hitherto evinced, I shall proceed to give my account of the argument proposed.

That we mistake not, I only premise that I take schism in this argument in the notion and sense of the Scripture precisely, wherein alone it will reach the conscience, and bear the weight of inferring damnation from it.

1. Then, I wholly deny the major proposition as utterly false, in what sense soever that expression, "True church of Christ," is taken. Take it for the catholic church of Christ, I deny that any one who is once a true member of it can utterly forsake its communion. No living member of that body of Christ can perish; and on supposition it could do so, it would be madness to call that crime schism. Nor is this a mere denial of the assertion, but such as is attended with an invincible truth for its maintenance.

Take it for the *general visible church* of Christ; the voluntary forsaking of its communion, which consists in the profession of the same faith, is not schism but apostasy, and the thing itself is to be removed from the question in hand. And as for apostates from the faith of the gospel, we question not their damnation; it sleepeth not. Who ever called a Christian that turned Jew or Mohammedan a schismatic?

Take it for a *particular church* of Christ, I deny,—

(1.) That separation from a particular church, as such, as merely separation, is schism, or ought to be so esteemed; though, perhaps, such separation may proceed from schism, and be also attended with other evils.

(2.) That, however, separation upon just cause and ground from any church is no schism, this is granted by all persons living. Schism is causeless, say all men, however concerned. And herein is a truth uncontrollable: Separation upon just cause is a duty, and therefore cannot be schism, which is always a sin. Now, there are five hundred things in the church of Rome, whereof every one, grafted as they are there into the stock and principle of imposition on the practice and confession of men, is a sufficient cause of separation from any particular church in the world, yea, from all of them, one after another, should they all consent unto the same thing, and impose it in the same manner, if there be any truth in that maxim, " It is better to obey God than man."

2. I wholly deny the minor proposition also, if spoken in reference to the church of Rome, though I willingly acknowledge our separation to be voluntary from them, no more being done than I would do over again this day, God assisting me, were I called unto it. But separation, in the sense contended about, must be from some state and condition of Christ's institution, from communion with a church which we held by his appointment; otherwise it will not be pleaded that it is a schism, at least not in a gospel sense. Now, though our forefathers, in the faith we profess, lived in subjection to the pope of Rome, or his subordinate engines, yet they were not so subject to them in any way or state instituted by Christ; so that the relinquishment of that state can possibly be no such separation as to be termed schism: for I wholly deny that the Papacy, exercising its power in its supreme and subordinate officers, which with them is their church, is a church at all of Christ's appointment, or any such thing; and when they prove it is so, I will be of it. So that when our forefathers withdrew their neck from his tyrannical yoke, and forsook the practice of his abominations in the worship of God, they forsook no church of Christ's institution, they relinquished no communion of Christ's appointment. A man may possibly forsake Babylon, and yet not forsake Zion.

[As] for the aggravations of the sin of schism from some ancient writers,—Austin and Optatus, men interested in the contests about it; Leo and Innocent, gaining by the notion of it then growing in the world; Thomas Aquinas, and such vassals of the Papacy; we are not concerned in them: what the Lord speaks of it, that we judge concerning it. It is true of the catholic church always, that out of it is no salvation, it being the society of them that shall be saved; and of the visible church in general, in some sense and cases, seeing "with the heart man believeth unto righteousness, and with the mouth confession is made unto salvation;" but of a particular church in no sense, unless that of contempt of a known duty,—and to imagine Peter to speak of any such thing is a fancy.

The consequence of this divesting the Roman synagogue of the privileges of a true church in any sense, arising in the thoughts of some to a denial of that *ministry* which we have at this day in England, must, by the way, a little be considered. For my part (be it spoken without offence), if any man hath nothing to plead for his ministry but merely that successive ordination which he hath received through the church of Rome, I cannot see a stable bottom of owning him so to be; I do not say, if he will plead nothing else, but if he hath nothing else to plead. He may have that which indeed constitutes him a minister, though he will not own that so it doth. Nor doth it come here into inquiry, whether there were not a true ministry in some all along under the Papacy, distinct from it, as were the thousands in Israel in the days of Elijah, when in the ten tribes, as to the public worship, there was no true ministry at all. Nor is it said that any have their ministry from Rome; as though the office, which is an ordinance of Christ, were instituted by Antichrist. But the question is, Whether this be *a sufficient and good basis and foundation* of any man's interest in the office of the ministry, that he hath received ordination in a succession, through the administration of, not the woman flying into the wilderness under the persecution of Antichrist, not of the two witnesses prophesying all along under the Roman apostasy, not from them to whom we succeed in doctrine, as the Waldenses, but the beast itself, the persecuting church of Rome, the pope and his adherents, who were certainly administrators of the ordination pleaded for; so that in *doctrine* we should succeed the *persecuted woman*, and in *office* the *persecuting beast*. I shall not plead this at large, professedly disclaiming all thoughts of rejecting those ministers as papal and antichristian who yet adhere to this ordination, being many of them eminently gifted of God to dispense the word, and submitted unto by his people in the administration of the ordinances, and are right worthy ministers of the gospel of Christ; but,—

I shall only remark something on the plea that is insisted on by them who would (if I mistake not) keep up in this particular what God would have pulled down. They ask us, "Why not ordination from the church of Rome as well as the Scripture?" in which inquiry I am sorry that some do still continue. We are so far from having the Scriptures from the church of Rome, by any authority of it as such, that it is one cause of daily praising God, that by his providence he kept them from being either corrupted or destroyed by them. It is true, the Bible was kept among the people that lived in those parts of the world where the pope prevailed; so was the Old Testament by the Jews; the whole by the eastern Christians; by none so corrupted as by those of the papal territory. God forbid we should say we had the Scriptures from the church of Rome, as such! If we had, why do we not keep them as she delivered them to us, in the Vulgar translation, with the apocryphal additions? The ordination pleaded for is from the authority of the church of Rome, as such. The Scriptures were by the providence of God preserved under the Papacy for the use of his people; and had they been found by chance, as it were, like the law of old, they had been the same to us that now they are. So that of these things there is not the same reason.

It is also pleaded that the granting true ordination to the church of Rome doth not prove that to be a *true* church. This I profess I understand not. They who ordained had no power so to do but as they were officers of that church. As such they did it; and if others had ordained who were not officers of that church, all would confess that action to be null. But they who will not be contented that Christ hath appointed the office of the ministry to be continued in his churches; that he continues to dispense the gifts of his Spirit for the execution of that office when men are called thereunto; that he prepares the hearts of his people to desire and submit unto them in the Lord; that as to the manner of entrance upon the work, they may have it according to the mind of Christ to the utmost, in all circumstances, so soon as his churches are shaken out of the dust of Babylon with his glory shining on them, and the tabernacle of God is thereby once more placed with men,—shall have leave, for me, to derive their interest in the ministry through that dark passage, wherein I cannot see one step before me. If they are otherwise qualified and accepted as above, I shall ever pay them that honour which is due to elders labouring in the word and doctrine.

CHAPTER VII.

Of a particular church; its nature—Frequently mentioned in Scripture—Particular congregations acknowledged the only churches of the first institution—What ensued on the multiplication of churches—Some things premised to clear the unity of the church in this sense—Every believer ordinarily obliged to join himself to some particular church—Many things in instituted worship answering a natural principle—Perpetuity of the church in this sense—True churches at first planted in England—How they ceased so to be—How churches may be again re-erected—Of the union of a particular church in itself—Foundation of that union twofold—The union itself—Of the communion of particular churches one with another—Our concernment in this union

III. I NOW descend to the last consideration of a church, in the most usual acceptation of that name in the New Testament,—that is, of a *particular instituted church*. A church in this sense I take to be *a society of men called by the word to the obedience of the faith in Christ, and joint performance of the worship of God in the same individual ordinances, according to the order by Christ prescribed.* This general description of it exhibits its nature so far as is necessary to clear the subject of our present disquisition. A more accurate definition would only administer farther occasion of contesting about things not necessary to be determined as to the inquiry in hand. Such as this was the church at Jerusalem that was persecuted, Acts viii. 1,—the church whereof Saul made havoc, verse 3,—the church that was vexed by Herod, chap. xii. 1. Such was the church at Antioch, which assembled together in one place, chap. xiv. 27; wherein were sundry prophets, chap. xiii. 1, as that at Jerusalem consisted of elders and brethren, chap. xv. 22,—the apostles, or some of them, being there then present, which added no other consideration to that church than that we are now speaking of. Such were those many churches wherein elders were ordained by Paul's appointment, chap. xiv. 23; as also the church of Cæsarea, chap. xviii. 22, and at Ephesus, chap. xx. 17, 28; as was that of Corinth, 1 Cor. i. 2, vi. 4, xi. 18, xiv. 4, 5, 12, 19, 2 Cor. i. 1; and those mentioned, Rev. i., ii., iii.;—all which Paul calls the " churches of the Gentiles," Rom. xvi. 4, in contradistinction to those of the Jews; and calls them indefinitely "the churches of Christ," verse 16; or "the churches of God," 2 Thess. i. 4; or " the churches," 1 Cor. vii. 17, 2 Cor. viii. 18, 19, 23, 24, and in sundry other places. Hence we have mention of many churches in one country,—as in Judea, Acts ix. 31; in Asia, 1 Cor. xvi. 19; in Macedonia, 2 Cor. viii. 1; in Galatia, Gal. i. 2; the seven churches of Asia, Rev. i. 11; and unto τὰς πόλεις, Acts xvi. 4, αἱ ἐκκλησίαι answers, verse 5, in the same country.

I suppose that, in this description of a particular church, I have not only the consent of them of all sorts with whom I have now to do as to what remains of this discourse, but also their acknowledgment that these were the only kinds of churches of the first institution. The reverend authors of the Jus Divinum Ministerii [Evangelici] Anglicani,[1] p. 2, cap. vi., tell us that " in the beginning of Christianity the number of believers, even in the greatest cities, was so few as that they might all meet ἐπὶ τὸ αὐτό, in one and the same place; and these are called the church of the city; and the angel of such a city was congregational, not diocesan;"—which discourse exhibits that state of a particular church which is now pleaded for, and which shall afterward be evinced, allowing no other, no not in the greatest cities. In a rejoinder to that treatise, so far as the case

---

[1] A work published by the Provincial Assembly of London, in 4to, 1654.—Ed.

of episcopacy is herein concerned, by a person well known by his labours in that cause, this is acknowledged to be so. "Believers," saith he, "in great cities were not at first divided into parishes, whilst the number of Christians was so small that they might well assemble in the same place," Ham.[1] Vind., p. 16. Of the believers of one city meeting in one place, being one church, we have the like grant, p. 18. "In this particular church," he says, "there was one bishop, which had the rule of it, and of the believers in the villages adjacent to that city; which as it sometimes was not so, Rom. xvi. 5, so for the most part it seems to have been the case: and distinct churches, upon the growth of the number of believers, were to be erected in several places of the vicinage."

And this is the state of a particular instituted church which we plead for. Whether in process of time, believers multiplying, those who had been of one church met in several assemblies, by a settled distribution of them, to celebrate the same ordinances specifically, and so made many churches, or met in several places in parties, still continuing one body, and were governed in common by the elders, whom they increased and multiplied in proportion to the increase of believers; or whether that one or more officers, elders, or bishops, of that first single congregation, taking on him or them the care of those inhabiting the city wherein the church was first planted, designed and sent some fitted for that purpose, upon their desire and choice, or otherwise, to the several lesser companies of the region adjacent, which, in process of time, became dependent on and subject to the officer or officers of that first church from whence they came forth, —I dispute not. I am satisfied that the first plantation of churches was as hath been pleaded; and I know what was done afterward, on the one hand or the other, must be examined, as to our concernment, by what ought to have been done. But of those things afterward.

Now, according to the course of procedure hitherto insisted on, a declaration of the unity of the church in this sense, what it is, wherein it doth consist, with what it is to be guilty of the breach of that unity, must ensue; and this shall be done after I have premised some few things previously necessary thereunto.

I say, then,—

1. A man may be a member of the catholic church of Christ, be united to him by the inhabitation of his Spirit, and participation of life from him, who, upon the account of some providential hinderance, is never joined to any particular congregation, for the participation of ordinances, all his days.

2. In like manner may he be a member of the church considered as professing visibly, seeing that he may do all that is of him re-

---

[1] Dr Hammond's Vindication of the Dissertations concerning Episcopacy.—ED.

quired thereunto without any such conjunction to a visible particular church. But yet,—

3. I willingly grant that every believer is obliged, as in a part of his duty, to join himself to some one of those churches of Christ, that therein he may abide, in "doctrine and fellowship, and in breaking of bread, and in prayers," according to the order of the gospel, if he have advantage and opportunity so to do; for,—

(1.) There are some duties incumbent on us which cannot possibly be performed but on a supposition of this duty being previously required and submitted unto, Matt. xviii. 15–17.

(2.) There are some ordinances of Christ, appointed for the good and benefit of those that believe, which they can never be made partakers of if not related to some such society; as public admonition, excommunication, participation of the sacrament of the Lord's supper.

(3.) The care that Jesus Christ hath taken that all things be well ordered in these churches,—giving no direction for the performance of any duty of worship merely and purely of sovereign institution, but only in them and by them who are so joined,—sufficiently evinces his mind and our duty herein, Rev. ii. 7, 11, 29, iii. 6, 13, 22; 1 Cor. xi.

(4.) The gathering, planting, and settling of such churches by the apostles, with the care they took in bringing them to perfection, leaving none whom they converted out of that order, where it was possible for them to be reduced unto it, is of the same importance, Acts xiv. 23; Tit. i. 5.

(5.) Christ's institution of officers for them, Eph. iv. 11, 1 Cor. xii. 28; calling such a church his "body," verse 27; exactly assigning to every one his duty in such societies, in respect of the place he holds in them; with his care for their preservation from confusion and for order,—evince from whom they are, and what is our duty in reference unto them.

(6.) The judging and condemning them by the Holy Ghost as disorderly, blamable persons, who are to be avoided, who walk not according to the rules and order appointed in these churches; his care that those churches be not scandalized or offended; with innumerable other considerations,—evince their institution to be from heaven, not of men, or any prudential considerations of them whatever.

That there is an instituted worship of God, to be continued under the New Testament until the second coming of Christ, I suppose needs not much proof. With those with whom it doth so I am not now treating, and must not make it my business to give it evidence by the innumerable testimonies which might be alleged to that purpose. That for the whole of his worship, matter, or manner, or any part of it, God hath changed his way of proceeding, and will now allow the will and prudence of man to be the measure and rule of his honour and glory therein, contrary to what he did or would allow under the law, is so prejudicial to the perfection of the gospel, infinite wisdom and all-sufficiency of Christ, and so destructive to the whole obligation of the second commandment, having no ground in the Scripture, but being built merely on the conceit of men, suited to one carnal interest or other, I shall unwillingly debate it. That, as to this particular under consideration, there were particular churches instituted by the authority of Jesus Christ, owned and approved by him; that officers for them were of his appointment, and furnished with gifts from him for the execution of their employment; that rules, cautions, and instructions for the due settlement of those churches were given by him; that those churches were made the only seat of that worship which in particular he expressed his will to have continued until he came,—is of so much light in Scripture that he must wink hard that will not see it.

1. That either he did not *originally* appoint these things, or he did not give out the gifts of his Spirit in reference to the right ordering of them, and exalting of his glory in them; or that having done so then, yet that his institutions have an end, being only for a season, and that it may be known when the efficacy of any of his institutions ceaseth; or that he doth not now dispense the gifts and graces of his Spirit to render them useful,—is a difficult task for any man to undertake to evince.

There is, indeed, in the institutions of Christ, much that answers a *natural principle* in men, who are on many accounts formed and fitted for society. A confederation and consultation to carry on any design wherein the concernment of the individuals doth lie, within such bounds and in such order as lie in a ready way to the end aimed at, is exceeding suitable to the principles whereby we are acted and guided as men. But he that would hence conclude that there is no more but this, and the acting of these principles, in this church-constitution whereof we speak, and that therefore men may be cast into any prudential form, or appoint other ways and forms of it than those mentioned in the Scripture as appointed and owned, takes on himself the demonstrating that all things necessarily required to the constitution of such a church-society are commanded by the law of nature, and therefore allowed of and approved only by Christ, and so to be wholly moral, and to have nothing of instituted worship in them. And also, he must know that when, on that supposition, he hath given a probable reason why never any persons in the world fixed on such societies in all essential things as those, seeing they are natural, that he leaves less to the prudence of men, and to the ordering and disposing of things concerning them, than those who make them of pure institution, all whose circumstances cannot be derived from themselves, as those of things purely moral may.   But this is not of my present consideration.

2. Nor shall I consider whether *perpetuity* be a property of the church of Christ in this sense; that is, not whether a church that was once so may cease to be so,—which it is known I plead for in the instance of the church of Rome, not to mention others,—but whether, by virtue of any promise of Christ, there shall always be somewhere in the world a visible church, visibly celebrating his ordinances. Luke i. 33, " He shall reign over the house of Jacob for ever, and of his kingdom there shall be no end," is pleaded to this purpose; but that any more but the spiritual reign of Christ in his catholic church is there intended is not proved.   Matt. xvi. 18, " Upon this rock will I build my church," is also urged; but to intend any but true believers, and that as such, in that promise, is wholly to enervate it, and to take away its force and efficacy.   Matt. xviii. 19, 20, declares the presence of Christ with his church wherever it be, not that a church in the regard treated of shall be.   To the same purpose are other expressions in the Scripture.   As I will not deny this in general, so I am unsatisfied as to any particular instance for the making of it good.

It is said that *true churches were at first planted* in England. How, then, or by what means, did they cease so to be? how, or by what act, did God unchurch them?   They did it themselves meritoriously, by apostasy and idolatry; God legally, by his institution of a law of rejection of such churches.   If any shall ask, "How, then, is it possible that any such churches should be raised anew?" I say, that the catholic church mystical and that visibly professing being preserved entire, he that thinketh there needs a miracle for those who are members of them to join in such a society as those now spoken of, according to the institution of Christ, is a person delighting in needless scruples.

Christ hath promised that where two or three are gathered together in his name, he will be in the midst of them, Matt. xviii. 20. It is now supposed, with some hope to have it granted, that the Scripture, being the "power of God unto salvation," Rom. i. 16, hath a sufficient efficacy and energy in itself, as to its own kind, for the conversion of souls; yea, let us, till opposition be made to it, take it for granted that by that force and efficacy it doth mainly and principally evince its own divinity, or divine original.   Those who are contented, for the honour of that word which God delighteth to magnify, to grant this supposition, will not, I hope, think it impossible that though all church-state should cease in any place, and yet the

Scripture by the providence of God be there in the hand of individuals preserved, two or three should be called, converted, and regenerated by it. For my part, I think he that questions it must do it on some corrupt principle of a secondary dependent authority in the word of God as to us; with which sort of men I do not now deal. I ask whether these converted persons may not possibly come together, or assemble themselves, in the name of Jesus? May they not, upon his command, and in expectation of the accomplishment of his promise, so come together with resolution to do his will, and to exhort one another thereto? Zech. iii. 10; Mal. iii. 16. Truly, I believe they may, in what part of the world soever their lot is fallen. Here lie all the difficulties, whether, being come together in the name of Christ, they may do what he hath commanded them or no? whether they may exhort and stir up one another to do the will of Christ? Most certain it is that Christ will give them his presence, and therewithal his authority, for the performance of any duty that he requireth at their hands. Were not men angry, troubled, and disappointed, there would be little difficulty in this business. But of this elsewhere.

3. Upon this supposition, that particular churches are *institutions of Jesus Christ,* which is granted by all with whom I have to do, I proceed to make inquiry into their union and communion, that so we may know wherein the bonds of them do consist.

There is a *double foundation,* fountain, or cause of the union of such a church,—the one *external,* procuring, commanding; the other *internal,* inciting, directing, assisting. The first is the institution of Jesus Christ, before mentioned, requiring peace and order, union, consent, and agreement, in and among all the members of such a church; all to be regulated, ordered, and bounded by the rules, laws, and prescripts, which from him they have received for their walking in those societies. The latter is that love without dissimulation which always is, or which always ought to be, between all the members of such a church, exerting itself in their respective duties one towards another in that holy combination whereunto they are called and entered for the worship of God, whether they are those which lie in the level of the equality of their common interest of being church-members, or those which are required of them in the several differences whereby, on any account whatever, they are distinguished one from another amongst themselves; for " love is the bond of perfectness," Col. iii. 14.

Hence, then, it appears what is the union of such a church, and what is the communion to be observed therein, by the appointment of Jesus Christ. The joint consent of all the members of it, in obedience to the command of Christ, from a principle of love, to walk together in the universal celebration of all the ordinances of the worship of God, instituted and appointed to be celebrated in such a church, and to perform all the duties and offices of love which, in reference to one another, in their respective stations and places, are by God required of them, and doing so accordingly, is the union inquired after. See Phil. ii. 1-3, iv. 1-3; 1 Cor. i. 10; 2 Cor. xiii. 11; Rom. xv. 5, 6.

Whereas there are in these churches some rulers, some ruled; some eyes, some hands in this body; some parts visibly comely, some uncomely, upon the account of that variety of gifts and graces which are distributed to them,—in the performance of duties, a regard is to be had to all the particular rules that are given with respect to men in their several places and distributions. Herein doth the union of a particular church consist; herein have the members of it communion among themselves, and with the whole.

4. I shall farther grant and add hereunto, that, over and above the *union* that is between the members of several particular churches, by virtue of their interest in the church catholic, which draws after it a necessity for the occasional exercise of duties of love one towards another; and that communion they have, as members of the general church visible, in the profession of the faith once delivered unto the saints; there is a *communion* also to be observed between these churches, as such, which is sometimes, or may be, exerted in their assemblies by their delegates, for declaring their sense and determining things of joint concernment unto them. Whether there ought to be an ordinary combination of the officers of these churches, invested with power for the disposal of things and persons that concern one or more of them, in several subordinations, by the institution of Christ; as it is not my judgment that so there is, so it belongs not unto my present undertaking at all to debate.

That which alone remains to be done, is to consider what is our concernment as to the breach of this union, which we profess to be appointed by Jesus Christ; and that both as we are Protestants and as also farther differenced, according to the intimations given at the entrance of this discourse. What hath already been delivered about the nature of schism and the Scripture notion of it might well suffice as to our vindication in this business from any charge that we are or seem obnoxious unto; but because I have no reason to suppose that some men will be so favourable unto us as to take pains for the improvement of principles, though in themselves clearly evinced, on our behalf, the application of them to some present cases, with the removal of objections that lie against my intendment, must be farther added.

Some things there are which, upon what hath been spoken, I shall assume and suppose as granted "in thesi," until I see them otherwise disproved than as yet I have done.

Of these the first is, That the departing or *secession of any man or men* from any particular church, as to that communion which is peculiar to such a church, which he or they have had therewith, is nowhere called schism, nor is so in the nature of the thing itself (as the general signification of the word is restrained by its Scripture use), but is a thing to be judged and receive a title according to the causes and circumstances of it.

Secondly, *One church refusing to hold that communion with another* which ought to be between them is not schism, properly so called.

Thirdly, *The departure of any man or men from the society or communion of any church whatever,*—so it be done without strife, variance, judging, and condemning of others,—because, according to the light of their consciences, they cannot in all things in them worship God according to his mind, cannot be rendered evil but from circumstances taken from the persons so doing, or the way and manner whereby and wherein they do it.

Unto these I add, that if any one can show and evince that we have departed from and left the communion of any particular church of Christ, with which we ought to walk according to the order above mentioned, or have disturbed and broken the order and union of Christ's institution, wherein we are or were inwrapped, we put ourselves on the mercy of our judges.

The consideration of what is the charge on any of us on this account was the first thing aimed at in this discourse; and, as it was necessary from the rules of the method wherein I have proceeded, comes now, in the last place, to be put to the issue and trial; which it shall in the next chapter.

CHAPTER VIII.

Of the church of England—The charge of schism in the name thereof proposed and considered—Several considerations of the church of England—In what sense we were members of it—Of Anabaptism—The subjection due to bishops —Their power examined—Its original in this nation—Of the ministerial power of bishops—Its present continuance—Of the church of England, what it is— Its description—Form peculiar and constitutive—Answer to the charge of schism, on separation from it in its episcopal constitution—How and by what means it was taken away—Things necessary to the constitution of such a church proposed and offered to proof—The second way of constituting a national church considered—Principles agreed on and consented unto between the parties at variance on this account—Judgment of Amyraldus in this case —Inferences from the common principles before consented unto—The case of schism, in reference to a national church in the last sense, debated—Of particular churches, and separation from them—On what accounts justifiable—No necessity of joining to this or that—Separation from some so called, required— Of the church of Corinth—The duty of its members—Austin's judgment of the practice of Elijah—The last objection waived—Inferences upon the whole.

THAT which first presents itself is a plea against us, in the name of the church of England, and those intrusted with the reiglement thereof, as it was settled and established some years since; the sum whereof, if I mistake not, amounts to thus much:—

"You were some time members and children of the church of England, and lived in the communion thereof, professing obedience thereunto, according to its rules and canons. You were in an orderly subjection to the archbishops, bishops, and those acting under them in the hierarchy, who were officers of that church. In that church you were baptized, and joined in the outward worship celebrated therein. But you have now voluntarily, and of your own accord, forsaken and renounced the communion of this church; cast off your subjection to the bishops and rulers; rejected the form of worship appointed in that church, that great bond of its communion; and set up separate churches of your own, according to your pleasures: and so you are properly schismatics."

This I say, if I mistake not, is the sum of the charge against us, on the account of our late attempt for reformation, and reducing of the church of Christ to its primitive institution; which we profess our aim in singleness of heart to have been, and leave the judgment of it unto God.

To acquit ourselves of this imputation, I shall declare,—

1. How far we own ourselves to have been, or to be, members or "children" (as they speak) "of the church of England," as it is called or esteemed.

2. What was the subjection wherein we or any of us stood, or might be supposed to have stood, to the prelates or bishops of that church. And then I shall,—

3. Put the whole to the issue and inquiry, whether we have broken any bond or order which, by the institution and appointment of Jesus Christ, we ought to have preserved entire and unviolated; not doubting but that, on the whole matter in difference, we shall find the charge managed against us to be resolved wholly into the prudence and interest of some men, wherein our consciences are not concerned.

As to the first proposal, the several considerations that the church of England may fall under will make way for the determination of our relation thereunto.

1. There being in this country of England much people of God, many of his elect, called and sanctified by and through the Spirit and blood of Christ, with the " washing of water by the word," so made true living members of the mystical body or catholic church of Christ, holding him as a spiritual head, receiving influences of life and grace from him continually, they may be called, though improperly, the church of England; that is, that part of Christ's catholic church militant which lives in England. In this sense it is the de-

sire of our souls to be found and to abide members of the church of England, to keep with it, whilst we live in this world, the " unity of the Spirit in the bond of peace." Jerusalem which is above is the mother of us all, and one is our Father, which is in heaven; one is our Head, Sovereign, Lord, and Ruler, the dearly-beloved of our souls, the Lord Jesus Christ. If we have grieved, offended, troubled the least member of this church, so that he may justly take offence at any of our ways, we profess our readiness to lie at his or their feet for reconciliation, according to the mind of Christ. If we bear not love to all the members of the church of England in this sense, without dissimulation (yea, even to them amongst them who, through mistakes and darkness, have on several accounts designed our harm and ruin); if we rejoice not with them and suffer not with them, however they may be differenced in and by their opinions or walkings; if we desire not their good as the good of our own souls, and are not ready to hold any communion with them, wherein their and our light will give and afford unto us peace mutually; if we judge, condemn, despise any of them, as to their persons, spiritual state, and condition, because they walk not with us,—let us be esteemed the vilest schismatics that ever lived on the face of the earth. But as to our membership in the church of England on this account, we stand or fall to our own Master.

2. The rulers, governors, teachers, and body of the people of this nation of England, having, by laws, professions, and public protestations, cast off the tyranny, authority, and doctrine of the church of Rome, with its head the pope, and jointly assented unto and publicly professed the doctrine of the gospel, as expressed in their public confession, variously attested and confirmed, declaring their profession by that public confession, preaching, laws, and writings suitable thereunto, may also be called on good account the church of England. In this sense we profess ourselves members of the church of England, and professing and adhering to that doctrine of faith, in the unity of it, which was here established and declared, as was before spoken. As to the attempt of some, who accuse us for everting of fundamentals by our doctrine of election by the free grace of God, of effectual redemption of the elect only, conversion by the irresistible efficacy of grace, and the associate doctrines, which are commonly known, we suppose the more sober part of our adversaries will give them little thanks for their pains therein; if for no other reason, yet at least because they know the cause they have to manage against us is weakened thereby. Indeed, it seems strange to us that we should be charged with schism from the church of England, for endeavouring to reform ourselves as to something relating to the worship of God, by men everting and denying so considerable a

portion of the doctrine of that church, which we sacredly retain entire, as the most urgent of our present adversaries do. In this sense, I say, we still confess ourselves members of the church of England; nor have we made any separation from it, but do daily labour to improve and carry on the light of the gospel which shines therein, and on the account whereof it is renowned in the world.

3. Though I know not how proper that expression of "children of the church" may be under the New Testament, nor can by any means consent unto it, to be the urging of any obedience to any church or churches whatsoever on that account, no such use being made of that consideration by the Holy Ghost, nor any parallel unto it insisted on by him; yet, in a general sense, so far as our receiving our regeneration and new birth, through the grace of God, by the preaching of the word and the saving truths thereof here professed, with the seal of it in our baptism, may be signified by that expression, we own ourselves to have been, and to be, children of the church of England, because we have received all this by the administration of the gospel here in England, as dispensed in several assemblies therein, and are contented that this concession be improved to the utmost.

Here, indeed, we are left by them who renounce the baptism they have received in their infancy, and repeat it again amongst themselves. Yet I suppose that he who, upon that single account, will undertake to prove them schismatical may find himself entangled. Nor is the case with them exactly as it was with the Donatists. They do the same thing with them, but not on the same principles. The Donatists rebaptized those who came to their societies, because they professed themselves to believe that all administration of ordinances not in their assemblies was null, and that they were to be looked on as no such thing. Our Anabaptists do the same thing, but on this plea, that though baptism be, yet infant baptism is not, an institution of Christ, and so is null from the nature of the thing itself, not the way of its administration. But this falls not within the verge of my defence.

In these several considerations we were, and do continue, members of the church of God in England; and as to our failing herein, who is it that convinces us of sin?

The second thing inquired after is, what subjection we stood in, or were supposed to have stood in, to the bishops? Our subjection being regulated by their power, the consideration of this discovers the true state of that.

They had and exercised in this nation a twofold power, and consequently the subjection required of us was twofold:—

1. A power delegated from the supreme magistrate of the nation,

conferred on them, and invested in them, by the laws, customs, and usages of this commonwealth; and exercised by them on that account. This not only made them barons of the realm and members of parliament, and gave them many dignities and privileges, but also was the sole fountain and spring of that jurisdiction which they exercised by ways and means such as themselves will not plead to have been purely ecclesiastical and of the institution of Jesus Christ. In this respect we did not cast off our subjection to them, it being our duty to "submit ourselves to every ordinance of man, for the Lord's sake." Only, whenever they commanded things unlawful in themselves or unto us, we always retreated to the old safe rule, "Whether it be right to hearken unto you more than unto God, judge ye." On this foundation, I say, was all the jurisdiction which they exercised among and over the people of this nation built. They had not leave to exercise that which they were invested in on another account, but received formally their authority thereby. The tenure whereby their predecessors held this power before the Reformation, the change of the tenure by the laws of this land, the investiture of the whole original right thereof in another person than formerly by the same means, the legal concession and delegation to them made, the enlarging or contracting of their jurisdiction by the same laws, the civil process of their courts in the exercise of their authority, sufficiently evince from whence they had it. Nor was any thing herein any more of the institution of Jesus Christ than the courts are in Westminster Hall. Sir Edward Coke, who knew the laws of his country, and was skilled in them to a miracle, will satisfy any in the rise and tenor of episcopal jurisdiction: "De jure regis eccles." What there is of primitive institution giving colour and occasion to this kind of jurisdiction, and the exercise of it, shall farther (God assisting) be declared, when I treat of the state of the first churches, and the ways of their degeneracy. Let them, or any for them, in the meantime, evince the jurisdiction they exercised, in respect whereunto our subjection in the first kind was required, to derive its original from the pure institution of Christ in the gospel, or to be any such thing as it was, in an imagined separation from the human laws whereby it was animated, and more will be asserted than I have had the happiness as yet to see. Now, I say that the subjection to them due on this account we did not cast off; but their whole authority, power, and jurisdiction was removed, taken away, and annulled, by the people of the land assembled in parliament.

"But this," they reply, "is the state of the business in hand: The parliament, as much as in them lay, did so, indeed, as is confessed, and by so doing made the schism; which you by adhering to them, and joining with them in your several places, have made yourselves also guilty of."

But do these men know what they say, or will it ever trouble the conscience of a man in his right wits to be charged with schism on this account? The parliament made alteration of nothing but what they found established by the laws of this nation; pleading that they had power committed to them to alter, abrogate, and annul laws, for the good of the people of the land. If their making alterations in the civil laws and constitutions, in the political administrations of the nation, be schism, we have very little security but that we may be made new schismatics every third year, whilst the constitution of a triennial parliament doth continue. In the removal, then, of all episcopal jurisdiction, founded on the laws and usages of this nation, we are not at all concerned; for the laws enforcing it do not press it as a thing necessary on any other account, but as that which themselves gave rise and life unto. But should this be granted, that the office was appointed by Christ, and the jurisdiction impleaded annexed by him thereunto; yet this, whilst we abide at diocesans, with the several divisions apportioned to them in the nation, will not suffice to constitute a national church, unless some union of those diocesans, or of the churches whereunto they related, into one society and church, by the same appointment, be proved; which, to my present apprehension, will be no easy work for any one to undertake.

2. " Bishops had here a power, as ministers of the gospel, to preach, administer the sacraments, to join in the ordination of ministers, and the like duties of church-officers." To this we say, Let the individuals of them acquit themselves, by the qualifications mentioned in the epistles to Timothy and Titus, with a sedulous exercise of their duty in a due manner, according to the mind of Christ, to be such indeed, and we will still pay them all the respect, reverence, duty, and obedience, which as such, by virtue of any law or institution of Christ, they can claim. Let them come forth with weapons that are not carnal, evidencing their ministry to the consciences of believers, acting in a spirit and power received from Christ, and who are they that will harm them?

I had once formerly said thus much: " Let the bishops attend the particular flocks over which they are appointed, preaching the word, administering the holy ordinances of the gospel in and to their own flock, there will not be contending about them." It was thought meet to return, by one concerned: " I shall willingly grant herein my suffrage, let them discharge them (and I beseech all who have any way hindered them at length to let and quietly permit them), on condition he will do this as carefully as I. I shall not contend with him concerning the nature of their task. Be it, as he saith, 'the attending to the particular churches over which they are appointed' (the bishop of Oxford over that flock or portion to which he was and is appointed, and so all others in like manner); be it their 'preaching and their administering the holy ordinances of the gospel in and to their own flock,' and whatever else of duty and ' ratione officii' belongs to a rightly-constituted bishop; and let all that have disturbed this course, so duly settled in this church, and in all churches of Christ since the apostles' planting them, discern their error, and return to that peace and unity of the church from whence they have causelessly and inexcusably departed."

Though I was not then speaking of the bishops of England, yet I am contented with the application to them, there being amongst them men of piety and learning, whom I exceedingly honour and reverence. Amongst all the bishops, he of Oxford is, I suppose, peculiarly instanced in, because it may be thought that, living in this place, I may belong to his jurisdiction. But in the condition wherein I now am, by the providence of God, I can plead an exemption on the same foot of account as he can his jurisdiction; so that I am not much concerned in his exercise of it as to my own person. If he have a particular flock at Oxon, which he will attend according to what before I required, he shall have no let or hinderance from me; but seeing he is, as I hear he is, a reverend and learned person, I shall be glad of his neighbourhood and acquaintance. But to suppose that the diocese of Oxon, as legally constituted and bounded, is his particular flock or church; that such a church was instituted by Christ, or hath been in being ever since the apostles' times; that, in his presidency in this church, he is to set up courts and exercise a jurisdiction in them, and therewith a power over all the inhabitants of this diocese or shire (excepting the exempt peculiar jurisdiction), although gathered into particular congregations, and united by a participation of the same ordinances; and all this by the will and appointment of Jesus Christ,—is to suppose what will not be granted. I confess, as before, there was once such an order in this place, and that it is now removed by laws, on which foundation alone it stood before; and this is that wherein I am not concerned. Whether we have causelessly and inexcusably departed from the unity of the church is the matter now in inquiry. I am sure, unless the unity can be fixed, our departure will not be proved. A *law* unity I confess; an *evangelical* I am yet in the disquisition of. But I confess it will be to the prejudice of the cause in hand, if it shall be thought that the determination of it depends on the controversy about episcopacy; for if so, it might be righteously expected that the arguments produced in the behalf and defence thereof should be particularly discussed. But the truth is, I shall easily acknowledge all my labour to no purpose, if I have to deal only with men who suppose that if it be granted that bishops, as commonly esteemed in this nation, are of the appointment of Christ, it will thence follow that we have a national church of Christ's appointment; between which, indeed, there is no relation or connection. Should I grant, as I said, diocesan bishops, with churches answerable to their supportment, particled into several congregations, with their inferior officers, yet this would be remote enough from giving subsistence and union to a national church.

What, then, it is which is called the church of England, in respect whereto we are charged with schism, is nextly to be considered.

Now, there are two ways whereby we may come to the discovery of what is intended by the church of England, or there are two ways whereby such a thing doth arise:—

1. " Descendendo;" which is the way of the Prelates
2. " Ascendendo;" which is the way of the Presbyterians.

For the first, to constitute a national church by *descent*, it must be supposed that all church power is vested in national officers, namely, archbishops, and from them derived to several diocesans by a distribution of power, limited in its exercise, to a certain portion of the nation, and by them communicated by several engines to parochial priests in their several places. A man with half an eye may see that here are many things to be proved.

Thus, their first church is national, which is distributed into several greater portions, termed provinces; those again into others, now called *dioceses;* and those again subdivided into *parochial or particular congregations.* Now, the union of this church consisteth in the due observance of the same worship specifically by all the members of it, and subjection, according to rules of their own appointment (which were called commonly *canons,* by way of distinction), unto the rulers before mentioned, in their several capacities. And this is that which is the peculiar form of this church. That of the *church catholic, absolutely so called,* is its unity with Christ and in itself, by the one Spirit whereby it is animated; that of the *church catholic visibly professing,* the unity of the faith which they do profess, as being by them professed; that of a *particular church,* as such, its observance and performance of the same ordinances of worship numerically, in the confession of the same faith, and subjection to the same rules of love for edification of the whole. Of this *national* [*church*], as it is called, the unity consists in the subjection of one sort of officers unto another, within a precinct limited, originally, wholly on an account foreign to any church-state whatever. So that it is not called the church of England from its participation of the nature of the catholic church, on the account of its most noble members; nor yet from its participation of the nature of the visible church in the world, on the account of its profession of the truth,— in both which respects we profess our unity with it; nor yet from its participation of the nature of a particular church, which it did not in itself, nor as such, but in some of its particular congregations; but from a peculiar form of its own, as above described, which is to be proved to be of the institution of Jesus Christ.

In this description given of their church-state with whom we have now to do, I have purposely avoided the mention of things odious and exposed to common obloquy, which yet were the very ties and ligaments of their order, because the thing, as it is in itself, being nakedly represented, we may not be prejudiced in judging of the strength and utmost of the charge that lies against any of us on the account of a departure from it.

The communion of this church, they say, we have forsaken, and broken its unity; and therefore are schismatics.

I answer in a word: Laying aside so much of the jurisdiction of it [as was] mentioned before, and the several ways of its administration for which there is no colour or pretence that it should relate to any gospel institution; passing by, also, the consideration of all those things which the men enjoying authority in, or exercising the pretended power of, this church, did use all their authority and power to enjoin and establish, which we judge evil;—let them prove that such a national church as would remain with these things pared off, that is in its best estate imaginable, was ever instituted by Christ, or the apostles in his name, in all the things of absolute necessity to its being and existence, and I will confess myself to be what they please to say of me.

That there was such an order in things relating to the worship of God established by the law of the land, in and over the people thereof; that the worship pleaded for was confirmed by the same law; that the rulers mentioned had power, being by the magistrates assembled, to make rules and canons to become binding to the good people of the commonwealth, when confirmed by the supreme authority of the nation, and not else; that penalties were appointed to the disturbers of this order by the same law,—I grant: but that any thing of all this, as such,—that is, as a part of this whole, or the whole itself,— was instituted by the will and appointment of Jesus Christ, that is denied. Let not any one think that because we deny the constitution pleaded about to have had the stamp of the authority of Jesus Christ, that therefore we pulled it down and destroyed it by violence. It was set up before we were born, by them who had power to make laws to bind the people of this nation, and we found men in an orderly legal possession of that power, which, exerting itself several ways, maintained and preserved that constitution, which we had no call to eradicate. Only, whereas they took upon them to act in the name of Christ also, and to interpose their orders and

authority in the things of the worship of God, we entreated them
that we might pass our pilgrimage quietly in our native country (as
Israel would have gone through the land of Edom, without the disturbance of its inhabitants), and worship God according to the light
which he had graciously imparted to us; but they would not hearken.
But herein also was it our duty to keep the word of Christ's patience.
Their removal and the dissolution of this national church arose, and was
carried on, as hath been declared, by other hands, on other accounts.

Now, it is not to any purpose to plead the authority of the church
for many of the institutions mentioned; for neither hath any church
power, or can have, to institute and appoint the things whereby it
is made to be so,—as these things are the very form of the church
that we plead about,—nor hath any church any authority but what
is answerable to its nature. If itself be of a civil prudential constitution, its authority also is civil, and no more. Denying their church,
in that form of it which makes it such, to be of the institution of
Christ, it cannot be expected that we should grant that it is, as such,
invested with any authority from Christ; so that the dissolution of the
unity of this church, as it had its rise on such an account, proceeded
from an alteration of the human constitution whereon it was built;
and how that was done was before declared. Then let them prove,—

1. That *ordinary officers are before the church*, and *that* in "ecclesia instituta," as well as "instituenda;" which must be the foundation of their work. (We confess extraordinary officers were before
the church, nor, considering the way of men's coming to be joined
in such societies, was it possible it should be otherwise; but as for
ordinary officers, they were an exurgency from a church, and serve
to the completion of it, Acts xiv. 23; Tit. i. 5.)

2. That Christ hath appointed any *national officers*, with a plenitude of ordinary power, to be imparted, communicated, and distributed to other recipient subjects, in several degrees, within one
nation, and not elsewhere; I mean, such an officer or officers who, in
the first instance of their power, should, on their own single account,
relate unto a whole nation.

3. That he hath instituted any *national church* as the proper
correlatum of such an officer. Concerning which, also, I desire to be
informed, whether a catalogue of those he hath so instituted be to
be obtained, or their number be left indefinite? whether they have
limits and bounds prescribed to them by him, or are left to be commensurate to the civil dominion of any potentate, and so to enjoy
or suffer the providential enlargements or straits that such dominions
are continually subject unto? whether we had seven churches here
in England during the heptarchy of the Saxons, and one in Wales,
or but one in the whole? if seven, how came they to be one? if but

one, why those of England, Scotland, and Ireland were not one also, especially since they have been under one civil magistrate? or whether the difference of the civil laws of these nations be not the only cause that there are three churches? and if so, whether from thence any man may not discern whereon the unity of the church of England doth depend?

Briefly; when they have proved metropolitan, diocesan bishops in a firstness of power by the institution of Christ; a national church by the same institution, in the sense pleaded for; a firstness of power in the national officers of that national church to impose a form of worship upon all being within that nation, by the same institution, which should contain the bond of the union of that church; also, that every man who is born, and in his infancy baptized, in that nation, is a member of that national church, by the same institution; and shall have distinguished clearly in and about their administrations, and have told us what they counted to be of ecclesiastical power, and what they grant to be a mere emanation of the civil government of the nation,—we will then treat with them about the business of schism. Until then, if they tell us that we have forsaken the church of England in the sense pleaded for by them, I must answer, "That which is wanting cannot be numbered." It is no crime to depart from nothing. We have not left to be that which we never were. Which may suffice both us and them as to our several respective concernments of conscience and power. It hath been from the darkness of men, and ignorance of the Scriptures, that some have taken advantage to set up a product of the prudence of nations in the name of Jesus Christ; and on that account to require the acceptance of it. When the tabernacle of God is again well fixed amongst men, these shadows will flee away. In the meantime, we owe all these disputes, with innumerable other evils, to the apostasy of the Roman combination; from which we are far, as yet, from being clearly delivered.

I have one thing more to add upon the whole matter, and I shall proceed to what is lastly to be considered.

The church of England, as it is called (that is, the people thereof), separated herself from the church of Rome. To free herself from the imputation of schism in so doing, as she (that is, the learned men of the nation) pleaded the errors and corruptions of that church, under this especial consideration of their being imposed by tyrants; so also by professing her design to do nothing but to reduce religion and the worship of God to its original purity, from which it was fallen. And we all jointly justify both her and all other reformed churches in this plea.

In her design to reduce religion to its primitive purity, she always professed that she did not take her direction from the Scripture only, but also from the councils and examples of the first four or five centuries; to which she laboured to conform her reformation. Let the question now be, Whether there be not corruptions in this church of England, supposing such a national church-state to be instituted? what, I beseech you, shall bind my conscience to acquiesce in what is pleaded from the first four or five centuries, consisting of men that could and did err, more than that did hers which was pleaded from the nine or ten centuries following? Have not I liberty to call for reformation according to the Scripture only? or at least to profess that my conscience cannot be bound to any other? The sum is,—The business of schism from the church of England is a thing built purely and simply on political considerations, so interwoven with them, so influenced from them, as not to be separated. The famous advice of Mæcenas to Augustus, mentioned in Dio Cassius, is the best authority I know against it.

Before we part with this consideration, I must needs prevent one mistake, which perhaps, in the mind of some, may arise upon the preceding discourse; for whereas sundry ordinances of the worship of God are rightly to be administered only in a church, and ministers do evidently relate thereunto, the denying of a national church-state seems to deny that we had either ministers or ordinances here in England. The truth is, it seems so to do, but it doth not; unless you will say, that unless there be a national church-state there is no other, which is too absurd for any one to imagine. It follows, indeed, that there were no national church-officers, that there were no ordinances numerically the same, to be administered in and to the nation at once; but that there was not another church-state in England, and on the account thereof ordinances truly administered by lawful ministers, doth not follow. And now, if by this discourse I only call this business to a review by them who are concerned to assert this national church, I am satisfied. That the church of England is a true church of Christ, they have hitherto maintained against the Romanists, on the account of the doctrine taught in it, and the successive ordination of its officers, through the church of Rome itself, from the primitive times. About the constitution and nature of a national church they have had with them no contention; therein the parties at variance were agreed. The same grounds and principles, improved with a defence of the external worship and ceremonies established on the authority of the church, they managed against the Nonconformists and Separatists at home. But their chief strength against them lay in arguments more forcible, which need not be repeated. The constitution of the church now impleaded deserves, as I said, the review; hitherto it hath been unfurnished of any considerable defensative.

Secondly, There is another way of constituting a national church, which is insisted on by some of our brethren of the presbyterian way. This is, that such a thing should arise from the particular congregations that are in the nation, united by sundry associations and subordinations of assemblies in and by the representatives of those churches; so that though there cannot be an assembly of all the members of those churches in one place for the performance of any worship of God, nor is there any ordinance appointed by Christ to be so celebrated in any assembly of them (which we suppose necessary to the constitution of a particular church), yet there may be an assembly of the representatives of them all, by several elevations, for some end and purpose.

"In this sense," say some, "a church may be called *national*, when all the particular congregations of one nation, living under one civil government, agreeing in doctrine and worship, are governed by their greater and lesser assemblies" (Jus Divinum Minist. Anglic., p. 12). But I would be loath to exclude every man from being a member of the church in England,—that is, from a share in the profession of the faith which is owned and professed by the people of God in England,—who is not a member of a particular congregation. Nor does subjection to one civil government, and agreement in the same doctrine and worship specifically, either jointly or severally, constitute one church, as is known even in the judgment of these brethren. It is the last expression, of " greater and lesser assemblies," that must do it. But as to any such institution of Christ, as a standing ordinance, sufficient to give unity, yea, or denomination to a church, this is the τὸ κρινόμενον. And yet this alone is to be insisted on; for, as was showed before, the other things mentioned contribute nothing to the form nor union of such a church.

It is pleaded that there are prophecies and promises of a national church that should be under the New Testament: as Ps. lxxii. 10–12; Isa. xlix. 23, lx. 10, 16. That it is foretold and promised that many, whole nations, shall be converted to the faith of the gospel, and thereby become the people of God, who before were no people, is granted; but that their way of worship shall be by national churches, governed by lesser and greater assemblies, doth not appear. And when the Jews shall be converted, they shall be a national church as England is; but their way of worship shall be regulated according to the institution of Christ in the gospel. And therefore the publishers of the Life of Dr Gouge have expressed his judgment, found in a paper in his study, that the Jews on their calling shall be gathered together into churches, and not be scattered, as now they are. A nation may be said to be converted, from the professed subjection to the gospel of so many in it as may give demonstration to the whole; but the way of worship for those so converted is peculiarly instituted. It is said, moreover, that [as] the several congregations in one city are called a "church," as in Jerusalem, Acts viii. 1, xii. 1, 5, xv. 4, 22, so also may all the churches in a nation be called a "national church." But this is τὸ ἐν ἀρχῇ· nor is that allowed to be made a medium in another case, which at the same time is "sub judice" in its own. The like, also, may be said of the church of Ephesus, Acts xx. 17; Rev. ii. 1. Nor is it about a mere denomination that we contend, but the union and form of such a church; and if more churches than one were together called a church, it is from their participation of the nature of the general visible church, not of that which is particular, and the seat of ordinances. So where Paul is said to "persecute the church of God," Gal. i. 13, it is spoken of the professors of the faith of Christ in general, and not to be restrained to the churches of Judea, of whom he speaks, verses 22, 23, seeing his rage actually reached to Damascus, a city of another nation, Acts xxii. 5, 6, and his design was πρὸς τὸ γένος. That by the "church," mentioned 1 Cor. xii. 28, x. 32, Eph. iii. 21, is intended the whole visible church of Christ, as made up into one body or church, by a collection of all particular churches in the world by lesser and greater assemblies (a thing that never was in the world, nor ever will be), is denied, and not yet, by any that I know, proved. Not that I am offended at the name of the "church of England;" though I think all professors, as such, are rather to be called so than all the congregations. That all professors of the truth of the gospel, throughout the world, are the visible church of Christ, in the sense before explained, is granted. So may, on the same account, all the professors of that truth in England be called the church of England. But it is the institution of lesser and greater assemblies, comprising the representatives of all the churches in the world, that must give being and union to the visible church in the sense pleaded for, throughout the world, or in this nation, and that bound to this relation by virtue of the same institution that is to be proved.

But of what there is, or seems to be, of divine institution in this order and fabric, what of human prudent creation, what in the matter or manner of it I cannot assent unto, I shall not at present enter into the consideration; but shall only, as to my purpose in hand, take up some principles which lie in common between the men of this persuasion and myself, with some others otherwise minded. Now, of these are the ensuing assertions:—

1. No man can possibly be a member of a national church in this sense, but by virtue of his being a member of some particular church in the nation, which concurs to the making up of the national church; as a man doth not *legally* belong to any county in the nation, unless he belong to some hundred or parish in that county. This is evident

from the nature of the thing itself. Nor is it pleaded that we are one national church, because the people of the nation are generally baptized and do profess the true faith; but because the particular congregations in it are ruled, and so consequently the whole, by lesser and greater assemblies. I suppose it will not be, on second thoughts, insisted on that particular congregations, agreeing solemnly in doctrine and worship, under one civil government, do constitute a national church; for if so, its form and unity as such must be given it merely by the civil government.

2. No man can recede from this church, or depart from it, but by departing from some particular church therein. At the same door that a man comes in, he must go out. If I cease to be a member of a national church, it is by the ceasing or abolishing of that which gave me original right thereunto; which was my relation to the particular church whereof I am.

3. To make men members of any particular church or churches, their own *consent* is required. All men must admit of this who allow it is free for a man to choose where he will fix his habitation.

4. That as yet, at least since possibly we could be personally concerned who are now alive, no such church in this nation hath been formed. It is impossible that a man should be guilty of offending against that which is not. We have not separated from a national church in the presbyterian sense, as never having seen any such thing, unless they will say we have separated from what should be.

5. As to the state of such a church as this, I shall only add to what hath been spoken before the judgment of a very learned and famous man in this case, whom I the rather name, because professedly engaged on the Presbyterians' side. It is Moses Amyraldus, the present professor of divinity at Saumur; whose words are these that follow:—" Scio nonnunquam appellari particularem ecclesiam communionem, ac veluti confœderationem plurium ejusmodi societatum, quas vel ejusdem linguæ usus, vel eadem reipublicæ forma" (the true spring of a national church), " una cum ejusdem disciplinæ regimine consociavit. Sic appellatur ecclesia Gallicana, Anglicana Germanica particularis, ut distinguatur ab universali illa Christianorum societate; quæ omnes Christiani nominis nationes complectitur. At uti supradiximus, ecclesiæ nomen non proprie convenire societati omnium Christianorum, eo modo quo convenit particularibus Christianorum cœtibus; sic consequens est, ut dicamus, ecclesiæ nomen non competere in eam multarum ecclesiarum particularium consociationem eodem plane modo. Vocetur ergo certe ecclesiarum quæ sunt in Gallia communio inter ipsas, et ecclesia, si ecclesia est multarum ecclesiarum confœderatio, non si nomen ecclesiæ ex usu Scrip-

turæ sacræ accipiatur. Paulus enim varias ecclesias particulares quæ erant in Achaia, ecclesias Achaiæ nuncupat, non ecclesiam Achaiæ vel ecclesiam Achaicam," Amyral. Disput. de Ecclesiæ Nom. et Defin. thes. xxviii.

These being, if I mistake not, things of mutual acknowledgment (for I have not laid down any principles peculiar to myself and those with whom I consent in the way of the worship of God, which yet we can justly plead in our own defence), this whole business will be brought to a speedy issue. Only, I desire the reader to observe that I am not pleading the right, liberty, and duty of gathering churches in such a state of professors as that of late, and still amongst us,— which is built on other principles and hypotheses than any as yet I have had occasion to mention,—but am only, in general, considering the true notion of schism, and the charge managed against us on that single account, which relates not to gathering of churches, as simply considered. I say, then,—

First, either we have been members by our own *voluntary consent*, according to the mind of Christ, of some particular congregations in such a national church, and that as " de facto" part of such a church, or we have not. If we have not been so (as it is most certain we have not), then we have not as yet broken any bond, or violated any unity, or disturbed any peace or order, of the appointment of Jesus Christ ; so that whatever of trouble or division hath followed on our way and walking is to be charged on them who have turned every stone to hinder us [in] our liberty. And I humbly beg of them who, acting on principles of reformation according to the (commonly called) presbyterian platform, do accuse us for separation from the church of England, that they would seriously consider what they intend thereby. Is it that we are departed from the faith of the people of God in England? They will not sustain any such crimination. Is it that we have forsaken the church of England as under its episcopal constitution? Have they not done the same? Have they not rejected their national officers, with all the bonds, ties, and ligaments of the union of that pretended church? Have they not renounced the way of worship established by the law of the land? Do they not disavow all obedience to them who were their legal superiors in that constitution? Do they retain either matter or form, or any thing but the naked name of that church? And will they condemn others in what they practise themselves? As for a church of England in their new sense (which yet in some respects is not new, but old), for what is beyond a voluntary consociation of particular churches, we have not as yet had experience of it.

That we shall be accused of schism for not esteeming ourselves made members of a particular church, against our wills, by buying or hiring a habitation within such a precinct of ground, we expect not, especially considering what is delivered by the chief leaders of them with whom now we are treating, whose words are as followeth:— " We grant that living in parishes is not sufficient to make a man a member of a particular church. A Turk, or pagan, or idolater, may live within the precincts of a parish, and yet be no member of a church. A man must, therefore, in order of nature, be a member of the church visible, and then, living in a parish and making profession of Christianity, may claim admission into the society of Christians within those bounds, and enjoy the privileges and ordinances which are there dispensed," Ans. of Commit., p. 105. This is also pursued by the authors of Jus Divinum Ministerii Anglicani, pp. 9, 10, where, after the repetition of the words first mentioned, they add, that "all that dwell in a parish, and constantly hear the word, are not yet to be admitted to the sacraments;" which excludes them from being " fideles," or church-members, and makes them at best as the catechumeni of old, who were never esteemed members of the church.

If we have been so members by our own voluntary consent, and do not continue so to be, then this congregation wherein we are so members was reformed according to the mind of Christ (for I speak now to them that own reformation, as to their light) or it was not. If it were reformed, and a man were a member of it so reformed by his own voluntary consent, I confess it may be difficult to see how a man can leave such a congregation without their consent in whose power it is to give it him, without giving offence to the church of God. Only, I say, let all by-respects be laid aside on the one hand, and on the other all regard to repute and advantage, let love have its perfect work, and no church, knowing the end of its being and constitution to be the edification of believers, will be difficult and tenacious as to the granting a dismission to any member whatever that shall humbly desire it, on the account of applying himself to some other congregation, wherein he supposes and is persuaded that he may be more effectually built up in his most holy faith.

I confess this to be a case of the greatest difficulty that presents itself to my thoughts, in this business: Suppose a man to be a member of a particular church, and that church to be a true church of Christ, and granted so by this person, and yet, upon the account of some defect which is in, or at least he is convinced and persuaded to be in, that church, whose reformation he cannot obtain, he cannot abide in that church to his spiritual advantage and edification; suppose the church, on the other side, cannot be induced to consent to his secession and relinquishment of its ordinary external communion, and that that person is hereby entangled;—what course is to be taken? I

profess, for my part, I never knew this case fall out wherein both
parties were not blamable;—the person seeking to depart, in making
that to be an indispensable cause of departure from a church which
is far short of it; and the church, in not condescending to the man's
desire, though proceeding from infirmity or temptation. In general,
the rule of forbearance and condescension in love, which should salve
the difference, is to give place to the rule of obeying God in all
things according to our light. And the determining in this case depending on circumstances in great variety, both with reference to
the church offending and the person offended, he that can give one
certain rule in and upon the whole shall have much praise for his
invention. However, I am sure this cannot be rationally objected
by them who, esteeming all parishes, as such, to be churches, do yet
allow men on such occasions to change their habitations, and consequently their church relations. "Men may be relieved by change
of dwelling," Subcom. of Div., p. 52. And when a man's leaving
the ordinary external communion of any particular church for his
own edification, to join with another whose administration he is persuaded, in some things more or fewer, is carried on more according
to the mind of Christ, is, as such, proved to be schism, I shall acknowledge it.

As, then, the not giving a man's self up unto any way, and submitting to any establishment, pretended or pleaded to be of Christ,
which he hath not light for, and which he was not by any act of his
own formerly engaged in, cannot, with any colour or pretence of
reason, be reckoned unto him for schism, though he may, if he persist in his refusal, prejudice his own edification; so no more can a
man's peaceable relinquishment of the ordinary communion of one
church, in all its relations, to join with another, be so esteemed.

For instance of the first case: Suppose, by the law of this nation, the
several parochial churches of the land, according to arbitrary distributions made of them, should be joined in classical associations; and
those again, in the like arbitrary disposal, into provincial; and so
onward (which cannot be done without such interveniences as will
exonerate conscience from the weight of pure institution);—or sup
pose this not to be done by the law of the land, but by the voluntary
consent of the officers of the parochial churches, and others joining
with them: the saints of God in this nation who have not formerly
been given up unto or disposed of in this order by their own voluntary consent; nor are concerned in it any farther than by their habitation being within some of these different precincts that, by public
authority or consent of some amongst them, are combined as above;
nor do believe such associations to be the institutions of Christ, whatever they prove to be in the issue,—I say, they are, by their dissent

and refusal to subject themselves to this order, not in the least liable to the charge of schism, whatever they are who, neglecting the great duty of love and forbearance, would by any means whatever impose upon them a necessity of so doing; for, besides what they have to plead as to the non-institution of any such ordinary associations, and investiture of them with power and authority in and over the churches, they are not guilty of the disturbance of any order wherein they were stated according to the mind of Christ, nor of the neglect of any duty of love that was incumbent on them.

For the latter: Suppose a man stated in a particular church, wherewith he hath walked for a season; he discovers that some, perhaps, of the principles of its constitution are not according to the mind of Christ, something is wanting or redundant, and imposed in practice on the members of it, which renders the communion of it, by reason of his doubts and scruples, or, it may be, clear convictions, not so useful to him as he might rationally expect it would be, were all things done according to the mind of Christ; that also he hath declared his judgment as he is able, and dissatisfaction;—if no reformation do ensue, this person, I say, is doubtless at liberty to dispose of himself, as to particular church-communion, to his own best advantage.

But now suppose this congregation, whereof a man is supposed to be a member, is not reformed, will not nor cannot reform itself (I desire that it may be minded with whom I have to do,—namely, those who own a necessity of reformation as to the administration of ordinances, in respect to what hath been hitherto observed in most parochial assemblies. Those I have formerly dealt withal are not to be imposed on with this principle of reformation; they acknowledge none to be needful. But they are not concerned in our present inquiry. Their charge lies all in the behalf of the church of England, not of particular assemblies or parishes; which it is not possible that, according to their principle, they should own for churches, or account any separation from any of them to be blameworthy, but only as it respecteth the constitutions of the church national in them to be observed. If any claim arise on that hand as to parochial assemblies, I should take liberty to examine the foundation of the plea, and doubt not but that I may easily frustrate their attempts. But this is not my present business. I deal, as I said, with them who own reformation; and I now suppose the congregation, whereof a man is supposed to be a member on any account whatever, not to be reformed);—in this case, I ask whether it be schism or no for any number of men to reform themselves, by reducing the practice of worship to its original institution, though they be the minor part lying within the parochial precincts, or for any of them to join themselves with others for that end and purpose not living within those precincts? I shall boldly say this schism is commanded by the Holy Ghost, 1 Tim. vi. 5; 2 Tim. iii. 5; Hos. iv. 15. Is this yoke laid upon me by Christ, that, to go along with the multitude where I live, that hate to be reformed, I must forsake my duty and despise the privileges that he hath purchased for me with his own precious blood? Is this a unity of Christ's institution, that I must for ever associate myself with wicked and profane men in the worship of God, to the unspeakable detriment and disadvantage of my own soul?

I suppose nothing can be more *unreasonable* than once to imagine any such thing.

However, not to drive this business any farther, but to put it to its proper issue: When it is proved that this is the will and appointment of Jesus Christ, that every believer who liveth within such a precinct allotted by civil constitutions, wherein the people or inhabitants do, or may usually, meet for the celebration of the worship of God, or which they have light for, or on any account whatever do make profession of, how profane soever that part of them be from whom the whole is denominated, how corrupt soever in their worship, how dead soever as to the power of godliness, must abide with them and join with them in their administrations and worship, and that indispensably, this business may come again under debate. In the meantime, I suppose the people of God are not in any such subjection. I speak not this as laying down this for a principle, that it is the duty of every man to separate from that church wherein evil and wicked men are tolerated (though that opinion must have many other attendancies before it can contract the least affinity with that of the same sound, which was condemned in the Donatists); but this only I say, that where any church is overborne by a multitude of men wicked and profane, so that it cannot reform itself, or will not, according to the mind of Christ, a believer is so far at liberty that he may desert the communion of that society without the least guilt of schism. But this state of things is now little pleaded for.

It is usually objected about the church of Corinth, that there was in it many disorders and enormous miscarriages, divisions, and breaches of love; miscarriages through drink at their meetings, gross sins, the incestuous person tolerated, false doctrine broached, the resurrection denied;—and yet Paul advises no man to separate from it, but all to perform their duty in it.

But how little our present plea and defensative is concerned in this instance, supposed to lie against it, very few considerations will evince:—

First, the church of Corinth was undoubtedly *a true church*, lately instituted according to the mind of Christ, and was not fallen from that privilege by any miscarriage, nor had suffered any thing destructive to its being; which wholly differences between the case proposed, in respect of many particulars, and the instance produced. We confess the abuses and evils mentioned had crept into the church; and do thence grant that many abuses may do so into any of the best of the churches of God. Nor did it ever enter into the heart of any man to think that so soon as any disorders fall out or abuses creep into it, it is instantly the duty of any to fly out of it, like Paul's mariners out of the ship when the storm grew hazardous; it being the duty of all the members of such a church, untainted with the evils and corruptions of it, upon many accounts, to attempt and labour the remedy of those disorders, and rejection of those abuses to the uttermost; which was that which Paul advised the Corinthians all and some[1] unto; in obedience whereunto they were recovered. But yet this I say, had the church of Corinth continued in the condition before described,—that notorious, scandalous sins had gone unpunished, unreproved, drunkenness continued and practised in the assemblies, men abiding by the denial of the resurrection, so overturning the whole gospel, and the church refusing to do her duty, and exercise her authority to cast all those disorderly persons, upon their obstinacy, out of her communion,—it had been the duty of every saint of God in that church to have withdrawn from it, to come out from among them, and not to have been partaker of their sins, unless they were willing to partake of their plague also, which on such an apostasy would certainly ensue.

I confess Austin, in his single book against the Donatists, Post Collationem, cap. xx., affirms that Elijah and Elisha communicated with the Israelites in their worship, when they were so corrupted as in their days, and separated not from their sacraments (as he calls them), but only withdrew sometimes for fear of persecution;—a mistake unworthy so great and wise a person as he was. The public worship of those ten tribes, in the days of those prophets, was idolatrous, erected by Jeroboam, confirmed by a law by Omri, and continued by Ahab. That the prophets joined with them in it is not to be imagined. But earnestness of desire for the attaining of any end sometimes leaves no room for the examination of the mediums, offering their service to that purpose.

Let us now see the sum of the whole matter, and what it is that we plead for our discharge as to this crime of schism, allowing the term to pass in its large and usual acceptation, receding, for the sake of the truth's farther ventilation, from the precise propriety of the word annexed to it in the Scripture. The sum is, We have broken no bond

---

[1] *All and some,* a corruption of an Anglo-Saxon phrase, meaning *all together,* one and all.—ED.

of unity, no order instituted or appointed by Jesus Christ,—have causelessly deserted no station that ever we were in, according to his mind; which alone can give countenance to an accusation of this nature. That on pure grounds of conscience we have withdrawn, or do withhold ourselves from partaking in some ways, engaged into upon mere grounds of prudence, we acknowledge.

And thus, from what hath been said, it appears in what a fair capacity, notwithstanding any principle or practice owned by us, we are in to live peaceably, and to exercise all fruits of love towards those who are otherwise minded.

There is not the least necessity on us, may we be permitted to serve God according to our light, for the acquitting ourselves from the charge which hath made such a noise in the world, to charge other men with their failings, great or small, in or about the ways and worship of God. This only is incumbent on us, that we manifest that we have broken no bond, no obligation or tie to communion, which lay upon us by the will and appointment of Jesus Christ, our Lord and Master. What is prudentially to be done in such a nation as this, in such a time as this, as to the worship of God, we will treat with men at farther leisure, and when we are lawfully called thereto.

It may be some will yet say (because it hath been often said), "There is a difference between reforming of churches already gathered and raised, and raising of churches out of mere materials. The first may be allowed, but the latter tends to all manner of confusion."

I have at present not much to say to this objection, because, as I conceive, it concerns not the business we have in hand; nor would I have mentioned it at all, but that it is insisted on by some on every turn, whether suited for the particular cause for which it is produced or no. In brief, then,—

1. I know no other *reformation* of any church, or any thing in a church, but the reducing of it to its primitive institution, and the order allotted to it by Jesus Christ. If any plead for any other reformation of churches, they are, in my judgment, to blame.

And when any society or combination of men (whatever hitherto it hath been esteemed) is not capable of such a reduction and renovation, I suppose I shall not provoke any wise and sober person if I profess I cannot look on such a society as a church of Christ, and thereupon advise those therein who have a due right to the privileges purchased for them by Christ, as to gospel administrations, to take some other peaceable course to make themselves partakers of them.

2. Were I fully to handle the things pointed to in this objection, I must manage principles which, in this discourse, I have not been occasioned to draw forth at all or to improve. Many things of great weight and importance must come under debate and consideration

before a clear account can be given of the case stated in this objection; as,—

(1.) The *true* nature of an instituted church under the gospel, as to the matter, form, and all other necessary constitutive causes, is to be investigated and found out.

(2.) The nature and form of such a church is to be *exemplified from the Scripture* and the stories of the first churches, before sensibly infected with the poison of that apostasy which ensued.

(3.) The *extent of the apostasy* under Antichrist, as to the ruining of instituted churches, making them to be Babylon, and their worship fornication, is duly and carefully to be examined.

" Hic labor, hoc opus."

Here lie our disorder and division; hence is our darkness and pollution of our garments, which is not an easy thing to free ourselves of: though we may arise, yet we shall not speedily shake ourselves out of the dust.

(4.) By what way and means God *begat anew and kept alive his elect* in their several generations, when antichristian darkness covered the earth and thick darkness the nations, supposing an intercision of instituted ordinances, so far as to make a nullity in them as to what was of simple and pure institution; what way might be used for the fixing the tabernacle of God *again* with men, and the setting up of church-worship according to his mind and will. And here the famous case of the United Brethren of Bohemia would come under consideration; who, concluding the whole Papacy to be purely antichristian, could not allow of the ordination of their ministers by any in communion with it, and yet, being persuaded of a necessity of continuing that ordinance in a way of succession, sent some to the Greek and Armenian churches; who, observing their ways, returned with little satisfaction; so that at last, committing themselves and their cause to God, they chose them elders from among themselves, and set them apart by fasting and prayer: which was the foundation of all those churches, which, for piety, zeal, and suffering for Christ, have given place to none in Europe.

(5.) What was the *way of the first Reformation* in this nation, and what *principles* the godly learned men of those days proceeded on; how far what they did may be satisfactory to our consciences at the present, as to our concurrence in them, who from thence have the truth of the gospel derived down to us; whether ordinary officers be before or after the church, and so whether a church-state is preserved in the preservation of officers, by a power foreign to that church whereof they are so, or the office be preserved, and consequently the officers inclusively, in the preservation and constitution of a church;—these, I say, with sundry other things of the like importance, with inferences from them, are to be considered to the bottom before a full resolution can be given to the inquiry couched in this objection, which, as I said, to do is not my present business.

This task, then, is at its issue and close. Some considerations of the manifold miscarriages that have ensued for want of a due and right apprehension of the thing we have now been exercised in the consideration of shall shut it up:—

1. It is not impossible that some may, from what hath been spoken, begin to apprehend that they have been too hasty in judging other men. Indeed, none are more ready to charge highly than those who, when they have so done, are most unable to make good their charge. " Si accusâsse sufficiat, quis erit innocens?" What real schisms in a moral sense have ensued among brethren, by their causeless mutual imputation of schism in things of institution, is known. And when men are in one fault, and are charged with another wherein they are not, it is a ready way to confirm them in that wherein they are. There is more darkness and difficulty in the whole matter of instituted worship than some men are aware of; not that it was so from the beginning, whilst Christianity continued in its naked simplicity, but it is come occasionally upon us by the customs, darkness, and invincible prejudices that have taken hold on the minds of men by a secret diffusion of the poison of that grand apostasy. It were well, then, that men would not be so confident, nor easily persuaded that they presently know how all things ought to be, because they know how they would have some things to be, which suit their temper and interest. Men may easily perhaps see, or think they see, what they do not like, and cry out *schism!* and *separation!* but if they would a little consider what ought to be in this whole matter, according to the mind of God, and what evidences they have of the grounds and principles whereon they condemn others, it might make them yet swift to hear, but slow to speak, and take off from the number of teachers among us. Some are ready to think that all that join not with them are schismatics, and they are so because they go not with them; and other reason they have none, being unable to give any solid foundation of what they profess. What the cause of unity among the people of God hath suffered from this sort of men is not easily to be expressed.

2. In all differences about religion, to drive them to their *rise* and *spring,* and to consider them as stated originally, will ease us of much trouble and labour. Perhaps many of them will not appear so formidable as they are represented. He that sees a great river is not instantly to conclude that all the water in it comes from its first rise and spring; the addition of many brooks, showers, and land-floods, have perhaps swelled it to the condition wherein it is. Every difference in religion is not to be thought to be as big at its rise as it appears to be when it hath passed through many generations, and hath

received additions and aggravations from the disputings and contendings of men, on the one hand and the other engaged. What a flood of abominations doth this business of schism seem to be, as rolling down to us through the writings of Cyprian, Austin, and Optatus, of old, the schoolmen, decrees of popish councils, with the contrivances of some among ourselves, concerned to keep up the swelled notion of it! Go to its rise, and you will find it to be, though bad enough, yet quite another thing than what, by the prejudices accruing by the addition of so many generations, it is now generally represented to be.

The great maxim, "To the law and to the testimony," truly improved, would quickly cure all our distempers. In the meantime, let us bless God that though our outward man may possibly be disposed of according to the apprehension that others have of what we do or are, our consciences are concerned only in what he hath appointed. How some men may prevail against us, before whom we must stand or fall according to their corrupt notion of schism, we know not. The rule of our consciences in this, as in all other things, is eternal and unchangeable. Whilst I have an uncontrollable faithful witness that I transgress no limits prescribed to me in the word, that I do not willingly break or dissolve any unity of the institution of Jesus Christ, my mind as to this thing is filled with perfect peace. Blessed be God, that hath reserved the sole sovereignty of our consciences in his hand, and not in the least parcelled it out to any of the sons of men, whose tender mercies being oftentimes cruelty itself, they would perhaps destroy the soul also, when they do so to the body, seeing they stay there, as our Saviour witnesseth, because they can proceed no farther! Here, then, I profess to rest, in this doth my conscience acquiesce: Whilst I have any comfortable persuasion, on grounds infallible, that I hold the head, and that I am by faith a member of the mystical body of Christ; whilst I make profession of all the necessary saving truths of the gospel; whilst I disturb not the peace of that particular church whereof by my own consent I am a member, nor do raise up nor continue in any causeless differences with them, or any of them, with whom I walk in the fellowship and order of the gospel; whilst I labour to exercise faith towards the Lord Jesus Christ, and love towards all the saints,—I do keep the unity which is of the appointment of Christ. And let men say, from principles utterly foreign to the gospel, what they please or can to the contrary, I am no schismatic.

3. Perhaps the discovery which hath been made, how little we are many of us concerned in that which, having mutually charged it on one another, hath been the greatest ball of strife and most effectual engine of difference and distance between us, may be a means to reconcile in love them that truly fear God, though engaged in several ways, as to some particulars. I confess I have not any great hope of

much success on this account; for let principles and ways be made as evident as if he that wrote them carried the sun in his hand, yet whilst men are forestalled by prejudices, and have their affections and spirits engaged suitably thereunto, no great alteration in their minds and ways, on the clearest conviction whatever, is to be expected. All our hearts are in the hand of God; and our expectations of what he hath promised are to be proportioned to what he can effect, not to what of outward means we see to be used.

4. To conclude; what vain janglings men are endlessly engaged in, who will lay their own false hypotheses and preconceptions as a ground of farther procedure, is also in part evident by what hath been delivered. Hence, for instance, is that doughty dispute in the world, whether a schismatic doth belong to the church or no? which for the most part is determined in the negative; when it is impossible a man should be so, but by virtue of his being a church-member. A church is that " alienum solum," wherein that evil dwelleth. The most of the inquiries that are made and disputed on, whether this or that sort of men belong to the church or no, are of the same value and import. He belongs to the *church catholic* who is united to Christ by the Spirit, and none other. And he belongs to the *church general visible* who makes profession of the faith of the gospel, and destroys it not by any thing of a just inconsistency with the belief of it. And he belongs to a *particular church* who, having been in due order joined thereunto, hath neither voluntarily deserted it nor been judicially ejected out of it. Thus, one may be a member of the church catholic who is no member of the general visible church nor of a particular church; as an elect infant, sanctified from the womb, dying before baptism. And one may be a member of the church general visible who is no member of the church catholic nor of a particular church; as a man making profession of the true faith, yet not united to Christ by the Spirit, nor joined to any particular visible church;—or he may be also of the catholic church, and not of a particular, as also of a particular church, and not of the catholic. And a man may be,—every true believer walking orderly ordinarily is,—a member of the church of Christ in every sense insisted on;—of the catholic church, by *a union with Christ, the head;* of the visible general church, by his *profession of the faith;* and of a particular congregation, by his *voluntarily associating* himself therewith, according to the will and appointment of our Lord Jesus Christ.

A

REVIEW OF THE TRUE NATURE OF SCHISM,

WITH

A VINDICATION OF THE CONGREGATIONAL CHURCHES IN ENGLAND
FROM THE IMPUTATION THEREOF,

UNJUSTLY CHARGED ON THEM BY MR D. CAWDREY,

PREACHER OF THE WORD AT BILLING, IN NORTHAMPTONSHIRE.

———

Δοῦλον Κυρίου οὐ δεῖ μάχεσθαι.——2 Tim. ii. 24.

Δεῖ τὸν ἐπίσκοπον ἀνέγκλητον εἶναι, ὡς Θεοῦ οἰκονόμον, μὴ αὐθάδη, μὴ ὀργίλον,
μὴ πάροινον, μὴ πλήκτην, μὴ αἰσχροκερδῆ.——Tit. i. 7.

———

OXFORD: 1657.

PREFATORY NOTE.

THE preceding treatise was too important to pass without a reply. Dr Hammond, engaged at the time in another controversy with Owen, respecting the orthodoxy of Grotius, appended to one of his pamphlets " A Reply to some Passages of the Reviewer," (Owen), " in his late Book on Schism." Giles Firmin, a Nonconformist divine and physician, much respected for his personal worth and attainments, published, in 1658, a work entitled, " Of Schism, Parochial Congregations, and Ordination by Imposition of Hands; wherein Dr Owen's Discovery of the True Nature of Schism is briefly and friendly examined." Dr Owen did not feel it necessary to offer any reply to these reviews of his work. Mr Daniel Cawdrey, however, a Presbyterian minister at Great Billing, in Northamptonshire, in a pamphlet entitled " Independency a Great Schism," assailed both the principles and the character of Dr Owen in no very measured terms. Much would not have been lost to the world if Cawdrey also had been left without an answer; for he does not seem to have managed the discussion to any good purpose. Owen very conclusively repels the charge of inconsistency with which Cawdrey had reproached him, and urges some additional considerations in support of the general argument contained in his first treatise on schism. He earnestly disclaims the sentiment imputed to him, that he held no church except his own to be a true church of Christ, and closes in a strain of calm and dignified rebuke to the petty and offensive spirit in which his opponent had discussed his statements.

In the beginning of the second chapter there will be found, what Owen very rarely gives us,—an allusion to his personal history. So far as it goes, it is a piece of autobiography replete with interest; for it narrates the circumstances in which he was led to embrace Congregational views. In the midst of a keen dispute and the heavy cares of public life, the heart of our author seems to open to us under the remembrances of his youth, and there is some tenderness of feeling in the allusion to his father, whom he describes as " a Nonconformist all his days, and a painful labourer in the vineyard of the Lord."

In all his treatises on schism, Owen adheres with steadiness and decision to his profession as an Independent. He makes, however, in the beginning of the ninth chapter, a statement that deserves some attention : " For my part, so we could once agree in the matter of our churches, I am under some apprehension that it were no impossible thing to reconcile the whole difference as to a Presbyterian church or a single congregation," p. 258. He intimates that he would " offer, ere long, to the consideration of godly men, something that may provoke others of better abilities and more leisure to endeavour to carry on so good a work." A purpose announced in these terms can hardly be restricted to the mere difference in regard to the eldership, of which he has been speaking, but must include the whole difference between Presbytery and Independency. To have reconciled these two systems, or rather the Christians respectively attached to them, would certainly have been " a good work," though many will doubt its practicability. The sentiment shows, at least, the generous and catholic spirit Owen breathed, so superior to the tendency with which weak minds, on such a change as he made, are apt to adopt the extreme position in their new views. Are those works he published long afterwards, " The Inquiry into Evangelical Churches," and " The True Nature of a Gospel Church," in which Presbyterians think they find a confirmation of their views on some points, a fulfilment of the promise quoted above ? Some difficulties in understanding them would be explained if they were.—ED.

TO THE READER.

CHRISTIAN READER,

It is now about three weeks since that there was sent unto me a book entitled, "Independency a Great Schism;" as the frontispiece farther promiseth, undertaken to be managed against something written by me in a treatise about the true nature of schism, published about a year ago; with an addition of a charge of inconstancy in opinion upon myself. Of the one and the other the ensuing discourse will give a farther and full account. Coming unto my hands at such a season, wherein, as it is known, I was pressed with more than ordinary occasions of sundry sorts, I thought to have deferred the examination of it until farther leisure might be obtained, supposing that some fair advantage would be administered by it to a farther Christian debate of that discovery of truth and tender of peace which in my treatise I had made. Engaging into a cursory perusal of it, I found the reverend author's design and discourse to be of that tendency and nature as did not require nor would admit of any such delay. His manifold mistakes in apprehending the intention of my treatise and of the severals of it; his open presumption of his own principles as the source and spring of what pretends to be argumentative in his discourse, arbitrarily inferring from them, without the least attempt of proof, whatever tenders its assistance, to cast reproach on them with whom he hath to do; his neglect in providing a defence for himself, by any principles not easily turned upon him, against the same charge which he is pleased to manage against me; his avowed laying the foundation of his whole fabric in the sand of notoriously false suppositions,—quickly delivered me from the thoughts of any necessity to delay the consideration of what he tendered to make good the title of his discourse. The open and manifest injury done not only to myself,—in laying things to my charge which I know not, lading me with reproaches, tending to a rendering of me odious to all the ministers and churches in the world not agreeing with me in some few things concerning gospel administrations,—but also to all other churches and persons of the same judgment with myself, called for a speedy account of the true state of the things contended about.

Thou hast therefore here, Christian reader, the product (through the grace of Him who supplieth seed to the sower) of the spare hours of four or five days; in which space of time this ensuing discourse was begun and finished. Expect not, therefore, any thing from it but what is necessary for the refutation of the book whereunto it is opposed; and as to that end and purpose, I leave it to thy strictest judgment. Only, I shall desire thee to take notice, that having kept myself to a bare defence, I have resolvedly forborne all re-charge on the presbyterian way, either as to the whole of it (whence, by way of distinction, it is so called), or as to the differences in judgment and practice of them who profess that way among themselves;

which at this day, both in this and the neighbour nation, are more and greater than any that our author hath as yet been able to find amongst them whom he doth principally oppose.   As the ensuing sheets were almost wrought off at the press, there came to my hand a vindication of that eminent servant of God, Mr John Cotton, from the unjust imputations and charge of the reverend person with whom I have now to do, written by himself not long before his death.   The opportunity of publishing that discourse with the ensuing being then lost, I thought meet to let the reader know that a short season will furnish him with it.   Farewell, and love, truth, and peace.

CHRIST CHURCH COLLEGE, OXON,
       July 9, 1657.

A VINDICATION

OF THE

TREATISE ABOUT THE TRUE NATURE OF SCHISM, ETC.

CHAPTER I.

THE present state of things in the Christian world will, on a slight consideration, yield this account of controversies in religion, that when they are driven to such an issue as, by foreign coincidences, to be rendered the interest of parties at variance, there is not any great success to be obtained by a management of them, though with never so much evidence and conviction of truth. An answering of the profession that is on us, by a good and lawful means, the paying of that homage and tribute we owe to the truth, the tendering of assistance to the safeguarding of some weaker professors thereof from the sophisms and violence of adversaries, is the most that, in such a posture of things, the most sober writers of controversies can well aim at.

The winning over of men to the truth we seek to maintain, where they have been pre-engaged in an opposition unto it, without the alteration of the outward state of things whence their engagements have insensibly sprung and risen, is not ordinarily to be expected. How far I was from any such thoughts in the composing and publishing my treatise of the nature of schism, I declared in sundry passages in the treatise itself. Though the thing contended about, whatsoever is pretended to the contrary, will not be found amongst the most important heads of our religion, yet knowing how far, on sundry accounts, the stated fixed interest of several sorts of men engageth them to abide by the principles they own in reference thereunto, I was so far from hoping to see speedily any visible fruits of the efficacy of the truth I had managed, that I promised myself a vigorous opposition, until some urgent providence or time, altering the frame of men's spirits, should make way for its acceptance. Freely I left in the hand of Him, whose truth I have good security

I had in weakness maintained, to dispose of it, with its issues and events, at his pleasure. I confess, knowing several parties to be concerned in an opposition to it, I was not well able to conjecture from what hand the first assault of it would arise. Probability cast it on them who looked on themselves [as] in the nearest proximity of advantage by the common notion of schism opposed. The truth is, I did apprehend myself not justly chargeable with want of charity, if I thought that opposition would arise from some other principles than mere zeal for a supposed truth; and, therefore, took my aim in conjecturing at the prejudices that men might fear themselves and interests obnoxious unto by a reception and establishment of that notion of schism which I had asserted. Men's contentedness to make use of their quietness in reference to Popery, Socinianism, Arminianism, daily vented amongst us, unless it were in some declamatory expressions against their toleration, which cost no more than they are worth, shaken off by a speedy engagement against my treatise, confirmed such thoughts in me. After, therefore, it had passed in the world for some season, and had found acceptance with many learned and godly persons, reports began to be raised about a design for a refutation of it. That so it should be dealt withal I heard was judged necessary at sundry conventions; what particular hand it was likely the task would fall upon, judging myself not concerned to know, I did not inquire. When I was informed how the disposal of the business did succeed, as I was not at all surprised in reference to the party in general from which it did issue, so I did relieve myself, under my fears and loathing to be engaged in these contests, by these ensuing considerations:—1. That I was fully persuaded that what I had written was, for the substance of it, the truth of God; and being concerned in it only on truth's account, if it could be demonstrated that the sentence I had asserted was an unlawful pretender thereunto, I should be delivered from paying any farther respect or service to that whereunto none at all was due. 2. That in the treatise itself so threatened, I had laid in provision against all contending about words, expressions, collateral assertions, deductions, positions, all and every thing, though true, that might be separated from the life or substance of the notion or truth pleaded for. 3. That whereas the whole weight of the little pile turned on one single hinge, and that visible and conspicuous, capable of an ocular demonstration as to its confirmation or refutation, I promised myself that any man who should undertake the demolishing of it would be so far from passing that by, and setting himself to the superstruction, that subsists on its single strength and vigour, that indeed finding that one thing necessary for him, he would solely attempt that, and therein rest. This I knew was evident to any considering person that should but view the treatise, that if that foundation were cast down, the whole superstructure would fall with its own weight; but if left standing, a hundred thousand volumes against the rest of the treatise could not in the least prejudice the cause undertaken to be managed in it. Men might, indeed, by such attempts, manifest my weakness and want of skill, in making inferences and deductions from principles of truth wherein I am not concerned, but the truth itself contended for would still abide untouched. 4. Having expressly waived man's day and judgment, I promised myself security from a disturbance by urging against me the authority of any of old or late; supposing that, from the eviction of their several interests, I had emancipated myself from all subjection to their bare judgments in this cause. 5. Whereas I had confined myself to a bare defensative of some, not intending to cast others from the place which, in their own apprehensions, they do enjoy (unless it was the Roman party), I had some expectations that peace-loving, godly men would not be troubled that an apparent immunity from a crime was, without their prejudice or disadvantage, manifested in behalf of their brethren, nor much pain themselves to re-enforce the charge accounted for; so that the bare notion of schism, and the nature of it, abstracted from the consideration of persons, would come under debate. Indeed, I questioned whether, in that friendly composure of affections which, for sundry years, hath been carrying on between sober and godly men of the presbyterian and congregational judgment, any person of real godliness would interest himself to blow the coal of dissension and engage in new exasperations. I confess, I always thought the plea of Cicero for Ligarius against Tubero most unreasonable,—namely, that if he had told (as he calls it) "*an honest and merciful lie*" in his behalf, yet it was not the part of a man to refel it, especially of one who was accused of the same crime; but yet I must needs say, a prompt readiness to follow most questionable accusations against honest defensatives from good men, unjustly accused by others of the same crime, I did not expect. I added this also in my thoughts, that the facility of rendering a discourse to the purpose on the business under consideration was obviated by its being led out of the common road, wherein common-place supplies would be of little use to any that should undertake it; not once suspecting that any man of learning and judgment would make a return unto it out of vulgar discourses about ministers' calling, church-government, or the like. How far these and the like considerations might be a relief unto my thoughts, in my fears of farther controversial engagements, having the pressure of more business upon me than any one man I know of my calling in the whole nation, I leave it to the judgment of them who love truth and peace. But what little confidence I ought, in the present posture of the minds of men, to have placed in any or all of them, the discourse under consideration hath instructed me. That any one thing hath fallen out according to my expectations and conjectures, but only its being a product of the men of the persuasions owned therein, I am yet to seek. The truth is, I cannot blame my adversary, "viis et modis," to make good the opposition he is engaged in. It concerns him and his advisers beyond their interest in the appearing skirts of this controversy. Perhaps, also, an adjudged necessity of endeavouring a disreputation to my person and writings was one ingredient in the undertaking; if so, the whole frame was to be carried on by correspondent mediums. But let the principles and motives to this discourse be what they will, it is now made public, there being a warmer zeal acting therein than in carrying on some other things expected from the same hand.

To what may seem of importance in it, I shall with all possible plainness give a return. Had the reverend author of it thought good to have kept within the bounds by me fixed, and candidly debated the notion proposed, abstracting from the provocations of particular applications, I should most willingly have taken pains for a farther clearing and manifesting of the truth contended about.

But the whole discourse wherewith I have now to do is of another complexion, and the design of it of another tendency, yea, so managed sometimes, that I am ready to question whether it be the product and fruit of his spirit whose name it bears; for though he be an utter stranger to me, yet I have received such a character of him as would raise me to an expectation of any thing from him rather than such a discourse.

The reader will be able to perceive an account of these thoughts in the ensuing view of his treatise.

1. I am, without any provocation intended, and I hope given, *reviled* from one end of it to the other, and called, partly in downright terms, partly by oblique intimations, whose reflections are not to be waived, Satan, atheist, sceptic, Donatist, heretic, schismatic, sectary, Pharisee, etc.; and the closure of the book is merely an attempt to blast my reputation, whereof I shall give a speedy account.

2. The professed design of the whole is to prove "Independency," as he is pleased to call it,—which what it is he declares not, nor (as he manages the business) do I know,—to be a " great *schism*," and that Independents (by whom it is full well known whom he intends) are " *schismatics*," " sectaries," the " troublers of England," so that it were happy for the nation if they were out of it; or discovering sanguinary thoughts in reference unto them. And these kinds of discourses fill up the book, almost from one end to the other.

3. No Christian care doth seem to have been taken, nor good

conscience exercised, from the beginning to the ending, as to imputation of any thing *unto me* or *upon me*, that may serve to help on
the design in hand.

Hence, I think, it is repeated near a hundred times, that I deny
their ministers to be ministers, and their churches to be churches,
—that I deny all the reformed churches in the world but only " our
own" (as he calls them) to be true churches; all which is notoriously untrue, contrary to my known judgment, professedly declared on all occasions, contrary to express affirmations in the book
he undertakes to confute, and the whole design of the book itself.
I cannot easily declare my surprisal on this account. What am I to
expect from others, when such reverend men as this author shall, by
the power of prejudice, be carried beyond all bounds of moderation
and Christian tenderness in offending? I no way doubt but that
Satan hath his design in this whole business. He knows how apt
we are to fix on such provocations, and to contribute thereupon to
the increase of our differences. Can he, according to the course of
things in the world, expect any other issue, but that, in the necessary defensative I am put upon, I should not waive such reflections
and retortions on him and them with whom I have to do, as present
themselves with as fair pleas and pretences unto me as it is possible
for me to judge that the charges before mentioned (I mean of
schism, heresy, and the like) did unto him? for as to a return of
any thing·in its own nature false and untrue as to matter of fact, to
meet with that of the like kind wherewith I am entertained, I suppose the devil himself was hopeless to obtain it. Is he not filled
with envy to take notice in what love without dissimulation I walk
with many of the presbyterian judgment; what Christian inter-
course and communion I have with them in England, Scotland,
Holland, France; fearing that it may tend to the furtherance of
peace and union among the churches of Christ? God assisting, I
shall deceive his expectations; and though I be called schismatic and
heretic a thousand times, it shall not weaken my love or esteem of
or towards any of the godly ministers or people of that way and
judgment with whom I am acquainted, or have occasion of converse.

And as for this reverend author himself, I shall not fail to pray
that none of the things whereby he hath, I fear, administered advantage unto Satan to attempt the exasperations of the spirits of brethren one against another, may ever be laid to his charge. For my
own part, I profess in all sincerity that such was my unhappiness,
or rather happiness, in the constant converse which, in sundry places,
I have with persons of the presbyterian judgment, both of the
English and Scottish nation, utterly of another frame of spirit than
that which is now showed, that until I saw this treatise, I did not

believe that there had remained in any one godly, sober, judicious person in England, such thoughts of heart in reference to our present differences as are visible and legible therein.

" Tantæne animis cœlestibus iræ ? "

I hope the reverend author will not be offended if I make bold to tell him that it will be no joy of heart to him one day, that he hath taken pains to cast oil on those flames, which it is every one's duty to labour to extinguish.

But that the whole matter in difference may be the better stated and determined, I shall first pass through with the general concernments of the book itself, and then consider the several chapters of it, as to any particulars in them that may seem to relate to the business in hand. It may possibly not a little conduce towards the removal of those obstructions unto peace and love, laid in our way by this reverend author, and to a clearer stating of the controversy pretended to be ventilated in his discourse, to discover and lay aside those mistakes of his, which, being interwoven with the main discourse from the beginning to the end, seem as principles to animate the whole, and to give it that life of trouble whereof it is partaker. Some of them were, as absolutely considered, remarked before. I shall now renew the mention of them, with respect to that influence which they have into the argumentative part of the treatise under consideration.

1. First, then, it is strenuously supposed all along, *that I deny all or any churches in England to be true churches of Christ,* except only the churches gathered in the congregational way and upon their principles; then, that I deny all the reformed churches beyond the seas to be true churches of Christ. This supposition being laid as the foundation of the whole building, a confutation of my treatise is fixed thereon; a comparison is instituted between the Donatists and myself; arguments are produced to prove their churches to be true churches, and their ministers true ministers; the charge of schism on this bottom is freely given out and asserted; the proof of my schismatical separation from hence deduced; and many terms of reproach are returned as a suitable reply to the provocation of this opinion. How great a portion of a small treatise may easily be taken up with discourses relating to these heads is easy to apprehend. Now, lest all this pains should be found to be useless and causelessly undergone, let us consider how the reverend author proves this to be my judgment. Doth he evince it from any thing delivered in that treatise he undertakes to confute? doth he produce any other testimonies out of what I have spoken, delivered, or written elsewhere, and on other occasions, to make it good? This, I suppose, he thought not of, but took it for granted that either I was of that judgment, or it was fit

I should be so, that the difference between us might be as great as he desired to have it appear to be.

Well, to put an end to this controversy, seeing he would not believe what I told the world of my thoughts herein in my book of schism, I now inform him again that all these surmises are fond and untrue. And truly, for his own sake, with that respect which is due to the reputation of religion, I here humbly entreat him not to entertain what is here affirmed with unchristian surmises, which the apostle reckons amongst the works of the flesh, as though I were of another mind, but durst not declare it; as more than once, in some particulars, he insinuates the state of things with me to be. But blessed be the God of my salvation and of all my deliverances, I have yet liberty to declare the whole of my judgment in and about the things of his worship! Blessed be God, it is not as yet in the power of some men to bring in that their conceited happiness into England, which would, in their thoughts, accrue unto it by my removal from my native soil, with all others of my judgment and persuasion! We are yet at peace, and we trust that the Lord will deliver us from the hands of men whose tender mercies are cruel. However, be it known unto them, that if it be the will of the Lord, upon our manifold provocations, to give us up to their disposal, who are pleased to compass us with the ornaments of reproaches before mentioned, that so we might fall as a sacrifice to rage or violence, we shall, through his assistance and presence with us, dare to profess the whole of that truth and those ways of his which he hath been pleased to reveal unto us.

And if, on any other account, this reverend person suppose I may foster opinions and thoughts of mine own and their ways which I dare not own, let him at any time give me a command to wait upon him, and as I will freely and candidly answer to any inquiries he shall be pleased to make, after my judgment and apprehensions of these things, so he shall find that (God assisting) I dare own, and will be ready to maintain, what I shall so deliver to him. It is a sufficient evidence that this reverend author is an utter stranger to me, or he would scarce entertain such surmises of me as he doth. Shall I call in witnesses as to the particular under consideration? One evidence, by way of instance, lies so near at hand that I cannot omit the producing of it. Not above fourteen days before this treatise came to my hands, a learned gentleman, whom I had prevailed withal to answer in the Vespers of our Act, sent me his questions by a doctor of the presbyterian judgment, a friend of his and mine. The first question was, as I remember, to this purpose: "Utrum ministri ecclesiæ Anglicanæ habeant validam ordinationem?" I told the doctor, that since the questions were to pass under my approbation, I must needs confess myself scrupled at the limitation of the subject of the question in that term, "Ecclesia Anglicana," which would be found ambiguous and equivocal in the disputation, and therefore desired that he would rather supply it with "Ecclesiarum Reformatarum," or some other expression of like importance; but as to the thing itself aimed at,—namely, the assertion of the ministry of the godly ministers in England,—I told him, and so now do the reverend author of this treatise, that I shall as willingly engage in the defence of it, with the lawfulness of their churches, as any man whatever. I have only in my treatise questioned the institution of a national church, which this author doth not undertake to maintain, nor hath the least reason so to do, for the asserting of true ministers and churches in England; I mean those of the presbyterian way. What satisfaction now this reverend author shall judge it necessary for him to give me for the public injury which voluntarily he hath done me, in particular for his attempt to expose me to the censure and displeasure of so many godly ministers and churches as I own in England, as a person denying their ministry and church station, I leave it to himself to consider. And by the declaration of this mistake, how great a part of his book is waived, as to my concernments therein, himself full well knows.

2. A second principle of like importance which he is pleased to make use of as a thing granted by me, or at least which he assumes as that which ought so to be, is, that whatever the presbyterian ministers and churches be, I have *separated* from them, as have done all those whom he calls Independents. This is another fountain out of which much bitter water flows. Hence we must needs be thought to condemn their ministry and churches. The Brownists were our fathers, and the Anabaptists are our elder brothers; we make a harlot of our mother, and are schismatics and sectaries from one end of the book to the other : "quod erat demonstrandum." But doth not this reverend author know that this is wholly denied by us? Is it not disproved sufficiently in that very treatise which he undertakes to answer ?

He grants, I suppose, that the separation he blames must respect some union of Christ's institution: for any other, we profess ourselves unconcerned in its maintenance or dissolution, as to the business in hand. Now, wherein have we separated from them as to the breach of any such union? For an individual person to change from the constant participation of ordinances in one congregation, to do so in another, barely considered in itself, this reverend author holds to be no separation. However, for my part, who am forced to bear all this wrath and storm, what hath he to lay to my charge? I condemn not their churches in general to be no churches, nor any one that I am acquainted withal in particular; I never disturbed, that

I know of, the peace of any one of them, nor separated from them : but having already received my punishment, I expect to hear my crime by the next return.

3. He supposeth throughout that I deny not only the *necessity of a successive ordination,* but, as far as I can understand him, the *lawfulness* of it also. By ordination of ministers, many, upon a mistake, understand only the imposition of hands that is used therein. Ordination of ministers is one thing, and imposition of hands another, differing as whole and part. Ordination in Scripture compriseth the whole authoritative translation of a man from among the number of his brethren into the state of an officer in the church. I suppose he doth not think that this is denied by me, though he tells me, with the same Christian candour and tenderness which he exerciseth in every passage almost of his book, of making myself a minister, and I know not what. I am, I bless the Lord, extremely remote from returning him any of his own coin in satisfaction for this love. For that part of it which consists in the imposition of hands by the presbytery (where it may be obtained according to the mind of Christ), I am also very remote from managing any opposition unto it. I think it necessary by virtue of *precept,* and that [it ought] to be continued in a way of *succession.* It is, I say, according to the mind of Christ, that he who is to be ordained unto office in any church receive imposition of hands from the elders of that church, if there be any therein; and this is to be done in a way of succession, that so the churches may be perpetuated. That alone which I oppose is the denying of this successive ordination through the authority of Antichrist. Before the blessed and glorious Reformation, begun and carried on by Zuinglius, Luther, Calvin, and others, there were, and had been, two estates of men in the world professing the name of Christ and the gospel, as to the outward profession thereof; —the one of them in glory, splendour, outward beauty, and order, calling themselves *the church,* the *only* church in the world, the *catholic* church,—being in deed and in truth, in that state wherein they so prided themselves, the mother of harlots, the beast, with his false prophet; the other party, poor, despised, persecuted, generally esteemed and called heretics, schismatics, or, as occasion gave advantage for their farther reproach, Waldenses, Albigenses, Lollards, and the like. As to the claim of a successive ordination drawn from the apostles, I made bold to affirm that I could not understand the validity of that successive ordination, as successive, which was derived down unto us from and by the first party of men in the world.

This reverend author's reply hereunto is like the rest of his discourse. Page 118, he tells me, " This casts dirt in the face of their ministry, as do all their good friends the sectaries;" and that he hath much ado to forbear saying, "The Lord rebuke thee." How he doth forbear it, having so expressed the frame of his heart towards me, others will judge. The Searcher of all hearts knows that I had no design to cast dirt on him, or any other godly man's ministry in England. Might not another answer have been returned without this wrath? This is so, or it is not so, in reference to the ministry of this nation. If it be not so, and they plead not their successive ordination from Rome, there is an end of this difference. If it be so, can Mr C. hardly refrain from calling a man Satan for speaking the truth? It is well if we know of what spirit we are.

But let us a little farther consider his answer in that place. He asketh first, "Why may not this be a sufficient foundation for their ministry as well as for their baptism?" If it be so, and be so acknowledged, whence is that great provocation that arose from my inquiry after it? For my part, I must tell him that I judge their baptism good and valid, but, to deal clearly with him, not on that foundation. I cannot believe that that idolater, murderer, man of sin, has had, since the days of his open idolatry, persecution, and enmity to Christ, any authority, more or less, from the Lord Jesus committed to him in or over his churches. But he adds, secondly, that "had they received their ordination from the woman flying into the wilderness, the two witnesses, or Waldenses, it had been all one to me and my party; for they had not their ordination from the people (except some extraordinary cases), but from a presbytery, according to the institution of Christ." So, then, ordination by a presbytery is, it seems, opposed by me and my party. But I pray, sir, who told you so? When, wherein, by what means, have I opposed it? I acknowledge myself of no party. I am sorry so grave a minister should suffer himself to be thus transported, that every answer, every reply, must be a reflection, and that without due observation of truth and love. That those first reformers had their ordination from the people is acknowledged; I have formerly evinced it by undeniable testimony: so that the proper succession of a ministry amongst the churches that are their offspring runs up no higher than that rise. Now, the good Lord bless them in their ministry, and the successive ordination they enjoy, to bring forth more fruit in the earth, to the praise of his glorious grace! But upon my disclaiming all thoughts of rejecting the ministry of all those who yet hold their ordination on the account of its successive derivation from Rome, he cries out, "Egregiam vero laudem!" and says, "that yet I secretly derive their pedigree from Rome." Well, then, he doth not so. Why, then, what need these exclamations? We are as to this matter wholly agreed. Nor shall I at present farther pursue his discourse in that place; it is almost totally composed and made up of scornful revilings, reflections, and such other ingredients of the whole.

He frequently and very positively affirms, without the least hesitation, that I have "renounced my own ordination;" and adds hereunto, that "whatever else they pretend, unless they renounce their ordination, nothing will please me;" and that "I condemn all other churches in the world as no churches." But who, I pray, told him these things? Did he inquire so far after my mind in them as, without breach of charity, to be able to make such positive and express assertions concerning them? A good part of his book is taken up in the repetition of such things as these, drawing inferences and conclusions from the suppositions of them, and warming himself by them into a great contempt of myself and "party," as he calls them. I am now necessitated to tell him that all these things are false, and utterly, in part and in whole, untrue, and that he is not able to prove any one of them. And whether this kind of dealing becomes a minister of the gospel, a person professing godliness, I leave it to himself to judge. For my own part, I must confess that as yet I was never so dealt withal by any man, of what party soever, although it hath been my unhappiness to provoke many of them. I do not doubt but that he will be both troubled and ashamed when he shall review these things. That whole chapter which he entitles, "Independentism is Donatism," as to his application of it unto me or any of my persuasion, is of the same importance, as I have sufficiently already evinced. I might instance in sundry other particulars, wherein he ventures, without the least check or supposition, to charge me with what he pleaseth that may serve the turn in hand. So that it may serve to bring in, "He and his party are schismatics, are sectaries, have separated from the church of God, are the cause of all our evils and troubles," with the like terms of reproach and hard censures, lying in a fair subserviency to a design of widening the difference between us, and mutually exasperating the spirits of men professing the gospel of Jesus Christ one against another, nothing almost comes amiss. His sticking upon by-matters, diverting from the main business in hand, answering arguments by reflections, and the like, might also be remarked. One thing wherein he much rejoiceth, and fronts his book with the discovery he hath made of it,—namely, concerning my change of judgment as to the difference under present debate, which is the substance and design of his appendix,—must be particularly considered, and shall be, God assisting, in the next chapter accordingly.

CHAPTER II.

An answer to the appendix of Mr C.'s charge.

THOUGH, perhaps, impartial men will be willing to give me an acquitment from the charge of altering my judgment in the matters of our present difference, upon the general account of the co-partnership with me of the most inquiring men in this generation, as to things of no less importance; and though I might, against this reverend brother, and others of the same mind and persuasion with him, at present relieve myself sufficiently by a recrimination in reference to their former episcopal engagements, and sundry practices in the worship of God them attending; pleading in the meantime the general issue of changing from error to truth (which that I have done as to any change I have really made, I am ready at any time to maintain to this author): yet it being so much insisted upon by him as it is, and the charge thereof, in the instance given, accompanied with so many evil surmisings and uncharitable reflections, looking like the fruits of another principle than that whereby we ought in the management of our differences to be ruled, I shall give a more particular account of that which hath yielded him this great advantage. The sole instance insisted on by him is a small treatise, published long ago by me, entitled, "The Duty of Pastors and People Distinguished," wherein I profess myself to be of the presbyterian judgment. " Excerpta" out of that treatise, with animadversions and comparisons thereon, make up the appendix, which was judged necessary to be added to the book, to help on with the proof that Independency is a great schism. Had it not been, indeed, needful to cause the person to suffer as well as the thing, some suppose this pains might have been spared. But I am not to prescribe to any what way it is meet for them to proceed in for the compassing of their ends aimed at. The best is, here is no new thing produced, but what the world hath long since taken notice of, and made of it the worst they can. Neither am I troubled that I have a necessity laid upon me to give an account of this whole matter. That little treatise was written by me in the year 1643, and then printed: however, it received the addition of a year in the date affixed to it by the printers; which, for their own advantage, is a thing usual with them. I was then a young man myself, about the age of twenty-six or twenty-seven years. The controversy between Independency and Presbytery was young also, nor, indeed, by me clearly understood, especially as stated on the congregational side. The conceptions delivered in the treatise were not (as appears in the issue) suited to the opinion of

ANSWER TO THE APPENDIX OF MR C.'S CHARGE.   223

the one party nor of the other, but were such as occurred to mine own naked consideration of things, with relation to some differences that were then upheld in the place where I lived. Only, being unacquainted with the congregational way, I professed myself to own the other party, not knowing but that my principles were suited to their judgment and profession, having looked very little farther into those affairs than I was led by an opposition to Episcopacy and ceremonies. Upon a review of what I had there asserted, I found that my principles were far more suited to what is the judgment and practice of the congregational men than those of the presbyterian. Only, whereas I had not received any farther clear information in these ways of the worship of God, which since I have been engaged in, as was said, I professed myself of the presbyterian judgment, in opposition to democratical confusion; and, indeed, so I do still, and so do all the congregational men in England that I am acquainted withal. So that when I compare what then I wrote with my present judgment, I am scarce able to find the least difference between the one and the other; only, a misapplication of names and things by me gives countenance to this charge. Indeed, not long after, I set myself seriously to inquire into the controversies then warmly agitated in these nations. Of the congregational way I was not acquainted with any one person, minister or other; nor had I, to my knowledge, seen any more than one in my life. My acquaintance lay wholly with ministers and people of the presbyterian way. But sundry books being published on either side, I perused and compared them with the Scripture and one another, according as I received ability from God. After a general view of them, as was my manner in other controversies, I fixed on one to take under peculiar consideration and examination, which seemed most methodically and strongly to maintain that which was contrary, as I thought, to my present persuasion. This was Mr Cotton's book of the Keys. The examination and confutation hereof, merely for my own particular satisfaction, with what diligence and sincerity I was able, I engaged in. What progress I made in that undertaking I can manifest unto any by the discourses on that subject and animadversions on that book, yet abiding by me. In the pursuit and management of this work, quite beside and contrary to my expectation, at a time and season wherein I could expect nothing on that account but ruin in this world, without the knowledge or advice of, or conference with, any one person of that judgment, I was prevailed on to receive that and those principles which I had thought to have set myself in an opposition unto. And, indeed, this way of impartial examining all things by the word, comparing causes with causes and things with things, laying aside all prejudicate respects unto persons or present traditions, is a course that I would admonish all to beware of who would avoid the danger of being made Independents. I cannot, indeed, deny but that it was possible I was advantaged in the disquisition of the truth I had in hand from my former embracing of the principles laid down in the treatise insisted on. Now, being by this means settled in the truth, which I am ready to maintain to this reverend and learned author, if he or any other suppose they have any advantage hereby against me as to my reputation,—which alone is sought in such attempts as this,—or if I am blamably liable to the charge of inconstancy and inconsistency with my own principles, which he thought meet to front his book withal, hereupon I shall not labour to divest him of his apprehension, having abundant cause to rejoice in the rich grace of a merciful and tender Father, that, men seeking occasion to speak evil of so poor a worm, tossed up and down in the midst of innumerable temptations, I should be found to fix on that which I know will be found my rejoicing in the day of the Lord Jesus.

I am necessitated to add somewhat also to a surmise of this reverend man, in reference to my episcopal compliances in former days, and strict observation of their canons. This, indeed, I should not have taken notice of, but that I find others besides this author pleasing themselves with this apprehension, and endeavouring an advantage against the truth I profess thereby. How little some of my adversaries are like to gain by branding this as a crime is known; and I profess I know not the conscience that is exercised in this matter. But to deliver them once for all from involving themselves in the like unchristian procedure hereafter, let them now know, what they might easily have known before, namely, that this accusation is false, a plain calumny,—a lie. As I was bred up from my infancy under the care of my father, who was a Nonconformist all his days, and a painful labourer in the vineyard of the Lord, so ever since I came to have any distinct knowledge of the things belonging to the worship of God, I have been fixed in judgment against that which I am calumniated withal; which is notoriously known to all that have had any acquaintance with me. What advantage this kind of proceeding is like to bring to his own soul or the cause which he manageth, I leave to himself to judge.

Thus, in general, to take a view of some particular passages in the appendix destined to this good work: The first section tries, with much wit and rhetoric, to improve the pretended alteration of judgment to the blemishing of my reputation, affirming it to be from truth to error; which, as to my particular, so far as it shall appear I am concerned (I am little moved with the bare affirmation of men, especially if induced to it by their interest), I desire him to let me know when and where I may personally wait upon. him to be convinced of it. In the meantime, so much for that section. In the second, he declares what my judgment was in that treatise about the distance between pastors and people, and of the extremes that some men on each hand run into; and I now tell him that I am of the same mind still, so that that note hath little availed him. In the third, he relates what I delivered, "That a man not solemnly called to the office of the ministry, by any outward call, might do, as to the preaching of the gospel in a collapsed church-state." Unto this he makes sundry objections,—that my discourse is dark, not clear, and the like; but remembering that his business was not to confute that treatise only, but to prove from it my inconstancy and inconsistency with myself, he says I am changed from what I then delivered. This is denied; I am punctually of the same judgment still. But he proves the contrary by a double argument :—1. " Because I have renounced my ordination ;" 2. " Because I think now, that not only in a complete church-state, but when no such thing can be charged, gifts and consent of the people are enough to make a man a preacher in office;"—both untrue and false in fact. I profess I am astonished to think with what frame of spirit, what neglect of all rules of truth and love, this business is managed. In the fourth section, he chargeth me to have delivered somewhat in that treatise about the personal indwelling of the Holy Ghost in believers; and my words to that purpose are quoted at large. What then ? am I changed in this also? No; but "that is an error, in the judgment of all that be orthodox." But that is not the business in hand, but the alteration of my judgment ; wherefore he makes a kind of exposition upon my words in that treatise, to show that I was not then of the mind that I have now delivered myself to be of in my book of schism. But I could easily answer the weakness of his exceptions and pretended expositions of my former assertions, and evidence my consistency in judgment with myself in this business ever since. But this, he saith, is an error which he gathered out of my book of schism; and somebody hath sent him word from Oxford that I preached the same doctrine at St Mary's. I wish his informer had never more deceived him. It is most true I have done so, and since printed at large what then I delivered, with sundry additions thereunto ; and if this reverend author shall think good to examine what I have published on that account (not in the way in this treatise proceeded in, which in due time will be abhorred of himself and all good men, but with candour, and a spirit of Christian ingenuity and meekness), I shall acknowledge myself obliged to him. And, in the meantime, I desire him to be cautious of large expressions concerning all the orthodox, to oppose that opinion, seeing evidences of the contrary lie at hand in great plenty; and let him learn from hence how little his insulting in his book on this account is to be valued. Sect. 5, he shows that I then proved "the name of priests not to be proper, or to be ascribed to the ministers of the gospel; but that now" (as is supposed in scorn) "I call the ministers of their particular congregations parochial priests." Untrue! In the description of the pre-latical church, I showed what they esteemed and called "parish ministers" amongst them. I never called the presbyterian ministers of particular congregations "parochial priests." Love, truth, and peace; these things ought not thus to be. Sect. 6, he labours to find some difference in the tendency of several expressions in that treatise; which is not at all to the purpose in hand, nor true, as will appear to any that shall read the treatise itself. In sect. 7–11, he takes here and there a sentence out of the treatise and examines it, interlacing his discourse with untrue reflections, surmises, and prog-nostications, and in particular, pp. 238, 239. But what doth all this avail him in reference to his design in hand? Not only before, but even since his exceptions to the things then delivered, I am of the same mind that I was, without the least alteration; and in the reviewing of what I had then asserted, I find nothing strange to me but the sad discovery of what frame of spirit the charge proceeded from. Sect. 12 doth the whole work; there I acknowledge myself to be of the presbyterian judgment, and not of the independent or congregational! Had this reverend author thought meet to have confined his charge to this one quotation, he had prevented much evil that spreads itself over the rest of his discourse, and yet have attained the utmost of what he can hope for from the whole; and hereof I have already given an account. But he will yet proceed, and, sect. 13, inform his reader that in that treatise I aver that two things are required in a teacher, as to formal ministerial teaching,— 1. Gifts from God; 2. Authority from the church. Well! what then? I am of the same mind still. But now "I cry down ordination by presbytery." "What! and is not this a great alteration and sign of inconstancy?" Truly, sir, there is more need of humiliation in yourself than triumphing against me, for the assertion is most un-true, and your charge altogether groundless; which I desire you would be satisfied in, and not be led any more, by evil surmises, to wrong me and your own soul. He adds, sect. 14, two cautions, which in that treatise I give to private Christians in the exercise of their gifts; and closeth the last of them with a juvenile epiphonema, divinely spoken, and like a true Presbyterian. And yet there is not one word in either of these cautions that I do not still own and allow; which confirms the unhappiness of the charge. Of all that is substantial in any thing that follows, I affirm the same as to all that which is gone before. Only, as to the liberty to be allowed unto them which meet in private, who cannot in conscience join in the celebration of public ordinances as they are performed amongst us, I confess myself to be otherwise minded at present than the words there quoted by this author do express. But this is nothing to the difference between Presbytery and Independency. And he that can glory that in fourteen years he hath not altered or improved in his conception of some things of no greater importance than that mentioned shall not have me for his rival. And this is the sum of Mr C.'s appendix; the discourse whereof being carried on with such a temper of spirit as it is, and suited to the advantage aimed at by so many evil surmises, false suggestions, and uncharitable reflections, I am persuaded the taking of that pains will one day be no joy of heart unto him.

CHAPTER III.

A review of the charger's preface.

His first chapter consists, for the most part, in a repetition of my words, or so much of the discourse of my first chapter as he could wrest, by cutting off one and another parcel of it from its coherence in the whole, with the interposure of glosses of his own, to serve him to make biting reflections upon them with whom he hath to deal. How unbecoming such a course of procedure is for a person of his worth, gravity, and profession, perhaps his δεύτεραι φροντίδες have by this time convinced him. If men have a mind to perpetuate controversies unto an endless, fruitless reciprocation of words and cavils; if to provoke to easy and facile retortions, if to heighten and aggravate differences beyond any hope of reconciliation,—they may do well to deal after this manner with the writings of one another. Mr C. knows how easy it were to make his own words dress him up in all those ornaments wherein he labours to make me appear in the world, by such glosses, inversions, additions, and interpositions, as he is pleased to make use of; but "meliora speramus." Such particulars as seem to be of any importance to our business in hand may be remarked as we pass through it. Page 1, he tells us the Donatists had two principles,—"1. That they were the only church of Christ, in a corner of Africa; and left no church in the world but their own. 2. That none were truly baptized, or entered members of the church of Christ, but by some minister of their party." These principles, he says, are again improved by men of another party, whom, though yet he name not, it is evident whom he intends; and, p. 3, he requires my judgment of those principles.

Because I would not willingly be wanting in any thing that may tend to his satisfaction, though I have some reason to conjecture at my unhappiness in respect of the event, I shall with all integrity give him my thoughts of the principles expressed above.

Then, if they were considered in reference to the Donatists, who owned them, I say they were wicked, corrupt, erroneous principles, tending to the disturbance of the communion of saints, and everting all the rules of love that our Lord Jesus Christ hath given to his disciples and servants to observe. If he intend my judgment of them in reference to the churches of England which he calls Independent, I am sorry that he should think he hath any reason to make this inquiry. I know not that man in the world who is less concerned in obtaining countenance to those principles than I am. Let them who are so ready, on all occasions or provocations, to cast abroad the solemn forms of reproach, " schismatics," " sectaries," " heretics," and the like, search their own hearts as to a conformity of spirit unto these principles. It is not what men say, but what men do, that they shall be judged by. As the Donatists were not the first who in story were charged with schism, no more was their schism confined to Africa. The agreement of multitudes in any [evil] principles makes it in itself not one whit better, and in effect worse. For my part, I acknowledge the churches in England, Scotland, and France, Helvetia, the Netherlands, Germany, Greece, Muscovia, etc., as far as I know of them, to be true churches. Such, for aught I know, may be in Italy or Spain; and what pretence or colour this reverend person hath to fix a contrary persuasion upon me, with so many odious imputations and reflections of being " one of the restorers of all lost churches," and the like, I profess I know not. These things will not be peace in the latter end. "Shall the sword devour for ever?" I dare not suppose that he will ask, Why then do I separate from them? He hath read my book of schism, wherein I have undeniably proved that I separated from none of them; and I am loath to say, though I fear before the close of my discourse I shall be compelled to it, that this reverend author hath answered a matter before he understood it, and confuted a book whose main and chief design he did not once apprehend. The rest of this chapter is composed of reflections upon me from my own words, wrested at his pleasure, and added to according to the purpose in hand, and the taking for granted unto that end that they are in the right, we in the wrong; that their churches are true churches, and yet not esteemed so by me; that we have separated from those churches; with such like easy suppositions. He is troubled that I thought the mutual chargings of each other with schism between the Presbyterians and Independents was as to its heat abated, and ready to vanish; wherein he hath invincibly compelled me to acknowledge my mistake: and I assure him I am heartily sorry that I was mistaken; it will not be somebody's joy one day that I was so. He seems to be offended with my notion of schism, because, if it be true, it will carry it almost out of the world, and bless the churches with everlasting peace. He tells me that a learned doctor said "my book was one great schism." I hope that is but one doctor's opinion, because, being nonsense, it is not fit it should be entertained by many. In the process of his discourse he culls out sundry passages, delivered by me in reference to the great divisions and differences that are in the world among men professing the name of Christ, and applies them to the difference between the Presbyterians and Independents, with many notable lashes in his way, when they were very little in my thoughts; nor are the things spoken by me in any tolerable measure applicable to them. I suppose no rational man will expect that I should follow our reverend author in such ways and paths as these; it were easy, in so doing, to enter into an endless maze of words to little purpose, and I have no mind to deal with him as he hath done by me. I like not the copy so well as to write by it. So his first chapter is discussed and forgiven.

CHAPTER IV.

Of the nature of schism.

THE second chapter of my book, whose examination this author undertakes in the second of his, containing the foundation of many inferences that ensue, and in particular of that description of schism which he intends to oppose, it might have been expected that he should not have culled out passages at his pleasure to descant upon, but either have transcribed the whole, or at least under one view have laid down clearly what I proposed to confirmation, that the state of the controversy being rightly formed, all might understand what we say and whereof we do affirm. But he thought better of another way of procedure, which I am now bound to allow him in; the reason whereof he knows, and other men may conjecture.

The first words he fixes on are the first of the chapter, "The thing whereof we treat being a disorder in the instituted worship of God." Whereunto he replies, "It is an ill sign or omen, to stumble at the threshold in going out. These words are ambiguous, and may have a double sense; either that schism is to be found in matter of instituted worship only, or only in the differences made in the time of celebrating instituted worship; and neither of these is yet true or yet proved, and so a mere begging of the thing in question: for," saith he, " schism may be in and about other matter besides instituted worship."

What measure I am to expect for the future from this entrance or beginning is not hard to conjecture. The truth is, the reverend author understood me not at all in what I affirmed. I say not that schism in the church is either about instituted worship or only in the time of worship, but that the thing I treat of is a disorder in the instituted worship of God; and so it is, if the being and constitution of any church be a part of God's worship. But when men are given to disputing, they think it incumbent on them to question every word and expression that may possibly give them an advantage. But we must, now we are engaged, take all in good part as it comes.

Having, nextly, granted my request of standing to the sole determination of Scripture in the controversy about the nature of schism, he insists on the Scripture use and notion of the word, according to what I had proposed: only, in the metaphorical sense of the word, as applied unto civil and political bodies, he endeavours to make it appear that it doth not only denote the difference and division that falls among them in judgment, but their secession also into parties; which though he proves not from any of the instances produced, yet that he may not trouble himself any farther in the like kind of needless labour, I do here inform him, that if he suppose that I deny that to be a schism where there is a separation, and that *because there is a separation*, as though schism were in its whole nature exclusive of all separation, and lost its being when separation ensued, he hath taken my mind as rightly as he has done the whole design of my book, and my sense in his first animadversions on this chapter. But yet, because this is not proved, I shall desire him not to make use of it for the future, as though it were so. The first place urged is that of John vii. 43, " There was a schism among the people." It is not pretended that here was any separation. Acts xiv. 4, " The multitude of the city was divided,"—that is, in their judgment about the apostles and their doctrine; but not only so, for οἱ μὲν ἦσαν is spoken of them, which expresses their separation into parties. What weight this new criticism is like to find with others, I know not: for my part, I know the words enforce not the thing aimed at, and the utmost that seems to be intended by that expression is the siding of the multitude, some with one, some with another, whilst they were all in a public commotion; nor doth the context require any more. The same is the case, Acts xxiii. 7, where the Pharisees and Sadducees were divided about Paul, whilst abiding in the place where the sanhedrim sat, being divided into parties long before. And in the testimony cited in my margin for the use of the word in other authors, the author makes even that διεμερίσθησαν εἰς τὰ μέρη to stand in opposition only to ὡμονόησαν,—nor was it any more. There was not among the people of Rome such a separation as to break up the corporation or to divide the government, as is known from the story. The place of his own producing, Acts xix. 9, proves, indeed, that then and there there was a separation; but, as the author confesses in the margin, the word there used to express it hath no relation to σχίσμα. Applied to ecclesiastical things, the reverend author confesses with me that the word is only used in 1 Cor. xi. 18, 19; and, therefore, that from thence the proper use and importance of it is to be learned. Having laid down the use of the word, to denote difference of mind and judgment, with troubles ensuing thereupon, amongst men met in some one assembly, about the compassing of a common end and design, I proceed to the particular accommodation of it to church-rents and schism, in that solitary instance given of it in the church of Corinth. What says our author hereunto? Says he, p. 26, "This is a forestalling the reader's judgment by a mere begging of the thing in question. As it hath in part been proved from the Scripture itself, where it is used for separation into parties in the political use of the word, why it may not so be used in the ecclesiastical sense, I see no reason." But if this be the way of begging the question, I confess I know not what course to take to prove what I intend. Such words are used sometimes in warm disputes causelessly; it were well they were placed where there is some pretence for them. Certainly they will not serve every turn. Before I asserted the use of the word, I instanced in all the places where it is used, and evinced the sense of it from them. If this be begging, it is not that lazy trade of begging which some use, but such as a man had as good professedly work as follow. How well he hath disproved this sense of the word from Scripture we have seen. I am not concerned in his seeing no reason why it may not be used in the ecclesiastical sense, according to his conception; my inquiry was how it was used, not how it might be used in this reverend author's judgment. And this is the substance of all that is offered to overthrow that principle, which, if it abide and stand, he must needs confess all his following pains to be to no purpose, " He sees no reason but it may be as he says!"

After the declaration of some such suspicions of his as we are now wonted unto, and which we cannot deny him the liberty of expressing, though I profess he does it unto my injury, he says, "This is the way, on the one hand, to free all church-separation from schism; and, on the other, to make all particular churches more or less inschismatical." Well, the first is denied; what is offered for the confirmation of the second? Saith he, " What one congregation almost is there in the world where there are not differences of judgment, whence ensue many troubles, about the compassing of one common end and design? I doubt whether his own be free therefrom." If any testimony may remove his scruple, I assure him, through the grace of God, hitherto it hath been so, and I hope it is so with multitudes of other churches; those with whom it is otherwise, it will appear at last to be more or less blamable on the account of schism.

Omitting my farther explication of what I had proposed, he passes unto p. 27 [102] of my book, and thence transcribes these words: " They had differences among themselves about unnecessary things. On these they engaged in disputes and sidings even in their solemn assemblies. Probably much vain jangling, alienation of affections, exasperation of spirit, with a neglect of due offices of love, ensued hereupon." Whereunto he subjoins, " That the apostle charges this upon them is true, but was that all? were there not divisions into parties as well as in judgments? We shall consider that ere long." But I am sorry he hath waived this proper place for the consideration of this important assertion. The truth is, " hic pes figendus," if he remove not this position, he labours in vain for the future. I desire also to know what he intends by " divisions into parties." If he intend that some were of one party, some of another, in these divisions and differences, it is granted; there can be no difference in judgment amongst men, but they must on that account be divided into parties. But if he intend thereby that they divided into several churches, assemblies, or congregations, any of them setting up new churches on a new account, or separating from the public assemblies of the church whereof they were, and that their so doing is reproved by the apostle under the name of schism, then I tell him that this is that indeed whose proof is incumbent on him. Fail he herein, the whole foundation of my discourse continues firm and unshaken. The truth is, I cannot meet with any one attempt to prove this, which alone was to be proved, if he intended that I should be any farther concerned in his discourse than only to find myself reviled and abused.

Passing over what I produce to give light and evidence unto my assertion, he proceeds to the consideration of the observations and inferences I make upon it, p. 29 [103] and onward.

The first he insists upon is, " That the thing mentioned is entirely in one church, amongst the members of one particular society. No mention is there in the least of one church divided against another, or separated from another."

1. To this he replies,—" That the church of Corinth was a collective church, made up of many congregations, and that I myself confess they had solemn assemblies, not one assembly only; that I beg the question, by taking it for one single congregation." But I suppose one particular congregation may have more than one solemn as-

sembly, even as many as are the times wherein they solemnly assemble.

2. I supposed I had proved that it was " only one congregation," that used to assemble in one place, that the apostle charged this crime upon; and that this reverend author was pleased to overlook what was produced to that purpose, I am not to be blamed.

3. Here is another discovery that this reverend person never yet clearly understood the design of my treatise nor the principles I proceed upon. Doth he think it is any thing to my present business whether the church of Corinth were such a church as Presbyterians suppose it to be, or such a one as the Independents affirm it? Whilst all acknowledge it to be one church, be that particular church of what kind it will, if the schism rebuked by the apostle consisted in division in it, and not in separation from it, as such, I have evinced all that I intended by the observation under consideration. Yet this he again pursues, and tells me, that " there were more particular churches in and about Corinth, as that at Cenchrea; and that their differences were not confined to the verge of one church (for there were differences abroad out of the church); and says, that at unawares I confess that they disputed from house to house, and in the public assemblies." But I will assure the reverend author I was aware of what I said. Is it possible he should suppose that by the "verge of one church" I intended the meeting-place, and the assembly therein? Was it at all incumbent on me to prove that they did not manage their differences in private as well as in public? Is it likely any such thing should be? Did I deny that they sided and made parties about their divisions and differences? Is it any thing to me, or to any thing I affirm, how, where, and when, they managed their disputes and debated their controversies? It is true, there is mention of a church at Cenchrea, but is there any mention that that church made any separation from the church of Corinth, or that the differences mentioned were between the members of these several churches? Is it any thing to my present design though there were twenty particular congregations in Corinth, supposing that, on any consideration, they were one church? I assure you, sir, I am more troubled with your not understanding the business and design I manage, than I am with all your reviling terms you have laden me withal.

Once for all, unless you prove that there was a separation from that church of Corinth (be it of what constitution it may by any be supposed), as such, into another church, and that this is reproved by the apostle under the name of schism, you speak not one word to invalidate the principle by me laid down. And for what he adds, " That for what I say, 'There was no one church divided against another, or separated from another,' it is assumed, but not proved, unless by a negative, which is invalid," he wrests my words. I say not there was *no such thing*, but that there was *no mention of any such thing;* for though it be as clear as the noonday that indeed there was no such thing, it sufficeth my purpose that there was no mention of any such thing, and therefore no such thing reproved under the name of schism. With this one observation I might well dismiss the whole ensuing treatise, seeing of how little use it is like to prove as to the business in hand, when the author of it indeed apprehends not the principle which he pretends to oppose. I shall once more tell him, that he abide not in his mistake, that if he intend to evert the principle here by me insisted on, it must be by a demonstration that the schism charged on the Corinthians by Paul consisted in the separation from, and relinquishment of, that church whereof they were members, and congregating into another not before erected or established; for this is that which the reformed churches are charged to do by the Romanists in respect of their churches, and accused of schism thereupon. But the differences which he thinks good to manage and maintain with and against the Independents do so possess the thoughts of this reverend author, that whatever occurs to him is immediately measured by the regard which it seems to bear, or may possibly bear, thereunto, though that consideration were least of all regarded in its proposal.

The next observation upon the former thesis that he takes into his examination, so far as he is pleased to transcribe it, is this: " Here is no mention of any particular man or number of men separating from the assembly of the whole church, or subducting of themselves from its power; only, they had groundless, causeless differences amongst themselves."[1] Hereunto our author variously replies, and says, first, " Was this all? were not separations made, if not from that church, yet in that church, as well as divisions? Let the Scripture determine. 1 Cor. i. 12, iii. 4, ' I am a disciple of Paul,' said one, 'And I a disciple of Apollos,' said another. In our language, ' I am a member of such a minister's congregation,' says one; ' Such a man for my money;' and so a third. And hereupon they most probably separated themselves into such and such congregations; and is not separation the ordinary issue of such envyings?"

I doubt not but that our reverend author supposeth that he hath here spoken to the purpose and matter in hand; and so, perhaps, may some others think also. I must crave leave to enter my dissent upon the account of the ensuing reasons; for,—1. It is not separation *in* the church, by men's divisions and differences, whilst they continue members of the same church, that I deny to be here charged under

---

[1] If the reader turn to p. 103, he will find slight differences between the sentence as originally given and as it stands here. It is given, however, in both instances, according to the original editions of the treatises; and the difference, therefore, does not arise from inaccuracy in the subsequent printing of them.—Ed.

the name of schism, but such a separation *from* the church as was before described. 2. The disputes amongst them about Paul and Apollos, the instruments of their conversion, cannot possibly be supposed to relate unto ministers of distinct congregations among them. Paul and Apollos were not so, and could not be figures of them that were; so that those expressions do not at all answer those which he is pleased to make parallel unto them. 3. Grant all this, yet this proves nothing to the cause in hand. Men may cry up, some the minister of one congregation, some of another, and yet neither of them separate from the one or other, or the congregations themselves fall into any separation. Wherefore, 4. He says, " Probably they separated into such and such congregations." But this is most improbable; for,—(1.) There is no mention at all of those many congregations that are supposed; but rather the contrary, as I have declared, is expressly asserted. (2.) There is no such thing mentioned or intimated; nor, (3.) Are they in the least rebuked for any such thing, though the forementioned differences, which are a less evil, are reproved again and again under the name of schism. So that this most improbable improbability, or rather vain conjecture, is a very mean refuge and retreat from the evidence of express Scripture; which in this place is alone inquired after. Doth, indeed, the reverend author think, will he pretend so to do, that the holy apostle should so expressly, weightily, and earnestly reprove their dissensions in the church whereof they were members, and yet not speak one word or give the least intimation of their separation from the church, had there indeed been any such thing? I dare leave this to the conscience of the most partially addicted person under heaven to the author's cause, who hath any conscience at all; nor dare I dwell longer on the confutation of this fiction, though it be, upon the matter, the whole of what I am to contend withal. But he farther informs us that " there was a separation to parties in the church of Corinth, at least as to one ordinance of the Lord's supper, as appears chap. xi. 18, 20–22; and this was part of their schism, verse 16. And not long after they separated into other churches, slighting and undervaluing the first ministers and churches as nothing, or less pure than their own; which we see practised sufficiently at this day." *Ans.* Were not this the head and seat of the first part of the controversy insisted on, I should not be able to prevail with myself to cast away precious time in the consideration of such things as these, being tendered as suitable to the business in hand. It is acknowledged that there were differences amongst them, and disorders in the administration of the Lord's supper; that therein they used " respect of persons,"—as the place quoted in the margin by our author, James ii. 1–4, manifests that they were ready to do in other places. The disorder the apostle blames in the administration of the ordinance was, "when they came together in the church," 1 Cor. xi. 18, when they "came together in one place," verse 20, there they "tarried not one for another," as they ought, verse 33, but coming unprepared, some having eaten before, some being hungry, verse 21, all things were managed with great confusion amongst them, verse 22. And if this prove not that the schism they were charged withal consisted in a separation from that church with which they came together in one place, we are hopeless of any farther evidence to be tendered to that purpose. That there were disorders amongst them in the celebration of the Lord's supper is certain; that they separated into several congregations on that account, or one from another, or any from all, is not, in the least intimation, signified; but the plain contrary shines in the whole state of things, as there represented. Had that been done, and had so to do been such an evil as is pleaded (as causelessly to do it is no small evil), it had not passed unreproved from him who was resolved, in the things of God, not to "spare" them. 2. That they afterward fell into the separation aimed at to be asserted our reverend author affirms, that so he may make way for a reflection on the things of his present disquietment. But as we are not as yet concerning ourselves in what they did afterward, so when we are, we shall expect somewhat more than bare affirmations for the proof of it, being more than ordinarily confident that he is not able, from the Scripture, nor any other story of credit, to give the least countenance to what he here affirms. But now, as if the matter were well discharged, when there hath not one word been spoken that in the least reaches the case in hand, he saith,—3. "By way of supposition that there was but one single congregation at Corinth, yet," saith he, "the apostle dehorts the brethren from schism, and writes to more than the church of Corinth, chap. i. 2." *Ans.* I have told him before, that though I am full well resolved that there was but one single congregation at Corinth in those days, yet I am not at all convinced, as to the proposition under confirmation, to assert any such thing, but will suppose the church to be of what kind my author pleaseth, whilst he will acknowledge it to be the particular church of Corinth. I confess the apostle dehorts the brethren from schism, even others as well as those at Corinth,—so far as the church of God, in all places and ages, is concerned in his instructions and dehortations,—when they fall under the case stated, parallel with that which is the ground of his dealing with them at Corinth. But what that schism was from which he dehorts them, he declares only in the instance of the church of Corinth; and thence is the measure of it to be taken in reference to all dehorted from it. Unto the third observation added by me he makes no return, but only lays down some exceptions to the exemplification given of the whole matter, in another schism that fell out in that church about forty years after the composure of this, which was the occasion of that excellent epistle unto them from the church of Rome, called the epistle of Clement, dissuading them from persisting in that strife and contention, and pressing them to unity and agreement among themselves. Some things our reverend author offers as to this instance, but so as that I cannot but suppose that he consulted not the epistle on this particular occasion; and therefore now I desire him that he would do so, and I am persuaded he will not a second time give countenance to any such apprehension of the then state of the church, as though there were any separation made from it by any of the members thereof doing or suffering the injury there complained of, about which those differences and contentions arose. I shall not need to go over again the severals of that epistle. One word mentioned by myself, namely, μετηγάγετε, he insists on, and informs us that it implies a separation into other assemblies; which, he says, I waived to understand. I confess I did so in this place; and so would he also, if he had once consulted it. The speech of the church of Rome is there to the church of Corinth, in reference to the elders whom they had deposed. The whole sentence is, Ὁρῶμεν γὰρ ὅτι ἐνίους ὑμεῖς μετηγάγετε καλῶς πολιτευομένους ἐκ τῆς ἀμέμπτως αὐτοῖς τετιμημένης λειτουργίας· and the words immediately going before are, Μακάριοι οἱ προοδοιπορήσαντες πρεσβύτεροι οἵτινες ἔγκαρπον καὶ τελείαν ἔσχον τὴν ἀνάλυσιν, οὐ γὰρ εὐλαβοῦνται μή τις αὐτοὺς μεταστήσῃ ἀπὸ τοῦ ἱδρυμένου αὐτοῖς τόπου· then follows that ὁρῶμεν γάρ. Our author, I suppose, understands Greek, and so I shall spare my pains of transcribing Mr Young's Latin translation, or adding one in English of mine own; and if he be pleased to read these words, I think we shall have no more of his μετηγάγετε.

If a fair opportunity call me forth to the farther management of this controversy, I shall not doubt but from that epistle and some other pieces of undoubted antiquity, as the epistles of the churches of Vienne and Lyons, of Smyrna, with some public records of those days, as yet preserved (worthy all of them to be written in letters of gold), to evince that state of the churches of Christ in those days, as will give abundant light to the principles I proceed upon in this whole business.

And thus have I briefly vindicated what was proposed as the precise Scripture notion of schism; against which, indeed, not any one objection hath been raised that speaks directly to the thing in hand. Our reverend author being full of warm affections against the Independents, and exercised greatly in disputing the common principles which either they hold or are supposed so to do, measures every thing that is spoken by his apprehension of those differences wherein, as he thinks, their concernment doth lie. Had it not been for some such prejudice (for I am unwilling to ascribe it to more blamable principles), it would have been almost impossible that he should have once imagined that he had made the least attempt towards the eversion of what I had asserted, much less that he had made good the title of his book, though he scarce forgets it, or any thing concerning it but its *proof*, in any one whole leaf of his treatise. It remains, then, that the nature and notion of schism, as revealed and described in the Scripture, was rightly fixed in my former discourse; and I must assure this reverend author that I am not affrighted from the embracing and maintaining of it with those scare-crows of "new light," "singularity," and the like, which he is pleased frequently to set up to that purpose. The discourse that ensues in our author concerning a parity of reason, to prove that if that be schism, then much more is separation so, shall afterward, if need be, be considered, when I proceed to show what yet farther may be granted without the least prejudice of truth, though none can necessitate me to recede from the precise notion of the name and thing delivered in the Scripture. I confess I cannot but marvel that any man undertaking the examination of that treatise, and expressing so much indignation at the thoughts of my discourse that lieth in this business, should so slightly pass over that whereon he knew I laid the great weight of the whole. Hath he so much as endeavoured to prove that that place to the Corinthians is not the only place wherein there is, in the Scripture, any mention of schism in an ecclesiastical sense, or that the church of Corinth was not a particular church? Is any thing of importance offered to impair the assertion, that the evil reproved was within the verge of that church, and without separation from it? And do I need any more to make good to the utmost that which I have asserted? But of these things afterward.

In all that follows to the end of this chapter, I meet with nothing of importance that deserves farther notice. That which is spoken is for the most part built upon mistakes; as, that when I speak of a member or the members of one particular church, I intend only one single congregation, exclusively to any other acceptation of that expression, in reference to the apprehension of others; that I deny the reformed churches to be true churches, because I deny the church of Rome to be so, and deny the institution of a national church, which yet our author pleads not for. He would have it for granted that because schism consists in a difference among church-members, therefore he that raises such a difference, whether he be a member of that church wherein the difference is raised, or of any other, or no (suppose he be a Mohammedan or a Jew), is a schismatic; pleads for the old definition of schism, as suitable to the Scripture, after the whole foundation of it is taken away; wrests many of my expressions,—as that in particular, in not making the matter of schism to be things relating to the worship of God,—to needless discourses about doctrine and discipline, not apprehending what I intended by that expression, of "the worship of God;" and I suppose it not advisable to follow him in such extravagancies. The usual aggravations of schism he thought good to re-enforce; whether he hoped that I would dispute with him about them I cannot tell. I shall now assure him that I will not, though, if I may have his good leave to say so, I lay much more weight on those insisted on by myself, wherein I am encouraged by his approbation of them.

CHAPTER V.

THE third chapter of my treatise, consisting in the preventing and removing such objections as the precedent discourse might seem liable and obnoxious unto, is proposed to examination by our reverend author in the third chapter of his book, and the objections mentioned undertaken to be managed by him; with what success, some few considerations will evince.

The first objection by me proposed was taken from the common apprehension of the nature of schism, and the issue of stating it as by me laid down,—namely, hence it would follow that the "separation of any man or men from a true church, or of one church from others, is not schism." But now waiving, for the present, the more large consideration of the name and thing,—which yet in the process of my discourse I do condescend upon, according to the principle laid down,—I say that, in the precise signification of the word, and description of the thing as given by the Holy Ghost, this is true. No such separation is in the Scripture so called, or so accounted: whether it may not in a large sense be esteemed as such, I do not dispute; yea, I afterward grant it so far as to make that concession the bottom and foundation of my whole plea for the vindication of the reformed churches from that crime. Our reverend author re-enforces the objection by sundry instances: as,—1. "That he hath disproved that sense or precise signification of the word in Scripture;" how well, let the reader judge. 2. "That supposing that to be the only sense mentioned in that case of the Corinthians, yet may another sense be intimated in Scripture, and deduced by regular and rational consequence." Perhaps this will not be so easy an undertaking, this being the only place where the name is mentioned or thing spoken of in an ecclesiastical sense; but when any proof is tendered of what is here affirmed, we shall attend unto it. It is said, indeed, that "if separation in judgment in a church be a schism, much more to separate from a church." But our question is about the precise notion of the word in Scripture, and consequences from thence, not about consequents from the nature of things; concerning which, if our author had been pleased to have stayed a while, he would have found me granting as much as he could well desire. 3. 1 John ii. 19 is sacrificed, ἀμετρίᾳ τῆς ἀνθολκῆς, and interpreted of schism; where (to make one venture in imitation of our author) all orthodox interpreters and writers of controversies expound it of apostasy, neither will the context or arguing of the apostle admit of another exposition. Men's wresting of Scripture to give countenance to inveterate errors is one of their worst concomitants. So, then, that separation from churches is oftentimes evil is readily granted. Of what nature that evil is, with what are the aggravations of it, a judgment is to be made from the pleas and pretences that its circumstances afford. So far as it proceeds from such dissensions as before were mentioned, so far it proceeds from schism; but in its own nature, absolutely considered, it is not so.

To render my former assertions the more unquestionably evident, I consider the several accounts given of men's blamable departures from any church or churches mentioned in Scripture, and manifest that none of them come under the head of schism. "Apostasy, irregularity of walking, and professed sensuality," are the heads whereinto all blamable departures from the churches in the Scripture are referred.

That there are other accounts of this crime our author doth not assert; he only says, that "all or some of the places" I produce as "instances of a blamable separation from a church do mind the nature of schism as precedaneous to the separation." Whatever the matter is, I do not find him speaking so faintly and with so much caution through his whole discourse as in this place: "All or some do it; they mind the nature of schism; they mind it as precedaneous to the separation." So the sum of what he aims at in contesting about the exposition of those places of Scripture is this: "Some of them do mind" (I know not how) "the nature of schism, which he never once named as precedaneous to separation; therefore, the precise notion of schism in the Scripture doth not denote differences and divisions in a church only." "Quod erat demonstrandum." That I should spend time in debating a consideration so remote from the state of the controversy in hand, I am sure will not be expected by such as understand it.

Page 77 [p. 122] of my treatise I affirm, "That for a man to withdraw or withhold himself from the communion external and visible of any church or churches, on the pretension or plea, be it

true or otherwise, that the worship, doctrine, or discipline instituted
by Christ is corrupted among them, with which corruption he dares
not defile himself, it is nowhere in the Scripture called schism; nor is
that case particularly exemplified or expressly supposed, whereby a
judgment may be made of the fact at large, but we are left upon the
whole matter to the guidance of such general rules and principles as
are given us for that end and purpose." Such is my meanness of
apprehension, that I could not understand but that either this assertion must be subscribed unto as of irrefragable verity, or else that instances to the contrary must have been given out of the Scripture;
for on that hinge alone doth this present controversy (and that by
consent) turn itself. But our reverend author thinks good to take
another course (for which his reasons may easily be conjectured), and
excepts against the assertion itself in general, first, as "ambiguous
and fallacious," and then also intimates that he will scan the words in
particular. " Mihi jussa capessere [fas est]." 1. He says that " I tell
not whether a man may separate where there is corruption in some
one of these only, or in all of them; nor, 2. How far some or all of
these must be corrupted before we separate." *Ans.* This is no small
vanity under the sun, that men will not only measure themselves by
themselves, but others also by their own measure. Our author is
still with his finger in the sore, and therefore supposes that others
must needs take the same course. Is there any thing in my assertion whether a man may separate from any church or no? any thing
upon what corruption he may lawfully so do? any thing of stating
the difference betwixt the Presbyterians and Independents? do I at
all fix it on this foot of account when I come so to do? I humbly
beg of this author, that if I have so obscurely and intricately delivered myself and meaning that he cannot come to the understanding of my design nor import of my expressions, he would favour me
with a command to explain myself before he engage into a public
refutation of what he doth not so clearly apprehend. Alas! I do not
in this place in the least intend to justify any separation, nor to
show what pleas are sufficient to justify a separation, nor what corruption in the church separated from is necessary thereunto, nor at
all regard the controversy his eye is always on; but only declare what
is not comprised in the precise Scripture notion of schism, as also
how a judgment is to be made of that which is so by me excluded,
whether it be good or evil. Would he have been pleased to have
spoken to the business in hand, or any thing to the present purpose,
it must not have been by an inquiry into the grounds and reasons
of separation, how far it may be justified by the plea mentioned, or
how far not; when that plea is to be allowed, and when rejected;
but this only was incumbent on him to prove,—namely, that such a

separation upon that plea, or the like, is called schism in the Scripture, and as such a thing condemned. What my concernment is in the ensuing observations, that " the Judaical church was as corrupt as ours,—that if a bare plea, true or false, will serve to justify men, all separatists may be justified," he himself will easily perceive. But, however, I cannot but tell him by the way, that he who will dogmatize in this controversy from the Judaical church, and the course of proceedings amongst them, to the direction and limitation of duty as to the churches of the gospel,—considering the vast and important differences between the constitutions of the one and the other, with the infallible obligation to certain principles, on the account of the typical institution in that primitive church, when there neither was nor could be any more in the world,—must expect to bring other arguments to compass his design than the analogy pretended. [As] for the justification of separatists of the reason, if it will ensue upon the examination for separation, and the circumstances of the separating, whereunto I refer them, let it follow, and let who will complain.

But to fill up the measure of the mistake he is engaged in, he tells us, p. 75, that " this is the pinch of the question, whether a man or a company of men may separate from a true church, upon a plea of corruption in it, true or false, and set up another church as to ordinances, renouncing that church to be a true church. This," saith he, " is plainly our case at present with the doctor and his associates." Truly, I do not know that ever I was necessitated to a more sad and fruitless employment in this kind of labour and travail. Is that the question in present agitation? is any thing, word, tittle, or iota spoken to it? Is it my present business to state the difference between the Presbyterians and Independents? Do I anywhere do it upon this account? Do I not everywhere positively deny that there is any such separation made? Nay, can common honesty allow such a state of a question, if that were the business in hand, to be put upon me? Are their ordinances and churches so denied by me as is pretended? What I have often said must again be repeated: the reverend author hath his eye so fixed on the difference between the Presbyterians and the Independents, that he is at every turn led out of the way, into such mistakes as it was not possible he should otherwise be overtaken withal. This is, perhaps, " mentis gratissimus error;" but I hope it would be no death to him to be delivered from it. When I laid down the principles which it was his good will to oppose, I had many things under consideration as to the settling of conscience in respect of manifold oppositions, and, to tell him the truth, least valued that which he is pleased to manage and to look upon as my sole intendment. If it be not possible to deliver him from this strong imagination, that carries the images and species of

Independency always before his eyes, we shall scarce speak "ad idem" in this whole discourse. I desire, then, that he would take notice, that as the state of the controversy he proposes doth no more relate to that which peculiarly is pretended to lie under his consideration than any other thing whatever that he might have mentioned; so when the peculiar difference between him and the Independents comes to be managed, scarce any one term of his state will be allowed.

Exceptions are, in the next place, attempted to be put in to my assertion, that there is no example in the Scripture of any one church's departure from the union which they ought to hold with others, unless it be in some of their departures from the common faith, which is not schism; much with the same success as formerly. Let him produce one instance, and " en herbam."[1] I grant the Roman church, on a supposition that it is a church (which yet I utterly deny), to be a *schismatical* church, upon the account of the *intestine divisions* of all sorts; on what other accounts other men urge them with the same guilt, I suppose he knows by this that I am not concerned. Having finished this exploit, because I had said " *if* I were unwilling I did not understand how I might be compelled to carry on the notion of schism any farther," he tells me, " though I be unwilling, he doubts not but to be able to compel me." But who told him I was unwilling so to do? Do I not immediately, without any compulsion, very freely fall upon the work? Did I say I was unwilling? Certainly it ought not to be thus. Of his abilities in other things I do not doubt; in this discourse he is pleased to exercise more of something else.

There is but one passage more that needs to be remarked, and so this chapter also is dismissed. He puts in a caveat, that I limit not schism to the worship of God, upon these words of mine: " The consideration of what sort of union in reference to the worship of God" (where he inserts in the repetition, " mark that!"), " as instituted by Jesus Christ, is the foundation of what I have farther to offer;" whereto he subjoins, " The design of this is, that he may have a fair retreat when he is charged with breach of union in other respects, and so with schism, to escape by this evasion. This breach of union is not in reference to the worship of God in one assembly met to that end." I wish we had once an end of these mistakes and false, uncharitable surmises. By the " worship of God" I intend the whole compass of institutions, and their tendency thereunto; and I know that I speak properly enough. In so doing I have no such design as I am charged withal, nor do I need it. I walk not in fear of this author's forces, that I should be providing beforehand to secure my retreat. I have passed the bounds of the precise notion of schism before insisted on, and yet doubt not but, God assisting, to make

---

[1] " I am cast to the ground, I own myself conquered."—Ed.

good my ground.   If he judge I cannot, let him command my *personal attendance* on him at any time, to be driven from it by him. Let him by any means prove against me, at any time, a breach of any union instituted by Jesus Christ, and I will promise him that with all speed I will retreat from that state or thing whereby I have so done.   I must profess to this reverend author that I like not the cause he manages one whit the better for the way whereby he manageth it.   We had need watch and pray that we be not led into temptation, seeing we are in some measure not ignorant of the devices of Satan.

Now, that he may see this door of escape shut up, that so he may not need to trouble himself any more in taking care lest I escape that way, when he intends to fall upon me with those blows, which as yet I have not felt, I shall shut it fast myself, beyond all possibility of my opening it again.   I here, then, declare unto him, that whenever he shall prove that I have broken any union of the institution of Jesus Christ, of what sort soever, I will not, in excuse of myself, insist on the plea mentioned, but will submit to the discipline which shall be thought meet by him to be exercised towards any one offending in that kind.   Yet truly, on this engagement, I would willingly contract with him, that in his next reply he should not deal with me as he hath done in this, neither as to my person nor as to the differences between us.

CHAPTER VI.

HAVING declared and vindicated the Scripture proper notion of schism, and thence discovered the nature of it, with all its aggravations, with the mistakes that men have run into who have suited their apprehensions concerning it unto what was their interests to have it thought to be, and opened a way thereby for the furtherance of peace among professors of the gospel of Jesus Christ; for the farther security of the consciences of men unjustly accused and charged with the guilt of this evil, I proceeded to the consideration of it in the usual common acceptation of the word and thing, that so I might obviate whatever, with any tolerable pretence, is insisted on, as deduced by a parity of reason from what is delivered in the Scripture, in reference to the charge managed by some or other against all sorts of Protestants.   Hereupon I grant that it may be looked on in general as διαίρεσις ἑνότητος, "a breach of union," so that it be granted also that that union be a union of the institution of Jesus Christ.   To find out, then, the nature of schism under the consideration of the condescension made, and to discover wherein the guilt of it doth consist, it is necessary that we find out what that union is, and wherein it doth consist, whereof it is the breach and interruption, or is supposed so to be, over and above the breach above mentioned and described. Now, this union being the union of the church, the several acceptations of the "church" in Scripture are to be investigated, that the union inquired after may be made known. The "church" in Scripture being taken either for the church catholic, or the whole number of elect believers in the world (for we lay aside the consideration of that part of this great family of God which is already in heaven from this distinction), or else for the general visible body of those who profess the gospel of Christ, or for a particular society joining together in the celebration of the ordinances of the New Testament instituted by Christ, to be so celebrated by them, the union of it, with the breach of that union in these several respects, with the application of the whole to the business under consideration, was to be inquired after; which also was performed.

I began with the consideration of the catholic invisible church of Christ, and the union thereof. Having declared the rise of this distinction, and the necessity of it from the nature of the things themselves, as to the matter of this church, or the church of Christ as here militant on earth, I affirm and evince it to be *all and only elect believers.* The union of this church consists in the inhabitation of the same Spirit in all the members of it, uniting them to the head, Christ Jesus, and therein to one another. The breach of this union I manifested to consist in the loss of that Spirit, with all the peculiar consequences and effects of him in the hearts of them in whom he dwells. This I manifest, according to our principles, to be impossible, and upon a supposition of it, how remote it would be from schism, under any notion or acceptation of the word; so closing that discourse with a charge on the Romanists of their distance from an interest in this church of Jesus Christ.

Our reverend author professes that he hath but little to say to these things. Some exceptions he puts in unto some expressions used in the explication of my sense in this particular. That which he chiefly insists upon, is the accommodation of that promise, Matt. xvi. 18, "Upon this rock I will build my church," to the church in this sense; which he concludes to belong to the visible church of professors. Now, as I am not at all concerned, as to the truth of what I am in confirmation of, to which of these it be applied, so I am far from being alone in that application of it to the catholic church which I insist upon. All our divines that from hence prove the perseverance of all individual believers,—as all do that I have met withal who write on that subject,—are of the same mind with me. Moreover, the church is built on this rock in its individuals, or I know not how it is so built. The building on Christ doth not denote a mere relation of a general body to his truth, that it shall always have an existence, but the union of the individuals with him, in their being built on him, to whom the promise is made. I acknowledge it for as unquestionable a truth as any we believe, that Christ hath had, and ever shall have, to the end of the world; a visible number of those that profess his name and subjection to his kingdom, because of the necessary consequence of profession upon believing; but that that truth is intended in this promise, any farther but in respect of this consequence, I am not convinced. And I would be loath to say that this promise is not made to every particular believer, and only unto them, being willing to vindicate to the saints of God all those grounds of consolation which he is so willing they should be made partakers of.

As to the union of this church and the breach of it, our reverend author hath a little to say. Because there may be "some decays in true grace in the members of this church," he affirms, "that in a sort there may be said to be a breach in this union; and so, consequently, a schism in this body." He seemed formerly to be afraid lest all schism should be thrust out of the world; if he can retrieve it on the account of any true believer's failing in grace, or falling for a season, I suppose he needs not fear the loss of it whilst this world continues. But it is fit wise and learned men should take the liberty of calling things by what names they please, so they will be pleased withal not to impose their conceptions and use of terms on them who are not able to understand the reasons of them. It is true, there may be a schism among the members of this church, but not as members of this church, nor with reference to the union thereof. It is granted that schism is the breach of *union*, but not of *every union*, much less not a breach of that, which if it were a breach of, it were not schism. However, by the way, I am bold to tell this reverend author that this doctrine of his concerning schism in the catholic invisible church, by the failing in grace in any of the members of it for a season, is a new notion; which as he cannot justify to us, because it is false, so I wonder how he will justify it to himself, because it is "new." And what hath been obtained by the author against my principles in this chapter I cannot perceive. The nature of the church in the state considered is not opposed; the union asserted not disproved; the breach of that union is denied, as I suppose, no less by him than myself. That the instances that some saints, as members of this church, may sometimes fail in grace, more or less, for some season, and that the members of this church, though not as members of this church, yet on other considerations, may be guilty of schism, concern not the business under debate, himself I hope is satisfied.

CHAPTER VII.

OUR progress, in the next place, is to the consideration of the *catholic church visible.* Who are the members of this church, where-of it is constituted, what is required to make them so, on what ac-count men visibly professing the gospel may be esteemed justly divested of the privilege of being members of this church, with sundry respects of the church in that sense, are in my treatise discussed. The union of this church, that is proper and peculiar unto it as such, I declared to be the profession of the saving doctrines of the gospel, not everted by any of the miscarriages, errors, or oppositions to it, that are there recounted. The breach of this union I manifest to consist in apostasy from the profession of the faith, and so to be no schism, upon whomsoever the guilt of it doth fall; pleading the immunity of the Protestants, as such, from the guilt of the breach of this union, and charging it upon the Romanists, in all the ways whereby it may be broken, an issue is put to that dis-course.

What course our reverend author takes in the examination of this chapter, and the severals of it, wherein the strength of the contro-versy doth lie, is now to be considered. Doth he deny this church to be a collection of all that are duly called Christians in respect of their profession? to be that great multitude who, throughout the world, profess the doctrine of the gospel and subjection to Jesus Christ? Doth he deny the union of this church, or that whereby that great multitude are incorporated into one body as visible and professing, to be the profession of the saving doctrines of the gospel, and of subjection to Jesus Christ according to them? Doth he deny the dissolution of this union, as to the interest of any member by it in the body, to be by apostasy from the profession of the gospel? Doth he charge that apostasy upon those whom he calls Indepen-dents, as such? or if he should, could he tolerably defend his charge? Doth he prove that the breach of this union is, under that formality, properly schism? Nothing less, as far as I can gather. Might not, then, the trouble of this chapter have been spared? Or shall I be necessitated to defend every expression in my book, though nothing at all to the main business under debate, or else Independency must go for "a great schism?" I confess this is a somewhat hard law, and such as I cannot proceed in obedience unto, without acknowledg-ing his ability to compel me to go on farther than I am willing; yet I do it with this engagement, that I will so look to myself, that he shall never have that power over me any more, nor will I, upon any compulsion of useless, needless cavils and exceptions, do so again. So that in his reply he now knows how to order his affairs, so as to be freed from the trouble of a rejoinder.

His first attempt in this chapter is upon a short discourse of mine in my process, which I profess not to be needful to the purpose in hand, relating to some later disputes about the *nature* of this church; wherein some had affirmed it to be a *genus* to particular churches, which are so many distinct *species* of it; and others, that it was a *totum* made up of particular churches as its parts;—both which in some sense I denied; partly, out of a desire to keep off all debates about the things of God from being inwrapped and agitated in and under philosophical notions and feigned terms of art, which hath exceedingly multiplied controversies in the world and rendered them endless, and doth more or less straiten or oppose every truth that is so dealt withal; partly, because I evidently saw men deducing false consequents from the supposition of such notions of this church. For the first way, our reverend author lets it pass, only with a remark upon my dissenting from Mr Hooker of New England, which he could not but note by the way, although he approves what I affirm. A worthy note! as though all the brethren of the presbyterian way were agreed among themselves in all things of the like importance, or that I were in my judgment inthralled to any man or men, so that it should deserve a note when I dissent from them. Truly, I bless God I am utterly unacquainted with any such frame of spirit or bondage of mind as must be supposed to be in them whose dissent from other men is a matter of such observation. One is my Master, to whom alone my heart and judgment are in subjection. For the latter, I do not say absolutely that particular churches are not the parts of the catholic visible [church] in any sense, but that they are not so parts of it as such, so that it should be constituted and made up by them and of them, for the order and purpose of an instituted church, for the celebration of the worship of God and institutions of Christ, according to the gospel; which when our author proves that it is, I shall acknowledge myself obliged to him. He says, indeed, that " it was once possible that all the members of the catholic church should meet together to hear one sermon," etc. But he is to prove that they were bound to do so as that catholic church, and not that it was possible for all the members of it under any other notion or consideration so to convene. But he says they are bound to do so still, but that the multitude makes it impossible. " Credat Apella," that Christ hath bound his church to that which himself makes impossible! Neither are they so bound. They are bound, by his own acknowledgment, to be members of particular churches; and in that capacity are they bound so to convene, those churches being, by the will of God, appointed for the seat of ordinances. And so what he adds in the next place, of particular churches being bound, according to the institution of Christ, to assemble for the celebration of ordinances, is absolutely destructive of the former figment. But he would know a reason why forty or more, that are not members of one particular church, but only of the catholic, meeting together, may not join together in all ordinances, as well as they may meet to hear the word preached, and often do. To which I answer, that it is because Jesus Christ hath appointed particular churches, and there is more required to them than the occasional meeting of some, any, or all if possible, of the members of the catholic church, as such, will afford.

His reflections upon myself added in that place are now grown so common that they deserve not any notice. In his ensuing discourse, if I may take leave to speak freely to our reverend author, he wrangles about terms and expressions, adding to and altering those by me used in this business at his pleasure, to make a talk to no purpose. The sum of what he pretends to oppose is,—That this *universal church*, or the universality of professors considered as such, neither formally as members of the church catholic mystically elect, nor as members of any particular church, have, as such, any church-form of the institution of Christ, by virtue whereof they should make up one instituted church, for the end and purpose of the celebration of the ordinances of the gospel therein. If he suppose he can prove the contrary, let him cease from cavilling at words and by-expressions,—which is a facile task for any man to engage in, and no way useful, but to make controversies endless,—and answer my reasons against it, which here he passeth over, and produce his testimonies and arguments for that purpose. This trivial ventilation of particular passages cut off from their influence into the whole is not worth a nut-shell, but is a business fit for them who have nothing else to employ themselves about.

Coming to consider the *union* that I assign to this church, after whose breach an inquiry is to be made,—which is the main and only thing of his concernment as to the aim he hath proposed to himself, —he passeth it over very slightly, taking no notice at all of my whole discourse from p. 116 to p. 133 [pp. 138–145] of my treatise, wherein I disprove the pretensions of other things to be the union or bond of union to this church. He fixes a very little while on what I assign to be that union. This, I say, is " profession of the faith of the gospel, and subjection to Jesus Christ according to it." To which he adds, that they are bound to more than this, namely, " to the exercise of the same specific ordinances, as also to love one another, to subjection to the same discipline, and, where it is possible, to the exercise of the same numerical worship." All this was expressly affirmed by me before; it is all virtually contained in their " profession," so far as the things mentioned are revealed in the gospel. Only, as to the celebrating of the same numerical ordinances, I cannot grant that they are obliged hereunto, as formally considered members of that church; nor shall, until our reverend author shall think meet to prove that particular congregations are not the institutions of Jesus Christ. But hereupon he affirms that that is a strange assertion used by me, p. 117 [p. 139], namely, "That if there be not an institution for the joining in the same numerical ordinances, the union of this church is not really a church union." This is no more but what was declared before, nor more than what I urged the testimony of a learned Presbyterian for; no more but this, that the universality of Christians throughout the world are not, under such an institution as that, to assemble together for the celebration of the same numerical ordinances, the pretence of any such institution being supplied by Christ's acknowledged institution of particular churches for that purpose.

What I have offered in my treatise as evidence that Protestants are not guilty of the breach of this union, and that where any are, their crime, is not schism but apostasy, either as to profession or conversation, I leave to the judgment of all candid, sober, and ingenuous readers. For such as love strife, and debates, and disputes, whereof the world is full, I would crave of them, that if they must choose me for their adversary, they would allow me to answer in person, "vivâ voce," to prevent this tedious trouble of writing; which, for the most part, is fruitless and needless. Some exceptions our author lays in against the properties of the profession by me required as necessary to the preservation of this union. As to the first, of "professing all necessary saving truths of the gospel," he excepts that the apostles were ignorant of many necessary truths of the gospel for a season, and some had never heard of the Holy Ghost, Acts xix. 2, and yet they kept the union of the catholic church. And yet our author, before he closeth this chapter, will charge the breach of this union on some whose errors cannot well be apprehended to lie in the denial of any necessary truth of the gospel that is indispensably necessary to salvation! As to his instance of the apostles, he knows it is one thing not to know clearly and distinctly for some season some truths "in hypothesi," and another to deny them, being sufficiently and clearly revealed "in thesi." And for those in the Acts, it is probable they were ignorant of the dispensations of the Holy Ghost, with his marvellous effects under the gospel, rather than of the person of the Holy Ghost; for even in respect of the former, it is absolutely said that "the Holy Ghost was not yet, because that Jesus was not yet glorified." I shall not pursue his other exceptions, being sorry that his judgment leads him to make them; that which alone bears any aspect to the business in hand, he insists on, p. 99, in these words:

" I have intimated, and partly proved, that there may be a breach of union with respect to the catholic church upon other considerations" (namely, besides the renunciation of the profession of the gospel); " as, first, There is a bond that obliges every member of this church to join together in exercising the same ordinances of worship. When, then, any man shall refuse to join with others, or refuse others to join with him, here is a breach of love and union among the members of the catholic church, and in the particular churches, as parts of the catholic."

The reader must pardon me for producing and insisting on these things, seeing I do it with this profession, that I can fix on nothing else so much to the purpose in hand; and yet how little these are so cannot but be evident, upon a slight view, to the meanest capacities: for,—1. He tells us that "there may be a breach of union with respect to the catholic church upon other considerations;" not that there may be a breach of the union of the catholic church. 2. That there is a bond binding men to the exercise of ordinances; so there is, binding man to all holiness;—and yet he denies the vilest profane persons to break that bond or this union. 3. That there may be a breach of union among the members of the church; but who knows it not that knows all members of particular churches are also members of this church general? Our inquiry is after the union of the catholic church visible, what it is, how broken, and what the crime or evil is whereby it is broken; also, what obligations lie on the members of that church, as they stand under any other formal considerations. What is the evil they are any of them guilty of in not answering these obligations, we were not at all inquiring; nor doth it in this place concern us so to do. And in what he afterward tells us of some proceedings contrary to the practice of the universal church, he intends, I suppose, all the churches in the world wherein the members of the universal church have walked or do so: for the universal church, as such, hath no practice as to celebration of ordinances; and if he suppose it hath, let him tell us what it is, and *when that practice was.* His appeal to the primitive believers and their small number will not avail him: for although they should be granted to be the then catholic visible church (against which he knows what exceptions may be laid from the believers amongst the Jews, such as Cornelius, to whom Christ had not as yet been preached as the Messiah come and exhibited), yet as such they joined not in the celebration of ordinances, but (as yet they were) as a particular congregation; yea, though all the apostles were amongst them,—the foundation of all the churches that afterward were called.

He concludes this chapter with an exception to my assertion, that "if the catholic church be a political body, it must have a visible political head," which nothing but the pope claims to be. Of this he says,—" 1. There is no necessity; for," saith he, " he confesses the commonwealth of the Jews was a political body, and God, who is invisible, was their political head. 2. Jesus Christ is a visible head, yea, sometimes more, ' visus,' seen of men whilst on earth; though now for a time, in majesty (as some great princes do), he hath withdrawn himself from the sight of men on earth, yet is he seen of angels and saints in heaven." *Ans.* 1. I confess God was the king and ruler of the Jews; but yet, that they might be a visible political body, the invisible God appointed to them, under him, a visible head; as the pope blasphemously pretends to be appointed under Jesus Christ. 2. Jesus Christ is in his human nature still visible; as to his person, wherein he is the head of his church, he ever was, and is still, invisible. His present absence is not upon the account of majesty, seeing in his majesty he is still present with us; and as to his bodily absence, he gives other accounts than that here insinuated. Now, it sufficeth not to constitute a visible political body, that the head of it in any respect may be seen, unless as their head he is seen. Christ is visible, as this church is visible;—he in his laws, in his word; that in its profession, in its obedience. But I marvel that our reverend author, thus concluding for Christ to be the political head of this church, as a church, should at the same time contend for such subjects of this head as he doth, p. 96,— namely, persons " contradicting their profession of the knowledge of God by a course of wickedness, manifesting principles of profaneness, wherewith the belief of the truth they profess hath an absolute inconsistency," as I expressly describe the persons whose membership in this church, and relation thereby to Christ their head, he pleads for. Are, indeed, these persons any better than Mohammedans as to church privileges? They are, indeed, in some places, as to providential advantages of hearing the word preached; but woe unto them on that account! it shall be more tolerable for Mohammedans in the day of Christ than for them. Shall their baptism avail them? Though it were valid in its administration,—that is, was celebrated in obedience to the command of Christ,—is it not null to them? Is not their circumcision uncircumcision? Shall such persons give their children any right to church privileges? Let them, if you please, be so subject to Christ as rebels and traitors are subject to their earthly princes. They ought, indeed, to be so, but are they so? Do they own their authority? are they obedient to them? do they enjoy any privilege of laws? or doth the apostle anywhere call such persons as live in a course of wickedness, manifesting principles utterly inconsistent with the profession of the gospel, "Brethren?" God forbid we should once imagine these things so to be! And so much for that chapter.

CHAPTER VIII.

Of Independentism and Donatism.

THE title of our author's book is, "Independency a Great Schism;" of this chapter, that it may be the better known what kind of schism it is, "Independentism is Donatism." Men may give what title they please to their books and chapters, though perhaps few books make good their titles. I am sure this doth not as yet, " nisi accusâsse sufficiat." Attempts of proof we have not as yet met withal; what this chapter will furnish us withal we shall now consider. He, indeed, that shall weigh the title, "Independentism is Donatism," and then, casting his eye upon the first lines of the chapter itself, find that the reverend author says he cannot but " acknowledge what I plead for the vindication of Protestants from the charge of schism, in their separation from Rome, as the catholic church, to be rational, solid, and judicious," will perhaps be at a loss in conjecturing how I am like to be dealt withal in the following discourse. A little patience will let him see that our author lays more weight upon the title than the preface of this chapter, and that, with all my fine trappings, I am enrolled in the black book of the Donatists; but, " Quod fors feret, feramus æquo animo;" or as another saith, "Debemus optare optima, cogitare difficillima, ferre quæcunque erunt." As the case is fallen out, we must deal with it as we can. First, he saith, " he is not satisfied that he not only denies the church of Rome (so called) to be a particular church, p. 119 [p. 154], but also affirms it to be no church at all." That he is not satisfied with what I affirm òf that synagogue of Satan, where he hath his throne, I cannot help it, though I am sorry for it.

I am not, also, without some trouble that I cannot understand what he means by placing my words so as to intimate that I say not only that the church of Rome is no particular church, but also that it is no church at all; as though it might, in his judgment or mine, be *any church,* if it be not a *particular church:* for I verily suppose neither he nor I judge it to be that catholic church whereto it pretends. But yet, as I have no great reason to expect that this reverend author should be satisfied in any thing that I affirm, so I hope that it is not impossible but that, without any great difficulty, he may be reconciled to himself, affirming the very same thing that I do, p. 113 [p. 137]. It is of Rome in that sense wherein it claims itself to be a church that I speak: and in that sense he says it is no church of Christ's institution; and so, for my part, I account it no church at all. But he adds, that he is "far more unsatisfied that I undertake the cause of the Donatists, and labour to exempt them from schism, though I allow them guilty of other crimes." But do I indeed undertake the cause of the Donatists? do I plead for them? Will he manifest it by saying more against them in no more words than I have done? Do I labour to exempt them from schism? Are these the ways of peace, love, and truth, that the reverend author walks in? Do I not condemn all their practices and pretensions from the beginning to the end? Can I not speak of their cause in reference to the catholic church and its union, but it must be affirmed that I plead for them? But yet, as if righteousness and truth had been observed in this crimination, he undertakes, as of a thing granted, to give my grounds of doing what he affirms me to have done. "The first is," as he says, "his singular notion of schism, limiting it only to differences in a particular assembly. Secondly, his jealousy of the charge of schism to be objected to himself and party, if separating from the true churches of Christ be truly called schism." *Ans.* What may I expect from others, when so grave and reverend a person as this author is reported to be shall thus deal with me? Sir, I have no singular notion of schism, but embrace that which Paul hath long since declared; nor can you manifest any difference in my notion from what he hath delivered. Nor is that notion of schism at all under consideration in reference to what I affirm of the Donatists (who, in truth, were concerned in it, the most of them to the utmost), but the union of the church catholic and the breach thereof. Neither am I jealous or fearful of the charge of schism from any person living on the earth, and least of all from men proceeding in church affairs upon the principles you proceed on. Had you not been pleased to have supposed what you please, without the least ground, or colour, or reason, perhaps you would have as little satisfied yourself in the charge you have undertaken to manage against me, as you have done many good men, as the case now stands, even of your own judgment in other things.

Having made this entrance, he proceeds in the same way, and, p. 164, lays the foundation of the title of his book and this chapter, of his charge of Donatism, in these words: "This lies in full force against him and his party, who have broken the union of our churches, and separated themselves from all the protestant churches in the world not of their own constitution, and that as no true churches of Christ." This, I say, is the foundation of his whole ensuing discourse, all the ground that he hath to stand upon in the defence of the invidious title of this chapter; and what fruit he expects from this kind of proceeding I know not. The day will manifest of what sort this work is. Although he may have some mistaken apprehensions to countenance his conscience in the first part of his assertion, as that it may be forgiven to inveterate prejudice, though it be false,—namely, that I and my party (that is the phraseology this author, in his love to unity, delights in) have broken the union of their churches (which we have no more done than they have broken the union of ours, for we began our reformation with them on even terms, and were as early at work as they),—yet what colour, what excuse can be invented to alleviate the guilt of the latter part of it, that we have separated from all the reformed churches, as no churches? And yet he repeats this again, p. 106, with especial reflection on myself. "I wonder not," saith he, "that the doctor hath unchurched Rome, for he hath done as much to England and all foreign protestant churches, and makes none to be members of the church but such as are, by covenant and consent, joined to some of their congregations." Now, truly, though all righteous laws of men in the world will afford recompense and satisfaction for calumniating accusations and slanders of much less importance than this here publicly owned by our reverend author, yet, seeing the gospel of the blessed God requires to forgive and pass by greater injuries, I shall labour, in the strength of his grace, to bring my heart unto conformity to his will therein; notwithstanding which, because by his providence I am in that place and condition that others also that fear his name may be some way concerned in this unjust imputation, I must declare that this is open unrighteousness, wherein neither love nor truth hath been observed. How little I am concerned in his following parallel of Independentism and Donatism,—wherein he proceeds with the same truth and candour,—or in all that follows thereupon, is easy for any one to judge. He proceeds to scan my answers to the Romanists, as in reference to their charge of schism upon us, and says, "I do it suitably to my own principles;" and truly if I had not, I think I had been much to blame. I refer the reader to the answers given in my book; and if he like them not, notwithstanding this author's exceptions, I wish he may fix on those that please him better; in them there given my conscience doth acquiesce.

But he comes, in the next place, to *arguments;* wherein if he prove more happy than he hath done in *accusations,* he will have great cause to rejoice. By a double argument, as he says, he will prove that there may be schism besides that in a particular church. His first is this: "Schism is a breach of union; but there may be a breach of union in the catholic visible church." His second this: "Where there are differences raised in matter of faith professed, wherein the union of the catholic church consists, there may be a breach of union; but there may be differences in the catholic, or among the members of the catholic church in matter of faith professed: *ergo.*" Having thus laid down his arguments, he falls to conjecture what I will answer, and how I will evade. But it will quickly appear that he is no less unhappy in arguing and conjecturing than he is and was in accusing. For, to consider his first argument, if he will undertake to make it good as to its form, I will, by the same way of arguing, engage myself to prove what he would be unwilling to find in a regular conclusion. But as to the matter of it,—First, Is schism every breach of union? or is every breach of union schism? Schism, in the ecclesiastical notion, is granted to be, in the present dispute, *the breach of the union of a church,* which it hath by the institution of Christ, and this not of *any* union of Christ's institution, but of one certain kind of union; for, as was proved, there is a union whose breach can neither, in the language of the Scripture, nor in reason, nor common sense, be called or accounted schism, nor ever was by any man in the world, nor can be, without destroying the particular nature of schism, and allowing only the general notion of any separation, good or bad, in what kind soever. So that, secondly, It is granted not only that there may be *a breach of union in the catholic church,* but also that there may be *a breach of the union of the catholic church* by a denial or relinquishment of the profession wherein it consists; but that this breach of union is schism, because schism is a breach of union, is as true as that every man who hath two eyes is every thing that hath two eyes. For his second, it is of the same importance with the first. There may be differences in the catholic church, and breaches of union among the members of it, which are far enough from the breach of the union of that church as such. Two professors may fall out and differ, and yet, I think, continue both of them professors still. Paul and Barnabas did so; Chrysostom and Epiphanius did so; Cyril and Theodoret did so. That which I denied was, that the breach of the union of the catholic church as such is schism. He proves the contrary, by affirming there may be differences among the members of the catholic church, that do not break the union of it as such. " But," he says, " though there be apostasy or heresy, yet there may be schism also;" but not in respect of the breach of the same union, which only he was to prove. Besides evil surmises, reproaches, false criminations, and undue suggestions, I find nothing wherein my discourse is concerned to the end of this chapter. Page 109, upon the passage of mine, " We are thus come off from this part of schism, for the relinquishment of the catholic church, which we have not done, and so to do is not schism, but a sin of another nature and importance," he adds, that " the ground I go upon why separation from a true church" (he must mean the catholic church, or he speaks nothing at all to the business in hand) "is no schism is that afore-mentioned, that a schism in the Scripture notion is only a division of judgment in a particular assembly." But who so blind as they that will not see? The ground I proceeded on evidently, openly, solely, was taken from the nature of the catholic church, its union, and the breach of that union; and if "obiter" I once mention that notion, I do it upon my confidence of its truth, which I here again tender myself in a readiness to make good to this reverend author, if at any time he will be pleased to command my personal attendance upon him to that purpose. To repeat more of the like mistakes and surmises, with the wranglings that ensue on such false suppositions, to the end of this chapter, is certainly needless. For my part, in and about this whole business of separation from the catholic church, I had not the least respect to Presbyterians or Independents, as such, nor to the differences between them; which alone our author, out of his zeal to the truth and peace, attends unto. If he will fasten the guilt of schism on any on the account of separation from the catholic church, let him prove that that church is not made up of the universality of professors of the gospel throughout the world, under the limitations expressed; that the union of it as such doth not consist in the profession of the truth; and that the breach of that union, whereby a man ceases to be a member of that church, is schism. Otherwise, to tell me that I am a " sectary," a " schismatic," to fill up his pages with vain surmises and supposals, to talk of a difference and schism among the members of the catholic church, or the like impertinences, will never farther his discourse among men, either rational, solid, or judicious. All that ensues, to the end of this chapter, is about the ordination of ministers; wherein, however, he hath been pleased to deal with me in much bitterness of spirit, with many clamours and false accusations. I am glad to find him, p. 120, renouncing ordination from the authority of the church of Rome as such, for I am assured that by so doing he can claim it no way from, by, or through Rome; for nothing came to us from thence but what came in and by the authority of that church.

CHAPTER IX.

WE are now gathering towards what seems of most immediate concernment as to this reverend author's undertaking,—namely, to treat of the nature of a particular church, its union, and the breach of that union. The description I give of such a church is this: " It is a society of men called by the word to the obedience of the faith in Christ, and joint performance of the worship of God in the same

individual ordinances, according to the order by Christ prescribed."
This I profess to be a general description of its nature, waiving all
contests about accurate definitions, which usually tend very little to
the discovery or establishment of truth. After some canvassing of
this description, our author tells us that he grants it to be the definition of a particular church, which is more than I intended it for;
only he adds, that according to this description, their churches are as
true as ours; which, I presume, by this time he knows was not the
thing in question. His ensuing discourse of the will of Christ that
men should join not all in the same individual congregation, but in
this or that, is by me wholly assented unto, and the matter of it contended for by me as I am able. What he is pleased to add about
explicit covenanting, and the like, I am not at all, for the present,
concerned in. I purposely waived all expressions concerning it, one
way or other, that I might not involve the business in hand with any
unnecessary contests; it is possible somewhat hereafter may be spoken
to that subject, in a tendency unto the reconciliation of the parties
at variance. His argument, in the close of the section, for a presbyterian church, from Acts xx. 17, " because there is mention of more
elders than one in that church, and therefore it was not one single
congregation," I do not understand. I think no one single congregation is wholly completed according to the mind of Christ unless there
be more elders than one in it. There should be " *elders in every
church;*" and, for my part, so we could once agree practically in the
matter of our churches, I am under some apprehension that it were
no impossible thing to reconcile the whole difference as to a presbyterian church or a single congregation. And though I be reproved
anew for my pains, I may offer, ere long, to the candid consideration
of godly men, something that may provoke others of better abilities
and more leisure to endeavour the carrying on of so good a work.
Proceeding to the consideration of the unity of this church, he takes
notice of three things laid down by me, previously to what I was
farther to assert; all which he grants to be true, but yet will not let
them pass without his animadversions.

The first two are, that,—" 1. A man may be a member of the catholic invisible church, and, 2. Of the visible catholic church, and yet not
be joined to a particular church." These, as I said, he owns to be true,
but asks how I can "reconcile this with what I said before,—namely,
that the members of the catholic visible church are initiated into the
profession of the faith by baptism." But where lies the difference?
Why, saith he, " baptism, according to his principles, is an ordinance
of worship only to be enjoyed in a particular church, whilst he will
grant (what yet he doth deny, but will be forced to grant) that a minister is a minister to more than his own church, even to the catholic

church, and may administer baptism out of a particular church, as Philip did to the eunuch." *Ans.* How well this author is acquainted with my principles hath been already manifested; as to his present mistake I shall not complain, seeing that some occasion may be administered unto it from an expression of mine, at least as it is printed, of which I shall speak afterward. For the present, he may be pleased to take notice that I am so far from confining baptism subjectively to a particular congregation, that I do not believe that any member of a particular church was ever regularly baptized. Baptism precedes admission into church membership, as to a particular church; the subjects of it are professing believers and their seed; as such they have right unto it, whether they be joined to any particular church or no. Suitable to this judgment hath been my constant and uninterrupted practice. I desire also to know who told him that I deny a minister to be *a minister to more than his own church*, or averred that he may perform ministerial duty only in and towards the members of his own congregation; for so much as men are appointed the objects of the dispensation of the word, I grant a man, in the dispensations of it, to act ministerially towards not only the members of the catholic church, but the visible members of the world also, in contradistinction thereunto.

The third thing laid down by me, whereunto also he assents, is, " That every believer is obliged to join himself to some one of those churches, that therein he may abide in ' doctrine and fellowship, and in breaking of bread, and in prayers:'" but my reasons whereby I prove this he says he likes not so well; and truly I cannot help it. I have little hope he should like any thing well which is done by me. Let him be pleased to furnish me with better, and I shall make use of them; but yet when he shall attempt so to do, it is odds but that one or other will find as many flaws in them as he pretends to do in mine. But this, he saith, he shall make use of, and that he shall make advantage of, and I know not what; as if he were playing a prize upon a stage. The third reason is that which he likes worst of all, and I like the business the better that what he understands least that he likes worst; it is, " That Christ hath given no direction for any duty of worship merely and purely of sovereign institution, but only to them and by them who are so joined." Hereupon he asks:—1. " Is baptism a part of worship?" *Ans.* Yes, and to be so performed *by them*,—that is, a minister *in* or *of them*. I fear my expression in this place led him to his whole mistake in this matter. 2. " Prayer and reading of the word in private families, are they no duty of worship?" *Ans.* Not merely and purely of sovereign institution. 3. " Is preaching to convert heathens a duty of worship?" Not, as described, in all cases. When it is, it is to be performed by a minister; and so he knows my answer to his next invidious inquiry, relating to my own person.

Against my fourth reason, taken from the apostle's care to leave none out of this order who were converted, where it was possible, he gives in the instance of the eunuch, and others converted where there were not enough to engage in such societies,—that is, in them with whom it was impossible. My fifth is from Christ's providing of officers for these churches. This also, he saith, is " weak as the rest: for, first, Christ provided officers at first for the catholic church,—that is, the apostles; secondly, All ordinary officers are set first in the catholic church, and every minister is first a minister to the catholic church; and if," saith he, " he deny this, he knows where to find a learned antagonist." *Ans.* But see what it is to have a mind to dispute. Will he deny that Christ appointed officers for particular churches? or if he should have a mind to do it, will his arguments evince any such thing? Christ appointed apostles, catholic officers; therefore, he did not appoint officers for particular churches, though he commanded that "elders should be ordained in every church"! Pastors and teachers are set first in the catholic church; therefore, Christ hath not ordained officers for particular churches! But this is is the way with our author. If any word offer itself, whence it is possible to draw out the mention of any thing that is, or hath at any time been, in difference between Presbyterians and Independents, that presently is run away withal. For my part, I had not the least thought of the controversy which, to no purpose at all, he would here lead me to. But yet I must tell him that my judgment is, that ordinary officers are firstly to be ordained in particular churches; and as I know where to find a "learned antagonist" as to that particular, so I do in respect of every thing that I affirm or deny in the business of religion; and yet I bless the Lord I am not in the least disquieted or shaken in my adherence to the truth I profess.

My last reason, he saith, is "fallacious and inconsequent;" and that because he hath put an inference upon it never intended in it. Now, the position that these reasons were produced to confirm being true, and so acknowledged by himself, because it is a truth that indeed I lay some more than ordinary weight upon, it being of great use in the days wherein we live, I would humbly entreat this reverend author to send me his reasons whereby it may be confirmed; and I shall promise him, if they be found of more validity than those which, according to my best skill, I have already used, he shall obtain many thanks and much respect for his favour.

What he remarks upon or adds to my next discourse, about instituted worship in general, I shall not need to insist on; only, by the way, I cannot but take notice of that which he calls "a chief piece of Independency;" and that is, "that those who are joined in church fellowship are so confined that they cannot, or may not, worship God in the same ordinances in other churches." How this comes to be "a chief piece of Independency," I know not. It is contrary to the known practice of all the churches of England that I am acquainted with which he calls Independents. For my part, I know but one man of that mind, and he is no child in these things.

For the ensuing discourse, about the intercision of ordinances, it being a matter of great importance, and inquired into by me merely in reference to the Roman apostasy, it needs a more serious disquisition than any thing at present administered by our author will give occasion unto; possibly, in convenient time, I may offer somewhat farther towards the investigation of the mind of God therein. Every thing in this present contest is so warped to the petty differences between Presbyterians and Independents, that no fair progress nor opportunity for it can be afforded. If, it may be, in my next debate of it, I shall waive all mention of those meaner differences, and as, I remember, I have not insisted on them in what I have already proposed to this purpose, so possibly the next time I may utterly escape. For the present, I do not doubt but the Spirit of God in the Scripture is furnished with sufficient authority to erect new churches, and set up the celebration of all ordinances, on supposition that there was an intercision of them. To declare the way of his exerting his authority to this purpose, with the obviating of all objections to the contrary, is not a matter to be tossed up and down in this scambling chase; and I am not a little unhappy that this reverend person was in the dark as to my design and aim all along, which hath entangled this dispute with so many impertinences. But, however, I shall answer a question which he is pleased to put to me in particular. He asks me, then, "Whether I do not think in my conscience that there were no true churches in England until the Brownists our fathers, the Anabaptists our elder brothers, and ourselves, arose and gathered new churches?" With thanks for the civility of the inquiry in the manner of its expression, I answer, No; I have no such thoughts. And his pretence of my insinuation of any such thing is most vain, as also is his insultation thereupon. Truly, if men will, in all things, take liberty to speak what they please, they have no reason but to think that they may, at one time or other, hear that which will displease.

Having investigated the nature of a particular church, I proceed, in my treatise of schism, to inquire after the union of it, wherein it doth consist, and what is the breach thereof. The sum is, "The joint consent of the members to walk together in celebration of the same numerical ordinances, according to the mind of Jesus Christ, is that wherein the union of such a church doth consist." This is variously excepted against; and I know not what disputes about an implicit and explicit covenant, of specificating forms, of the practice of New and Old England, of admission of church-members, of the right of the members of the catholic church to all ordinances, of the miscarriage of the Independents, of church matriculations, and such like things, not once considered by me in my proposal of the matter in hand, are fallen upon. By the way, he falls upon my judgment about the inhabitation of the Spirit, calls it an error, and says so it hath been reputed by all that are orthodox; raising terrible suspicions and intimations of judgments on our way from God by my falling into that error; when yet I say no more than the Scripture saith in express terms forty times; for which I refer him to what I have written on that subject, wherein I have also the concurrence of Polanus, Bucanus, Dorchetus, with sundry others, Lutherans and Calvinists. It may be, when he hath seriously weighed what I have offered to the clearing of that glorious truth of the gospel, he may entertain more gentle thoughts both concerning it and me.

The rest of the chapter I have passed through once and again, and cannot fix on any thing worthy of farther debate. A difference is attempted to be found in my description of the union of a particular church, in this and another place. Because in one place I require the consent of the members to walk together, in another mention only their so doing,—when the mention of that only was necessary in that place, not speaking of it absolutely, but as it is the difference of such a church from the church catholic,—some impropriety of expression is pretended to be discovered ("id populus curat scilicet"); which yet is a pure mistake of his, not considering unto what especial end and purpose the words are used. He repeats sundry things as in opposition to me, that are things laid down by myself and granted! Doth he attempt to prove that the union of a church is not rightly stated? He confesseth the form of such a church consists in *the observance and performance of the same ordinances of worship numerically.* I ask, is it not the command of Christ that believers should so do? Is not their obedience to that command their consent so to do? Are not particular churches instituted of Christ? Is it not the duty of every believer to join himself to some one of them? Was not this acknowledged above? Can any one do so without his consenting to do so? Is this consent any thing but his voluntary submission to the ordinances of worship therein? As an express consent and subjection to Christ in general is required to constitute a man a member of the church catholic visible; so if the Lord Jesus hath appointed any particular church for the celebration of his ordinances, is not their consent who are to walk in them necessary thereunto? But the topic of an explicit covenant presenting itself with an advantage to take up some leaves could not be waived, though nothing at all to the purpose in hand. After this, my confession, made in as much condescension unto compliance as I could well imagine, of the use of greater assemblies, is examined and excepted against, as "being in my esteem," he saith, "though it be not so indeed, a matter of prudence only." But I know full well that he knows not what esteem or disesteem I have of sundry things of no less importance. The consideration of my "postulata," proposed in a preparation to what was to be insisted on in the next chapter, as influenced from the foregoing dissertations, alone remains, and indeed alone deserves our notice.

My first is this: "The departing of any man or men from any particular church, as to the communion peculiar to such a church, is nowhere called schism, nor is so in the nature of the thing itself; but is a thing to be judged and receive a title according to the circumstances of it." To this he adjoins, "This is not the question. A simple secession of a man or men, upon some just occasion, is not called schism; but to make causeless differences in a church, and then separating from it as no church, denying communion with it, hath the nature and name of schism in all men's judgments but his own." *Ans.* What question doth our reverend author mean? I fear he is still fancying of the difference between Presbyterians and Independents, and squaring all things by that imagination. Whether it be a question stated to his mind or no I cannot tell; but it is an assertion expressive of mine own, which he may do well to disprove if he can. Who told him that raising causeless differences in a church, and then separating from it, is not in my judgment schism? May I possibly retain hopes of making myself understood by this reverend author? I suppose though that a pertinacious abiding in a mistake is neither schism nor heresy; and so this may be passed over.

My second is: "One church refusing to hold that communion with another which ought to be between them is not schism, properly so called." The reply hereunto is twofold:—1. "That one church may raise differences in and with another church, and so cause schism." 2. "That the Independents deny any communion of churches but what is prudential; and so, that communion cannot be broken." To the first I have spoken sufficiently before; the latter is but a harping on the same string. I am not speaking of Independent churches, nor upon the principles of Independents, much less on them which are imposed on them. Let the reverend author suppose or aver what communion of churches he pleaseth, my position holds in reference to it; nor can he disprove it. However, for my part, I am not acquainted with those Independents who allow no communion of churches but what is prudential; and yet it is thought that I know as many as this reverend author doth.

Upon the last proposal we are wholly agreed, so that I shall not need to repeat it; only he gives me a sad farewell at the close of the chapter, which must be taken notice of. "Is not," saith he, "the design of this book to prove, if he could, and condemn us as no churches? Let the world be judge." And I say, let all the saints of God judge; and Jesus Christ will judge whether I have not outrageous injury done me in this imputation. "But," saith he, "unless this be proved, he can never justify his separation." Sir, when your and our brethren told the bishops they thanked God they were none of them, and defied the prelatical church, did they make a separation or no? were they guilty of schism? I suppose you will not say so, nor do I; yet have I done any such thing in reference to you or your churches? I have no more separated from you than you have done from me; and as for the distance which is between us upon our disagreement about the way of reformation, let all the churches of God judge on which side it hath been managed with more breach of love, —on yours or mine. Let me assure you, sir, through the mercy of God in Jesus Christ, I can freely forgive unto you all your reproaches, revilings, hard censurings, and endeavours to expose me to public obloquy, and yet hope that I may have, before we die, a place in your heart and prayers.

CHAPTER X.

Independency no schism.

WE are come now to the chapter that must do the work intended, or else "operam et oleum perdidimus." "Independentism a Great Schism," is the title of it. What this Independentism is he doth neither here declare, nor in any other part of his book; nor do I know what it is that he intends by it. I hear, indeed, from him that it is a "schism," a "sect;" but of what peculiar import, or wherein it consists, he hath not declared. I suppose he would have it taken for separation from true churches; but neither doth the notion of the name, though individiously broached, and disavowed by them to whom it is ascribed, import any such thing, nor is the thing itself owned by them with whom he pretends to have to do. I find, indeed, that he tells us that all sectaries are Independents,—Anabaptists, Seekers, Ranters, Quakers. Doth he expect that I should undertake their defence? What if it should appear that I have done more against them than our reverend author, and many of his brethren joined with him? He may, perhaps, be willing to load myself and those which he is pleased to call my "associates," my "party," I know not what, with their evils and miscarriages; but is this done as becomes a

Christian, a minister, a brother? What security hath he that, had he been the only judge and disposer of things in religion in this nation, if I and my associates had been sent to plant churches among the Indians, he should have prevented eruption of the errors and abominations which we have been exercised withal in this generation, unless he had sent for Duke d'Alva's instruments to work his ends by? and, indeed, there is scarce any sect in the nation but had they their desires, they would take that course. This may be done by any that are uppermost, if they please. But how shall we know what it is he intends by Independentism? All, it may be, that are not Presbyterians are Independents. Among these some professedly separate both from them and us (for there are none that separate from them but withal they separate from us, that I know of), because, as they say, neither theirs nor ours are true churches. We grant them to be true churches, but withal deny that we separate from them. Is it possible at once to defend both these sects of men? Is it possible at once with the same arguments to charge them? The whole discourse, then, of our reverend author being uniform, it can concern but one of these sects of Independents; which it is, any man may judge that takes the least view of his treatise. He deals with them that unchurch their churches, unminister their ministers, disannul their ordinances, leaving them churchless, officerless, and in the like sad condition. Is this Independentism a schism? Though that it is properly so called he cannot prove, yet I hope he did not expect that I should plead for it. What I shall do in this case, I profess, well I know not. I here deny that I unminister their ministers, unchurch their churches. Hath this author any more to say to me or those of my persuasion? Doth not this whole discourse proceed upon a supposition that it is otherwise with them with whom he hath to do? Only, I must tell him by the way, that if he suppose by this concession that I justify and own their way, wherein they differ from the congregational ministers in England, to be of Christ's institution, or that I grant all things to be done regularly among them and according to the mind of Christ, therein I must profess he is mistaken. In brief, by Independentism he intends a separation from true churches, with condemning them to be no churches, and their ministers no ministers, and their ordinances none or antichristian. Whatever becomes of the nature of schism, I disavow the appearing as an advocate in the behalf of this Independentism. If by Independentism he understand the peaceable proceeding of any of the people of God in this nation, in the several parts of it, to join themselves, by their free consent, to walk together in the observation and celebration of all the ordinances of Christ appointed to be observed and celebrated in particular churches, so to reform themselves from the disorders wherein they were entangled,—being not able in some things to join in that way of reformation which many godly ministers, commonly called Presbyterians, have engaged in and seek to promote, without judging and condemning them as to the whole of their station or ordinances;—if this, I say, be intended by Independentism, when the reverend author shall undertake to prove it schism, having not in this book spoken one word or tittle to it, his discourse will be attended unto. This whole chapter, then, being spent against them who deny them to be true churches and defend separation, I marvel what can be said unto it by me, or how I come to be concerned in it, who grant them true churches and deny separation.

But our reverend author, knowing that if this bottom be taken from under him, he hath no foundation for any thing he asserts, thought it not sufficient to charge me over and over with what is here denied, but at length attempts to make it good from mine own words; which if he do effect and make good, I confess he changes the whole nature and state of the dispute in hand. Let us see, then, how he answers this undertaking.

From those words of mine, "The reformation of any church, or any thing in it, is the reducing of it to its primitive institution," approving the assertion as true, he labours to evince that I deny their churches to be true churches. How so, I pray? "Why, we erect new churches out of no churches; and it had been happy for England if we had all gone to do this work among the Indians." What will prove England's happiness or unhappiness the day will manifest; this is but man's day and judgment; He is coming who will not judge by the seeing of the eye, nor by the hearing of the ear. In the meantime we bless God, and think all England hath cause to bless God, whatever become of us, that he and our brethren of the same mind with him in the things of God have their liberty to preach the gospel and carry on the work of reformation in their native soil, and are not sent into the ends of the earth, as many of ours have been. But how doth our gathering of churches deny them to be true churches? Doth our granting them to be true churches also grant that all the saints in England are members of their churches? It is notoriously known that it is and was otherwise, and that when they and we began to reform, thousands of the people of God in these nations had no reason to suppose themselves to belong to one particular church rather than another. They lived in one parish, heard in another, removed up and down for their advantage, and were in bondage on that account all their days.

But he says, "In some words following I discover my very heart." I cannot but by the way tell him, that it is a sufficient evidence of his unacquaintedness with me, that he thinks there is need of searching and raking my words to discover my very heart in any thing that belongs (though in never so remote a distance) to the worship of God. All that know me, know how open and free I am in these things, how ready on all occasions to declare my whole heart; it is neither fear nor favour can influence me unto another frame. But what are the words that make this noble discovery? They are these that follow: "When any society or combination of men (whatever hitherto it hath been esteemed) is not capable of such a reduction and revocation" (that is, to its primitive institution), "I suppose I shall never provoke any wise or sober person if I profess I cannot look on such a society as a church of Christ." His reply hereunto is the hinge upon which his whole discourse turneth, and must therefore be considered. Thus then he: "Is not this, reader, at once to unchurch all the churches of England since the Reformation? for it is known during the reign of the prelates they were not capable of that reduction; and what capacity our churches are now in for that reduction, partly by want of power and assistance from the magistrate, without which some dare not set upon a reformation, for fear of a premunire, partly by our divisions amongst ourselves, fomented by he knows whom, he cannot but see as well as we lament." And hereupon he proceeds with sundry complaints of my dealing with them. And now, Christian reader, what shall we say to these things? A naked supposition, of no strength nor weight, that will not hold in any thing or case,—namely, that a thing is not to be judged capable of that which by some external force it is withheld from,—is the sole bottom of all this charge! The churches of England were capable of that reduction to their primitive institution under the prelates, though in some things hindered by them from an actual reducement; so they are now, in sundry places where the work is not so much as attempted. The sluggard's field is capable of being weeded. The present pretended want of capacity from the non-assistance of the magistrate, whilst perfect liberty for reformation is given, and the work in its several degrees encouraged, will be found to be a sad plea for some when things come to be tried out by the rule of the gospel. And for our divisions, I confess I begin to discover somewhat more by whom they are fomented than I did four days ago. For the matter itself, I desire our reverend author to take notice that I judge every church capable of a reduction to its primitive institution; which, all outward hinderances being removed, and all assistances granted that are necessary for reformation according to the gospel, may be reduced into the form and order appointed unto a particular church by Jesus Christ. And where any society is not so capable, let them call themselves what they please, I shall advise those therein who have personally a due right to the privileges purchased for them by Jesus Christ, in the way of their administration by him appointed, to take some other peaceable course to make themselves partakers of them; and for giving this advice, I neither dread the anger nor indignation of any man living in the world. And so I suppose by this time the author knows what has become of his "quod erat demonstrandum;" and here, in room of it, I desire him to accept of this return.

Those who, in the judgment of charity, were and continue members of the church catholic invisible, by virtue of their union with Christ, the head thereof; and members of the general visible church, by their due profession of the saving truths of the gospel, and subjection to Christ Jesus, their King and Saviour, according to them; and do walk in love and concord in the particular churches whereof, by their own consent and choice, they are members, not judging and condemning other particular churches of Christ, where they are not members, as they are such, as to their station and privileges, being ready for all instituted communion with them as revealed; are not, according to any gospel rule, nor by any principles acknowledged amongst Christians, to be judged or condemned as guilty of schism;— but such are all they for whom, under any consideration whatever, I have pleaded as to their immunity from this charge in my treatise of schism: therefore, they are not to be judged so guilty. If you please, you may add, " Quod erat demonstratum."

I shall not digress to a recharge upon this reverend author, and those of the same profession with him, as to their mistakes and miscarriages in the work of reformation, nor discuss their ways and principles, wherein I am not satisfied as to their procedure. I yet hope for better things than to be necessitated to carry on the defensative of the way wherein I walk by opposing theirs. It is true, that he who stands upon mere defence is thought to stand upon none at all; but I wait for better things from men than their hearts will yet allow them to think of. I hope the reverend author thinks that as I have reasons wherewith I am satisfied as to my own way, so I have those that are of the same weight with me against him. But whatever he may surmise, I have no mind to foment the divisions that are amongst us; hence I willingly bear all his imputations without retortion I know in part how the case is in the world. The greatest chargers have not always the most of truth; witness Papists, Lutherans, Prelatists, Anabaptists. I hope I can say in sincerity I am for peace, though others make themselves ready for war.

But we must proceed a little farther, though, as to the cause by me undertaken to be managed, causelessly. The discourse of our author from the place fixed on, wherein he faintly endeavours to make good the foundation of this chapter, which I have already considered, consists of two parts:—1. His animadversions on some *principles* which I lay down, as necessary to be stated aright and determined, that the question about *gathering churches* may be clearly and satisfactorily debated. Some of them, he says, have been handled by others; which if it be a rule of silence to him and me, it might have prevented this tedious debate. Whatever his thoughts may be of my pamphlet, I do not fear to affirm of his treatise that I have found nothing in it, from the beginning to the ending, but what hath lien neglected on booksellers' stalls for above these seven years. For the rest of those principles which he excepts against as he thinks meet, I leave their consideration to that farther inquiry which, the Lord assisting, I have destined them unto. The way of gathering churches upon a supposition of their antecedency to officers, he says, is very pretty; and he loads it with the difficulty of men's coming to be baptized in such a case. But as I can tell him of that which is neither true nor pretty in the practice of some whom he knows, or hath reason so to do, so I can assure him that we are not concerned in his objection about baptism; and with them who may possibly be so, it is a ridiculous thing to think it an objection. And for that part of my inquiry, whether the church be before ordinary officers, or they before it, as light as he is pleased to make of it, it will be found to lie very near the bottom of all our differences, and the right stating of it to conduce to the composure and determination of them. His charges and reflections, which he casts about in his passage, are not now to be farther mentioned; we have had them over and over,—indeed we have had little else. If strong, vehement, passionate affirmations, complaints, charges, false imputations, and the like, will amount to a demonstration in this business, he hath demonstrated *Independentism* to be a *great schism*.

He shuts up his discourse as he began it, reciting my words by adding, interposing, perverting, commenting, inquiring; he makes them speak what he pleases, and compasses the ends of his delight upon them. What contentment he hath received in his so doing I know not, nor shall I express what thoughts I have of such a course of procedure. This only I shall say, it is a facile way of writing treatises and proving whatever men have a mind unto.

My last task is, to look back to the beginning of this last chapter, and to gather up in our passage what may seem to respect the business in hand; and so the whole matter will be dismissed. The plea insisted on for immunity from the charge of schism, with reference to the episcopal government of the church of England, and the constitution which, under it, it is pretended to have had, he passes over; though, on sundry accounts, his concernments lie as deeply in it as in any thing pleaded in that treatise. The things he is pleased to take notice of, as far as they tend in the least to the issue of the debate between us, shall be reviewed. Considering the several senses wherein that expression, "The church of England," may be taken, I manifest in my treatise in which of them, and how far, we acknowledge ourselves to have been, and to continue, *members of the church of England.* The first is as it comprises the *elect believers* in England. What the unity of the church in this sense is was before evinced. Our desire to be found members of this church, with our endeavour to keep the unity of it in the bond of peace, was declared. I am grieved to repeat our reverend author's exceptions to this declaration. Says he, " Unless he think there are no members of this church in England but those that are of his formed particular churches, I fear he will be found to break the union that ought to be between them." And why so, I pray? The union of the members of the church in this sense consists in their joint union to and with Christ, their head, by one Spirit. What hath the reverend author to charge upon me with reference thereunto? Let him speak out to the utmost. Yea, I have some reason to think that he will scarce spare where he can strike. God forbid that I should think all the members of the catholic church in England to be comprised, either jointly or severally, in their churches or ours, seeing it cannot be avoided; but you will keep up those notes of division. I doubt not but there be many thousands of them who walk neither with you nor us. He adds, that " by gathering saints of the first magnitude, we do what lies in us to make the invisible church visible." It is confessed we do so; yea, we know that that church which is invisible in some respects, and under one formal consideration, is visible as to its profession which it makes unto salvation. This, with all that lies in us, we draw them out unto. What he adds about the churches being elect, and the uncomely parts of it, which they may be for a season who are elect believers (because it must be spoken), are useless cavils. For the scornful rejection of what I affirm concerning our love to all the members of this church, and readiness to tender them satisfaction in case of offence, with his insinuation of my want of modesty and truth in asserting these thoughts, because he will one day know that the words he so despises were spoken in sincerity, and with reverence of the great God, and out of love to all his saints, I shall not farther vindicate them. Such hay and stubble must needs burn.

My next profession of our relation to the church of England [was] in respect of that denomination given to the body of professors in this nation cleaving to the doctrine of the gospel, here preached and established by law as the public profession of this nation. But he tells me,—1. "That many independent churches of this nation are grossly apostatized from that doctrine, and so are heretical." 2. " That the worship was professed, and protested, and established, as well as the doctrine, and that we are all departed from it, and so are schismatical; for we hold communion with them," he says, " in the same doctrine, but not in the same worship." *Ans.* 1. His first exception ariseth from the advantage he makes use of from his large use of the word " Independent;" which will serve him, in his sense, for what end he pleaseth. In the sense before declared his charge is denied. Let him prove it by instance, if he be able. Surely God hath not given orthodox men leave to speak what they please, without due regard to love and truth. 2. As to the worship established in this nation by law (he means the way of worship, for the substantials of it we are all agreed in), I suppose he will not say a relinquishment of the practice of it is schism. If he do, I know what use some men will make of his affirmation, though I know not how he will free himself from being schismatical. For his renewed charge of schism, I cannot, I confess, be moved at it, proceeding from him who neither doth nor will know what it is. His next endeavour is, to make use of another concession of mine, concerning our receiving of our regeneration and new birth by the preaching of the word in England, saying, " Could they make use of our preaching," etc. But the truth is, when the most of us, by the free grace of God, received our new birth through the preaching of the word, neither they nor we, as to the practice of our ways, were in England; so that their concernment, as such, in the concession is very small: and we hope, since, in respect of others, our own ministry hath not been altogether fruitless, though we make no comparison with them.

In rendering of the next passage, which is concerning Anabaptists and Anabaptism, I shall not contend with him; he hath not in the least impaired the truth of what I assert in reference to them and their way. I cannot but take notice of that passage, which, for the substance of it, hath so often occurred, and that is this, " Doth not himself labour in this book to prove that the administration of ordinances in our assemblies is null, our ordination null and antichristian?" for the proof of which suggestion he refers his reader to p. 197 [p. 172] of my book. I confess, seeing this particular quotation, I was somewhat surprised, and began to fear that some expression of mine (though contrary to my professed judgment) might have given countenance to this mistake, and so be pleaded as a justification of all the uncharitableness, and something else, wherewith his book is replenished; but turning to the place, I was quickly delivered from my trouble, though I must ingenuously confess I was cast into another, which I shall not now mention.

Page 167, we arrive at that which alone almost I expected would have been insisted on, and, quite contrary thereto, it is utterly waived,—namely, the whole business of a national church; upon which account, indeed, all the pretence of the charge this reverend author is pleased to manage doth arise. Take that out of the way, and certainly *they* and *we* are upon even terms; and if we will be judged by them who were last in possession of the reiglement of that church, upon supposition that there is such a church still, they are no more interested in it than we, yea, are as guilty of schism from it as we. But that being set aside, and *particular churches* only remaining, it will be very difficult for him to raise the least pretence of his great charge. But let us consider what he thinks meet to fasten on in that discourse of mine about a national church. The first thing is, my inquiry whether the denial of the institution of a national church (which he pleads not for) doth not deny, in consequence, that we had either ordinances or ministry amongst us? to which I say, that though it seems so to do, yet indeed it doth not, because there was then another church-state, even that of particular churches, amongst us. With many kind reflections of "my renouncing my ministry, and rejecting of my jejune and empty vindication of their ministry" (which yet is the very same that himself fixes on), he asks me "how I can in my conscience believe that there were any true ministers in this church in the time of its being national?" and so proceeds to infer from hence my denying of all ministry and ordinances among them. Truly, though I were more to be despised than I am (if that be possible), yet it were not common prudence for any man to take so much pains to make me his enemy whether I will or no. He cannot but know that I deny utterly that ever we had indeed, whatever men thought, a national church; for I grant no such thing as a national church, in the present sense contended about. That in England, under the rule of the prelates, when they looked on the church as national, there were true churches and true ministers, though in much disorder, as to the way of entering into the ministry and dispensing of ordinances, I grant freely: which is all this reverend author, if I understand him, pleads for; and this, he says, I was unwilling to acknowledge, lest I should thereby condemn myself as a schismatic. Truly, in the many sad differences and divisions that are in the world amongst Christians, I have not been without sad and jealous thoughts of heart, lest, by any doctrine or practice of mine, I should occasionally contribute any thing unto them; if it hath been otherwise with this author, I envy not his frame of spirit. But I must freely say, that having together with them weighed the reasons for them, I have been very little moved with the clamorous accusations and insinuations of this author. In the meantime, if it be possible to give him satisfaction, I here let him know that I assent unto that sum of all he hath to say as to the church of England,—namely, " That the true and faithful ministers, with the people in their several congregations, administering the true ordinances of Jesus Christ, whereof baptism is one, was and is the true church-state of England;" from which I am not separated. Nor do I think that some addition of human prudence, or imprudence, can disannul the ordinances of Jesus Christ, upon the disavower made of any other national church-state, and the assertion of this, to answer all intents and purposes. I suppose now that the reverend author knows that it is incumbent on him to prove that we have been members of some of these particular churches in due order, according to the mind of Christ, to all intents and purposes of church membership, and that we have, in our individual persons, raised causeless differences in those particular churches whereof we were members respectively, and so separated from them with the condemnation of them; or else, according to his own principles, he fails in his brotherly conclusion, ἰδοὺ Ῥόδος, ἰδοὺ πήδημα. I suppose the reader is weary of pursuing things so little to our purpose. If he will hear any farther that Independents are schismatics; that the setting up of their way hath opened a door to all evils and confusions; that they have separated from all churches, and condemn all churches in the world but their own; that they have hindered reformation and the setting up of the presbyterian church; that being members of our churches, as they are members of the nation, because they are born in it, yet they have deserted them; that they gather churches, which they pretend to be "spick and span new," they have separated from us; that they countenance Quakers and all other sectaries; that they will reform a national church whether men will or no, though they say that they only desire to reform themselves, and plead for liberty to that end;—if any man, I say, have a mind to read or hear of this any more, let him read the rest of this chapter, or else converse with some persons whom I can direct him to, who talk at this wholesome rate all the day long.

What seems to be my particular concernment I shall a little farther attend unto. Some words (for that is the manner of managing this controversy) are culled out from pp. 259, 260 [p. 198], to be made the matter of farther contest. Thus they lie in my treatise: " As the not giving a man's self up unto any way, and submitting to any establishment, pretended or pleaded to be of Christ, which he hath not light for, and which he was not by any act of his own formerly engaged in, cannot, with any colour or pretence of reason, be reckoned to him for schism, though he may, if he persist in his refusal, prejudice his own edification; so no more can a man's peaceable relinquishment of the ordinary communion of one church, in all its relations, be so esteemed." These words have as yet, unto me, a very harmless aspect;—but our reverend author is sharp-sighted, and sees I know not what monsters in them; for, first, saith he, " Here he seems to me to be a very sceptic in his way of Independency." Why so, I pray? " This will gratify all sects, Quakers and all, with a toleration." How, I pray? It is schism, not toleration, we are treating about. " But this leaves them to judge, as well as others, of what is and what is not according to the mind of Christ." Why, pray, sir, who is appointed to judge finally for them? " Why, then, should they be denied their liberty?" But is that the thing under consideration? Had you concluded that their not submitting to what they have not light for its institution is not properly schism, you should have seen how far I had been concerned in the inference; (but excursions unto Quakers, etc., are one topic of such discourses.) But now he asks me one question, it seems, to try whether I am a sceptic or no. " Whether," saith he, " does he believe his own way to be the only true way of Christ (for he hath instituted but one way), having run from and renounced all other ways in this nation?" I promise you this is a hard question, and not easily answered. If I *deny* it, he will say I am a sceptic, and other things also will be brought in. If I *affirm* it, it may be he will say that I condemn their churches for no churches, and the like. It is good to be wary when a man hath to deal with wise men. How if I should say that our way and their way is, for the substance of them, one way, and so I cannot say that my way is the only true way exclusively to theirs? I suppose this may do pretty well. But I fear this will scarce give satisfaction, and yet I know not well how I can go any farther. Yet this I will add: I do indeed believe that wherein their way and our way differ, our way is according to the mind of Christ, and not theirs; and this I am ready at any time (God assisting) personally to maintain to him. And as for my running from ways of religion, I dare again tell him these reproaches and calumnies become him not at all. But he proceeds. " If so," saith he, " is not every man bound to come into it, and not upon every conceived new light to relinquish it?" Truly, I think Mr C. himself is bound to come into it, and yet I do not think that his not so doing makes him a schismatic; and as for relinquishment, I assert no more than what he himself concludes to be lawful.

And thus, Christian reader, I have given thee a brief account of all things of any importance that I could meet withal in this treatise, and of many which are of very little. If thou shalt be pleased to compare my treatise of schism with the refutation of it, thou wilt quickly see how short this is of that which it pretends to; how untouched my principles do abide; and how the most material parts of my discourse are utterly passed by, without any notice taken of them. The truth is, in the way chosen by this reverend author to proceed in, men may multiply writings to the world's end without driving any controversy to an issue. Descanting and harping on words, making exceptions to particular passages, and the like, is an easy and facile, and, to some men, a pleasant labour. What small reason our author had to give his book the title it bears, unless it were to discover his design, I hope doth by this time appear. Much of the proof of it lies in the repeated asseverations of it, " It is so, and it is so." If he shall be pleased to send me word of one argument tending that way that is not founded in an evident mistake, I will promise him, if I live, a reconsideration of it.

In the meantime, I humbly beg of this reverend author that he would review, in the presence of the Lord, the frame of spirit wherein he wrote this charge; as also, that he would take into his thoughts all the reproaches and all that obloquy he hath endeavoured to load me causelessly and falsely withal. As for myself, my name, reputation, and esteem with the churches of God, to whom he hath endeavoured to render me odious, I commit the whole concernment of them to Him whose presence, through grace, I have hitherto enjoyed, and whose promise I lean upon, that he will " never leave me nor forsake me." I shall not complain of my usage (but what am I?)—of the usage of many precious saints and holy churches of Jesus Christ,—to Him that lives and sees, any farther than by begging that it may not be laid to his charge. And if so mean a person as I am can in any way be serviceable to him, or to any of the churches that he pleads for, in reference to the gospel of Christ, I hope my life will not be dear to me that it may effect it; and I shall not cease to pray that both he and those who promoted this work in his hand may at length consider the many calls of God that are evident upon them, to lay aside these unseemly animosities, and to endeavour a coalition in love with all those who in sincerity call upon the name of the Lord Jesus Christ, their Lord and ours.

For the distances themselves that are between us, wherein we are not as yet agreed; what is the just state of them, the truth and war-rantableness of the principles whereupon we proceed, with the necessity of our practice in conformity thereunto; in what we judge our brethren to come short of, or wherein to go beyond the mind of Jesus Christ; with a farther ventilation of this business of schism,— I have some good grounds of expectation that possibly, ere long, we may see a fair discussion of these things, in a pursuit of truth and peace.

AN ANSWER

TO

A LATE TREATISE OF MR CAWDREY

ABOUT

THE NATURE OF SCHISM.

Δεῖ τὸν ἐπίσκοπον ἀνέγλητον εἶναι, ὡς Θεοῦ οἰκονόμον, μὴ αὐθάδη, μὴ ὀργίλον, μὴ πάροινον, μὴ πλήκτην, μὴ αἰσχροκερδῆ.—Tit. i. 7.

OXFORD: 1658.

PREFATORY NOTE.

The two foregoing treatises had appeared in 1657, and in the year following our author had to reply to another work by his opponent Cawdrey, " Independency further Proved to be a Schism." The latter had been previously engaged in a controversy on the subject of church government with Mr John Cotton, an eminent Congregationalist of New England, to whose work on "The Keys of the Kingdom of Heaven," Cawdrey had replied in his " Vindiciæ Clavium," and in another work, " The Inconsistency of the Independent Way with Scripture and Itself." A manuscript by Cotton in defence of his book had been committed to Owen, who cherished a respect for his memory, as it was the perusal of his work, " The Keys of the Kingdom of Heaven," which led our author to reconsider and modify his views respecting the nature and polity of the church. To meet the last assault of Cawdrey he gave the manuscript of Cotton to the press, and accompanied it with a lengthy preface in vindication of himself from the charges of his opponent. The disproof of the alleged contradictions with which he was reproached is complete, but it cannot be said that there is much of novelty or importance in the statements contained in this treatise. After a lapse of twenty-two years, Dr Owen had again to vindicate his denomination from the same charge of schism, in very different circumstances, and against a more adroit and accomplished adversary. Accordingly, with the different works of Owen on the subject of schism, we have connected his pamphlet on the same subject in reply to Stillingfleet, though the interval just specified ensued before he broke a lance in controversy with the learned Dean of St Paul's. —Ed.

AN ANSWER

TO

A LATE TREATISE ABOUT THE NATURE OF SCHISM.

CHRISTIAN READER,

I HAVE not much to say unto thee concerning the ensuing treatise,—it will speak for itself with all impartial men; much less shall I insist on the commendation of its author, who also being dead ἔτι λαλεῖται, and will be so, I am persuaded, whilst Christ hath a church upon the earth. The treatise itself was written sundry years ago, immediately upon the publishing of Mr Cawdrey's accusation against him. I shall not need to give an account whence it hath been that it saw the light no sooner; it may suffice that, in mine own behalf and that of others, I do acknowledge that, in the doing of sundry things seeming of more importance, this ought not to have been omitted. The judgment of the author approving of this vindication of himself as necessary, considering the place he held in the church of God, should have been a rule unto us for the performance of that duty, which is owing to his worth and piety in doing and suffering for the truth of God. It is now about seven months ago since it came into my hands; and since I engaged myself unto the publication of it, my not immediate proceeding therein being sharply rebuked by a fresh charge upon myself from that hand under which this worthy person so far suffered as to be necessitated to the ensuing defensative, I have here discharged that engagement. The author of the charge against him, in his epistle to that against me, tells his reader that " it is thought that it was intended by another (and now promised by myself) to be published, to cast a slur upon him." So are our intentions judged, so our ways, by thoughts and reports! Why a vindication of Mr Cotton should cast a slur upon Mr Cawdrey, I know not. Is he concerned in spirit or reputation in the acquitment of a holy, reverend person, now at rest with Christ, from imputations of inconstancy and self-contradiction? Is there not room enough in the world to bear the good names of Mr Cotton and Mr Cawdrey, but that if one be vindicated the other must be slurred? He shall find now, by experience, what assistance he found from Him who loved him to bear his charge and to repel it, without any such reflection on his accuser as might savour of an intention to slur him. " Mala mens, malus animus." The measure that men fear from others they have commonly meted out unto them beforehand. He wishes those " that intend to rake in the ashes of the dead to consider whether they shall deserve any thanks for their labour." How *the covering of the dead* with their own comely garments comes to be *a raking into their ashes*, I know not. His name is alive, though he be dead. It was that, not his person, that was attempted to be wounded by the charge against him. To pour forth that balm for its healing, now he is dead, which himself provided whilst he was alive, without adding or diminishing one syllable, is no raking into his ashes; and I hope the δεύτεραι φροντίθες of the reverend author will not allow him to be offended that this friendly office is performed to a dead brother, to publish this his defence of his own innocency, written in obedience to a prime dictate of the law of nature, against the wrong which was not done him in secret.

But the intendment of this prefatory discourse being my own concernment in reference to a late tract of Mr Cawdrey's, bearing on its title and superscription a vindication from my " unjust clamours and false aspersions," I shall not detain the reader with any farther discourse of that which he will find fully debated in the ensuing treatise itself, but immediately address myself to that which is my present peculiar design. By what ways and means the difference betwixt us is come to that issue wherein now it stands stated in the expressions before mentioned, I shall not need to repeat. Who first let out those waters of strife, who hath filled their streams with bitterness, clamour, and false aspersions, is left to the judgment of all that fear the Lord, who shall have occasion at any time to reflect upon those discourses. However, it is come to pass, I must acknowledge, that the state of the controversy between us is now degenerated into such a useless strife of words as that I dare publicly own engagements into studies of so much more importance unto the interest of truth, piety, and literature, as that I cannot, with peace in my own retirement, be much farther conversant therein. Only, whereas I am not in the least convinced that Mr Cawdrey hath given satisfaction to my former expostulations about the injuries done me in his other treatise, and hath evidently added to the number and weight of them in this, I could not but lay hold of this opportunity, given by my discharging a former promise, once more to remind him of some miscarriages, exceedingly unbecoming his profession and calling, which I shall do in a brief review of his epistle and treatise: upon the consideration whereof, without charging him or his way with schism in great letters on the title-page of this book, I doubt not but it will appear that the guilt of the crime he falsely, unjustly, and uncharitably chargeth upon others, may be laid more equitably at his own door; and that the shortness of the covering used by him and others to hide themselves from the inquisition made after them for schism, upon their own principles, will not be supplied by such outcries as those he is pleased to use after them who are least of all men concerned in the matter under contest, there being no solid medium whereby they may be impleaded. And in this discourse I shall, as I suppose, put an end to my engagement in this controversy. I know no man whose patience will enable him to abide always in the consideration of things to so little purpose. Were it not that men bear themselves on high by resting on the partial adherence of many to their dictates, it were impossible they should reap any contentment in their retirements from such a management of controversies as this: " Independency is a great schism, it hath made all the divisions amongst us." " Brownists, Anabaptists, and all sectaries, are Independents." " They deny our ministers and churches; they separate from us; all errors come from among them." " This I have been told," and, " That I have heard;"—[which] is the sum of this treatise. Who they are of whom he speaks; how they came into such a possession of all church-state in England, that all that are not with them are schismatics; how, " de jure" or " de facto," they came to be so instated; what claim they can make to their present stations without schism, on their own principles; whether, granting the church of England, as constituted when they and we began that which we call Reformation, to have been a true instituted church, they have any power of rule in it but what hath been got by violence; what that is purely theirs hath any pretence of establishment from the Scripture, antiquity, and the laws of this land; —I say, with these and the like things, which are incumbent on him to clear up before his charges with us will be of any value, our author troubleth not himself. But to proceed to the particulars by him insisted on.

1. He tells the reader in his epistle that his unwillingness to this rejoinder was heightened by the necessity he found of *discovering some personal weaknesses and forgetfulnesses in me, upon my denial of some things which were known to be true, if he should proceed therein.* For what he intimates of the unpleasantness that it is to him to discover things of that importance in me, when he professeth his design to be to impair my authority so far that the cause I own may receive no countenance thereby, I leave it to Him who will one day reveal the secrets of all hearts, which at present are open and naked unto Him. But how, I pray, are the things by me denied known to be true? Seeing it was unpleasant and distasteful to him to insist upon them, men might expect that his evidence of them was not only open, clear, undeniable, and manifest as to its truth, but cogent as to their publication. The whole insisted on is, "If there be any truth in reports," "hic nigræ succus loliginis, hæc est ærugo mera." Is this a bottom for a minister of the gospel to proceed upon to such charges as those insinuated? Is not the course of nature set on fire at this day by reports? Is any thing more contrary to the royal law of charity than to take up reports as the ground of charges and accusations? Is there any thing more unbecoming a man,—laying aside all considerations of Christianity,—than to suffer his judgment to be tainted, much more his words and public expressions in charging and accusing others to be regulated, by reports? And whereas we are commanded to speak evil of no man, may we not on this ground speak evil of all men, and justify ourselves by saying, "It is so, if reports be true?" The prophet tells us that a combination for his defaming and reproach was managed among his adversaries: Jer. xx. 10, "I heard the defaming of many, fear on every side. Report, say they, and we will report it." If they can have any to go before them in the transgression of that law, which He who knows how the tongues of men are "set on fire of hell" gave out to lay a restraint upon them, "Thou shalt not raise a false report," Exod. xxiii. 1, they will second it, and spread it abroad to the utmost, for his disadvantage and trouble. Whether this procedure of our reverend author come not up to the practice of their design, I leave to his own conscience to judge. Should men suffer their spirits to be heightened by provocations of this nature, unto a recharge from the same offensive dunghill of reports, what monsters should we speedily be transformed into! But this being far from being the only place wherein appeal is made to reports and hear-says by our author, I shall have occasion, in the consideration of the severals of them, to re-assume this discourse. For what he adds about the space of time wherein my former reply was drawn up, because I know not whether he had heard any report insinuated to the contrary to what I affirmed, I shall not trouble him with giving evidence thereunto, but only add, that here he hath the product of half that time, which I now interpose upon the review of my transcribed papers; only, whereas it is said that Mr Cawdrey is an ancient man, I cannot but wonder he should be so easy of belief. Aristotle, Rhetor. lib. ii. cap. 18, tells us, Οἱ πρεσβύτεροι, ἄπιστοι δι' ἐμπειρίαν, and not apt to believe, whence on all occasions of discourse προστιθέασιν ἀεὶ τὸ ἴσως καὶ τάχα· but he believes all that comes to hand with an easy faith, which he hath totally in his own power to dispose of at pleasure. That I was in passion when I wrote my review is his judgment; but this is but man's day; we are in expectation of that wherein "the world shall be judged in righteousness." It is too possible that my spirit was not in that frame, in all things, wherein it ought to have been; but that the reverend author knows not. I have nothing to say to this but that of the philosopher, Ἐάν τίς σοι ἀπαγγείλῃ ὅτι ὁ δεῖνά σε κακῶς λέγει, μὴ ἀπολογοῦ πρὸς τὰ λεχθέντα, ἀλλ' ἀποκρίνου ὅτι ἀγνόει, τὰ γὰρ ἄλλα προσιόντα μοι κακὰ ἐπεὶ οὐκ ἂν ταῦτα μόνα ἔλεγεν, Epic., cap. xlviii. Much, I confess, was not spoken by me (which he afterward insisteth on) to the argumentative part of his book; which as in an answer I was not to look for, so to find had been a difficult task. As he hath nothing to say unto the differences among themselves, both in judgment and practice, so how little there is in his recrimination of the differences among us,—as, that one and the same man differeth from himself, which charge he casts upon Mr Cotton and myself,—will speedily be manifested to all impartial men. For the treatise itself, whose consideration I now proceed unto, that I may reduce what I have to say unto it into the bounds intended, in confining my defensative unto this preface to the treatise of another, I shall refer it unto certain heads, that will be comprehensive of the whole, and give the reader a clear and distinct view thereof.

I shall begin with that which is least handled in the two books of this reverend author, though the sum of what was pleaded by me in my treatise of schism. For the discovery of the true nature of schism, and the vindication of them who were falsely charged with the crime thereof, I laid down two principles as the foundation of all that I asserted in the whole cause insisted on, which may briefly be reduced to these two syllogisms:—

1. If in all and every place of the New Testament where there is mention made of schism, name or thing, in an ecclesiastical sense, there is nothing intended by it but a *division* in a particular church, then that is the proper Scripture notion of schism in the ecclesiastical sense; but in all and every place, etc.: *ergo.* The proposition being clear and evident in its own light, the assumption was confirmed in my treatise by an induction of the several instances that might any way seem to belong unto it.

2. My second principle was raised upon a concession of the general nature of schism, restrained with one necessary limitation, and amounts unto this argument:—If schism in an ecclesiastical sense be the breach of a union of Christ's institution, then they who are not guilty of the breach of a union of Christ's institution are not guilty of schism; but so is schism: *ergo.*

The proposition also of this syllogism, with its inference, being unquestionable, for the confirmation of the assumption, I considered the nature of all church-union as instituted by Christ, and pleaded the innocency of those whose defence, in several degrees, I had undertaken, by their freedom from the breach of any church-union. Not finding the reverend author, in his first answer, to speak clearly and distinctly to either of those principles, but to proceed in a course of perpetual diversion from the thing in question, with reflections, charges, etc.,—all rather, I hope, out of an unacquaintedness with the true nature of argumentation than any perverseness of spirit, in cavilling at what he found he could not answer,—I earnestly desired him, in my review, that we might have a fair and friendly meeting, personally to debate those principles which he had undertaken to oppose, and so to prevent trouble to ourselves and others, in writing and reading things remote from the merit of the cause under agitation. What returns I have had hitherto the reader is now acquainted withal from his rejoinder, the particulars whereof shall be farther inquired into afterward.

The other parts of his two books consist in his charges upon me about my judgment in sundry particulars, not relating in the least, that I can as yet understand, unto the controversy in hand. As to his excursions about Brownists, Anabaptists, Seekers, rending the peace of their churches, separating from them, the errors of the Separatists, and the like, I cannot apprehend myself concerned to take notice of them; to the other things an answer shall be returned and a defence made, so far as I can judge it necessary. It may be our author seeks a relief from the charge of schism that lies upon him and his party (as they are called) from others, by managing the same charge against them who, he thinks, will not return it upon them; but for my part, I shall assure him that were he not, in my judgment, more acquitted upon my principles than upon his own, I should be necessitated to stand upon even terms with him herein. But to have advantages from want of charity, as the Donatists had against the Catholics, is no argument of a good cause.

In the first chapter there occurs not any thing of real difference, as to the cause under agitation, that should require a review, being spent wholly in things ἔξω τοῦ πράγματος, and therefore I shall briefly animadvert on what seems of most concernment therein, on the manner of his procedure. His former discourse, and this also, consisting much of my words perverted by adding in the close something that might wrest them to his own purpose, he tells me, in the beginning of his third chapter, that " this is to turn my testimony against myself; which is," as he saith, " an allowed way of the clearest victory," which it seemeth he aimeth at; but nothing can be more remote from being defended with that pretence than this way of proceeding. It is not of urging a testimony from me against me that I complained, but the perverting of my words, by either heading or closing of them with his own, quite to other purposes than those of their own intendment;—a way whereby any man may make other men's words to speak what he pleaseth; as Mr Biddle, by his leading questions, and knitting of scriptures to his expressions in them, makes an appearance of constraining the word of God to speak out all his Socinian blasphemies.

In this course he still continues, and his very entrance gives us a pledge of what we are to expect in the process of his management of the present business. Whereas I had said, that, " considering the various interests of parties at difference, there is no great success to be promised by the management of controversies, though with never so much evidence and conviction of truth;" to the repetition of my words he subjoins the instance of " sectaries, not restrained by the clearest demonstration of truth;" not weighing how facile a task it is to supply " Presbyterians" in their room; which in his account is, it seems, to turn his testimony against himself, and, as he somewhere phraseth it, " to turn the point of his sword into his own bowels." But " nobis non tam licet esse disertis;" neither do we here either learn or teach any such way of disputation.

His following leaves are spent, for the most part, in slighting the notion of schism by me insisted on, and in reporting my arguments for it, pp. 8, 9, 12, in such a way and manner as argues that he either never understood them or is willing to pervert them. The true nature and importance of them I have before laid down, and shall not now again repeat; though I shall add, that his frequent repetition of his disproving that principle, which it appears that he never yet contended withal in its full strength, brings but little advantage to his cause with persons whose interest doth not compel them to take up things on trust. How well he clears himself from the charge of reviling and using opprobrious, reproachful terms, although he profess himself to have been astonished at the charge, may be seen in his justification of himself therein, pp. 16–19, with his re-enforcing every particular expression instanced in; and yet he tells me, for inferring that he discovered sanguinary thoughts in reference unto them whose removal from their native soil into the wilderness he affirms England's happiness would have consisted in, that he hath " much ado to forbear once more to say, ' The Lord rebuke thee.'" For my part, I have received such a satisfactory taste of his spirit and way, that as I shall not from henceforth desire him to keep in any thing that he can hardly forbear to let out, but rather to use his utmost liberty, so I must assure him that I am very little concerned, or not at all, in what he shall be pleased to say or to forbear for the time to come; himself hath freed me from that concernment.

The first particular of value insisted on, is his charge upon me for *the denial of all the churches of England to be true churches of Christ, except the churches gathered in a congregational way.* Having frequently, and without hesitation, charged this opinion upon me in his first answer, knowing it to be very false, I expostulated with him about it in my review.　Instead of accepting the satisfaction tendered in my express denial of any such thought or persuasion, or tendering any satisfaction as to the wrong done me, he seeks to justify himself in his charge, and so persisteth therein.　The reasons he gives for his so doing are not unworthy a little to be remarked.

The first is this: He "supposed me to be an Independent," and therefore made that charge; the consequent of which supposition is much too weak to justify this reverend author in his accusation.　Doth he suppose that he may without offence lay what he pleases to the charge of an Independent?　But he saith, secondly, that he "took the word Independent generally, as comprehending Brownists, and Anabaptists, and other sectaries."　But herein also he doth but delude his own conscience, seeing he personally speaks to me and to my design in that book of schism which he undertook to confute; which also removes his third intimation, that he "formerly intended any kind of Independence," etc.　The rest that follow are of the same nature, and, however compounded, will not make a salve to heal the wound made in his reputation by his own weapon.　For the learned author called "vox populi," which he is pleased here to urge, I first question whether he be willing to be produced to maintain this charge; and if he shall appear, I must needs tell him (what he here questions whether it be so or no) that he is a very liar.　For any principles in my treatise whence a denial of their ministers and churches may be regularly deduced, let him produce them if he can; and if not, acknowledge that there had been a more Christian and ingenuous way of coming off an engagement into that charge than that by him chosen to be insisted on. "Animos et iram ex crimine sumunt."　And again we have "vox populi" cited on the like occasion, p. 34, about my refusal to answer whether I were a minister or not; which as the thing itself, of such a refusal of mine, on any occasion in the world (because it must be spoken), is "purum putum mendacium," so it is no truer that that was "vox populi" at Oxford, which is pretended.　That which is "vox populi" must be public; "publicum" was once "populicum."　Now, set aside the whispers of, it may be, two or three ardelios,[1] notorious triflers, whose lavish impertinency will deliver any man from the danger of being slandered by their tongues, and there will be little ground left for the report that is fathered on "vox populi."　And I tell him here once again,—which is a sufficient answer, indeed, to his whole first chapter,—that I do not deny presbyterian churches to be true churches of Jesus Christ, nor the ministers of them to be true ministers, nor do maintain a nullity in their ordination, as to what is the proper use and end of salvation[2] (taking it in the sense wherein by them it is taken), though I think it neither administered by them in due order, nor to have in itself that force and efficacy, singly considered, which by many of them is ascribed unto it.　Thus much of my judgment I have publicly declared long ago; and I thought I might have expected, from persons professing Christianity, that they would not voluntarily engage themselves into an opposition against me, and, waiving my judgment, which I had constantly published and preached, have gathered up reports from private and table discourses, most of them false and untrue, all of them uncertain, the occasions and coherences of those discourses from whence they have been raised and taken being utterly lost, or at present by him wholly omitted.　His following excursions, about a successive ordination from Rome, wherein he runs cross to the most eminent lights of all the reformed churches, and their declared judgments, with practice, in re-ordaining those who come unto them with that Roman stamp upon them, I shall not farther interest myself in, nor think myself

---

[1] *Ardelio*, a busy-body, a meddler; a term borrowed from Phædrus, lib ii. fab. 5.—ED.
[2] Vid. Gerard. loc. Com. de Minist. Ecclesiast. sect. 11, 12.

concerned so to do, until I see a satisfactory answer given unto Beza and others on this very point. And yet I must here again profess that I cannot understand that distinction, of deriving ordination from the church of Rome, but not from the Roman church. Let him but seriously peruse these ensuing words of Beza, and tell me whether he have any ground of a particular quarrel against me upon this account:—

"Sed præterea quænam ista est, quæso, ordinaria vocatio, quam eos habuisse dicis, quos Deus paucis quibusdam exceptis, excitavit? Certe papistica. Nam hæc tua verba sunt; hodie si episcopi Gallicanarum ecclesiarum se et suas ecclesias a tyrannide episcopi Romani vindicare velint, et eas ab omni idololatria et superstitione repurgare, non habent opus alia vocatione ab ea quam habent. Quid ergo? Papisticas ordinationes,—in quibus neque morum examen præcessit, neque leges ullæ servatæ sunt inviolabiliter ex divino jure in electionibus et ordinationibus præscriptæ, in quibus puri etiam omnes canones impudentissime violati sunt: quæ nihil aliud sunt, quam fœdissima Romani prostibuli nundinatio, quâvis meretricum mercede, quam Deus templo suo inferri prohibuit, inquinatior: quibus denique alii non ad prædicandum sed pervertendum evangelium: alii non ad docendum, sed ad rursus sacrificandum, et ad abominandum βδέλυγμα sunt ordinati,— usque adeo firmas tecum esse censebimus, ut quoties tali cuipiam pseudoepiscopo Deus concesserit, ad verum Christianismum transire, omnis illa istiusmodi ordinationis impuritas simul expurgata censeatur? Imo quia sic animum per Dei gratiam mutavit, quo ore, quo pudore, qua conscientia papismum quidem detestabitur, suam autem inordinatissimam ordinationem non ejurabit? aut si, ejuret, quomodo ex illius jure auctoritatem dicendi habebit? Nec tamen nego quin tales, si probe doctrinam veram tenere, si honestis moribus præditi, si ad gregem pascendum apti comperiantur, ex pseudoepiscopis novi pastores, legitimè designentur." Thus he, who was thought then to speak the sense of the churches of Geneva and France, in his book against Saravia about the divers orders of ministers in the church.

His plea for the church-authority of the pope, notwithstanding his being an idolater, a murderer, the man of sin, an adversary of Christ, because a civil magistrate doth not by any moral crime, or those whereof the pope is guilty, lose his jurisdiction and authority, considering the different principles, grounds, ends, laws, rules, privileges, of the authority of the one and the other, and the several tenures whereby the one doth hold and the other pretends to hold his power, is brought in to serve the turn in hand, and may be easily laid aside. And when he shall manifest that there is appointed by Christ one single high priest or prelate in the house of God, the whole church, and that office to be confined to one nation, one blood, one family, propagated by natural generation, without any provision of relief by any other way, person, or family, in case of miscarriage; and when he shall have proved that such an officer as the pope of Rome, in any one particular that constituteth him such an officer, was once instituted by Christ,—I shall farther attend unto his reason for his authority from that of the high priest's among the Jews, which was not lost, as to its continuance in the family of Aaron, notwithstanding the miscarriage of some individual persons vested therewithal. In the close of the chapter he re-assumes his charge of my renouncing my own ordination, which, with great confidence, and without the least scruple, he had asserted in his answer. Of that assertion he now pretends to give the reasons, whereof the first is this:—

1. "*The world looks on him as an Independent of the highest note; therefore, he hath renounced his ordination, and therefore I dare to say so.*" So much for that reason. I understand neither the logic nor morality of this first reason.

2. He *knows from good hands that some of the brethren have renounced their*

ordination; therefore, he durst say positively that I have renounced mine, Prov. xii. 18.

3. He hath heard that *I dissuaded others from their ordination;* and therefore he durst say I renounced my own. And yet I suppose he may possibly dissuade some from episcopal ordination; but I know it not, no more than he knows what he affirms of me, which is false.

4. He concludes from the principles in my book of schism, because I said that to insist upon *a succession of ordination from antichrist and the beast of Rome would, if I mistake not, keep up in this particular what God would have pulled down,* therefore I renounced my ordination, when he knows that I avowed the validity of ordination on another account.

5. If all this will not do, he tells me of something that was said at a *public meeting* (at dinner, it seems) with the canons of Christ Church,—namely, that *I valued not my ordination by the bishop of Oxford any more than a crumb upon my trencher;* which words, whether ever they were spoken or no, or to what purpose, òr in reference to what ordination (I mean of the two orders), or in what sense, or with what limitation, or as part of what discourse, or in comparison of what else, or whether solely in reference to the Roman succession,—in which sense I will have nothing to do with it,—I know not at all, nor will concern myself to inquire, being greatly ashamed to find men professing the religion of Jesus Christ so far forgetful of all common rules of civility and principles of human society as to insist upon such vain, groundless reports as the foundation of accusations against their brethren. Nor do I believe that any one of the reverend persons quoted will own this information, although I shall not concern myself to make inquiry into their memories concerning any such passage or discourse.

Much relief, for the future, against these and the like mistakes may be afforded, from an easy observation of the different senses wherein the term of *ordination* is often used. It is one thing when it is taken largely, for the whole appointment of a man to the ministry,—in which sense I desire our author to consider what is written by Beza among the Reformed, and Gerhard among the Lutheran divines, to omit innumerable others,—another thing when taken for the imposition of hands, whether by bishops or presbyters; concerning which single act, both as to its order and efficacy, I have sufficiently delivered my judgment, if he be pleased to take notice of it. I fear, indeed, that when men speak of an " ordained ministry,"— which, in its true and proper sense, I shall with them contend for,—they often relate only to that solemnity, restraining the authoritative making of ministers singly thereunto, contrary to the intention and meaning of that expression in Scripture, antiquity, and the best reformed divines, both Calvinists and Lutherans; and yet it is not imaginable how some men prevail, by the noise and sound of that word, upon the prejudiced minds of partial, unstudied men. A little time may farther manifest, if it be not sufficiently done already, that another account is given of this matter by Clemens, Tertullian, Cyprian, Origen, Justin Martyr, and generally all the first writers of the Christians, besides the councils of old and late, with innumerable protestant authors of the best note, to the same purpose.

This, I say, is the ground of this mistake: Whereas sundry things concur to *the calling of ministers,* as it belongs to the church of God, the pillar and ground of truth, the spouse of Christ, Ps. xlv. 9, and mother of the family, or her that tarrieth at home, Ps. lxviii. 12, unto whom all ministers are stewards, 1 Cor. iv. 1, even in the house of God, 1 Tim. iii. 15; and sundry qualifications are indispensably previously required in the persons to be called; overlooking the necessity of the qualifications required, and omitting the duty and authority of the church, Acts i. 15–26, vi. 2–6, xiii. 2, 3, xiv. 23, the act of them who are not the whole church, Eph. iv. 11, 12, but only a part of it, 1 Cor. iii. 5. 2 Cor. i. 24, 1 Pet.

v. 3, as to ministry, consisting in the approbation and solemn confirmation of what is supposed to go before, hath in some men's language gotten the name of " ordination," and an interpretation of that name, to such an extent as to inwrap in it all that is indispensably necessary to the constitution or making of ministers: so that where that is obtained, in what order soever, or by whomsoever administered, who have first obtained it themselves, there is a lawful and sufficient calling to the ministry! Indeed, I know no error about the institutions of Christ attended with more pernicious consequences to the church of God than this, should it be practised according to the force of the principle itself. Suppose six, eight, or ten men, who have themselves been formerly ordained, but now perhaps, not by any ecclesiastical censure, but by an act of the civil magistrate, are put out of their places for notorious ignorance and scandal, should concur and ordain a hundred ignorant and wicked persons like themselves to be ministers, must they not, on this principle, be all accounted ministers of Christ, and to be invested with all ministerial power, and so be enabled to propagate their kind to the end of the world? And, indeed, why should not this be granted, seeing the whole bulk of the papal ordination is contended for as valid? whereas it is notoriously known that sundry bishops among them (who perhaps received their own ordination as the reward of a whore), being persons of vicious lives, and utterly ignorant of the gospel, did sustain their pomp and sloth by selling " holy orders," as they called them, to the scum and refuse of men. But of these things more in their proper place.

Take then, reader, the substance of this chapter in this brief recapitulation:— 1. " He denies our churches to be true churches, and our ministers true ministers;" 2. " He hath renounced his own ordination;" 3. " When some young men came to advise about their ordination, he dissuaded them from it;" 4. " He saith he would maintain against all the ministers of England there was in Scripture no such thing as ordination;" 5. " That when he was chosen a parliament-man, he would not answer whether he was a minister or not;"—all which are notoriously untrue, and some of them, namely, the last two, so remote from any thing to give a pretence or colour unto them, that I question whether Satan have impudence enough to own himself their author. And yet, from hear-says, reports, rumours, from table-talk, " vox populi," and such other grounds of reasoning, this reverend author hath made them his own; and by such a charge he hath, I presume, in the judgment of all unprejudiced men, discharged me from farther attending to what he shall be prompted from the like principles to divulge, for the same ends and purposes which hitherto he hath managed, for the future. For my judgment about their ministry and ordination, about the nature and efficacy of ordination, the state and power of particular churches, my own station in the ministry, which I shall at all times, through the grace and assistance of our Lord Jesus Christ, freely justify against men and devils, it is so well known that I shall not need here farther to declare it. For the true nature and notion of schism, alone by me inquired after in this chapter, as I said, I find nothing offered thereunto. Only, whereas I restrained the ecclesiastical use of the word " schism" to the sense wherein it is used in the places of Scripture that mention it with relation to church affairs,—which that it ought not to be so, nothing but asseverations to the contrary are produced to evince,—this is interpreted to extend to all that I would allow as to the nature of schism itself, which is most false; though I said, if I would proceed no farther, I might not be compelled so to do, seeing in things of this nature we may crave allowance to think and speak with the Holy Ghost. However, I expressly comprised in my proposition all the places wherein the nature of schism is delivered, under what terms or words soever. When, then, I shall be convinced that such discourses as those of this treatise, made up of diversions into things wholly foreign to the inquiry by me insisted on in the investigation of the true notion and nature of schism, with long talks about Anabaptists, Brownists, Sectaries, Independents, Presbyterians, ordination, with charges and reflections grounded on this presumption, [prove] that this author and his party (for we will no more contend about that expression) are "in solidum" possessed of all true and orderly church-state in England, so that whosoever are not of them are "schismatics," and I know not what besides, he being

—— "gallinæ filius albæ,
Nos viles pulli nati infelicibus ovis," Juv., xiii. 141,

I shall farther attend unto them.

I must farther add, that I was not so happy as to foresee that, because I granted the Roman party before the Reformation to have made outwardly a profession of the religion of Christ,—although I expressed them to be really a party combined together for all ends of wickedness, and, in particular, for the extirpation of the true church of Christ in the world, having no state of union but what the Holy Ghost calls "Babylon," in opposition to "Zion,"—our reverend author would conclude, as he doth, p. 34, that I allowed them to be a true church of Christ; but it is impossible for wiser men than I to see far into the issue of such discourses, and therefore we must take in good part what doth fall out. And if the reverend author, instead of having his zeal warmed against me, would a little bestir his abilities to make out to the understandings and consciences of uninterested men, that, all ecclesiastical power being vested in the pope and councils, by the consent of that whole combination of men called the Church of Rome, and flowing from the pope in its execution to all others,—who, in the derivation of it from him, owned him as the immediate fountain of it, which they sware to maintain in him, and this in opposition to all church-power in any other persons whatsoever,—it was possible that any power should be derived from that combination but what came expressly from the fountain mentioned; I desire our author would consider the frame of spirit that was in this matter in them who first laboured in the work of reformation, and to that end peruse the stories of Lasitius[1] and Regenuolscius[2] about the churches of Bohemia, Poland, and those parts of the world, especially the latter, from pp. 29, 30, and forward.   And as to the distinction used by some between the Papacy and the church of Rome, which our author makes use of to another purpose than those did who first invented it (extending it only to the consideration of the possibility of salvation for individual persons living in that communion before the Reformation), I hope he will not be angry if I profess my disability to understand it.   All men cannot be wise alike.   If the Papacy comprise the pope, and all papal jurisdiction and power, with the subjection of men thereunto; if it denote all the idolatries, false worship, and heresies of that society of men,—I do know that all those are confirmed by church-acts of that church, and that, in the *church-public sense* of that church, no man was a member of it but by virtue of the union that consisted in that Papacy, it being placed always by them in all their definitions of their church; as also, that there was neither church-order, nor church-power, nor church-act, nor church-confession, nor church-worship amongst them, but what consisted in that Papacy.

Now, because nothing doth more frequently occur than the objection of the difficulty of placing the dispensation of baptism on a sure foot of account, in case of the rejection of all authoritative influence from Rome into the ministry of the reformed churches, with the insinuation of a supposition of the non-baptization of all such as derive not a title unto it by that means, they who do so being supposed

1 Joannes Lasitius wrote a large work on the Bohemian Brethren. The eighth book of this work, under the title, "Historiæ de Origine et Rebus Gestis Fratrum Bohemorum," etc., was published by Comenius in 1649.—ED.

2 Regenuolscius, or rather, according to his true name, Wingerscius, was the author of "Systema Historico-Chronologicum Ecclesiarum Slavonicarum."—ED.

to stand upon an unquestionable foundation, I shall a little examine the grounds of their security, and then compare them with what they have to plead who refuse to acknowledge the deriving any sap or nourishment from that rotten corrupt stock.

It is, I suppose, taken for granted that an unbaptized person can never effectually baptize, let him receive what other qualifications soever that are to be superadded as necessary thereunto. If this be not supposed, the whole weight of the objection, improved by the worst supposition that can be made, falls to the ground. I shall also desire, in the next place, that as we cannot make the popish baptism better than it is, so, that we would not plead it to be better, or any other than they profess it to be, nor pretend that though it be rotten or null in the foundation, yet by continuance and time it might obtain validity and strength. When the claim is by succession from such a stock or root, if you suppose once a total intercision in the succession from that stock or root, there is an utter end put to that claim. Let us now consider how the case is with them from whom this claim is derived.

1. It is notoriously known that, amongst them, the *validity* of the sacraments depends upon *the intention of the administrator*. It is so with them as to every thing they call a sacrament. Now, to take one step backwards, that baptism will by some of ours be scarce accounted valid which is not administered by a lawful minister. Suppose now that some pope, ordaining a bishop in his stable to satisfy a whore, had not an intention to make him a bishop (which is no remote surmise), he being no bishop rightly ordained, all the priests by him afterward consecrated were indeed no priests, and so, indeed, had no power to administer any sacraments: and so, consequently, the baptism that may lie, for aught we know, at the root of that which some of us pretend unto, was originally absolutely null and void, and could never by tract of time be made valid or effectual, for, like a muddy fountain, the farther it goes, the more filthy it is. Or, suppose that any priest, baptizing one who afterwards came to be pope, from whom all authority in that church doth flow and is derived, had no intention to baptize him, what will become of all that ensues thereon?

It is endless to pursue the uncertainties and entanglements that ensue on this head of account, and sufficiently easy to manifest that whosoever resolves his interest in gospel privileges into this foundation can have no assurance of faith, nay, nor tolerably probable conjecture that he is baptized, or was ever made partaker of any ordinance of the gospel. Let them that delight in such troubled waters sport themselves in them. For my own part,—considering the state of that church for some years if not ages, wherein the fountains of all authority amongst them were full of filth and blood, their popes, upon their own confession, being made, set up, and pulled down, at the pleasure of vile, impudent, domineering strumpets, and supplying themselves with officers all the world over of the same spirit and stamp with themselves, and that for the most part for hire, being in the meantime all idolaters to a man,—I am not willing to grant that their good and upright intention is necessary to be supposed as a thing requisite unto my interest in any privilege of the gospel of Christ.

2. It is an ecclesiastical determination, of irrefragable authority amongst them, that whosoever he be that administers baptism, so he use *the matter and form*, that baptism is good and valid, and not to be reiterated; yea, Pope Nicholas, in his resolutions and determinations upon the inquiry of the Bulgarians (whose decrees are authentic and recorded in their councils, tom. ii. Crab. p. 144), declares the judgment of that church to the full. They tell him that many in their nation were baptized by an unknown person, a Jew or a Pagan, they knew not whether, and inquire of him whether they were to be rebaptized or no; whereunto he answers: "Si in nomine S.S. Trinitatis, vel tantum in Christi nomine, sicut in

Actis apostolorum legimus, baptizati sunt, unum quippe idemque est, ut S. Ambrosius expressit, constat eos denuo non esse baptizandos." If they were baptized in the name of the Trinity, or of Christ, they are not to be baptized again. Let a blasphemous Jew or Pagan do it, so it be done, the work is wrought, grace conveyed, and baptism valid! The constant practice of women baptizing amongst them is of the same import   And what doth Mr Cawdrey think of this kind of baptism? Is it not worth the contending about, to place it in the derived succession of ours? Who knows but that some of these persons, baptized by a counterfeit impostor, on purpose to abuse and defile the institutions of our blessed Saviour, might come to be baptizers themselves, yea, bishops or popes, from whom all ecclesiastical authority was to be derived? and what evidence or certainty can any man have that his baptism doth not flow from this fountain.

3. Nay, upon the general account, if this be required as necessary to the administration of that ordinance, that he that doth baptize be rightly and effectually *baptized himself*, who can in faith bring an infant to any to be baptized, unless he himself saw that person rightly baptized?

As to the matter of baptism, then, we are no more concerned than as to that of ordination. By what ways or means soever any man comes to be a minister according to the mind of Jesus Christ, by that way and means he comes to have the power for a due administration of that ordinance; concerning which state of things our author may do well to consult Beza in the place mentioned. Many other passages there are in this chapter that might be remarked, and a return easily made according to their desert of untruth and impertinency; but the insisting on such things looks more like children's playing at push-pin than the management of a serious disputation. Take an instance. Page 23, he seems to be much offended with my commending him, and tells me, as Jerome said of Rufinus, "I wrong him with praises;" when yet the utmost I say of him is, that "I had received a better character of him than he had given of himself in his book," p. 10 [214]; and that "his proceeding was unbecoming his worth, gravity, and profession," p. 46 [227], or "so grave and reverend a person as he is reported to be," p. 121 [234]; wherein, it seems, I have transgressed the rule, Μήποτ᾽ εὖ ἔρδειν γέροντα.

The business of his second chapter is, to make good his former charge of my inconstancy and inconsistency with myself as to my former and present opinions, which he had placed in the frontispiece of his other treatise. The impertinency of this chapter had been intolerable, but that the loose discourses of it are relieved by a scheme of my self-contradictions, in the close. His design, he professeth, in his former discourse, was, not to blast my reputation or to " cause my person to suffer, but to prevent the prevalency of my way by the authority of my person;" that is, it was not his intention, it was only his intention for such a purpose! I bless my God I have good security, through grace, that whether he, or others like-minded with himself, intend any such thing or no, in those proceedings of his and theirs, which seemed to have in their own nature a tendency thereunto, my reputation shall yet be preserved in that state and condition as is necessary to accompany me in the duties and works of my generation, that I shall, through the hand of God, be called out unto. And, therefore, being prepared in some measure to go through good report and bad report, I shall give him assurance that I am very little concerned in such attempts, from whatever intention they do proceed; only, I must needs tell him that he consulted not his own reputation with peaceable, godly men, whatever else he omitted, in the ensuing comparing of me to the seducers in Jude, called " wandering planets," for their inconstancy and inconsistency with themselves,—according to the exposition that was needful for the present turn.

But seeing the scheme at the close must bear the weight of this charge, let us briefly see what it amounts unto, and whether it be a sufficient basis of the super-struction that is raised upon it. Hence it is that my inconsistency with myself must be remarked in the title-page of his first treatise; from hence must my authority (which what it is I know not) be impaired, and myself be compared to cursed apostates and seducers, and great triumph be made upon my self-inconsistency.

The contradictions pretended are taken out of two books, the one written in the year 1643, the other in 1657, and are as follow:—

| He spake of Rome as a " collapsed, corrupted church-state," p. 40 [p. 37.] | He says, " Rome we account no church at all," p. 156 [p. 155.] |

" Crimen inauditum, C. Cæsar." "Is it meet that any one should be tolerated that is thus wofully inconsistent with himself? What! speak of Rome as a *collapsed church* in Italy, and within thirteen or fourteen years after to say it is *no church at all.*" Well! though I may say there is indeed no contradiction between these assertions, seeing in the latter place I speak of Rome as that church is stated by themselves, when yet I acknowledge there may be corrupted churches both in Rome and Italy, in the same treatise; yet I do not find that in the place directed unto, I have in terms, or in just consequence, at all granted the church of Rome to be a collapsed church; nay, the church of Rome is not once mentioned in the whole page, nor as such is spoken of. And what shall we think of this proceeding? But yet I will not so far offend against my sense of my own weakness, ignorance, and frailty, as to use any defensative against this charge. Let it pass at any rate that any sober man, freed from pride, passion, self-fulness, and prejudice, shall be pleased to put upon it:—

—— ὁδὶ ὁρῶν τοῦς νόμους
Λίαν ἀκριβῶς, συκοφάντης φαίνεται.

But the second instance will make amends, and take more of the weight of this charge upon its shoulders. Take it, then, as it lies in its triple column:—

| " Gifts in the person and consent of people are warrant enough to make a man a preacher, in an extraordinary case only," pp. 15, 40 [pp. 18, 37]. | Denying our ordination to be sufficient, he says " he may have that which indeed constitutes him a minister, —namely, gifts and submission by the people," p. 198 [p. 172]. | " I am punctually of the same mind still," p. 40 [p. 226]. Yet had said in his first book, p. 46 [p. 43], "As to formal teaching is required, 1. Gifts; 2. Authority from the church,"—if he do not equivocate. |

I must confess I am here at a stand to find out the pretended contradiction, especially laying aside the word " only" in the first column, which is his, and not mine. By a " preacher," in the first place, I intend a " minister." Gifts, and consent or submission of the people, I affirm in both places to be sufficient to constitute a man a minister in extraordinary cases,—that is, when imposition of hands by a presbytery may not be obtained in due order, according to the appointment of Jesus Christ. That the consent and submission of the people, which include election, have nothing of authority in them, I never said. The superadded act of the imposition of hands by a presbytery, when it may be regularly obtained, is also necessary. But that there is any contradiction in my words (although, in truth, they are not my words, but an undue collection from them), or in this author's inference from them, or any colour of equivocation, I profess I cannot discern. In this place Mr Cawdrey, οὐκ ἴδεν, ἀλλ᾽ ἐδόκησεν ἰδεῖν διὰ νύκτα σελήνην. Pass we to the third:—

| He made the union of Christ and believers to be mystical, p. 21 [p. 129]. | He makes the union to be personal, pp. 94, 95 [p. 22]. |

I wish our reverend author, for his own sake, had omitted this instance, because I am enforced, in my own necessary defence, to let him know that what he assigns to me in his second column is notoriously false, denied and disproved by me in the very place and treatise wherein I have handled the doctrine of the indwelling of the Spirit; and whether he will hear or forbear, I cannot but tell him that this kind of dealing is unworthy his calling and profession. His following deductions and inferences, whereby he endeavours to give countenance to this false and calumnious charge, arise from ignorance of the doctrine that he seeks to blemish and oppose. Though the same Spirit dwell in Christ and us, yet *he* may have him in *fulness*, *we* in *measure;*—fulness and measure relating to his communication of graces and gifts, which are arbitrary to him; indwelling, to his person. That the Spirit animates the catholic church, and is the author of its spiritual life by a voluntary act of his power, as the soul gives life to the body by a necessary act, by virtue of its union,—for [that] life is " actus vivificantis in vivificatum per unionem utriusque,"—is the common doctrine of divines. But yet the soul being united to the body as " pars essentialis suppositi," and the Spirit dwelling in the person as a free inhabitant, the union between Christ and the person is not of the same kind with the union of soul and body. Let our author consult Zanchy on the second of the Ephesians, and he will not repent him of his labour; or, if he please, an author whom I find him often citing, namely, Bishop Hall, about union with Christ. And for my concernment in this charge, I shall subjoin the words from whence it must be taken, p. 133 of my book of Perseverance.[1]

" 1. The first signal issue and effect which is ascribed to this indwelling of the Spirit is union; not a personal union with himself, which is impossible. He doth not assume our nature, and so prevent our personality, which would make us one person with him; but dwells in our persons, keeping his own, and leaving us our personality infinitely distinct. But it is a spiritual union, the great union mentioned so often in the Gospel, that is the sole fountain of our blessedness, our union with the Lord Christ, which we have thereby.

" Many thoughts of heart there have been about this union; what it is, wherein it doth consist, the causes, manner, and effects of it. The Scripture expresses it to be very eminent, near, durable; setting it out for the most part by similitudes and metaphorical illustrations, to lead poor weak creatures into some useful, needful acquaintance with that mystery, whose depths, in this life, they shall never fathom. That many, in the days wherein we live, have miscarried in their conceptions of it is evident. Some, to make out their imaginary union, have destroyed the person of Christ; and, fancying a way of uniting man to God by him, have left him to be neither God nor man. Others have destroyed the person of believers; affirming that, in their union with Christ, they lose their own personality, —that is, cease to be men, or at least those are [or ?] these individual men.

" I intend not now to handle it at large, but only,—and that I hope, without offence,—to give in my thoughts concerning it, as far as it receiveth light from, and relateth unto, what hath been before delivered concerning the indwelling of the Spirit, and that without the least contending about other ways of expression." So far there, with much more to the purpose. And in the very place of my book of schism referred to by this author, I affirm, as the head of what I assert, that by the indwelling of the Spirit, *Christ personal* and his church do become one *Christ mystical*, 1 Cor xii. 12; the very expression insisted on by him in my former treatise. And so you have an issue of this self-contradiction; concerning which, though reports be urged for some other things, Mr Cawdrey might have said what Lucian doth of his true history, Γράφω τοίνυν περὶ ὧν μήτ' εἶδον, μήτ' ἔπαθον, μήτε παρ' ἄλλων ἐπυθόμην.

1 See vol. xi. of Owen's works, chap. viii.

Let us, then, consider the fourth, which is thus placed:—

1. "In extraordinary cases, every one that undertakes to preach the gospel must have an immediate call from God," p. 28 [p. 28.]	2. Yet required no more of before but " the gifts and consent of the people, which are ordinary and mediate calls," p. 15 [p. 18], neither is here any need or use of an immediate call, p. 53 [p. 48.]	3. To assure a man that he is extraordinarily called, he gives three ways: " 1. Immediate revelation ; 2. Concurrence of Scripture rule; 3. Some outward acts of providence ; "—the two last whereof are mediate calls, p. 30 [p. 29.]

All that is here remarked and cast into three columns, I know not well why, is taken out of that one treatise of " The Duty of Pastors and People;" and could I give myself the least assurance that any one would so far concern himself in this charge as to consult the places from whence the words are pretended to be taken, to see whether there be any thing in them to answer the cry that is made, I should spare myself the labour of adding any one syllable towards their vindication, and might most safely so do, there being not the least colour of opposition between the things spoken of.   In brief, extraordinary cases are not all of one sort and nature; in some an extraordinary call may be required, in some not.   Extraordinary calls are not all of one kind and nature neither.   Some may be immediate from God, in the ways there by me described; some calls may be said to be extraordinary, because they do in some things come short of or go beyond the ordinary rule that ought to be observed in well-constituted churches.   Again: concurrence of Scripture rules and acts of outward providence may be such sometimes as are suited to an *ordinary*, sometimes to an *extraordinary call;* all which are at large unfolded in the places directed unto by our author, and all laid in their own order, without the least shadow of contradiction.   But it may sometimes be said of good men, as the satirist said of evil women, "Fortem animum præstant rebus quas turpiter audent?"   Go we to the next:—

1. " The church government from which I desire not to wander is the presbyterial."	2. He now is engaged in the independent way.	3. Is settled in that way, which he is " ready to maintain, and knows it will be found his rejoicing in the day of the Lord Jesus."

" Hinc mihi sola mali labes."   This is that inexpiable crime that I labour under. An account of this whole business I have given in my review, so that I shall not here trouble the reader with a repetition of what he is so little concerned in. I shall only add, that whereas I suppose Mr Cawdrey did subscribe unto the three articles at his ordination, were it of any concernment to the church of God or the interest of truth, or were it a comely and a Christian part to engage in such a work, I could manifest contradictions between what he then solemnly subscribed to and what he hath since written and preached, manifold above what he is able to draw out of this alteration of my judgment.   Be it here, then, declared, that whereas I some time apprehended the *presbyterial, synodical* government of churches to have been fit to be received and walked in (then when I knew not but that it answered those principles which I had taken up, upon my best inquiry into the word of God), I now profess myself to be satisfied that I was then under a mistake, and that I do now own, and have for many years lived in, the way and practice of that called *congregational*.   And for this alteration of judgment, of all men I fear least a charge from them, or any of them, whom within a few years we saw reading the service-book in their surplices, etc.; against which things they do now inveigh and declaim.   What influence the perusal of Mr Cotton's book of the Keys had on my thoughts in this business I have formerly declared.   The answer to it (I suppose that written by himself) is now recommended to me by this author, as that which would have perhaps prevented my change; but I must needs tell him, that as I have perused that book, many years ago, without the effect intimated, so they must be things written with another frame of spirit, evidence of truth, and manner of reasoning, than any I can find in that book, that are likely for the future to lay hold upon my reason and understanding. Of my settlement in my present persuasion I have not only given him an account formerly, but, with all Christian courtesy, tendered myself in a readiness personally to meet him, to give him the proofs and reasons of my persuasions; which he is pleased to decline, and return, in way of answer, that "I complimented him after the mode of the times," when no such thing was intended; and thereupon my words of desiring liberty to wait upon him are expressed, but the end and purpose for which it was desired are concealed in an "etc." But he adds another instance:—

| "Men ought not to cut themselves from the communion of the church, to rend the body of Christ, and break the sacred bond of charity," p. 48 [p. 45.] | He says, "separation is no schism, nor schism any breach of charity," pp. 48, 49 [pp. 110, 111.] | "There is not one word in either of these cautions that I do not still own and allow," p. 44 [p. 226] sure not without equivocation. |

I have before owned this caution as consistent with my present judgment, as expressed in my book of schism, and as it is indeed; wherein lies the appearance of contradiction I am not able to discern. Do not I, in my book of schism, declare and prove that men ought not to cut themselves from the communion of the church; that they ought not to rend the body of Christ; that they ought not to break the sacred bonds of charity? Is there any word or tittle in the whole discourse deviating from these principles? How and in what sense separation is not schism, that the nature of schism doth not consist in a breach of charity, the treatise instanced will so far declare, as withal to convince those that shall consider what is spoken, that our author scarce keeps close either to truth or charity in his framing of this contradiction. The close of the scheme lies thus:—

| "I conceive they ought not at all to be allowed the benefit of private meeting who wilfully abstain from the public congregations." | "As for liberty to be allowed to those that meet in private, I confess myself to be otherwise minded." |

I remember that about fifteen years ago, meeting occasionally with a learned friend, we fell into some debate about the liberty that began then to be claimed by men, differing from what had been, and what was then likely to be, established. Having at that time made no farther inquiry into the grounds and reasons of such liberty than what had occurred to me in the writings of the Remonstrants, all whose plea was still pointed towards the advantage of their own interest, I delivered my judgment in opposition to the liberty pleaded for, which was then defended by my learned friend. Not many years after, discoursing the same difference with the same person, we found immediately that we had changed stations,— I pleading for an indulgence of liberty, he for restraint. Whether that learned and worthy person be of the same mind still that then he was or no, directly I know not; but this I know, that if he be not, considering the compass of circumstances that must be taken in to settle a right judgment in this case of liberty, and what alterations influencing the determination of this case we have had of late in this nation, he will not be ashamed to own his change, being a person who despises any reputation but what arises from the embracing and pursuit of truth. My change I here own; my judgment is not the same, in this particular, as it was fourteen years ago: and in my change I have good company, whom I need not to name. I shall only say, my change was at least twelve years before the "Petition and Advice," wherein the parliament of the three nations is come up to my judgment. And if Mr Cawdrey hath any thing to object to my present judgment, let him, at his next leisure, consider the treatise that I wrote in the year 1648 about toleration, where he will find the whole of it expressed. I suppose he will be doing, and that I may almost say of him, as Polyeuctus did of Speusippus, Τὸ μὴ δύνασθαι ἡσυχιάν ἄγειν ὑπὸ τῆς τύχης ἐν πεντασυρίγγῳ νόσῳ δεδεμένον. And now, Christian reader, I leave it to thy judgment whether our author had any just cause of all his outcries of my inconstancy and self-contradiction, and whether it had not been advisable for him to have passed by this seeming advantage for the design he professed to manage, rather than to have injured his own conscience and reputation to so little purpose.

Being sufficiently tired with the consideration of things of no relation to the cause at first proposed (but, " This saith he, this the Independents, this the Brownists and Anabaptists," etc.), I shall now only inquire after that which is set up in opposition to any of the principles of my treatise of schism before mentioned, or any of the propositions of the syllogisms wherein they are comprised at the beginning of this discourse; remarking in our way some such particular passages as it will not be to the disadvantage of our reverend author to be reminded of. Of the nature of the thing inquired after, in the third chapter I find no mention at all; only, he tells me by the way that the doctor's assertion, that "my book about schism was one great schism," was not nonsense, but usual rhetoric; wherein profligate sinners may be called by the name of sin, and therefore a book about schism may be called a schism. I wish our author had found some other way of excusing his doctor than by making it worse himself.

In the fourth chapter he comes to the business itself; and if, in passing through that, with the rest that follow, I can fix on any thing rising up with any pretence of opposition to what I have laid down, it shall not be omitted. For things by myself asserted, or acknowledged on all hands, or formerly ventilated to the utmost, I shall not again trouble the reader with them. Such are the positions about the general nature of schism in things national and political, antecedently considered to the limitation and restriction of it to its ecclesiastical use; the departure from churches, voluntary or compelled, etc.;—all which were stated in my first treatise, and are not directly opposed by our author. Such, also, is that doughty controversy he is pleased to raise and pursue about the seat and subject of schism, with its restriction to the instituted worship of God, pp. 18, 19; so placed by me to distinguish the schism whereof we speak from that which is national, as also from such differences and breaches as may fall out amongst men, few or more, upon civil and national accounts;—all which I exclude from the enjoyment of any room or place in our consideration of the true nature of schism, in its limited ecclesiastical sense. The like, also, may be affirmed concerning the ensuing strife of words about *separation* and *schism*, as though they were, in my apprehension of them, inconsistent: which is a fancy no better grounded than sundry others which our reverend author is pleased to make use of. His whole passage, also, receives no other security than what is afforded to it by turning my universal proposition into a particular. What I say of all places in the Scripture where the name or thing of schism is used in an ecclesiastical sense, as relating to a gospel church, he would restrain to that one place of the Corinthians, where alone the word is used in that sense. However, if that one place be all, my proposition is universal. Take, then, my proposition in its extent and latitude, and let him try once more, if he please, what he hath to object to it, for as yet I find no instance produced to alleviate its truth. He much, also, insists that there may be a separation *in* a church where there is no separation *from* a church; and saith this was at first by me denied. That it was denied by me he cannot prove; but that the contrary was proved by me is evident to all impartial men that have considered my treatise, although I cannot allow that the separation in the church of Corinth was carried to that height as is by him pretended,—namely, as to separate from the ordinance of the Lord's supper. Their disorder and division about and in its administration are reproved, not their separation from it. Only, on that supposition made, I confess I was somewhat surprised with the delivery of his judgment in reference to many of his own party, whom he condemns of schism for not administering the Lord's supper to all the congregation with whom they pray and preach. I suppose the greatest part of the most godly and able ministers of the presbyterian way in England and Scotland are here cast into the same condition of schismatics with the Independents; and the truth is, I am not yet without hopes of seeing a fair coalescency in love and church-communion between the reforming Presbyterians and Independents, though for it they shall with some suffer under the unjust imputation of schism.

But it is incredible to think whither men will suffer themselves to be carried "studio partium," and ἀμετρίᾳ ἀνθολκῆς. Hence have we the strange notions of this author about schism: decays in grace are schism, and errors in the faith are schism; and schism and apostasy are things of the same kind, differing only in degree, because the one leads to the other, as one sin of one kind doth often to another,—drunkenness to whoredom, and envy and malice to lying; and differences about civil matters, like that of Paul and Barnabas, are schism; and this, by one blaming me for a departure from the sense of antiquity, unto which these insinuations are so many monsters. Let us, then, proceed.

That Acts xiv. 4, xix. 9, 18, are pertinently used to discover and prove the nature of schism in an evangelically-ecclesiastical sense, or were ever cited by any of the ancients to that purpose, I suppose our author, on second consideration, will not affirm. I understand not the sense of this argument: " ' The multitude of the city was divided, and part held with the Jews, and part with the apostles;' therefore, schism in a gospel church-state is not only a division in a church," or that it is a separation into new churches, or that it is something more than the breach of the union appointed by Christ in an instituted church. Much less doth any thing of this nature appear from Paul's separating the disciples whom he had converted to the faith from the unbelieving, hardened Jews; an account whereof is given us, Acts xix. 9. So, then, that in this chapter there is any thing produced "de novo" to prove that the precise Scripture notion of schism, in its ecclesiastical sense, extends itself any farther than differences, divisions, separations in a church, and that a particular church, I find not; and do once more desire our author, that if he be otherwise minded, to spare such another trouble to ourselves and others as that wherein we are now engaged, he would assign me some time and place to attend him for the clearing of the truth between us.

Of schism, Acts xx. 30, Heb. x. 25, Jude 19. there is no mention; nor are those places interpreted of any such thing by any expositors, new or old, that ever I yet saw; nor can any sense be imposed on them inwrapping the nature of schism with the least colour or pretence of reason.

But now, by our author schism and apostasy are made things of one kind, differing only in degrees, p. 107; so confounding schism and heresy, contrary to the constant sense of all antiquity. Acts xx. 30, the apostle speaks of men "speaking perverse things, to draw away disciples,"—that is, teaching them false doctrines, contrary to the truths wherein they had been by him instructed, in his revealing unto them "the whole counsel of God," verse 27. This by the ancients is called heresy, and is contradistinguished from schism by them constantly; so Austin a hundred times. To draw men from the church by drawing them into pernicious errors, false doctrine being the cause of their falling off, is not schism, nor so called in Scripture, nor by any of the ancients that ever yet I observed. That the design of the apostle, in the Epistle to the Hebrews, is to preserve and keep them from apostasy unto Judaism, besides that it is attested by a cloud of witnesses, is too evident from the thing itself to be denied. Chap. x. 25, he warns them of a common entrance into that fearful condition which he describes, verse 26. Their neglect of the Christian assemblies was the door of their apostasy to Judaism. What is this to schism? Would we charge a man with that crime whom we saw neglecting our assemblies, and likely to fall into Judaism? Are there not more forcible considerations to deal with him upon? and doth not the apostle make use of them? Jude 19 hath been so far spoken unto already that it may not fairly be insisted on again. "Parvas habet spes Troja, si tales habet."

In the entrance of the fifth chapter he takes advantage from my question, p. 147 [p. 263], "Who told him that raising causeless differences in a church, and then separating from it, is not in my judgment schism?" where the first part of the assertion included in that interrogation expresseth the *formal nature* of schism, which is not destroyed, nor can any man be exonerated of its guilt, by the subsequent crime of separation, whereby it is aggravated. 1 John ii. 19 is again mentioned to this purpose of schism, to as little purpose; so also is Heb. x. 25. Both places treat of apostates, who are charged and blamed under other terms than that of schism. There is in such departures, as in every division whatever of that which was in union, somewhat of the general nature of schism; but that particular crime and guilt of schism, in its restrained, ecclesiastical sense, is not included in them.

In his following discourse he renews his former charges of denying their ordinances and ministry, of separating from them, and the like. As to the former part of this charge I have spoken in the entrance of this discourse; for the latter, of separating from them, I say we have no more separated from them than they have from us. Our right to the celebration of the ordinances of God's worship, according to the light we have received from him, is, in this nation, as good as theirs; and our plea from the gospel we are ready to maintain against them, according as we shall at any time be called thereunto. If any of our judgment deny them to be churches, I doubt not but he knows who comes not behind in returnal of charges on our churches. Doth the reverend author think or imagine that we have not, in our own judgment, more reason to deny their churches and to charge them with schism, though we do neither, than they have to charge us therewith and to deny our churches? Can any thing be more fondly pretended than that he hath proved that we have separated from them? upon which, p. 105, he requires the performance of my promise to retreat from the state wherein I stand upon the establishment of such proof. Hath he proved the due administration of ordinances amongst them whom he pleads for? Hath he proved any church-union between them as such and us? Hath he proved us to have broken that union? What will not self-fulness and prejudice put men upon!

How came they into the sole possession of all church-state in England, so that whoever is not of them and with them must be charged to have separated from them? Mr Cawdrey says, indeed, that the episcopal men and they agree in substantials, and differ only in circumstantials, but that they and we differ in substantials. But let him know they admit not of his compliances; they say he is a schismatic, and that all his party are so also. Let him answer their charge solidly upon his own principles, and not think to own that which he hath the weakest claim imaginable unto, and was never yet in possession of. We deny that, since the gospel came into England, the *presbyterian* government, as by them stated was ever set up in England, but in the wills of a party of men; so that here, as yet, unless as it lies in particular congregations, where our right is as good as theirs, none have separated from it that I know of, though many cannot consent unto it. The first ages we plead ours, the following were unquestionably *episcopal*.

In the beginning of chapter the sixth he attempts to disprove my assertion, that the union of the church catholic visible, which consists in the "professing of the saving doctrine of the gospel," etc., is broken only by apostasy. To this end he confounds apostasy and schism, affirming them only to differ in degrees; which is a new notion, unknown to antiquity, and contrary to all sound reason. By the instances he produceth to this purpose he endeavours to prove that there are things which break this union, whereby this union is not broken. Whilst a man continues a member of that church, which he is by virtue of the union thereof and his interest therein, by no act doth he, or can he, break that union.

The partial breach of that union, which consists in the profession of the truth, is *error* and heresy, and not *schism*. Our author abounds here in new notions, which might easily be discovered to be as fond as new, were it worth while to consider them; of which in brief before. Only, I wonder why, giving way to such thoughts as these, he should speak of men with contempt under the name of *notionists*, as he doth of Dr Du Moulin; but the truth is, the doctor hath provoked him. And were it not for some considerations that are obvious to me, I should almost wonder why this author should sharpen his leisure and zeal against me, who scarce ever publicly touched the grounds and foundations of that cause which he hath so passionately espoused, and pass by him who, both in Latin and English, hath laid his axe to the very root of it, upon principles sufficiently destructive to it, and so apprehended by the best learned in our author's way that ever these nations brought forth. But, as I said, reasons lie at hand why it was more necessary to give me this opposition; which yet hath not altered my resolution of handling this controversy in another manner, when I meet with another manner of adversary.

Page 110, he fixes on the examination of a particular passage about the disciples of John, mentioned Acts xix. 2, 3, of whom I affirmed that it is probable they were rather ignorant of the miraculous dispensations of the Holy Ghost than of the person of the Holy Ghost; alleging to the contrary, that the words are " more plain and full than to be so eluded, and, for aught appears, John did not baptize into the name of the Holy Ghost." I hope the author doth not so much dwell at home as to suppose this to be a *new notion* of mine. Who almost of late, in their critical notes, have not either (at least) considered it or confirmed it? Neither is the question into whose name they were expressly baptized, but in what doctrine they were instructed. He knows who denies that they were at all actually baptized, before they were baptized by Paul. Nor ought it to be granted, without better proof than any which as yet hath been produced, that any of the saints under the Old Testament were ignorant of *the being of the Holy Ghost;* neither do the words require the sense by him insisted on. Ἀλλ' οὐδὲ εἰ Πνεῦμα ἅγιόν ἐστιν, ἠκούσαμεν, do no more evince the person of the Holy Ghost to be included in them than in those other, John vii. 39, Οὔπω ἦν Πνεῦμα ἅγιον. The latter, in the proper sense, he will not contend for; nor can, therefore, the expression being uniform, reasonably for the former. Speaking of men openly and notoriously wicked, and denying them to be members of any church whatever, he bids me answer his arguments to the contrary from 1 Cor. v. 7, 2 Thess. iii. 14; and I cannot but desire him that he would impose that task on them that have nothing else to do: for my own part, I shall not entangle myself with things to so little purpose. Having promised my reader to attend only to that which looks toward the merit of the case, I must crave his pardon that I have not been able to make good my resolution. Meeting with so little, or nothing at all, which is to that purpose, I find myself entangled in the old diversions that

we are now plentifully accustomed unto; but yet I shall endeavour to recompense
this loss by putting a speedy period to this whole trouble, despairing of being able
to tender him any other satisfaction whilst I dwell on this discourse. In the
meantime, to obviate all strife of words, if it be possible, for the future, I shall
grant this reverend author that, in the general large notion of schism, which his
opposition to that insisted on by me hath put him upon, I will not deny but that
he and *I* are both *schismatics*, and any thing else shall be so that he would have to
be so, rather than to be engaged in this contest any farther. In this sense he
affirms that there was a schism between Paul and Barnabas, and so one of them
at least was a schismatic; as also, he affirms the same of two lesser men, though
great in their generation, Chrysostom and Epiphanius. So error and heresy, if he
please, shall be schism from the catholic church; and scandal of life shall be schism.
And his argument shall be true, that schism is a breach of union in a church of
Christ's institution; therefore, in that which is so only by call, not to any end of
joint worship as such;—of any union, that which consists in the profession of the
saving truths of the gospel; and so there may be a schism in the catholic church.
And so those Presbyterians that reform their congregations, and do not administer
the sacraments to all promiscuously, shall be guilty of schism; and, indeed, as to
me, what else he pleaseth, for my inquiry concerns only *the precise limited nature
of schism*, in its evangelically-ecclesiastical sense.

Neither shall I at present (allotting very few hours to the despatch of this business, which yet I judge more than it deserves) consider the scattered ensuing
passages about ordination, church-government, number of elders, and the like;
which all men know not at all to belong unto the main controversy which was by
me undertaken, and that they were, against all laws of disputation, plucked violently into this contest by our reverend author. One thing I cannot pass by, and it
will, upon the matter, put a close to what I shall at present offer to this treatise.
Having said that " Christ hath given no direction for the performance of any duty
of worship of sovereign institution, but only in them and by them" (meaning particular churches), he answers, that " if he would imply that a minister in or of a
particular church may perform those ordinances without those congregations, he
contradicts himself, by saying a particular church is the seat of all ordinances."
But why so, I pray? May not a particular church be the seat of all ordinances
subjectively, and yet others be the object of them, or of some of them? " But,"
saith he, " if he mean those ordinances of worship are to be performed only by a
minister of a particular congregation, what shall become of the people?" I suppose they shall be instructed and built up according to the mind of Christ; and
what would people desire more? But whereas he had before said that I " denied
a minister to be a minister to more than his own church," and I had asked him
" who told him so," adding that explication of my judgment, that for " so much
as men are appointed the objects of the dispensation of the word, I grant a minister, in the dispensation of it, to act ministerially towards not only the members of
the catholic church, but the visible members of the world also in contradistinction
thereunto;" he now tells me a story of passages between the learned Dr Wallis
and myself, about his question in the Vespers, 1654,—namely, that as to that question, " An potestas ministri evangelici ad unius tantum ecclesiæ particularis mem-
bra extendatur?" I said that Dr Wallis had brought me a challenge, and that, if
I did dispute on that question, I must dispute " ex animo." Although I grant
that a minister, as a minister, may preach the word to more than those of his own
congregation, yet knowing the sense wherein the learned Dr Wallis maintained
that question, it is not impossible but I might say, if I did dispute I must do it
" ex animo." For his bringing me a challenge, I do not know that either he did
so or that I put that interpretation on what he did; but I shall crave leave to say,

that if the learned Dr Wallis do find any ground or occasion to bring a challenge unto me, to debate any point of difference between us, I shall not waive answering his desire, although he should bring Mr Cawdrey for his second.   For the present I shall only say, that as it is no commendation to the moderation or ingenuity of any one whatever thus to publish to the world private hear-says, and what he hath been told of private conferences; so if I would insist on the same course, to make publication of what I have been told hath been the private discourse of some men, it is not unlikely that I should occasion their shame and trouble.   Yet in this course of proceeding a progress is made out in the ensuing words, and Mr Stubbes (who is now called my " amanuensis," who some five years ago transcribed about a sheet of paper for me, and not one line before or since) is said to be employed, or at least encouraged, by me to write against the learned Dr Wallis, his Thesis being published.   This is as true as much of that that went before, and as somewhat of that that follows after; and whereas it is added, that I said what he had written on that subject was " a scurrilous, ridiculous piece," it is of the same nature with the rest of the like reports.   I knew that Mr Stubbes was writing on that subject, but not until he had proceeded far in it.   I neither employed him nor encouraged him in it, any otherwise than the consideration of his papers, after he had written them, may be so interpreted; and the reason why I was not willing he should proceed, next to my desire of continuance of peace in this place, was, his using such expressions of me, and some things of mine, in sundry places of his discourse, as I could not modestly allow to be divulged.   The following words to the same purpose with them before mentioned, I remember not, nor did ever think to be engaged in the consideration of such transgressions of the common rules of human society as those now passed through.   Reports, hear-says, talks, private discourse between friends, allegations countenanced by none of these, nor any thing else, are the weapons wherewith I am assaulted!   " I have heard," " I am told," " if reports be true," " it was ' vox populi' at Oxford," ." is it not so ?"   " I presume he will not deny it," are the ornaments of this discourse!   Strange! that men of experience and gravity should be carried, by the power of these temptations, not only to the forgetfulness of the royal law of Christ, and all gospel rules of deportment towards his professed disciples, but also be engaged into ways and practices contrary to the dictates of the law of nature, and such as sundry heathens would have abhorred.   For my own part, had not God by his providence placed me in that station wherein others also that fear him are concerned in me, I should not once turn aside to look upon such heaps as that which I have now passed over.   My judgment on most heads and articles of Christian religion is long since published to the world, and I continue, through the grace and patience of God, preaching in public answerably to the principles I do profess; and if any man shall oppose what I have delivered, or shall so deliver, in print, or the pulpit, or in divinity lectures, as my judgment, I shall consider his opposition, and do therein as God shall guide. With evil surmises, charges upon hear-says and reports, attended with perpetual excursions from the argument in hand, I shall no more contend.

Some few observations on scattered passages will now speedily issue this discourse.   Page 112, to that assertion of mine, that " if Rome be no particular church, it is no church at all, for the catholic church it is not," he replies, that " though it be not such a particular congregation as I intend, yet it may be a particular patriarchal church."   But,—1. Then, it seems, it is a particular church; which grants my inference. 2. It was a particular church of Christ's institution that I inquired after. Doth our author think that Christ hath appointed any patriarchal churches? A patriarchal church, as such, is such from its relation to a patriarch; and he can scarce be thought to judge patriarchs to be of divine institution who hath cast off and abjured episcopacy.

The Donatists are mentioned again, p. 113; and I am again charged with an attempt to vindicate them from schism. My thoughts of them I have before declared to the full, and have no reason to retract any thing from what was then spoken, or to add any thing thereunto. If it may satisfy our author, I here grant they were schismatics, with what aggravations he pleaseth; and wherein their schism consisted I have also declared. But he says, I undertake to exempt some others from schism (I know whom), that suffer with them, in former and after ages, under the same imputation. I do so, indeed; and I suppose our author may guess at whom I intend,—himself, amongst others! I hope he is not so taken up in his thoughts with charging schism on others as to forget that many, the greatest part and number of the true churches of Christ, do condemn him for a schismatic, a Donatistical schismatic. I suppose he acknowledges the church of Rome to be a true church; the Lutheran I am persuaded he will not deny, nor perhaps the Grecian, to be so; the Episcopal church of England he contends for;—and yet all these, with one voice, cry out upon him for a schismatic. And as to the plea of the last, how he can satisfy his conscience as to the rejection of his lawful superiors, upon his own principles, without pretending any such crime against them as the Donatists did against Cæcilianus, I profess I do not understand. New mention is made of episcopal ordination, p. 120, and they are said to have had their successive ordination from Rome who ordained therein. So, indeed, some say, and some otherwise. Whether they had or no is nothing to me; I lay no weight upon it. They held, I am sure, that place in England, that without their approbation no man could publicly preach the gospel. To say they were presbyters, and ordained as presbyters, I know not what satisfaction can arise unto conscience thereby. Party and argument may be countenanced by it. They profess they ordained as bishops; that for their lives and souls they durst not ordain but as such. So they told those whom they ordained, and affirm they have open injury done them by any one's denial of it. As it was, the best is to be made of it. This shift is not handsome. Nor is it ingenuous, for any one that hath looked into antiquity, to charge me with departing from their sense in the notion of schism, declared about the third and fourth ages, and at the same time to maintain an equality between bishops and presbyters, or to say that bishops ordained as presbyters, not as bishops. Nor do I understand the excellency of that order which we see in some churches, where they have two sorts of elders, the one made so by ordination without election, and the other by election without ordination; those who are ordained casting off all power and authority of them that ordained them, and those who are elected immediately rejecting the greatest part of those that chose them.

Nor did I, as is pretended, plead for their presbyterian way in the year [16]46; all the ministers almost in the county of Essex know the contrary, one especially, being a man of great ability and moderation of spirit, and for his knowledge in those things not behind any man I know in England of his way, with whom in that year, and the next following, I had sundry conferences at public meetings of ministers as to the several ways of reformation then under proposal. But the frivolousness of these imputations hath been spoken of before, as also the falseness of the calumny which our author is pleased to repeat again about my turning from ways in religion.

My description of a particular church he once more blames as applicable to the catholic church invisible, and to the visible catholic church (I suppose he means as such), when a participation in the same ordinances numerically is assigned as its difference. He asks whether it becomes my ingenuity to interpret the capability of a church's reduction to its primitive constitution by its own fitness and capacity to be so reduced, rather than by its external hinderances or furtherances; but with what ingenuity or modesty that question is asked, I profess I understand not. And, p. 134, he hath this passage (only I take notice of his introduction to his answer, with thanks for the civility of the inquiry in the manner of its expression):—" My words were these: ' Whether our reverend author do not in his conscience think there was no true church in England till,' etc.; which puts me into suspicion that the reverend doctor was offended that I did not always (for oft I do) give him that title of the 'reverend author,' or the 'doctor,' which made him cry out he was never so dealt withal by any party as by me; though, upon review, I do not find that I gave him any uncivil language, unbeseeming me to give or him to receive; and I hear that somebody hath dealt more uncivilly with him in that respect, which he took very ill."

Let this reverend author make what use of it he please, I cannot but again tell him that these things become neither him nor any man professing the religion of Jesus Christ, or that hath any respect to truth or sobriety. Can any man think that in his conscience he gives any credit to the insinuation which here he makes, that I should thank him for calling me " reverend author" or " reverend doctor," or be troubled for his not using these expressions? Can the mind of an honest man be thought to be conversant with such mean and low thoughts? For the title of " reverend," I do give him notice that I have very little valued it ever since I have considered the saying of Luther, " Nunquam periclitatur religio nisi inter reverendissimos;" so that he may, as to me, forbear it for the future, and call me as the Quakers do, and it shall suffice. And for that of " doctor," it was conferred on me by the university in my absence, and against my consent, as they have expressed it under their public seal, nor doth any thing but gratitude and respect unto them make me once own it; and freed from that obligation, I should never use it more, nor did I use it until some were offended with me, and blamed me for my neglect of them. And for that other whom he mentions, who before this gave so far place to indignation as to insinuate some such thing, I doubt not but by this time he hath been convinced of his mistake therein, being a person of another manner of ability and worth than some others with whom I have to do; and the truth is, my manner of dealing with him in my last reply, which I have since myself not so well approved of, requires the passing by such returns. But you will say, then, why do I preface this discourse with that expression, " With thanks for the civility of the inquiry in the manner of its expression?" I say, this will discover the iniquity of this author's procedure in this particular. His inquiry was, " Whether I did not in my conscience think that there were no true churches in England until the Brownists our fathers, the Anabaptists our elder brothers, and ourselves, arose and gathered new churches?" Without once taking notice or mentioning his titles that he says he gave me, I used the words in a sense obvious to every man's first consideration, as a reproof of the expressions mentioned. That which was the true cause of my words our author hides in an " etc.;" that which was not by me once taken notice of is by him expressed to serve an end of drawing forth an evil surmise and suspicion, that hath not the least colour to give it countenance. Passing by all indifferent readers, I refer the honesty of this dealing with me to the judgment of his own conscience. Setting down what I neither expressed nor took notice of, nor had any singular occasion in that place so to do, the words being often used by him, hiding and concealing what I did take notice of and express, and which to every man's view was the occasion of that passage, that conclusion or unworthy insinuation is made, which a good man ought to have abhorred.

Sundry other particulars there are, partly false and calumniating, partly impertinent, partly consisting in mistakes, that I ought at the first view to have made mention of; but, on several accounts, I am rather willing here to put an end to the reader's trouble and my own.

A

BRIEF VINDICATION OF THE NONCONFORMISTS
FROM THE CHARGE OF SCHISM,

AS IT WAS MANAGED AGAINST THEM IN A SERMON PREACHED BEFORE THE LORD MAYOR
BY DR STILLINGFLEET, DEAN OF ST PAUL'S.

"Coitio Christianorum merito sane illicita, si illicitis par ; merito damnanda, si quis de ea queritur eo titulo quo de factionibus querela est. In cujus perniciem aliquando convenimus ? Hoc sumus congregati quod et dispersi ; hoc universi quod et singuli ; neminem lædentes, neminem contristantes ; quum probi, cum boni coeunt, cum pii, cum casti congregantur, non est factio dicenda, sed curia."—
Tertul.

PREFATORY NOTE.

In 1680, when the nation was under strong fears lest, with the help and favour of the Court, Popery should resume its old domination in Britain, the celebrated Stillingfleet, at that time Dean of St Paul's, preached a sermon on the 2d of May before the Lord Mayor of London. It was published under the title, "On the Mischief of Separation." His object was to prove the Nonconformists guilty of schism, on the ground that they admitted the Church of England to be a true church of Christ, and yet lived in a state of dissent and separation from it. His text was Phil. iii. 16.

Perhaps no sermon has ever given rise to a controversy in which a greater number of writers has appeared on both sides; and among these were names signally eminent for worth and learning. Besides the following pamphlet by Owen, Baxter published his "Answer to Dr Stillingfleet's Charge of Separation," in terms of vehement invective against the injustice with which he had treated Dissent. John Howe addressed to the offending Dean "A Letter written from the Country to a Person of Quality in the City," protesting with all his characteristic mildness and candour, but most firmly, against the insinuations of Stillingfleet. Vincent Alsop also took the field, in a work brimful of wit and humour to the very title-page, "The Mischief of *Impositions*." Mr Barret of Nottingham, in allusion to the "Irenicum," written by Stillingfleet when rector of Sutton, to reconcile conflicting sects by proving that no form of church-government could plead divine authority in its favour, published, "The Rector of Sutton Committed with the Dean of St Paul's," etc. Besides these authors, to whom Stillingfleet replies in his "Unreasonableness of Separation," Mr John Troughton of Bicester published "An Apology for the Nonconformists; showing their reasons both for their not conforming and for their preaching publicly, though forbidden by law: with an Answer to Dr Stillingfleet's Sermon and his Defence of it, 1681." An account of the work in which Stillingfleet replied to the first five of these antagonists will be found in a prefatory note to Owen's answer to it, vol. xv. p. 183, of Owen's works. But Stillingfleet had to encounter fresh attacks: —"More Work for the Dean," by Mr Thomas Wall; Mr Barret's second "Attempt to Vindicate the Principles of the Nonconformists, not only by Scripture, but by Dr Stillingfleet's Rational Account;" the "Modest and Peaceable Inquiry," by Mr Lob; Baxter's "Second True Defence of the mere Nonconformists;" Humphrey's "Answer to Dr Stillingfleet's Book, as far as it concerned the Peaceable Design;" and "The Rational Defence of Nonconformity," in 1689, by Mr Gilbert Rule.

To the rescue of the Dean from this host of opponents, there advanced, with his vizor down and name withheld, Dr Sherlock, in his "Discourse about Church Unity, being a Defence of Dr Stillingfleet's 'Unreasonableness of Separation,' in answer to several late pamphlets, but principally to Dr Owen and Mr Baxter, 1681." This work was followed up by "A Continuation and Vindication of the Defence of Dr Stillingfleet, in answer to Mr Baxter, Mr Lob, and others." Mr Long of Exeter, wandering from the points in debate into most offensive personalities against Baxter, published "The Unreasonableness of Separation, the Second Part; or, a farther impartial account of the history, nature, and pleas, of the present separation from the Church of England, with special remarks on the life and actions of Richard Baxter, 1682." Richard Hook, D.D., vicar of Halifax, was the author of the "Nonconformist Champion, his Challenge Accepted; or, an answer to Mr Baxter's Petition for Peace, with remarks on his Holy Commonwealth, his Sermon to the House of Commons, his Nonconformist's Plea, and his Answer to Dr Stillingfleet, 1682." The famous Sir Roger L'Estrange could not refrain from taking part in this curious mêlée with all his coarse but clever wit, of which the title of his work is a specimen, "The Casuist Uncased, in a Dialogue betwixt Richard and Baxter, with a moderator between them for quietness' sake."

The sermon which embroiled so many able men in disputes that lasted for ten years may well excite curiosity; and yet it would be difficult to say why it should have roused such a storm of controversy, resounding over the breadth of a kingdom. It is calm and measured in its tone, and contains no reckless invective, no impeachment of motives, no envenomed intensity of language. Its strength lay in its calmness, and in the extreme plausibility with which the case of the Church of England is stated against Dissenters. That the latter should admit it to be a church of Christ, and yet hold themselves justified in their nonconformity; and that the common grounds of objection to the Established Church should refer to the terms on which men were admitted to *office* in it, and did not, as the Dean alleged, affect their admission to *membership*, were points which such a controversialist could handle most effectively for his own cause. That Nonconformists, who had suffered so much in resisting popish encroachment, should be exhibited as practically the friends of Popery in opposing the Church of England, reputed to be the chief defence against it; while they, on the other hand, had been warning the nation for years against the vantage-ground which Popery had in the constitution and rites of the English Church; and that all this should have been done, not in the vulgar abuse which refutes itself, but in downright and deliberate logic, was sufficiently galling, and fitted to bring upon them no small odium from the temper of the nation, roused at the time by the fear of popish aggression and ascendency. It was, in truth, an attempt not merely to spike the best guns of Dissent, but to turn them against itself.

This "Vindication" by Owen in reply is all that could be wished, in strength of reasoning, civility of language, and crushing effect. There is a passage of eloquent pathos at the close, in allusion to the long sufferings of the Nonconformists.—Ed.

A BRIEF VINDICATION OF THE NONCONFORMISTS

FROM THE CHARGE OF SCHISM.

IT was no small surprise unto many, first to hear of, and then to see in print, the late sermon of the Rev. Dean of St Paul's, preached at Guildhall, May 2, 1680, being the first Sunday in Easter term, before the Lord Mayor, etc.

Whatever there might be of truth in it, yet they judged the time both of the one and the other, the preaching and printing of it, to be somewhat unseasonable; for they say that this is a time wherein the agreement of all Protestants, so far as they have attained, is made more than ordinarily necessary. And whereas the Nonconformists do agree in religion with all the sober protestant people of the nation, which is the church of England, they do suppose that ordinary prudence would advise unto a forbearance of them in those few things wherein they dissent, not indeed from the body of the protestant people, but from some that would impose them on their consciences and practices. Who knows not that the present danger of this nation is from Popery, and the endeavours that are used both to introduce it and enthrone it, or give it power and authority among us? And it is no part of the popish design to take away and destroy those things wherein the Nonconformists do dissent from the present ecclesiastical establishment, but rather to confirm them. Their contrivance is, to ruin and destroy the religion of the body of the Protestants in this kingdom, wherein the Nonconformists are one with them, and equally concerned with any of them. Wherefore it cannot but be grievous unto them, as well as useless unto the common interest of the protestant religion, that at such a time and season they should be reflected on, charged, and severely treated, on the account of those lesser differences which in no way disenable them from being useful and serviceable unto the government and nation, in the defence and preservation of the protestant religion. And that it is their resolution so to be, they have given sufficient evidence, equal at least with that given by any sort of people in the nation. Yea, of their diligence in opposition unto Popery, and their readiness to observe the direction of the magistrates therein, whilst the plot hath been in agitation, they suppose the honourable person unto whom this sermon is dedicated can and will bear them witness.

In these circumstances, to be required severely to change their judgments and practices, as it were "momento turbinis," immediately and in an instant, or else to be looked on and treated as adversaries, many do think as unseasonable as to command a good part of an army, when it is actually engaged against an enemy, to change all their order, postures, discipline, and advantages, or immediately to depart out of the field. And they do withal suppose that such a sudden change is least of all to be expected to be wrought by such severe charges and reflections as are made on all Nonconformists in this discourse. Such like things as these do men talk concerning the season of the preaching and publishing of this sermon; but in such things every man is to be left unto his own prudence, whereof he may not esteem himself obliged to give an account.

For my part, I judge it not so unseasonable as some others do; for it is meet that honest men should understand the state of those things wherein they are greatly and deeply concerned. Nonconformists might possibly suppose that the common danger of all Protestants had reconciled the minds of the conforming ministry unto them, so as that they were more than formerly inclined unto their forbearance; and I was really of the same judgment myself. If it be not so, it is well they are fairly warned what they have to expect, that they may prepare themselves to undergo it with patience. But we shall pass by these things, and attend a little unto the consideration of the sermon itself.

The design of this discourse seems to consist in these three things, or to aim at them:—

1. To prove all the Nonconformists to be guilty of schism and a sinful separation from the church of England.

2. To aggravate their supposed guilt and crime, both in its nature and all the pernicious consequences of it that can be imagined.

3. To charge them, especially their ministers, with want of sincerity and honesty in the management of their dissent from the church of England, with reference unto the people that hear them.

What there is of truth in these things, or what there may be of mistake in them, it is the duty of Nonconformists to try and examine. But some few things must have a previous consideration before we come to the merits of the cause itself:—

1. The reverend author of this discourse affirms, that in the preaching of this sermon he was " far from intending to stir up the magistrates and judges unto a persecution of dissenters, as some ill men

have reported," Epist. Ded. Without this information, I confess I could not but judge it would have been as liable unto a supposition of such a design as the actings of the Nonconformists, in the management of their cause, are unto that of insincerity in the judgment of this reverend author; for,—

(1.) It was not preached unto Nonconformists, perhaps not one of them being present; so that the intention of preaching it could not be their conviction. They were not likely either to hear the charge or the reasons of it.

(2.) It was preached unto them who were no way guilty of the pretended crime reproved, but peculiarly to such as were intrusted with the execution of the penal laws against them that were supposed guilty, magistrates and judges; which in another would have but an ill aspect. If a man should go unto a justice of the peace, and complain that his neighbour is a thief, or a swearer, or a murderer, though he should give the justice never so many arguments to prove that his neighbour did very ill in being so and doing so, yet his business would seem to be the execution of the law upon him. But let the will of God be done; Nonconformists are not much concerned in these things.

We are likewise informed, in the same epistle, that there are "no sharp and provoking expressions" on the persons of any. It is, indeed, beneath the gravity and dignity of this reverend author to bring reviling or railing accusations against any; neither will he, I am sure, give countenance to such a practice in others, which is seldom used but by men of very mean consideration: but I am not satisfied that he hath not used even great severity in reflections on a whole party of men, and that unprovoked; nor do I know how persons, on a religious account, can be more severely reflected on,—and that not only as unto their opinions and practices, but also as unto the sincerity of their hearts and honesty of their designs,—than the Nonconformists are in this sermon.

I have seen a collection made of such reflections, by the hand of a person of honour, a member of the church of England, with his judgment upon them; wherein they appear to me not to be a true resemblance or representation of Christian love and charity.

2. A great part of this discourse being such as became a popular auditory, consisting in generals on all hands acknowledged, as, the good of union, the evil of schism and causeless separation, etc.,—which will indifferently serve any party, until it be determined where the original fault and mistake doth lie,—I shall not at all take notice of it, though it be so dressed as to be laid at the door of Nonconformists, in a readiness for an application unto their disadvantage; but nothing that, by way of argument, testimony, or instance, is pro-

duced to prove the charge mentioned, and the consequents of it, shall be omitted.

3. Some few things may be taken notice of in the passage of the author unto his text. Of that nature is his complaint, p. 2: "There is just cause for many sad reflections, when neither the miseries we have felt nor the calamities we fear, neither the terrible judgments of God upon us, nor the unexpected deliverance vouchsafed unto us, nor the common danger we are yet in, have abated men's hearts, or allayed their passions, or made them more willing to unite with our established church and religion; but, instead of that, some stand at a greater distance, if not [in] defiance." It is acknowledged willingly by us that the warnings and calls of God unto this nation have been great and marvellous, and yet continue so to be; but it is worthy our inquiry, whether this be to be looked on as the only end and design of them, that the Nonconformists do immediately in all things comply with the established church and religion, and are evidences of God's displeasure because they do not so, when He who searcheth their hearts doth know that they would do it were it not for fear of His displeasure? What if it should be the design of God in them to call the nation, and so the church of England, unto repentance and reformation? which, when all is done, is the only way of reconciling all protestant dissenters. What if God should in them testify against all the atheism, profaneness, sensuality, that abound in this nation, unto the public scandal of it, with the dread and terror of those by whom they are duly considered, the persons guilty of them being no way proceeded against by any discipline of the church, nor any reformation of the church itself from such horrible pollutions once attempted? Every man who knows any thing of Christ, of his law, gospel, rule, and discipline,—of the nature, end, and use of them, with the worship of God to be performed in them and by them; and doth withal consider the terror of the Lord, unto whom an account is to be given of these things; must acknowledge that, both in persons and things, there is a necessity of reformation among us, on the utmost peril of the displeasure of Christ Jesus: yet no such reformation is so much as endeavoured in a due manner. It is no encouragement unto conscientious men to unite themselves absolutely and in all things unto such a church as doth not, as will not, or as cannot, reform itself, in such a degenerate state as that which many churches in the world are at this day openly and visibly fallen into. And, to deal plainly with our brethren (if they will allow us to call them so),—that they may know what to expect, and, if it be the will of God, be directed unto the only true way of uniting all Protestants in the only bands of evangelical union, order, and communion,— unless those who are concerned will endeavour, and until they are

enabled in some measure to effect, a reformation in the ministry and people, as unto their relation to the church, as also in some things in the worship of God itself, it is vain to expect that the Nonconformists should unite with the church, however established. And may we not think that those many warnings and calls of God may have some respect unto those abominations that are found in the nation, yea, such as, without a due reformation of them, will issue in our desolation? I do know that with the Nonconformists also there are " sins against the LORD their God;" and it will be a great addition unto their sins, as also an aggravation of their guilt, if they comply not with the " warnings of God," as they are here expressed by this reverend author, so as to reform whatever is amiss in them, and return wholly unto God from all their wanderings. But as unto those things which are usually charged on them, they are such as interest, hatred, and the desire of their ruin, suggest unto the minds of their adversaries, or are used by some against their science and conscience to further that end, without the least pretence to be raised from any thing in them,—their opinions, practices, or conversation in the world. Doth atheism abound among us?—it is from the differences in religion made by Nonconformists! Is there danger of Popery?—it is because of the Nonconformists! Are the judgments of God coming on the nation?—it is for Nonconformity! So was it of old with the Christians: " Si Tybris ascendit in mænia, si Nilus non ascendit in arva, si cœlum stetit, si terra movit, si fames, si lues, statim, ' Christianos ad leonem!'"

4. The immediate introduction unto the opening of his text is an account of the differences and divisions that were in the primitive churches, occasioned by the Judaizing Christians, who contended for the observation of the ceremonies of the law. But some things may be added unto his account, which are necessary unto the right stating of that case, as it may have any respect unto our present differences. And we may observe,—

(1.) That those with and concerning whom the apostle dealeth in his epistle were principally those of the Jewish church and nation who had owned the gospel, professed faith in Christ Jesus, had received (many of them) spiritual gifts, or " tasted of the powers of the world to come," and did join in the worship of God in the assemblies of the Christians. I only mention this, because some places quoted usually in this matter do relate directly unto the unbelieving Jews, which went up and down to oppose the preaching of Christ and the gospel, in rage and fury, stirring up persecution everywhere against them that were employed in it.

(2.) This sort of persons were freely allowed by the apostle to continue in the use of those rites and ceremonies which they esteemed themselves obliged unto by virtue of Moses' law, granting them in all other things the privilege of believers, and such as whom they would not in any thing offend. So do James and the elders of the church declare themselves, Acts xxi. 20, etc. Yea,—

(3.) Out of tenderness unto them, and to prevent all offence to be taken by them at the liberty of the Gentiles, they did order that the believers of the Gentiles should forbear for a season the use of their natural liberty in some few things, whereby the other were, in their common meetings, as in eating and drinking together, usually scandalized; giving them, also, unto the same end, direction concerning one thing evil in itself, whose long usage and practice among the Gentiles had obliterated a sense of its guilt, wherewith they could not but be much offended.

(4.) With this determination or state of things, thus settled by the apostles, no doubt but that a multitude of the Jewish believers did rest content and satisfied; but certain it is that with many of them it was otherwise: they were no way pleased that they were left unto the freedom of their own judgment and practice in the use and observance of the legal ceremonies, but they would impose the observation of them on all the churches of the Gentiles wherever they came. Nothing would serve their turn but that all other churches must observe their ceremonies, or they would not admit them unto communion with them. And, in the pursuit of this design, they prevailed for a season on whole churches to forego the liberty wherewith Christ hath made them free, and to take on them the yoke of bondage which they imposed on them; as it was with the churches of the Galatians.

I have mentioned these things only to show how remote we are from any access unto those opinions and practices which caused the first divisions in Christian churches, and among all sorts of believers. We agree with our brethren in the faith of the gospel, as the Gentiles did with the believing Jews; we have nothing to impose in religion on the consciences or practices of any other churches or persons; we are not offended that others, be they many or few, should use their own choice, liberty, and judgment, in the government, discipline, worship, and ceremonies, of pretended order, nor do envy them the advantages which they have thereby; we desire nothing but what the churches of the Gentiles desired of old, as the only means to prevent division in them,—namely, that they might not be imposed on to observe those things which they were not satisfied that it was the mind of Christ they should observe, for he had taken all the churches under his own power, requiring that they should be taught to do and observe all that he commanded them, and nothing else, that we know of. We desire no more of our governors, rulers, brethren (if they think so) in the ministry, but that we be not, with outward force and destructive penalties, compelled to comply with and practise in the worship of God such things as, for our lives, and to save ourselves from the greatest ruin, we cannot conceive that it is the mind of Christ that we should do and observe;—that, whilst we are peaceable and useful in our places, firmly united unto the body of the Protestants in this nation (which, as this author tells us, is the church of England), in confession of the same faith and common interest, for the maintenance and preservation of that one religion which we profess, we be not deprived of that liberty which God and nature, Christ and the gospel, the example of the primitive churches, and the present protestant interest of this nation, do testify to be our due.

These things being premised, because I have no design to except against any thing in the discourse of the reverend author of this sermon wherein the merit of the cause is not immediately concerned, nor to seek for advantages from expressions, nor to draw a saw of contention about things not necessary unto that defence of our innocency which alone I have undertaken (as is the way of the most in the management of controversies), I shall pass on unto the charge itself, or the consideration of the arguments and reasons whereon all Nonconformists are charged with schism, etc.

But yet because there are some things insisted on by the author, in the progress of his discourse, according as he judged the method to be most convenient for the managing of his charge, which I judge not so convenient unto the present defence, I shall speak briefly unto them, or some of them, before I proceed unto what is more expressly argumentative; as,—

1. He chargeth the Nonconformist ministers for concealing their opinions and judgments from the people about the lawfulness of their communion with the church, and that for ends easily to be discerned (that is, their own advantage); that is, they do indeed judge that it is lawful for the people to hold communion with the church of England, but will not let them know so much, lest they should forsake their ministry:—

Pages 19, 20, "I do not intend to speak of the terms upon which persons are to be admitted among us to the exercise of the function of the ministry, but of the terms of lay-communion; that is, those which are necessary for all persons to join in our prayers and sacraments, and other offices of divine worship. I will not say there hath been a great deal of art to confound these two (and it is easy to discern to what purpose it is), but I dare say the people's not understanding the difference of these two cases hath been a great occasion of the present separation; for, in the judgment of some of the most impartial men of the dissenters at this day, although they think the case of the ministers very hard, on account of subscriptions and declarations required of them, yet they confess very little is to be said on the behalf of the people, from whom none of those things are required. So that the people are condemned in their separation by their own teachers; but how they can preach lawfully to a people who commit a fault in hearing them I do not understand."

And the same thing is yet managed with more severity, pp. 37, 38, in words that I shall at large transcribe:—

"I dare say if most of the preachers at this day, in the separate meetings, were soberly asked their judgment, whether it were lawful for the people to join with us in the public assemblies, they would not deny it: and yet the people that frequent them generally judge otherwise; for it is not to be supposed that faction among them should so commonly prevail beyond interest, and, therefore, if they thought it were lawful for them to comply with the laws, they would do it. But why, then, is this kept up as such a mighty secret in the breasts of their teachers? why do they not preach to them in their congregations? Is it for fear they should have none left to preach to?—that is not to be imagined of mortified and conscientious men. Is it lest they should seem to condemn themselves, whilst they preach against separation in a separate congregation?

"This, I confess, looks oddly, and the tenderness of a man's mind in such a case may, out of mere shamefacedness, keep him from declaring a truth which flies in his face while he speaks it.

"Is it that they fear the reproaches of the people, which some few of the most eminent persons among them have found they must undergo if they touch upon this subject? (for, I know not how it comes to pass, that the most godly people among them can the least endure to be told of their faults;) but is it not as plainly written by St Paul, 'If I yet pleased men, I should not be the servant of Christ,'[1] as, 'Woe be unto me if I preach not the gospel?' If they, therefore, would acquit themselves like honest and conscientious men, let them tell the people plainly that they look on our churches as true churches, and that they may lawfully communicate with us in prayers and sacraments; and I do not question but in time, if they find it lawful, they will judge it to be their duty: for it is the apostle's command here, 'Whereto we have already attained, let us walk by the same rule, let us mind the same thing.'"

A crime this is which, if true, is not easily to be expiated; nor can men give greater evidence of their own hypocrisy, insincerity, and government by corrupt ends and designs, than by such abominable arts and contrivances. So, if it should prove not to be true, it can-

[1] Gal. i. 10.

not but be looked on as animated by such an evil surmise as is of no small provocation in the sight of God and men.

This reverend author makes a distinction about communion with the church, p. 20, between what is required of ministers and that which is called "lay-communion," which is the foundation of this charge:—

" I do not confound bare suspending communion in some particular rites, which persons do modestly scruple, and using it in what they judge to be lawful, with either total or at least ordinary forbearance of communion in what they judge to be lawful, and proceeding to the forming of separate congregations,—that is, under other teachers and by other rules than what the established religion allows. And this is the present case of separation which I intend to consider, and to make the sinfulness and mischief of it appear."

But he knows that by the communion and uniting ourselves unto the church, which is pressed either on ministers or people, a total submission unto the rule, as established in the Book of Canons and Rubric of the Liturgy, is required of them all. When this is once engaged in, there is no suspending of communion in particular rites to be allowed; they who give up themselves hereunto must observe the whole rule to a tittle. Nor is it in the power of this reverend author, who is of great dignity in the church, and as like as any man I know to be inclined thereunto, to give indulgence unto them in their abstinence from the least ceremony enjoined. Wherefore, the question about lay-communion is concerning that which is absolute and total, according unto all that is enjoined by the laws of the land, or by the canons, constitutions, and orders of the church. Hereby are they obliged to bring their children to be baptized with the use of the aerial sign of the cross; to kneel at the communion; to the religious observation of holidays; to the constant use of the liturgy in all the public offices of the church, unto the exclusion of the exercise of those gifts which Christ continues to communicate for its edification; to forego all means of public edification besides that in their parish churches, where, to speak with modesty, it is ofttimes scanty and wanting; to renounce all other assemblies wherein they have had great experience of spiritual advantage unto their souls; to desert the observation of many useful gospel duties, in their mutual watch that believers of the same church ought to have one over another; to divest themselves of all interest of a voluntary consent in the discipline of the church and choice of their own pastors; and to submit unto an ecclesiastical rule and discipline which not one in a thousand of them can apprehend to have any thing in it of the authority of Christ or rule of the gospel: and other things of the like nature may be added.

This being the true state of lay-communion, which will admit of no indulgence if the rule be observed, I must say that I do not believe that there are six nonconformist ministers in England that do believe this communion to be lawful for the people to embrace; and, on the other hand, they cease not to instruct them wherein their true communion with the church of England doth consist,—namely, in faith and love, and all the fruits of them, unto the glory of God.

I heartily wish these things had been omitted, that they had not been spoken;—not to cover any guilt in the Nonconformists, whose consciences are unto them a thousand witnesses against such imputations; but whereas the ground of them is only surmises and suspicions, and the evil charged of the highest nature that any men can involve themselves in the guilt of, it argues such a frame of spirit, such a habit of mind, as evidenceth men to be very remote from that Christian love and charity which, on all hands, we sometimes pretend unto. Of the same nature is another charge of the like want of sincerity, p. 46: "Those," saith he, "who speak now most against the magistrate's power in matters of religion had ten substantial reasons for it when they thought the magistrates on their own side;" for which is quoted an "Answer unto Two Questions," 1659;[1]—that is, they change their opinions according to their interest. I know not directly whom he intends. Those who are commonly called Independents expressed their apprehension of the magistrate's power in and about religion in their Confession, made 1659.[2] That any of them have, on what hath ensued, changed their opinion therein I know not. And, for my part, I have on this occasion perused the answer unto the two questions directed unto, and do profess myself at this day to be of the same judgment with the author of them, as it is expressed in that paper. There are things, not easily to be numbered, wherein we acknowledge the magistrate's power and duty in matters of religion, as much as ever was in the godly kings of Judah of old, or was at first claimed by the first Christian emperors. Yet there are some who, although they are fed and warmed, promoted and dignified, by the effects of the magistrate's power in and about religion, will not allow that any thing is ascribed unto him, unless we grant that it is in his rightful power, and his duty, to coerce and punish with all sorts of mulcts, spoiling of goods, imprisonments,

---

[1] Stillingfleet alludes to one of Owen's tracts under this title. See this vol., p. 507.—Ed.

[2] The first edition of the Savoy Confession,—so called from an old building in the Strand founded by an Earl of Savoy,—was printed in 1659. In doctrine it agrees with the Westminster Confession. A chapter on "the institution of churches" was substituted in the Savoy Declaration for those chapters on the power of synods, church censures, marriage, divorce, and the magistrate's power in regard to religion, which are to be found in the Westminster Confession. The chapter substituted details the principles of Congregationalism.—Ed.

banishments, and in some cases death itself, such persons as hold the Head and all the fundamental principles of Christian religion entire, whose worship is free from idolatry, whose conversations are peaceable and useful, unless in all things they comply with themselves, when possibly some of them may be as useful in and unto the church of God as those that would have them so dealt withal. And it may be, common prudence would advise a forbearance of too much severity in charges on others for changing their opinions, lest a provocation unto a recrimination on them that make them should arise of changing their opinions also, not without an appearing aspect to their own interests; but we have some among the Nonconformists who are so accustomed, not only unto such undue charges as that here insisted on, but unto such unjust accusations, false reports, malicious untruths, concerning them, their words, doctrines, and practices,— which, being invented by a few ill men, are trumpeted abroad with triumph by many,—as that they are come to a resolution never to concern themselves in them any more.

2. As unto the state of the question, we are told that " he speaks not of the separation or distinct communion of whole churches from each other; which, according to the Scripture, antiquity, and reason, have a just right and power to govern and reform themselves. By whole churches, I mean the churches of such nations, which, upon the decay of the Roman empire, resumed their just right of government to themselves, and, upon their owning Christianity, incorporated into one Christian society, under the same common ties and rules of order and government," p. 16.

I do suppose that particular churches or congregations are hereby exempted from all guilt of schism in not complying with rules of communion imposed on them by other churches. I am sure, according unto the principles of Nonconformists, they are so; for they judge that particular or congregational churches, stated with their officers according to the order of the gospel, are entire churches, that have a just right and power to govern and reform themselves. Until this be disproved,—until it be proved either that they are not churches because they are congregational, or that, although they are churches, yet they have not power to govern and reform themselves,—they are free from the guilt of schism in their so doing.

But the reverend author seems, in the ensuing discourse, to appropriate this right and power unto national churches, whose rise he assigns unto the dissolution of the Roman empire, and the alteration of the church government unto that of distinct kingdoms and provinces. But this is a thing that fell out so long after the institution of churches and propagation of Christian religion, that we are not at all concerned in it; especially considering that the occasion and means of the constitution of such churches was wholly foreign unto religion and the concerns of it.

The right and power of governing and reforming themselves here spoken of is that which is given by Christ himself unto his churches; nor do I know where else they should have it. Wherefore, those national provincial churches, which arose upon the dissolution of the Roman empire, must first be proved to be of his institution before they can be allowed to have their power given them by Jesus Christ. In what kings, potentates, and other supreme magistrates, might do to accommodate the outward profession of religion unto their rule and the interest thereof, we are not at all concerned, nor will give interruption unto any of them, whilst they impose not the religious observation of their constitutions unto that end upon our consciences and practice. Our sole inquiry is, what our Lord Jesus Christ hath ordained; and which, if we are compliant withal, we shall fear neither this nor any other charge of the like nature.

But to give strength hereunto it is added: "Just as several families united make one kingdom, which at first had a distinct and independent power; but it would make strange confusion in the world to reduce kingdoms back again to families, because at first they were made up of them," p. 17; which is again insisted on, p. 31. But the case is not the same; for if, indeed, God had appointed no other civil government in the world but that of families, I should not much oppose them who would endeavour peaceably to reduce all government thereunto. But whereas we are certain that God, by the light of the law of nature, by the ends and uses of the creation of man, and by express revelation in his word, hath, by his own authority, appointed and approved other sorts of civil government in kingdoms and common-weals, we esteem it not only a madness to endeavour a reduction of all government into families, as unto the possibility of the thing, but a direct opposition unto the authority, command, and institution of God. So, if these national churches were of the immediate institution of Christ himself, we should no more plead the exemption of particular churches from any power given them by Christ as such, than we do to exempt private families from the lawful government of public magistrates. And we must also add, that whatever be their original and constitution, if all their governors were as the apostles, yet have they no power but what is for edification, and not for destruction. If they do or shall appoint and impose on men what tends unto the destruction of their souls, and not unto their edification, as it is fallen out in the church of Rome, not only particular churches, but every individual believer is warranted to withdraw from their communion: and hereon we ground the lawfulness of our separation from the church of Rome, without any need of a retreat unto the late device of the power of provincial churches to reform themselves. Let none mistake themselves herein; believers are not made for churches, but churches are appointed for believers. Their edification, their guidance and direction in the profession of the faith and performance of divine worship in assemblies, according to the mind of God, is their use and end; without which they are of no signification. The end of Christ in the constitution of his churches was, not the moulding of his disciples into such ecclesiastical shapes as might be subservient unto the power, interest, advantage, and dignity, of them that may in any season come to be over them, but to constitute a way and order of giving such officers unto them as might be in all things useful and subservient unto their edification; as is expressly affirmed, Eph. iv. 11–16.

As it should seem, an opinion opposite unto this notion of national churches is examined and confuted, p. 17: "And it is a great mistake, to make the notion of a church barely to relate to acts of worship, and, consequently, that the adequate notion of a church is an assembly for divine worship,—by which means they appropriate the name of churches to particular congregations,—whereas, if this hold true, the church must be dissolved as soon as the congregation is broken up; but if they retain the nature of a church when they do not meet together for worship, then there is some other bond that unites them, and whatever that is, it constitutes the church." I am far from pretending to have read the writings of all men upon this subject, nay, I can say I have read very few of them, though I never avoided the reading of any thing written against the way and order which I approve of; wherefore there may be some, as far as I know, who have maintained this notion of a church, or that it is only an assembly for divine worship; but for my part, I never read nor heard of any who was of this judgment. Assemblies for divine worship we account indispensably necessary for the edification of the churches; but that this is that which gives them their constitution and formeth that which is the bond of their union, none of the Nonconformists, as I know of, do judge; for it will not only hence follow, as the reverend author observes, "that the church is dissolved when the congregation is broken up" (on which account churches at this time would be dissolved almost every week, whether they would or no), but that any sort of persons, who have no church relation unto one another, meeting occasionally for divine worship, do constitute a church, which it may be within an hour they cease to be. It is not, therefore, on this account that we appropriate the name of churches unto particular congregations; there is quite another way and means, another bond of union, whereby particular churches are constituted, which hath been sufficiently declared. But if the meaning of the "appropriating the name of churches unto particular congregations" be, that those societies which have not, or which cannot have, assemblies for divine worship, are not churches properly so called, it is a thing of another consideration, that need not here be insisted on. But when such societies as whose bounds and limits are not of divine institution, as were those of the national church of the Jews; no, nor yet of the prudence and wisdom of men, as were the distribution of the ancient church into patriarchates and dioceses; but a mere natural and necessary consequent of that prevailing sword which, on the dissolution of the Roman empire, erected distinct kingdoms and dominions, as men were able,—such societies as are not capable of any religious assemblies for divine worship, and the ministration of Christian discipline in them,—such as are forced to invent and maintain a union by ways and means, and officers and orders, which the Scripture knows nothing of,—are proved to be churches of Christ's institution, I shall embrace them as such. In the meantime, let them pass at their own proper rate and value, which the stamp of civil authority hath put upon them. What is farther discoursed by the author on this subject, proceeding no farther but why may it not be so and so, we are not concerned in.

3. Pages 23, 24, there is a distribution of all dissenters into two parties:—(1.) Such as say, "That although they are in a state of separation from our church, yet this separation is no sin." (2.) Such as say, "That a state of separation would be sin, but, notwithstanding their meeting in different places, yet they are not in a state of separation." The difference of these two parties seems to me to be only in the different ways of expressing themselves,—the one granting the use of the word "separation" in this case, which others will not admit; for their practice, so far as I can observe, is one and the same, and therefore their principles must be so also, though they choose several ways of expressing them. Both sorts intended do plead that in sundry things they have communion with the church of England; and in some things they have not, nor can have it so. Some knowing the word "separation" to be of an indifferent signification, and to be determined as unto its sense by what it is applied unto, do not contend but that, if any will have it so, the state wherein they are should be denominated from their dissent unto those things wherein they cannot hold communion with the church of England, and so are not offended if you call it a state of separation; howbeit this hinders not but that they continue their communion with the church of England, as was before mentioned. Others seem to take "separation" in the same sense with "schism," which is always evil, or at least they pretend it is their right to have the denomination of their state taken from what they agree in with the

church of England, and not from their dissent in other things from it; and therefore they continue in a practice suitable unto that dissent. Wherefore, I judge that there is no need of this distinction, but both parties intended are equally concerned in the charge that is laid against them for their dissent in some things from the church.

These things being premised, that we may not be diverted from the substance of the cause in hand, as they would otherwise occur unto us in our progress, I shall proceed unto the consideration of the charge itself laid against the Nonconformists, and the arguings whereby it is endeavoured to be confirmed.

The charge is, "That all the Nonconformists, of one sort or another,—that is, Presbyterians and Independents,—are guilty of sin, of a sinful separation from the church of England;" and therefore, as they live in a known sin, so they are the cause thereby of great evils, confusion, disturbances among ourselves, and of danger unto the whole protestant religion: whence it is meet that they should, etc.

The matter of fact being thus far mutually acknowledged, that there is such a stated difference between the church of England and the Nonconformists, the next inquiry naturally should be on these two heads:—

1. Who or what is the cause of this difference or distance? without which we cannot judge aright on whom the blame of it is to be charged; for that all men are not presently to be condemned for the withdrawing from the communion of any church, because they do so, without a due examination of the causes for which they do it, will be acknowledged by all Protestants. In plain terms, our inquiry is, Whether the cause hereof be, on the one hand, the imposition of terms of communion, without any obligation in conscience to make that imposition so much as pleaded or pretended from the nature of the things imposed; or the refusal of compliance with those impositions, under a profession that such a compliance would be against the light of conscience and the best understanding in them who so refuse which they can attain of the mind and will of God in the Scripture?

2. Whereas the parties at difference do agree in all substantial parts of religion, and in a common interest as unto the preservation and defence of the protestant religion, living alike peaceably under the same supreme authority and civil government, Whether the evils and inconveniences mentioned are necessary and inseparable effects of such a difference; or whether they do not wholly owe themselves unto passions, corrupt affections, and carnal interests of men, which ought on all hands to be mortified and subdued? For as, it may be, few wise men,—who know the nature of conscience, how delicate and tender it is, what care is required in all men to keep it as a precious

jewel, whose preservation from defilements and affronts God hath committed unto us, under the pain of his eternal displeasure; how unable honest men are to contravene the light of their own minds, in things of the smallest importance, for any outward advantages whatever; how great care, diligence, and accuracy ought to be used in all things relating unto the worship of God, about which he so frequently declares his jealousy, and displeasure against those who in any thing corrupt or debase it, with sundry other things of the like nature,—will admire that these differences are not ended among us by an absolute acquiescency of the one party in the judgments, dictates, and impositions of the other: so, upon the supposition before mentioned, —of an agreement in all the foundations of religion, in all things, from themselves and God's appointment, necessary unto salvation; of that union of affections which our joint interest in the unity of the faith doth require; and of that union of interest which both parties have in the preservation of the protestant religion, and that of obedience and subjection unto the same civil government; and on the satisfaction which the dissenting parties have in that the others do enjoy all those great advantages which the public profession of religion in this kingdom is accompanied withal, not in the least pretending to or contending for any share therein,—many wise men do and cannot but admire that the inconveniences and evils pretended should ensue on this difference as it is stated among us, and that the dissenters should be pursued with so much vehemency as they have been, even unto their ruin. But we must proceed in the way and method here proposed unto us.

First, the foundation whereon the reverend author manageth his charge of schism, with all its consequents, against the Nonconformists, is taken from the words of his text, and declared, pp. 10–14 of his book. I shall not transcribe his words, principally because I would not oblige myself to take notice of any thing that is ἔξω τοῦ πράγματος, which, in such discourses, do commonly administer occasion of unnecessary strife. The force of the argument, unto the best of my understanding, consists in the things that follow:—1. That all churches and the members of them, by virtue of the apostolical precept contained in the text, ought to walk according unto rule. 2. That the rule here intended is nŏt the rule of charity and mutual forbearance in the things wherein they who agree in the foundation are differently minded or otherwise than one another. But, 3. This was a standing rule for agreement and uniformity in practice in church order and worship, which the apostles had given and delivered unto them. 4. That this rule they did not give only as *apostles*, but as governors of the church, as appears from Acts xv. 5. Wherefore, what the apostles so did, *that* any church hath power to do, and ought to do, namely, to establish a rule of all practice in their communion. 6. That not to comply with this rule in all things is schism, the schism whereof Nonconformists are guilty. This, to the best of my understanding, is the entire force of the argument insisted on, and that proposed unto the best advantage for the apprehension of its force and strength, etc.

Let us, therefore, hereon a little inquire whether this will bear the weight of so great a charge as that which is built upon it and resolved into it, with all the dismal consequents pretended to ensue thereon; and we shall not pass by, in so doing, any thing that is offered to give an especial enforcement unto the charge itself. But in our entrance into the consideration of these things, I must needs say it is somewhat surprising unto me to see a charge wherein the consciences, reputation, liberty, etc., of so many are concerned, founded on the exposition of a text which no sober expositor that I know of did ever find out, propose, or embrace. But if it be true and according unto the mind of the Holy Ghost, this ought to be no disparagement unto it, though it be applied unto such an end. This is that which we are to examine. I say, therefore,—

1. We no way doubt but that the apostles did give rules of faith, obedience, and worship, not only unto private Christians, but to whole churches also; which we find recorded in the Scripture. Unto all these rules we do declare our assent and consent with an entire conformity; and do hope that with indifferent, unbiassed persons this is enough to free us from the charge of schism. 2. For the rule here intended, some take it to be the rule of *faith* in general, or divine revelation; some, to be the rule of *charity* and brotherly condescension; some, to be the particular rule here laid down, of *walking together in the different measures* of faith, light, and knowledge, which we do attain unto. The apostle, in the foregoing verses, having given an account of the glorious excellencies of the mysteries of the gospel, and of his own endeavour after the full attainment of them, yet affirms that he had not attained unto that perfection in the comprehension of them which he designed and aimed at. Herein, in the instance of himself, he declares the condition of the best believers in this life; which is not a full measure and perfection in the comprehension of the truths of the gospel, or enjoyment of the things themselves contained in them: but withal he declares their duty, in pressing continually, by all means, after that measure of attainment which is proposed unto their acquisition. Hereupon he supposes what will certainly ensue on the common pursuit of this design: which is, that men will come unto different attainments, have different measures of light and knowledge, yea, and different conceptions or opinions about these things; some will be " otherwise minded" than other some will

be, in some things only.   3. Hereupon he gives direction how they
should walk and behave themselves in this state and condition; and
unto those who have attained that measure whence, in comparison
of others, they may be styled "perfect," that they press on unanimously towards the end proposed; and as for those who in any
things differed from others, he encourageth them to wait on the teach-
ings of God, in that use of the means of instruction which they enjoyed.   And having prescribed to each supposed party their especial
duties as such, he lays down the duty of them both in common;
which is, that in and with respect unto what they had attained, they
should "walk by the same rule," namely, which he had now laid
down, and "mind the same thing," as he had before enjoined them.
Wherefore, these words of the apostle are so far from being a foundation to charge them with schism who, agreeing in the substance of
the doctrine of the gospel, do yet dissent from others (probably the
greater part of the church are intended) in some things, that they
enjoin a mutual forbearance among those who are so differently
minded.   4. But our author affirms that it cannot be a rule of
charity and mutual forbearance that is intended, because the apostle
had spoken of that just before.   But it is apparent that he speaks
these words with reference unto what he had said just before; and
if this be that which those who are "otherwise minded" are not
obliged unto, then are they not obliged at all to "walk by the rule"
intended; which is not the mind of the apostle.   So himself declares
out of Cajetan, that "the apostle subjoins the last words to the former, lest the persons he there speaks unto should think themselves
excused from going as far as they can in the same rule," p. 37.
    But "a rule," he says, "it is limiting and determining the prac-
tice, requiring uniformity in observing the same standing rule."   The
Nonconformists hereon do say, that if the apostles, or any one apostle,
did appoint such a rule as this intended, let it be produced with any
probability of proof to be theirs, and they are all ready to subscribe
and conform unto it.   On supposition that any rule of this nature
was appointed by the apostles and declared unto the churches, as
the reverend author I suppose doth intimate that it was (though I
dare not affix a determinate sense unto his words in this place), all
that can be required of us is, that we do conform and walk according
unto that rule so appointed and declared by them.   This we are
always ready to do.   Sundry general rules we find in the Scripture
given unto us, relating unto the constitution and edification of
churches, to their order, and worship, and government; sundry particular rules for ministers and others, how they should behave themselves in church societies and assemblies, are also laid down therein;
—all which we embrace, and submit unto the authority of Christ in

them. And if any other government or particular rule can be produced given by them, which is not recorded in the Scripture, so it can be proved to be theirs, we will engage to conform unto it.

5. If the rule pretended to be given by the apostles be of any use in this case, or can give any force unto the argument in hand, it must be such a one as appointed and required things to be observed in the worship of God that were never divinely appointed, imposing the observation of them on the consciences and practice of all the members of the church, under penalties spiritual and temporal; a rule constituting national churches, with a government and discipline suited unto that constitution, with modes and ceremonies of worship nowhere intimated in the Scripture, nor any way necessary in the light of reason. Such a rule, I say, it must be, since, although I should grant (which yet I do not) that the consequent is good, that because the apostles made rules for the practice of the church, that believers were bound in conscience to submit unto, therefore ordinary governors of the church may do so also, yet it will by no means follow that because the apostles appointed a rule of one sort, present church governors may appoint those of another. We know full well, and it is on all hands agreed, what is the rule that our conformity is required unto. If this be done from any rule given by the apostles, it must be a rule of the same nature or to the same purpose; otherwise, by a pretence of their pattern or example, rules may be made directly contrary unto and destructive of all the rules they ever really gave; as it is actually fallen out in the church of Rome. But,—

6. We deny that the apostles made or gave any such rules to the churches present in their days, or for the use of the churches in future ages, as should appoint and determine outward modes of worship, with ceremonies in their observation, stated feasts and fasts, beyond what is of divine institution, liturgies or forms of prayer, or discipline to be exercised in law courts, subservient unto a national ecclesiastical government. What use, then, they are or may be of, what benefit or advantage may come to the church by them, what is the authority of the superior magistrate about them, we do not now inquire or determine. Only we say, that no rule unto these ends was ever prescribed by the apostles; for,—

(1.) There is not the least intimation of any such rule to be given by them in the Scripture. There are in it, as was before observed, many express rules, both general and particular, about churches, their faith, worship, and men's walking in them, thoroughly sufficient to direct the duty and practice of all believers in all cases and occurrences relating to them: but of any such rule as that here pretended there is no mention; which certainly, if it had been given, and of the importance which now it is pleaded to be of,—such as that without it neither peace, nor unity, nor order, can be preserved in churches, —some intimation at least would have been made of it therein. Especially, we may judge it would have been so, seeing sundry things (every thing, so far as we can understand) wherein the edification of the church is any way concerned are recorded in it, though of little or no use in comparison of what so great and general a rule would be of. Besides, there is that doctrine delivered, and those directions given by them, in the Scripture, concerning the liberty of believers and forbearance of dissenters, as is inconsistent with such a rule and the imposition of it.

(2.) The first churches after their times knew nothing of any such rule given by them; and, therefore, after they began to depart from the simplicity of the gospel in any things, as unto worship, order, and rule, or discipline, they fell into a great variety of outward observances, orders, and ceremonies, every church almost differing in some thing or other from others, in some such observations, yet all " keeping the unity of the faith in the bond of peace." This they would not have done if the apostles had prescribed any one certain rule of such things that all must conform unto, especially considering how scrupulously they did adhere unto every thing that was reported to be done or spoken by any of the apostles, were the report true or false.

(3.) In particular, when a difference fell out amongst them in a business of this nature, namely, in a thing of outward order, nowhere appointed by the authority of Christ,—namely, about the observation of Easter,—the parties at variance appealed on the one side to the practice of Peter, on the other to the practice of John (both vainly enough): yet was it never pretended by any of them on either side that the apostles had constituted any rule in the case; and therefore it is not probable that they esteemed them to have done so in things of an alike nature, seeing they laid more weight on this than on any other instance of the like kind.

(4.) It is expressly denied, by good and sufficient testimony among them, that the apostles made any law or rule about outward rites, ceremonies, times, and the like. See Socrat., lib. v. cap. 21.

However, then, the apostles might, by their epistles and presence with the churches, reform abuses that were creeping or had crept in among them, and set things in order among them, with renewed directions for their walking; and though all Christians were obliged unto the observation of those rules, as all those still are unto whom they are applicable in their circumstances; yet all this proves nothing of their appointing such a general rule as is pretended: and such a rule alone would be pleadable in this case; and yet not this neither, until either it were produced in a scheme of canons, or it were proved that because they had power to make such a rule, so others may do the like, adding unto what they prescribed, leaving place unto others to add to their rule by the same right, and so endlessly.

The truth is, if God would be pleased to help us, on all hands, to lay aside prejudices, passions, secular interests, fears, and every other distempered affection, which obstruct our minds in passing a right judgment on things of the nature treated on, we [should] find in the text and context spoken unto a sacred truth divinely directive of such a practice as would give peace and rest unto us all; for it is supposed that men, in a sincere endeavour after acquaintance with the truths and mysteries of the gospel, with an enjoyment of the good things represented and exhibited in them, may fall, in some things, into different apprehensions about what belongs unto faith and practice in religion. But whilst they are such as do not destroy or overthrow the foundation, nor hinder men from "pressing towards the mark for the prize of the high calling of God in Christ Jesus," that which the apostle directs unto them who are supposed to be ignorant of or to mistake in the things wherein they do differ from others, is only that they wait for divine instruction in the use of the means appointed for that end, practising in the meantime according to what they have received. And as unto both parties, the advice he gives them is, that "whereunto they have attained," wherein they do agree,—which were all those principles of faith and obedience which were necessary unto their acceptance with God,—they should "walk by the same rule, and mind the same thing;" that is, "forbearing one another" in the things wherein they differ: which is the substance of what is pleaded for by the Nonconformists.

And that this is the meaning and intention of the apostle in this place is evident from the prescription of the same rule in an alike case, Rom. xiv. This the reverend author saw,—namely, that the rule there laid down is such as expressly requires mutual forbearance in such cases, where men are unsatisfied in conscience about any practice in religion; which seems, in the same case, to be quite another rule than that which he supposeth to be intended in this place to the Philippians. But hereunto he answers, that "the apostle did act like a prudent governor, and in such a manner as he thought did most tend to the propagation of the gospel and the good of particular churches. In some churches that consisted mostly of Jews, as the church of Rome at this time did, and where they did not impose the necessity of keeping the law on the Gentile Christians (as we do not find they did at Rome), the apostle was willing to have the law buried as decently and with as little noise as might be; and, therefore, in this case he persuades both parties to forbearance and charity in

avoiding the judging and censuring of one another, since they had
an equal regard unto the honour of God in what they did. But in
those churches where the false apostles made use of this pretence of
the Levitical law being still in force, to divide the churches and to
separate the communion of Christians, the apostle bids them beware
of them and their practices, as being of a dangerous and pernicious
consequence," pp. 14, 15. First, No man ever doubted of the prudence of the apostle as a governor, though in this place he acts only
as a teacher divinely inspired, instructing the churches in the mind of
God as unto the differences that were among them. Secondly, The
difference then among the Romans was about the observation of the
Mosaical ceremonies and worship; that is, so far as they might be
observed in the countries of the Gentiles, out of the limits of the
church, the land of Canaan. It could not be, therefore, concerning
such things as whose discharge and practice was confined unto the
temple or that land, which yet the Jews of Jerusalem adhered unto,
Acts xxi. 20–24. Their controversy, therefore, was principally about
meats and drinks, days of feasting or fasting, and the like, all founded
on a supposed necessity of circumcision. Thirdly, It is well observed
by our author, that the Judaizing Christians (which, in all probability, at this time were the greatest number at Rome, the Gentile
church not making any great increase before the coming of the
apostle thither) did not impose the necessity of keeping the law on
the Gentile Christians; at least not in that manner as was done by
the false teachers who troubled the churches of the Galatians and
others, so as to eject them who complied not with them out of
church-communion, and from all hopes of salvation: but yet both
parties continued in their different practices; which, through want
of instruction what was their duty in such cases, produced many inconveniences among them, as judging or despising one another, contrary to the rule of Christian love and charity. In this state the
apostle prescribes unto them the rule of their duty; which is, plainly,
to bear with one another, to love one another, and, according to the
nature of charity, to believe all things,—to believe that each party was
accepted with God, whilst they served him according unto the light
which they had received. And as it is to be thought that, upon the
giving of this rule and direction, they utterly laid aside all the animosities in judging and despising one another which they had been
guilty of; so it is certain that they continued in their different practice a long time after without any rebuke or reproof; yea, some
learned men do judge, and that not on grounds to be despised, that
the parties who differed were gathered into distinct churches, and so
continued to walk, even to the days of Adrian the emperor, when
the last and final destruction of the whole nation of the Jews did

befall them; after which those who were not hardened to the utmost gave off all expectation of any respect to be had with God of their old institutions. I do not know how the present case between the church of England and the Nonconformists could have possibly been more plainly and distinctly stated and exemplified, in any thing that the churches were capable of or liable unto in those days, than it is in this case here stated and determined by the apostle; in whose direction, rule, and determination we do fully acquiesce. But, Fourthly, It is true also which this reverend author observes, that when the false apostles, or any other Judaizing teachers pretending to authority, did impose the observation of the rites and ceremonies of the Levitical law on any churches, unto their disturbance and division, the apostle looks hereon as that which so far altered the case that he gives other rules and directions about it. And if such impositions might be yet forborne in the like case, especially as accompanied with the severe supplement and addition of all sorts of outward penalties, to be inflicted on them who cannot comply with them, an open door would appear into all that agreement, peace, and quietness among us which are desired.

I have treated thus far of these things, not to manage a controversy with this author or any other, but only to show that there is no ground to be taken from this text or its context to give countenance unto the severe censure of schism and all the evil consequents of it, as maintained by ill arts and practices, upon the Nonconformists.

The procedure of our author in the management of his charge, is in a way of proving, from the assertions and concessions of the several parties whereinto he hath distinguished Nonconformists, that they have no just cause to withhold full communion from the church of England, especially in its parochial assemblies. And as unto the first party, whom he affirms to grant that they are in a state of separation, he quotes some sayings out of a discourse of a nameless author, concerning Evangelical Love, Church-Peace, and Unity;[1] and together with some concessions of his, he adds his judgment, that communion in ordinances must be only in such churches as Christ himself instituted by unalterable rules, which were only particular and congregational churches. As I remember, that author hath at large declared in his discourse what communion believers ought to have with the church, or all churches,—the church in every sense wherein that name is used in the Scripture. But I shall not trouble myself to inquire into his assertions or concessions; nor at present can I do so, not having that book with me where I now am. My business is only to examine, on this occasion, what this reverend

---

[1] See a work by our author under this title, published in 1672, vol. xv. p. 57.—ED.

author excepteth against or opposeth unto his assertion about congregational churches, and the answering his charge of schism, notwithstanding this plea of the institution of particular churches for
the celebration of divine ordinances. This he doth p. 25: " Granting
this to be true, how doth it hence appear not to be a sin to separate
from our parochial churches, which, according to their own concessions, have all the essentials of true churches? And what ground
can they have to separate and divide those churches, which, for all
that we can see, are of the same nature with the churches planted
by the apostles at Corinth, Philippi, or Thessalonica?"

Ans. 1. We will allow at present that the parochial churches, at
least some of them, in this nation are true churches; that is, that
they are not guilty of any such heinous errors in doctrine or idolatrous practice in worship as should utterly deprive them of the being
and nature of churches. Yet we suppose it will not be made a rule,
that communion may not be withheld or withdrawn from any church
in any thing, so long as it continues, as unto the essence of it, to be
so. This author knows that testimonies may be produced out of very
learned protestant writers to the contrary.

2. We do not say, it is not pleaded, that because " communion in
ordinances must be only in such churches as Christ himself hath instituted," etc., that therefore it is lawful and necessary to separate
from parochial churches; but it may be pleaded thence, that if it be
on other grounds necessary to so separate or withhold communion
from them, it is the duty of them who do so to join themselves in or
unto some other particular congregations.

The reasons why the Nonconformists cannot join in that communion with those parochial churches which were before described are
quite of another nature, which are not here to be pleaded; however,
some of them may be mentioned, to deliver us from this mistake,
that the ground of separation from them is the institution of particular congregational churches. And they are such as these:—

(1.) There are many things in all parochial churches that openly
stand in need of reformation. What these are, both with respect
unto persons and things, hath been before intimated, and shall be
farther declared if occasion require. But these parochial churches
neither do, nor indeed can, nor have power in themselves to reform
the things that ought, by the rule of the Scripture, to be reformed;
for none among us will plead that they are intrusted with power for
their own government and reformation. In this case we judge it
lawful for any man peaceably to withdraw communion from such
churches, [and] to provide for his own edification in others.

(2.) That there are many things, in the constant and total communion of parochial churches, imposed on the consciences and prac-

tices of men, which are not according to the mind of Christ. The things of this nature I shall not here mention in particular.

(3.) There is no evangelical church discipline administered in such parochial churches, which yet is a necessary means unto the edification of the churches, appointed by Christ himself, and sacredly attended unto by the primitive churches; and we dare not renounce our interest in so blessed an ordinance of Christ in the gospel.

(4.) The rule and government which such parochial churches are absolutely under, in the room of that rule and discipline which ought to be in and among themselves,—namely, that by the courts of bishops, chancellors, commissaries, etc.,—is unknown to the Scriptures, and in its administration is very remote from giving a true representation of the authority, wisdom, love, and care of Christ to his church; which is the sole end of all church rules and discipline. The yoke hereof many account themselves not obliged to submit unto.

(5.) There is in such churches a total deprivation of the liberty of the people, secured unto them by the rules and practices of several ages from the beginning, of choosing their own pastors; whereby they are also deprived of all use of their light and knowledge of the gospel in providing for their own edification.

(6.) It cannot be denied but that there is want of due means of edification in many of those parochial churches, and yet provision is made by the government that those churches are under that none shall, by any way, provide themselves of better means for that great end of all church-society.

It is on these and the like reasons that the Nonconformists cannot join in total communion, such as the rule pleaded for requireth, with parochial churches. In this state, as was said, the Lord Christ having instituted particular congregations, requiring all believers to walk in them, it is the duty of those who are necessitated to decline the communion of parochial churches, as they are stated at present, to join themselves in and unto such congregations as wherein their edification and liberty may be better provided for according unto rule.

But hereon the reverend author proceeds to oppose such particular congregations or churches, I think, as unto their original and necessity; for so he speaks, pp. 25, 26: "But I must needs say farther, I have never yet seen any tolerable proof that the churches planted by the apostles were limited to congregations." Howbeit, this seems to be so clear and evident in matter of fact, and so necessary from the nature of the thing itself, that many wise men, wholly unconcerned in our controversies, do take it for a thing to be granted by all with-

out dispute.   So speaks Chief-Justice Hobart,[1] p. 149, in the case of
Colt and Glover *cont.* Bishop Coventry and Litchfield: "And we
know well that the primitive church, in its greatest purity, was but
voluntary congregations of believers, submitting themselves to the
apostles, and after to other pastors; to whom they did minister of
their temporals as God did move them." Of the same judgment are
those who esteem the first government of the church to be democratical. So speaks Paulus Sarpius: "In the beginning, the government of the holy church had altogether a democratical form, all the
faithful intervening in the chiefest deliberations. Thus we see that
all did intervene at the election of Matthias unto the apostleship, and
in the election of the six deacons; and when St Peter received Cornelius, a heathen centurion, unto the faith, he gave an account of it
to all the church; likewise in the council celebrated in Jerusalem,
the apostles, the priests, and the other faithful brethren did intervene,
and the letters were written in the name of all these three orders.
In success of time, when the church increased in number, the faithful retiring themselves to the affairs of their families, and having left
those of the congregation, the government retained only in the
ministers, and became aristocratical, saving the election, which was
popular." And others also of the same judgment may be added.

But let us hear the reasoning of this learned author against this
apprehension; this he enters upon, p. 26: "It is possible at first
there might be no more Christians in one city than could meet in
one assembly for worship; but where doth it appear that when they
multiplied into more congregations, they did make new and distinct
churches, under new officers, with a separate power of government?
Of this, I am well assured, there are no marks or footsteps in the
New Testament nor the whole history of the primitive church. I do
not think it will appear credible to any considerate man that the
five thousand Christians in the church of Jerusalem made one stated
and fixed congregation for divine worship, not if we make all the
allowances for strangers which can be desired; but if this were
granted, where are the unalterable rules that as soon as the company became too great for one particular assembly, they must become
a new church, under peculiar officers and an independent authority?
It is very strange that those who contend so much for the Scripture
being a perfect rule of all things pertaining to worship and discipline should be able to produce nothing in so necessary a point."

I answer,—1. It is possible that an impartial account may, ere

---

[1] Sir Henry Hobart, Lord Chief-Justice of the Court of Common Pleas, published, in
1650, a work under the title of "Reports in the Reign of King James I., with some
few Cases in the Reign of Queen Elizabeth." The fifth edition was revised and corrected by Lord Ch. Nottingham, 1724.—Ed.

long, be given of the state and ways of the first churches after the decease of the apostles; wherein it will be made to appear how they did insensibly deviate in many things from the rule of their first institution, so as that, though their mistakes were of small moment, and not prejudicial unto their faith and order, yet occasion was administered to succeeding ages to increase those deviations, until they issued in a fatal apostasy. An eminent instance hereof is given us in the discourse of Paulus Sarpius about matters beneficiary, lately made public in our own language.[1]

2. The matter of fact herein seems to me evidently to be exemplified in the Scripture; for although, it may be, there is not express mention made that these or those particular churches did divide themselves into more congregations with new officers, yet are there instances of the erection of new particular congregations in the same province, as distinct churches, with a separate power of government. So the first church in the province of Judea was in Jerusalem; but when that church was complete, as to the number of them who might communicate therein unto their edification, the apostles did not add the believers of the adjacent towns and places unto that church, but erected other particular congregations all the country over. So there were different churches in Judea, Galilee, and Samaria,—that is, many in each of them, Acts ix. 31. So the apostle mentions the churches of God that were in Judea, 1 Thess. ii. 14, and nowhere speaks of them as one church, for worship, order, and government. So he speaks again, that is constantly, Gal. i. 22, "I was unknown by face unto the churches of Judea." And that these churches were neither national nor diocesan, but particular congregations, is, as I suppose, sufficiently evident. So was it in the province of Galatia. There is no mention of any church therein that should be comprehensive of all the believers in that province; but many particular churches there were, as it is testified chap. i. 2. So was it also in Macedonia. The first church planted in that province was at Philippi, as it is declared Acts xvi.; and it was quickly brought into complete order, so as that when the apostle wrote unto it, there were in it the "saints" whereof it was constituted, with "bishops and deacons," Phil. i. 1. But that church being so complete, the apostle appointed other particular congregational churches in the same province, which had officers of their own, with a power of government; these he mentions and calls "The churches of Macedonia," 2 Cor. viii. 1, 23. Wherefore we need no more directions in this matter than what are given us by the apostle's authority, in the name and authority of Jesus Christ, nor are concerned in the prac-

[1] Appended to the edition of Paul Sarpi's "History of the Council of Trent," published in 1676, will be found also his "Treatise of Beneficiary Matters."—ED.

tice of those who afterward took another course, of adding believers from other places unto the church first planted, unless it were in case of a disability to enjoy church-communion among themselves elsewhere. Whatever, therefore, is pretended unto the contrary, we have plain Scripture evidence and practice for the erecting particular distinct congregations, with power for their own rule and edification, in the same province, be it as small as those that were of Samaria or Galilee. It cannot, surely, be said that these churches were national, whereof there were many in one small province of a small nation, nor yet metropolitical or diocesan; nor, I suppose, will it be denied but that they were intrusted with power to rule and govern themselves in all ordinary cases, especially when in every one of them elders were ordained; which the apostles were careful to see done, Acts xiv. 23. This is the substance of what we plead as unto particular congregations.

3. It is not probable that any of the first churches did, for a long time, increase in any city unto such a number as might exceed the bounds of a particular church or congregation; for such they might continue to be, notwithstanding a multiplication of bishops or elders in them, and occasional distinct assemblies for some acts of divine worship. And it seems if they did begin to exceed in number beyond a just proportion for their edification, they did immediately erect other churches among them or near them. So, whereas there was a mighty increase of believers at Corinth, Acts xviii. 10, there was quickly planted a distinct church at Cenchrea, which was the port of the city, Rom. xvi. 1. And notwithstanding the great number of five thousand that were converted at Jerusalem upon the first preaching of the gospel, yet were they so disposed of or so dispersed, that some years after this there was such a church only there as did meet together in one place as occasion did require, even the whole multitude of the brethren, who are called the "church" in distinction from the "apostles and elders," who were their governors, Acts xv. 4, 12, xxi. 22. Nor was that church of any greater number when they all departed afterward and went out into Pella, a village beyond Jordan, before the destruction of the people, city, and temple. And though many alterations were before that time introduced into the order and rule of the churches, yet it appears that when Cyprian was bishop of the church at Carthage, the whole community of the members of that church did meet together to determine of things that were for their common interests, according unto what was judged to be their right and liberty in those days; which they could not have done had they not all of them belonged unto the same particular church and congregation. But these things may be pleaded elsewhere if occasion be given thereunto. But yet,—

4. I must say that I cannot discern the least necessity of any positive rule or direction in this matter, nor is any such thing required by us on the like occasion; for this distribution of believers into particular congregations is that which the nature of the thing itself, and the duty of men with respect unto the end of such churches, do indispensably require. For what is the end of all churches, for which they are instituted? is it not the edification of them that do believe? They will find themselves mistaken who suppose that they were designed to be subservient unto the secular interest of any sort of men. What are the means appointed of Christ in such churches for that end? Are they not "doctrine and fellowship, breaking of bread, and prayers,"—that is, the joint celebration of the ordinances of Christ in the gospel, in preaching the word, administering the sacraments, mutual watchfulness over one another, and the exercise of that discipline which he hath appointed unto his disciples? I desire to know whether there be any need of a new revelation to direct men who are obliged to preserve churches in their use unto their proper end, to take care of such things as would obstruct and hinder them in the use of means unto the end of their edification? Whereas, therefore, it is manifest that, ordinarily, these means cannot be used in a due manner but in such churches as wherein all may be acquainted with what all are concerned in, the very institution itself is a plain command to plant, erect, and keep all churches in such a state as wherein this end may be attained. And, therefore, if believers in any place are so few, or so destitute of spiritual gifts, as not to be able of themselves jointly to observe these means for their edification, it is their duty not to join by themselves in a church-state, but to add themselves as members unto other churches; and so when they are so many as that they cannot orderly communicate together in all these ordinances, in the way of their administration appointed in the Scripture, unto the edification of them, it is their duty, by virtue of the divine institution of churches, to dispose of their church-state and relation into that way which will answer the ends of it,—that is, into more particular churches or congregations.

I speak not these things in opposition unto any other church-state which men may erect or establish out of an opinion of its usefulness and conveniency, much less against that communion which ought to be among those particular churches, or their associations for their common rule and government in and by their officers; but only to manifest that those Nonconformists who are supposed to adhere unto the institution of particular churches in a peculiar way, do not thereby deserve the imputation of so great and intolerable a guilt as they are here charged withal. And whereas I have hereby discharged all that

I designed with respect unto the first sort of Nonconformists, as they are here distinguished, I might here give over the pursuit of this argument; but because I seek after truth and satisfaction also in these things, I shall a little farther consider what is offered by this reverend author unto the same purpose with what we have passed through. So, therefore, he proceeds, pp. 26, 27, "If that of which we read the clearest instance in Scripture must be the standard of all future ages, much more might be said for limiting churches to private families than to particular congregations; for do we not read of the church that was in the house of Priscilla and Aquila at Rome, of the church that was in the house of Nymphas at Colosse, and in the house of Philemon at Laodicea? Why, then, should not churches be reduced to particular families, when by that means they may fully enjoy the liberty of their consciences and avoid the scandal of breaking the laws? But if, notwithstanding such plain examples, men will extend churches to congregations of many families, why may not others extend churches to those societies which consist of many congregations?"

I answer,—1. Possibly a church may be in a family, or consist only of the persons that belong to a family: but a family, as a family, neither is nor can be a church; for as such it is constituted by natural and civil relations. But a church hath its form and being from the voluntary spiritual consent of those whereof it consists unto church-order: "They gave," saith the apostle, "their own selves to the Lord, and unto us by the will of God," 2 Cor. viii. 5. Neither is there any mention at all in the Scripture of the constitution of churches in private families, so as that they should be limited thereunto.

2. What is spoken of the church in the houses of Aquila, Nymphas, and Philemon, doth not at all prove that there was a particular church in each of their houses, consisting only of their own families as such; but only that there was a church which usually assembled in their respective houses. Wherefore,—

3. There is no such example given of churches in private families in the whole Scripture as should restrain the extent of churches from congregations of many families. And the inquiry hereon, that "if men will extend churches to congregations of many families, why may not others extend churches unto societies which consist of many congregations," hath not any force in it; for they who extended churches unto congregations of many families were the apostles themselves, acting in the name and authority of Jesus Christ. It cannot be proved that ever they stated, erected, or planted any one church, but it was composed of many persons out of many families; nor that ever they confined a church unto a family, or taught that families, though all of them believers and baptized, were churches on the

account of their being families. "So others may extend churches unto those societies which consist of many congregations;"—yet not so as those who cannot comply or join with them should thereon be esteemed schismatics, seeing such societies were not appointed by Christ and his apostles. If such societies be so constituted as that there is but a probable plea that they are ordained by Christ, there may be danger in a dissent from them merely on this account, that they consist of many congregations; but this is not our case, as hath been before declared.

The remainder of this section consists in an account of the practice of the churches in some things in following ages. This though of importance in itself, and deserving a full inquiry into, yet belongeth not unto our present case, and will, it may be, in due time be more fully spoken unto.

Those supposed of the first way and judgment, who grant a separation from the established form of the church of England, are dismissed with one charge more on and plea against their practice, not without a mixture of some severity in expression, p. 30: "But suppose the first churches were barely congregated, by reason of the small number of believers at that time, yet what obligation lies upon us to disturb the peace of the church we live in, to reduce churches to their infant state?" which is pressed with sundry considerations in the two following pages. But we say,—1. That the first churches were not "congregated by reason of the small number of believers," but because the Lord Christ had limited and determined that such a state of his churches should be under the New Testament, as best suited unto all the ends of their institution. 2. That which is called the "infant state of churches" was, in truth, their sole perfect estate; —what they grew up unto afterward, most of them, we know well enough; for leaving, as it is called, their "infant state" by degrees, they brought forth at last "The man of sin." 3. No obligation lies upon us from hence to "disturb the peace" of any church; nor do we do so, let what will be pretended to the contrary. If any such disturbance do ensue upon the differences that are between them and us, as far as I know, the blame will be found lying upon them who [are] not [only] satisfied that they may leave the first state of the churches, under a pretence of its infancy, and bring them into a greater perfection than was given them by Christ and his disciples, but compel others also to forego their primitive constitution, and comply with them in their alteration thereof.

The remainder of the discourse of this section, so far as I can understand, proceeds on this principle, that the sole reason and cause of our nonconformity is this persuasion of the divine institution of particular churches; but all men know that this is otherwise. This of all things is least pleaded, and commonly in the last place, and but by some, among the causes and reasons of our withholding communion, so far as we do so, from the church of England, as unto the way and manner wherein it is required of us. Those reasons have been pleaded already, and may yet be so farther in due time. For the rest of the discourse, we do not, we cannot, believe that the due and peaceable observation of the institutions of Christ doth of itself give any disturbance unto any churches or persons whatever, nor that a peaceable endeavour to practise ourselves according unto those institutions, without imposing that practice on them, can be justly blamable. We do not, we cannot, believe that our refusal of a total compliance with a rule for order, discipline, worship, and ceremonies in the church, not given by Christ and his apostles, but requiring of us sundry things either in themselves or as required of us directly contrary unto, or inconsistent with, the rules and directions given us by them unto those ends (as, in our judgment and light of our consciences, is done in and by this rule), is either schism or blamable separation. We do judge ourselves obliged to preserve peace and unity among Christians by all the means that Christ hath appointed for that end,—by the exercise of all graces, the performance of all duties, the observation of all rules and directions given us for that end; but we do not, we cannot, believe that to neglect the means of our own edification, appointed unto us by Christ himself, to cast away the liberty wherewith he hath made us free, and to destroy our own souls for ever by acting against his authority in his word, and our own consciences guided thereby, in a total complying with the rule proposed unto us, is a way or means for the attaining of that end. And we do believe that, in the present state of the differences among us, an issue whereof is not suddenly to be expected in an absolute agreement in opinion and judgment about them, the rule of the Scripture, the example of the first churches, the nature of Christian religion, and the present interest of the protestant religion among us, do call for mutual forbearance, with mutual love, and peaceable walking therein. And we begin to hope, that whereas it is confessed that the foundations of Christian religion are preserved entire among us all, and it is evident that those who dissent from the present ecclesiastical establishments, or any of them, are as ready to do and suffer what they shall be lawfully called unto in the defence and for the preservation of the protestant religion, wise men will begin to think that it is better for them to take up quietly in what the law hath provided for them, and not turmoil themselves and others in seeking to put an end unto these differences by force and compulsion; which by these ways they will never whilst they live attain unto. And we do suppose that many of them who do cordially own and seek the preservation of the protestant religion in this nation,—men, I mean, of authority, power, and interest,— will be no more instrumental to help one part [to] ruin and destroy another, unduly weakening the whole interest of Protestantism thereby; but, considering how little the concern of themselves or their posterity can be in these lesser differences, in comparison of what it is in the whole protestant cause, will endeavour their utmost to procure an equal liberty (though not equal outward advantages) for all that are firm and stable in their profession of that protestant religion which is established by law in this kingdom. I know that learned and eloquent men, such as this author is, are able to declaim against mutual forbearance in these things, with probable pleas and pretences of evil consequents which will ensue thereon; and I do know that others, though not with equal learning or eloquence, do declare and set forth the inequality, unrighteousness, and destructive events of a contrary course, or the use of force and compulsion in this cause;—but it must be granted that the evil consequences pretended on a mutual forbearance do follow from the corrupt affections and passions of men, and not from the thing itself; but all the evils which will follow on force and compulsion do naturally arise from the thing itself.

I shall close this part of my discourse with an observation on that wherewith it is closed by this author, in his management of it. Saith he, " To withdraw from each other into separate congregations tempts some to spiritual pride, and scorn and contempt of others, as of a more carnal and worldly church than themselves; and provokes others to lay open the follies, and indiscretions, and immoralities of those who pretend to so much purity and spirituality above their brethren," pp. 32, 33. If there be any unto whom this is such a temptation as is mentioned in the first place, and being so, doth prevail upon them, it is their sin, arising from their own lusts, by which every man is tempted, and is not at all occasioned by the thing itself. And for the other part, let those who delight in that work proceed as they shall see cause; for if they charge upon us things that are really foolish, indiscreet, and immoral, as in many things we sin all, we hope we shall learn what to amend, and to be diligent therein, as for other reasons, so because of our observers. But if they do what some have done, and others yet continue to do,—fill their discourses with false, malicious defamations, with scorn, contempt, railing, and revilings, scandalous unto Christian religion, like a sermon lately preached before my Lord Mayor, and since put in print (I intend not that under consideration),—we are no way concerned in what they do or say, nor do, as we know of, suffer any disadvantage thereby; yea, such persons are beneath the offence and

contempt of all men pretending unto the least wisdom and sobriety.

For what remains of this discourse, I esteem not myself concerned
to insist on the examination of it; for I would not so express my judgment in these things as some are here represented to declare themselves, and I know that those who are principally reflected on are
able to defend both their principles and practices. And besides, I
hear (in the retirement wherein I live, and wherein I die daily) that
some of those most immediately concerned have returned an answer
unto this part of the discourse under consideration. I shall, therefore, only observe some few things that may abate the edge of this
charge; for although we judge the defence of the truth which we
profess to be necessary when we are called thereunto, yet at present,
for the reasons intimated at the entrance of this discourse, we should
choose that it might not be brought under debate. But the defence
of our innocency, when the charge against us is such as in itself tends
to our distress and ruin, is that alone which is our present design,
and which wise men, no way concerned in our nonconformity, for the
sake of the protestant religion and public peace of the nation, have
judged necessary.

The principal strength of this part of the reverend author's discourse consists in his application of the reasons of the [Westminster]
Assembly against those who desired forbearance, in distinct communion from the rule sought then to be established, unto those who
now desire the same forbearance from the church of England. I
will not immerse myself in that controversy, nor have any contention with the dead. This only I say, that the case then between the
Presbyterians and those who dissented from them is so vastly different from that now between the church of England and the Nonconformists, and that in so many material instances and circumstances, that no light can be communicated unto the right determination of the latter from what was pleaded in the former. In
brief, those who pleaded then for a kind of uniformity or agreement
in total communion did propose no one of those things, as the condition of it, which are now pleaded as the only reasons of withholding the same kind of conformity from the church of England, and
the non-imposition of any such things they made the foundation of
their plea for the compliance of others with them; and those on the
other side, who pleaded for liberty and forbearance in such a case as
wherein there were no such impositions, did it mostly on the common liberty which, as they judged, they had with their other brethren
to abide by the way which they had declared and practised long
before any rule was established unto its prejudice. And these things
are sufficient to give us, as unto the present case under debate, an

absolute unconcernment in what was then pleaded on the one side or the other, and so it shall be here dismissed.

The especial charge here managed against the Nonconformists is, that they allow that to " live [in] a state of separation from such churches as many at least of ours are is a sin;" yet that themselves so do, which is manifest in their practice.   But it may be said,— 1. That this concession respects only parochial churches, and that some of them only ; but the conformity in general required of us respects the constitution, government, discipline, worship, and communion of the national church and diocesan churches therein. 2. Persons who thus express themselves are to be allowed the interpretation of their own minds, words, and expressions; for if they do judge that such things do belong unto a state of separation from any churches, as, namely, a causeless renouncing of all communion with them, a condemnation of them as no church, and on that ground setting up churches against them, which they know themselves not to be guilty of, they may both honestly and wisely deny themselves to be in a state of separation, nor will their present practice prove them so to be.   And, on the other hand, those who do acknowledge a separation as unto distinct local presential communion with the church of England, yet do all of them deny those things which, in the judgment of those now intended, are necessary to constitute a state of separation.   But on this account, I cannot see the least contradiction between the principles and practice of these brethren, nor wherein they are blameworthy in their concessions, unless to be in too much earnestness to keep up all possible communion with the church of England.   " Forgive them that wrong."   Yet I say not this as though those who are here supposed to own a state of separation were not as zealous also for communion in faith, love, and doctrine of truth with the body of Protestants in this nation as they are. 3. That which animates this part of the discourse, and which is the edge of this charge, is, that " the ministers do conceal from the people what their judgment is about the lawfulness of communion with the church of England."   How this can be known to be so, I cannot understand; for that it is their judgment that they may do so is proved only, so far as I know, from what they have written and published in print unto that purpose.   And certainly what men so publish of their own accord, they can have no design to conceal from any, especially not from them who usually attend on their ministry, who are most likely to read their books with diligence.   But this hath been spoken unto before.

In these things we seek for no shelter nor countenance from what is pleaded by any concerning the obliging power of an " erroneous conscience," which the reverend author insists on, pp. 42–44; for we acknowledge no rule of conscience in those things which concern churches, their state, power, order, and worship, but divine revelation only,—that is, the Scripture, the written word of God,—and sure enough we are not deceived in the choice of our rule, so as that we desire no greater assurance in any concerns of religion. And by the Scripture as our rule, we understand both the express words of it, and whatever may, by just and lawful consequence, be educed from them. This rule we attend unto, and inquire into the mind of God in it, with all the diligence we are able, and in the use of all the means that are usually and truly pleaded as necessary unto the attainment of a right understanding thereof; and if any one can inform us of any thing required of us thereby which yet we have not received, we shall with all readiness comply therewithal. We have no prejudices, no outward temptations, that should bias our minds and inclinations unto those principles, and practices on them, which we judge ourselves guided and directed unto by this rule; but all such considerations as might be taken from the most moderate desires, even of food and raiment, do lie against us. We are hereon fully satisfied that we have attained that knowledge in the mind of God about these things as will preserve us from evil or sin against him, from being hurtful or useless unto the rest of mankind, if we submit unto the light and conduct of it. Wherefore, we seek no relief in, we plead no excuse from, the obligation of an erroneous conscience, but do abide by it that our consciences are rightly informed in these things; and then it is confessed on all hands what is their power, and what their force to oblige us, with respect unto all human commands.

I know not of any farther concern that the Nonconformists have in the discourse of this reverend author, unless it be in the considerations which he proposeth unto them, and the advice which he gives them in the close of it. I shall only say, concerning the one and the other, that having weighed them impartially, unto the best of my understanding, I find not any thing in them that should make it the duty of any man to invent and constitute such a rule of church communion as that which is proposed unto the Nonconformists for their absolute compliance withal, nor any thing that should move the Nonconformists unto such compliance, against the light of their consciences and understanding in the mind of Christ; which alone are the things in debate between us. But if the design of the author, in the proposal of these considerations and the particulars of his advice, be, that we should take heed to ourselves, that during these differences among us we give no offence unto others, so far as it is possible, nor entertain severe thoughts in ourselves of them from whom we differ, we shall be glad that both he and we should be found in the due observance of such advice. One head of his advice

I confess might be, if I am not mistaken, more acceptable with some of the Nonconformists, if it had not come in the close of such a discourse as this is; and it is, that " they should not be always complaining of their hardships and persecution," p. 54: for they say, after so many of them have died in common jails; so many have endured long imprisonments, not a few being at this day in the same durance; so many have been driven from their habitations into a wandering condition, to preserve for a while the liberty of their persons; so many have been reduced unto want and penury by the taking away of their goods, and from some the very instruments of their livelihood; after the prosecutions which have been against them in all courts of justice in this nation, on informations, indictments, and suits, to the great charge of all of them who are so persecuted, and ruin of some; after so many ministers and their families have been brought into the utmost outward straits which nature can subsist under; after all their perpetual fears and dangers wherewith they have been exercised and disquieted,—they think it hard they should be complained of for complaining by them who are at ease. It may be remembered what one speaks very gravely in the Comedian,—

> " Sed, Demea, hoc tu facito cum animo cogites,
> Quàm vos facillime agitis, quàm estis maxume
> Potentes, dites, fortunati, nobiles ;
> Tam maxume vos æquo animo æqua noscere
> Oportet, si vos voltis perhiberi probos."—
> [Ter. Ad. iii., iv., 54.]

Indeed, men who are encompassed with an affluence of all earthly enjoyments, and in the secure possession of the good things of this life, do not well understand what they say when they speak of other men's sufferings. This I dare undertake for all the Nonconformists: let others leave beating them, and they shall all leave complaining. She is thought but a curst[1] mother who beats her child for crying, and will not cease beating until the child leave crying; which it cannot do whilst it is continually beaten. Neither do I know that the Nonconformists are "always complaining of their sufferings," nor what are their complaints that they make, nor to whom; yea, I do suppose that all impartial men will judge that they have borne their sufferings with as much patience and silence as any who have gone before them in the like state and condition. And they do hope that men will not be angry with them if they cry unto God for deliverance from those troubles which they judge they undergo for his sake. Thankful, also, they are unto God and men for any release they have received from their sufferings; wherein their chief respect amongst men hitherto is unto the king himself. But that they

---

[1] Not our English "cursed," but an adjective, said to be derived from the Dutch " korst," signifying crusty, ill-tempered.—ED.

should be very thankful to those who esteem all their past and present sufferings to be light, and do really endeavour to have them continued and increased (among whom I do not reckon this reverend author, for I do not know that I can truly do so), is not to be expected.

I shall add no more, but that whereas the Nonconformists intended in this defence are one, or do completely agree, with the body of the people in this nation that are Protestants, or the church of England, in the entire doctrine of faith and obedience, in all the instances whereby it hath been publicly declared or established by law,—which agreement in the unity of faith is the principal foundation of all other union and agreement among Christians, and without which every other way or means of any such union or agreement is of no worth or value, and which if it be not impeached is in itself a sufficient bond of union, whatever other differences may arise among men, and ought to be so esteemed among all Christians;—and whereas they are one with the same body of the people, that is, in its magistracy and those who are under rule, in one common interest, for the maintenance and preservation of protestant religion, whereunto they are secured by a sense of their duty and safety, and without whose orderly and regular concurrence in all lawful ways and actings unto that end it will not be so easily attained as some imagine;—and whereas also they are one with them in all due legal subjection unto the same supreme power amongst us, and are equally ready with any sort of persons of their respective qualities or condition in the nation to contribute their assistance unto the preservation of its peace and liberty;—and whereas in their several capacities they are useful unto the public faith and trust of the nation, the maintenance and increase of the wealth and prosperity of it;—considering what evidences there are of the will of God in the constitution of our natures, under the conduct of conscience, in immediate subordination unto himself; the different measures of light, knowledge, and understanding which he communicates unto men; as also of the spirit, rule, and will of Jesus Christ, with the example of the apostles and the primitive churches for mutual forbearance, in such different apprehensions of and practices about religion, as no way intrencheth on the unity of faith, or any good of public society;—I cannot but judge (in which persuasion I now live, and shall shortly die) that all writings tending to exasperate and provoke the dissenting parties one against another are at this day highly unseasonable; and all endeavours, of what sort soever, to disquiet, discourage, trouble, punish, or distress such as dissent from the public rule, in the way before described, are contrary to the will of God, obstructive of the welfare of the nation, and dangerous unto the protestant religion.

TRUTH AND INNOCENCE VINDICATED;

IN

A SURVEY OF A DISCOURSE CONCERNING ECCLESIASTICAL POLITY, AND THE AUTHORITY OF THE CIVIL MAGISTRATE OVER THE CONSCIENCES OF SUBJECTS IN MATTERS OF RELIGION.

———

Non partûm studiis agimur ; sed sumsimus arma,
Consiliis inimica tuis, discordia vecors.
Οὐδὲν ἄτερ γραφῆς.—CLEMENS ALEXAND.

———

LONDON: 1669.

PREFATORY NOTE.

SAMUEL PARKER, author of the " Discourse of Ecclesiastical Polity, and of the Power of the Magistrate in Matters of Religion," to which Owen supplied the following answer, was a noted character in his day. When a student in Wadham College, Oxford, he was a Puritan of the strictest fashion; but as worldly advancement was his ruling motive, he changed his views, and recommended himself to the Court by his abject subserviency to its arbitrary measures. He was made Bishop of Oxford in 1686, and when the Fellows of Magdalen College distinguished themselves by their magnanimous resistance to the encroachment on their privileges attempted by the Crown, and Hough, who had obtained their almost unanimous suffrages to the vacant office of President, had been forcibly ejected, Parker was thrust upon them, as a fit tool for promoting the despotic and popish views of James II. It was natural that such a man should harbour the deepest malice against Nonconformists,—a malice in which the usual rancour of apostasy mingled as an ingredient of especial bitterness.

We refer to the Life of Owen, vol. i., p. lxxxviii., for an account of the controversy to which Parker's book gave rise, and for a just appreciation of the merits of Owen's work in reply to it. Besides Owen's work, several anonymous answers to Parker appeared, under such titles as the following:—" Insolence and Impudence Triumphant; Envy and Fury Enthroned; The Mirror of Malice and Madness," etc., 1670; " Toleration Discussed in Two Dialogues," 1670; " Animadversions on a New Book entitled Ecclesiastical Polity," 1670; and, " A Free Inquiry into the Causes of that very great Esteem the Nonconformists are in with their Followers," 1673.

Parker in 1671 replied to Owen, in " A Defence and Continuation of the Ecclesiastical Polity," and in a preface to Bishop Bramhall's " Vindication of the Episcopal Clergy," written in a characteristic strain of mingled ribaldry and bombast. In 1672, Marvell published his famous " Rehearsal Transprosed." Marvell was immediately assailed in a host of pamphlets:—" The Transproser Rehearsed;" " Rosemary and Bayes;" " Gregory Father Greybeard with his Vizor off;" " A Common-place Book out of the Rehearsal Transprosed;" " S'too him Bayes," etc. Parker's own pamphlet in reply to him bore the title, " A Reproof to the Rehearsal Transprosed, in a Discourse to its Author."

The genius of Marvell, however, carried all before him in the second part of his work, published in 1673. The title of it, with the exception of an oath prefixed to the threat quoted in it, is subjoined, as an illustration of the intensity of feeling excited by the dispute, and of the dread which the friends of Parker entertained for the keen weapons of the Puritan wit:—" The Rehearsal Transprosed, the second part : occasioned by two letters; the first printed by a nameless author, entitled ' A Reproof,' etc.; the second left for me at a friend's house, dated November 3, 1673, subscribed 'J. G.,' and concluding with these words, 'If thou darest to print any lie or libel against Dr Parker, ... I will cut thy throat.'" Marvell, undeterred by these profane threats and ravings, dealt such a blow to his main opponent as made him the laughing-stock of every circle, and compelled him for a time to hide his shame in rural obscurity.

Owen in the following work confines himself to a refutation of the slavish and extravagant notions respecting magistratical authority and the royal prerogative which the minion of the Court had not shrunk from propounding. The work is a complete magazine of sound argumentation on such questions as the power of the magistrate, the rights of conscience, and the iniquity of persecution. If Marvell had the credit of silencing Parker in a torrent of caustic ridicule, which, though not untainted with the coarseness of the age, has rendered his " Rehearsal" a source of interest and amusement to many who, taking no interest in ecclesiastical disputes, have been drawn to the perusal of it simply by its literary merit, still we may claim for Owen the praise of establishing, on a basis of able argument, the rights and privileges of which such abettors of arbitrary power as Parker sought to deprive their countrymen. Owen writes in that spirit of calm self-possession and dignity which never under any provocations deserted him, and, compared with the " Rehearsal Transprosed," his treatise will be accounted dull. Frequently, however, he brightens and relieves the tenor of his reasonings by strokes of effective sarcasm, which it may be questioned if even the genius of Marvell has surpassed. Parker's views are ludicrously reduced to an absurdity by the supposition of an edict for the settlement of religion, drawn up according to his own principles, and almost in his own words. See page 382. And again, after showing that Parker virtually claimed for the civil magistrate an authority which God only possesses over the conscience, Owen alludes to the preposterous argument that the magistrate should now inflict penalties for errors in religion, in room of what the excommunicated suffered in the days of the apostles at the hands of the devil, p. 406. " This work," he remarks, in a sally of exquisite humour, " the devil now ceasing to attend unto, he would have the magistrate to take upon him to supply his place and office, by punishments of his own appointment and infliction: and so at last, to be sure of giving him full measure, he hath ascribed two extremes unto him about religion,—namely, to act the part of God and the devil!" For an estimate of the more solid qualities and general merits of the following work, the reader is again commended to the critique on it, in the " Life of Owen."—ED.

A SURVEY

OF

A DISCOURSE CONCERNING ECCLESIASTICAL POLITY.

REVIEW OF THE PREFACE.

AMONG the many disadvantages which those who plead in any sense for liberty of conscience are exposed unto, it is not the least that in their arguings and pleas they are enforced to admit a supposition that those whom they plead for are indeed really mistaken in their apprehensions about the matters concerning which they yet desire to be indulged in their practice: for unless they will give place to such a supposition, or if they will rigidly contend that what they plead in the behalf of is absolutely the truth, and that obedience thereunto is the direct will and command of God, there remains no proper field for the debate about indulgence to be managed in; for things acknowledged to be such are not capable of an indulgence, properly so called, because the utmost liberty that is necessary unto them is their right and due in strict justice and law. Men, therefore, in such discourses, speak not to the nature of the things themselves, but to the apprehensions of them with whom they have to do. But yet against this disadvantage every party which plead for themselves are relieved by that secret reserve that they have in the persuasion of the truth and goodness of what they profess, and desire to be indulged in the practice of; and this, also, as occasion doth offer itself, and in defence of themselves from the charge of their adversaries, they openly contend and avow. Neither was it judged formerly that there was any way to deprive them of this reserve and relief but by a direct and particular debate of the matters specially in difference, carried on unto their conviction by evidence of truth, managed from the common principles of it. But after trial made, this way to convince men of their errors and mistakes, who stand in need of indulgence with respect unto the outward administration of the powers that they are under, is found, as it should seem, tedious, unreasonable, and ineffectual. A new way, therefore, to this purpose is fixed on, and it is earnestly pleaded that there needs no other argument or medium to prove men to be mistaken in their apprehensions, and to miscarry in their practice of religious duties, than that at any time or in any place they stand in need of indulgence. To dissent, at all adventures, is a crime, and he whom others persecute, tacitly at least, confesseth himself guilty; for it is said that the law of the magistrate being the sole rule of obedience in religious worship, their non-compliance with any law by him established, evidencing itself in their desire of exemption, is a sufficient conviction, yea, a self-acknowledgment, not only of their errors and mistakes in what they apprehend of their duty in these things, and of their miscarriages in what they practise, but also that themselves are persons turbulent and seditious, in withdrawing obedience from the laws which are justly imposed on them. With what restrictions and limitations, or whether with any or no, these assertions are maintained, we shall afterward inquire.

The management of this plea (if I greatly mistake him not) is one of the principal designs of the author of that discourse, a brief survey whereof is here proposed. The principle which he proceeds herein upon himself, it seems, knew to be novel and uncouth, and therefore thought it incumbent on him that both the manner of its handling, and the other principles that he judged meet to associate with it or annex unto it, should be of the same kind and complexion. This design hath at length produced us this discourse; which, of what use it may prove to the church of God, what tendency it may have to retrieve or promote love and peace among Christians, I know not. This I know, that it hath filled many persons of all sorts with manifold surprisals, and some with amazement. I have, therefore, on sundry considerations, prevailed with myself, much against my inclinations, for the sake of truth and peace, to spend a few hours in the examination of the principal parts and seeming pillars of the whole fabric. And this I was in my own mind the more easily induced unto, because there is no concernment either of the church or state in the things here under debate, unless it be that they should be vindicated from having any concern in the things and opinions here pleaded and argued. For as to the present church, if the principles and reasonings here maintained and managed are agreeable unto her sentiments, and allowed by her, yet there can be no offence given in their examination, because she hath nowhere yet declared them so to be. And the truth is, if they are once owned and espoused by her, to the ends for which they are asserted, as the Christians of old triumphed in the thoughts of him who first engaged in ways of violence against them among the nations in the world, so the Nonconformists will have no small relief to their minds in their sufferings, when they understand these to be the avowed principles and grounds on which they are to be persecuted and destroyed. And for the power of ecclesiastical jurisdiction belonging to the kings of this nation, as it hath been claimed and exercised by them in all ages since the establishment of Christian religion among us, as it is declared in the laws, statutes, and customs of the kingdom, and prescribed unto an acknowledgment in the oaths of allegiance and supremacy, it hath not the least concern in the matter here in question; yea, it is allowed, acknowledged, and pleaded for, by those whom this author designs to oppose. Whatever, then, shall be spoken of this subject, it is but a bare ventilation of private opinions, and those such as which, if one doctor's judgment may advance into the reputation of probability, so that some may venture to act upon them, yet are they not so far thereby secured as to have sanctuary given them even from private men's examinations. Herein, then, I suppose, a liberty may be exercised without just offence to any; and our disquisition after the truth of the principles and theorems that will come under consideration may be harmlessly accompanied with a moderate plea in the behalf of their innocency who are invidiously traduced, contemptuously reproached, unduly charged and calumniated, beyond, I am sure, any ordinary examples or precedents, among men of any sort, rank, degree, difference, or profession in the world. Yea, this seems to be called for by the light and law of nature, and to be useful, yea, needful to public tranquillity, beyond what in this present hasty review shall be attempted.

For the author of this discourse, he is to me utterly unknown; neither do I intend either to make any inquiry after him, or hastily to fix a credit unto any reports concerning either who he is or of what consideration in the world. I am not concerned to know what, it seems, he was concerned to conceal. Nor do I use to consider reasons, arguments, or writings under a relation to any persons; which contributes nothing to their worth or signification. Besides, I know how deceitful reports are in such matters, and no way doubt but that they will betray persons of an over-easy credulity into those mistakes about the writer of this survey which he is resolved to avoid with reference to the author of the discourse itself. Only, the character that in the entrance of it he gives of himself, and such other intimations of his principles as he is pleased to communicate, I suppose he will be willing we should take notice of, and that we may do so without offence.

Thus, in the entrance of his preface, he tells us that he is "a person of such a tame and softly humour, and so cold a complexion, that he thinks himself scarce capable of hot and passionate impressions," though I suppose he avow himself, p. 4, to be chafed into some heat and briskness with that evenness and steadiness of expression which we shall be farther accustomed unto. But in what here he avers of himself, he seems to have the advantage of our Lord Jesus Christ, who, upon less provocations than he hath undertaken the consideration of (for the Pharisees with whom he had to deal were gentlemen, he tells us, unto those with whom himself hath to do), as he saith, "fell into a hot fit of zeal, yea, into a height of impatience, which made him act with a seeming fury and transport of passion," p. 7. And if that be indeed his temper which he commends in himself, he seems to me to be obliged for it unto his constitution and complexion, as he speaks, and not to his age, seeing his juvenile expressions and confidence will not allow us to think that he suffers under any defervescency of spirit by his years. The philosopher tells us that old men, in matters dubious and weighty, are not over-forward to be positive, but ready to cry, *ἴσως καὶ τάχα*, perhaps, and it may be so; and this *δι᾽ ἐμπειρίαν*, because they have experience of the uncertainty of things in this world; as, indeed, those who know what entanglements all human affairs are attended withal, what appearing causes and probable reasons are to be considered and examined about them, and how all rational determinations are guided and influenced by unforeseen emergencies and occasions, will not be over-forward to pronounce absolutely and peremptorily about the disposal of important affairs. But, as the same author informs us, *Οἱ νέοι εἰδέναι πάντα οἴονται καὶ διϊσχυρίζονται*, "Young men suppose that they know all things, and are vehement in their asseverations:" from which frame proceeded all those dogmatical assertions of what is politic and impolitic in princes, of what will establish or ruin governments, with the contempt of the conceptions of others about things conducing to public peace and tranquillity, which so frequently occur in our author. This makes him smile at as serious consultations for the furtherance of the welfare and prosperity of this nation as, it may be, in any age or juncture of time have been upon the wheel, preface, p. 48. These considerations made it seem to me that, in an ordinary course, he hath time enough before him to improve the notions he hath here blessed the world with a discovery of, if, upon second thoughts, he be equally enamoured of them unto what now he seems to be.

I could, indeed, have desired that he had given us a more clear account of that religion which in his judgment he doth most approve. His commendation of the church of England sufficiently manifesteth his interest to lie therein, and that, in pursuit of his own principles, he doth outwardly observe the institutions and prescriptions of it; but the scheme he hath given us of religion, or religious duties,— wherein there is mention neither of sin nor a Redeemer, without which no man can entertain any one true notion of Christian religion,—would rather bespeak him a philosopher than a Christian. It is not unlikely but that he will pretend he was treating of religion as religion in general, without an application of it to this or that in particular; but to speak of religion as it is among men in this world, or ever was since the fall of Adam, without a supposition of sin, and the way of a relief from the event of it mentioned, is to talk of chimeras,—things that neither are, ever were, or will be. On the other hand, the profit and advantage of his design falls clearly on the papal interest; for whereas it is framed and contrived for the advantage, security, and unquestionableness of absolute compliers with the present possessors of power, it is evident that, in the state of Europe, the advantage lies incomparably on that hand. But these things are not our concernment. The designs which he manageth in his discourse, the subject-matter of it, the manner how he treats those with whom he hath to do, and deports himself therein, are by himself exposed to the judgment of all, and are here to be taken into some examination. Now, because we have in his preface a perfect representation of the things last mentioned throughout the whole, I shall, in the first place, take a general view and prospect of it.

And here I must have regard to the judgment of others. I confess, for my own part, I do not find myself at all concerned in those invectives, tart and upbraiding expressions, those sharp and twinging satires against his adversaries, which he avoweth or rather boasteth himself to have used. If this unparalleled heap of revilings, scoffings, despiteful reproaches, sarcasms, scornful, contemptuous expressions, false criminations, with frequent intimations of sanguinary affections towards them, do please his fancy and express his morality to his own satisfaction, I shall never complain that he hath used his liberty, and do presume that he judgeth it not meet that it should be restrained. It is far from my purpose to return him any answer in the like manner to these things; to do it

> " —— opus est mangone perito
> Qui Smithfieldensi polleat eloquio."

Yet some instances of prodigious excesses in this kind will, in our process, be reflected on; and it may be the repetition of them may make an appearance, unto some less considerate readers, of a little harshness in some passages of this return. But as nothing of that nature in the least is intended,—nothing that might provoke the author in his own spirit, were he capable of any "hot impressions," nothing to disadvantage him in his reputation or esteem,—so what is spoken, being duly weighed, will be found to have nothing sharp or unpleasant in it, but what is unavoidably infused into it from the discourse itself, in its approach unto it to make a representation of it.

It is of more concernment to consider with what frame and temper of spirit he manageth his whole cause and debate; and this is such as that a man who knows nothing of him but what he learns from this discourse would suppose that he hath been some great commander

> " In campis Gurgustidoniis,
> Ubi Bombamachides Cluninstarydisarchides
> Erat imperator summus; Neptuni nepos,"
> [Plaut. Mil. I. i. 13,]

associate unto him who with his breath blew away and scattered all the legions of his enemies, as the wind doth leaves in autumn.

Such confidence in himself and his own strength; such contempt of all his adversaries, as persons " silly, ignorant, illiterate;" such boastings of his achievements, with such a face and appearance of scorning all that shall rise up against him; such expressions " animi gladiatorii," doth he march withal as no man, sure, will be willing to stand in his way, unless he think himself to have lived, at least quietly, long enough. Only, some things there are which I cannot but admire in his undertaking and management of it; as, first, that such a man of arms and art as he is should harness himself with so much preparation, and enter the lists with so much pomp and glory, to combat such pitiful, poor, baffled ignoramuses as he hath chosen to contend withal, especially considering that he knew he had them bound hand and foot, and cast under his strokes at his pleasure. Methinks it had more become him to have sought out some giant in reason and learning, that might have given him at least " par animo periculum," as Alexander said in his conflict with Porus, a danger big enough to exercise his courage, though through mistake it should, in the issue, have proved but a windmill. Again; I know not whence it is, nor by what rules of errantry it may be warranted, that, being to conflict with such pitiful triflers, he should, before he come near to touch them, thunder out such terrible words, and load them with so many reproaches and contemptuous revilings; as if he designed to scare them out of the lists, that there might be no trial of his strength nor exercise of his skill.

But leaving him to his own choice and liberty in these matters, I am yet persuaded that if he knew how little his adversaries esteem themselves concerned in or worsted by his revilings, how small advantage he hath brought unto the cause managed by him, with what severity of censures, that I say not indignation, his proceedings herein are reflected on by persons sober and learned, who have any respect to modesty or sobriety, or any reverence for the things of God as debated among men, he would abate somewhat of that self-delight and satisfaction which he seems to take in his achievement.

Neither is it in the matter of *dissent* alone from the established forms of worship that this author and some others endeavour, by their revilings and scoffings, to expose Nonconformists to scorn and violence, but a semblance at least is made of the like reflections on their whole profession of the gospel and their worship of God; yea, these are the special subjects of those swelling words of contempt, those sarcastical, invidious representations of what they oppose, which they seem to place their confidence of success in. But what do they think to effect by this course of procedure? Do they suppose that by crying out, " canting phrases, silly nonsense, metaphors," they shall shame the Nonconformists out of the profession of the gospel, or make them forego the course of their ministry, or alienate one soul from the truth taught and professed amongst them? They know how their predecessors in the faith thereof have been formerly entertained in the world. St Paul himself, falling among the gentlemen philosophers of those days, was termed by them σπερμολόγος, a " babbler," or one that *canted*, his doctrine despised as silly and foolish, and his phrases pretended to be unintelligible. These things move not the Nonconformists, unless it be to a compassion for them whom they see to press their wits and parts to so wretched an employment. If they have any thing to charge on them with respect to gospel truths,—as, that they own, teach, preach, or publish, any doctrines or opinions that are not agreeable thereunto and to the doctrine of the ancient and late (reformed) churches, let them come forth, if they are men of learning, reading, and ingenuity, and, in ways used and approved from the beginning of Christianity for such ends and purposes, endeavour their confutation and conviction;—let them, I say, with the skill and confidence of men, and according to all the rules of method and art, state the matters in difference between themselves and their adversaries, confirm their own judgments with such reasons and arguments as they think pleadable in their behalf, and oppose the opinions they condemn with testimonies and reasons suited to their eversion. The course at present steered and engaged in, to carp at phrases, expressions, manners of the declaration of men's conceptions, collected from, or falsely fathered upon, particular persons, thence intimated to be common to the whole party of Nonconformists (the greatest guilt of some whereof, it may be, is only their too near approach to the expressions used in the Scripture to the same purpose, and the evidence of their being educed from thence), is unmanly, unbecoming persons of any philosophic generosity, much more Christians and ministers; nay, some of the things or sayings reflected on and carped at by a late author are such as those who have used or asserted them dare modestly challenge him, in their defence, to make good his charge in a personal conference,—provided it may be scholastical or logical, not dramatic or romantic. And surely were it not for their confidence in that tame and patient humour which this author so tramples upon, p. 15, they could not but fear that some or other, by these disingenuous proceedings, might be provoked to a recrimination, and to give in a charge against the cursed oaths, debaucheries, profaneness, various immoralities, and sottish ignorance, that are openly and notoriously known to have taken up their residence among some of those persons, whom the railleries of this and some other authors are designed to countenance and secure.

Because we may not concern ourselves again in things of this nature, let us take an instance or two of the manner of the dealing of our author with the Non-conformists, and those as to their preaching and praying, which of all things they are principally maligned about. For their preaching, he thus sets it out, p. 75: "Whoever among them can invent any new language presently sets up for a man of new discoveries; and he that lights upon the prettiest nonsense is thought by the ignorant rabble to unfold new gospel mysteries; and thus is the nation shat-tered into infinite factions with senseless and fantastic phrases: and the most fatal miscarriage of them all lies in abusing Scripture expressions, not only without but in contradiction to their sense; so that had we but an act of parliament to abridge preachers the use of fulsome and luscious metaphors, it might perhaps be an effectual cure of all our present distempers. Let not the reader smile at the oddness of the proposal; for were men obliged to speak sense as well as truth, all the swelling mysteries of fanaticism would then sink into flat and empty non-sense, and they would be ashamed of such jejune and ridiculous stuff as their ad-mired and most profound notions would appear to be." Certainly there are few who read these expressions that can retain themselves from smiling at the pitiful, fantastic souls that are here characterized, or from loathing their way of preach-ing here represented. But yet if any should, by a surprisal, indulge themselves herein, and one should seriously inquire what it is that stirred those humours in them, it may be they could scarce return a rational account of their commotions; for when they have done their utmost to countenance themselves in their scorn and derision, they have nothing but the bare assertions of this author for the proof of what is here charged on those whom they deride. And how if these things are most of them, if not all of them, absolutely false? how if he be not able to prove any of them by any considerable avowed instance? how if all the things intended, whether they be so or no as here represented, depend merely on the judgment and fancy of this author, and it should prove in the issue that they are no such rules, measures, or standards of men's rational expressions of their con-ceptions, but that they may be justly appealed from? And how if sundry things so odiously here expressed be proved to have been sober truths, declared in words of wisdom and sobriety? what if the things condemned as "fulsome metaphors" prove to be scriptural expressions of gospel mysteries? what if the principal doctrines of the gospel, about the grace of God, the mediation of Christ, of faith, justification, gospel obedience, communion with God, and union with Christ, are esteemed and stigmatized by some as "swelling mysteries of fanaticism," and the whole work of our redemption by the blood of Christ, as expressed in the Scripture, be deemed metaphorical? In brief, what if all this discourse concerning the preachings of Nonconformists be, as unto the sense of the words here used, false, and the crimes in them injuriously charged upon them? what if the metaphors they are charged with are no other but their expression of gospel mysteries, "not in the words which man's wisdom teacheth, but which the Holy Ghost teacheth, comparing spi-ritual things with spiritual? As these things may and will be made evident when particulars shall be instanced in, so when, I say, these things are discovered and laid open, there will be a composure, possibly, of those affections and disdainful thoughts which those swelling words may have moved in weak and inexperienced minds. It may be, also, it will appear that, upon a due consideration, there will be little subject-matter remaining to be enacted in that law or act of parliament which he moves for; unless it be from that uncouth motion, that men may be "obliged to speak sense as well as truth," seeing hitherto it hath been supposed that every proposition that is either true or false hath a proper and determined sense; and if sense it have not, it can be neither. I shall only crave leave to say, that as to the doctrines which they preach, and the manner of their preaching, or the way of expressing those doctrines or truths which they believe and teach, the Nonconformists appeal from the rash, false, and invidious charge of this author, to the judgment of all learned, judicious, and pious men in the world; and are ready to defend them against himself, and whosoever he shall take to be his patrons or his associates, before any equal, competent, and impartial tribunal under heaven. It is far from me to undertake the absolute defence of any party of men, or of any man because he is of any party whatever, much less shall I do so of all the individual persons of any party, and least of all as to all their expressions, private opinions, and peculiar ways of declaring them, which too much abound among persons of all sorts. I know there is no party but have weak men belonging to it, nor any men amongst them but have their weaknesses, failings, and mistakes; and if there are none such in the church of England,—I mean those that universally comply with all the observances at present used therein,—I am sure enough that there are so amongst all other parties that dissent from it. But such as these are not principally intended in these aspersions, nor would their adversaries much rejoice to have them known to be and esteemed of all what they are. But it is others whom they aim to expose unto contempt; and in the behalf of them, not the mistakes, misapprehensions, or undue expressions of any private persons, these things are pleaded.

But let us see if their prayers meet with any better entertainment. An account of his thoughts about them he gives us, p. 19: "It is the most solemn strain of their devotion, to vilify themselves with large confessions of the heinousest and most aggravated sins. They will freely acknowledge their offences against all the commands, and that with the foulest and most enhancing circumstances; they can rake together and confess their injustice, uncleanness, and extortion, and all the publican and harlot sins in the world: in brief, in all their confessions they stick not to charge themselves with such large catalogues of sin, and to amass together such a heap of impieties, as would make up the completest character of lewdness and villany; and if their consciences do really arraign them of all those crimes whereof they so familiarly indict themselves, there are no such guilty and unpardonable wretches as they. So, then, their confessions are either true or false. If false, then they fool and trifle with the Almighty; if true, then I could easily tell them the fittest place to say their prayers in."

I confess this passage, at its first perusal, surprised me with some amazement. It was unexpected to me that he who designed all along to charge his adversaries with Pharisaism, and to render them like unto them, should instance in *their confession of sin* in their prayers, when it is even a *characteristical note* of the Pharisees that in their prayers they made no confession of sin at all; but it was far more strange to me that any man durst undertake the reproaching of poor sinners with the deepest acknowledgment of their sins before the holy God that they are capable to conceive or utter. Is this, thought I, the spirit of the men with whom the Nonconformists do contend, and upon whose instance alone they suffer? Are these their apprehensions concerning God, sin, themselves, and others? Is this the spirit wherewith the children of the church are acted? Are these things suited to the principles, doctrines, practices, of the church of England? Such reproaches and reflections, indeed, might have been justly expected from those poor deluded souls who dream themselves perfect and free from sin; but to meet with such a treaty from them who say or sing, "O God, the father of heaven, have mercy upon us, miserable sinners," at least three times a-week, was some surprisal. However, I am sure the Nonconformists need return no other answer, to them who reproach them for vilifying themselves in their confessions to God, but that of David to Michal, "It is before the LORD; and we will yet be more vile than thus, and will be base in our own sight." Our author makes no small stir with the pretended censures of some whom he opposes,—namely, that they should "esteem themselves and their party to be the elect of God, all others to be reprobates,—themselves and theirs to be godly, and all others ungodly;" wherein I am satisfied that he unduly chargeth those whom he intends to reflect upon. However, I am none of them. I do not judge any party to be all the elect of God, or all the elect of God to be confined unto any party. I judge no man living to be a reprobate, though I doubt not but that there are living men in that condition. I confine not holiness or godliness to any party,—not to the church of England, nor to any of those who dissent from it; but am persuaded that in all societies of Christians that are under heaven that hold the Head, there are some really fearing God, working righteousness, and accepted with him. But yet neither my own judgment nor the reflections of this author can restrain me from professing that I fear that he who can thus trample upon men, scoff at and deride them for the deepest confessions of their sins before God which they are capable of making, is scarce either well acquainted with the holiness of God, the evil of sin, or the deceitfulness of his own heart, or did not in his so doing take them into sufficient consideration. The church of England itself requires its children to "acknowledge their manifold sins and wickednesses, which from time to time they have grievously committed by thought, word, and deed, against the divine Majesty;" and what in general others can confess more, I know not. If men that are, through the light of God's Spirit and grace, brought to an acquaintance with the deceitful workings of sin in their own hearts and the hearts of others, considering aright the terror of the Lord, and the manifold aggravations wherewith all their sins are attended, do more particularly express these things before and to the Lord, when indeed nor they nor any other can declare the thousandth part of the vileness and unworthiness of sin and sinners on the account thereof, shall they be now despised for it, and judged to be men meet to be hanged? If this author had but seriously perused the confessions of Austin, and considered how he traces his sin from his nature in the womb, through the cradle, into the whole course of his life, with his marvellous and truly ingenuous acknowledgments and aggravations of it, perhaps the reverence of so great a name might have caused him to suspend this rash, and I fear impious discourse.

For the particular instances wherewith he would countenance his sentiments and censures in this matter, there is no difficulty in their removal. Our Lord Jesus Christ hath taught us to call the most secret workings of sin in the heart, though resisted, though controlled and never suffered to bring forth, by the names of those sins which they lie in a tendency unto; and men in their confessions respect more the pravity of their natures and the inward working and actings of sin than the outward perpetrations of it, wherein perhaps they may have little concernment in the world: as Job, who pleaded his uprightness, integrity, and righteousness against the charge of all his friends, yet when he came to deal with God, he could take that prospect of his nature and heart as to vilify himself before him, yea, to "abhor himself in dust and ashes."

Again; ministers, who are the mouths of the congregation to God, may and ought to acknowledge, not only the sins whereof themselves are personally guilty, but those also which they judge may be upon any of the congregation. This assuming of the persons of them to whom they speak, or in whose name they speak, is usual even to the sacred writers themselves. So speaks the apostle Peter,

1 Epist. iv. 3, "For the time past of our lives may suffice us to have wrought the will of the Gentiles, when we walked in lasciviousness, lusts, excess of wine, revellings, banquetings, and abominable idolatries." He puts himself amongst them, although the time past of his life, in particular, was remote enough from being spent in the manner there described; and so it may be with ministers when they confess the sins of the whole congregation. And the dilemma of this author about the truth or falsehood of these confessions will fall as heavy on St Paul as on any Nonconformist in the world; for besides the acknowledgment that he makes of the former sins of his life, when he was "injurious, a blasphemer, and persecutor" (which sins I pray God deliver others from), and the secret working of indwelling sin, which he cries out in his present condition to be freed from, he also, when an apostle, professeth himself the "chiefest of sinners." Now, this was either true or it was not: if it was not true, God was mocked; if it were, our author could have directed him to the fittest place to have made his acknowledgments in. What thinks he of the confessions of Ezra, of Daniel, and others, in the name of the whole people of God; of David concerning himself, whose self-abasements before the Lord, acknowledgments of the guilt of sin in all its aggravations and effects, far exceed any thing that Nonconformists are able to express?

As to his instances of the confession of "injustice, uncleanness, and extortion," it may be, as to the first and last, he would be put to it to make it good by express particulars; and I wish it be not found that some have need to confess them who cry at present they are not of these publicans. Uncleanness seems to bear the worst sound, and to lead the mind to the worst apprehensions of all the rest; but it is God with whom men have to do in their confessions, and before him, "What is man, that he should be clean? and he that is born of a woman, that he should be righteous? Behold, he putteth no trust in his saints; yea, the heavens are not clean in his sight. How much more abominable and filthy is man, who drinketh iniquity like water," Job xv. 14–16. And the whole church of God in their confession cry out, "We are all as an unclean thing, and all our righteousnesses are as filthy rags," Isa. lxiv. 6. There is a pollution of flesh and spirit which we are still to be cleansing ourselves from whilst we are in this world.

But to what purpose is it to contend about these things? I look upon this discourse of our author as a signal instance of the power of prejudice and passions over the minds of men: for, setting aside the consideration of a present influence from them, I cannot believe that any one that professeth the religion taught by Jesus Christ and contained in the Scripture can be so ignorant of the terror of the Lord; so unaccustomed to thoughts of his infinite purity, severity, and holiness; such a stranger to the accuracy, spirituality, and universality of the law; so unacquainted with the sin of nature, and the hidden deceitful workings of it in the hearts, minds, and affections of men; so senseless of the great guilt of the least sin, and the manifold inexpressible aggravations wherewith it is attended; so unexercised to that self-abasement and abhorrency which becomes poor sinners in their approaches to the holy God, when they consider what they are in themselves; so disrespective of the price of redemption that was paid for our sins, and the mysterious way of cleansing our souls from them by the blood of the Son of God,—as to revile, despise, and scoff at men for the deepest humblings of their souls before God, in the most searching and expressive acknowledgments of their sins, that they do or can make at any time.

The like account may be given of all the charges that this author manageth against the men of his indignation; but I shall return at present to the preface under consideration.

In the entrance of his discourse, being, as it seems, conscious to himself of a strange and wild intemperance of speech in reviling his adversaries, which he had either used or intended so to do, he pleads sundry things in his excuse or for his justification. Hereof the first is his zeal for the reformation of the church of England, and the settlement thereof with its forms and institutions. These, he saith, are "countenanced by the best and purest times of Christianity, and established by the fundamental laws of this land" (which yet, as to the things in contest between him and Nonconformists, I greatly doubt of, as not believing any fundamental law of this land to be of so late a date). To see this "opposed by a wild and fanatic rabble, rifled by folly and ignorance, on slender and frivolous pretences, so often and so shamefully baffled, yet again revived by the pride and ignorance of a few peevish, ignorant, and malapert preachers, brain-sick people" (all which gentle and peaceable expressions are crowded together in the compass of a few lines), is that which hath "chafed him into this heat and briskness." If this be not to deal with gainsayers in a "spirit of meekness;" if herein there be not an observation of the rules of speaking evil of no man, despising no man, of not saying "Raca" to our brother, or calling of him "fool;" if here be not a discovery how remote he is from self-conceit, elation of mind, and the like immoralities,—we must make inquiry after such things elsewhere: for, in this whole ensuing treatise, we shall scarce meet with any thing more tending to our satisfaction. For the plea itself made use of, those whom he so tramples on do highly honour the reformation of the church of England, and bless God for it continually, as that which hath had a signal tendency unto his glory, and usefulness to the souls of men. That as to the outward rites of worship and discipline contested about, it was in all things conformed unto the great rule of them, our author doth not pretend; nor can he procure it in those things, whatever he says, any "countenance from the best and purest times of Christianity." That it was every way perfect in its first edition, I suppose will not be affirmed; nor, considering the posture of affairs at the time of its framing, both in other nations and in our own, was it like it should so be. We may rather admire that so much was then done according to the will of God, than that there was no more. Whatever is wanting in it, the fault is not to be cast on the first reformers, who went as far as well in those days could be expected from them. Whether others who have succeeded in their place and room have since discharged their duty in perfecting what was so happily begun is "sub judice," and there will abide after this author and I have done writing. That as to the things mentioned, it never had an absolute quiet possession or admittance in this nation,—that a constant and no inconsiderable suffrage hath, from first to last, been given in against it,—cannot be denied; and for any "savage worrying" or "rifling of it" at present, no man is so barbarous as to give the least countenance to any such thing. That which is intended in these exclamations [explanations?] is only a desire that those who cannot comply with it as now established, in the matters of discipline and worship before mentioned, may not merely for that cause be worried and destroyed, as many have already been.

Again, the chief glory of the English Reformation consisted in the purity of its doctrine, then first restored to the nation. This, as it is expressed in the articles of religion, and in the publicly-authorized writings of the bishops and chief divines of the church of England, is, as was said, the glory of the English Reformation. And it is somewhat strange to me, that whilst one writes against *original sin*, another preaches up *justification by works*, and scoffs at *the imputation of the righteousness of Christ* to them that believe; yea, whilst some can openly dispute against the *doctrine of the Trinity*, the *Deity of Christ*, and *the Holy Ghost;* whilst instances may be collected of some men's impeaching all the articles almost throughout,—there should be no reflection in the least on these things. Only those who dissent from some outward methods of worship must be made the object of all this wrath and indignation.

"Quis tulerit Gracchos de seditione querentes?"
[Juv., ii. 24.]

Some men's guilt in this nature might rather mind them of pulling the beam out of their own eyes than to act with such fury to pull out the eyes of others for the motes which they think they espy in them. But hence is occasion given to pour out such a storm of fury, conveyed by words of as great reproach and scorn as the invention of any man, I think, could suggest, as is not lightly to be met withal. Might our author be prevailed with to mind the old rule, "Mitte male loqui, dic rem ipsam," these things might certainly be debated with less scandal, less mutual offences and provocations.

Another account of the reasons of his intemperance in these reproaches, supplying him with an opportunity to increase them in number and weight, he gives us, pp. 6, 7 of his preface; which, because it may well be esteemed a summary representation of his way and manner of arguing in his whole discourse, I shall transcribe:—

"I know," says he, "but one single instance in which zeal, or a high indignation, is just and warrantable, and that is when it vents itself against the arrogance of haughty, peevish, and sullen religionists, that, under higher pretences of godliness, supplant all principles of civility and good-nature; that strip religion of its outside, to make it a covering for spite and malice; that adorn their peevishness with a mark of piety, and shroud their ill-nature under the demure pretences of godly zeal, and stroke and applaud themselves as the only darlings and favourites of Heaven; and, with a scornful pride, disdain all the residue of mankind as a rout of worthless and unregenerate reprobates. Thus, the only hot fit of zeal we find our Saviour in was kindled by an indignation against the pride and insolence of the Jews, when he whipped the buyers and sellers out of the outward court of the temple; for though they bore a blind and superstitious reverence towards that part of it that was peculiar to their own worship, yet as for the outward court, the place where the Gentiles and proselytes worshipped, that was so unclean and unhallowed that they thought it could not be profaned by being turned into an exchange of usury. Now, this insolent contempt of the Gentiles, and impudent conceit of their own holiness, provoked the mild spirit of our blessed Saviour to such an height of impatience and indignation as made him, with a seeming fury and transport of passion, whip the tradesmen thence, and overthrow their tables."

What truth, candour, or conscience, hath been attended unto in the insolent reproaches here heaped up against his adversaries is left to the judgment of God and all impartial men; yea, let judgment be made and sentence be passed according to the ways, course of life, conversation, usefulness amongst men, readiness to serve the common concerns of mankind, in exercising loving-kindness in the earth, of those who are thus injuriously traduced, compared with any in the approbation and commendation of [those by] whom they are covered with these reproaches, and there lives not that person who may not be admitted to pronounce concerning the equity and righteousness, or iniquity, of these intemperances. However, it is nothing with them with whom he hath to do to be judged in man's day; they stand at the judgment-seat of Christ, and have not so learned him as to relieve themselves by false or fierce recriminations. The measure of the covering provided for all these excesses of unbridled passion is that alone which is now to be taken. The case expressed, it seems, is the only single instance in which zeal is "just and warrantable." How our author came to be assured thereof, I know not; sure I am that it doth neither comprise in it, nor hath any aspect on, the ground, occasion, or nature of the zeal of Phinehas, or of Nehemiah, or of David, or of Joshua, and, least of all, of our Saviour, as we shall see. He must needs be thought to be over-intent upon his present occasion, when he forgot not one or two, but indeed all instances of just and warrantable zeal that are given us in the only sacred repository of them.

For what concerns the example of our blessed Saviour, particularly insisted on, I wish he had offended one way only in the report he makes of it ; for let any sober man judge, in the first place, whether those expressions he useth, of the " hot fit of zeal " that he was in, of the " height of impatience " that he was provoked unto, the " seeming fury and transport of passion" that he acted withal, do become that reverence and adoration of the Son of God which ought to possess the hearts and guide the tongues and writings of men that profess his name. But whatever other men's apprehensions may be, as it is not improbable but that some will exercise severity in their reflections on these expressions, for my part, I shall entertain no other thoughts but that our author, being engaged in the composition of an invective declamation, and aiming at a grandeur of words, yea, to fill it up with tragical expressions, could not restrain his pen from some extravagant excess when the Lord Christ himself came in his way to be spoken of.

However, it will be said the instance is pertinently alleged, and the occasion of the exercise of the zeal of our blessed Saviour is duly represented. It may be some will think so ; but the truth is, there are scarce more lines than mistakes in the whole discourse to this purpose. What *court* it was of the temple wherein the action remembered was performed is not here particularly determined ; only it is said to be the " outward court, wherein the Gentiles and proselytes worshipped, in opposition to that which was peculiar to the worship of the Jews." Now, of old, from the first erection of the temple, there were two courts belonging unto it, and no more: the inward court, wherein were the *brazen altar*, with all those utensils of worship which the priests made use of in their sacred offices; and the outward court, whither the people assembled, as for other devotions, so to behold the priests exercising their function, and to be in a readiness to bring in their own especial sacrifices, upon which account they were admitted to the altar itself. Into this outward court, which was a dedicated part of the temple, all Gentiles who were proselytes of righteousness,—that is, who, being circumcised, had taken upon them the observation of the law of Moses, and thereby joined themselves to the people of God,—were admitted, as all the Jewish writers agree. And these were all the courts that were at first sanctified, and were in use when the words were spoken by the prophet which are applied to the action of our Saviour,— namely, " My house shall be called a house of prayer, but ye have made it a den of thieves." Afterward, in the days of the Herodians, another court was added, by the immuring of the remainder of the hill, whereinto a promiscuous entrance was granted unto all people. It was, therefore, the ancient outward court whereinto the Jews thought that Paul had brought Trophimus the Ephesian, whom they knew to be uncircumcised. I confess some expositors think that it was this latter area from whence the Lord Christ cast out the buyers and sellers, but their conjecture seems to be altogether groundless; for neither was that court ever absolutely called " the temple," nor was it esteemed sacred, but common or profane, nor was it in being when the prophet used the words mentioned concerning the temple. It was, therefore, the other ancient outward court, common to the Jews and proselytes of the Gentiles, that is intended; for as there the salt and wood were stored that were daily used in their sacrifices, so the covetous priests, knowing that many who came up to offer were wont to buy the beasts they sacrificed at Jerusalem, to prevent the charge and labour of bringing them from far, to further, as they pretended, their accommodation, appropriated a market to themselves in this court, and added a trade in money, relating it may be thereunto, and other things, for their advantage. Hence the Lord Christ twice drove them, once at the beginning, and once at the end of his ministry in the flesh; not with "a seeming transport of fury," but with that evidence of the presence of God with him, and majesty of God upon him, that it is usually reckoned amongst one of the miracles that he wrought, considering the state of all things at that time amongst the Jews. And the reason why he did this, and the occasion of the exercise of his zeal, is so express in the Scripture, as I cannot but admire at the invention of our author, who could find out another reason and occasion of it; for it is said directly that he did it because of their wicked profanation of the house of God, contrary to his express institution and command. Of a regard to the Jews' "contempt of the Gentiles" there is not one word, not the least intimation; nor was there in this matter the least occasion of any such thing.

These things are not pleaded in the least to give countenance to any in their proud, supercilious censures and contempt of others; wherein if any person living have outdone our author, or shall endeavour so to do, he will not fail, I think, to carry away the prize in this unworthy contest. Nor is it to apologize for them whom he charges with extravagancies and excesses in this kind. I have no more to say in their behalf but that, as far as I know, they are falsely accused and calumniated, though I will not be accountable for the expressions of every weak and impertinent person. Where men, indeed, sin openly in all manner of transgressions against the law and gospel; where a spirit of enmity to holiness and obedience unto God discovers and acts itself constantly on all occasions; in a word, where men wear sin's livery,—some are not afraid to think them sin's servants. But as to that elation of mind in self-conceit wherewith they are charged, their contempt of other men upon the account of party, which he imputes unto them, I must expect other proofs than the bare assertion of this author before I join with him in the management of his accusations. And no other answer shall I return to the ensuing leaves, fraught with bitter reproaches, invectives, sarcasms, far enough distant from truth and all sobriety ; nor shall I, though in their just and necessary vindication, make mention of any of those things which might represent them persons of another complexion. If this author will give those whom he probably most aims to load with these aspersions leave to confess themselves poor and miserable sinners in the sight of God, willing to bear his indignation against whom they have sinned, and to undergo quietly the severest rebukes and revilings of men, in that they know not but that they have a providential permissive commission from God so to deal with them; and add thereunto that they yet hope to be saved by Jesus Christ, and in that hope endeavour to give up themselves in obedience to all his commands,—it contains that description of them which they shall always, and in all conditions, endeavour to answer. But I have only given these remarks upon the preceding discourse to discover upon what feeble grounds our author builds for his own justification in his present engagement.

Page 13 of his preface, he declares his *original design* in writing this discourse, —which was to "represent to the world the lamentable folly and silliness of those men's religion with whom he had to do;" which he farther expresses and pursues with such a lurry[1] of virulent reproaches as I think is not to be paralleled in any leaves but some others of the same hand; and in the close thereof he supposeth he hath evinced that, in comparison of them, "the most insolent of the Pharisees

---

[1] A word occurring more than once in Owen's writings, though not noticed in such dictionaries as those of Webster and Richardson. It seems to mean "a disturbance, or tumult." See Halliwell's "Dictionary of Archaic and Provincial Words," where he quotes Cotton using the word in this sense.—ED.

were gentlemen, and the most savage of the Americans philosophers." I must confess myself an utter stranger unto that generous disposition and philosophic nobleness of mind which vent themselves in such revengeful, scornful wrath, expressed in such rude and barbarous railings, against any sort of men whatever, as that here manifested in, and those here used by this author. If this be a just delineation and character of the spirit of a gentleman, a due portraiture of the mind and affections of a philosopher, I know not who will be ambitious to be esteemed either the one or the other. But what measures men now make of gentility I know not. Truly noble generosity of spirit was heretofore esteemed to consist in nothing more than remoteness from such pedantic severities against, and contemptuous reproaches of, persons under all manner of disadvantages, yea, impossibilities to manage their own just vindication, as are here exercised and expressed in this discourse; and the principal pretended attainment of the old philosophy was a sedateness of mind, and a freedom from turbulent passions and affections under the greatest provocations: which if they are here manifested by our author, they will give the greater countenance unto the character which he gives of others, the judgment and determination whereof is left unto all impartial readers.

But in this *main design* he professeth himself prevented by "the late learned and ingenious discourse, The Friendly Debate;"[1] which, to manifest, it may be, that his rhetorical faculty is not confined to invectives, he spendeth some pages in the splendid encomiums of. There is no doubt, I suppose, but that the author of that discourse will, on the next occasion, requite his panegyric, and return him his commendations for his own achievements with advantage. They are like enough to agree, like those of the poet:—

> " Discedo Alcæus puncto illius, ille meo quis?
> Quis nisi Callimachus?"
> [Hor. Ep., ii. 2, 99.]

For the present, his account of the excellencies and successes of that discourse minds me of the dialogue between Pyrgopolynices and Artotrogus:—

> "*Pyrg.* Ecquid meministi? *Art.* Memini; centum in Ciliciâ,
> Et quinquaginta centum Sycolatron dæ,
> Triginta Sardi, sexaginta Macedones,
> Sunt homines tu quos occidisti uno die.
> *Pyrg.* Quanta isthæc hominum summa est?
> *Art.* Septem millia.
> *Pyrg.* Tantum esse oportet; rectè rationem tenes.
> *Art.* At nullos habeo scriptos, sic memini tamen."
> [Plaut. Mil. Glor., i. 1, 42.]

Although the particular instances he gives of the man's successes are prodigiously ridiculous, yet the casting up of the sum-total to the completing of his victory sinks them all out of consideration. And such is the account we have here of the Friendly Debate. This and that it hath effected; which though unduly asserted as to the particular instances, yet altogether comes short of that absolute victory and triumph which are ascribed unto it. But I suppose that, upon due consideration, men's glorying in those discourses will be but as the crackling of thorns in the fire,—noise and smoke, without any real and solid use or satisfaction. The great design of the author, as is apparent unto all, was to render the sentiments

---

[1] The work to which Owen refers is entitled, "A Friendly Debate between a Conformist and a Nonconformist, in two parts," London, 1669. It is understood to have been written by Dr Simon Patrick, who was afterwards successively Bishop of Chichester and of Ely. He died in 1691, and his memory is still respected for his Paraphrase and Critical Commentaries on the books of the Old Testament, and other works of a theological and devotional character. The "Debate" was resented by the Nonconformists as harsh and unjust in its strictures; and even on the other side, the eminent Judge Hale wrote to Baxter in strong disapproval of it.—Ed.

and the expressions of his adversaries ridiculous, and thereby to expose their persons to contempt and scorn.

> " Egregiam verò laudem et spolia ampla !"
> [Æn., iv. 93.]

And to this end his way of writing by dialogues is exceedingly suited and accommodated ; for although ingenious and learned men, such as Plato and Cicero, have handled matters of the greatest importance in that way of writing, candidly proposing the opinions and arguments of adverse parties in the persons of the dialogists, and sometimes used that method to make their design of instruction more easy and perspicuous, yet it cannot be denied that advantages may be taken from this way of writing to represent both persons, opinions, and practices, invidiously and contemptuously, above any other way ; and therefore it hath been principally used by men who have had that design. And I know nothing in the skilful contrivance of dialogues, which is boasted of here with respect unto the Friendly Debate, as also by the author of it in his preface to one of his worthy volumes, that should free the way of writing itself from being supposed to be peculiarly accommodated to the ends mentioned. Nor will these authors charge them with want of skill and art in composing of their dialogues, who have designed nothing in them but to render things uncouth and persons ridiculous, with whom themselves were, in worth and honesty, no way to be compared.

An instance hereof we have in the case of Socrates. Sundry in the city being weary of him, for his uprightness, integrity, and continual pressing of them to courses of the like nature ; some, also, being in an especial manner incensed at him and provoked by him ; amongst them they contrived his ruin. That they might effect this design, they procured Aristophanes to write a dialogue, his comedy, which he entitled Νεφέλαι, " The Clouds ;" wherein Socrates is introduced and personated, talking at as contemptible and ridiculous a rate as any one can represent the Nonconformists to do, and yet withal to commend himself as the only man considerable amongst them. Without some such preparation of the people's minds, his enemies thought it impossible to obtain his persecution and destruction. And they failed not in their projection. Aristophanes, being poor, witty, and, as is supposed, hired to this work, lays out the utmost of his endeavours so to frame and order his dialogues, with such elegancy of words and composure of his verses, with such a semblance of relating the words and expressing the manner of Socrates, as might leave an impression on the minds of the people. And the success of it was no way inferior to that of the Friendly Debate; for though at first the people were somewhat surprised with seeing such a person so traduced, yet they were after a while so pleased and tickled with the ridiculous representation of him and his philosophy, wherein there was much of appearance and nothing of truth, that they could make no end of applauding the author of the Dialogues. And though this was the known design of that poet, yet that his dialogues were absurd and inartificial I suppose will not be affirmed, seeing few were ever more skilfully contrived. Having got this advantage of exposing him to public contempt, his provoked malicious adversaries began openly to manage their accusation against him. The principal crime laid to his charge was *nonconformity*, or that he did not comply with the religion which the supreme magistrate had enacted; or, as they then phrased it, " he esteemed not them to be gods whom the city so esteemed." By these means, and through these advantages, they ceased not until they had destroyed the best and wisest person that ever that city bred in its heathen condition, and whereof they quickly repented themselves. The reader may see the whole story exactly related in Ælian., lib. ii ; Var. Histor., cap. 13. Much of it also may be collected from the Apologies of Xenophon and Plato in behalf of Socrates, as also Plutarch's

Discourse concerning his Genius. To this purpose have dialogues very artificially written been used, and are absolutely the most accommodate of all sorts of writing unto such a design. Hence Lucian, who aimed particularly to render the things which he disliked ridiculous and contemptible, used no other kind of writing; and I think his Dialogues will be allowed to be artificial, though sundry of them have no other design but to cast contempt on persons and opinions better than himself and his own. And this way of dealing with adversaries in points of faith, opinion, and judgment, hath hitherto been esteemed fitter for the stage than a serious disquisition after truth, or confutation of error. Did those who admire their own achievements in this way of process but consider how easy a thing it is for any one, deposing that respect to truth, modesty, sobriety, and Christianity, which ought to accompany us in all that we do, to expose the persons and opinions of men, by false, partial, undue representations, to scorn and contempt, they would perhaps cease to glory in their fancied success. It is a facile thing to take the wisest man living, and after he is lime-twigged with ink and paper, and gagged with a quill, so that he can neither move nor speak, to clap a fool's coat on his back, and turn him out to be laughed at in the streets. The Stoics were not the most contemptible sort of philosophers of old, nor will be thought so by those who profess their religion to consist in morality only, and yet the Roman orator, in his pleading for Muræna, finding it his present interest to cast some disreputation upon .Cato, his adversary in that cause, who was addicted to that sect, so represented their dogmas that he put the whole assembly into a fit of laughter ; whereunto Cato only replied, that he made others laugh, but was himself ridiculous. And, it may be, some will find it to fall out not much otherwise with themselves by that time the whole account of their undertaking is well cast up.

Besides, do these men not know that if others would employ themselves in a work of the like kind, by way of retortion and recrimination, that they would find real matter, amongst some whom they would have esteemed sacred, for an ordinary ingenuity to exercise itself upon unto their disadvantage ? But what would be the issue of such proceedings ? who would be gainers by it ? Every thing that is professed among them that own religion, all ways and means of their profession, being by their mutual reflections of this kind rendered ridiculous, what remains but that men fly to the sanctuary of atheism to preserve themselves from being scoffed at and despised as fools ? On this account alone I would advise the author of our late Debates to surcease proceeding in the same kind, lest a provocation unto a retaliation should befall any of those who are so foully aspersed.

But, as I said, what will be the end of these things, namely, of mutual virulent reflections upon one another ? Shall this " sword devour for ever ? and will it not be bitterness in the latter end?" for, as he said of old of persons contending with revilings,—

> "Εστι γὰρ ἀμφοτέροισιν ὀνείδεα μυθήσασθαι
> Πολλὰ μάλ᾽· οὐδ᾽ ἂν νηῦς ἑκατόζυγος ἄχθος ἄρριτο.
> Στρεπτὴ δὲ γλῶσσ᾽ ἐστὶ βροτῶν, πολέες δ᾽ ἔνι μῦθοι,
> Παντοῖοι· ἐπέων δὲ πολὺς νομὸς ἔνθα καὶ ἔνθα.
> Ὁπποῖόν κ᾽ εἴπησθα ἔπος, τοῖόν κ᾽ ἐπακούσαις.
>
> [Il., xx. 246-250.]

Great store there are of such words and expressions on every hand, and every provoked person, if he will not bind his passion to a rule of sobriety and temperance, may at his pleasure take out and use what he supposeth for his turn. And let not men please themselves with imagining that it is not as easy, though perhaps not so safe, for others to use towards themselves haughty and contemptuous expressions, as it is for them to use them towards others. But shall this wrath never be allayed? Is this the way to restore peace, quietness, and satisfaction to the minds of men? Is it meet to use her language in this nation concerning the present differences about religion:—

> " Nullus amor populis, nec fœdera sunto.
> Littora littoribus contraria, fluctibus undas
> Imprecor, arma armis : pugnent ipsique nepotes !"
> [Æn., iv. 624-628.]

Is agreement in all other things, all love and forbearance, unless there be a centring in the same opinions absolutely, become criminal, yea detestable? Will this way of proceeding compose and satisfy the minds of men? If there be no other way for a *coalescence* in love and unity, in the bond of peace, but either that the Nonconformists do depose and change in a moment, as it were, their thoughts, apprehensions, and judgments, about the things in difference amongst us, which they cannot, which is not in their power to do; or that in the presence, and with a peculiar respect unto the eye and regard of God, they will act contrary unto them, which they ought not, which they dare not, no not upon the present instruction,—the state of these things is somewhat deplorable.

That alone which, in the discourses mentioned, seemeth to me of any consideration, if it have any thing of truth to give it countenance, is, that the Nonconformists, under pretence of preaching *mysteries and grace*, do neglect the pressing of *moral duties*, which are of near and indispensable concernment unto men in all their relations and actions, and without which religion is but a pretence and covering for vice and sin. A crime this is, unquestionably, of the highest nature, if true, and such as might justly render the whole profession of those who are guilty of it suspected. And this is again renewed by our author, who, to charge home upon the Nonconformists, reports the saying of Flacius Illyricus, a Lutheran, who died a hundred years ago, namely, that " bona opera sunt perniciosa ad salutem ; " though I do not remember that any such thing was maintained by Illyricus, though it was so by Amsdorfius against Georgius Major. But is it not strange how any man can assume to himself and swallow so much confidence as is needful to the management of this charge? The books and treatises published by men of the persuasion traduced, their daily preaching, witnessed unto by multitudes of all sorts of people, the open avowing of their duty in this matter, their principles concerning sin, duty, holiness, virtue, righteousness, and honesty, do all of them proclaim the blackness of this calumny, and sink it, with those who have taken, or are able to take, any sober cognizance of these things, utterly beneath all consideration. Moral duties they do esteem, commend, count as necessary in religion as any men that live under heaven. It is true, they say that on a supposition of that performance whereof they are capable without the assistance of the grace and Spirit of God, though they may be good in their own nature and useful to mankind, yet they are not available unto the salvation of the souls of men; and herein they can prove that they have the concurrent suffrage of all known churches in the world, both those of old and these at present. They say, moreover, that for men to rest upon their performances of these moral duties for their justification before God, is but to set up their own righteousness through an ignorance of the righteousness of God, for we are freely justified by his grace; neither yet are they sensible of any opposition to this assertion.

For their own discharge of the work of the ministry, they endeavour to take their rule, pattern, and instruction, from the precepts, directions, and examples of them who were first commissioned unto that work, even the apostles of our Lord Jesus Christ, recorded in the Scripture, that they might be used and improved unto that end. By them are they taught to endeavour the declaring unto men all the counsel of God concerning his grace, their obedience, and salvation; and having the word of reconciliation committed unto them, they do pray their hearers "in Christ's stead to be reconciled unto God." To this end do they declare the "unsearchable riches of Christ," and comparatively determine to know nothing in this world but "Christ and him crucified,"—whereby their preaching becometh principally the word or doctrine of the cross, which by experience they find to be a "stumbling-block" unto some, and "foolishness" unto others; by all means endeavouring to make known "what is the riches of the glory of the mystery of God in Christ, reconciling the world unto himself;" praying withal for their hearers, that "the God of our Lord Jesus Christ, the Father of glory, would give unto them the spirit of wisdom and revelation in the knowledge of him," that "the eyes of their understanding being enlightened," they may learn to know "what is the hope of his calling, and what the riches of the glory of his inheritance in the saints." And in these things are they "not ashamed of the gospel of Christ, which is the power of God unto salvation."

By this dispensation of the gospel do they endeavour to ingenerate in the hearts and souls of men "repentance toward God, and faith toward our Lord Jesus Christ." To prepare them also hereunto they cease not, by the preaching of the law, to make known to men "the terror of the Lord," to convince them of the nature of sin, of their own lost and ruined condition by reason of it, through its guilt, as both original in their natures and actual in their lives; that they may be stirred up to "flee from the wrath to come," and to "lay hold on eternal life." And thus, as God is pleased to succeed them, do they endeavour to lay the great foundation, Jesus Christ, in the hearts of their hearers, and to bring them to an interest in him by believing. In the farther pursuit of the work committed unto them, they endeavour more and more to declare unto, and instruct their hearers in, all the mysteries and saving truths of the gospel; to the end that, by the knowledge of them, they may be wrought unto obedience, and brought to conformity to Christ,—which is the end of their declaration. And in the pursuit of their duty there is nothing more that they insist upon, as far as ever I could observe, than an endeavour to convince men that that faith or profession that doth not manifest itself, which is not justified by works, which doth not purify the heart within, that is not fruitful in universal obedience to all the commands of God, is vain and unprofitable; letting them know that though we are saved by grace, yet we are the "workmanship of God, created in Christ Jesus unto good works, which he hath before ordained that we should walk in them,"—a neglect whereof doth uncontrollably evict men of hypocrisy and falseness in their profession: that, therefore, these things, in those that are adult, are indispensably necessary to salvation. Hence do they esteem it their duty continually to press upon their hearers the constant observance and doing of "whatsoever things are honest, whatsoever things are just, whatsoever things are pure, whatsoever things are lovely, whatsoever things are of good report;" letting them know that those who are called to a participation of the grace of the gospel have more, higher, stronger obligations upon them to righteousness, integrity, honesty, usefulness amongst men, in all moral duties, throughout all relations, conditions, and capacities, than any others whatever.

For any man to pretend, to write, [to] plead that this they do not, but indeed do discountenance morality and the duties of it, is to take a liberty of saying what he pleases for his own purpose, when thousands are ready from the highest experience to contradict him. And if this false supposition should prove the soul that animates any discourses, let men never so passionately admire them and expatiate in the commendation of them, I know some that will not be their rivals in their ecstasies. For the other things which those books are mostly filled withal, setting aside frivolous, trifling exceptions about modes of carriage and common phrases of speech, altogether unworthy the review or perusal of a serious person, they consist of such exceptions against expressions, sayings, occasional reflections on texts of Scripture, invectives, and impertinent calling over of things past and bygone, as the merit of the cause under contest is no way concerned in. And if any one would engage in so unhandsome an employment as to collect such fond speeches, futilous expressions, ridiculous expositions of Scripture, smutty passages, weak and impertinent discourses, yea, profane scurrilities, which some others, whom for their honour's sake and other reasons I shall not name, have in their sermons and discourses about sacred things been guilty of, he might provide matter enough for a score of such dialogues as the Friendly Debates are composed of.

But to return: that the advantages mentioned are somewhat peculiar unto dialogues, we have a sufficient evidence in this, that our author having another special design, he chose another way of writing suited thereunto. He professeth that he hath neither hope nor expectation to convince his adversaries of their crimes or mistakes, nor doth endeavour any such thing. Nor did he merely project to render them contemptible and ridiculous (which to have effected, the writing of dialogues in his management would have been most accommodate); but his purpose was to expose them to persecution, or to the severity of penal laws from the magistrates, and if possible, it may be, to popular rage and fury, The voice of his whole discourse is the same with that of the Jews concerning St Paul, "Away with such fellows from the earth, for it is not fit that they should live." Such an account of his thoughts he gives us, p. 253. Saith he, "The only cause of all our troubles and disturbances" (which what they are he knows not nor can declare), "is the inflexible perverseness of about a hundred proud, ignorant, and seditious preachers; against whom if the severity of the laws were particularly levelled, how easy would it be," etc.

"Macte novâ virtute puer: sic itur ad astra."
[Æn., ix. 641.]

But I hope it will appear, before the close of this discourse, that our author is far from deserving the reputation of infallible in his politics, whatever he may be thought to do in his divinity. It is sufficiently known how he is mistaken in his calculation of the numbers of those whom he designs to brand with the blackest marks of infamy, and whom he exposeth in his desires to the severities of law for their ruin. I am sure it is probable that there are more than a hundred of those whom he intends, who may say unto him as Gregory of Nazianzum introduceth his father speaking to himself,

"Nondum tot sunt anni tui, quot jam in sacris nobis sunt peracti victimis,"

who have been longer in the ministry than he in the world. But suppose there were but a hundred of them, he knows, or may know, when there was such a disparity in the numbers of them that contested about religion, that it was said of them, "All the world against Athanasius, and Athanasius against the world," who yet was in the right against them all, as they must acknowledge who frequently say or sing his "Quicunque vult."

But how came he so well acquainted with them all and every one as to pronounce of them that they are "proud, ignorant, and seditious?" Allow him the liberty,—which I see he will take whether we allow it him or no,—to call whom he pleaseth "seditious," upon the account of real or supposed principles not compliant with his thoughts and apprehensions, yet that men are "proud and ignorant," how he can prove but by particular instances from his own acquaintance with them, I know not. And if he should be allowed to be a competent judge of knowledge and ignorance in the whole compass of wisdom and science,—which, it may be, some will except against,—yet unless he had personally conversed with them all, or were able to give sufficient instances of their ignorance from actings, writings, or expressions of their own, he would scarce be able to give a tolerable account of the honesty of this his peremptory censure. And surely this must needs be looked on as a lovely, gentle, and philosophic humour, to judge all men proud and ignorant who are not of our minds in all things, and on that ground alone.

But yet, let them be as ignorant as can be fancied, this will not determine the difference between them and their adversaries. One unlearned Paphnutius[1] in the Council of Nice stopped all the learned fathers, when they were precipitately casting the church into a snare; and others, as unlearned as he, may honestly attempt the same at any time. And for our author's projection for the obtaining of quiet by severe dealings with these men in an especial manner, one of the same nature failed in the instance mentioned; for when Athanasius stood almost by himself in the eastern empire for a profession in religion which the supreme magistrate and the generality of the clergy condemned, it was thought the levelling of severity in particular against him would bring all to a composure. To this purpose, after they had again and again charged him to be proud and seditious, they vigorously engaged in his prosecution, according to the projection here proposed, and sought him near all the world over, but to no purpose at all, as the event discovered; for the truth which he professed having left its root in the hearts of multitudes of the people, on the first opportunity they returned again to the open avowing of it.

But to return from this digression: this being the design of our author, not so much to expose his adversaries to common contempt and laughter as to ruin and destruction, he diverted from the beaten path of dialogues, and betook himself unto that of rhetorical invective declamations; which is peculiarly suited to carry on and promote such a design. I shall, therefore, here leave him for the present, following the triumphal chariot of his friend, singing, "Io triumphe!" and casting reflections upon the captives that he drags after him at his chariot wheels; which will doubtless supply his imagination with a pleasing entertainment, until he shall awake out of his dream, and find all the pageantry that his fancy hath erected round about him to vanish and disappear.

His next attempt is upon *atheists*, wherein I have no concern, nor his principal adversaries, the Nonconformists. For my part, I have had this advantage by my own obscurity and small consideration in the world, as never to converse with any persons that did or durst question the being or providence of God, either really or in pretence. By common reports and published discourses, I find that there are not a few in these days who, either out of pride and ostentation or in a real compliance with their own darkness and ignorance, do boldly venture to dispute the things which we adore; and, if I am not greatly misinformed, a charge of this prodigious licentiousness and impiety may, from pregnant instances, be brought near the doors of some who on other occasions declaim against it. For practical atheism, the matter seems to be unquestionable; many live as though they believed neither God nor devil in the world but themselves. With neither sort am I concerned to treat at present, nor shall I examine the invectives of our author against them, though I greatly doubt whether ever such a kind of defence of the being of God was written by any man before him. If a man would make a judgment upon the genius and the way of his discourse, he might possibly be tempted to fear that it is persons rather than things that are the object of his indignation; and it may be the fate of some to suffer under the infamy of atheism, as it is thought Diagoras did of old, not for denying the Deity, nor for any absurd conceptions of mind concerning it, but for deriding and contemning them who, without any interest in or sense of religion, did foolishly, in idolatrous instances, make a pretence of it in the

---

[1] See Cave's Lives of the Fathers; Life of Athanasius, sec. iii. 2.—ED.

world. But whatever wickedness or miscarriages of this nature our author hath observed, his zeal against them were greatly to be commended, but that it is not in that only instance wherein he allows of the exercise of that virtue. Let it, then, be his anger or indignation, or what he pleases, that he may not miss of his due praises and commendation. Only I must say, that I question whether to charge persons inclined to atheism with profaning Jonson and Fletcher, as well as the holy Scriptures, be a way of proceeding probably suited to their conviction or reduction.

It seems, also, that those who are here chastised do vent their atheism in scoffing, drollery, and jesting, and such like contemptible efforts of wit, that may take for a while amongst little and unlearned people, and immediately evaporate. I am more afraid of those who, under pretences of sober reason, do vent and maintain opinions and principles that have a direct tendency to give an open admission unto atheism in the minds of men, than of such fooleries. When others' fury and raving cruelties succeeded not, he alone prevailed "qui solus accessit sobrius ad perdendam rempublicam." One principle contended for as rational and true, which, if admitted, will insensibly seduce the mind unto and justify a practice ending in atheism, is more to be feared than ten thousand jests and scoffs against religion, which, methinks, amongst men of any tolerable sobriety, should easily be buried under contempt and scorn. And our author may do well to consider whether he hath not, unwittingly I presume, in some instances, so expressed and demeaned himself as to give no small advantage to those corrupt inclinations unto atheism which abound in the hearts of men. Are not men taught here to keep the liberty of their minds and judgments to themselves, whilst they practise that which they approve not nor can do so? which is directly to act against the light and conviction of conscience. And yet an associate of his in his present design, in a modest and free conference, tells us that "there is not a wider step to atheism than to do any thing against conscience;" and informs his friend that "dissent out of grounds that appear to any founded on the will of God is conscience." But against such a conscience, the light, judgment, and conviction of it, are men here taught to practise; and thereby, in the judgment of that author, are instructed unto atheism! And, indeed, if once men find themselves at liberty to practise contrary to what is prescribed unto them in the name and authority of God, as all things are which conscience requires, it is not long that they will retain any regard of him or reverence unto him. It hath hitherto been the judgment of all who have inquired into these things, that the great concern of the glory of God in the world, the interest of kings and rulers, of all governments whatever, the good and welfare of private persons, lies in nothing more than in preserving conscience from being debauched in the conducting principles of it, and in keeping up its due respect to the immediate sovereignty of God over it in all things. Neither ever was there a more horrid attempt upon the truth of the gospel, all common morality, and the good of mankind, than that which some of late years or ages have been engaged in, by suggesting, in their casuistical writings, such principles for the guidance of the consciences of men as in sundry particular instances might set them free, as to practice, from the direct and immediately influencing authority of God in his word. And yet I doubt not but it may be made evident that all their principles in conjunction are scarce of so pernicious a tendency as this one general theorem, that men may lawfully act in the worship of God, or otherwise, against the light, dictates, or convictions of their own consciences. Exempt conscience from an absolute, immediate, entire, universal dependence on the authority, will, and judgment of God, according to what conceptions it hath of them, and you disturb the whole harmony of divine providence in the government of the world, and break the first link of that great chain whereon all religion and government in the world do depend. Teach men to be like Naaman the Syrian, to believe only in the God of Israel, and to worship him according to his appointment, by his own choice and from a sense of duty, yet also to bow in the house of Rimmon, contrary to his light and conviction, out of compliance with his master; or, with the men of Samaria, to fear the Lord but to worship their idols,—and they will not fail, at one time or other, rather to seek after rest in restless atheism than to live in a perpetual conflict with themselves, or to cherish an everlasting sedition in their own bosoms.

I shall not much reflect upon those expressions which our author is pleased to vent his indignation by, such as "religious rage and fury, religious villany, religious lunacies, serious and conscientious villanies, wildness of godly madness, men led by the Spirit of God to disturb the public peace, the world filled with a buzz and noise of the Divine Spirit, sanctified fury, sanctified barbarism, pious villanies, godly disobedience, sullen and cross-grained godliness," with innumerable others of the like kind; which, although perhaps he may countenance himself in the use of, from the tacit respect that he hath to the persons whom he intends to vilify and reproach, yet in themselves, and to others who have not the same apprehensions of their occasion, they tend to nothing but to beget a scorn and derision of all religion and the profession of it,—a humour which will not find where to rest or fix itself, until it come to be swallowed up in the abyss of atheism.

We are at length arrived at the last act of this tragical preface; and as in our progress we have rather heard a great noise and bluster than really encountered either true difficulty or danger, so now I confess that weariness of conversing with so many various sounds of the same signification, the sum of all being "knaves, villains, fools," will carry me through the remainder of it with some more than ordinary precipitation, as grudging an addition in this kind of employment to those few minutes wherein the preceding remarks were written or dictated.

There are two or three heads which the remainder of this prefatory discourse may be reduced unto: First, a magnificent proclamation of his own achievements,—what he hath proved, what he hath done, especially in representing the "inconsistence of liberty of conscience with the first and fundamental laws of government." And I am content that he please himself with his own apprehensions, like him who admired at the marvellous feats performed in an empty theatre; for it may be that, upon examination, it will be found that there is scarce in his whole discourse any one argument offered that hath the least seeming cogency towards such an end. Whether you take "liberty of conscience" for liberty of judgment, which himself confesseth uncontrollable, or liberty of practice upon indulgence, which he seems to oppose, an impartial reader will, I doubt, be so far from finding the conclusion mentioned to be evinced, as he will scarcely be able to satisfy himself that there are any premises that have a tendency thereunto. But I suppose he must extremely want an employment who will design himself a business in endeavouring to dispossess him of his self-pleasing imagination. Yea, he seems not to have pleaded his own cause absurdly at Athens, who, giving the city the news of a victory when they had received a fatal defeat, affirmed that public thanks were due to him for affording them two days of mirth and jollity before the tidings came of their ill success, which was more than they were ever likely to see again in their lives! And there being as much satisfaction in a fancied as a real success, though useless and failing, we shall leave our author in the highest contentment that thoughts of this nature can afford him. However, it may not be amiss to mind him of that good old counsel, "Let not him that girdeth on his armour boast himself as he that putteth it off."

Another part of his oration is, to decry the folly of that brutish apprehension, that men can possibly live peaceably and quietly if they enjoy the liberty of their consciences; where he fears not to affirm that it is more eligible to tolerate the highest debaucheries than liberty for men to worship God according to what they apprehend he requires! whence some severe persons would be too apt, it may be, to make a conjecture of his own inclinations, for it is evident that he is not absolutely insensible of self-interest in what he doth or writes. But the contrary to what he asserts being a truth at this day written with the beams of the sun in many nations of Europe, let envy, malice, fear, and revenge suggest what they please otherwise, and the nature of the thing itself denied being built upon the best, greatest, and surest foundations and warranty that mankind hath to build on or trust unto for their peace and security, I know not why its denial was here ventured at, unless it were to embrace an opportunity once more to give vent to the remainders of his indignation by revilings and reproaches, which I had hoped had been now exhausted.

But these things are but collateral to his principal design in this close of his declamation, and this is, the removal of an objection, that "liberty of conscience would conduce much to the improvement of trade in the nation." It is known that many persons of great wisdom and experience, and who, as it is probable, have had more time to consider the state and proper interest of this nation, and have spent more pains in the weighing of all things conducing thereunto, than our author hath done, are of this mind and judgment. But he at once strikes them and their reasons dumb by drawing out his Gorgon's head, that he hath proved it inconsistent with government, and so it must needs be a foolish and silly thing to talk of its usefulness to trade. " Verum, ad populum phaleras." If great blustering words, dogmatical assertions, uncouth, unproved principles, accompanied with a pretence of contempt and scorn of all exceptions and oppositions to what is said, with the persons of them that make them, may be esteemed proofs, our author can prove what he pleaseth, and he is to be thought to have proved whatever he affirms himself so to have done. If sober reason, experience, arguments derived from commonly-acknowledged principles of truth, if a confirmation of deductions from such principles by confessed and commonly approved instances, are necessary to make up convincing proofs in matters of this nature and importance, we are yet to seek for them, notwithstanding any thing that hath been offered by this author, or, as far as I can conjecture, is likely so to be. In the meantime, I acknowledge many parts of his discourse to be singularly remarkable. His insinuation " that the affairs of the kingdom are not in a fixed and established condition, that we are distracted amongst ourselves with a strange variety of jealousies and animosities," and such like expressions, as, if divulged in a book printed without licence, would, and that justly, be looked on as seditious, are the foundations that he proceedeth upon. Now, as I am confident that there is very little ground, or none at all, for these insinuations, so the public disposing of the minds of men to fears, suspicions, and apprehensions of unseen dangers by such means, becomes them only who care not what disadvantage they cast others, nay, their rulers under, so they may compass and secure their own private ends and concerns.

But yet, not content to have expressed his own real or pretended apprehensions, he proceeds to manifest his scorn of those, or his smiling at them, who " with mighty projects labour for the improvement of trade;" which the council appointed, as I take it, by his majesty, thence denominated, is more concerned in than the Nonconformists, and may do well upon this information, finding themselves liable to scorn, to desist from such a useless and contemptible employment. They may now know that to erect and encourage trading combinations is only to build so many nests of faction and sedition; for he says, " There is not any sort of people so inclinable to seditious practices as the trading part of a nation," and that " their pride and arrogance naturally increase with the improvement of their stock." Besides, "the fanatic party," as he says, "live in these greater societies, and it is a very odd and preposterous folly to design the enriching of that sort of people; for wealth doth but only pamper and encourage their presumption, and he is a very silly man, and understands nothing of the follies, passions, and inclinations of human nature, who sees not that there is no creature so ungovernable as a wealthy fanatic."

It cannot be denied but that this modern policy runs contrary to the principles and experience of former ages. To preserve industrious men in a peaceable way of improving their own interests, whereby they might partake, in their own and family concerns, of the good and advantages of government, hath been by the weak and silly men of former generations esteemed the most rational way of inducing their minds unto peaceable thoughts and resolutions; for as the wealth of men increaseth, so do their desires and endeavours after all things and ways whereby it may be secured, that so they may not have spent their labour and the vigour of their spirits, with reference unto their own good and that of their posterity, in vain. Yea, most men are found to be of Issachar's temper, who, when he saw that "rest was good, and the land pleasant," wherein his own advantages lay, "bowed his shoulder to bear, and became a servant unto tribute." "Fortes" and "miseri" have heretofore been only feared, and not such as found satisfaction to their desires in the increases and successes of their endeavours. And as Cæsar said he feared not those fat and corpulent persons, Antony and Dolabella, but those pale and lean discontented ones, Brutus and Cassius, so men have been thought to be far less dangerous or to be suspected in government who are well clothed with their own wealth and concerns, than such as have nothing but themselves to lose, and, by reason of their straits and distresses, do scarce judge them worth the keeping.

And hath this gentleman really considered what the meaning of that word "trade" is, and what is the concernment of this nation in it? or is he so fond of his own notions and apprehensions as to judge it meet that the vital spirits and blood of the kingdom should be offered in sacrifice unto them? Solomon tells us that the "profit of the earth is for all, and the king himself is served by the field;" and we may truly in England say the same of trade. All men know what respect unto it there is in the revenues of the crown, and how much they are concerned in its growth and promotion. The rents of all, from the highest to the lowest that have an interest in the soil, are regulated by it, and rise and fall with it; nor is there any possibility to keep them up to their present proportion and standard, much less to advance them, without the continuance of trade in its present condition at least, nay, without a steady endeavour for its increase, furtherance, and promotion. Noblemen and gentlemen must be contented to eat their own beef and mutton at home if trade decay; to keep up their ancient and present splendour, they will find no way or means. Corporations are known to be the most considerable and significant bodies of the common people, and herein lies their being and bread. To diminish or discountenance their trade is to starve them, and discourage all honest industry in the world. It was a sad desolation that not long since befell the great city by fire; yet, through the good providence of God, under the peaceable government of his majesty, it is rising out of its ashes with a new signal beauty and lustre. But that consumption and devastation of it which the pursuit of this counsel will inevitably produce would prove fatal and irreparable. And as the interests of all the several parts of the commonwealth do depend on the trade of the people amongst ourselves, so the honour, power, and security of the whole, in reference unto foreign nations, are resolved also into the same principles: for as our soil is but small in comparison of some of our neighbours', and the numbers of our people no way to be compared with theirs, so if we should forego the advantages of trade, for which we have opportunities, and unto which the people of this nation have inclinations above any country or nation in the world, we should quickly find how unequal the competition between them and us would be; for even our naval force, which is the honour of the king, the security of his kingdoms, the terror of his enemies, oweth its rise and continuance unto that preparation of persons employed therein which is made by the trade of the nation.   And if the counsel of this author should be followed, to suspend all thoughts of the supportment, encouragement, and furtherance of trade, until all men, by the severities of penalties, should be induced to a uniformity in religion, I doubt not but our envious neighbours would as readily discern the concernment of their malice and ill-will therein as Hannibal did his in the action of the Roman general, who, at the battle of Cannæ, according to their usual discipline (but fatally at that time misapplied), caused, in the great distress of the army, his horsemen to alight and fight on foot, not considering the advantage of his great and politic enemy as things then stood ; who immediately said, " I had rather he had delivered them all bound unto me," though he knew there was enough done to secure his victory.

A SURVEY OF THE FIRST CHAPTER.

[Inconsistent expressions of Parker in regard to the power of the magistrate and the rights of conscience—The design of his discourse to prove the magistrate's authority to govern the consciences of his subjects in affairs of religion—This doctrine inconsistent with British law—Ascribes more power to the magistrate than to Christ—Contrary to the history of the royal prerogative—Alleged necessity of the principle to public peace and order—Evils alleged to spring from liberty of conscience—The principle of Parker no real preventive to these evils—Various pleas refuted.[1]]

THE author of this discourse seems, in this first chapter, to design the stating of the controversy which he intendeth to pursue and handle (as he expresseth himself, p. 11); as also, to lay down the main foundations of his ensuing superstructure.   Nothing could be more regularly projected, nor more suited to the satisfaction of ingenious inquirers into the matters under debate; for those who have any design in reading beyond a present divertisement of their minds or entertainment of their fancies, desire nothing more than to have the subject-matter which they exercise their thoughts about clearly and distinctly proposed, that a true judgment may be made concerning what men say and whereof they do affirm.   But I fear our author hath fallen under the misadventure of a failure in these projections, at least as unto that certainty, clearness, and perspicuity in the declaration of his conceptions and expression of his assertions and principles, without which all other ornaments of speech, in

---

[1] No contents to the different sections of this treatise appear in the previous editions. We have prefixed a brief table of them to each section, as far as possible in the words of our author.—ED.

matters of moment, are of no use or consideration. His language is good and proper; his periods of speech laboured, full, and even; his expressions poignant towards his adversaries, and, singly taken, appearing to be very significative and expressive of his mind. But I know not how it is come to pass that, what either [whether?] through his own defect as to a due comprehension of the notions whose management he hath undertaken, or out of a design to cloud and obscure his sentiments, and to take the advantage of loose, declamatory expressions, it is very hard, if possible, to gather from what he hath written either what is the true state of the controversy proposed to discussion, or what is the precise, determinate sense of those words wherein he proposeth the principles that he proceeds upon.

Thus, in the title of the book he asserts " the power of the magistrate over the consciences of men;" elsewhere [he] confines " the whole work and duty of conscience to the inward thoughts and persuasions of the mind, over which the magistrate hath no power at all." " Conscience itself," he sometimes says, " is every man's opinion;" sometimes he calls it an " imperious faculty;"—which surely are not the same. Sometimes he pleads for " the uncontrollable power of magistrates over religion and the consciences of men;" sometimes asserts their " ecclesiastical jurisdiction" as the same thing, and seemingly all that he intends;—whereas, I suppose, no man ever yet defined "ecclesiastical jurisdiction" to be " an uncontrollable power over religion and the consciences of men." The magistrate's "power over religion" he asserts frequently, and denieth outward worship to be any part of religion, and at last pleads upon the matter only for his power over outward worship. Every *particular virtue* he affirms to be such, because it is "a resemblance and imitation of some of the divine attributes;" yet [he] also teacheth that there may be more virtues, or new ones that were not so, and that to be virtue in one place which is not so in another. Sometimes he pleads that the magistrate hath power to impose "any religion on the consciences of his subjects that doth not countenance vice or disgrace the Deity," and then anon pleads for it in indifferent things and circumstances of outward worship only. Also, that the magistrate may " oblige his subjects' consciences" to the performance of moral duties, and other duties in religious worship, under penalties, and yet " punisheth none for their crime and guilt," but for the example of others. And many other instances of the like nature may be given.

Now, whatever dress of words these things may be set off withal, they savour rankly of crude and undigested notions, not reduced unto such a consistency in his mind as to suffer him to speak evenly, steadily, and constantly to them. Upon the whole matter, it may not be unmeetly said of his discourses, what Tully said of Rullus's oration about the agrarian law: " Concionem ..... advocari jubet: summâ cum expectatione concurritur.   Explicat orationem sanè longam, et verbis valdè bonis.   Unum erat quod mihi vitiosum videbatur, quod tantâ ex frequentiâ inveniri nemo potuit, qui intelligere posset, quid diceret.   Hoc ille utrum insidiarum causâ fecerit, an hoc genere elo-quentiæ delectetur, nescio.   Tamen, siqui acutiores in concione stete-runt, de lege agraria nescio quid voluisse eum dicere, suspicabantur." [De Lege Agr., ii. 5]   Many good words it is composed of, many sharp reflections are made on others, a great appearance there is of reason ; but besides that it is plain that he treats of the Nonconformists and the magistrate's power, and would have this latter exercised about the punishment or destruction of the former (which almost every page expresseth), it is very hard to gather what is the case he speaks unto, or what are the principles he proceeds upon.

The entrance of his discourse is designed to give an account of the great difficulty which he intends to assail, of the controversy that he will handle and debate, and of the difference which he will com-pose.   Here, if anywhere, accuracy, perspicuity, and a clear, distinct direction of the minds of the reader unto a certain just apprehension of the matter in question and difference, ought to be expected; for if the foundation of discourses of this nature be laid in terms general, ambiguous, loose, rhetorical, and flourishing, giving no particular, de-terminate sense of the controversy (for so this is called by our author), all that ensues in the pursuit of what is so laid down must needs be of the same complexion.   And such appears to be the declamatory entrance of this chapter; for instead of laying a solid foundation to erect his superstructure upon, the author seems in it only to have built a castle in the air, that makes a goodly appearance and show, but is of no validity or use.   Can he suppose that any man is the wiser or the more intelligent, in the difference about liberty of conscience, the power and duty of magistrates in granting or denying an indulgence unto the exercise of it, by reading an elegant parabolical discourse of " two supreme powers, the magistrate and conscience, contesting for sovereignty, in and about" no man knows what?   What conscience is, what liberty of conscience, what it is pleaded for to extend unto, who are concerned in it, whether its plea be resolved absolutely into its own nature and constitution, or into that respect which it hath to another common rule of the minds and conceptions of men in and about the worship of God, is not declared; nor is it easily discernible what he allows and approves of in his own discourse, and what he introduceth to reflect upon, and so reject.   Page 5, he tells us that " conscience is subject and accountable to God alone, that it owns no superior but the Lord of consciences ;" and, p. 7, " that those who make it accountable to none but God alone do in effect usurp their prince's crown, defy his authority, and acknowledge no governor but themselves"! If it be pleaded that, in the first place, not what is, but what is unduly pretended, is declared, his words may be as well so expounded in all his ascriptions unto magistrates also,—namely, that it is not with them as he asserts, but only it is unduly pretended so to be,—as to any thing that appears in the discourse. The distinct consideration of the principles of conscience and the outward exercise of it can alone here give any show of relief. But as no distinction of that nature doth as yet appear, and, if rested on, ought to have been produced by any one who understood himself, and intended not to deceive or entangle others, so when it is brought on the stage, its inconsistency to serve the end designed shall be evinced. But that a plea for the consciences of private men (submitting themselves freely and willingly to the supreme power and government of magistrates in all things belonging to public peace and tranquillity) to have liberty to express their obedience unto God in the exercise of his outward worship, should receive such a tragical description, of a "rival supreme power set up against the magistrate, to the usurpation of his crown and dignity," is a new way of stating controversies, whether in divinity or policy, which this author judgeth conducing to his design and purpose; and I shall say no more but that those who delight in such a way of writing, and do receive light and satisfaction thereby, do seem to be exercised in a logic that I was never acquainted withal, and which I shall not now inquire after.

What seems to be of real difficulty in this matter, which is so rhetorically exaggerated, our blessed Saviour hath stated and determined in one word. "Give," saith he, "unto Cæsar the things that are Cæsar's, and to God the things that are God's;" and this he did when he gave his disciples command not only to think, judge, and believe according to what he should propose and reveal unto them, but also to observe and do in outward practices whatever he should command them. As he requires all subjection unto the magistrate in things of his proper cognizance,—that is, all things necessary to public peace and tranquillity in this world, the great end of his authority; so he asserts also that there are things of God which are to be observed and practised, even all and every one of his own commands, in a neglect whereof, on any pretence or account, we give not unto God that which is his. And he doubted not but that these things, these distinct respects to God and man, were exceedingly well consistent, and together directive to the same end of public good. Wherefore, passing through the flourishes of this frontispiece with the highest unconcernment, we may enter the fabric itself, where, possibly, we may find him declaring directly what it is that he asserts in this matter and contendeth for; and this he doth, p. 10: "And, therefore, it is the design of this discourse, by a fair and impartial debate, to compose all these differences, and adjust all these quarrels and contentions, and settle things upon their true and proper foundations; first, by proving it to be absolutely necessary to the peace and government of the world, that the supreme magistrate of every commonwealth should be vested with a power to govern and conduct the consciences of subjects in affairs of religion."

I am sure our author will not be surprised, if, after he hath reported the whole party whom he opposeth as a company of "silly, foolish, illiterate persons," one of them should so far acknowledge his own stupidity as to profess that, after the consideration of this declaration of his intention and mind, he is yet to seek for the direct and determinate sense of his words, and for the principle that he designs the confirmation of. I doubt not but that the magistrate hath all that power which is absolutely necessary for the preservation of public peace and tranquillity in the world; but if men may be allowed to fancy what they please to be necessary unto that end, and thence to make their own measures of that power which is to be ascribed unto him, no man knows what bounds will be fixed unto that ocean wherein the leviathans they have framed in their imaginations may sport themselves. Some will, perhaps, think it necessary to this purpose that the magistrate should have power to declare and determine whether there be a God or no; whether, if there be, it be necessary he should be worshipped or no; whether any religion be needful in, or useful to, the world; and if there be, then to determine what all subjects shall believe and practise from first to last in the whole of it. And our author hopes that some are of this mind. Others may confine it to lesser things, according as their own interest doth call upon them so to do, though they are not able to assign a clear distinction between what is subjected unto him and what may plead an exemption from his authority. He, indeed, who is the fountain and original of all power hath both assigned its proper end, and fully suited it to the attainment thereof; and if the noise of men's lusts, passions, and interests, were but a little silenced, we should quickly hear the harmonious consenting voice of human nature itself declaring the just proportion that is between the grant of power and its end, and undeniably expressing it in all the instances of it: for as the principle of rule and subjection is natural to us, concreated with us, and indispensably necessary to human society, in all the distinctions it is capable of, and the relations whence those distinctions arise; so nature itself, duly attended unto, will not fail, by the reason of things, to direct us unto all that is essential unto it and necessary unto its end. Arbitrary fictions of ends of govern-

.ment, and what is necessary thereunto, influenced by present interest, and arising from circumstances confined to one place, time, or nation, are not to be imposed on the nature of government itself, which hath nothing belonging unto it but what inseparably accompanieth mankind as sociable.

But to let this pass; the authority here particularly asserted is a "power in the supreme magistrate to govern and guide the consciences of his subjects in affairs of religion." Let any man duly consider these expressions, and if he be satisfied by them as to the sense of the controversy under debate, I shall acknowledge that he is wiser than I,—which is very easy for any one to be. What are the "affairs of religion" here intended, all or some; whether in religion or about it; what are the "consciences of men," and how exercised about these things; what it is to "govern and conduct" them; with what "power," by what means, this may be done,—I am at a loss, for aught that yet is here declared. There is a guidance, conduct, yea, government of the consciences of men, by instructions and directions, in a due proposal of rational and spiritual motives, for those ends, such as is that which is vested in and exercised by the guides of the church, and that in subjection to and dependence on Christ alone, as hath been hitherto apprehended, though some now seem to have a mind to change their master, and to take up "præsente Numine," who may be of more advantage to them. That the magistrate hath also power so to govern and conduct the consciences of his subjects in his way of administration,—that is, by ordering them to be taught, instructed, and guided in their duty,—I know none that doth deny: so did Jehoshaphat, 2 Chron. xvii. 7–9. But it seems to be a government and guidance of another nature that is here intended. To deliver ourselves, therefore, from the deceit and entanglement of these general expressions, and that we may know what to speak unto, we must seek for a declaration of their sense and importance from what is elsewhere, in their pursuit, affirmed and explained by their author.

His general assertion is, as was observed, "That the magistrate hath power over the consciences of his subjects in religion," as appears in the title of his book; here, p. 10, that power is said to be "to govern and conduct their consciences in religious affairs;" p 13, that "religion is subject to his dominion, as well as all other affairs of state;" p. 27, that "it is a sovereignty over men's consciences in matters of religion, and this universal, absolute, and uncontrollable." Matters of religion are as uncontrollably subject to the supreme power as all other civil concerns: "He may, if he please, reserve the exercise of the priesthood to himself," p. 32;—that is, what now in religion corresponds unto the ancient priesthood, as the ordering bishops and priests, administering sacraments, and the like; as the Papists in Queen Elizabeth's time did commonly report, in their usual manner, that it was done by a woman amongst us, by a fiction of such principles as begin, it seems, now to be owned.   That if this "power of the government of religion be not universal and unlimited, it is useless," p. 35; that this "power is not derived from Christ, nor any grant of his, but is antecedent to his coming, or any power given unto him or granted by him," p. 40.   "Magistrates have a power to make that a particular of the divine law which God had not made so," p. 80, and "to introduce new duties in the most important parts of religion: so that there is a public conscience, which men are in things of a public concern (relating to the worship of God) to attend unto, and not to their own; and if there be any sin in the command, he that imposed it shall answer for it, and not I, whose whole duty it is to obey," p. 308.   Hence, the command of "authority will warrant obedience, and obedience will hallow my actions and excuse me from sin," ibid.   Hence it follows, that whatever the magistrate commands in religion, his authority doth so immediately affect the consciences of men that they are bound to observe it, on the pain of the greatest sin and punishment; and he may appoint and command whatever he pleaseth in religion, "that doth not either countenance vice or disgrace the Deity," p. 85.   And many other expressions are there of the general assertion before laid down.

This, therefore, seems to me, and to the most impartial considerations of this discourse that I could bring unto it, to be the doctrine or opinion proposed and advanced for the quieting and composing of the great tumults described in its entrance,—namely, that the supreme magistrate in every nation hath power to order and appoint what religion his subjects shall profess and observe, or what he pleaseth in religion, as to the worship of God required in it, provided that he " enjoineth nothing that doth countenance vice or disgrace the Deity;" and thereby binds their consciences to profess and observe that which is by him so appointed (and nothing else are they to observe), making it their duty in conscience so to do, and the highest crime or sin to do any thing to the contrary, and that whatever the precise truth in these matters be, or whatever be the apprehensions of their own consciences concerning them.   Now, if our author can produce any law, usage, or custom of this kingdom, any statute or act of parliament, any authentic record, any acts or declarations of our kings, any publicly-authorized writing, before or since the Reformation, declaring, asserting, or otherwise approving, the power and authority described to belong unto, to be claimed or exercised by, the kings of this nation, I will faithfully promise him never to write one word against it, although I am sure I shall never be of that mind.   And, if I mistake not, in a transient reflection on these principles, compared with those which the church of England hath formerly pleaded against them who opposed her constitutions, they are utterly by them cast out of all consideration; and this one notion is advanced in the room of all the foundations which, for so many years, her defenders (as wise and as learned as this author) have been building upon. But this is not my concernment to examine; I shall leave it unto them whose it is, and whose it will be made appear to be, if we are again necessitated to engage in this dispute.

For the present be it granted that it is the duty and in the power of every supreme magistrate to order and determine what religion, what way, what modes in religion, shall be allowed, publicly owned, and countenanced, and by public revenue maintained in his dominions;—that is, this is allowed with respect to all pretensions of other sovereigns, or of his own subjects. With respect unto God, it is his truth alone, the religion by him revealed, and the worship by him appointed, that he can so allow or establish. The rule that holds in private persons with respect to the public magistrate holds in him with respect unto God. "Illud possumus quod jure possumus." It is also agreed that no men, no individual person, no order or society of men, are, either in their persons or any of their outward concerns, exempted, or may be so, on the account of religion, from his power and jurisdiction; nor any causes that are liable unto a legal, political disposal and determination. It is also freely acknowledged that whatever such a magistrate doth determine about the observances of religion, and under what penalties soever, his subjects are bound to observe what he doth so command and appoint, unless by general or especial rules their consciences are obliged to a dissent or contrary observation, by the authority of God and his word. In this case they are to keep their souls entire in their spiritual subjection unto God, and quietly and peaceably to bear the troubles and inconveniences which on the account thereof may befall them, without the least withdrawing of their obedience from the magistrate. And in this state of things, as there is no necessity or appearance of it that any man should be brought into such a condition as wherein sin on the one hand or the other cannot be avoided, so that state of things will probably occur in the world, as it hath done in all ages hitherto, that men may be necessitated to sin or suffer.

To wind up the state of this controversy, we say, that antecedent to the consideration of the power of the magistrate, and all the influence that it hath upon men or their consciences, there is a superior determination of what is true, what false in religion, what right and what wrong in the worship of God, wherein the guidance of the consciences of men doth principally depend, and whereinto it is ultimately resolved.   This gives an obligation or liberty unto them antecedent unto the imposition of the magistrate, of whose commands, and our actual obedience unto them in these things, it is the rule and measure.   And I think there is no principle, no common presumption of nature, nor dictate of reason, more evident, known, or confessed than this, that whatever God commands us, in his worship or otherwise, that we are to do; and whatever he forbids us, that we are not to do, be the things themselves in our eye great or small.

Neither is there any difference, in these things, with respect unto the way or manner of the declaration of the will of God.   Whether it be by *innate common light* or by revelation, all is one; the authority and will of God in all is to be observed.   Yea, a command of God, made known by revelation (the way which is most contended about), may suspend, as to any particular instance, the greatest command that we are obliged unto by the law of nature in reference unto one another; as it did in the precept given to Abraham for the sacrificing of his son.   And we shall find our author himself setting up the supremacy of conscience in opposition unto and competition with that of the magistrate (though with no great self-consistency), ascribing the pre-eminence and prevalency in obligation unto that of conscience, and that in the principal and most important duties of religion and human life.   Such are all those moral virtues which have in their nature a resemblance of the divine perfections, wherein he placeth the substance of religion.   With respect unto these, he so setteth up the throne of conscience as to affirm that if any thing be commanded by the magistrate against them, " to disobey him is no sin, but a duty."   And we shall find the case to be the same in matters of mere revelation; for what God commands, that he commands, by what way soever that command be made known to us; and there is no consideration that can add any thing to the obligatory power and efficacy of infinite authority.   So that where the will of God is the formal reason of our obedience, it is all one how or by what means it is discovered unto us.   Whatever we are instructed in by innate reason or by revelation, the reason why we are bound by it is neither the one nor the other, but the authority of God in both.

But we must return unto the consideration of the sentiments of our author in this matter, as before laid down.   The authority ascribed to the civil magistrate being as hath been expressed, it will be very hard for any one to distinguish between it and the sovereignty that the Lord Christ himself hath in and over his church; yea, if there be any advantage on either side, or a comparative pre-eminence, it will be found to be cast upon that of the magistrate.   Is the Lord Christ the lord of the souls and consciences of men? hath he dominion over them, to rule them in the things of the worship of God?

—it is so with the magistrate also; he hath "a universal power over the consciences of his subjects." Doth the Lord Christ require his disciples to do and observe in the worship of God whatever he commanded them?—so also may the magistrate, "the rule and conduct of conscience in these matters belonging unto him," provided that he command nothing that may "countenance vice or disgrace the Deity;" which, with reverence be it spoken, our Lord Jesus Christ himself, not only on the account of the perfection and rectitude of his own nature, but also of his commission from the Father, could not do. Is the authority of Christ the formal reason making obedience necessary to his commands and precepts?—so is the authority of the magistrate in reference unto what he requires. Do men, therefore, sin if they neglect the observance of the commands of Christ in the worship of God, because of his immediate authority so to command them binding their consciences?—so do men sin if they omit or neglect to do what the magistrate requires in the worship of God, because of his authority, without any farther respect. Hath the Lord Christ instituted two sacraments in the worship of God, that is, "outward visible signs," or symbols, "of inward invisible or spiritual grace?"—the magistrate, if he please, may institute and appoint twenty under the name of "significant ceremonies," that is, "outward visible signs of inward spiritual grace," which alone is the significancy contended about. Hath the magistrate this his authority in and over religion and the consciences of men from Jesus Christ? No more than Christ hath his authority from the magistrate, for he holds it by the law of nature, antecedent to the promise and coming of Christ. Might Christ in his own person administer the holy things of the church of God? Not in the church of the Jews, for he "sprang of the tribe of Judah, concerning which nothing was spoken as to the priesthood;" only he might in that of the gospel, but hath judged meet to commit the actual administration of them to others. So it is with the magistrate also.

Thus far, then, Christ and the magistrate seem to stand on even or equal terms. But there are two things remaining that absolutely turn the scale, and cast the advantage on the magistrate's side; for, first, Men may do and practise many things in the worship of God which the Lord Christ hath nowhere nor by any means required. Yea, to think that his word, or the revelation of his mind and will therein, is "the sole and adequate rule of religious worship," is reported as an "opinion foolish, absurd, and impious, and destructive of all government." If this be not supposed, not only the whole design of our author in this book is defeated, but our whole controversy also is composed and at an end. But, on the other hand, no man must do or practise any thing in that way but what is prescribed, appointed, and commanded by the magistrate, upon pain of sin, schism, rebellion, and all that follow thereon. To leave this unasserted is all that the Nonconformists would desire in order unto peace. Comprehension and indulgence would ensue thereon. Here, I think, the magistrate hath the advantage. But that which follows will make it yet more evident; for, secondly, Suppose the magistrate require any thing to be done and observed in the worship of God, and the Lord Christ require the quite contrary in a man's own apprehension, so that he is as well satisfied in his apprehension of his mind as he can be of any thing that is proposed to his faith and conscience in the word of God; in this case he is to obey the magistrate, and not Christ, as far as I can learn, unless all confusion and disorder be admitted an entrance into the world. Yea, but this seems directly contrary to that rule of the apostles, which hath such an evidence and power of rational conviction attending it, that they refer it to the judgment of their adversaries, and those persons of as perverse, corrupt minds and prejudicate engagements against them and their cause as ever lived in the world,—namely, " Whether it be right to obey God or man, judge ye." But we are told that " this holds only in greater matters," the logic (by the way) of which distinction is as strange as its divinity; for if the formal reason of the difference intimated arise from the comparison between the authority of God and man, it holds equally as to all things, small or great, that they may be oppositely concerned in. Besides, who shall judge what is small or what is great in things of this nature? " Cave ne titubes." Grant but the least judgment to private men themselves in this matter, and the whole fabric tumbles. If the magistrate be judge of what is great and of what is little, we are still where we were, without hope of delivery. And this, to me, is a notable instance of the pre-eminence of the magistrate above Christ in this matter. Some of the old Irish have a proverbial speech amongst them, " That if Christ had not been Christ when he was Christ, Patrick had been Christ," but it seems now, that taking it for granted that he was Christ, yet we have another that is so also, that is lord over the souls and consciences of men; and what can be said more of him " who sits in the temple of God, and shows himself to be God?"

As we formerly said, Nonconformists, who are unacquainted with the mysteries of things of this nature, must needs desire to know whether these be the avowed principles of the church of England, or whether they are only inventions to serve a present turn of the pursuit of some men's designs. Are all the old pleas of the "*jus divinum*" *of episcopacy, of example and direction apostolical, of a parity of reason between the condition of the church whilst under extraordinary officers and whilst under ordinary, of the power of the church to appoint ceremonies* for decency and order, *of the consistency of Christian liberty with the necessary practice of indifferent things, of the pattern of the churches of old,* which (whether duly or otherwise we do not now determine) have been insisted on in this cause, swallowed all up in this abyss of magistratical omnipotency, which plainly renders them useless and unprofitable? How unhappy hath it been that the Christian world was not sooner blessed with this great discovery of the only way and means of putting a final end unto all religious contests! that he should not until now appear,

" Qui genus humanum ingenio superavit, et omnes
Præstinxit, stellas exortus ut ætherius sol!"
[Lucret. of Epicurus, iii. 1056.]

But every age produceth not a Columbus. Many indeed have been the disputes of learned men about the power of magistrates in and concerning religion. With us it is stated in the recorded actings of our sovereign princes, in the oath of supremacy, and the acts of parliament concerning it, with other authentic writings explanatory thereof. Some have denied him any concern herein; our author is none of them, but rather is like the frenetic gentleman, who, when he was accused, in former days, for denying the corporeal presence of Christ in the sacrament, replied, in his own defence, that he "believed him to be present, booted and spurred as he rode to Capernaum." He hath brought him booted and spurred, yea, armed cap-a-pie, into the church of God, and given all power into his hands, to dispose of the worship of God according to his own will and pleasure; and that not with respect unto outward order only, but with direct obligation upon the consciences of men.

But, doubtless, it is the wisdom of sovereign princes to beware of this sort of enemies,—persons who, to promote their own interest, make ascriptions of such things unto them as they cannot accept of without the utmost hazard of the displeasure of God. Is it meet that, to satisfy the desires of any, they should invade the prerogative of God, or set themselves down at his right hand, in the throne of his only-begotten Son? I confess they are no way concerned in what others, for their advantage' sake, as they suppose, will ascribe unto them, which they may sufficiently disown by scorn and silence; nor can their sin involve them in any guilt. It was not the vain acclamation of the multitude unto Herod, "The voice of a god, and not of a man," but his own arrogant satisfaction in that blasphemous assignation of divine glory to him, that exposed him to the judgment and vengeance of God. When the princes of Israel found, by the answer of the Reubenites, that they had not transgressed against the law of God's worship in adding unto it or altering of it, which they knew would have been a provocation not to have been passed over without a recompense of revenge, they replied unto them, "Now ye have delivered the children of Israel out of the hand of the LORD;" and it is to be desired that all the princes of the Israel of God in the world, all Christian potentates, would diligently watch against giving admission unto any such insinuations as would deliver them into the hand of the Lord.

For my own part, such is my ignorance that I know not that any magistrate from the foundation of the world, unless it were Nebuchadnezzar, Caius Caligula, Domitian, and persons like to them, ever claimed, or pretended to exercise, the power here assigned unto them. The instances of the laws and edicts of Constantine in the matters of religion and the worship of God, of Theodosius and Gratian, Arcadius, Marcian, and other emperors of the east, remaining in the Code and Novels; the Capitular of the western emperors, and laws of Gothish kings; the right of ecclesiastical jurisdiction inherent in the imperial crown of this nation, and occasionally exercised in all ages, —are of no concernment in this matter: for no man denies but that it is the duty of the supreme magistrate to protect and further the true religion and right worship of God, by all ways and means suited and appointed of God thereunto. To encourage the professors thereof, to protect them from wrong and violence, to secure them in the performance of their duties, is doubtless incumbent on them. Whatever, under pretence of religion, brings actual disturbance unto the peace of mankind, they may coerce and restrain. When religion, as established in any nation by law, doth or may interest the professors of it, or guides in it, in any privileges, advantages, or secular emoluments, which are subject and liable, as all human concerns, to doubts, controversies, and litigious contests, in their security and disposal, all these things depend merely and solely on the power of the magistrate, by whose authority they are originally granted, and by whose jurisdictive power both the persons vested with them and themselves are disposable. But for an absolute power over the consciences of men, to bind or oblige them formally thereby to do whatever they shall require in the worship of God, so as to make it their sin, deserving eternal damnation, not so to do, without any consideration whether the things are true or false, according to the mind of God or otherwise, yea, though they are apprehended by them who are so obliged to practise them to be contrary to the will of God,—that this hath hitherto been claimed by any magistrate, unless such as those before mentioned, I am yet to seek. And the case is the same with respect unto them who are not satisfied that what is so prescribed unto them will be accepted with God; for whereas, in all that men do in the worship of God, they ought to be fully persuaded of its acceptableness to God in their own minds, seeing "whatsoever is not of faith is sin," he that "doubteth" is in a very little better capacity to serve God on such injunctions than he who apprehendeth them to be directly contrary to his mind.

If an edict were drawn up for the settlement of religion and religious worship in any Christian nation, according to the principles and directions before laid down, it may be there would be no great strife in the world by whom it should be first owned and espoused; for it must be of this importance:—

"Whereas we have a universal and absolute power over the consciences of all our subjects in things appertaining to the worship of God, so that, if we please, we can introduce new duties, never yet heard of, in the most important parts of religion (p. 80), and may impose on them, in the practice of religion and divine worship, what we please, so that, in our judgment, it do not countenance vice nor disgrace the Deity (p. 85): and whereas this power is naturally inherent in us; not given or granted unto us by Jesus Christ, but belonged to us or our predecessors before ever he was born; nor is expressed in the Scripture, but rather supposed; and this being such as that we ourselves, if we would, whether we be man or woman" (here France must be excepted by virtue of the Salique law, though the whole project be principally calculated for that meridian), "might exercise the special offices and duties of religion in our own person, especially that of the priesthood, though we are pleased to transfer the exercise of it unto others: and whereas all our prescriptions, impositions, and injunctions, in these things, do immediately affect and bind the consciences of our subjects, because they are ours, whether they be right or wrong, true or false, so long as in our judgment they neither, as was said, countenance vice nor disgrace the Deity, we do enact and ordain as followeth:"

(Here, if you please, you may intersert the scheme of religion given us by our author in his second chapter, and add unto it, "That because sacrifices were a way found out by honest men of old to express their gratitude unto God thereby, so great and necessary a part of our religious duty, it be enjoined that the use of them be again revived, seeing there is nothing in them that offends against the bounds prescribed to the power to be expressed, and that men in all places do offer up bulls and goats, sheep and fowls, to God," with as many other institutions of the like nature as shall be thought meet.) Hereunto add,—

"Now, our express will and pleasure is, that every man may and do think and judge what he pleaseth concerning the things enjoined and enacted by us; for what have we to do with their thoughts and judgments? They are under the empire and dominion of conscience, which we cannot invade if we would. They may, if they please, judge them inconvenient, foolish, absurd, yea, contrary to the mind, will, and law of God. Our only intention, will, and pleasure is, to bind them to the constant observation and practice of them, and that under the penalties of hanging and damnation."

I know not any expression in such an impious and futilous edict that may not be warranted out of the principles of this discourse, the main parts of it being composed out of the words and phrases of it, and those used, to the best of my understanding, in the sense fixed to them by our author.

Now, as was said before, I suppose Christian princes will not be earnest in their contests who shall first own the authority intimated, and express it in a suitable exercise; and if any one of them should put forth his hand unto it, he will find that

—— " Furiarum maxima juxta
Accubat, et manibus prohibet contingere mensas."—[Æn., vi. 605.]

There is one who lays an antecedent claim to a sole interest in this power, and that bottomed on other manner of pretensions than any which as yet have been pleaded in their behalf; for the power and authority here ascribed unto princes is none other but that which is claimed by the pope of Rome, with some few enlargements, and appropriated unto him by his canonists and courtiers. Only here "the old gentleman" (as he is called by our author) hath the advantage, in that, beside the precedency of his claim, it being entered on record at least six or seven hundred years before any proctor or advocate appeared in the behalf of princes, he hath forestalled them all in the pretence of infallibility: which, doubtless, is a matter of singular use in the exercise of the power contended about; for some men are so peevish as to think that thus to deal with religion and the consciences of men belongs to none but him who is absolutely, yea, essentially so,—that is, infallible. For, as we have now often said (as, contrary to their design, men in haste oftentimes speak the same things over and over), as to all ecclesiastical jurisdiction over persons and causes ecclesiastical, and the sovereign disposal of all the civil and political concernments of religion, which is vested in the imperial crown of this nation, and by sundry acts of parliament is declared so to be, I shall be always ready to plead the right of our kings, and all Christian kings whatever, against the absurd pleas and pretences of the pope; so, as to this controversy between him and such princes as shall think meet to contend with him about it, concerning the power over the consciences of men before described, I shall not interpose myself in the scuffle, as being fully satisfied they are contending about that which belongs to neither of them.

But what reason is there why this power should not be extended unto the inward thoughts and apprehensions of men about the wor-

ship of God, as well as the expression of them in pure, spiritual acts
of that worship? The power asserted, I presume, will be acknowledged to be from God, though I can scarce meet with the communication and derivation of it from him in this discourse. But whereas
it is granted on all hands that " the powers that be are of God," and
that none can have authority over another unless it be originally
" given him from above," I desire to be informed why the other part
of the power mentioned,—namely, over the thoughts, judgments, and
apprehensions of men, in the things of the worship of God,—should
not be invested in the magistrate also; that so, he having declared
what is to be believed, thought, and judged in such things, all men
should be obliged so to believe, think, and judge: for this power God
can give, and hath given it unto Jesus Christ. I presume it will be
said that this was no way needful for the preservation of peace in
human society, which is the end for which all this power is vested in
the magistrate; for let men believe, think, and judge what they
please, so long as their outward actings are, or may be, overruled,
there is no danger of any public disturbance. But this seems to be
a mighty uneasy condition for mankind,—namely, to live continually
in a contradiction between their judgments and their practices; which
in this case is allowed to be incident unto them. Constantly to judge
one way best and most according to the mind of God in his worship,
and constantly to practise another, will, it is to be feared, prove like
the conflicting of vehement vapours with their contrary qualities,
that at one time or other will produce an earthquake. How, then,
if men, weary of this perplexing, distorting condition of things in
their minds, should be provoked to run to excesses and inordinate
courses for their freedom and rest, such as our author excellently dis-
plays in all their hideous colours and appearances, and which are
really pernicious to human policy and society? were it not much
better that all these inconveniences had been prevented in the first
instance, by taking care that the faith, thoughts, persuasions, and
judgments of all subjects about the things of God, should be absolutely bound up unto the declared conceptions of their rulers in these
matters? Let it not be pretended that this is impossible, and contrary to the natural liberty of the minds of men as rational creatures,
guiding and determining themselves according to their own reason
of things and understandings; for do but fix the declared will of
the ruler in the room and place of divine revelation (which is no
hard matter to do, which some actually do universally, and our
author as to a great share and proportion), and the obligation sought
after to prevent all inconveniences in government falls as full and
directly upon the minds, thoughts, and judgments of men, as upon
any of their outward actions. And this, for the substance of it, is

now pleaded for, seeing it is pretended that in all things dubious, where men cannot satisfy themselves that it is the will of God that they should do a thing or no, the declaration of the magistrate determines not only their practice but their judgment also, and gives them that full persuasion of their minds which is indispensably required unto their acting in such things, and that faith which frees them from sin; for " he that doubteth is damned if he eat."

But it will be said that there will be no need hereof; for let men think and judge what they please, whilst they are convinced and satisfied that it is their duty not to practise any thing outwardly in religion but what is prescribed by their rulers, it is not possible that any public evil should ensue upon their mental conceptions only. We observed before that the condition described is exceedingly uneasy; which, I suppose, will not be denied by men who have seriously considered what it is either to judge or practise any thing that lies before them with reference unto the judgment of God. And that which should tie men up to rest perpetually in such a restless state is, as it seems, a mere conviction of their duty. They ought to be, and are supposed to be, convinced that it is their duty to maintain the liberty of their minds and judgments, but to submit in their outward practice universally to the laws of men that are over them; and this sense and conviction of duty is a sufficient security unto public tranquillity in all that contrariety and opposition of sentiments unto established religion and forms of worship that may be imagined. But if this be so, why will not the same conviction and sense of duty restrain them who do peaceably exercise the worship of God, according to the light and dictates of their consciences, from any actings whatever that may tend to the disturbance of the public peace? Duty, nakedly considered, is even, as such, the greatest obligation on the minds of men; and the great security of others in their actings ariseth from thence. But the more it is influenced and advantaged by outward considerations, the less it is assaulted and opposed by things grievous and perplexing in the way of the discharge of it, the more efficacious will be its operations on the minds of men, and the firmer will be the security unto others that thence ariseth. Now, these advantages lie absolutely on the part of them who practise, or are allowed so to do, according to their own light and persuasion in the worship of God, wherein they are at rest and full satisfaction of mind; and not on theirs who all their days are bound up to a perverse, distorted posture of mind and soul, in judging one thing to be best and most pleasing unto God, and practising of the contrary. Such a one is the man that, of all others, rulers have need, I think, to be most jealous of; for what security can be had of him who hath inured himself unto a continual contradiction between his faith and his practice? For my part, I should either expect no other measure from him in any other thing, nor ever judge that his profession and ways of acting are any sufficient indications of his mind (which takes away all security from mankind), or fear that his convictions of light and knowledge, as he apprehends, would, at one time or other, precipitate him into attempts of irregularity and violence, for his own relief.

—— " Hic niger est, hunc tu Romane caveto."

It will be said, perhaps, that we need not look farther for the disturbance of public peace from them who practise outwardly any thing in the worship of God but what is prescribed, established, and enjoined, seeing that every such practice is such a disturbance itself. I say, this pretence is miserably ridiculous and contemptible, and contrary to the common experience of mankind. If this were so, the whole world for three hundred years lived in one continual disturbance and tumult upon the account of Christian religion, whose professors constantly practised and performed that in the worship of God which was so far from being established or approved by public authority, that it was proscribed and condemned under penalties of all sorts, pecuniary, corporeal, and sanguinary or capital; but we see no such matter ensued, nor the least disquietment unto the world, but what was given unto it by the rage of bloody persecutors, that introduced the first convulsions into the Roman empire, which were never well quieted, but ended in its dissolution. The experience, also, of the present and next preceding ages casts this frivolous exception out of consideration. And as such a practice, even against legal prohibitions, though it be by the transgression of a penal law, is yet in itself and [by] just consequence remote enough from any disturbance of government (unless we should suppose that every non-observance of a penal statute invalidates the government of a nation, which were to fix it upon such a foundation as will not afford it the steadiness of a weather-cock); so being allowed by way of exemption, it contains no invasion upon or intrusion into the rights of others, but, being accompanied with the abridgment of the privileges of none, or the neglect of any duty required to the good of the commonwealth, it is as consistent with, and may be as conducing to, public good and tranquillity, as any order of religious things in the world, as shall be elsewhere demonstrated.

It remains, therefore, that the only answer to this consideration is, that men who plead for indulgence and liberty of conscience in the worship of God, according to his word and the light which he hath given them therein, have indeed no conscience at all, and so are not to be believed as to what they profess against sinister and evil practices. This flail I know no fence against but this only, that they have as good and better grounds to suspect him to have no conscience at all who, upon unjust surmises, shall so injuriously charge them, as finding him in a direct transgression of the principal rules that conscience is to be guided and directed by, than he hath to pronounce such a judgment concerning them and their sincerity in what they profess. And whether such mutual censures tend not to the utter overthrow of all peace, love, and security amongst mankind, it is easy to determine. Certainly, it is the worst game in the world for the public, to have men bandying suspicions one against another, and thereon managing mutual charges of all that they do surmise, or what else they please to give the countenance of surmise unto.

I acknowledge the notion insisted on,—namely, "That whilst men reserve to themselves the freedom and liberty of judging what they please, or what seems good unto them, in matters of religion and the worship of God, they ought to esteem it their duty to practise in all things according to the prescription of their rulers, though every way contrary unto and inconsistent with their own judgments and persuasions, unless it be in things that countenance vice or disgrace the Deity" (whereof yet, it may be, it will not be thought meet that they themselves should judge for themselves and their own practice, seeing they may extend their conceptions about what doth so unto such minute instances as would frustrate the whole design),—is exceedingly accommodated to the corrupt lusts and affections of men, and suited to make provision for their security in this world by an exemption from the indispensable command of professing the truth communicated and known unto them ; a sense of the obligation whereof hath hitherto exposed innumerable persons in all ages to great difficulties, dangers, and sufferings, yea, to death, the height and sum of all: for whereas men have been persuaded that " with the heart man believeth unto righteousness, and with the mouth confession is made unto salvation," the latter clause is in many cases hereby sufficiently superseded, and the troublesome duty seeming to be required in it is removed out of the way. It will not, it may be, be so easy to prove that in the religion of the Mohammedans there is any thing enjoined in practice that will directly fall under the limitations assigned unto the compliance with the commands of superiors contended for; and, therefore, let a man but retain his own apprehensions concerning Jesus Christ and the gospel, it may be lawful for him, yea, be his duty, to observe the worship enjoined by the law of Mohammed, if his lot fall to live under the power of the Grand Seignior or any sovereign prince of the same persuasion! But the case is clear in the religion of the Papists, which is under the protection of the greatest number of supreme magistrates in Europe. It will not be pretended, I suppose, by our author, that there is any thing in the confession of the church of Rome, or imposed by it on the practices of men, that directly gives countenance unto any immorality, especially as the sense of that term is by him stated; and it is no easy matter for ordinary men to prove and satisfy themselves that there is aught in their modes of worship of such a tendency as to cast disgrace upon the Deity, especially considering with how much learning and diligence the charge of any such miscarriage is endeavoured to be answered and removed,—all which pleas ought to be satisfied before a man can make sedately a determinate judgment of the contrary. Let, then, men's judgments be what they will in the matters of difference between Protestants and Papists, it is, on this hypothesis, the duty of all that live under the dominion of sovereign popish princes outwardly to comply with and practise that religious worship that is commanded by them and enjoined! The case is the same, also, as to the religion of the Jews!

Now, as this casts a reflection of incredible folly and inexpiable guilt upon all protestant martyrs, in casting away their own lives and disobeying the commands of their lawful sovereigns, so it exposeth all the Protestants in the world who are still in the same condition of subjection to the severe censures of impiety and rebellion, and must needs exasperate their rulers to pursue them to destruction, under pretence of unwarrantable obstinacy in them: for if we wholly take off the protection of conscience in this matter, and its subjection to the authority of God alone, there is no plea left to excuse dissenting Protestants from the guilt of such crimes as may make men justly cry out against them, as the Jews did against St Paul, "Away with such fellows from the earth; for it is not fit that they should live!" or, "Protestantes ad leones!" according to the old cry of the Pagans against the primitive Christians. But if this should prove to be a way of teaching and justifying the grossest hypocrisy and dissimulation that the nature of man is capable of, a means to cast off all regard unto the authority of God over the ways and lives of men, all the rhetoric in the world shall never persuade me that God hath so moulded and framed the order and state of human affairs that it should be any way needful to the preservation of public peace and tranquillity. Openness, plainness of heart, sincerity in our actions and professions, generous honesty, and a universal respect in all things to the supreme Rector of all, the great Possessor of heaven and earth, with an endeavour to comply with his present revealed mind and future judgment, are far better foundations for and ligaments of public peace and quietness. To make this the foundation of our political superstructure, that "divisum imperium cum Jove Cæsar habet," God hath immediate and sole power over the minds and inward thoughts of men, but the magistrate

over the exercise of those thoughts, in things especially belonging to
the worship of God, and in the same instances, seems not to prognos-
ticate a stable or durable building.   The prophet was not of that
mind of old, who, in the name of God, blamed the people for willingly walking after the commandment of their ruler in concerns of
worship not warranted by divine appointment; nor was Daniel so,
who, notwithstanding the severe prohibition made against his praying in his house, continued to do so three times a-day.

But besides all this, I do not see how this hypothesis is necessarily subservient to the principal design of the author, but it may
be as well improved to quite distant, yea, contrary ends and purposes.   His design, plainly, is to have one fabric of religion erected,
one form of external worship enacted and prescribed, which all men
should be compelled by penalties to the outward profession and observance of.   These penalties he would have to be such as should
not fail of their end,—namely, of taking away all professed dissent
from his religious establishment; which, if it cannot be effected without the destruction and death of multitudes, they also are not to be
forborne.   Now, how this ensues from the forementioned principle
I know not; for a supreme magistrate, finding that the minds of
very many of his subjects are, in their judgments and persuasions,
engaged in a dissent unto the religion established by him, or somewhat in it, or some part of it, especially in things of practical worship, though he should be persuaded that he hath so far a power
over their consciences as to command them to practise contrary to
their judgment, yet, knowing their minds and persuasions to be
out of his reach and exempted from his jurisdiction, why may he
not think it meet and conducing to public tranquillity and all the
ends of his government, even the good of the whole community
committed to his charge, rather to indulge them in the quiet and
peaceable exercise of the worship of God according to their own
light, than always to bind them up unto that unavoidable disquietment which will ensue upon the conflict in their minds between
their judgments and their practices, if he should oblige them as is
desired?   Certainly, as in truth and reality, so according to this principle, he hath power so to do; for to fancy him [to have] such a power
over the religion and consciences of his subjects as that he should
be inevitably bound, on all occurrences, and in all conditions of
affairs, to impose upon them the necessary observation of one form
of worship, is that which would quickly expose him to inextricable
troubles.   And instances of all sorts might be multiplied to show the
ridiculous folly of such a conception.   Nay, it implies a perfect contradiction to what is disputed before; for if he be obliged to settle
and impose such a form on all, it must be because there was a neces-

sity of somewhat antecedent to his imposition, whence his obligation to impose it did arise. And, on such a supposition, it is in vain to inquire after his liberty or his power in these things, seeing by his duty he is absolutely determined; and whatever that be which doth so determine him and put an obligation upon him, it doth indispensably do the same on his subjects also, which, as it is known, utterly excludes the authority pleaded for.

This principle, therefore, indeed asserts his liberty to do what he judgeth meet in these matters, but contains nothing in it to oblige him to judge that it may not be meet and most conducing unto all the ends of his government to indulge unto the consciences of men peaceable (especially if complying with him in all the fundamentals of the religion which himself professeth) the liberty of worshipping God according to what they apprehend of his own mind and will. And let an application of this principle be made to the present state of this nation, wherein there are so great multitudes of persons peaceable, and not unuseful unto public good, who dissent from the present establishment of outward worship, and have it not in their power either to change their judgments or to practise contrary unto them; and as it is in the power of the supreme magistrate to indulge them in their own way, so it will prove to be his interest, as he is the spring and centre of public peace and prosperity.

Neither doth it appear that, in this discourse, our author hath had any regard either to the real principles of the power of the magistrate as stated in this nation, or to his own, which are fictitious, but yet such as ought to be obligatory to himself. His principal assertion is, "That the supreme magistrate hath power to bind the consciences of men in matters of religion;" that is, by laws and edicts to that purpose. Now, the highest and most obligatory way of the supreme magistrate's speaking in England is by acts of parliament; it is therefore supposed that what is so declared in or about matters of religion should be obligatory to the conscience of this author; but yet quite otherwise, page 59, he sets himself to oppose and condemn a public law of the land, on no other ground than because it stood in his way, and seemed incompliant with his principles : for whereas the law of 2 and 3 Edward VI., which appointed two weekly days for abstinence from flesh, had been, amongst other reasons, prefaced with this, "That the king's subjects having now a more clear light of the gospel, through the infinite mercy of God" (such "canting" language was then therein used), "and thereby the king's majesty perceiving that one meat of itself was not more holy than another," etc., "yet considering that due abstinence was a means to virtue, and to subdue men's bodies to their souls and spirits," etc. ; and it being after found (it should seem by a farther degree of light) that those expressions, meeting with the inveterate opinions of some newly brought out of Popery, had given countenance to them to teach or declare that something of religion was placed therein, thereon, by the law made 5 Eliz., adding another weekly day to be kept with the former for the same purpose, the former clause was omitted, and mention only made therein of the civil and politic reasons inducing the legislators thereunto, and withal a penalty of inflicting punishment on those who should affirm and maintain that there was any concernment of conscience and religion in that matter. This provision hath so distasted our author, that forgetting, it seems, his own design, he reproaches it with the title of "jejunium Cecilianum,"[1] and thinks it so far from obliging his conscience to acquiesce in the determination therein made, that he will not allow it to give law to his tongue or pen! But ("vexet censura columbas") it seems they are the fanatics only that are thus to be restrained.

Moreover, on occasion hereof, we might manifest how some other laws of this land do seem carefully to avoid that imposition on conscience which, against law and reason, he pleadeth for. For instance, in that of 21 Jac., touching usury, and the restraint of it unto the sum therein established, it was provided, "That no words in this act contained shall be construed or expounded to allow the practice of usury in point of religion and conscience." And why did not the supreme magistrate in that law determine and bind the consciences of men by a declaration of their duty in a point of religion, seeing whither way soever the determination had been made, neither would immorality have been countenanced nor the Deity disgraced? But, plainly, it is rather declared that he hath not cognizance of such things with reference to the consciences of men, to oblige them or set them at liberty, but only power to determine what may be practised in order to public profit and peace. And, therefore, the law would neither bind nor set at liberty the consciences of men in such cases; which is a work for the supreme Lawgiver only.

Neither, as it hath been before observed, do the principles here asserted and contended for either express or represent the supremacy of the kings of this nation in matters ecclesiastical, as it is stated and determined by themselves in parliament, but rather so as to give great offence and scandal to the religion here professed, and advantage to the adversaries thereof; for after there appeared some ambiguity in those words of the oath, enacted 1 Eliz., of "testifying the queen to be supreme governor, as well in all spiritual or ecclesiastical things or causes as in temporal," and many doubts and scruples had ensued thereon, as though there were assigned to her a power over the

[1] In allusion, doubtless, to Cecil, Lord Burleigh, the celebrated prime minister of Elizabeth.—ED.

consciences of her subjects in spiritual things, or that she had a power herself to order and administer spiritual things, in 5 Eliz. it is enacted, by way of explanation, that the oaths aforesaid shall be expounded in such form as is set forth in the admonition annexed to the queen's injunctions, published in the first year of her reign; where, disclaiming the power of the ministry of divine offices in the church, or the power of the priesthood here by our author affixed to the supreme magistrate, her power and authority is declared to be a sovereignty over all manner of persons born within this realm, whether they be ecclesiastical or temporal, so that no foreign power hath, or ought to have, any superiority over them. And so is this supremacy stated in the articles, anno 1562,—namely, an authority to rule all estates and degrees committed to the charge of the supreme magistrate by God, whether they be ecclesiastical or temporal, and to restrain the stubborn or evil-doers. Of the things contended for by our author,—the authority of the priesthood, and power over the consciences of men in matters of religion,— there is not one word in our laws, but rather they are both of them rejected and condemned.

I have yet laid the least part of that load upon this principle, which, if it be farther pressed, it must expect to be burdened withal, and that from the common suffrage of Christians in all ages. But yet, that I may not transgress against the design of this short and hasty discourse, I shall proceed no farther in the pursuit of it, but take a little survey of what is here pleaded in its defence. Now, this is undertaken and pursued in the first chapter, with the two next ensuing, where an end is put to this plea: for if I understand any thing of his words and expressions, our author in the beginning of his fourth chapter cuts down all those gourds and wild vines that he had been planting in the three preceding; for he not only grants but disputes also for an obligation on the consciences of men antecedent and superior unto all human laws and their obligation! His words are as followeth, p. 115: "It is not because subjects are in any thing free from the authority of the supreme power on earth, but because they are subject to a superior in heaven, and they are only then excused from the duty of obedience to their sovereign when they cannot give it without rebellion against God: so that it is not originally any right of their own that exempts them from a subjection to the sovereign power in all things; but it is purely God's right of governing his own creatures that magistrates then invade when they make edicts to violate or control his laws. And those who will take off from the consciences of men all obligations antecedent to those of human laws, instead of making the power of princes supreme, absolute, and uncontrollable, they utterly enervate all their authority, and set their subjects at perfect liberty from all their commands."

I know no men that pretend to exemption from the obligation of human laws but only on this plea, that God by his law requires them to do otherwise; and if this be so, the authority of such laws as to the consciences of men is superseded, by the confession of this author. Allow, therefore, but the principles here expressed,—namely, that men have a superior Power over them in heaven, whose laws and the revelation of whose will concerning them is the supreme rule of their duty, whence an obligation is laid upon their consciences of doing whatever is commanded, or not doing what is forbidden by him, which is superior unto, and actually supersedes, all human commands and laws that interfere therewith,—and I see neither use of nor place for that power of magistrates over the consciences of men which is so earnestly contended for. And our author, also, in his ensuing discourse in that chapter, placeth all the security of government in the respect that the consciences of men have to the will and command of God, and which they profess to have; which in all these chapters he pleads to be a principle of all confusion! But it is the first chapter which alone we are now taking a view of.

The only argument therein insisted on to make good the ascription unto the magistrate of the power over religion and the consciences of men before described, is "the absolute and indispensable necessity of it unto public tranquillity; which is the principal and most important end of government." In the pursuit of this argument, sometimes, yea often, such expressions are used concerning the magistrate's power as, in a tolerable construction, declare it to be what no man denies nor will contend about: but it is necessary that they be interpreted according to the genius and tenor of the opinion contended for; and, accordingly, we will consider them. This alone, I say, is that which is here pleaded, or is given in as the subject of the ensuing discourse. But, after all, I think that he who shall set himself seriously to find out how any thing here spoken hath a direct and rational cogency towards the establishment of the conclusion before laid down will find himself engaged in no easy undertaking. We were told, I confess, at the entrance (so as that we may not complain of a surprisal) that we must expect to have invectives twisted with arguments, and some such thing seems here to be aimed at; but if a logical chemist come and make a separation of the elements of this composition, he will find, if I mistake not, a heap of the drossy invective, and scarce the least appearance of any argument ore. Instead of sober, rational arguing,

—— " crimina rasis
Librat in antithetis;"—— Pers. i. 85,

great aggravations of men's miscarriages in the pursuit of the dictates of their consciences, either real or feigned, edged against and fiercely reflected upon those whom he makes his adversaries, and these the same for substance, repeated over and over in a great variety of well-placed words, take up the greatest part of his plea in this chapter, especially the beginning of it, wherein alone the controversy, as by himself stated, is concerned.

But if the power and authority over religion and the consciences of men here ascribed unto supreme magistrates be so indispensably necessary to the preservation of public tranquillity as is pretended, a man cannot but wonder how the world hath been in any age past kept in any tolerable peace and quietness, and how it is anywhere blessed with those ends of government at this day; for it will not be an easy task for our author, or any one else, to demonstrate that the power mentioned hath ever been either claimed or exercised by any supreme magistrate in Christendom, or that it is so at this day. The experience of past and present ages is, therefore, abundantly sufficient to defeat this pretence, which is sufficiently asserted, without the least appearance of proof or argument to give it countenance or confirmation, or they must be very charitable to him, or ignorant in themselves, who will mistake invectives for arguments. The remembrance, indeed, of these severities I would willingly lay aside, especially because the very mention of them seems to express a higher sense of and regret concerning them than I am in the least subject unto, or something that looks like a design of retaliation; but as these things are far from my mind, so the continual returns that almost in every page I meet with of high and contemptuous reproaches will not allow that they be always passed by without any notice or remark.

It is, indeed, indispensably necessary that public peace and tranquillity be preserved; but that there is any thing in point of government necessary hereunto, but that God have all spiritual power over the consciences of men, and rulers political power over their actings, wherein public peace and tranquillity are concerned, the world hath not hitherto esteemed, nor do I expect to find it proved by this author. If these things will not preserve the public peace, it will not be kept if one should rise from the dead to persuade men unto their duty. The power of God over the consciences of men I suppose is acknowledged by all who own any such thing as conscience, or believe there is a God over all. That, also, in the exercise of this authority, he requires of men all that obedience unto rulers that is any way needful or expedient unto the preservation of the ends of their rule, is a truth standing firm on the same foundation of universal consent, derived from the law of creation; and his positive commands to that purpose have an evidence of his will in this matter not liable to exception or control. This conscience unto God our author confesseth (as we have observed in his fourth chapter) to be the great preservation and security of government and governors, with respect unto the ends mentioned; and if so, what becomes of all the pretences of disorder and confusion that will ensue unless this power over men's consciences be given to the magistrate, and taken as it were out of the hands of God? Nor is it to be supposed that men will be more true to their consciences, supposing the reiglement of them in the hand of men, than when they are granted to be in the hand and power of God; for both at present are supposed to require the same things. Certainly, where conscience respects authority, as it always doth, the more absolute and sovereign it apprehends the authority by which it is obliged, the greater and more firm will be the impression of the obligation upon it; and in that capacity of pre-eminence it must look upon the authority of God, compared with the authority of man. Here, then, lies the security of public peace and tranquillity, as it is backed by the authority of the magistrate, to see that all outward actions are suitable unto what conscience toward God doth in this matter openly and unquestionably require.

The pretence, indeed, is, that the placing of this authority over the consciences of men in the supreme ruler doth obviate and take away all grounds and occasions of any such actings on the account of religion as may tend unto public disturbance; for suppose conscience, in things concerning religion and the worship of God, subject to God alone, and the magistrate require such things to be observed in the one or the other as God hath not required, at least in the judgments and consciences of them of whom the things prescribed are required, and to forbid the things that God requires to be observed and done, in this case, it is said, they cannot or will not comply in active obedience with the commands of the magistrate. But what if it so fall out? Doth it thence follow that such persons must needs rebel and be seditious, and disturb the public peace of the society whereof they are members? Wherefore is it that they do not do or observe what is required of them by the magistrate in religion or the worship of God, or that they do what he forbids? Is it not because of the authority of God over their minds and consciences in these things? and why should it be supposed that men will answer the obligations laid by God on their consciences in one thing and not in another, in the things of his worship and not of obedience unto civil power, concerning which his commands are as express and evident as they can be pretended to be in the things which they avow their obligation unto?

Experience is pretended to the contrary. It is said again and again that "men, under pretence of their consciences unto God in religion, have raised wars and tumults, and brought all things into confusion, in this kingdom and nation especially; and what will words avail against the evidence of so open an experience to the contrary?" But what if this also should prove a false and futilous pretence? Fierce and long wars have been in this nation of old, upon the various titles of persons pleading their right unto supreme government in the kingdom against one another; so also have there been about the civil rights and privileges of the subjects in the confusions commonly called "The barons' wars." The late troubles, disorders, and wars amongst us must bear the weight of this whole charge. But if any one will take the pains to review the public writings, declarations, treatises, whereby those tumults and wars were begun and carried on, he will easily discern that liberty of conscience in practice, or the exemption of it from the power of the magistrate, as to the rule and conduct of it, now ascribed unto him in the latitude, by sober persons defended or pleaded for, had neither place in nor influence into the beginnings of those troubles. And when such confusions are begun, no man can give assurance or conjecture where they shall end.

Authority, laws, privileges, and I know not what things, wherein private men, of whom alone we treat, have no pretence of interest, were pleaded in those affairs. He that would judge aright of these things must set aside all other considerations, and give his instance of the tumults and seditions that have ensued on the account of men's keeping their consciences entire for God alone, without any just plea or false pretence of authority, and the interest of men in the civil concerns of nations.

However, it cannot be pretended that *liberty of conscience* gave the least occasion unto any disorders in those days, for indeed there was none but only that of opinion and judgment, which our author placeth out of the magistrate's cognizance and dispose, and supposeth it is a thing wherein the public peace neither is nor can be concerned. It is well if it prove so; but this liberty of judgment, constantly pressed with a practice contrary to its own determinations, will, I fear, prove the most dangerous posture of the minds of men, in reference to public tranquillity, that they can be well disposed into. However, we may take a little nearer view of the certain remedy provided for all these evils by our author, and satisfy ourselves in some inquiries about it. Shall, then, according to this expedient, the supreme magistrate govern, rule, and oblige unto obedience the consciences of his subjects universally in all things in religion and the worship of God, so that, appoint what he please, forbid what he please, subjects are bound in conscience to observe them and yield obedience accordingly? His answer, as far as I can gather his meaning, is, that he may and must do so in all things, taking care that what he commands shall neither countenance vice nor disgrace the

Deity; and then the subjects are obliged according to the inquiry. But there seems another limitation to be given to this power, p. 37, where he affirms that the " Lord Christ hath given severe injunctions to secure the obedience of men to all lawful superiors, except where they run directly cross to the interest of the gospel;" and elsewhere he seems to give the same privilege of exemption where a religion is introduced that is idolatrous or superstitious. I would, then, a little farther inquire, who shall judge whether the things commanded in religion and the worship of God be idolatrous and superstitious? whether they cross directly the interest of the gospel? whether they countenance vice and disgrace the Deity or no? To say that the magistrate is to judge and determine hereof is the highest foppery imaginable; for no magistrate, unless he be distracted, will enjoin such a religion to observance as he judgeth himself to fall under the [dis]qualifications mentioned, and when he hath done so declare that so they do, and yet require obedience unto them. Besides, if this judgment be solely committed unto him indeed, in the issue there neither is nor can be any question for a judgment to be passed upon in this matter, for his injunction doth quite render useless all disquisitions to that purpose. The judgment and determination hereof, therefore, is necessarily to be left unto the subjects from whom obedience is required. So it lies in the letter of the proposal; they must obey in all things but such; and, therefore, surely must judge what is such and what is not. Now, who shall fix bounds to what they will judge to fall under one or other of these limitations? If they determine, according to the best light they have, that the religious observances enjoined by the magistrate do directly cross the interest of the gospel, they are absolved by our author from any obligation in conscience to their observation; and so we are just as before, and this great engine for public tranquillity vanisheth into air and smoke.

Thus this author himself, in way of objection, supposeth a case of a magistrate enjoining, as was said, a religion superstitious and idolatrous. This he acknowledgeth to be an inconvenience, yet such as is far beneath the mischiefs that ensue upon the exemption of the consciences of men in religion from the power of the magistrate! which I confess I cannot but admire at, and can give reasons why I do so admire it, which also may be given in due season. But what, then, is to be done in this case? He answers, " It is to be borne." True, but how? Is it to be so borne as to practise and observe the things so enjoined, though superstitious and idolatrous? Though his words are dubious, yet I suppose he will not plainly say so, nor can he, unless he will teach men to cast off all respect unto the authority of God, and open such a door to atheism as his rhetorical, prefatory invective will not be able to shut. The bearing, then, intended, must be by patient suffering in a refusal to practise what is so commanded, and observing the contrary commands of God. But why in this case ought they to suffer *quietly* for refusing a compliance with what is commanded, and for their observance of the contrary precepts of the gospel? Why, they must do so because of the command of God, obliging their consciences unto obedience to the magistrate in all things wherein the public peace is concerned; and so that is absolutely secured. Is it not evident to him that hath but half an eye that we are come about again where we were before? Let this be applied to all the concernments of religion and religious worship, and there will arise, with respect unto them, the same security which in this case is deemed sufficient, and all that human affairs are capable of; for if in greater matters men may refuse to act according to the magistrate's command, out of a sense of the authority of God obliging them to the contrary, and yet their civil peaceableness and obedience be absolutely secured from the respect of their consciences to the command of God requiring it, why should it not be admitted that they may and will have the same respect to that command when they dissent from the magistrate's constitution in lesser things, on the same account of the authority of God requiring the contrary of them? Shall we suppose that they will cast off the authority of God requiring their obedience, on the account of their dissatisfaction in lesser things of the magistrate's appointment, when they will not do so for all the violence that may be offered unto them in things of greater and higher importance? The principle, therefore, asserted is as useless as it is false, and partakes sufficiently of both these properties to render it inconsiderable and contemptible; and he that can reconcile these things among themselves or make them useful to the author's design will achieve what I dare not aspire unto.

I know not any thing that remains in the first chapter deserving our farther consideration; what seems to be of real importance, or to have any aspect towards the cause in hand, may undergo some brief remarks, and so leave us at liberty to a farther progress. In general, a supposition is laid down, and it is so vehemently asserted as is evident that it is accompanied with a desire that it should be taken for granted,—namely, that if the consciences of men be not regulated, in the choice and practice of religion, by the authority of the magistrate over them, they will undoubtedly run into principles and practices inconsistent with the safety of human society, and such as will lead them to seditions and tumults; and hence (if I understand him, a matter I am continually jealous about, from the looseness of his expressions, though I am satisfied I constantly take his words in the sense which is received of them by the most intelligent persons) he educeth all his reasonings, and not from a mere dissent from the magistrate's injunctions, without the entertainment of such principles or an engagement into such practices. I cannot, I say, find the arguments that arise from a mere supposition that men, in some things relating to the worship of God, will or do practise otherwise than the magistrate commands, which are used to prove the inconsistency of such a posture of things with public tranquillity; which yet alone was the province our author ought to have managed. But there is another supposition added,—that where conscience is in any thing left unto its own liberty to choose or refuse in the worship of God, there it will embrace, sure enough, such wicked, debauched, and seditious principles as shall dispose men unto commotions, rebellions, and all such evils as will actually evert all rule, order, and policy amongst men. But now this supposition will not be granted him, in reference unto them who profess to take up all their profession of religion from the command of God or the revelation of his will in the Scripture, wherein all such principles and practices as those mentioned are utterly condemned; and the whole profession of Christianity being left for three hundred years without the rule, guidance, and conduct of conscience now contended for, did not once give the least disturbance unto the civil governments of the world. Disturbances, indeed, there were, and dreadful revolutions of governments, in those days and places when and where the professors of it lived; but no concerns of religion being then involved in or with the civil rights and interests of men, as the professors of it had no engagements in them, so from those alterations and troubles no reflection could be made on their profession. And the like peace, the like innocency of religion, the like freedom from all possibility of such imputations as are now cast upon it, occasioned merely by its intertexture with the affairs, rights, and laws of the nations, and the interests of its professors as such therein, will ensue when it shall be separated from that relation wherein it stands to this world, and left at the pure, naked tendency of the souls of men to another, and not before.

But what says our author? " If for the present the minds of men happen to be tainted with such furious and boisterous conceptions of religion as incline them to stubbornness and sedition, and make them unmanageable to the laws of government, shall not a prince be allowed to give check to such unruly and dangerous persuasions?" I answer, That such principles which, being professed and avowed, are in their own nature and just consequence destructive to public peace and human society, are all of them directly opposite to the light of human nature, that common reason and consent of mankind wherein and whereon all government is founded, with the prime fundamental laws and dictates of the Scripture, and so may and ought to be re strained in the practices of the persons that profess them; and with reference unto them the magistrate "beareth not the sword in vain:" for human society being inseparably consequent unto, and an effect of, the law of our nature, or concreated principles of it, which hath subdued the whole race of mankind, in all times and places, unto its observance; opinions, persuasions, principles opposite unto it, or de-structive of it, manifesting themselves by any sufficient evidence or in overt acts, ought to be no more allowed than such as profess an enmity to the being and providence of God himself. For men's in-clinations, indeed, as in themselves considered, there is no competent judge of them amongst the sons of men; but as to all outward actions that are of the tendency described, they are under public inspection, to be dealt withal according to their demerit.

I shall only add, that the mormo here made use of is not now first composed or erected; it hath, for the substance of it, been flourished by the Papists ever since the beginning of the Reformation. Neither did they use to please themselves more in or to dance more merrily about any thing than this calf: " Let private men have their con-sciences exempted from a necessary obedience to the prescriptions of the church, and they will quickly run into all pernicious fancies and persuasions." It is known how this scare-crow hath been cast to the ground, and this calf stamped to powder, by divines of the church of England. It is no pleasant thing, I confess, to see this plea revived now with respect to the magistrate's authority, and not the pope's; for I fear that when it shall be manifested, and that by the consent of all parties, that there is no pleadable argument to bottom this pre-tension for the power of the magistrate upon, some, rather than forego it, will not be unwilling to recur to the fountain from whence it first sprang, and admit the pope's plea as meet to be revived in this case. And, indeed, if we must come at length, for the security of public peace, to deprive all private persons of the liberty of judging what is right and wrong in religion in reference to their own practice, or what is their duty towards God about his worship, and what is not, there are innumerable advantages attending the design of devolving the absolute determination of these things upon the pope, above that of committing it to each supreme magistrate in his own dominions; for besides the plea of at least better security in his determinations than in that of any magistrate, if not his infallibility, which he hath so long talked of, and so sturdily defended, as to get it a great re-putation in the world, the delivering up of the faith and consciences of all men unto him will produce a seeming agreement, at least of incomparably a larger extent than the remitting of all things of this nature to the pleasure of every supreme magistrate, which may probably establish as many different religions in the world as there are different nations, kingdoms, or commonwealths.

That which alone remains seeming to give countenance to the assertions before laid down, is our author's assignation of the priesthood by natural right unto the supreme magistrate, which in no alteration of religion he can be divested of, but by virtue of some positive law of God, as it was for a season in the Mosaical institution and government. But these things seem to be of no force; for it never belonged to the priesthood to govern or to rule the consciences of men with an absolute, uncontrollable power, but only in their name, and for them, to administer the holy things which by common consent were admitted and received amongst them. Besides, our author, by his discourse, seems not to be much acquainted with the rise of the office of the priesthood amongst men; as shall be demonstrated if farther occasion be given thereunto. However, by the way, we may observe what is his judgment in this matter. The magistrate, we are told, hath not his ecclesiastical authority from Christ, and yet this is such as that the power of the priesthood is included therein, the exercise whereof, "as he is pleased to transfer to others, so he may, if he please, reserve it to himself," p. 32; whence it follows, not only that it cannot be given by Christ unto any other, for it is part of the magistrate's power, which he hath not limited or confined by any subsequent law, nor can there be a co-ordinate subject of the same power of several kinds; so that all the interest or right any man or men have in or unto the exercise of it is but transferred to them by the magistrate; and therefore they act therein in his name and by his authority only; and hence the bishops, as such, are said to be "ministers of state," p. 49. Neither can it be pretended that this was indeed in the power of the magistrate before the coming of Christ, but not since; for he hath, as we are told, all that he ever had, unless there be a restraint put upon him by some express prohibition of our Saviour, p. 41,—which will hardly be found in this matter. I cannot, therefore, see how, in the exercise of the Christian priesthood, there is (on these principles) any the least respect unto Jesus Christ or his authority: for men have only the exercise of it transferred to them by the magistrate, by virtue of a power inherent in him antecedent unto any concessions of Christ; and, therefore, in his name and authority they must act in all the sacred offices of their functions. It is well if men be so far awake as to consider the tendency of these things.

At length Scripture proofs for the confirmation of these op'nions are produced, pp. 35, 36; and the first pleaded is that promise, that "kings shall be nursing fathers unto the church." It is true this is promised, and God accomplish it more and more! but yet we do not desire such nurses as beget the children they nurse. The proposing, prescribing, commanding, binding religion on the consciences of men, is rather the *begetting* of it than its *nursing*. To take care of the church and religion, that it receive no detriment, by all the ways and means appointed by God and useful thereunto, is the duty of the magistrates: but it is so also, antecedently to their actings unto this purpose, to discern aright which is the church whereunto this promise is made; without which they cannot duly discharge their trust nor fulfil the promise itself. The very words, by the rules of the metaphor, do imply that the church and its religion, and the worship of God observed therein, are constituted, fixed, and regulated by God himself, antecedently unto the magistrate's duty and power about it. They are to nurse that which is committed to them, and not what themselves have framed or begotten. And we contend for no more but a rule concerning religion and the worship of God antecedent unto the magistrate's interposing about it, whereby both his actings in his place, and those of subjects in theirs, are to be regulated. Mistakes herein have engaged many sovereign princes, in pursuit of their trust as nursing fathers to the church, to lay out their strength and power for the utter ruin of it; as may be evidenced in instances too many of those who, in a subserviency to and by the direction of the papal interest, have endeavoured to extirpate true religion out of the world. Such a nursing mother we had some time in England, who, in pursuit of her care, burned so many bishops and other holy men to ashes.

He asks farther, "What doth the Scripture mean when it styles our Saviour the King of kings, and maketh princes his vicegerents here on earth?" I confess, according to this gentleman's principles, I know not what it means in so doing. Kings, he tells us, have not their authority in and over religion and the consciences of men from him, and therefore in the exercise of it cannot be his vicegerents; for none is the vicegerent of another in the exercise of any power and authority, if he have not received that power and authority from him. Otherwise the words have a proper sense, but nothing to our author's purpose. It is his power over them, and not theirs over the consciences of their subjects, that is intended in the words. Of no more use, in this controversy, is the direction of the apostle, that we "should pray for kings, that under them we may lead a quiet and peaceable life;" for no more is intended therein but that, under their peaceable and righteous administration of human affairs, we may live in that godliness and honesty which is required of us. Wherefore, then, are these weak attempts made to confirm and prove what is not? Those, or the most of them, whom our author in this discourse treats with so much severity, do plead that it is the duty of all supreme magistrates to find out, receive, embrace, and promote, the truths of the gospel, with the worship of God appointed therein; confirming, protecting, and defending them, and those that embrace them, by their power and authority: and in the discharge of this duty they are to use the liberty of their own judgments, informed by the ways that God hath appointed, independently of the dictates and determinations of any other persons whatever.   They affirm, also, that to this end they are intrusted with supreme power over all persons in their respective dominions; who on no pretence can be exempted from the exercise of that power, as occasion, in their judgments, shall require it to be exercised: as also, that all causes wherein the profession of religion in their dominions is concerned, which are determinable in "foro civili," by coercive umpirage or authority, are subject unto their cognizance and power.   The sovereign power over the consciences of men, to institute, appoint, and prescribe religion and the worship of God, they affirm to belong unto Him alone who is the "author and finisher of our faith, who is the head over all things to the church."   The administration of things merely spiritual in the worship of God is, they judge, derived immediately from him to the ministers and administrators of the gospel, possessed of their offices by his command and according to his institution.   As to the external practice of religion, and religious worship as such, it is, they say, in the power of the magistrate to regulate all the outward civil concernments of it, with reference unto the preservation of public peace and tranquillity, and the prosperity of his subjects; and herein also they judge that such respect is to be had to the consciences of men as the Scripture, the nature of the thing itself, and the right of the Lord Christ to introduce his spiritual kingdom into all nations, do require.

That which seems to have imposed on the mind of this author is, that if the magistrate may make laws for the regulating of the outward profession of religion, so as public peace and tranquillity may be kept, added to what is his duty to do in the behalf of the truth, then he must have the power over religion and the consciences of men by him ascribed unto him; but there is no privity of interest between these things.   The laws which he makes to this purpose are to be regulated by the word of God and the good of the community over which, in the name of God, he doth preside; and whence he will take his warranty to forbid men the exercise of their consciences in the duties of spiritual worship, whilst the principles they profess are suited to the light of nature and the fundamental doctrines of the gospel, with the peace of mankind, and their practices absolutely consistent with the public welfare, I am yet to seek; and so, as far as I can yet perceive, is the author of the discourse under consideration.

It will not arise, from a parity of reason, from the power that he hath
to restrain cursed swearing and blasphemies by penal coercions; for
these things are no less against the light of nature, and no less condemned by the common suffrage of mankind (and the persons that
contract the guilt of them may be no less effectually brought to
judge and condemn themselves), than are the greatest outrages that
may be committed in and against human society. That the gospel will give no countenance hereunto he seems to acknowledge, in
his assignation of several reasons why the use of the power, and
exercise of it in the way of compulsion by penalties, pleaded for by
him, is not mentioned therein. That " Christ and his apostles behaved themselves as subjects; that he neither took nor exercised any
sovereign power; that he gave his laws to private men as such, and
not to the magistrate; that the power that then was was in bad
hands," are pleaded as excuses for the silence of the gospel in this
matter.   But, lest this should prove farther prejudicial to his present
occasion, he adds, p. 42, " The only reason why the Lord Christ
bound not the precepts of the gospel upon men's consciences by any
secular compulsories was, not because compulsion was an improper
way to put his laws in execution, for then he had never established
them with more enforcing sanctions, but only because himself was not
vested with any secular power, and so could not use those methods
of government which are proper to its jurisdiction." This in plain
English is, that if Christ had had power, he would have ordered the
gospel to have been propagated as Mohammed hath done his Alcoran;
an assertion untrue and impious, contrary to the whole spirit and
genius of the gospel and of the author of it, and the commands and
precepts of it.   And it is fondly supposed that the Lord Christ suited
all the management of the affairs of the gospel unto that state and
condition in this world wherein he emptied himself, and took upon
him the form of a servant, making himself of no reputation, that he
might be obedient unto death, the death of the cross.   He lays the
foundation of the promulgation and propagation of it in the world
in the grant of all power unto him in heaven and earth.   " All
power," saith he to his apostles, " is given unto me in heaven and
in earth. Go ye therefore, and teach all nations, baptizing them in the
name of the Father, and of the Son, and of the Holy Ghost: teaching
them to observe all things whatsoever I have commanded you," Matt.
xxviii. 18–20.   He is considered, in the dispensation of the gospel, as
he who is " head over all things to the church," the " Lord of lords,
and King of kings," whom our author acknowledgeth to be his vicegerents.   On this account the gospel, with all the worship instituted
therein and required thereby, is accompanied with a right to enter
into any of the kingdoms of the earth, and spiritually to make the

inhabitants of them subject to Jesus Christ, and so to translate them out of the power of darkness into the kingdom of the Son of God; and this right is antecedent and paramount to the right of all earthly kings and princes whatever, who have no power or authority to exclude the gospel out of their dominions, and what they exercise of that kind is done at their peril.

The "penalties that he hath annexed to the final rejection of the gospel and disobedience thereunto" are pleaded by our author to justify the magistrate's power of binding men to "the observation of his commands in religion on temporal penalties, to be by him inflicted on them." Unto that is the discourse of this chapter arrived, which was designed unto another end. I see neither the order, method, nor projection of this procedure, nor know

"Amphora cum cœpit institui, cur urceus exit."
[Altered from Hor. ad Pison. 21.]

However, the pretence itself is weak and impertinent. Man was originally made under a law and constitution of eternal bliss or woe. This state, with regard to his necessary dependence on God and respect to his utmost end, was absolutely unavoidable unto him. All possibility of attaining eternal happiness by himself he lost by sin, and became inevitably obnoxious to eternal misery and the wrath to come. In this condition the Lord Jesus Christ, the supreme Lord of the souls and consciences of men, interposeth his law of relief, redemption and salvation, the great means of man's recovery, together with the profession of the way and law hereof. He lets them know that those by whom it is refused shall perish under that wrath of God which before they were obnoxious unto, with a new aggravation of their sin and condemnation, from the contempt of the relief provided for them and tendered to them. This he applies to the souls and consciences of men, and to all the inward secret actings of them in the first place,—such as are exempted not only from the judicature of men, but from the cognizance of angels. This he doth by spiritual means, in a spiritual manner,—with regard to the subjection of the souls of men unto God, and with reference unto their bringing to him and enjoyment of him, or their being eternally rejected by him. Hence to collect and conclude that earthly princes,—who (whatever is pretended) are not the sovereign lords of the souls and consciences of men, nor do any of them, that I know of, plead themselves so to be; who cannot interpose any thing by their absolute authority that should have a necessary respect unto men's eternal condition; who have no knowledge of, no acquaintance with, nor can judge of, the principal things whereon it doth depend; from whose temporal jurisdiction and punishment the things of the gospel and the worship of God, as purely such, are by the nature of them (being spiritual and not of this world, though exercised in it, having their respect only unto eternity), and by their being taken into the sole disposal of the sovereign Lord of consciences, who hath accompanied his commands concerning them with his own promises and threatenings, plainly exempted,—should have power over the consciences of men, so to lay their commands upon them in these spiritual things as to back them with temporal, corporeal restraints and punishments, is a way of arguing that will not be confined unto any of those rules of reasoning which hitherto we have been instructed in. When the magistrate hath " an arm like God," and can " thunder with a voice like him;" when he " judgeth not after the sight of his eyes, nor reproveth after the hearing of his ears;" when he can "smite the earth with the rod of his mouth," and " slay the wicked with the breath of his lips;" when he is constituted a judge of the faith, repentance, and obedience of men, and of their efficacy in their tendency unto the pleasing of God here and the enjoyment of him hereafter; when spiritual things, in order to their eternal issues and effects, are made subject unto him;—in brief, when he is Christ let him act as Christ, or rather most unlike him, and guide the consciences of men by rods, axes, and halters (whereunto alone his power can reach), who in the meantime have an express command from the Lord Christ himself not to have their consciences influenced in the least by the consideration of these things.

Of the like complexion is the ensuing discourse, wherein our author, p. 43, having spoken contemptuously of the spiritual institutions of the gospel, as altogether " insufficient for the accomplishment of the ends whereunto they are designed,"—forgetting that they respect only the consciences of men, and are His institutions who is the Lord of their consciences, and who will give them power and efficacy to attain their ends, when administered in his name and according to his mind, and that because they are his,—would prove the necessity of temporal coercions and penalties in things spiritual, from the extraordinary effects of excommunication in the primitive times, in the " vexation and punishment of persons excommunicate, by the devil." This work the devil now ceasing to attend unto, he would have the magistrate to take upon him to supply his place and office, by punishments of his own appointment and infliction, and so at last, to be sure of giving him full measure, he hath ascribed two extremes unto him about religion,—namely, to act the part of God and the devil! But as this inference is built upon a very uncertain conjecture,—namely, that upon the giving up of persons to Satan in excommunication, there did any visible or corporeal vexation of them by his power ensue, or any other effects but what may yet be justly expected from an influence of his terror on the minds of men who are duly and regularly cast out of the visible kingdom of Christ by that censure,—and whereas, if there be any truth in it, it was confined unto the days of the apostles, and is to be reckoned amongst the miraculous operations granted to them for the first confirmation of the gospel, and the continuance of it all the time the church wanted the assistance of the civil magistrate is most unduly pretended, without any colour of proof or instance beyond such as may be evidenced to continue at this day;—supposing it to be true, the inference made from it, as to its consequence, on this concession, is exceeding weak and feeble; for the argument here amounteth to no more but this: God was pleased, in the days of the apostles, to confirm their spiritual censures against stubborn sinners, apostates, blasphemers, and such like heinous offenders, with extraordinary spiritual punishments (so in their own nature, or in the manner or way of their infliction); therefore, the civil magistrate hath power to appoint things to be observed in the worship of God, and forbid other things which the light and consciences of men, directed by the word of God, require the observation of, upon ordinary, standing, corporeal penalties, to be inflicted on the outward man, " quod erat demonstrandum."

To wind up this debate, I shall commit the umpirage of it to the church of England, and receive her determination in the words of one who may be supposed to know her sense and judgment as well as any one who lived in his days or since; and this is Dr Bilson, bishop of Winchester, a learned man, skilled in the laws of the land, and a great adversary unto all that dissented from church constitutions. This man, therefore, treating by way of dialogue, in answer to the Jesuits' Apology and Defence, in the third part, p. 293, thus introduceth Theophilus, a protestant divine, arguing with Philander, a Jesuit, about these matters:—" *Theoph.* As for the ' supreme head of the church,' it is certain that title was first transferred from the pope to King Henry the Eighth by the bishops of your side, not of ours. And though the pastors in King Edward's time might not well dislike, much less dissuade, the style of the crown, by reason the king was under years, and so remained until he died; yet as soon as it pleased God to place her majesty in her father's throne, the nobles and preachers, perceiving the words ' head of the church' (which is Christ's proper and peculiar honour) to be offensive unto many that had vehemently repelled the same in the pope, besought her highness the meaning of that word which her father had used might be expressed in some plainer, apter terms, and so was the prince called supreme governor of the realm,—that is, ruler and bearer of the sword, with lawful authority to command and punish, answerable to the word of God, in all spiritual or ecclesiastical things or causes, as well as in temporal, and no foreign prince or prelate to have any jurisdiction, superiority, pre-eminence, or authority to establish, prohibit, correct and chastise, with public laws or temporal pains, any crimes or causes ecclesiastical or spiritual within her realm. *Philand.* Calvin saith this is sacrilege and blasphemy. Look you, therefore, with what consciences you take that oath which your own master so mightily detesteth. *Theoph.* Nay, look you with what faces you allege Calvin, who maketh that style to be sacrilegious and blasphemous as well in the pope as in the prince; reason, therefore, you receive or refuse his judgment in both. If it derogate from Christ in the prince, so it doth in the pope. Yet we grant the sense of the word 'supreme,' as Calvin perceived it by Stephen Gardiner's answer and behaviour, is very blasphemous and injurious to Christ and his word, whether it be prince or pope that so shall use it." What this sense is he declares in the words of Calvin, which are as followeth, in his translation of them: " That juggler, which after was chancellor, I mean the bishop of Winchester, when he was at Rentzburge, neither would stand to reason the matter nor greatly cared for any testimonies of the Scripture, but said it was at the king's discretion to abrogate that which was in use and appoint new. He said the king might forbid priests' marriage; the king might bar the people from the cup in the Lord's supper; the king might determine this or that in his kingdom: and why? forsooth, the king had *supreme* power. This sacrilege hath taken hold on us, whilst princes think they cannot reign except they abolish all the authority of the church, and be themselves supreme judges, as well in doctrine as in all spiritual regimen." To which he subjoins: " This was the sense which Calvin affirmed to be sacrilegious and blasphemous, for princes to profess themselves to be supreme judges of doctrine and discipline; and, indeed, it is the blasphemy which all godly hearts reject and abomine in the bishop of Rome. Neither did King Henry take any such thing on him, for aught that we can learn. But this was Gardiner's stratagem to convey the reproach and shame of the Six Articles[1] from himself and his fellows, that were the authors of them, and to cast it on the king's supreme power. Had Calvin been told that ' supreme ' was first received to declare the prince to be superior to the prelates (which exempted themselves from the king's authority by their church liberties and immunities) as well as to the laymen of this realm, and not to be subject to the pope, the word would never have offended him." Thus far he; and if these controversies be any farther disputed, it is probable the next defence of what is here

---

[1] These Articles are well known by the name of the "Bloody Statute," 31 Henry VIII., cap. 14, entitled, "An Act for the Abolishing Diversity of Opinions in certain Articles concerning Christian Religion." They affirmed transubstantiation, communion in one kind, clerical celibacy, vows of chastity, private masses, and auricular confession.—ED.

pleaded will be in the express words of the principal prelates of this realm since the Reformation, until their authority be peremptorily rejected.

Upon my first design to take a brief survey of this discourse, I had not the least intention to undertake the examination of any particular assertions or reasonings that might fall under controversy, but merely to examine the general principles whereon it doth proceed. But passing through these things "currente calamo," I find myself engaged beyond my thoughts and resolutions; I shall therefore here put an end to the consideration of this chapter, although I see sundry things as yet remaining in it that might immediately be discussed with ease and advantage, as shall be manifest if we are called again to a review of them. I have neither desire nor design "serram reciprocare," or to engage in any controversial discourses with this author; and I presume himself will not take it amiss that I do at present examine those principles whose novelty justifies a disquisition into them, and whose tendency, as applied by him, is pernicious and destructive to so many quiet and peaceable persons who dissent from him. And yet I will not deny but that I have that valuation and esteem for that sparkling of wit, eloquence, and sundry other abilities of mind which appear in his writing, that if he would lay aside the manner of his treating those from whom he dissents, with revilings, contemptuous reproaches, personal reflections, sarcasms, and satirical expressions, and would candidly and perspicuously state any matter in difference, I should think that what he hath to offer may deserve the consideration of them who have leisure for such a purpose. If he be otherwise minded, and resolved to proceed in the way and after the manner here engaged in, as I shall in the close of this discourse absolutely give him my "salve æternumque vale," so I hope he will never meet with any one who shall be willing to deal with him at his own weapons.

A SURVEY OF THE SECOND CHAPTER.

[Alleged power of the magistrate over the conscience in matters of morality refuted—Distinction between moral virtue and grace—Meaning of the terms—Four propositions of Parker on grace and virtue considered—Agreement between the views of Parker and those of the Socinian Seidelius—Exceptions taken to these views—Power of the magistrate in reference to moral duties—The true ground of obligation to these duties.]

THE "summary" of this chapter must needs give the reader a great expectation, and the chapter itself no less of satisfaction, if what is in the one briefly proposed be in the other as firmly estab-

lished: for, amongst other things, a scheme of religion is promised,
reducing all its branches either to "moral virtues" or "instruments
of morality;"—which being spoken of Christian religion, is, as far as
I know, an undertaking new and peculiar unto this author, in whose
management all that read him must needs weigh and consider how
dexterously he hath acquitted himself; for as all men grant that
morality hath a great place in religion, so, that all religion is nothing
but morality many are now to learn. "The villany of those men's
religion that are wont to distinguish between grace and virtue" (that
is, moral virtue) is nextly traduced and inveighed against. I had
rather, I confess, that he had affixed the term of "villany" to the men
themselves whom he intended to reflect on than to their religion,
because, as yet, it seems to me that it will fall on Christianity, and
no other real or pretended religion that is or ever was in the world;
for if the professors of it have, in all ages, according to its avowed
principles, never before contradicted, made a distinction between
moral virtues (since these terms were known in the church) and
evangelical graces, if they do so at this day, what religion else can be
here branded with this infamous and horrible reproach I know not.
A farther inquiry into the chapter itself may possibly give us farther
satisfaction; wherein we shall deal as impartially as we are able, with
a diligent watchfulness against all prejudicate affections, that we may
discover what there is of sense and truth in the discourse, being ready
to receive whatever shall be manifested to have an interest in them.
The civil magistrate, we are also here informed, amongst many other
things that he may do, "may command any thing in the worship of
God that doth not tend to debauch men's practices or to disgrace
the Deity;" and that "all subordinate duties, both of morality and
religious worship" (such as elsewhere we are told the sacraments are),
"are equally subject to the determination of human authority."
These things, and sundry others represented in this summary, being
new, yea some of them, as far as I know, unheard of amongst Christians until within a few years last past, any reader may justify himself in the expectation of full and demonstrative arguments to be
produced in their proof and confirmation. What the issue will be,
some discovery may be made by the ensuing inquiry, as was said,
into the body of the chapter itself.

The design of this chapter, in general, is to confirm the power of
the magistrate over religion and the consciences of men, ascribed
unto him in the former, and to add unto it some enlargements not
therein insisted on. The argument used to this purpose is taken
from "the power of the magistrate over the consciences of men in
matters of morality," or with respect unto moral virtue; whence it
is supposed the conclusion is so evident unto his "power over their

consciences in matters of religious worship," that it strikes our author with wonder and amazement that it should not be received and acknowledged. Wherefore, to further the conviction of all men in this matter, he proceeds to discourse of moral virtue, of grace, and of religious worship, with his wonted reflections upon and reproaches of the Nonconformists for their ignorance about and villanous misrepresentation of these things; which seem more to be aimed at than the argument itself.

I must here wish again that our author had more perspicuously stated the things which he proposeth to debate for the subject of his disputation; but I find an excess of art is as troublesome sometimes as the greatest defect therein. From thence I presume it is that things are so handled in this discourse that an ordinary man can seldom discern satisfactorily what it is that directly and determinately he doth intend beyond reviling of Nonconformists; for in this proposition,—which is the best and most intelligible that I can reduce the present discourse unto,—" The supreme civil magistrate hath power over the consciences of men in morality, or with respect unto moral virtue," excepting only the subject of it, there is not one term in it that may not have various significations, and those such as have countenance given unto them in the ensuing disputation itself. But " contenti sumus hoc Catone," and make the best we can of what lies before us.

I do suppose that in the *medium* made use of in this argument, there is, or I am sure there may be, a controversy of much more importance than that principally under consideration. It, therefore, shall be stated and cleared in the first place; and then the concernment of the argument itself, in what is discoursed thereupon, shall be manifested. It is about *moral virtue* and *grace*, their coincidence or distinction, that we are in the first place to inquire; for without a due stating of the conception of these things, nothing of this argument nor what belongs unto it can be rightly understood. We shall, therefore, be necessitated to premise a brief explanation of these terms themselves, to remove as far as may be all ambiguity from our discourse.

First, then, the very name of *virtue*, in the sense wherein it is commonly used and received, comes from the schools of philosophy, and not from the Scripture. In the Old Testament we have " uprightness, integrity, righteousness, doing good and eschewing evil, fearing, trusting, obeying, believing in God, holiness," and the like; but the name of " virtue " doth not occur therein. It is true, we have translated אֵשֶׁת חַיִל, " a virtuous woman," and once or twice the same word " virtuously," Ruth iii. 11, Prov. xii. 4, xxxi. 10, 29; but that word signifies, as so used, " strenuous, industrious, diligent," and

hath no such signification as that we now express by "virtue." Nor
is it anywhere rendered ἀρετή by the LXX., although it may have
some respect unto it, as ἀρετή may be derived from ἄρης, and peculiarly denote the exercise of industrious strength, such as men use in
battle; for חַיִל is "vis, robur, potentia," or "exercitus" also. But
in the common acceptation of it, and as it is used by philosophers,
there is no word in the Hebrew or Syriac properly to express it.
The rabbins do it by מִדָּה, which signifies properly "a measure;"
for, studying the philosophy of Aristotle, and translating his Ethics
into Hebrew, which was done by Rabbi Meir, and finding his "vir-.
tue" placed in mediocrity, they applied מִדָּה to express it: so they call
Aristotle's Ethics סֵפֶר הַמִּדּוֹת, "The Book of Measures,"—that is, of
virtues; and מִדּוֹת טוֹבוֹת are "boni mores." Such a stranger is this
very word unto the Old Testament. In the New Testament ἀρετή
occurs four times; but it should not seem anywhere to be taken in
the sense now generally admitted. In some of the places it rather
denotes the excellency and praises that do attend virtue, than virtue
itself. So we render ἀρετάς "praises," 1 Pet. ii. 9, as the Syriac
doth also תֶּשְׁבּוּחְתֵּה, "praises;" and the same translation, Phil. iv. 8,
renders εἴ τις ἀρετή, "if there be any virtue," by עֲבָדָא דְשׁוּבְחָא,
"works glorious" or "praiseworthy," 1 Pet. ii. 19. It is a peculiar
gracious disposition and operation of mind, distinguished from "faith,
temperance, patience, brotherly-kindness, godliness, charity," etc.,
and so cannot have the common sense of the word there put upon it.

The word "moral" is yet far more exotic to the church and Scripture. We are beholden for it, if there be any advantage in its use,
merely to the schools of the philosophers, especially of Aristotle.
His doctrine περὶ ἠθῶν, commonly called his Ἠθικά or "Moralia," his
Morals, hath begotten this name for our use. The whole is expressed,
in Isocrates to Demonicus, by ἡ τῶν τρόπων ἀρετή, "the virtue of
manners." If, then, the signification of the words be respected as
usually taken, it is virtue in men's manners that is intended. The
schoolmen brought this expression with all its concerns, as they did
the rest of Aristotle's philosophy, into the church and divinity; and
I cannot but think it had been well if they had never done it, as all
will grant they might·have omitted some other things without the
least disadvantage to learning or religion. However, this expression
of "moral virtue" having absolutely possessed itself of the fancies
and discourses of all, and, it may be, of the understanding of some,
though with very little satisfaction when all things are considered, I
shall not endeavour to dispossess it or eliminate it from the confines
of Christian theology. Only, I am sure had we been left unto the
Scripture expressions of "repentance toward God, and faith toward
our Lord Jesus Christ, of the fear of God, of holiness, righteousness,

living unto God, walking with God, and before him," we might have been free from many vain, wordy perplexities, and the whole wrangle of this chapter in particular had been utterly prevented; for let but the Scripture express what it is to be religious, and there will be no contesting about the difference or no difference between grace and moral virtue.   It is said that " some judge those who have moral virtue to want grace, not to be gracious;" but say that men are " born of God, and do not commit sin," that they " walk before God and are upright," that they " cleave unto God with full purpose of heart," that they are " sanctified in Christ Jesus," and the like, and no man will say that they have not grace, or are not gracious, if they receive your testimony.   But having, as was said, made its entrance amongst us, we must deal with it as well as we can, and satisfy ourselves about its common acceptation and use.

Generally, moral virtues are esteemed to be the duties of the *second table:* for although those who handle these matters more accurately do not so straiten or confine them, yet it is certain that in vulgar and common acceptation (which strikes no small stroke in the regulating of the conceptions of the wisest men about the signification of words) nothing else is intended by "moral virtues," or "duties of morality," but the observation of the precepts of the second table; nor is any thing else designed by those divines who, in their writings, so frequently declare that it is not *morality alone* that will render men acceptable to God.   Others do extend these things farther, and fix the denomination of moral firstly upon the law or rule of all those habits of the mind and its operations which afterward thence they call moral.   Now, this moral law is nothing but the law of nature, or the law of our creation, which the apostle affirms to lie equally obligatory on all men, even all the Gentiles themselves, Rom. ii. 14, 15, and whereof the decalogue is summarily expressive. This moral law is, therefore, the law written in the hearts of all men by nature; which is resolved partly into the nature of God himself, which cannot but require most of the things of it from rational creatures, partly into that state and condition of the nature of things and their mutual relations wherein God was pleased to create and set them.   These things might be easily instanced and exemplified, but that we must not too much divert from our present occasion. And herein lies the largest sense and acceptation of the law moral, and consequently of moral virtues, which have their form and being from their relation and conformity thereunto.   Let it be, then, that moral virtues consist in the universal observance of the requisites and precepts of the law of our creation, and dependence on God thereby.   And this description, as we shall see, for the substance of it, is allowed by our author.

Now, these virtues, or this conformity of our minds and actions unto the law of our creation, may be, in the light and reason of Christian religion, considered two ways:—First, as with respect unto the substance or essence of the duties themselves, they may be performed by men in their own strength, under the conduct of their own reason, without any special assistance from the Spirit or sanctifying grace of Christ. In this sense they still bear the name of "virtues," and, for the substance of them, deserve so to do. Good they are in themselves, useful to mankind, and seldom, in the providence of God, go without their reward in this world. I grant, I say, that they may be obtained and acted without special assistance of grace evangelical, though the wiser heathens acknowledged something divine in the communication of them to men. Papinius speaks to that purpose:—

> " Diva Jovis solio juxta comes; unde per orbem
> Rara dari, terrisque solet contingere virtus.
> Seu Pater Omnipotens tribuit, sive ipsa capaces
> Elegit penetrare viros."——

But old Homer put it absolutely in the will of his god:—

> Ζεὺς δ᾽ ἀρετὴν ἄνδρεσσιν ὀφέλλει τε μινύθει τε
> Ὅππως κεν ἐθέλῃσι.—[Il. Υ., 242.]

Thus we grant moral virtue to have been in the heathen of old, for this is that alone whereby they were distinguished amongst themselves: and he that would exclude them all from any interest in moral virtue takes away all difference between Cato and Nero, Aristides and Tiberius, Titus and Domitian, and overthrows all natural difference between good and evil; which, besides other abominations that it would plentifully spawn in the world, would inevitably destroy all human society. But now, these moral virtues, thus performed, whatever our author thinks, are distinct from grace, may be without it, and in their present description, which is not imaginary, but real, are supposed so to be; and, if he please, he may exercise himself in the longsome disputes of Bellarmine, Gregory de Valentia, and others to this purpose innumerable,—not to mention reformed divines, lest they should be scornfully rejected as systematical. And this is enough, I am sure, to free their religion from villany who make a distinction between moral virtue and grace; and if our author is otherwise minded, and doth believe that there is grace evangelical wherever there is moral virtue, or that moral virtues may be so obtained and exercised without the special assistance of grace as to become a part of our religion and accepted with God, and will maintain his opinion in writing, I will promise him, if I live, to return him an answer, on one only condition, which is, that he will first answer what Augustine hath written against the Pelagians on this subject.

Again; these moral virtues, this observance of the precepts of the law of our creation, in a consonancy whereunto originally the image of God in us did consist, may now under the gospel be considered, as men are principled, assisted, and enabled to and in their performance by the grace of God, and as they are directed unto the especial end of living unto him in and by Jesus Christ. What is particularly required hereunto shall be afterward declared. Now, in this sense no man living ever distinguished between grace and virtue any otherwise than the cause and the effect are to be, or may be, distinguished; much less was any person ever so brutish as to fancy an inconsistency between them: for, take grace in one sense, and it is the efficient cause of this virtue, or of these virtues, which are the effects of it; and in another, they are all graces themselves, for that which is wrought in us by grace is grace, as that which is born of the Spirit is spirit.

To this purpose something may be spoken concerning *grace* also, the other term, whose ambiguity renders the discourse under consideration somewhat intricate and perplexed. Now, as the former term of "moral virtue" owes its original to the schools of philosophy, and its use was borrowed from them, so this of " grace " is purely scriptural and *evangelical*. The world knows nothing of it but what is declared in the word of God, especially in the gospel; for " the law was given by Moses, but grace and truth came by Jesus Christ." All the books of the ancient philosophers will not give us the least light into that notion of grace which the Scripture declares unto us. As, then, we allowed the sense of the former term, given unto it by its first coiners and users, so we cannot but think it equal that men be precisely tied up in their conceptions about grace unto what is delivered in the Scripture concerning it, as having no other rule either to frame them or judge of them; and this we shall attend unto. Not that I here design to treat of the nature of gospel grace in general; but whereas all the divines that ever I have read on these things, whether ancient or modern (and I have not troubled myself to consider whether they were systematical ones only, or otherwise qualified), allow some distinctions of this term to be necessary for the right understanding of those passages of Scripture wherein it is made use of, I shall mention that or those only which are so unto the right apprehension of what is at present under debate.

First, therefore, Grace in the Scripture is taken for the *free grace or favour of God towards sinners by Jesus Christ.* By this he freely pardoneth them their sins, justifieth and accepteth them, or makes them " accepted in the Beloved." This, certainly, is distinct from moral virtue. Secondly, It is taken for *the effectual working of the Spirit of God* in and upon the minds and souls of believers, thereby quickening them when they were "dead in trespasses and sins," regenerating of them, creating a new heart in them, implanting his image upon them. Neither, I presume, will this be called moral virtue. Thirdly, For the *actual supplies of assistance and ability given to believers*, so to enable them unto every duty in particular which in the gospel is required of them; for he "worketh in them both to will and to do of his own good pleasure." As yet the former distinction will appear necessary. Fourthly, For *the effects wrought and produced by this operation of God* and his grace in the hearts and minds of them that believe; which are either habitual, in the spiritual disposition of their minds, or actual, in their operation: all which are called "grace." It may be our author will be apt to think that I "cant," "use phrases," or "fulsome metaphors." But besides that I can confirm these distinctions, and the necessity of them, and the words wherein they are expressed, from the Scriptures and ancient fathers, I can give them him, for the substance of them, out of very learned divines,—whether systematical or no I know not; but this I know, they were not long since *bishops of the church of England.*

We are now, in the next place, to inquire into the mind of our author in these things; for, from his apprehensions about them, he frames a mighty difference between himself and those whom he opposeth, and from thence takes occasion and advantage afresh to revile and reproach them.

First, therefore, He declares his judgment, that the moral virtues which he treats of do "consist of men's observance of the law of nature, of the dictates of reason, and precepts thereof." Secondly, That "the substance, yea, the whole of religion, consists in these virtues or duties, so that by the observation of them men may attain everlasting happiness." Thirdly, That "there is no actual concurrence of present grace enabling men to perform these duties, or to exercise these virtues, but they are called grace on another account." Fourthly, That "his adversaries are so far from making virtue and grace to be the same, that they make them inconsistent."

And these things shall we take into a brief examination, according as indeed they do deserve.

The first of them he plainly and more than once affirms, nor shall I contend with him about it. So he speaks, p. 68: "The practice of virtue consists in living suitably to the dictates of reason and nature; and this is the substance and main design of all the laws of religion, to oblige mankind to behave themselves in all their actions as becomes creatures endowed with reason and understanding, and, in ways suitable to rational beings, to prepare and qualify themselves for the state of glory and immortality." This is a plain description both of the rule of moral virtues and of the nature of them.   The law of reason and nature is the rule; and their own nature, as acting or acted, consists in a suitableness unto rational beings acting to prepare themselves for the state of immortality and glory,—the first end of all virtue, no doubt.   We need not, therefore, make any farther inquiry into this matter, wherein we are agreed.

Secondly, That the *substance*, yea, the *whole* of religion, consists in these moral virtues he fully also declares, p. 69: " Moral virtue having the strongest and most necessary influence upon the end of all religion, namely, man's happiness, it is not only its most material and useful part, but the ultimate end of all its other duties" (though I know not how the practice of virtue in this life can be the ultimate end of other duties); " and all true religion can consist in nothing else but either the practice of virtue itself or the use of those means and instruments that contribute unto it."   So also, p. 70: " All duties of devotion, excepting only our returns of gratitude, are not essential parts of religion, but are only in order to it, as they tend to the practice of virtue and moral goodness, and their goodness is derived upon them from the moral virtues to which they contribute; and in the same proportion they are conducive to the ends of virtue, they are to be valued among the ministers of religion." So, then, the whole duty of man consists in being virtuous, and all that is enjoined beside is in order thereunto.   Hence we are told elsewhere that " outward worship is no part of religion."   Again, p. 76: " All religion must of necessity be resolved into enthusiasm or morality; the former is mere imposture, and therefore all that is true must be reduced to the latter."   But we need not insist on particulars, seeing he promoteth this to confirmation by the best of demonstrations,—that is, an induction of all particulars, which he calls "a scheme of religion;" wherein, yet, if any thing necessary be left out or omitted, this best of demonstrations is quickly turned into one of the worst of sophisms.   Therefore we have here, no doubt, a just and full representation of all that belongs to Christian religion; and it is as follows, p. 69: " The whole duty of man refers either to his Creator, or his neighbour, or himself.   All that concerns the two last is confessedly of a moral nature, and all that concerns the first consists either in praising of God or praying to him.   The former is a branch of the virtue of gratitude, and is nothing but a thankful and humble temper of mind, arising from a sense of God's greatness in himself and his goodness to us: so that this part of devotion issues from the same virtuous quality,—that is, the principle of all other resentments and expressions of gratitude; only, those acts of it that are terminated on God as their object are styled "religious;"—and therefore gratitude and devotion are not diverse things, but only differing names of the same thing, devotion being nothing else but the virtue of gratitude towards God. The latter, namely, prayer, is either put up in our own or other men's behalf. If for others, it is an act of that virtue we call kindness or charity; if for ourselves, the things we pray for, unless they be the comforts and enjoyments of this life, are some or other virtuous qualities;—and therefore the proper and direct use of prayer is, to be instrumental to the virtues of morality." It is of Christian religion that this author treats, as is manifest from his ensuing discourse, and the reason he gives why moral virtues are styled " graces." Now, I must needs say, that I look on this of our author as the rudest, most imperfect, and weakest scheme of Christian religion that ever yet I saw; so far from comprising an induction of all particulars belonging to it, that there is nothing in it that is constitutive of Christian religion, as such, at all. I wish he had given us a summary of the " credenda" of it, as he hath done of its " agenda," that we might have had a prospect of the body of his divinity. The ten commandments would, in my mind, have done twice as well on this present occasion, with the addition of the explication of them given us in the church catechism; but I am afraid that very catechism may, ere long, be esteemed fanatical also. One, I confess, I have read of before who was of this opinion, that all religion consisted in morality alone; but withal he was so ingenuous as to follow the conduct of his judgment in this matter unto a full renunciation of the gospel, which is certainly inconsistent with it. This was one Martin Seidelius, a Silesian, who gave the ensuing account of his faith unto Faustus Socinus and his society at Cracovia:—

" Cæterum ut sciatis cujus sim religionis, quamvis id scripto meo quod habetis, ostenderim, tamen hic breviter repetam. Et primum quidem doctrina de Messia, seu Rege illo promisso, ad meam religionem nihil pertinet; nam Rex ille tantum Judæis promissus erat, sicut et bona illa Canaan. Sic etiam circumcisio, sacrificia, et reliquæ ceremoniæ Mosis ad me non pertinent, sed tantum populo Judaico promissa, data, et mandata sunt. Neque ista fuerunt cultus Dei apud Judæos, sed inserviebant cultui divino, et ad cultum deducebant Judæos. Verus autem cultus Dei quem meam religionem appello est decalogus, qui est æterna Dei voluntas; qui decalogus ideo ad me pertinet, quia etiam mihi a Deo datus est, non quidem per vocem sonantem de cœlo sicut populo Judaico, at per creationem insita est menti meæ. Quia autem insitus decalogus, per corruptionem naturæ humanæ et pravis consuetudinibus, aliquâ ex parte obscuratus est, ideo ad illustrandum eum adhibeo vocalem decalogum, qui vocalis decalogus ideo etiam ad me, ad omnes populos pertinet, quia cum insito nobis decalogo consentit, imo idem ille decalogus est. Hæc est mea sententia de Messiâ seu Rege illo promisso, et hæc est mea religio, quam coram vobis ingenuè profiteor. Martin Seidelius Olavensis Silesius."

That is, "But that you may know of what religion I am, although it is expressed in that writing which you have already, yet I will here briefly repeat it. And, first of all, the doctrine of the Messiah or King that was promised doth not belong to my religion; for that King was promised to the Jews only, as was the good land of Canaan. So in like manner circumcision, sacrifices, and the rest of the ceremonies of Moses, belong not to me, but were promised, given, and granted unto the people of the Jews alone. Neither were they the worship of God among the Jews, but were only subservient unto divine worship, and led the Jews unto it" (the same opinion is maintained by our author concerning all exterior worship). "But the true worship, which I call my religion, is the decalogue; which is the eternal and immutable will of God" (and here also he hath the consent and concurrence of our author): "which decalogue doth therefore belong unto me, because it is given by God to me also; not, indeed, by a voice sounding from heaven, as he gave it to the people of the Jews, but it is implanted in my mind by nature. But because this implanted decalogue, by reason of the corruption of human nature and through depraved customs, is in some measure obscured, for the illustration of it I make use of the vocal decalogue; which therefore also belongs unto me and all people, because it consenteth with the decalogue written in our hearts, yea, is the same law with it. This is my opinion concerning the Messiah or the promised King, and this is my religion, which I freely acknowledge before you." So he. This is plain dealing. He saw clearly that if all religion and the worship of God consisted in *morality only*, there was neither need nor use of Christ nor the gospel; and accordingly, having no outward advantage by them, he discarded them. But setting aside his bold renunciation of Christ as promised, I see not any material difference between the religion of this man and that now contended for. The poor deluded souls among ourselves, who, leaving the Scripture, pretend that they are guided by the light within them, are, upon the matter, of the same religion: for that light being nothing but the dictates of reason and a natural conscience, it extends not itself beyond morality; which some of them understanding, we know what thoughts and apprehensions they have had of Christ and his gospel, and the worship of God instituted therein; for hence it is (and not as our author pretends, with a strange incogitancy concerning them and the Gnostics, that they assert the Scripture to be the only rule of religious worship) that they are fallen into these fond imaginations. And these are the effects which this principle doth naturally lead unto. I confess, then, that I do not agree with our author in and about this scheme of Christian religion; which I shall, therefore, first briefly put in my exceptions unto, and then offer him another in lieu of it.

First, then, This scheme seems to represent religion unto us as suited to the state of innocency, and that very imperfectly also; for it is composed to answer the former assertion of confining religion to moral virtues, which are granted to consist in our conformity unto and expression of the dictates of reason and the law of nature. Again, the "whole duty of man" is said to refer "either to his Creator, or his neighbour, or himself." Had it been said to God absolutely, another interpretation might have been put upon the words; but being restrained unto him as our Creator, all duties referring to our Redeemer are excluded, or not included, which certainly have some place in Christian religion. Our obedience therein is the " obedience of faith," and must answer the special objects of it. And we are taught in the church catechism to believe in God the Father, who made us and all the world; and in God the Son, who redeemed us and all mankind; and in God the Holy Ghost, who sanctifies us and all the elect people of God. Now, these distinct acts of faith have distinct acts of obedience attending them; whereas none here are admitted, or at least required, but those which fall under the first head. It is also very imperfect as a description of natural religion, or the duties of the law of nature: for the principal duties of it, such as fear, love, trust, affiance of and in God, are wholly omitted, nor will they be reduced unto either of the heads which all religion is here distributed into; for gratitude unto God hath respect formally and directly to the benefits we ourselves are made partakers of; but these duties are eternally necessary on the consideration of the nature of God himself, antecedent unto the consideration of his communicating of himself unto us by his benefits. Prayer proceeds from them, and it is an odd method, to reduce the cause under the head of its effect; and prayer itself is made at length not to be so much a moral virtue as somewhat instrumental to the virtues of morality.

Secondly, I cannot think we have here a complete representation of Christian religion, nor an induction of all its particulars, because we have neither supposition nor assertion of sin, or a Redeemer, or any duty with respect unto them. Gratitude and prayer, I confess, are two heads whereunto sundry duties of natural religion, without respect unto these things, may be reduced; but since the fall of Adam, there was never any religion in the world accepted with God that was not built and founded on the supposition of them, and whose principal duties towards God did not respect them. To prescribe now unto us a religion, as it respects God, without those duties which arise from the consideration of sin and a Redeemer, is to persuade us to throw away our Bibles. Sin, and the condition of all men on the account thereof; what God requires of them with reference thereunto; the way that God hath found out, proposed, and requires of us to make use of, that we may be delivered from that condition; with the duties necessary to that end,—do even constitute and make up that religion which the Scripture teacheth us, and which, as it summarily expresseth itself, consists in " repentance toward God and faith toward our Lord Jesus Christ," neither of which, nor scarce any thing that belongs unto them, appears in this scheme: so that,—

Thirdly, The most important duties of Christian religion are here not only omitted but excluded. Where shall we find any place here to introduce repentance, and, as belonging thereunto, conviction of sin, humiliation, godly sorrow, conversion itself to God? For my part, I will never be of that religion where these duties towards God have no place. Faith in our Lord Jesus Christ, with all that is necessary to it, preparatory for it, included in it, and consequential on it, are in like manner cast out of the verge of religious duties here schematized. An endeavour to flee from the wrath to come, to receive Jesus Christ, to accept of the atonement, to seek after the forgiveness of sins by him (that we may cant a little), and to give up our souls in universal obedience to all his commands, belong also to the duties of that religion towards God which the Scripture prescribeth unto us; but here they appear not in the least intimation of them. No more do the duties which, though generally included in the law of loving God above all, yet are prescribed and determined in the gospel alone; such are self-denial, readiness to take up the cross, and the like. Besides, all the duties wherein our Christian conflict against our spiritual adversaries doth consist, and, in especial, the whole of our duty towards God in the mortification of sin, can be of no consideration, there where no supposition of sin is made or allowed.

But there would be no end, if all exceptions of this nature, that readily offer themselves, might here have admittance. If this be the religion of our adversaries in these things, if this be a perfect scheme of its duties towards God and induction of all its particulars, let our author insult over and reproach them whilst he pleaseth who blame it as insufficient without grace and godliness, I would not be in the condition of them who trust their eternal concernment to mere observance of it, as knowing that there is no name under heaven given unto men whereby they may be saved, but only the name of Jesus Christ. It will be in vain pretended that it is not a description of Christian religion, but of religion as religion in general, that is here attempted; for besides that it is Christian religion, and that as used and practised by Christians, which is alone under consideration, and an introduction of religion here under any other notion would be grievously inconsistent and incoherent with the whole discourse, it is acknowledged by our author in the progress of his disputation, as was before observed, when he gives a reason why moral virtue is styled " grace," which is peculiar and appropriate to Christian religion alone.   Besides, to talk now of a religion in the world, which either hath been or may be since the fall of Adam, without respect unto sin, is to build castles in the air.   All the religion that God now requires, prescribes, accepts, that is or can be, is the religion of sinners, or of those who are such, and of them as such, though also under other qualifications.   On many accounts, therefore, this scheme of religion, or religious duties towards God, is exceedingly insufficient and imperfect.   To lay it, therefore, as a foundation whereon to stand and revile them who plead for a super-addition unto it of grace and godliness, is an undertaking from whence no great success is to be expected.

I can easily supply another *scheme of religion* in the room of this, which though it have not any such contexture of method, nor is set out with such gaudy words as those which our author hath at his disposal, yet I am confident, in the confession of all Christians, shall give a better account than what is here offered unto us both of the religion we profess and of the duties that God requires therein,—and this taken out of one epistle of St Paul, namely, that to the Romans; and I shall do it as things come to mind in the haste wherein I am writing.   He, then, gives us his scheme to this purpose: as, first, That all men sinned in Adam, came short of the glory of God, and rendered themselves liable to death and the whole curse of the law; then, that they do all, as left to themselves, accumulate their original sin and transgression with a world of actual sins and provocations of God; that against men in this condition God testifies his wrath and displeasure, both in his works and by his word.   Hence it necessarily follows that the first duty of man towards God is to be sensible of this condition, of the guilt of sin, with a fear of the wrath and judgment due to them.   Then he informs us that neither the Jews by the law, nor the Gentiles by the light of nature, could disentangle themselves from this state, or do that which is pleasing unto God, so as they might obtain forgiveness of sin and acceptance with him.   This bespeaks unto all the great duty towards God of their acknowledgment unto him of their miserable and helpless condition, with all those affections and subordinate duties wherewith it is attended.   In this state he declares that God himself, in his infinite wisdom, goodness, and grace, provided a remedy, a way of relief, on which he hath put such an impression of his glorious excellencies as may stir up the hearts of his creatures to endeavour a

return unto him from their apostasy; and that this remedy consists
in his setting forth Jesus Christ to be a propitiation through faith
in his blood, to declare his righteousness for the forgiveness of sin;
which he proposeth unto men for their receiving and acceptance.
This renders it the greatest duty of mankind towards God to believe
in the Son of God so set forth, to seek after an interest in him, or
being made partakers of him; for this is the great work that God
requires, namely, that we believe on him whom he hath sent. Again;
he declares that God justifieth them who so believe, pardoning their
sins, and imputing righteousness unto them; whereon innumerable
duties do depend, even all the obedience that Christ requires of us,
seeing in our believing in him we accept him to be our king, to rule,
govern, and conduct our souls to God. And all these are religious
duties towards God. He declares, moreover, that whereas men are
by nature dead in trespasses and sins, and stand in need of a new
spiritual life, to be born again, that they may live unto God, that
God in Jesus Christ doth, by his Spirit, quicken them and regenerate
them, and work in them a new principle of spiritual life; whence it
is their great duty towards God (in this religion of St Paul) to comply with, and to yield obedience unto, all the ways and methods that
God is pleased to use in the accomplishment of this work upon them,
the especial duties whereof are too many to be instanced in. But
he farther manifests, that notwithstanding the regeneration of men
by the Spirit and their conversion to God, there yet continues in
them a remainder of the principle of corrupted nature, which he
calls "the flesh," and "indwelling sin," that is of itself wholly
"enmity against God," and, as far [as] it abides in any, inclines the
heart and mind unto sin; which is to be watched against and opposed. And on this head he introduceth the great religious duty
towards God of our spiritual conflict against sin, and of the mortification of it; wherein those that believe are to be exercised all the
days of their lives, and wherein their principal duty towards God
doth consist, and without which they can perform no other in a due
manner. Moreover, he farther adds the great gospel privilege of the
communication of the Spirit of Christ unto believers, for their sanctification, consolation, and edification, with the duties of thankfulness towards God, joy and rejoicing in him, cheerfulness under
trials, afflictions, and persecutions, and sundry others that on that
account are required of us;—all religious duties towards God, in the
religion by him proposed unto us. Having laid these foundations,
and manifested how they all proceed from the eternal counsel and
free grace of God, in which it is our duty to admire, adore, and
praise him, he declareth how hereby, and on the account of these
things, we are bound unto all holiness, righteousness, godliness, honesty,

and usefulness in this world, in all relations and conditions whatsoever;—declaring our duties in churches, according to our especial interest in them, towards believers, and towards all men in the world
in our several relations; in obedience to magistrates and all superiors; in a word, in universal observance of the whole will and all the
commands of God. Now, whether any one will call this a "scheme"
or no, or allow it to have any thing of method in it or no, I neither
know nor care, but am persuaded that it makes a better, more
plain and intelligible, representation of the religious duties towards
God which Christian religion requires of us, unto all that suppose
this whole religion to depend on divine revelation, than that of our
author. But I find myself in a digression. The end of this discourse
was only to manifest the sentiments of our author on the second
head before laid down; which, I think, are sufficiently evinced.

The third is, That there is no actual work of present grace, either
to fit the persons of whom these duties of moral virtues are required
unto the performance of them or to work and effect them in them;
for although they are called "graces," and the "graces of the Spirit,"
in the Scripture, yet that is upon another account, as he declares himself, p. 72: "All that the Scripture intends by the 'graces of the Spirit'
are only virtuous qualities of the soul; that are therefore styled 'graces,'
because they are derived purely from God's free grace and goodness,
in that, in the first ages of Christianity, he was pleased, out of his infinite concern for its propagation, in a miraculous manner to inspire
its converts with all sorts of virtue."

"Virtuous qualities of the soul" is a very ambiguous expression.
Take these virtuous qualities for a new principle of spiritual life, consisting in the habitual disposition, inclination, and ability of mind unto
the things required of us in the will of God, or unto the acts of religious obedience, and it may express the graces of the Spirit; which are
yet far enough from being so called upon the account here mentioned.
But these virtuous qualities are to be interpreted according to the tenor
of the preceding discourses that have already passed under examination. Let now our author produce any one writer of the church of God,
from first to last, of any repute or acceptation, from the day that the
name of Christian was known in the world unto this wherein we live,
giving us this account why the fruits of the Spirit, the virtuous or gracious qualities of the minds of believers, are called "graces" that here
he gives, and I will give him my thanks publicly for his discovery; for
if this be the only reason why any thing in believers is called "grace,"
why virtues are graces,—namely, because God was pleased in the first
ages of Christianity miraculously to inspire its converts with all sorts
of virtue,—then there is no communication of grace unto any, no work
of grace in and upon any, in an ordinary way, through the ministry

of the gospel in these latter ages! The whole being and efficacy of grace, according to this notion, is to be confined unto the miraculous operations of God in gospel concernments in the first ages, whence a denomination in the Scripture is cast upon our virtues, when obtained and exercised by and in our own strength! Now, this plainly overthrows the whole gospel, and contains a Pelagianism that Pelagius himself never did nor durst avow.

Are these things, then, so indeed, that God did, from his free grace and goodness, miraculously inspire the first converts of Christianity with all sorts of virtues, but that he doth not still continue to put forth in any actually the efficacy of his grace, or make them gracious, holy, believing, obedient to himself, and to work in them all suitable actings towards himself and others? Then farewell Scripture, the covenant of grace, the intercession of Christ, yea, all the ancient fathers, councils, schoolmen, and most of the Jesuits themselves! Many have been the disputes amongst Christians about the nature of grace, the rule of its dispensation, the manner and way of its operation, its efficacy, concurrence, and co-operation in the wills of men; but that there is no dispensation of it, no operation but what was miraculous in the first converts of the gospel, was, I think, until now undiscovered. Nor can it be here pretended that the virtuous qualities of our minds and their exercise,—by which is intended all the obedience that God requireth of us, in principle and practice, that we may please him and come to the enjoyment of him,—are not said to be called graces *only* on the account mentioned; for as in respect of us they are not so termed at all, so if the term "only" be not understood, the whole discourse is impertinent and ridiculous: for those other reasons and accounts that may be taken in will render that given utterly useless unto our author's intention, and, indeed, are altogether inconsistent with it, and he hath given us no reason to suppose that he talks after such a weak and preposterous rate. This, then, is that which is here asserted: The qualities of our minds and their exercise, wherein the virtues pleaded about and affirmed to contain the whole substance of religion do consist, are not wrought in us by the grace or Spirit of God through the preaching of the gospel, but are only called " graces," as before. Now, though here be a plain contradiction to what is delivered but two pages before, namely, "that we pray for some or other virtuous qualities,"—that is, doubtless, to be wrought in us by the grace of God,—yet this present discourse is capable of no other interpretation but that given unto it. And, indeed, it seems to be the design of some men to confine all real gifts and graces of the Spirit of God to the first ages of the gospel, and the miraculous operations in it; which is to overthrow the whole gospel, the church, and the ministry of it, as to their use and efficacy, leaving men only the book of the Bible to philosophize upon, as shall be elsewhere demonstrated. Our author, indeed, tells us, that on the occasion of some men's writings in theology, "there hath been a buzz and a noise of the Spirit of God in the world." His expressions are exceedingly suited to pour contempt on what he doth not approve, not so to express what he doth himself intend. But I desire that he and others would speak plain and openly in this matter, that neither others may be deceived nor themselves have occasion to complain that they are misrepresented; a pretence whereof would probably give them a dispensation to deal very roughly, if not despitefully, with them with whom they shall have to do. Doth he, therefore, think or believe that there are not now any real gracious operations of the Spirit of God upon the hearts and minds of men in the world? that the dispensation of the Spirit is ceased, as well unto ordinary ministerial gifts, with its sanctifying, renewing, assisting grace, as unto gifts miraculous and extraordinary? that there is no work at all of God upon the hearts of sinners but that which is purely moral and persuasive by the word? that what is asserted by some concerning the efficacy of the grace of the Spirit, and concerning his gifts, is no more but "a buzz and a noise?" I wish he would explain himself directly and positively in these things, for they are of great importance; and the loose expressions which we meet with do give great offence unto some, who are apt to think that as pernicious a heresy as ever infested the church of God may be covered and cloaked by them.

But to return: in the sense that moral virtue is here taken, I dare boldly pronounce that there is *no villany in the religion of those men who distinguish between virtue and grace*,—that is, there is not in their so doing,—this being the known and avowed religion of Christianity. It is granted that wherever grace is, there is virtue; for grace will produce and effect all virtues in the soul whatever. But virtue, on the other side, may be where there is no grace; which is sufficient to confirm a distinction between them. It was so in sundry of the heathen of old; though now it be pretended that grace is nothing but an occasional denomination of virtue, not that it is the cause or principle of it. But the proofs produced by our author are exceedingly incompetent unto the end whereunto they are applied. For that place of the apostle, Gal. v. 22, 23, "The fruit of the Spirit is love, joy, peace, long-suffering, gentleness, goodness, faith, meekness, temperance," though our author should be allowed to turn "joy" into "cheerfulness," "peace" into "peaceableness," "faith" into "faithfulness," as he hath done, corruptly enough, to accommodate it to his purpose, yet it will no way reach his end, nor satisfy his intention; for doth it follow, that because the Spirit effects all these moral virtues in a new and gracious manner, and with a direction to a new and special end in believers, either that these things are nothing but mere moral virtues, not wrought in us by the grace of God (the contrary whereof is plainly asserted in calling them "fruits of the Spirit"), or that wherever there is moral virtue, though not so wrought by the Spirit, that there is grace also, because virtue and grace are the same? If these are the expositions of Scripture which we may expect from them who make such outcries against other men's perverting and corrupting of it, the matter is not like to be much mended with us, for aught I can see, upon their taking of that work into their own hands.

And indeed his quotation of this place is pretty odd. He doth not in the print express the words as he useth, and as he doth those of another scripture immediately, in a different character, as the direct words of the apostle, that no man may charge him with a false allegation of the text; yet he repeats all the words of it which he intends to use to his purpose, somewhat altering the expressions. But he hath had, I fear, some unhappiness in his explanations. By "joy" he would have "cheerfulness" intended; but what is meant by cheerfulness is much more uncertain than what is intended by joy. Mirth, it may be, in conversation is aimed at, or somewhat of that nature; but how remote this is from that spiritual joy which is recommended unto us in the Scripture, and is affirmed to be "unspeakable and full of glory," he that knows not is scarce meet to paraphrase upon St Paul's epistles. Neither is that "peace with God through our Lord Jesus Christ," which is wrought in the hearts of believers by the Holy Ghost, who "creates the fruit of the lips, peace, peace, unto them," a matter of any more affinity with a moral peaceableness of mind and affections. Our faith also in God, and our faithfulness in our duties, trusts, offices, and employments, are sufficiently distinct. So palpably must the Scripture be corrupted and wrested to be made serviceable to this presumption! He yet adds another proof to the same purpose,—if any man know distinctly what that purpose is,—namely, Titus ii. 11; where he tells us that the same apostle makes the "grace of God" to consist in gratitude towards God, temperance towards ourselves, and justice towards our neighbours. But these things are not so; for the apostle doth not say that the grace of God doth consist in these things, but that the "grace of God teacheth" us these things. Neither is the grace here intended any subjective or inherent grace, nor, to speak with our author, any "virtuous quality, or virtue;" but the love and grace of God himself in sending Jesus Christ, as declared in the gospel, as is manifest in the words and context beyond contradiction. And I cannot but wonder how our author, desirous to prove that the whole of our religion consists in moral virtues, and these only called "graces" because of the miraculous operations of God from his own grace in the first gospel converts, should endeavour to do it by these two testimonies; the first whereof expressly assigns the duties of morality, as in believers, to the operations of the Spirit; and the latter, in his judgment, makes them to proceed from grace.

Our last inquiry is into what he ascribes unto his adversaries in this matter, and how he deals with them thereupon. This, therefore, he informs us, p. 71: " 'It is not enough,' say they, 'to be completely virtuous, unless ye have grace too.' " I can scarce believe that ever he heard any one of them say so, or ever read it in any of their writings : for there is nothing that they are more positive in than that men cannot, in any sense, be *completely* virtuous unless they have grace; and so they cannot suppose them to be so who have it not. They say, indeed, that moral virtues, as before described, so far as they are attainable by, or may be exercised in the strength of, men's own wills and natural faculties, are not enough to please God and to make men accepted with him ; so that virtue as it may be without grace, and some virtues may be so for the substance of them, is not available unto salvation. And I had almost said, that he is no Christian that is of another mind. In a word, virtue is or may be without grace, in all or any of the acceptations of it before laid down. Where it is without the favour of God and the pardon of sin, where it is without the renewing of our natures and the endowment of our persons with a principle of spiritual life, where it is not wrought in us by present efficacious grace, it is not enough, nor will serve any man's turn with respect unto the everlasting concernments of his soul.

But he gives in his exceptions, p. 71: "But when," saith he, "we have set aside all manner of virtue, let them tell me what remains to be called grace, and give me any notion of it distinct from all morality, that consists in the right order and government óf our actions in all our relations, and so comprehends all our duty; and therefore if grace be not included in it, it is but a phantasm and an imaginary thing." I say, first, Where grace is, we cannot set aside virtue, because it will and doth produce and effect it in the minds of men ; but virtue may be where grace is not, in the sense so often declared. Secondly, Take moral virtue in the notion of it here received and explained by our author, and I have given sundry instances before of gracious duties that come not within the verge or compass of the scheme given us of it. Thirdly, The whole aimed at lies in this: That virtue that governs our actions in all our duties may be considered either as the duty we owe to the law of nature for the ends of it, to be performed in the strength of nature, and by the direction of it; or it may be considered as it is an especial effect of the grace of God in us, which gives it a new principle and a new end, and a new respect unto the covenant of grace wherein we walk with God;—the consideration whereof frustrates the intention of our author in this discourse.

But he renews his charge, p. 73: "So destructive of all true and real goodness is the very religion of those men that are wont to set grace at odds with virtue, and are so far from making them the same that they make them inconsistent; and though a man be exact in all the duties of moral goodness, yet if he be a graceless person (that is, void of I know not what imaginary godliness) he is but in a cleaner way to hell, and his conversion is more hopeless than the vilest and most notorious sinner's; and the morally righteous man is at a greater distance from grace than the profane; and better be lewd and debauched than live an honest and virtuous life, if you are not of the godly party,"—with much more to this purpose. For the "men that are wont to set grace at odds with virtue, and are so far from making them the same that they make them inconsistent," I wish our author would discover them, that he might take us along with him in his detestation of them. It is not unlikely, if all be true that is told of them, but that the Gnostics might have some principles not unlike this; but beside them, I never heard of any that were of this mind in the world. And, in truth, the liberty that is taken in these discourses is a great instance of the morality under consideration. But the following words will direct us where these things are charged; for some say that if " a man be exact in all the duties of moral goodness, yet if he be a graceless person, void of I know not what imaginary godliness, he is but in a cleaner way to hell." I think I know both what and who are intended, and that both are dealt withal with that candour we have been now accustomed unto. But, first, you will scarce find those you intend over-forward in granting that men may be " exact in all the duties of moral goodness," and yet be "graceless persons:" for taking moral virtues to comprehend, as you do, their duties towards God, they will tell you such persons cannot perform one of them aright, much less all of them exactly; for they can neither believe in God, nor trust him, nor fear him, nor glorify him, in a due manner.   [Secondly,] Take the duties of moral goodness for the duties of the law between man and man, and the observation of the outward duties of God's worship, and they say, indeed, that they may be so performed as that in respect of them men may be blameless, and yet be graceless; for that account, if they mistake not, the apostle Paul gives of himself, Phil. iii. 6–9. They do say, therefore, that many of these duties, so as to be useful in the world and blameless before men, they may perform who are yet graceless. Thirdly, This gracelessness is said to consist in being "void of I know not what imaginary godliness." No, no;—it is to be void of the Spirit of God, of the grace of Christ; not to be born again, not to have a new spiritual life in Christ; not to be united to him or ingrafted in him; not to be accepted and made an heir of God, and enabled to a due, spiritual, evangelical performance of all duties of obedience, according to the tenor of the covenant. These are the things intended. And as many with their "moral duties" may come short of them and be "graceless," so those to whom they are "imaginary" must reject the whole gospel of Christ as an imagination. And I must say (to give matter of a new charge), that, to the best observation that I have been able to make in the world, none have been, nor are, more negligent in the principal duties of morality than those who are aptest to exalt them above the gospel and the whole mystery of it; unless morality do consist in such a course of life and conversation as I will not at present characterize.

It is farther added, that the "conversion of such a one is more hopeless than the vilest and most notorious sinner's; and the morally righteous man," etc. Setting aside the invidious expression of what is here reflected upon, there is nothing more openly taught in the gospel. The Pharisees were a people *morally righteous*, whereon they "trusted in themselves that they were righteous;" and yet our Lord Jesus Christ told them that "publicans and harlots," the vilest and most notorious of sinners, entered before them into the kingdom of God. And where men trust to their own righteousness, their own duties, be they moral or what they will, there are no men farther from the way of the gospel than they; nay, our Saviour lets us know that, as such, the gospel is not concerned in them, nor they in it. "I came not," he says, "to call the righteous, but sinners to repentance,"—not men justifying or lifting up themselves in a conceit of their moral duties, but those who are burdened and laden with a sense of their sins; and so, in like manner, that "the whole have no need of a physician, but the sick." And St Paul declares what enemies they were to the righteousness of God who went about to set up their own righteousness, Rom. x. 3. Now, because moral duties are incumbent on all persons at all times, they are continually pressed upon all, from a sense of the authority and command of God, indispensably requiring all men's attendance unto them. Yet such is the deceitfulness of the heart of man and the power of unbelief, that oftentimes persons who, through their education or following convictions, have been brought to some observance of them, being not enlightened in their minds to discern their insufficiency unto the great end of salvation in and of themselves, are apt to take up with them and to rest in them, without ever coming to sincere repentance towards God, or faith in our Lord Jesus Christ; whereas others, the guilt of whose sins doth unavoidably press upon them, as it did on the publicans and sinners of old, are ofttimes more ready to look out after relief. And those who question these things do nothing but manifest their ignorance in the Scripture, and want of experience in the work of the ministry. But yet, upon the account of the charge mentioned, so unduly framed and impotently managed, our author makes an excursion into such an extravagancy of reproaches as is scarce exceeded in his whole book; part of it I have considered before in our view of his preface, and I am now so used to the noise and bluster wherewith he pours out the storm of his indignation, that I am altogether unconcerned in it, and cannot prevail with myself to give it any farther consideration.

These things, though not direct to the argument in hand, and which on that account might have been neglected, yet supposing that the author placed as much of his design in them as in any part of his discourse, I could not wholly omit the consideration of; not so much out of a desire for their vindication who are unduly traduced in them, as to plead for the gospel itself, and to lay a foundation of a farther defence of the truths of it, if occasion shall so require. And we have also here an insight into the judgment of our author, or his mistake in this matter. He tells us that it is better to tolerate debaucheries and immoralities than liberty of conscience for men to worship God according to their light and persuasion! Now, all religion, according to him, consisting in morality, to tolerate immoralities and debaucheries in conversation is plainly to tolerate atheism; which, it seems, is more eligible than to grant liberty of conscience unto them who differ from the present establishment only as to some things belonging to the outward worship of God!

These things being premised, the argument itself pleaded in this chapter is capable of a speedy despatch. It is to this purpose: "The magistrate hath power over the consciences of men in reference to morals or moral virtues, which are the principal things in religion; and therefore much more hath so in reference to the worship of God, which is of less importance." We have complained before of the ambiguity of these general terms, but it is to no purpose to do so any more, seeing that we are not like to be relieved in this discourse. Let us, then, take things as we find them, and satisfy ourselves on the intention of the author by that declaration which he makes of it up and down the chapter. But yet here we are at a loss also. When he speaks, or seems to speak, to this purpose, whether in the confirmation of the proposition, or the inferences whereof his arguments consist, what he says is cast into such an intertexture with invectives and reproaches, and expressed in such a loose, declamatory manner, as it is hard to discover or find out what it is that he intends. Suppose, therefore, in the first place, that a man should call his consequent into question,—namely, that because the magistrate hath power over the consciences of his subjects in morals, that therefore he hath so also in matters of instituted worship,—how would he confirm and vindicate it? Two things are all I can observe that are offered in the confirmation of it:—First, That "these things of morality, moral virtues, are of more importance in religion than the outward worship of God," which the amplitude of power before asserted is now reducing to a respect unto. Secondly, That "there is much more danger of his erring and mistaking in things of morality than in things of outward worship, because of their great weight and importance." These things are pleaded, p. 28, and elsewhere up and down. That any thing else is offered in the confirmation of this consequent I find not. And it may be some will think these proofs to be very weak and feeble, unable to sustain the weight that is laid upon them; for it is certain that the first rule,—that he that hath power over the greater hath so over the lesser,—doth not hold unless it be in things of the same nature and kind. And it is no less certain and evident that there is an especial and formal difference between these things,—namely, moral virtues and instituted worship; the one depending, as to their being and discovery, on the light of nature, and the dictates of that reason which is common to all, and speaks the same language in the consciences of all mankind; the other, on pure revelation, which may be and is variously apprehended. Hence it is, that whereas there is no difference in the world about what is virtue and what is not, there is no agreement about what belongs to divine worship and what doth not.

Again; *lesser* things may be exempted from that power and authority, by especial privilege or law, which hath the disposal of *greater* committed unto it, and intrusted with it; as the magistrate amongst us may take away the life of a man, which is the greatest of his concernments, the name of his all, for felony, but cannot take his estate or inheritance of land, which is a far less concernment unto him, if it be antecedently settled by law to other uses than his own. And if it cannot be proved that the disposal of the worship of God, as to what doth really and truly belong unto it, and all the parts of it, is exempted from all human power by special law and privilege, let it be disposed of as whoso will shall judge meet.

Nor is the latter consideration suggested to enforce this consequent of any more validity,—namely, "that there is more danger of the magistrate's erring or mistaking about moral virtue than about rites of worship," because that is of most concernment in religion; for it is true, that suppose a man to walk on the top of a high house or tower, on a plain floor, with battlements or walls round about him, there will be more danger of breaking his neck if he should fall from thence than if he should fall from the top of a narrow wall that had not the fourth part of the height of the house. But there would not be so much danger of falling: for from the top of the house, as circumstantiated, he cannot fall, unless he will wilfully and violently cast himself down headlong; and on the top of the wall, it may be, he cannot stand, with the utmost of his heed and endeavours. The magistrate cannot mistake about moral virtues, unless he will do it wilfully. They have their station fixed in the world on the same ground and evidence with the magistracy itself. The same evidence, the same common consent and suffrage of mankind, is given unto moral virtues, as is to any government in the world; and to suppose a supreme magistrate, a lawgiver, to mistake in these things, in judging whether justice, and temperance, or fortitude, be virtues or no, and that in his legislative capacity, is ridiculous. Neither Nero nor Caligula was ever in danger of any such misadventure. All the magistrates in the world at this day are agreed about these things. But as to what concerns the worship of God, they are all at variance. There is no such evidence in these things, no such common suffrage about them, as to free any absolutely from failings and mistakes; so that in respect of them, and not of the other, lies the principal danger of miscarrying as to their determination and administration. Supposing, therefore, the premises our author lays down to be true, his inference from them is feeble and obnoxious to various impeachments, whereof I have given some few instances only, which shall be increased if occasion require.

But the assertion itself which is the foundation of these consequences is utterly remote from accuracy and truth. It is said that "the magistrate hath power over the consciences of men in reference unto moral duties, which are the principal parts of religion." Our first and most difficult inquiry is after the meaning of this proposition; the latter, after its truth. I ask, then, first, Whether he hath power over the consciences of men with respect unto moral virtue, and over moral virtue itself as virtue and as a part of religion, or on some other account? If his power respect virtue as a part of religion, then it equally extends itself to all that is so, by virtue of a rule which will not be easily everted. But it doth not appear that it so extends itself as to plead an obliging authority in reference unto all duties; for let but the scheme of moral duties, especially those whose object is God, given us by our author, be considered, and it will quickly be discerned how many of them are exempted from all human cognizance and authority, and that from and by their nature, as well as their use in the world. And it is in vain to ascribe an authority to magistrates which they have no power to exert, or take cognizance whether it be obeyed or no. And what can they do therein with respect unto "gratitude to God," which holds the first place in the scheme of moral virtues here given in unto us? We are told, also, p. 83, "That in matters both of moral virtue and divine worship, there are some rules of good and evil that are of an eternal and unchangeable obligation, and these can never be prejudiced or altered by any human power, because the reason of their obligation arises from a necessity and constitution of nature, and therefore must be as perpetual as that; but then there are other rules of duty that are alterable according to the various accidents, changes, and conditions of human life, and depend chiefly upon contracts and positive laws of kingdoms." It would not be unworthy our inquiry to consider what rules of moral duty they are which are alterable and depend "on accidents and contracts;" but we might easily find work enough should we call all such fond assertions to a just examination. Neither doth the distinction here given us between various rules of moral virtue very well answer what we are told, p. 69,—namely, "that every particular virtue is therefore such, because it is a resemblance and imitation of some of the divine attributes;" which I suppose they are not whose rules and forms are alterable upon accidents and occasions. And we are taught also, p. 68, that the "practice of virtue consists in living suitably to the dictates of reason and nature;" which are rules not variable and changeable. There must be some new distinction to reconcile these things, which I cannot at present think of. That which I would enquire from hence is, Whether the magistrate have power over the consciences of men in reference unto those things in morality whose rules of good and evil are of an eternal obligation? That he hath not is evidently implied in this place. And I shall not enter into the confusion of the ensuing discourse, where the latter sort of rules for virtue, the other member of the distinction, are turned into various methods of executing laws about outward acts of virtue or vice, and the virtues themselves into outward expressions and significations of duty; for I have at present no contest with this author about his manner of writing, nor do intend to have. It is enough that here at once all the principal and most important virtues are vindicated to their own unalterable rules as such, and the consciences of men in reference unto them put under another jurisdiction. And what, then, becomes of this argument, "That the magistrate must have power over the consciences of men in matters of divine worship, because he hath so in things moral, which are of greater importance," when what is so of importance is exempted from his power?

Hence it sufficiently appears that the authority of the magistrate over men, with reference unto moral virtue and duty, doth not respect virtue as virtue, but hath some other consideration. Now what this is, is evident unto all. How moral virtues do belong unto religion, and are parts of it, hath been before declared. But God, who hath ordered all things in weight and measure, hath fore-designed them also to another end and purpose. For preparing mankind for political society in the world among themselves for a time, as well as for religious obedience unto himself, he inlaid his nature and composition with principles suited to both those ends, and appointed them to be acted with different respects unto them. Hence moral virtues, notwithstanding their peculiar tendency unto him, are appointed to be the instrument and ligament of human society also; —as the law of Moses had in it a typical end, use, and signification, with respect to Christ and the gospel; and a political use, as the instrument of the government of the nation of the Jews. Now, the power of the magistrate in respect to moral virtues is in their latter use,—namely, as they relate to human policy, which is concerned in the outward actings of them. This, therefore, is granted; and we shall inquire farther, whether any more be proved, namely, that the magistrate hath power over the outward actings of virtue and vice, so far as human society or public tranquillity is concerned in them, and on that account?

Secondly, It may be inquired, What is the power and authority over moral virtues which is here ascribed unto the civil magistrate, and over the consciences of men with respect unto them? Is it such as to make that to be virtue which was not virtue before, or which was vice, and oblige men in conscience to practise it as virtue? This would go a great way indeed, and answer somewhat of what is, or, as it is said, may be, done in the worship of God, when that is made a part of it which was not so before. But what name shall these new virtues be called by? A new virtue, both as to its acts and objects, will as much fly the imaginations of men as a sixth sense doth. It may be our author will satisfy us as to this inquiry; for he tells us, p. 80, that "he hath power to make that a particular of the divine law that God hath not made so." I wish he had declared himself how and wherein; for I am afraid this expression, as here it lies, is offensive. The divine law is divine, and so is every particular of it; and how a man can make a thing divine that is not so of itself, nor by divine institution, is hard to find out. It may be that only the subject-matter of the law, and not the law itself formally, is intended; and to make a thing a particular of the divine law is no more but to make the divine law require that in particular of a man which it did not require of him before. But this particular refers to the nature, essence, and being of the thing, or to the acting and occasion of it in particular. And if it be taken in the latter sense, there is no more ascribed unto the magistrate than is common with him to every man in the world : for every one that puts himself into new circumstances or new relations, doth so make that unto him to be a particular of the divine law which was not so before; for he is bound and obliged unto the actual performance of many duties which, as so circumstantiated, he was not bound unto before.

But somewhat else seems to be intended from the ensuing discourse : " They are fully empowered to declare new instances of virtue and vice, and to introduce new duties in the most important parts of religion." And yet I am still at the same loss ; for by his " declaring new instances of virtue and vice," I suppose he intends an authoritative declaration, such as that they have no other foundation, nor need none to make them what they are. They are new instances of virtue and vice, because so declared. And this suits unto the " introducing of new duties in the most important parts of religion,"—made duties by that introduction. I wish I could yet learn what these " new instances of virtue and vice" are or mean; whether they are new as virtues and vices, or as instances. For the first, would I could see a new practice of old virtues ! but, to tell you the truth, I care not for any of the new virtues that I have lately observed in the world, nor do I hope ever to see any better new ones.

If it be the *instances that are new*, I wish again I knew what were more in them than the actual and occasional exercise of old duties. Pages 79, 80, conduce most to extricate us out of these ambiguities. There we are informed that " the laws of every nation do distinguish and settle men's rights and properties, and that distinctly; with respect whereunto justice, that prime natural virtue, is in particular instances to be exercised. And, p. 84, it is farther declared, that " in the administration of justice there may be great difference in the constitution of penalties and execution of them." This, it seems, is that which is aimed at: The magistrate, by his laws, determines whether Titius have set his hedge upon Caius' ground, and whether Sempronius have rightly conveyed his land or house to his son or neighbour; whereby what is just and lawful in itself is accommodated to the use of political society. He determines, also, how persons guilty of death shall be executed, and by whom, and in what manner. Whence it must needs follow, that he hath power to assign new particulars of the divine law, to declare new bounds or hedges of right and wrong, which the law of God neither doth nor can limit, or hath power over the consciences of men with respect to moral virtues; which was to be demonstrated. Let us lay aside these swelling expressions, and we shall find that all that can be ascribed unto the civil magistrate in this matter is no more than to preserve property and peace by that rule and power over the outward actions of men which is necessary thereunto.

Having made some inquiry into the terms of "moral virtue" and the "magistrate's power," it remains only that we consider what respect this case hath unto the consciences of men, with reference unto them; and I desire to know whether all mankind be not obliged in conscience to the observation of all moral virtues antecedently to the command or authority of the magistrate, who doth only inspect their observation of them as to the concerns of public peace and tranquillity? Certainly, if all moral virtues consist in "living suitably to the dictates of reason," as we are told,—and in a sense rightly, if the rule of them all and every one, which gives them their formal nature, be the law of our creation, which all mankind enter the world under an indispensable obligation unto,—it cannot be denied but that there is such an antecedent obligation on the consciences of men as that inquired after.   But the things mentioned are granted by our author; nor can by any be denied without offering the highest outrage to Scripture, reason, and the common consent of mankind.   Now, if this obligation be thus on all men, unto all virtue as virtue, and this absolutely, from the authority of God over them and their consciences, how comes an inferior authority to interpose itself between that of God and their consciences, so as immediately to oblige them?   It is granted that when the magistrate commandeth and requireth the exercise of any moral duty, in a way suited unto public good and tranquillity, he is to be obeyed for conscience' sake, because he who is the Lord of conscience doth require men to be obedient unto him, whereon they are obliged in conscience so to be: but if the things required of them be in themselves moral duties, as they are such, their consciences are obliged to observe and exercise them from the command of God; and other obligation unto them, as such, they neither have nor can have.   But the direction and command for the exercise of them in these and those circumstances, for the ends of public good whereunto they are directed, belongs unto the magistrate, who is to be obeyed: for as in things merely civil, and which have nothing originally of morality in them, but secondarily only, as they tend to the preservation and welfare of human society, which is a thing morally good, the magistrate is to be obeyed for conscience' sake, and the things themselves, as far as they partake of morality, come directly under the command of God, which affects the conscience;—so in things that have an inherent and inseparable morality, and so respect God in the first place, when they come to have a civil sanction in reference to their exercise unto public political good, that sanction is to be obeyed out of conscience; but the antecedent obligation that was upon the conscience unto a due exercise of those duties, when made necessary by circumstances, is not superseded, nor any new one added thereunto.

I know what is said, but I find not as yet what is proved, from these things, concerning the uncontrollable and absolute power of the supreme magistrate over religion and the consciences of men. Some things are added indeed here, up and down, about circumstances of divine worship, and the power of ordering them by the magistrate; which though there may be some different conceptions about, yet they no way reach the cause under debate. But as they are expressed by our author, I know not of any one writer in and of the church of England that hitherto has so stated them as they are by him; for he tells us, p. 85, that "all rituals, ceremonies, postures, and manners of performing the outward expressions of devotion, that are not chargeable with countenancing vice or disgracing the Deity, are capable of being adopted into the ministries of divine service, and are not exempted from being subject to the determinations of human power." Whether they are so or no, the magistrate, I presume, is to judge, or all this flourish of words and concessions of power vanish into smoke. His command of them binds the consciences of men to observe them, according to the principle under consideration. Hence it must be absolutely in the power of every supreme magistrate to impose on the Christian subjects a greater number of ceremonious observances in the worship of God, and those of greater weight, than ever were laid upon the Jews; for who knows not that under the names of "rituals, ceremonies, postures, manners of performing all divine service," what a burdensome heap of things are imposed in the Roman church? whereunto, as far as I know, a thousand more may be added, not chargeable in themselves with either of the crimes which alone are allowed to be put in in bar or plea against them. And whether this be the liberty whereunto Jesus Christ hath vindicated his disciples and church, is left unto the judgment of sober men. Outward religious worship, we know, is to be performed by natural actions. These have their circumstances; and those ofttimes, because of the public concernment of the exercise of religion, of great importance. These may be ordered by the power and according to the wisdom of those in authority; but that they should make so many things as this assertion allows them to make to belong unto and to be parts of the worship of God, whereof not one is enjoined or required by him, and the consciences of men be thereby obliged unto their observance, I do not believe, nor is it here at all proved.

To close this discourse about the power of obliging the consciences of men; I think our author grants that conscience is immediately obliged to the observation of all things that are good in themselves, from the law of our creation. Such things as either the nature of God or our own requires from us, our consciences surely are obliged immediately by the authority of God to observe: nor can we have any dispensation for the non-performance of our duty from the interposition of the commands and authority of any of the sons of men; for this would be openly and directly to set up men against God, and to advance them or their authority above him or his. Things evidently deduced and necessarily following the first principles and dictates of nature are of the same kind with themselves, and have the authority of God no less enstamped on them than the other; and in respect unto them, conscience cannot by virtue of inferior commands plead an exemption.   Things of mere revelation do remain ; and concerning them I desire to know, whether we are not bound to observe and do whatever God in his revealed will commands us to observe and do, and to abstain from whatever he forbids, and this indispensably?   If this be denied, I will prove it with the same arguments whereby I can prove that there is a God and that we are his creatures, made to serve him; for the reason of these things is inseparable from the very being of God.   Let this be granted, and ascribe what ye will, or please, or can, to the supreme magistrate, and you shall not from me have the least contradiction.

A SURVEY OF THE THIRD CHAPTER.

[Liberty of conscience—The obligation to comply with its dictates not superseded by the authority of the magistrate—External worship an essential part of religion—External worship not left to be regulated by man—The rite of sacrifice shown to be of divine original—Alleged right of the magistrate to appoint ceremonies—Distinction between words and ceremonies as signs.]

THE third chapter entertains us with a magnificent grant of *liberty of conscience.*   The very first paragraph asserts a " liberty of conscience in mankind over all their actions, whether moral or strictly religious."   But lest this should prove a bedlam concession, that might mischief the whole design in hand, it is delivered to the power of a keeper; who yet, upon examination, is no less wild and extravagant than itself is esteemed absolutely to be.   This is, " That they have it as far as concerns their judgments, but not their practice;"—that is, they have liberty of conscience over their *actions* but not their *practices,* or *over their practices* but *not over their practices!* for, upon trial, their actions and practices will prove to be the same.   And I do not as yet well understand what is this liberty of conscience over men's actions.   Is it to do or not to do, as their consciences dictate to them? This is absolutely denied and opposed in the chapter itself. Is it to judge of their actions, as done, whether they be good or evil? This, conscience is at no liberty in; for it is determined to a judgment in that kind naturally and necessarily, and must be so whilst it hath the light of nature and word of God to regard, so far as a rule is capable of giving a measure and determination to things to be regulated by it,—that is, its moral actings are morally determined. What, then, this liberty of conscience over men's actions should be, when they can neither act freely according to their consciences what they are to do, nor abstain from what they are not to do, nor are at liberty to judge what they have done to be good or bad, I cannot divine.

Let us search after an explication of these things in the paragraph itself, whose contents are represented in the words mentioned. Here we are told that this liberty consists in " men's thinking of things according to their own persuasion, and therein asserting the freedom of their judgments." I would be loath to think that this liberty of men's consciences over all their moral actions should, at first dash, dwindle into a liberty in speculations,—that men may think what they will, opine as they please, in or about things that are not to be brought into practice; but yet, as far as I can perceive, I must think so, or matters will come to a worse issue.

But these things must be a little farther examined, and that very briefly. Here is mention of "liberty of conscience;" but what conscience is, or what that liberty is, is not declared. For conscience, it is called sometimes " the mind," sometimes " the understanding," sometimes "opinion," sometimes described by the "liberty of thinking," sometimes termed an "*imperious faculty;*" which things, without much discourse and more words than I can now afford to use, are not reconcilable among themselves. Besides, liberty is no proper affection of the mind or understanding. Though I acknowledge the mind and its actings to be naturally free from outward compulsion or coaction, yet it is capable of-such a determination from the things proposed unto it, and the manner of their proposal, as to make necessary the elicitation of its acts. It cannot but judge that two and three make five. It is the will that is the proper seat of *liberty;* and what some suppose to be the ultimate determination of the practical understanding is indeed *an act of the will.* It is so if you speak of liberty naturally and morally, and not of state and condition, which are here confounded. But suppose what you will to be conscience, it is moral actions or duties that are here supposed to be the objects of its actings. Now, what are or can be the thoughts or actings of the mind of man about moral actions, but about their virtue or their vice, their moral good or evil? Nor is a conclusion of what is a man's own duty in reference to the practice of them possibly to be separated from them. That, then, which is here asserted is, That a man may think, judge, or conceive such or such a thing to be his duty, and yet have thereby no obligation put upon him to perform it; for conscience, we are informed, hath nothing to do beyond the inward thoughts of men's minds!

To state this matter a little more clearly, let us take conscience in the most usual acceptation of it, and that which answers the experience of every man that ever looks into the affairs and concerns within; and so it is the practical judgment that men make of themselves and of their actions, or what they are to do and what they are not to do, what they have done or what they have omitted, with reference unto the judgment of God, at present declared in their own hearts and in his word, and to be fully executed at the last day: for we speak of conscience as it is amongst Christians, who acknowledge the word of God, and that for a double end; first, as the rule of conscience itself; secondly, as the declaration of the will of God, as to his approbation or rejecting of what we do or omit. Suppose, then, that a man make a judgment in his conscience, regulated by the word of God, and with respect unto the judgment of God concerning him, that such and such a thing is a duty, and whose performance is required of him, I desire to know whether any obligation be upon him from thence to act accordingly? It is answered, that "the territory of conscience is confined unto men's thoughts, judgments, and persuasions, and these are free" (Yea, no doubt); "but for outward actions there is no remedy, but they must be subject to the cognizance of human laws," p. 9. Who ever doubted of it? He that would have men so have liberty from outward actions as not to have those actions cognoscible by the civil power as to the end of public tranquillity, but to have their whole station firmed absolutely in the world upon the plea of conscience, would, no doubt, lay a foundation for confusion in all government. But what is this to the present inquiry, Whether conscience lay an obligation on men, as regulated by the word of God, and respecting him, to practise according to its dictates? It is true enough, that if any of its practices do not please or satisfy the magistrate, their authors must, for aught I know, stand to what will follow or ensue on them to their prejudice; but this frees them not from the obligation that is upon them in conscience unto what is their duty. This is that which must be here proved, if any thing be intended unto the purpose of this author,—namely, that notwithstanding the judgment of conscience concerning any duty, by the interposition of the authority of the magistrate to the contrary, there is no obligation ensues for the performance of that duty. This is the answer that ought plainly to be returned, and not a suggestion that outward actions must fall under the cognizance of the magistrate, which none ever doubted of, and which is nothing to the present purpose, unless he would have them so to fall under the magistrate's cognizance as that his will should be the supreme rule of them; which, I think, he cannot prove. But what sense the magistrate will have of the outward actions, wherein the discharge of man's duty doth consist, is of another consideration.

This, therefore, is the state of the present case applied unto religious worship: Suppose the magistrate command such things in religion as a man in his conscience, guided by the word and respecting God, doth look upon as unlawful and such as are evil, and sin unto him if he should perform them, and forbid such things in the worship of God as he esteems himself obliged in conscience to observe as commands of Christ; if he practise the things so commanded, and omit the things so forbidden, I fear he will find himself within doors continually at confession, saying, with trouble enough, " I have done those things which I ought not to have done, and I have left undone those things which I ought to have done, and there -is no health in me;" unless this author can prove that the commands of God respect only the minds of men, but not their outward actions, which are left unto the authority of the magistrate alone. If no more be here intended, but that whatever conscience may require of any, it will not secure them but that, when they come to act outwardly according to it, the civil magistrate may and will consider their actions, and allow them or forbid them, according to his own judgment, it were surely a madness to deny it, as great as to say the sun shineth not at noonday. If conscience to God be confined to thoughts, and opinions, and speculations about the general notions and notices of things, about true and false, and unto a liberty of judging and determining upon them what they are, whether they are so or no, the whole nature and being of conscience, and that to the reason, sense, and experience of every man, is utterly overthrown. If conscience be allowed to make its judgment of what is good or evil, what is duty or sin, and no obligation be allowed to ensue from thence unto a suitable practice, a wide door is opened unto atheism, and thereby the subversion of all religion and government in the world.

This, therefore, is the sum of what is asserted in this matter: Conscience, according to that apprehension which it hath of the will of God about his worship (whereunto we confine our discourse), obligeth men to act or forbear accordingly. If their apprehensions are right and true, just and equal, what the Scripture, the great rule of conscience, doth declare and require, I hope none, upon second thoughts, will deny but that such things are attended with a right unto a liberty to be practised, while the Lord Jesus Christ is esteemed the Lord of lords and King of kings, and is thought to have power to command the observance of his own institutions. Suppose their apprehensions to be such as may in those things, be they more or less, be judged not to correspond exactly with the great rule of conscience, yet supposing them also to contain nothing inconsistent with, or of a disturbing nature to, civil society and public tranquillity, nothing that gives countenance to any vice or evil, or is opposite to the principal truths and main duties of religion, wherein the minds of men in a nation do coalesce, nor to carry any politic entanglements along with them; and add thereunto the peaceableness of the persons possessed with those apprehensions, and the impossibility they are under to divest themselves of them;—and I say natural right, justice, equity, religion, conscience, God himself in all, and his voice in the hearts of all unprejudiced persons, do require that neither the persons themselves, on the account of their consciences, have violence offered unto them, nor their practices in pursuit of their apprehensions be restrained by severe prohibitions and penalties. But whereas the magistrate is allowed to judge and dispose of all outward actions in reference to public tranquillity, if any shall assert principles, as of conscience, tending or obliging unto the practice of vice, immorality, or sin, or to the disturbance of public society, such principles being all notoriously judged by Scripture, nature, the common consent of mankind, and inconsistent with the fundamental principles of human polity, may be, in all instances of their discovery and practice, coerced and restrained. But, plainly, as to the commands of conscience, they are of the same extent with the commands of God;—if these respect only the inward man, or the mind, conscience doth no more; if they respect outward actions, conscience doth so also.

From the liberty of conscience a proceed is made to Christian liberty, which is said to be " a duty or privilege founded upon the" (chimerical) " liberty of conscience" before granted. But these things stand not in the relation imagined. Liberty of conscience is of natural right, Christian liberty is a gospel privilege, though both may be pleaded in unwarrantable impositions on conscience. But these things are so described by our author as to be confounded: for the Christian liberty described in this paragraph is either restrained to matters of pure speculation, wherein the mind of man is left entirely free to judge of the truth and falsehood of things; or as it regards things that fall under laws and impositions, wherein men are left entirely free to judge of them, as they are objects of mere opinion. Now, how this differs from the liberty of conscience granted before I know not. And that there is some mistake in this description of

Christian liberty needs no other consideration to evince but this, namely, that Christian liberty, as our author tells us, is a privilege; but this is not so, being that which is equally common unto all mankind. This liberty is necessary unto human nature, nor can it be divested of it; and so it is not a privilege that includes a specialty in it. Every man cannot but think what he thinks, and judge what he judgeth, and that when he doth so, whether he will or no; for every thing when it is, and as it is, is necessary. In the use of what means they please, to guide, direct, and determine their thoughts, their liberty doth consist. This is equal in all, and natural unto all. Now, this inward freedom of our judgment is, it seems, our Christian liberty, consistent with any impositions upon men in the exercise of the worship of God, with an obligation on conscience unto their use and practice! a liberty, indeed, of no value, but a mere aggravation of bondage. And these things are farther discoursed, sect. iii., p. 95; wherein we are told, that " this prerogative of our Christian liberty is not so much any new favour granted in the gospel, as the restoration of the mind of man to its natural privilege, by exempting us from the yoke of the ceremonial law, whereby things in themselves indifferent were tied upon the conscience with as indispensable an obligation as the rule of essential goodness and equity, during the whole period of the Mosaic dispensation; which being corrected by the gospel, those indifferent things, that have been made necessary by a divine, positive command, returned to their own nature, to be used or omitted only as occasion shall direct."

It is true that a good part of our Christian liberty consists in our deliverance from the yoke of Mosaical institutions; but that this " is not so much a new favour granted in the gospel as the restoration of the mind of man to its natural privilege," is an assertion that runs parallel with many others in this discourse. This privilege, as all others of the gospel are, is spiritual, and its outward concerns and exercise are of no value where the mind is not spiritually made free by Christ. And it is uncertain what is meant by the " restoration of the mind to its natural privilege." If the privilege of the mind in its natural purity is intended, as it was before the entrance of sin, it is false; if any privilege [which] the mind of man, in its corrupt, depraved condition, is capable of, be designed, it is no less untrue. In things of this nature the mind in that condition is in bondage, and not capable of any liberty; for it is a thing ridiculous to confound the mere natural liberty of our wills, which is an affection inseparable from that faculty, with a moral or spiritual liberty of mind relating unto God and his worship. But this whole paragraph runs upon no small mistake,—namely, that the yoke of Mosaical institutions consisted in their impositions on the minds and judgments of men, with an opinion of the antecedent necessity of them; for although the words recited, "Things in themselves indifferent were tied upon the conscience with as indispensable an obligation as the rules of essential goodness and equity," may be restrained to their use, exercise, and observation, yet the conclusion of it, that "whatever our superiors impose upon us, whether in matters of religious worship or any other duties of morality, there neither is nor can be any intrenchment upon our Christian liberty, provided it be not imposed with an opinion of the antecedent necessity of the thing itself," with the whole scope of the argument insisted on, makes it evident to be the sense intended. But this is wide enough from the mark. The Jews were never obliged to judge the whole system of their legal institutions to be any way necessary antecedent unto their institution and appointment; nor were they obliged to judge their intrinsic nature changed by their institution: only, they knew they were obliged to their constant and indispensable practice, as parts of the worship of God, instituted and commanded by him who hath the supreme authority over their souls and consciences. There was, indeed, a bondage frame of spirit upon them in all things, especially in their whole worship of God, as the apostle Paul several times declares. But this is a thing of another nature, though our delivery from it be also a part of Christian liberty. This was no part of their inward no more than their outward bondage, that they should think, believe, judge, or esteem the things themselves enjoined them to be absolutely of any other nature than they were. Had they been obliged unto any such judgment of things, they had been obliged to deceive themselves, or to be deceived. But, by the absolute authority of God, they were indispensably bound in conscience to the actual observance and continual use of such a number of ceremonies, carnal ordinances, and outward observances, as, being things in themselves low and mean, called by the apostle "beggarly elements," and enjoined with so great strictness, and under so severe penalties,—many of them, of excision, or extermination from among the people,—so became an intolerable and insupportable yoke unto them. Neither doth the apostle Peter dispute about a judgment of their nature, but the necessity of their observation, when he calls them "a yoke which neither they nor their fathers were able to bear," Acts xv. 10. And when St Paul gives a charge to believers to "stand fast in the liberty wherewith Christ hath made them free," it is with respect to the outward observation of Mosaical rites, as by him instituted, and not as to any inward judgment of their minds concerning their nature antecedent unto that institution. His whole disputation on that subject respects only men's practice with regard unto an authoritative obligation thereunto, which he pleaded to be now expired and removed. And if this Christian liberty, which he built and proceeded upon, be of force to free, not our minds from the judgments that they had before of things in themselves, but our persons from the necessary practice and observance of things instituted of God, however antecedently indifferent in themselves, I think it is, at least, of equal efficacy to exempt us from the necessary practice of things imposed on us in the worship of God by men. For, setting aside the inequality of the imposing authority, which casts the advantage on the other side (for these legal impositions were imposed on the church by God himself; those now intended are such matters as our superiors of themselves impose on us in religious worship), the case is absolutely the same: for as God did not give the "law of commandments contained in ordinances" unto the Jews from the goodness of the things required therein antecedent to his command, which should make them necessary to be practised by them for their good, but did it of his own sovereign, arbitrary will and pleasure; so he obliged not the people themselves unto any other judgment of them, but that they were necessarily to be observed. And, setting aside the consideration of his command, they were things in their own nature altogether indifferent. So is it in the present case. It is pleaded that there is no imposition on the minds, consciences, or judgments of men, to think or judge otherwise of what is imposed on them than as their nature is and doth require; only they are obliged unto their usage, observance, and practice: which is to put us into a thousand times worse condition than the Jews, if instances of them should be multiplied, as they may lawfully be every year, seeing it much more quiets the mind, to be able to resolve its thoughts immediately into the authority of God under its yoke than into that of man. If, therefore, we are freed from the one by our Christian liberty, we are so much more from the other; so as that, "being made free by Christ," we should not be the "servants of men" in things belonging to his service and worship.

From this discovery here made of the nature of Christian liberty, our author makes some deductions, pp. 98, 99, concerning the nature of religious worship; wherein he tells us that "the whole substance of religious worship is transacted within the mind of man, and dwells in the heart and thoughts, the soul being its proper seat and temple, where men may worship their God as they please without offending their prince; and that external worship is no part of religion itself." I wish he had more clearly and distinctly expressed his mind in this matter, for his assertions, in the sense the words seem to bear, are prodigiously false, and such as will open a door to atheism, with all the villany and confusion in the world; for who would not think this to be his intention: Let men keep their minds and inward thoughts and apprehensions right for God, and then they may practise outwardly in religion what they please; one thing one day, another another; be Papists and Protestants, Arians and Homo-ousians, yea, Mohammedans and Christians, any thing, every thing, after the manner of the country and laws of the prince where they are and live;—the rule that Ecebolius[1] walked by of old? I think there is no man that owns the Scripture but will confess that this is, at least, if not a direct, yet an interpretative rejection of the whole authority of God. And may not this rule be quickly extended unto oaths themselves, the bonds and ligaments of human society? for whereas, in their own formal nature, they belong to the worship of God, why may not men pretend to keep up their reverence unto God in the internal part of them, or their esteem of him in their invocation of his name, but as to the outward part accommodate it unto what by their interest is required of them; so swearing with their tongues, but keeping their mind at liberty? If the principles laid down be capable of any other more tolerable sense, and such as may be exclusive of these inferences, I shall gladly admit it; at present, what is here deduced from them seems to be evidently included in them.

It is true, indeed, that natural, moral, or internal worship, consisting in faith, love, fear, thankfulness, submission, dependence, and the like, hath its constant seat and residence in the souls and minds of men; but that the ways whereby these principles of it are to be outwardly exercised and expressed, by God's command and appointment, are not also indispensably necessary unto us, and parts of his worship, is utterly false. That which principally in the Scripture comes under the notion of the worship of God, is the due observance of his outward institutions; which divines have, upon unquestionable grounds, contended to be commanded and appointed in general in the second commandment of the decalogue, whence all particular institutions in the several seasons of the church are educed, and resolved into the authority of God therein expressed. And that account which we have here given us of outward worship,—namely, that it is "no part of religion itself, but only an instrument to express the inward veneration of the mind by some outward action or posture of the body,"—as it is very difficultly to be accommodated unto the sacrifices of old or the present sacraments of the church, which were and are parts of outward worship, and, as I take it, of religion; so the being an instrument, unto the purpose mentioned, doth not exclude any thing from being also a part of religion and worship itself, if it be commanded by God to be performed in his

---

[1] Ecebolius was a sophist of Constantinople, a zealous Christian under Constantine the Great, and equally zealous as a Pagan under Julian.—ED.

service unto his glory. It is pretended that all outward worship is only "an exterior signification of honour;" but yet all the parts of it in their performance are acts of obedience unto God, and are the proper actings of faith, love, and submission of soul unto God; which if they are not his worship, and parts of religion, I know not what may be so esteemed. Let, then, outward worship stand in what relation it will to inward spiritual honour, where God requires it and commands it, it is no less necessary and indispensably to be performed than any part of inward worship itself, and is a no less important duty of religion; for any thing comes to be a part of religious worship outwardly to be performed, not from its own nature, but from its respect unto the commands of God, and the end whereunto it is by him designed. So the apostle tells us, that " with the heart man believeth unto righteousness, and with the mouth confession is made unto salvation," Rom. x. 10. Confession is but the " exterior signification" of the faith that is in our hearts; but yet it is no less necessary to salvation than faith itself is to righteousness. And those who regulate their obedience and religious worship by the commands of God, knowing that which way soever they are signified, by inbred light or superadded revelation, it is they which give their obedience its formal nature, making it religious, will not allow that place and use of the outward worship required by God himself which should exclude it from being religious, or a part of their religion.

But upon the whole matter our author affirms, " That in all ages of the world, God hath left the management of his outward worship unto the discretion of men, unless when to determine some particulars hath been useful to some other purpose," p. 100. "The management of outward worship" may signify no more but the due performance of it; and so I acknowledge that though it be not left unto men's discretion to observe or not observe it, yet it is, too, their duty and obedience, which are their discretion and their wisdom. But the management here understood is opposed to God's own determination of particular forms,—that is, his especial institutions; and hereof I shall make bold to say, that it was never in any age so left to the discretion of men. To prove this assertion, sacrifices are singled out as an instance. It is known and granted that these were the most solemn part of the outward worship of God for many ages, and that there was a general consent of mankind unto the use of them, so that however the greatest part of the world apostatized from the true, only, and proper object of all religious worship, yet they retained this mode and medium of it. These sacrifices, we are told, p. 101, " did not owe their original unto any divine institution, but were made choice of by good men as a fit way of imitating the grateful resentments of their minds." The argument alone, as far as I can find, fixed on to firm this assertion is, that those who teach the contrary, and say that this mode of worship was commanded, do say so without proof or evidence. Our author, for the most part, sets off his assertions at no less rate than as such without whose admittance all order and government, and almost every thing that is good amongst mankind, would be ruined and destroyed. But he hath the unhappiness to found them, ordinarily, not only on principles and opinions dubious and uncertain, but on such paradoxes as have been by sober and learned men generally decried. Such is this of the original of sacrifices, here insisted on. The divines of the church of Rome do generally contend that religion and sacrifices are so related that the one cannot be without the other. Hence, they teach [that] God would have required sacrifices in the state of innocency had mankind continued therein. And though the instance be ill laid and not proved, yet the general rule applied unto the religion of sinners is not easily to be evicted; for as in Christian religion we have a Sacrifice that is πρόσφατος καὶ ζῶσα, as to its efficacy, always " newly offered and living," so before the personal offering of it in the body of Christ, there was no season or age without a due representation of it in sacrifices typical and of mystical signification. And although there be no express mention in the Scripture of their institution (for these are ancient things), yet there is as good warrant for it as for offering and burning incense only with sacred fire taken from the altar, which was of a heavenly traduction, for a neglect whereof the priests were consumed with fire from before the Lord; that is, though an express command be not recorded for their institution and observation, yet enough may be collected from the Scripture that they were of a divine extract and original. And if they were arbitrary inventions of some men, I desire to have a rational account given me of their catholicism in the world, and one instance more of any thing not natural or divine that ever prevailed to such an absolute universal acceptance amongst mankind. It is not so safe, I suppose, to assign an arbitrary original unto any thing that hath obtained a universal consent and suffrage, lest men be thought to set their own houses on fire, on purpose to consume their neighbours'.

Besides, no tolerable colour can be given to the assertion that they were the " invention of good men." The first notice we have of them is in those of Cain and Abel, whereof one was a bad man and of the evil one, and yet must be looked on as the principal inventer of sacrifices, if this fiction be allowed. Some of the ancients, indeed, thought that Adam sacrificed the beasts to God whose skins his first garments were made of; and if so, he was very pregnant and sudden in his invention, if he had no direction from God. But more than all this, bloody sacrifices were types of Christ, from the foundation of the world; and Socinus himself, who and his followers are the principal assertors of this paradox, grants that Christ is called the "Lamb of God," with respect unto the sacrifices of old, even before the law, as he is termed "a Lamb slain from the foundation of the world," not only with respect unto the efficacy of his sacrifice, but to the typical representation of it. And he that shall deny that the patriarchs in their sacrifices had respect unto the promised Seed will endeavour the shaking of a pillar of the church's creed. Now, I desire to know how men, by their own invention or authority, could assign such an end unto their sacrifices, if they were not of divine prescription, if not designed of God thereunto.

Again, the apostle tells us, Abel offered his sacrifice by faith, Heb. xi. 4; and faith hath respect unto the testimony of God, revealing, commanding, and promising to accept our duty. Wherever any thing is done in faith, there an assent is included to this, "that God is true," John iii. 33; and what it doth is thereby distinguished from will-worship, that is resolved into the commandments and doctrines of men, which whoso rest on make void the commandment of God, Matt. xv. 3, 6. And the faith of Abel, as to its general nature, was "the substance of things hoped for, and the evidence of things not seen," Heb. xi. 1; which in this matter it could not be if it had neither divine command nor promise to rest upon. It is evident, therefore, that sacrifices were of a *divine original;* and the instance in them to prove that the "outward worship of God hath, in all ages, been left unto the prudence and management of men," is feeble, and such as will give no countenance unto what it is produced in the justification of. And herewith the whole discourse of our author on this subject falls to the ground; where I shall at present let it lie, though it might, in sundry particulars, be easily crumbled into useless asseverations and some express contradictions.

In the close of this chapter an application is made of what hath been before argued, or rather dictated, upon a particular controversy about "significant ceremonies." I am not willing to engage in any contests of that nature, seeing to the due handling of them a greater length of discourse would be necessary than I think meet at present to draw forth this survey unto. Only, seeing a very few words may serve to manifest the looseness of what is here discoursed, to that purpose I shall venture on the patience of the reader with an addition of them. We have, therefore, in the first place, a reflection on "the prodigious impertinency of the clamour against the institution of significant ceremonies, when it is the only use of ceremonies, as of all other outward expressions of religion, to be significant." I do somewhat admire at the temper of this author, who cannot express his dissent from others in controversial points of the meanest and lowest concernment, but with crying out, "prodigies," "clamours," "impertinencies," and the like expressions of astonishment in himself and contempt of others. He might reserve some of these great words for more important occasions. But yet I join with him thus far in what he pleads, that ceremonies instituted in the worship of God that are *not significant* are very *insignificant*, and such as deserve not the least contention about them. He truly, also, in the next words, tells us that all "outward worship is a sign of inward honour." It is so, both in civil things and sacred. All our question is, How these instituted ceremonies come to be significant, and what it is they signify, and whether it be lawful to assign a significancy to them in the worship of God, when indeed they have none of the kind intended? To free us from any danger herein he informs us, p. 108, " That all the magistrate's power of instituting significant ceremonies amounts to no more than a power of determining what shall or what shall not be visible signs of honour; and this can be no usurpation upon the consciences of men." This is new language, and such as we have not formerly been used unto in the church of England,— namely, that of the " magistrate's instituting significant ceremonies." It was of old, the " church's appointing ceremonies for decency and order." But all the terms of that assertion are metamorphosed; the " church" into the " magistrates;" " appointing," which respects exercise, into "institution," which respects the nature of the thing, and hath a singular use and sense in this matter (or let them pass for the same); and "order and decency" into "ceremonies significant." These things were indeed implied before, but not so fully and plainly expressed or avowed. But the " honour" here intended in this matter is the honour, which is given to God in his worship. This is the honour of faith, love, fear, obedience, spiritual and holy, in Jesus Christ. To say that the magistrate hath power to institute visible signs of this honour, to be observed in the outward worship of God, is upon the matter to say that he hath power to institute new sacraments, for so such things would be, and to say what neither is nor can be proved, nor is here either logically or any way regularly attempted so to be.

The comparing of the *ceremonies* and their signification, with *words* and their signification, will not relieve our author in this matter. Some things are naturally significant of one another: so effects are of causes; so is smoke of fire; and such were the signs of the weather mentioned by our Saviour, Matt. xvi. 2, 3. Thus, I suppose, ceremonies are not significant. They do not naturally signify the things whereunto they are applied; for if they did there would be no need of their institution, and they are here said to be *instituted by the magistrate*. Again, there are customary signs,—some, it may be, *catholic*, many *topical*,—that have prevailed by custom and usage to signify such things as they have no absolute natural coherence with or relation unto; such is *putting off the hat* in sign of reverence, with others innumerable. And both these sorts of signs may have some use about the service and worship of God, as might be manifested in instances. But the signs we inquire after are voluntary, arbitrary, and instituted, as our author confesseth; for we do not treat of appointing some ceremonies for order and decency, which our canons take notice of, but of instituting ceremonies for signification, such as neither naturally nor merely by custom and usage come to be significant, but only by virtue of their institution. Now, concerning these, one rule may be observed,—namely, that they cannot be of one kind and signify things of another, by virtue of any command and consent of men, unless they have an absolute authority both over the sign and thing signified, and can change their natures, or create a new relation between them. To take, therefore, things natural, that are outward and visible, and appoint them to be signs, not natural, nor civil, nor customary, but mystical, of things spiritual, supernatural, inward, and invisible, and as such to have them observed in the church or worship of God, is a thing which is not as yet proved to be lawful. Signify thus naturally they never can, seeing there is no natural relation between them; civilly, or by consent, they do not so, for they are things sacred which they are supposed to signify, and are so far from signifying by consent, that those who plead for their signification do not agree wherein it doth consist. They must, therefore, signify so mystically and spiritually, and "signa cum ad res divinas pertinent sunt sacramenta," says Austin;—these things are sacraments. And when men can give mystical and spiritual efficacy to any of their own institutions; when they can make a relation between such signs and the things signified by them; when they can make that teaching and instructing in spiritual things and the worship of God which he hath not made so or appointed, blessed or consecrated to that end; when they can bind God's promises of assistance and acceptance to their own inventions; when they can advance what they will into the same rank and series of things in the worship of God with the sacrifices of old, or other parts of instituted worship in the church, by God's command, and attended with his promise of gracious acceptance;—then, and not before, may they institute the "significant ceremonies" here contended for. Words, it is true, are signs of things, and those of a mixed nature, partly natural, partly by consent: but they are not of one kind and signify things of another; for, say the schoolmen, "Where words are signs of sacred things, they are signs of them as things, but not as sacred."

A SURVEY OF THE FOURTH CHAPTER.

[Conscience exempted from human authority, where there is an antecedent obligation from divine authority.]

In the fourth chapter we have no concern. The hypothesis whose confutation he hath undertaken, as it is in itself false, so it is rather suited to promote what he aims at than what he opposeth; and the principles which himself proceedeth on do seem to some to *border on*, if not to be *borrowed from* his, and those which are here confuted. And thence it is that the foundations which he lays down in the entrance of this discourse are as destructive of his own pretensions as of those against which they are by himself improved: for it is granted and asserted by him that there are actions and duties in and about which the consciences of men are not to be obliged by human authority, but have an antecedent obligation on them from the authority of God himself; " so that disobedience unto the contrary commands of human authority is no sin, but an indispensable duty." And although he seems at first to restrain things of this nature unto things natural, and of an essential rectitude,—that is, to the prime dictates of the law of nature,—yet he expressly extends it in instances unto the belief of the truth of the gospel, which is a matter of mere and pure revelation. And hereon he adds the formal and adequate reason of this exemption of conscience from human authority, and its obligation unto duty, before its consideration without it and against it; " which is, not because subjects are in any thing free from the authority of the supreme power on earth, but because they are subject to a superior in heaven; and they are then only excused from the duty of obedience to their sovereign, when they cannot give it without rebellion against God: so that it is not originally any right of their own that exempts them from a subjection to the sovereign power in all things, but it is purely God's right of governing his own creatures that magistrates then invade when they make edicts to violate or control his laws."

It is about religion and the worship of God that we are discoursing. Now, in these things no man ever thought that it was originally a right of subjects, as subjects, abstracting from the consideration of the authority of God, that should exempt them from a subjection to the sovereign power; for though some of the ancients discourse at large that it is of natural right and equity that every one should worship God as he would himself, yet they founded this equity in the nature of God and the authority of his commands. This exemption, then, ariseth merely, as our author observes, because they are subject to a superior power in heaven, which excuseth them from the duty of obedience to their superiors on earth, when they cannot give it without rebellion against God: whence it undeniably follows, that that supreme power in heaven exempted these things from all inferior powers on earth. Extend this, now, unto all things wherein men have, and ought to have, a regard unto that superior power in heaven, as it must be extended, or the whole is ridiculous (for that heavenly supremacy is made the formal reason of the exemption here granted), and all that our author hath been so earnestly contending for in the preceding chapters falls to the ground : for no man pleads exemption from subjection unto, yea, from giving active obedience unto, the authority and commands of the magistrate, even in things religious, but merely on the account of his subjection to the authority of God in heaven; and, where this is so, he is set at liberty by our author from all contrary commands of men. This is Bellarmine's "Tutissimum est," which, as King James observed, overthrows all that he had contended for in his five books De Justificatione.[1]

A SURVEY OF THE FIFTH CHAPTER.

[Alleged evils from the free exercise of conscience—Charges of Parker against Nonconformists—Mischief of different sects in a commonwealth—Duties of a prince in regard to divided interests in religion—Principle of toleration asserted.]

THE fifth chapter is at such variance with itself and what is elsewhere dictated in the treatise, that it would require no small labour to make any tolerable composition of things between them. This I shall not engage in, as not being of my present concernment. What seems to tend unto the carrying on of the design of the whole may be called unto some account. In the beginning of it he tells us that "a belief of the indifferency, or rather imposture, of all religions is made the most effectual, not to say the most fashionable, argument for liberty of conscience." For my part, I never read, I never heard of this pretence or argument, to be used to that purpose. It wants no such defence. Nay, the principle itself seems to me to be suited directly to oppose and overthrow it: for if there be no such thing in reality as religion in the world, it is certainly a very foolish thing to have differences perpetuated amongst men upon the account of conscience; which, without a supposition of religion, is nothing but a vain and empty name. But hence our author takes occasion to discourse of the use of religion and conscience in the government of affairs in the world; and proves in many words that " conscience unto God, with a regard to future eternal rewards or punishments, is the great ligament of human society, the security of government, the strongest bond of laws, and only support of rule; without which every man would first and last be guided by mere self-interest, which would reduce all power and authority to mere force and violence." To this purpose doth he discourse at large in one section of this chapter; and in another, with no less earnestness and elegancy of words, and repetition of various expressions of the same signification, that " the use and exercise of conscience will certainly overthrow all government, and fill the world with confusion"! In like manner, whereas we have been hitherto throughly instructed, as I thought, that men may think what they will in the matters of religion, and be of what persuasion they please, [and] no man can or ought to control them therein, here we are told that " no power nor policy can keep men peaceable until some persuasions are rooted out of their minds by severity of laws and penalties"! p. 145.   And whereas heretofore we were informed that " men might believe what they would," princes were concerned only in their outward practice, now are we assured that " above all things it concerns princes to look to the doctrines and articles of men's belief"! p. 147.   But these things, as was before intimated, are not of our concern.

Nor can I find much of that importance in the third and fourth paragraphs of this declamatory invective.   It is evident whom he regards and reflects upon, and with what false, unmanly, unchristian revilings he endeavours to traduce them.   He would have the world believe that there is a generation of men whose principles of religion teach them to be proud, peevish, malicious, spiteful, envious, turbulent, boisterous, seditious, and whatever is evil in the world; when others are all for candour, moderation, and ingenuity,—amongst whom, no doubt, he reckons himself for one, and gives in this discourse in evidence thereof.   But what are those doctrines and articles of men's belief, which dispose them inevitably to all the villanies that our author could find names for ?   A catalogue of them he gives us, pp. 147, 148.   Saith he, " What if they believe that princes are but the executioners of the decrees of the presbytery; and that in case of disobedience to their spiritual governors they may be excommunicated, and by consequence deposed ?   What if they believe that dominion is founded in grace, and therefore all wicked kings forfeit their crowns, and that it is in the power of the people of God to bestow them where they please ?   And what if others believe that to pursue their successes in villany and rebellion is to follow providence?" All the world knows what it is that hath given him the advantage of providing a covering for these monstrous fictions, and an account thereof hath been given elsewhere.   And what, now, if those intended do not believe these things, nor any one of them? What if they do openly disavow every one of them, as, for aught I ever heard or know, they do, and as I do myself? What if some of them are ridiculously framed into articles of faith, from the supposed practices of some individual persons? And what if men be of never so vile opinions about the pursuit of their successes, so they have none to countenance them in any unlawful enterprises; which, I think, must go before successes? What if only the Papists be concerned in these articles of faith, and they only in one of them, about the excommunication and deposition of princes, and that only some of them; and not one of those has any concern in them whom he intends to reproach? I say, if these things are so, we need look no farther for the principles of that religion which hath furnished him with all this candour, moderation, and ingenuity, and hath wrought him to such a quiet and peaceable temper, by teaching him that humility, charity, and meekness, which here bewray themselves.

Let it be granted, as it must and ought to be, that all principles of the minds of men, pretended to be from apprehensions of religion, that are in themselves inconsistent with any lawful government, in any place whatever, ought to be coerced and restrained; for our Lord Jesus Christ, sending his gospel to be preached and published in all nations and kingdoms of the world, then and at all times under various sorts of governments, all for the same end of public tranquillity and prosperity, did propose nothing in it but what a submission and obedience unto might be consistent with the government itself, of what sort soever it were. He came, as they used to sing of old, " to give men a heavenly kingdom, and not to deprive them or take from them their earthly temporal dominions." There is, therefore, nothing more certain than that there is no principle of the religion taught by Jesus Christ which either in itself, or in the practice of it, is inconsistent with any righteous government on the earth. And if any opinions can truly and really be manifested so to be, I will be no advocate for them nor their abettors. But such as these our author shall never be able justly to affix on them whom he opposeth, nor the least umbrage of them, if he do but allow the gospel and the power of Christ to institute those spiritual ordinances, and require their administration, which do not, which cannot, extend unto any thing wherein a magistrate, as such, hath the least concernment in point of prejudice; for if, on a false or undue practice of them, any thing should be done that is not purely spiritual, or that, being done, should be esteemed to operate upon any of the outward concerns, relations, interests, or occasions of men, they may be restrained by the power of him who presides over public good.

But besides these pretences, our author, I know not how, chargeth

also the humours, inclinations, and passions of some men as inconsistent with government, and always disposing men to fanaticism and
sedition; and on occasion thereof falls out into an excess of intemperance in reproaching them whom he opposeth, such as we have
not above once or twice before met with the like; and in particular,
he raves about that "zeal," as he calls it, for the glory of God, which
hath "turned whole nations into shambles, filled the world with
butcheries and massacres, and fleshed itself with slaughters of my-
riads of mankind." Now, omitting all other controversies, I shall
undertake to maintain this against any man in the world, that the
effects here so tragically expressed have been produced by the *zeal*
our author pleads for, in compelling all unto the same sentiments
and practices in religion, incomparably above what hath ensued upon
any other pretence in or about religion whatever. This, if need require, I shall evince with such instances, from the entering of Christianity into the world to this very day, as will admit of no competition with all those together which, on any account or pretence, have
produced the like effects. This it was and is that hath soaked the
earth with blood, depopulated nations, ruined families, countries,
kingdoms, and at length made innumerable Christians rejoice in the
yoke of Turkish tyranny, to free themselves from their perpetual
persecutions on the account of their dissent from the worship publicly established in the places of their nativity. And as for the
humours, inclinations, and passions of men, when our author will give
such rules and directions as whereby the magistrate may know how
to make a true and legal judgment of who are fit on their account
to live in his territories, and who are not, I suppose there will not
be any contest about them. Until then, we may leave them, as here
displayed and set up by our author, for every one to cast a cudgel at
them that hath a mind thereunto.

For to what purpose is it to consider the frequent occasions he
takes to discourse about the ill tempers and humours of men, or of
inveighing against them for being "morose and ungentle, unsociable,
peevish, censorious," with many other terms of reproach that do not
at present occur to my memory, nor are, doubtless, worth the searching after? Suppose he hath the advantage of a better natural temper, have more sedate affections, a more compliant humour, be more
remote from giving or receiving provocations, and have learned the
ways of courtly deportment, only was pleased to veil them all and
every one in the writing of this discourse, is it meet that they should
be persecuted and destroyed, be esteemed seditious, and I know not
what, because they are of a natural temper not so disposed to affabi-
lity and sweetness of conversation as some others are? For my part,
I dislike the humour and temper of mind characterized by our author,

it may be as much as he,—I am sure, I think, as much as I ought ; but to make it a matter of such huge importance as solemnly to introduce it into a discourse about religion and public tranquillity will not, it may be, on second thoughts, be esteemed over-considerately done. And it is not unlikely but that our author seems of as untoward a composition and peevish a humour to them whom he reflects upon as they do to him, and that they satisfy themselves as much in their disposition and deportment as he doth himself in his.

> " Nimirum idem omnes fallimur ; neque est quisquam,
> Quem non in aliqua re, videre Suffenum
> Possis."   [Catull., xxii. 18.]

Sect. v. pp. 155, 156, he inveighs against the events that attend the permission of *different sects of religion* in a commonwealth; and it is not denied but that some inconveniences may ensue thereon. But, as himself hath well observed in another place, we do not in these things inquire what is absolutely best, and what hath no inconvenience attending it ; but what is the best which, in our present condition, we can attain unto, and what in that state answers the duty that God requireth of us. Questionless, it were best that we should be all of one mind in these things of God, and it is no doubt also our duty on all hands to endeavour so to be ; but seeing, " de facto," this is not so, nor is it in the power of men, when and how they will, to depose those persuasions of their minds and dictates of their consciences from whence it is not so, on the one part or the other (although in some parts of our differences some may do so and will not, namely, in things acknowledged to be of no necessity antecedent to their imposition, and some would do so and cannot), it is now inquired, What is the best way to be steered in for the accomplishment of the desired end of peace and tranquillity for the future, and maintaining love, quietness, and mutual usefulness at present amongst men? Two ways are proposed to this purpose. The one is, to exercise mutual forbearance to each other whilst we are inevitably under the power of different persuasions in these things, producing no practices that are either injurious unto private men in their rights, or hurtful unto the state as to public peace; endeavouring, in the meantime, by the evidence of truth, and a conversation suited unto it, to win upon each other to a consent and agreement in the things wherein we differ. The other is, by severe laws, penalties, outward force, as imprisonments, mulcts, fines, banishments, or capital punishments, to compel all men out of hand to a uniformity of practice, whatever their judgments be to the contrary. Now, as the state of things is amongst us, which of these ways is most suitable to the law of our being and creation, the best principles of the nature of man, and those which have the most evident resemblance of divine perfections, the gospel, the spirit and letter of it, with the mind of its author, our Lord Jesus Christ,—which is most conducing to attain the end aimed at, in ways of a natural and genuine compliance with the things themselves of religion, conscience, and divine worship,—is left unto the judgment of God and all good men.

In the meantime, if men will make declamations upon their own surmises, jealousies, and suspicions of things which are either so indeed, that is, really surmised, or pretended to be so, for some private interests or advantages of their own, which no man can answer or remove; if they may fancy at their pleasure ghosts, goblins, fiends, walking sprights, seditions, drums, trumpets, armies, bears and tigers; every difference in religion, be it never so small, be the agreement amongst them that differ never so great; be it the visible, known, open interest of them that dissent from what is established to live quietly and peaceably, and to promote the good of the commonwealth wherein they live; do they profess that it is their duty, their principle, their faith and doctrine, to obey constantly their rulers and governors in all things not contrary to the mind of God, and pretend no such commands of his as should interfere in the least with their power in order to public tranquillity; do they offer all the security of their adherence to such declared principles as mankind is necessitated to be contented and satisfied with in things of their highest concernment; do they avow an especial sense of the obligation that is put upon them by their rulers when they are protected in peace; have they no concernment in any such political societies, combinations, interests, as might alone give countenance unto any such disturbance;—all is one, every different *opinion is press-money*, and *every sect is an army*, although they be all and every one of them Protestants, of whom alone we do discourse.   Other answer, therefore, I shall not return unto this part of our author's arguing than what he gave of old,—

> " Ne admittam culpam, ego meo sum promus pectori,
>   Suspicio est in pectore alieno sita.
>   Nam nunc ego te si surripuisse suspicer,
>   Jovi coronam de capite e Capitolio,
>   Quod in culmine astat summo, si non id feceris,
>   Atque id tamen mihi lubeat suspicarier;
>   Quî tu id prohibere me potes, ne suspicer."—[Plaut., Trin. i. 2, 44.]

Only, I may add, that sundry of the instances our author makes use of are false and unduly alleged; for what is here charged on differences in and about religion, in reference unto public tranquillity, might have been, yea, and was, charged on *Christian religion* for three hundred years, and is so by many still on *Protestancy*, as such; and that it were a very easy and facile task to set out the pernicious evils of a compelled agreement in the practice of religion, and those not fancied only or feigned, but such as do follow it, have followed it, and will follow it in the world.

An inquiry in this invective, tending to evince its reasonableness, is offered in p. 158,—namely, " Where there are divided interests in religion in the same kingdom, it is asked, how shall the prince behave himself towards them?" The answer thereunto is not, I confess, easy, because it is not easy to be understood what is intended by " divided interests in religion." We will, therefore, lay that aside, and consider what really is amongst us, or may be, according to what we understand by these expressions. Suppose, then, that in the same profession of protestant religion, some different ways and observances in the outward worship of God should be allowed, and the persons concerned herein have no other, cannot be proved to have any other interest, with respect unto religion, but to "fear God and honour the king," it is a very easy thing to return an answer to this inquiry: for, not entering into the profound political speculation of our author about " balancing of parties, or siding with this or that party," where the differences themselves constitute no distinct parties, in reference to civil government and public tranquillity, let the prince openly avow, by the declaration of his judgment, his constant practice, his establishing of legal rights, disposing of public favours in places and preferments, that way of religion which himself owns and approves; and let him indulge and protect others of the same religion, for the substance of it, with what himself professeth, in the quiet and peaceable exercise of their consciences in the worship of God, keeping all dissenters within the bounds allotted to them, that none transgress them to the invasion of the rights of others;—and he may have both the reality and glory of religion, righteousness, justice, and all other royal virtues; which will render him like to Him whose vicegerent he is; and he will undoubtedly reap the blessed fruits of them in the industry, peaceableness, and loyalty of all his subjects whatever.

There are sundry things, in the close of this chapter, objected against such a course of procedure, but those such as are all of them resolved into a supposition that they who in any place or part of the world desire liberty of conscience for the worship of God have indeed no conscience at all; for it is thereon supposed, without farther evidence, that they will thence fall into all wicked and unconscientious practices. I shall make, as I said, no reply to such surmises. Christianity suffered under them for many ages; Protestancy hath done so in sundry places for many years; and those who now may do so must, as they did, bear the effects of them as well as they are able. Only I shall say, first, Whatever is of real inconvenience in this pretension, on the supposition of liberty of conscience, is no way removed by taking away all different practices, unless ye could also obliterate all different persuasions out of the minds of men; which, although in one place he tells us ought to be done by severe penalties, yet in another he acknowledgeth that the magistrate hath no cognizance of any such things, who yet alone is the inflicter of all penalties. Nay, where different apprehensions are, the absolute prohibition of different answerable practices doth a thousand times more dispose the minds of men to unquietness than where they are allowed both together, as hath been before declared. And he that can obliterate out of and take away all different apprehensions and persuasions about the worship of God from the minds and consciences of men, bringing them to centre in the same thoughts and judgments absolutely, in all particulars about them,

"Dicendum est, Deus ille fuit, Deus, inclute Memmi!
Qui princeps vitæ rationem invenit eam;"—[Lucret., v. 8,]

he is God, and not man.

Secondly, It is granted that the magistrate may and ought to restrain all principles and outward practices that have any natural tendency unto the disturbance of the peace; which being granted, and all obligations upon dissenting parties being alone put upon them by the supreme legislative and executive power of the kingdoms and nations of the world, public tranquillity is, and will be, as well secured on that respect as such things are capable of security in this world. All the longsome discourse, therefore, which here ensues,—wherein all the evils that have been in this nation are charged on liberty of conscience, from whence not one of them did proceed, seeing there was no such thing granted until, upon other civil and political accounts, the flood-gates were set open unto the following calamities and confusions,—is of no use, nor unto any purpose at all: for until it can be demonstratively proved that those who do actually suffer, and are freely willing so to do (as far as the foregoing otherwise lawful advantages, open unto them as well as others, may be so called), and resolved to undergo what may farther, to their detriment, yea, to their ruin, be inflicted on them, to preserve their consciences entire unto some commands of God, have no respect unto others of as great evidence and light to be his (as are those which concern their obedience unto magistrates, compared with those which they avow about the worship of God); and that private men, uninterested in, and incapable of, any pretence unto public authority of any sort, do always think themselves warranted to do such things as others have done, pleading right and authority for their warranty; and until it be made manifest, also, that they have any other or greater interest than to enjoy their particular conditions and estates in peace, and to exercise themselves in the worship of God according as they apprehend his mind to be,—these declamations are altogether vain, and, as to any solid worth, lighter than a feather.

And I could desire if these controversies must be farther debated, that our author would omit the pursuit of those things which are really ἔξω τοῦ πράγματος, and, according to the ancient custom, attend ἄνευ προοιμίων καὶ παθῶν, without rhetorical prefaces or unreasonable passions, unto the merit of the cause. To this purpose I suppose it might not be amiss for him to consider a few sheets of paper lately published under the title of "A Case Stated," etc., wherein he will find the main controversy reduced to its proper heads, and a modest provocation unto an answer to what is proposed about it.

> —— " Illum aspice contra
> Qui vocat."

A SURVEY OF THE SIXTH CHAPTER.

[The word of God the sole rule of worship—The light of reason—Vocal revelation—Magistrate's power in regard to things *without* the church but *about* it—Testimonies from the ancient fathers as to the supreme authority of Scripture—Alleged instances from the Old Testament of the magistrate appointing religious rites—Parker's answers to certain objections considered—Doctrine of passive obedience refuted—Alleged right of the magistrate to punish his subjects if they will not comply with idolatry or superstition established by law—The true dignity and functions of the magistrate declared—Exhortation to toleration and charity.]

THE sixth chapter in this discourse,—which is the last that at the present I shall call to any account, as being now utterly wearied with the frequent occurrence of the same things in various dresses,—is designed to the confutation of a principle which is termed the "foundation of all Puritanism," and that wherein "the mystery of it" consisteth. Now this is, "That nothing ought to be established in the worship of God but what is authorized by some precept or example in the word of God, which is the complete and adequate rule of worship." Be it so that this principle is by some allowed, yea, contended for, it will not be easy to affix a guilt upon them on the account of its being so; for lay aside prejudices, corrupt interests, and passions, and I am persuaded that, at the first view, it will not seem to be foreign unto what is in a hundred places declared and taught in the Scripture. And certainly a man must be master of extraordinary projections who can foresee all the evil, confusion, and desolation in the world, which our author hath found out as inevitable consequences of its admittance. It hath, I confess, been formerly disputed with colourable arguments, pretences, and instances, on the one side and the other, and variously stated amongst learned men, by and on various distinctions, and with divers limitations. But the manner of our author is, that whatever is contrary to his apprehensions must presently overthrow all government and bring in all confusion into the world. Such huge weight hath he wonted himself to lay on the smallest different conceptions of the minds of men, where his own are not enthroned! Particularly, it is contended that there can be no peace in any churches or states whilst this principle is admitted; when it is easily demonstrable that without the admittance of it, as to its substance and principal end, all peace and agreement among churches are utterly impossible. The like also may be said of states; which, indeed, are not at all concerned in it, any farther than as it is a principal means of their peace and security where it is embraced, and that which would reduce rulers to a stability of mind in these things, after they have been tossed up and down with the various suggestions of men, striving every one to exalt their own imaginations. But seeing it is pretended and granted to be of so much importance, I shall, without much regard to the exclamations of this author, and the reproachful, contemptuous expressions, which, without stint or measure, he pours out upon the assertors of it, consider both what is the concern of his present adversaries in it and what is to be thought of the principle itself; so submitting the whole to the judgment of the candid reader. Only, I must add one thing to the position, without which it is not maintained by any of those with whom he hath to do, which may deliver him from combating the air in his next assault of it; and this is, That nothing ought to be established in the worship of God, as a part of that worship, or made constantly necessary in its observance, without the warranty before mentioned: for this is expressly contended for by them who maintain it, and who reject nothing upon the authority of it but what they can prove to be a pretended part of religious worship as such. And, as thus laid down, I shall give some farther account both of the principle itself and of the interest of the Nonconformists in it, because both it and they are together here reproached.

What then, I say, is the true sense and importance of that which our author designs to oppose, according to the mind of them who assert it? How impotent his attempts against it are for its removal shall briefly be declared. In the meantime, I cannot but in the first place tell him, that if by any means this principle, truly stated, as to the expressions wherein it is before laid down, and the formal terms whereof it consisteth, should be shaken or rendered dubious, yet that the way will not be much the plainer or clearer for the introduction of his pretensions. There are yet other general maxims

which Nonconformists adhere unto, and suppose not justly questionable, which they can firmly stand and build upon in the management of their plea, as to all differences between him and them ; and
because, it may be, he is unacquainted with them, I shall reckon
over some of them, for his information. And they are these that
follow:—

1. That whatever the Scripture hath indeed prescribed and appointed to be done and observed in the worship of God and the government of the church, that is indeed to be done and observed.
This, they suppose, will not be opposed; at least, they do not yet
know, notwithstanding any thing spoken or disputed in this discourse, any pretences on which it may honestly so be. It is also, as
I think, secured, Matt. xxviii. 20.

2. That nothing in conjunction with, nothing as an addition or supplement unto, what is so appointed ought to be admitted, if it be contrary either to the general rules or particular preceptive instructions
of the Scripture. And this also, I suppose, will be granted; and if it
be not freely, some are ready by arguments to extort the confession
of it from them that shall deny it.

3. That nothing ought to be joined with or added unto what in
the Scripture is prescribed and appointed in these things without
some cogent reason, making such conjunction or addition necessary.
Of what necessity may accrue unto the observation of such things by
their prescription, we do not now dispute, but at present only desire
to see the necessity of their prescription; and this can be nothing
but some defect, in substance or circumstance, matter or manner,
kind or form, in the institutions mentioned in the Scripture, as to
their proper ends. Now, when this is discovered, I will not, for my
part, much dispute by whom the supplement is to be made. In the
meantime, I do judge it reasonable that there be some previous reasons assigned unto any additional prescriptions in the worship of God
unto what is revealed in the Scripture, rendering the matter of those
prescriptions antecedently necessary and reasonable.

4. That if any thing or things in this kind shall be found necessary
to be added and prescribed, then that and those alone be so which
are most consonant unto the general rules of the Scripture given us
for our guidance in the worship of God, and the nature of those institutions themselves wherewith they are conjoined or whereunto
they are added. And this also I suppose to be a reasonable request,
and such as will be granted by all men who dare not advance their
own wills and wisdom above or against the will and wisdom of God.

Now, if, as was said, the general principle before mentioned
should by any means be duly removed, or could be so, or if entangled
or rendered dubious, yet, as far as I can learn, the Nonconformists

will be very far from supposing the matters in contest between them and their adversaries to be concluded. But as they look upon their concernments to be absolutely secured in the principles now mentioned, all which they know to be true and hope to be unquestionable, so the truth is, there is by this author very small occasion administered unto any thoughts of quitting the former more general thesis as rightly stated; but rather, if his ability be a competent measure of the merit of his cause, there is a strong confirmation given unto it in the minds of considering men, from the impotency and successlessness of the attempt made upon it. And that this may appear to the indifferent reader's satisfaction, I shall so far divert in this place from the pursuit of my first design as to state the principle aright, and briefly to call the present opposition of it unto a new account.

The sum, in general, of what this author opposeth with so much clamour is, That *divine revelation is the sole rule of divine religious worship;* an assertion that, in its latitude of expression, hath been acknowledged in and by all nations and people. The very heathen admitted it of old, as shall be manifested, if need require, by instances sufficient; for though they framed many gods, in their foolish, darkened imaginations, yet they thought that every one of them would be worshipped according to his own mind, direction, and prescription. So did, and I think do, Christians generally believe. Only, some have a mind to pare this generally-avowed principle, to curb it, and order it so, by distinctions and restrictions, that it may serve their turn and consist with their interest; for an opposition unto it nakedly, directly, and expressly, few have had the confidence yet to make. And the Nonconformists need not go one step farther in the expression of their judgments and principles in this matter; for who shall compel them to take their adversaries' distinctions (which have been invented and used by the most learned of them) of "substantial and accidental, proper and reductive, primitive and accessary, direct and consequential, intrinsic and circumstantial worship," and the like, for the most part, unintelligible terms, in their application unto the state of the question? If men have a mind, let them oppose this thesis as laid down; if not, let them let it alone: and they who shall undertake the confirmation of it will no doubt carry it through the briers of those unscriptural distinctions. And that this author may be the better instructed in his future work, I shall give him a farther account of the terms of the assertion laid down.

Revelation is either ἐνδιάθετος or προφορικός, and containeth every discovery or declaration that God hath made of himself or of his mind and will unto men. Thus it is comprehensive of that con-created light which is in all men concerning him and his will; for although we say that this is natural, and is commonly contradistinguished from revelation properly so called, which, for perspicuity's sake, we call revelation supernatural, yet whereas it doth not so necessarily accompany human nature but that it may be separated from it, nor is it educed out of our natural faculties by their own native or primogenial virtue, but is or was distinctly implanted in them by God himself, I place it under the general head of revelation. Hence, whatever is certainly from God, by the light of nature and instinct thereof declared so to be, is no less a certain rule of worship and obedience, so far forth as it is from him and concerneth those things, than any thing that comes from him by express vocal revelation. And this casts out of consideration a vain exception wherewith some men please themselves, as though the men of this opinion denied the admittance of what is from God, and by the light of nature discovered to be his mind and will. Let them once prove any thing in contest between them and their adversaries to be required, prescribed, exacted, or made necessary, by the light of nature, as the will of God revealed therein, and I will assure them that, as to my concern, there shall be an end to all difference about it. But yet, that I may add a little farther light into the sense of the Nonconformists in this matter, I say,—

1. That this inbred light of reason guides unto nothing at all in or about the worship of God, but what is more fully, clearly, and directly taught and declared in the Scripture. And this may easily be evinced, as from the untoward mixture of darkness and corruption that is befallen our primogenial, inbred principles of light and wisdom by the entrance of sin, so also from the end of the Scripture itself, which was to restore that knowledge of God and his mind which was lost by sin, and which might be as useful to man in his lapsed condition as the other was in his pure and uncorrupted estate. At present, therefore, I shall leave this assertion, in expectation of some instance, in matters great or small, to the contrary, before I suppose it be obnoxious to question or dispute.

2. As there can be no opposition nor contradiction between the light of nature and inspired vocal or scriptural revelation, because they are both from God, so if in any instance there should appear any such thing unto us, neither faith nor reason can rest in that which is pretended to be natural light, but must betake themselves for their resolution unto express revelation. And the reason hereof is evident,—because nothing is *natural light* but what is common to all men, and where it is denied, it is frustrated as to its ruling efficacy. Again; it is mixed, as we said before, and it is not every man's work to separate the chaff from the wheat, or what God hath implanted in the mind of man when he made him upright, and what is since soaked into the principles of his nature from his own inventions.

But this case may possibly very rarely fall out, and so shall not much be insisted on.

3. Our inquiry in our present contest is solely about *instituted worship*, which we believe to depend on supernatural revelation. The light of nature can no way relieve or guide us in it or about it, because it refers universally to things above and beyond that light; but only with reference unto those moral, natural circumstances, which appertain unto those actings or actions of men whereby it is performed, which we willingly submit unto its guidance and direction.

Again, *vocal revelation* hath come under two considerations:— First, As it was occasional. Secondly, As it became stated.

First, As it was occasional. For a long time God was pleased to guide his church in many concerns of his worship by fresh occasional revelations, even from the giving of the first promise unto Adam unto the solemn giving of the law by Moses; for although men had, in process of time, many *stated revelations*, that were preserved by tradition among them, as the first promise, the institution of sacrifices, and the like, yet as to sundry emergencies of his worship, and parts of it, God guided them by new occasional revelations. Now, those revelations being not recorded in the Scripture, as being only for present or emergent use, we have no way to know them but by what those to whom God was pleased so to reveal himself did practise, and which, on good testimony, found acceptance with him. Whatever they so did, they had especial warranty from God for; which is the case of the great institution of sacrifices itself. It is a sufficient argument that they were divinely instituted, because they were graciously accepted.

Secondly, Vocal revelation, as the rule of worship, became stated and invariable in and by the giving and writing of the law. From thence, with the allowances before mentioned, we confine it to the Scripture, and so unto all succeeding generations. I confess, many of our company, who have kept to us hitherto in granting divine revelation to be the sole principle and rule of religious worship, now leave us, and betake themselves to paths of their own. The postmisnical[1] Jews, after many attempts made that way by their predecessors, both before and after the conversation of our Lord Christ in the flesh, at length took up a resolution that all obligatory divine revelation was not contained in the Scripture, but was partly preserved by *oral tradition;* for although they added a multitude of observances unto what were prescribed unto their fathers by Moses, yet they would never plainly forego that principle, nor do to this day, that *divine revelation is the rule of divine worship.* Wherefore, to secure their

---

[1] The reference is to the Mishna, or the collection of oral traditions, which profess to be a comment on the laws of Moses. The collection of them is ascribed to Rabbi Jehudah Hakkadosh, A.D. 190, or 220.—ED.

principle and practice, and to reconcile them together (which are indeed at an unspeakable variance), they have fancied their oral law, which they assert to be of no less certain and divine original than the law that is written. On this pretence they plead that they keep themselves unto the forementioned principle, under the superstition of a multitude of self-invented observances. The Papists also here leave us, but still with a semblance of adhering to that principle, which carries so great and uncontrollable an evidence with it as that there are a very few, as was said, who have hitherto risen up in a direct and open opposition unto it; for whereas they have advanced a double principle for the rule of religious worship besides the Scripture,—namely, tradition, and the present determinations of their church, from thence educed,—they assert the first to be divine or apostolical, which is all one, and the latter to be accompanied with infallibility, which is the formal reason of our adherence and submission unto divine revelation : so that they still adhere in general unto the forementioned principle, however they have debauched it by their advancement of those other guides. But herein also we must do them right, that they do not absolutely turn loose those two rude creatures of their own, traditions and present church determinations, upon the whole face of religion, to act therein at their pleasure, but they secure them from whatever is determined in the written word, affirming them to take place only in those things that are not contrary to the word or not condemned in it; for in such, they confess, they ought not nor can take place,—which I doubt whether our author will allow of or no in reference to the power by him asserted.

By "religious worship," in the thesis above, we understand, as was said before, *instituted worship only*, and not that which is purely moral and natural; which, in many instances of it, hath a great coincidence with the light of nature, as was before discoursed.

We understand also *the solemn or stated worship* of the church of God. That worship, I say, which is solemn and stated for the church, the whole church, at all times and seasons, according to the rules of his appointment, is that which we inquire after. Hence, in this matter we have no concernment in the fact of this or that particular person which might be occasionally influenced by necessity, as David's eating of the shew-bread was, and which how far it may excuse or justify the persons that act thereon, or regulate their actions directly, I know not, nor am any way engaged to inquire.

This is the state of our question in hand, the mind of the assertion, which is here so hideously disguised and represented in its pretended consequences. Neither do I think there is any thing needful farther to be added unto it; but yet, for the clearing of it from mistakes, something may be discoursed which relates unto it. We say, then,—

First, That there are sundry things to be used in, about, and with those actions whereby the worship of God is performed, which yet are not sacred, nor do belong unto the worship of God as such, though that worship cannot be performed without them. The very breath that men breathe and the light whereby they see are necessary to them in the worship of God, and yet are not made sacred or religious thereby. Constantine said of old that he was "a bishop, but without the church;" not a sacred officer, but one that took care and had a supervisorship of things necessarily belonging to the performance of God's worship, yet no parts or adjuncts of it as such, for it was all still *without*. Now, all those things in or about the worship of God that belonged unto Constantine's episcopacy,—that is, the ordering and disposal of things *without* the church but *about* it, *without* worship but *about* it,—we acknowledge to be left unto common prudence, guided by the general rules of Scripture, by which the church is to walk and compose its actings. And this wholly supersedes the discourse of our author concerning the great variety of circumstances wherewith all human actions are attended; for, in one word, all such circumstances as necessarily attend human actions, as such, neither are sacred nor can be made so without an express institution of God, and are disposable by human authority: so that the long contest of our author on that head is altogether vain. So, then,—

Secondly, By " all the concernments of religious worship," which any affirm that they must be directed in by divine revelation or regulated by the Scripture, they intend all that is religious, or whatever belongs to the worship of God, as it is divine worship; and not what belongs unto the actions wherein and whereby it is performed, as they are actions.

Thirdly, That when any part of worship is instituted in special, and general rules are given for the practice of it, "hic et nunc," there the warranty is sufficient for its practice at its due seasons; and for those seasons, the nature of the thing itself, with what it hath respect unto, and the light of the general Scripture rules, will give them an acceptable determination.

And these few observations will abundantly manifest the impertinency of those who think it incumbent on any, by virtue of the principle before laid down, to produce express warranty in words of Scripture for every *circumstance* that doth attend and belong unto the actions whereby the worship of God is performed, which as they require not, so no such thing is included in the principle as duly stated. For particular circumstances that have respect to good order, decency, and external regulation of divine worship, they are all of them either circumstances of the actions themselves whereby divine worship is performed and exercised, and so in general they are natural and necessary, which in particular, or "actu exercito," depend on moral prudence; or religious rites themselves, added in and to the whole, or any parts of divine service,—which alone, in this question, come under inquiry.

I know there are usually sundry exceptions put in to this thesis, as before stated and asserted, and instances to the contrary are pretended, some whereof are touched upon by our author, p. 181, which are not now particularly and at large to be considered. But yet, because I am, beyond expectation, engaged in the explication of this principle, I shall set it so far forth right and straight unto farther examination as to give in such general observations as, being consistent with it and explanatory of it, will serve to obviate the most of the exceptions that are laid against it; as,—

1. Wherever in the Scripture we meet with any religious duty that had a preceding institution, although we find not expressly a consequent approbation, we take it for granted that it was approved; and so, on the contrary, where an approbation appears, an institution is concealed.

2. The question being only about religious duties, or things pertaining to or required in or about the worship of God, no exception against the general thesis can take place but such as consists in things directly of that nature. Instances in and about things civil and belonging merely to human conversation, or things natural, as signs and memorials one of another, are in this matter of no consideration.

3. Things extraordinary in their performance, and which, for aught we know, may have been so in their warranty or rule, have no place in our debate: for we are inquiring only after such things as may warrant a suitable practice in us without any farther authority, which is the end for which instances against this principle are produced; this actions extraordinary will not do.

4. Singular and occasional actions, which may be variously influenced and regulated by present circumstances, are no rule to guide the ordinary stated worship of the church. David's eating of the shew-bread, wherein he was justified because of his hunger and necessity, was not to be drawn into example of giving the shew-bread promiscuously to the people. And sundry instances to the same purpose are given by our Saviour himself.

5. There is nothing of any dangerous or bad consequence in this whole controversy, but what lies in the imposition on men's practices of the observation of uncommanded rites, making them necessary unto them in their observation. The things themselves are said in their own nature, antecedent to their injunction for practice, to be

indifferent, and indifferent as unto practice. What hurt would it be to leave them so? They cannot, say some, be omitted, for such and such reasons. Are there, then, reasons for their observation besides their injunction, and such as on the account whereof they are enjoined? Then are they indeed necessary in some degree before their injunction; for all reason for them must be taken from themselves. And things wholly indifferent have nothing in themselves, one more than another, why one should be taken and another left; for if one have the advantage of another in the reasons for its practice, it is no more indifferent, at least it is not comparatively so. Granting, therefore, things enjoined to be, antecedently to their injunction, equally indifferent in their own nature with all other things of the same or the like kind, which yet are rejected or not enjoined, and then to give reasons taken from themselves,—their decency, their conducingness to edification, their tendency to the increase of devotion, their significancy of this or that,—is to speak daggers and contradictions, and to say, "A thing is indifferent before the injunction of its practice; but yet if we had thought so, we would never have enjoined it, seeing we do so upon reasons." And, without doubt, this making necessary the practice of things in the worship of God, proclaimed to be indifferent in themselves, and no way called for by any antecedent reason, is an act of power.

6. Where things are instituted of God, and he himself makes an alteration in or of his own institutions, those institutions may be lawfully practised and observed until the mind of God for their alteration and abolition be sufficiently revealed, proposed, and confirmed unto them that are concerned in them; for as the making of a law doth not oblige until and without the promulgation of it, so as that any should offend in not yielding obedience unto it, so upon the abrogation of a law, obedience may be conscientiously and without sin yielded unto that law, until the abrogation, by what act soever it was made, be notified and confirmed. An instance hereof we have in the observation of Mosaical rites, in the forbearance of God, after the law of their institution was enervated and the obligation of it unto obedience really dissolved, at least the foundation of it laid, for the actual dissolution of it depended on the declaration of the fact wherein it was founded.

7. There may be a coincidence of things performed by sundry persons at the same time and in the same place, whereof some may have respect unto religious worship directly, and so belong unto it, and others only occasionally, and so not at all belong thereunto; as if, when the Athenians had been worshipping at their altars, St Paul had come, and reading the inscription of one of them, and thence taking occasion and advantage to preach "the unknown God" unto

them, their act was a part of religious veneration, his presence and observation of them, and laying hold of that occasion for his own purpose, was not so.

8. Many things which are mere natural circumstances, requisite unto the performance of all actions whatever in communities, and so to be ordered by prudence according unto general rules of the word of God, may seem to be adjuncts of worship, unless they are followed to their original, which will discover them to be of another nature.

9. Civil usages and customs observed in a religious manner,—as they are all to be by them that believe, and directed by them unto moral ends,—may have a show and appearance of religious worship, and so, according to the principle before stated, require express institution; but although they belong unto our living unto God in general, as do all things that we do, seeing "whether we eat or drink, we are to do all to the glory of God," and therefore are to be done in faith, yet they are, or may be, no part of instituted worship, but such actions of life as in our whole course we are to regulate by the rules of the Scripture, so far as they afford us guidance therein.

10. Many observances in and about the worship of God are recorded in the Scripture without especially reflecting any blame or crime on them by whom they were performed (as many great sins are historically only related, and left to be judged by the rule of the word in other places, without the least remark of displeasure on the persons guilty of them), and that by such whose persons were accepted of God; yea, it may be in that very service wherein, less or more, they failed in their observation, God being merciful to them, though not in all things prepared according to the preparation of the sanctuary; and yet the things themselves not to be approved or justified, but condemned of God. Such was the fact of Judas Maccabæus in his offering sacrifices for the sin of them that were dead; and that of instituting an anniversary feast in commemoration of the dedication of the altar.

This little search have I made into this "great mystery," as it is called, "of Puritanism," after which so mighty an outcry is raised by this author; and if it might be here farther pursued, it would, as stated by us in these general rules and explications, be fully manifested to be a principle in general admitted, until of late, by all sorts of men, some few only having been forced sometimes to corrupt it for the security of some especial interest of their own. And it were an easy thing to confirm this assertion by the testimonies of the most learned protestant writers that have served the church in the last ages. But I know how with many amongst us they are regarded, and that the citation of some of the most reverend names among them is not unlikely to prejudice and disadvantage the cause wherein their witness is produced. I shall not, therefore, expose them to the contempt of those, now they are dead, who would have been unwilling to have entered the lists with them in any kind of learning when they were alive. There is, in my apprehension, the substance of this assertion still retained among the Papists. Bellarmine himself lays it down as the foundation of all his controversies, and endeavours to prove: " Propheticos et apostolicos libros verum esse verbum Dei, et certam et stabilem regulam fidei," De Verbo Dei, lib. i. cap. 1;— " That the prophetical and apostolical books are the true word of God, a certain and stable rule of faith." [This] will go a great way in this matter; for all our obedience in the worship of God is the obedience of faith. And if the Scripture be the rule of faith, our faith is not, in any of its concerns, to be extended beyond it, no more than the thing regulated is to be beyond the rule.

Neither is this opinion of so late a date as our author and others would persuade their credulous followers. The full sense of it was spoken out roundly of old. So speaks the great Constantine (that an emperor may lead the way) in his oration to the renowned fathers assembled at Nice: Εὐαγγελικαὶ βίβλοι καὶ ἀποστολικαὶ, καὶ τῶν παλαιῶν προφητῶν θεσπίσματα σαφῶς ἡμᾶς ἃ 'χρὴ περὶ τοῦ θείου φρονεῖν ἐκπαιδεύουσι· τὴν πολεμοποιὸν οὖν ἀπελάσαντες ἔριν, ἐκ τῶν θεοπνεύστων λόγων λάβωμεν τῶν ζητουμένων τὴν λύσιν·—that is, " The evangelical and apostolical books and the oracles of the ancient prophets do plainly instruct us what we are to think of divine things. Laying aside, therefore, all hostile discord, let us resolve the things brought into question by the testimonies of the writings given by divine inspiration." We have here the full substance of what is pleaded for; and might the advice of this noble emperor be admitted, we should have a readier way to expedite all our present differences than as yet seems to be provided for us. The great Basil speaks yet more expressly than Constantine the Great, Lib. de Confes. Fid.: Φανερὰ ἔκπτωσις, καὶ ὑπερηφανίας κατηγορία, ἢ ἀθετεῖν τι τῶν γεγραμμένων, ἢ ἐπεισάγειν τῶν μὴ γεγραμμένων·—that is, " It hath the manifest guilt of infidelity and pride, to reject any thing that is written, or to add or introduce any thing that is not written;" which is the sum of all that in this matter is contended for. To the same purpose he discourseth, Epist. lxxx. ad Eustath.; where, moreover, he rejects all pretences of customs and usages of any sorts of men, and will have all differences to be brought for their determination to the Scripture. Chrysostom, in his Homily on Psalm xcv., speaks the same sense. Saith he, Καὶ τίς ὁ ταῦτα ἐγγυώμενος; Παῦλος. Οὐδὲν γὰρ δεῖ λέγειν ἀμάρτυρον, οὐδὲ ἀπὸ λογισμῶν μόνον· ἐάν τι γὰρ ἄγραφον λέγηται, ἡ διάνοια τῶν ἀκροατῶν σκάζει, πῆ μὲν ἐπινεύουσα, πῆ δὲ παραγραφομένη, καὶ ποτὲ μὲν τὸν λόγον ὡς ἔωλον ἀποστρεφομένη, ποτὲ δὲ ὡς πιθανὸν παραδεχομένη. Ὅταν δὲ ἔγγραφος ἡ μαρτυρία τῆς θείας φωνῆς προέλθῃ, καὶ τοῦ λέγοντος τὸν λόγον, καὶ τοῦ ἀκούοντος τὴν διάνοιαν ἐβεβαίωσε·—" Who is it that promiseth these things? Paul. For we are not to say any thing without testimony, nor upon our mere reasonings; for if any thing be spoken without Scripture (testimony), the mind of the hearers fluctuates, now assenting, anon hesitating, sometimes rejecting what is spoken as frivolous, sometimes receiving it as probable. But where the testimony of the divine voice comes forth from the Scripture, it confirmeth the word of the speaker and the mind of the hearer." It is even so. Whilst things relating to religion and the worship of God are debated and disputed by the reasonings of men, or on any other principles besides the express authority of the Scriptures, no certainty or full persuasion of mind can be attained about them. Men under such actings are as Lucian in his Menippus says he was between the disputations of the philosophers; sometimes he nodded one way, sometimes another, and seemed to give his assent backwards and forwards to express contradictions. It is in the testimony of the Scripture alone about the things of God that the consciences of those that fear him can acquiesce and find satisfaction. The same author, as in many other places, so in his 13th Homily on the Second Epistle to the Corinthians, expressly sends us to the Scripture to inquire after all things, as that which is the exact canon, balance, and rule of religion: Παρὰ τῶν γραφῶν ταῦτα πάντα πυνθάνεσθε. Among the Latins, Tertullian is express to the same purpose. In his book against Hermogenes, " Adoro," said he, " plenitudinem Scripturarum quæ mihi factorem manifestat et facta." Again, " Scriptum esse hoc doceat Hermogenis officina, aut timeat iræ illud adjicientibus aut detrahentibus destinatum;"—" I adore the fulness of the Scripture;" and, " Let Hermogenes prove what he saith to be written, or fear the woe denounced against them who add to or take from the word." And again, in his book, De Carne Christi, " Non recipio quod extra Scripturam de tuo infers;"—" I do not receive what you bring of your own without Scripture." So also in his book, De Præscriptionibus, " Nobis nihil ex nostro arbitrio indulgere licet; sed nec eligere quod aliquis de arbitrio suo induxerit. Apostolos Domini habemus authores, qui nec ipsi quicquam ex suo arbitrio quod inducerent elegerunt; sed acceptam a Christo disciplinam, fideliter nationibus assignaverunt;" —" It is not lawful for us" (in these things) " to indulge unto our own choice, nor to choose what any one brings in of his choosing. We have the apostles of our Lord for our example, who brought in nothing of their own minds or choice; but having received the discipline" (of Christian religion) " from Christ, they faithfully communicated it to the nations." Jerome is plain to the same purpose in sundry places. So Comment. in xxiii. Matth., " Quod de Scripturis authoritatem non habet, eadem facilitate contemnitur qua probatur;"—"That which hath not authority from the Scripture is as easily despised as asserted." Comm. in Hagg., cap. i., " Sed et alia quæ, absque authoritate et testimoniis Scripturarum, quasi traditione apostolica sponte reperiunt atque confingunt, percutit gladius Dei;" —" But those other things which, without authority or testimony of the Scriptures, they find out or feign of their own accord, as of apostolical tradition, the sword of God smites through." It were easy to produce twenty other testimonies out of the ancient writers of the church, giving sufficient countenance to the assertion contended about. What account our author gives of this principle is now, very briefly, to be considered.

First, therefore, pp. 174, 175, he reviles it as " a pretence wild and humorsome, which men must be absurd if they believe, or impudent if they do not, seeing it hath not the least shadow or foundation either from Scripture or reason;" though it be expressly asserted, either in its own terms, or confirmed by direct deductions, in and from above forty places of Scripture. And so much for that part of the assault.

The next chargeth it with infinite follies and mischiefs in those which allow it, and it is said that " there can never be an end of alterations and disturbances in the church whilst it is maintained;" the contrary whereof is true, confirmed by experience and evidence of the thing itself. The admittance of it would put an end to all disturbances; for let any man judge whether, if there be matters in difference, as in all these things there are and ever were, the bringing them to an issue and settled stability be not likelier to be effected by all men's consenting unto one common rule, whereby they may be tried and examined, than that every party should be left at liberty to indulge to their own affections and imaginations about them. And yet we are told, p. 178, " that all the pious villanies that ever have disturbed the Christian world have sheltered themselves in this grand maxim, that Jesus Christ is the only lawmaker to his church." I confess I could heartily desire that such expressions might be forborne; for let what pretence men please be given to them and colour put upon them, they are full of scandal to Christian religion. The maxim itself here traduced is as true as any part of the gospel; and it cannot be pretended that it is not the maxim itself, but the abuse of it (as all the principles of the gospel, through the blindness and lusts of men, have been abused), that is reflected on, seeing the design of the whole discourse is to evert the maxim itself. Now, whatever apprehensions our author may have of his own abilities, I am satisfied that they are no way competent to disprove this principle of the gospel, as will be evident on the first attempt he shall make to that purpose; let him begin the trial as soon as he pleaseth.

In the third section we have a heap of instances raked together to confront the principle in its proper sense before declared and vindicated, in no one whereof it is at all concerned; for the reasons of things in matters civil and religious are not the same. All political government in the world consists in the exercise of principles of natural right, and their just application to times, ages, people, occasions, and occurrences. Whilst this is done, government is acted regularly to its proper end; where this is missed, it fails. These things God hath left unto the prudence of men and their consent; wherein they cannot for the most part fail, unless they are absolutely given up unto unbridled lusts; and the things wherein they may fail are always convenient or inconvenient, good and useful or hurtful and destructive; not always, yea, very seldom, directly and in themselves morally good or evil. In such things men's ease and profit, not their consciences, are concerned. In the worship of God things are quite otherwise. It is not convenience or inconvenience, advantage or disadvantage, as to the things of this life, but merely good or evil, in reference to the pleasing of God and to eternity, that is in question. Particular applications to the manners, customs, usages of places, times, countries,—which is the proper field of human authority, liberty, and prudence in civil things (because their due, useful, and regular administration depends upon them),—have here no place: for the things of the worship of God, being spiritual, are capable of no variations from temporal, earthly varieties among men; have no respect to climates, customs, forms of civil government, or any thing of that nature; but, considering men quite under other notions, namely, of sinners and believers, with respect utterly unto other ends, namely, their living spiritually unto God here, and the eternal enjoyment of him hereafter, are not subject to such prudential accommodations or applications. The worship of God is, or ought to be, the same at all times, in all places, and amongst all people, in all nations; and the order of it is fixed and determined in all particulars that belong unto it. And let not men pretend the contrary until they can give an instance of any such defect in the institutions of Christ as that the worship of God cannot be carried on, nor his church ruled and edified, without an addition of something of their own for the supply thereof, which therefore should and would be necessary to that end antecedent unto its addition; and when they have so done, I will subscribe unto whatsoever they shall be pleased to add of that, or indeed any other kind. " Customs of churches," and " rules of decency," which our author here casts under the magistrate's power, are ambiguous terms, and in no sense express the hypothesis he hath undertaken the defence of. In the proper signification of the words, the things intended may fall under those natural circumstances wherein religious actions in the worship of the church may have their concern, as they are actions, and are disposable by human authority; but he will not, I presume, so soon desert his fundamental principle, of the magistrate's appointing things in and parts of religious worship, nowhere described or determined in the word of God, which alone we have undertaken to oppose. The instances he also gives us about actions in their own nature and use indifferent, as going to law or taking physic, are not in the least to his purpose. And yet if I should say that none of these actions are indeed indifferent in "actu exercito," as they speak, and in their individual performance, but have a moral good or evil, as an inseparable adjunct, attending them, arising out of respect to some rule, general or particular, of divine revelation, I know he cannot disprove it; and much more is not pleaded concerning religious worship.

But this principle is farther charged with "mischief equal to its folly;" which is proved by instances in sundry uninstituted observances, both in the Jewish and primitive Christian churches, as also in protestant churches abroad. I answer, that if this author will consent to umpire these differences by either the Old or New Testament, or by any protestant church in the world, we shall be nearer an end of them than, as far as I can see, yet otherwise we are. If he will not be bound neither to the example of the church of the Jews, nor of the churches of the New Testament, nor of the present protestant churches, it must be confessed that their names are here made use of only for a pretence and an advantage. Under the Old Testament we find that all that God required of his church was, that they should "remember the law of Moses his servant, which he commanded unto him in Horeb for all Israel, with the statutes and judgments," Mal. iv. 4. And when God had given out his institutions and the whole order of his worship, it being fixed in the church accordingly, it is added eight or ten times in one chapter that this was done: "As the LORD commanded Moses, so did he," Exod. xl. After this God gives them many strict prohibitions from adding any thing to what he had so commanded: as Deut. iv. 2, xii. 32; Prov. xxx. 6. And as he had in the decalogue rejected any worship not of his own appointment, as such, Exod. xx. 4, 5, so he made it afterward the rule of his acceptation of that people and what they did, or his refusal of them and it, whether it was by him commanded or no. So, in particular, he expressly rejects that which was so added as to days, and times, and places, though of the nearest affinity and cognation to what was appointed by himself, because it was invented by man, yea, by a king, 1 Kings xii. 33. And when, in process of time, many things of an uncertain original were crept into the observance of the church, and had firmed themselves with the notion of "traditions," they were all at once rejected in that word of the

blessed Holy One, " In vain do ye worship me, teaching for doctrines" (that is, what is in my worship to be observed) " the traditions
of men." For the churches of the New Testament, the foundation of
them is laid in that command of our Saviour, Matt. xxviii. 19, 20,
" Go ye therefore, and teach all nations, baptizing them in the
name of the Father, and of the Son, and of the Holy Ghost: teaching them to observe all things whatsoever I have commanded you:
and, lo, I am with you alway, even unto the end of the world."
That they should be taught to do or observe any thing but what
he commanded,—that his presence should accompany them in the
teaching or observation of any superadditions of their own,—we
nowhère find written, intimated, or exemplified by any practice of
theirs. Nor, however, in that juncture of time, the like whereunto
did never occur before, nor ever shall do again, during the expira-
tion and taking down of Mosaical institutions, before they became
absolutely unlawful to be observed, the apostles, according to the
liberty given them by our Lord Jesus Christ and direction of the
Holy Ghost, did practise some things compliant with both church-
states, did they, in any one instance, impose any thing on the practice of the churches in the worship of God, to be necessarily and for
a continuance observed among them, but what they had express
warrant, and authority, and command of our Lord Christ for. Counsel
they gave in particular cases, that depended upon present emergencies; directions for the regular and due observation of institutions,
and the application of general rules in particular practice; they also
taught a due and sanctified use of civil customs, and the proper use
of moral or natural symbols: but to impose any *religious* rites on
the constant practice of the church in the worship of God, making
them necessary to be always observed by that imposition, they did
not once attempt to do, or assume power for it to themselves. Yea,
when, upon an important difficulty, and to prevent a ruining scandal,
they were enforced to declare their judgment to the churches in some
points, wherein they were to abridge the practice of their Christian
liberty for a season, they would do it only in things made "necessary"
by the state of things then among the churches (in reference to the
great end of edification, whereby all practices are to be regulated),
before the declaration of their judgment for the restriction mentioned,
Acts xv. 23–29. So remote were they from assuming unto themselves
a dominion over the religion, consciences, or faith of the disciples of
Christ, or requiring any thing, in the constant worship of the church,
but what was according to the will, appointment, and command of
their Lord and Master. Little countenance, therefore, is our author
like to obtain unto his sentiments from the Scriptures of the Old and
New Testament, or the example either of the Jews or Christians
mentioned in them.

The instances he gives from the church of the Jews, or that may be given, are either civil observances, as the feast of purim; or moral conveniencies directed by general rules, as the building of synagogues; or customary signs suited to the nature of things, as wearing of sackcloth; or such as have no proof of their being approved, as the feast of dedication, and some monthly fasts taken up in the captivity;—from none of which any objection can be taken against the position before laid down. Those from the church of the New Testament had either a perpetual binding institution from the authority of Christ, as the Lord's-day Sabbath; or contain only a direction to use civil customs and observances in a holy and sanctified manner, as the love feasts and kiss of charity; or such as were never heard of in the New Testament at all, as the observation of Lent and Easter. He that out of these instances can draw a warranty for the power of the civil magistrate over religion and the consciences of men, to institute new duties in religion when he pleaseth, so these " do not countenance vice nor disgrace the Deity," which all his Christian subjects shall be bound in conscience to observe, or otherwise make good any of those particular conclusions, that therefore Christ is not the only lawgiver to his church, or that divine revelation is not the adequate rule of divine worship, or that men may add any thing to the worship of God, to be observed in it constantly and indispensably by the whole church, will manifest himself to have an excellency in argumentation beyond what I have ever yet met withal.

A removal of the argument taken from the perfection of the Scripture, and its sufficiency to instruct us in the whole counsel and will of God, concerning his worship and our obedience unto him, is nextly attempted; but with no engines but what have been discovered to be insufficient to that purpose a hundred times. It is alleged, "That what the Scripture commands in the worship of God is to be observed, that what it forbids is to be avoided;" which if really acknowledged, and a concernment of the consciences of men be granted therein, is sufficiently destructive of the principal design of our author. But, moreover, I say that it commands and forbids things by general rules, as well as by particular precepts and inhibitions; and that if what is so commanded be observed, and what is so forbidden be avoided, there is a direct rule remaining in it for the whole worship of God.

But this is said here to be of "substantial duties, but not of external circumstances;" and if it be so even of substantial duties, it perfectly overthrows all that our author hath been pleading in the first three chapters of his discourse. For external circumstances, of what nature those are which are disposable by human authority and prudence hath been now often declared, and needs not here to be repeated.

The sum of his apprehensions in this matter, about the perfection and sufficiency of the Scripture in reference to the worship of God, our author gives us, p. 189: "Any thing," saith he, "is lawful" (that is, in the worship of God) "that is not made unlawful by some prohibition; for things become evil, not upon the score of their being not commanded, but upon that of their being forbidden. And what the Scripture forbids not, it allows; and what it allows is not unlawful; and what is not unlawful may lawfully be done." This tale, I confess, we have been told many and many a time, but it hath been as often answered that the whole of it, as to any thing of reasoning, is captious and sophistical.

Once more, therefore; what is commanded in the worship of God is lawful, yea, is our duty to observe. All particular instances of this sort that are to have actual place in the worship of God were easily enumerated, and so expressly commanded; and why, among sundry things that might equally belong thereunto, one should be commanded, and another left at liberty without any institution, no man can divine. Of particular things not to be observed there is not the same reason. It is morally impossible that all instances of men's inventions, all that they can find out to introduce into the worship of God, at any time, in any age, and please themselves therein, should be beforehand enumerated and prohibited in their particular instances. And if, because they are not so forbidden, they may lawfully be introduced into divine worship, and imposed upon the practice of men, ten thousand things may be made lawful and be so imposed. But the truth is, although a particular prohibition be needful to render a thing evil in itself, a general prohibition is enough to render any thing unlawful in the worship of God. So we grant that what is not forbidden is lawful, but withal say that every thing is forbidden that should be esteemed as any part of divine worship that is not commanded; and if it were not, yet for want of such a command or divine institution, it can have neither use nor efficacy with respect to the end of all religious worship.

Our author speaks with his wonted confidence in this matter; yea, it seems to rise to its highest pitch, as also doth his contempt of his adversaries or whatever is or may be offered by them in the justification of this principle. "Infinite certainty" on his own part, p. 193, "baffled and intolerable impertinencies, weak and puny arguments, cavils of a few hot-headed and brain-sick people," with other opprobrious expressions of the like nature, filling up a great part of his leaves, are what he can afford unto those whom he opposeth. But yet I am not, for all this bluster, well satisfied, much less "infinitely certain," that he doth in any competent measure understand aright the controversy about which he treats with all this wrath and confidence; for the sum of all that here he pleads is no more but this, that "the circumstances of actions in particular are various, and as they are not, so they cannot be, determined by the word of God, and therefore must be ordered by human prudence and authority:" which if he suppose that any man denies, I shall the less wonder at his severe reflections upon them, though I shall never judge them necessary or excusable in any case whatever. Page 198, he imposeth it on others that lie under the power of this persuasion, "that they are obliged in conscience to act contrary to whatever their superiors command them in the worship of God;" which farther sufficiently evidenceth that either he understands not the controversy under debate, or that he believes not himself in what he saith; which, because the harsher imputation, I shall avoid the owning of in the least surmise.

Section 6, from the concession that the "magistrate may take care that the laws of Christ be executed,"—that is, command and require his subjects to observe the commands of Christ in that way and by such means as those commands, from the nature of the things themselves, and according to the rule of the gospel, may be commanded and required,—he infers that he hath himself power of making laws in religion! But why so? and how doth this follow? Why, saith he, "It is apparently implied, because whoever hath a power to see that laws be executed cannot be without a power to command their execution." Very good: but the conclusion should have been, "He cannot be without a power to make laws in the matter about which he looks to the execution;" which would be good doctrine for justices of the peace to follow. But what is here laid down is nothing but repeating of the same thing in words a little varied; as if it had been said, "He that hath power to see the laws executed, or a power to command their execution, he hath power to see the laws executed, or a power to command their execution;" which is very true. And this we acknowledge the magistrate hath, in the way before declared. But that, because he may do this, he may also make laws of his own in religion, it doth not at all follow from hence, whether it be true or no. But this is farther confirmed from "the nature of the laws of Christ, which have only declared the substance and morality of religious worship, and therefore must needs have left the ordering of its circumstances to the power and wisdom of lawful authority." "The laws of Christ" which are intended are those which he hath given concerning the worship of God. That these have "determined the morality of religious worship," I know not how he can well allow, who makes the law of nature to be the measure of morality and all moral religious worship. And for "the substance of religious worship," I wish it were well declared what is intended by it. For my part, I think that whatever is commanded by Christ, the observation of it is of the substance of religious worship; else, I am sure the sacraments are not so. Now, do but give men leave, as rational creatures, to observe those commands of Christ in such a way and manner as the nature of them requires them to be observed, as he hath himself in general rules prescribed, as the concurrent actions of many in society make necessary, and all this controversy will be at an end. When a duty, as to the kind of it, is commanded in particular, or instituted by Christ in the worship of God, he hath given general rules to guide us in the individual performance of it, as to the circumstances that the actions whereby it is performed will be attended withal. For the disposal of those circumstances according to those rules, prudence is to take place and to be used; for men, who are obliged to act as men in all other things, are not to be looked on as brutes in what is required of them in the worship of God.

But to institute mystical rites and fixed forms of sacred administrations, whereof nothing in the like kind doth necessarily attend the acting of instituted worship, is not to determine circumstances, but to ordain new parts of divine worship; and such injunctions are here confessed by our author, p. 191, to be " new and distinct commands by themselves," and to enjoin something that the Scripture nowhere commands: which when he produceth a warranty for, he will have made a great progress towards the determining of the present controversy.

Page 192, he answers an objection, consisting of two branches, as by him proposed, whereof the first is, " That it cannot stand with the love and wisdom of God not to take order himself for all things that immediately concern his own worship and kingdom." Now, though I doubt not at all but that God hath so done, yet I do not remember at present that I have read [of] any imposing the necessity hereof upon him in answer to his love and wisdom. I confess Valerianus Magnus, a famous writer of the church of Rome, tells us that never any one did so foolishly institute or order a commonwealth as Jesus Christ must be thought to have done, if he have not left one supreme judge to determine the faith and consciences of men in matters of religion and divine worship; and our author seems not to be remote from that kind of reasoning, who, without an assignment of a power to that purpose, contendeth that all things among men will run into confusion,—of so little concernment do the Scriptures and the authority of God in them to some seem to be. We do indeed thankfully acknowledge that God, out of his love and wisdom, hath ordered all things belonging to his worship and spiritual kingdom in the world; and we do suppose we need no other argument to evince this assertion but to challenge all men who are otherwise minded to give an instance of any defect in his institutions to that purpose. And this we are the more confirmed in, because those things which men think good to add unto them, they dare not contend that they are parts of his worship, or that they are added to supply any defect therein; neither did ever any man yet say that there is a defect in the divine institution of worship, which must be supplied by a minister's wearing a surplice. All, then, that is intended in this consideration, though not urged, as is here pretended, is, that God, in his goodness, love, and care towards his church, hath determined all things that are needful in or to his worship; and about what is not needful, men, if they please, may contend, but it will be to no great purpose.

The other part of the objection which he proposeth to himself is laid down by him in these words: " If Jesus Christ have not determined all particular rites and circumstances of religion, he hath discharged his office with less wisdom and fidelity than Moses, who ordered every thing appertaining to the worship of God, even as far as the pins or nails of the tabernacle." And hereunto in particular he returns in answer not one word, but only ranks it amongst idle and impertinent reasonings. And I dare say he wants not reasons for his silence; whether they be pertinent or no I know not: for setting aside the advantage that, it is possible, he aimed to make in the manner and terms of the proposal of this objection to his sentiments, it will appear that he hath not much to offer for its removal. We dispute not about the " rites and circumstances of religion," which are terms ambiguous, and, as hath been declared, may be variously interpreted, no more than we do about the " nails of the tabernacle," wherein there were none at all; but it is about the worship of God, and what is necessary thereunto. The ordering hereof, —that is, of the house of God and all things belonging thereunto,— was committed to Jesus Christ, " as a Son over his own house," Heb. iii. 1–6. In the discharge of his trust therein he was faithful, as was Moses, who received that testimony from God, that he was " faithful in all his house," upon his ordering all things in the worship of God as he commanded him, without adding any thing of his own thereunto, or leaving any thing uninstituted or undetermined which was to be of use therein. From the faithfulness of Christ, therefore, in and over the house of God, as it is compared with the faithfulness of Moses, it may be concluded, I think, that he ordered all things for the worship of God in the churches of the New Testament, as far as Moses did in and for the church of the Old, and more is not contended for; and it will be made appear that his commission in this matter was as extensive as that of Moses at the least, or he could not, in that trust and the discharge of it, have that pre-eminence above him which in this place is ascribed unto him.

Section 7, an account is given of the great variety of circumstances which do attend all human actions, whence it is impossible that they should be all determined by divine prescription. The same we say also; but add withal, that if men would leave these circumstances free, under the conduct of common prudence, in the instituted worship of God, as they are compelled so to do in the performance of moral duties, and as he himself hath left them free, it would be as convenient for the reasons and consciences of.men as an attempt to the contrary. Thus, we have an instance given us by our author in *the moral duty of charity*, which is commanded us of God himself; but the *times, seasons, manner, objects, measures* of it are left free, to be determined by human prudence upon emergencies and occasions. It may be now inquired whether the magistrate, or any other, can determine those circumstances by a law? or whether they are not, as by God, so by all wise men, left free, under the conduct of their reason and conscience who are obliged to do the duty itself by the command of God? And why may not the same rule and order be observed with respect to the circumstances that attend the performance of the duties of instituted worship? Besides, there are general circumstances that are capable of a determination,—such are time and place as naturally considered,—without such adjuncts as might give them a moral consideration, or render them good or evil; these the magistrate may determine: but for particular circumstances attending individual actions, they will hardly be regulated by a standing law. But none of these things have the least interest in our debate. To add things necessarily to be observed in the worship of God, no way naturally related unto the actions wherewith prescribed worship is to be performed, and then to call them circumstances thereof, erects a notion of things which nothing but interest can digest and concoct.

His eighth section is unanswerable. It contains such a strenuous reviling of the Puritans, and contemptuous reproaches of their writings, with such encomiums of their adversaries, as there is no dealing with it; and so I leave it. And so likewise I do his ninth, wherein, as he saith, he "upbraids the men of his contest with their shameful overthrows, and dares them to look those enemies in the face that have so lamentably cowed them by so many absolute triumphs and victories:" which kind of juvenile exultations on feigned suppositions will, I suppose, in due time receive an alloy from his own more advised thoughts and considerations. The instance wherewith he countenanceth himself in his triumphant acclamations unto the victory of his party is the book of Mr Hooker, and its being unanswered; concerning which I shall only say, that as I wish the same moderation, ingenuity, and learning unto all that engage in the same cause with him in these days, so if this author will mind us of any one argument in his longsome discourse not already frequently answered, and that in print long ago, it shall have its due consideration. But this kind of discourse, it may be, on second thoughts, will be esteemed not so comely. And I can mind him of those who boast as highly of some champions of their own against all Protestants, as he can do of any patron of those opinions which he contendeth for. But it doth not always fall out that those who have the most outward advantages and greatest leisure have the best cause and abilities to manage it.

The next sections treat concerning *superstition, will-worship,* and *Popery;* which, as he saith, having been charged by some on the church unduly, he retorts the crime of them upon the authors of that charge. I love not to strive, nor will I contend about words that may have various significations fixed on them. It is about things that we differ. That which is evil is so, however you call it, and whether you can give it any special name or no. That which is good will still be so, call it what and how men please. The giving of a bad or odious name to any thing doth not make itself to be bad or odious. The managing, therefore, of those appellations, either as to their charge or recharge, I am no way concerned in. When it is proved that men believe, teach, or practise otherwise than in duty to God they ought to do, then they do evil; and when they obey his mind and will in all things, then they do well, and in the end will have the praise thereof. In particular, I confess superstition, as the word is commonly used, denotes a vicious habit of mind with respect unto God and his worship, and so is not a proper denomination for the worship itself, or of any evil or crime in it; but yet, if it were worth contending about, I could easily manifest that, according to the use of the word by good authors, in all ages men have been charged with that crime from the kind and nature of the worship itself observed by them. And when St Paul charged the Athenians with an excess in superstition, it was from the multiplication of their gods, and thronging them together, right or wrong, in the dedication of their altars. But these things belong not at all to our present design. Let them who enjoin things unto an indispensable necessary observation in the worship of God, which are not by him prescribed therein, take care of their own minds that they be free from the vice of superstition, and they shall never be judged or charged by me therewith; though I must say that a multiplication of instances in this kind, as to their own observation, is the principal if not the only way whereby men who own the true and proper object of religious worship do or may manifest themselves to be influenced by that corrupt habit of mind, so that they may relate unto superstition as the effect to its cause. But the recrimination here insisted on, with respect unto them who refuse admittance unto or observance of things so enjoined, is such as ought to be expected from provocations and a desire of retortion. Such things usually taste of the cask, and are sufficiently weak and impertinent; for it is a mistake, that those charged do make, as it is here expressed, " any thing necessary not to be done," or put " any religion in the not doing of any thing," or the non-observance of any rites, orders, or ceremonies, any other than every one puts in his abstinence from what God forbids, which is a part of our moral obedience.

And the whole question in this matter is not, Whether, as it is here phrased, " God hath tied up his creatures to nice and pettish laws, laying a greater stress upon a doubtful or indifferent ceremony than upon the great duty of obedience?" but merely, Whether men are to observe in the worship of God what they apprehend he hath enjoined them, and to abstain from what he doth forbid, according to all the light that they have into his mind and will? which inquiry, as I suppose, may be [thus] satisfied,—that they are so to practise and so to abstain, without being liable to the charge of superstition. No man can answer for the minds of other men, nor know what depraved, vicious habits and inclinations they are subject unto. Outward actions are all that we are, in any case, allowed to pass judgment upon, and of men's minds as those actions are indications of them. Let men, therefore, observe and do in the worship of God whatever the Lord Christ hath commanded them, and abstain from what he hath forbidden, whether in particular instances or by general directive precepts and rules,—by which means alone many things are capable of falling under a prohibition, without the least thought of placing any worship of God in their abstinence from this or that thing in particular,—and I think they need not much concern themselves in the charge of superstition given in or out by any against them.

For what is discoursed, section 11, about will-worship, I cannot so far agree with our author as I could in what passed before about superstition; and that partly because I cannot discern him to be herein at any good agreement with himself: for " superstition," he tells us, "consists in the apprehensions of men, when their minds are possessed with weak and uncomely conceits of God," p. 201; here, that " will-worship consists in nothing else than in men's making their own fancies and inventions necessary parts of religion," which outward actings are not coincident with the inward frame and habit of mind before described. And I do heartily wish that some men could well free themselves from the charge of will-worship, as it is here described

by our author, though cautelously expressed, to secure the concernments of his own interest from it; for although I will not call the
things they contend to impose on others in the worship of God their
" fancies," yet themselves acknowledge them to be their " inventions."
And when they make them necessary to be observed in the whole worship of God, as public and stated, and forbid the celebration of that
worship without them; when they declare their usefulness and spiritual or mystical significancy in that worship or service, designing to
honour God in or by their use, setting up some of them to an exclusion of what Christ hath commanded,—if I cannot understand but
that they make them necessary parts of God's worship, as to the
actual observance of it, I hope they will not be angry with me, since
I know the worst they can possibly with truth charge upon me in
this matter is, that I am not so wise nor of so quick an understanding as themselves. Neither doth our author well remove his charge
from those whose defence he hath undertaken; for he doth it only
by this consideration, " that they do not make the things by them
introduced in the worship of God to be parts of religion; they are
not so," he saith, " nor are made so by them;"—for this hinders not
but that they may be looked on as parts of divine worship, seeing
we are taught by the same hand that " external worship is no part
of religion at all." And let him abide by what he closeth this section withal,—namely, that they make not any additions to the worship of God, but only provide that what God hath required be performed in an orderly and decent manner,—and, as to my concern,
there shall be an end of this part of our controversy.

The ensuing paragraphs about " Christian liberty, adding to the
commands of God, and Popery," are of the same nature with those
preceding about superstition and will-worship. There is nothing
new in them but words, and they may be briefly passed through.
For the charge of Popery, on the one side or other, I know nothing
in it, but that when any thing is enjoined or imposed on men's
practice in the worship of God, which is known to have been invented
in and by the papal church during the time of its confessed apostasy,
it must needs beget prejudices against it in the minds of them who
consider the ways, means, and ends of the fatal defection of that
church, and are jealous of a sinful compliance with it in any of those
things. The recharge on those who are said " to set up a pope in
every man's conscience, whilst they vest it with a power of counter-
manding the decrees of princes,"—if no more be intended by "coun-
termanding" but a refusal to observe their decrees and yield obedience to them in things against their consciences, which is all that can
be pretended,—if it fall not on this author himself, as in some cases it
doth, and which, by the certain conduct of right reason, must be ex-

tended to all wherein the consciences of men are affected with the authority of God, yet it doth on all Christians in the world that I know of, besides himself. [As] for "adding to the law of God," it is not charged on any that they add to his commands, as though they made their own divine, or part of his word and law; but only that they add in his worship to the things commanded by him: which being forbidden in the Scripture, when they can free themselves from it I shall rejoice, but as yet see not how they can so do. Nor are there any, that I know of, who "set up any prohibitions of their own," in or about the worship of God, or any thing thereunto pertaining, as is unduly and unrighteously pretended. There may be, indeed, some things enjoined by men which they do and must abstain from, as they would do from any other sin whatever; but their consciences are regulated by no prohibitions but those of God himself. And things are prohibited and made sinful unto them, not only when in particular, and by a specification of their instances, they are forbidden, but also when there lie general prohibitions against them on any account whatever. Some men, indeed, think that if a *particular prohibition* of any thing might be produced, they would acquiesce in it, whilst they plead an exemption of sundry things from being included in general prohibitions, although they have the direct formal reason attending them on which those prohibitions are founded: but it is to be feared that this also is but a pretence; for let any thing be particularly forbidden, yet if men's interest and superstition induce them to observe or retain it, they will find out distinctions to evade the prohibition and retain the practice. What can be more directly forbidden than the making or using of graven images in or about religious worship? and yet we know how little some men do acquiesce in that prohibition. And it was the observation of a learned prelate of this nation, in his rejection of the distinctions whereby they endeavoured to countenance themselves in their idolatry, that the particular instances of things forbidden in the second commandment are not principally intended, but the general rule of not adding any thing in the worship of God without his institution. "Non imago," saith he, "non simulachrum prohibetur; sed non facies tibi." What way soever, therefore, any thing becomes a sin unto any, be it by a particular or general prohibition, be it from the scandal that may attend its practice, unto him it is a sin. And it is a wild notion, that when any persons abstain from the practice of that in the worship of God which to them is sinful as so practised, they add prohibitions of their own to the commands of God.

The same is to be said concerning Christian liberty. No man, that I know of, makes "things indifferent to be sinful," as is pretended, nor can any man in his right wits do so; for none can entertain contradictory notions of the same thing at the same time, as these are, that the same things are indifferent, that is, not sinful, and sinful. But this some say, that things in their own nature indifferent, that is, absolutely so, may be yet relatively unlawful, because, with respect unto that relation, forbidden of God. To set up an altar of old for a civil memorial in any place was a thing indifferent; but to set up an altar to offer sacrifices on, where the tabernacle was not, was a sin. It is indifferent for a man that understands that language to read the Scripture in Latin or in English; but to read it in Latin unto a congregation that understands it not, as a part of God's worship, would be sin. Nor doth our Christian liberty consist alone in our judgment of the indifferency of things in their own nature, made necessary to practice by commands, as hath been showed; and if it doth so, the Jews had that privilege as much as Christians. And they are easily offended who complain that their Christian liberty, in the practice of what they think meet in the worship of God, is intrenched on by such as, leaving them to their pleasure, because of their apprehension of the will of God to the contrary, cannot comply with them in their practice.

The close of this chapter is designed to the removal of an objection, pretended to be weighty and difficult, but indeed made so merely by the novel opinions advanced by this author ; for, laying aside all respect unto some uncouth principles broached in this discourse, there is scarce a Christian child of ten years old but can resolve the difficulty pretended, and that according to the mind of God: for it is supposed that the magistrate may "establish a worship that is idolatrous and superstitious," and an inquiry is made thereon what the subject shall do in that case? Why, where lies the difficulty? "Why," saith he, "in this case they must be either rebels or idolaters. If they obey, they sin against God; if they disobey, they sin against their sovereign." According to the principles hitherto received in Christian religion, any one would reply and say, No: for it is certain that men must obey God, and not contract the guilt of such horrible sins as idolatry and superstition; but in so doing they are neither rebels against their ruler nor do sin against him. It is true, they must quietly and patiently submit to what they may suffer from him, but they are in so doing guilty of no rebellion or sin against him. Did ever any Christian yet so much as call it into question whether the primitive Christians were rebels, and sinned against their rulers, because they would not obey those edicts whereby they established idolatrous worship? or did any one ever think that they had a difficult case of conscience to resolve in that matter? They were, indeed, accused by the Pagans as rebels against the emperors; but no Christian ever yet thought their case to have been doubtful. But all this difficulty ariseth from the making of two Gods, where there ought to be but one; and this renders the case so perplexed, that, for my part, I cannot see directly how it is determined by our author. Sometimes he speaks as though it were the duty of subjects to comply with the establishment of idolatry supposed, as pp. 214, 215; for with respect, as I suppose, it is to the case as by him stated that he says, "Men must not withdraw their obedience;" and, "Better submit unto the unreasonable impositions of Nero or Caligula than to hazard the dissolution of the state." Sometimes he seems not to oblige them in conscience to practise according to the public prescription, but only pleads that the magistrate may punish them if they do not, and fain would have it thought that he may do so justly. But these things are certain unto us in this matter, and are so many κύριαι δόξαι in Christian religion:—That if the supreme magistrate command any thing in the worship of God that is idolatrous, we are not to practise it accordingly, because we must obey God rather than men. Nextly, That in our refusal of compliance with the magistrate's commands, we do neither rebel nor sin against him; for God hath not, doth not at any time, shut us up, in any condition, unto a necessity of sinning. Thirdly, That in case the magistrate shall think meet, through his own mistakes and misapprehensions, to punish, destroy, and burn them alive who shall not comply with his edicts, as did Nebuchadnezzar, or as they did in England in times of Popery, after all honest and lawful private ways of self-preservation used, which we are obliged unto, we are quietly and patiently to submit to the will of God in our sufferings, without opposing or resisting by force, or stirring up seditions or tumults, to the disturbance of public peace.

But our author hath elsewhere provided a full solution of this difficulty, chap. viii. p. 308, where he tells us, "That in cases and disputes of a public concern, private men are not properly 'sui juris;' they have no power over their actions; they are not to be directed by their own judgments, or determined by their own wills, but by the commands and determinations of the public conscience; and if there be any sin in the command, he that imposed it shall answer for it, and not I, whose duty it is to obey. The commands of authority will warrant my obedience; my obedience will hallow or at least excuse my action, and so secure me from sin, if not from error, because I follow the best guide and most probable direction I am capable of; and though I may mistake, my integrity shall preserve my innocence; and in all doubtful and disputable cases, it is better to err with authority than to be in the right against it." When he shall produce any one divine writer, any of the ancient fathers, any sober schoolmen or casuists, any learned modern divines, speaking at this rate, or giving countenance unto his direction given to men for the regulating of their moral actions, it shall be farther attended unto. I know some such thing is muttered amongst the pleaders for blind obedience upon vows voluntarily engaged into for that purpose. But as it is acknowledged by themselves that by those vows they deprive themselves of that right and liberty which naturally belong unto them, as unto all other men (wherein they place much of the merit of them); so by others those vows themselves, with all the pretended brutish obedience that proceeds from them, are sufficiently evidenced to be a horrible abomination, and such as make a ready way for the perpetration of all villanies in the world,—to which purpose that kind of obedience hath been principally made use of. But these things are extremely fond, and not only, as applied unto the worship of God, repugnant to the gospel, but also in themselves to the law of our creation, and that moral dependence on God which is indispensable unto all individuals of mankind. We are told in the gospel that "every man is to be fully persuaded in his own mind;" that "whatsoever is not of faith is sin;" that we are not to be (in such things) "the servants of men;" that other men's leading of us amiss, whoever they are, will not excuse us, "for if the blind lead the blind, both shall fall into the ditch," and he that followeth is as sure to perish as he that leadeth. The next guides of the souls and consciences of men are, doubtless, those who speak unto them in the name of God, or preachers of the gospel ; yet are all the disciples of Christ frequently warned to "take heed" that they be not deceived by any under that pretence, but diligently examining what is proposed unto them, they discern in themselves what is good and evil. Nor doth the great apostle himself require us to be followers of him any farther than he was a follower of Christ. They will find small relief who, at the last day, shall charge their sins on the commands of others, whatever hope to the contrary they are put into by our author. Neither will it be any excuse that we have done according to the precepts of men, if we have done contrary to those of God. Ephraim of old was "broken in judgment, because he willingly walked after the commandment," Hos. v. 11. But would not his "obedience hallow, or at least excuse, his action?" and would not the "authority of the king warrant his obedience?" or must Ephraim now answer for the sin, and not he only that imposed the command? But it seems that when Jeroboam sinned, who at that time had this goodly creature of the "public conscience" in keeping, he made Israel sin also, who obeyed him. It is, moreover, a brave attempt, to assert that "private men," with respect to any of their moral actions, "are not properly 'sui juris,' have no power over their actions, are not to be directed by their own judgments or determined by their own wills." This is Circe's rod, one stroke whereof turned men into hogs. For to what purpose serve their understandings, their judgments, their wills, if not to guide and determine them in their actions? I think he would find hard work that should go about to persuade men to put out their own eyes, or blind themselves, that they might see all by one public eye; and I am sure it is no less unreasonable to desire them to reject their own wills, understandings, and judgments, to be led and determined by a public conscience, considering especially that that public conscience itself is a mere "tragelaphus," which never had existence in "rerum natura."

Besides, suppose men should be willing to accept of this condition of renouncing their own understandings and judgments from being their guides as to their moral actions, I fear it will be found that indeed they are not able so to do. Men's understandings and their consciences are placed in them by him who made them, to rule in them and over their actions in his name, and with respect unto their dependence on him; and let men endeavour it whilst they please, they shall never be able utterly to cast off this yoke of God and destroy this order of things, which is by him inlaid in the principles of all rational beings. Men, whilst they are men, in things that have a moral good or evil in them or adhering to them, must be guided and determined by their own understandings whether they will or no; and if by any means they stifle the actings of them at present, they will not avoid that judgment which, according to them, shall pass upon them at the last day. But these things may elsewhere be farther pursued. In the meantime, the reader may take this case as it is determined by the learned prelate[1] before mentioned, in his dialogue about subjection and obedience, against the Papists, whose words are as follow. Part iii. p. 297:—"*Philand.* If the prince establish any religion, whatever it be, you must by your oath obey it. *Theoph.* We must not rebel and take arms against the prince, but with reverence and humility serve God before the prince; and that is nothing against our oath. *Philand.* Then is not the prince supreme. *Theoph.* Why so? *Philand.* Yourselves are superior, when you serve whom you list. *Theoph.* As though to serve God according to his will were to serve whom we list, and not whom princes and all others ought to serve. *Philand.* But you will be judges when God is well served, and when not. *Theoph.* If you can excuse us before God when you mislead us, we will serve him as you shall appoint us; otherwise, if every man shall answer for himself, good reason he be master of his own conscience in that which toucheth him so near, and no man shall excuse him for. *Philand.* This is to make every man supreme judge of religion. *Theoph.* The

---

[1] Dr Bilson. See page 407.

poorest wretch that is may be supreme governor of his own heart; princes rule the public and external actions of their countries, but not the consciences of men." This in his days was the doctrine of the church of England; and, as was observed before, no person who then lived in it knew better what was so.

The sole inquiry remaining is, Whether the magistrate, having established such a religion as is idolatrous or superstitious, may justly and lawfully punish and destroy his subjects for their non-compliance therewithal? This is that which, if I understand him, our author would give countenance unto, contrary to the common sense of all Christians, yea, of common sense itself; for whereas he interweaves his discourse with suppositions that men may mistake in religion and abuse it, all such interpositions are purely sophistical, seeing the case proposed to resolution, which ought in the whole to be precisely attended unto, is about the refusal to observe and practise a religion idolatrous or superstitious. Of the like nature is that argument which alone he makes use of here and elsewhere to justify his principles,—namely, the necessity of government, and how much better the worst government is and the most depraved in its administration than anarchy or confusion; for as this by all mankind is unquestioned, so I do not think there is any one among them who can tell how to use this concession to our author's purpose. Doth it follow that because magistrates cannot justly or righteously prescribe an idolatrous religion, and compel their subjects to the profession and obedience of it, and because the subjects cannot nor ought to yield obedience therein, because of the antecedent and superior power of God over them, therefore anarchy or confusion must be preferred before such an administration of government? Let the magistrate command what he will in religion, yet, whilst he attends unto the ends of all civil government, that government must needs be every way better than none, and is by private Christians to be borne with and submitted unto, until God in his providence shall provide relief. The primitive Christians lived some ages in the condition described, refusing to observe the religion required by law, and exercising themselves in the worship of God, which was strictly forbidden; and yet neither anarchy, nor confusion, nor any disturbance of public tranquillity did ensue thereon. So did the Protestants here in England in the days of Queen Mary, and some time before. The argument which he endeavours in these discourses to give an answer unto is only of this importance: If the supreme magistrate may command what religion he pleaseth, and enact the observation of it under destructive penalties, whereas the greatest part of magistrates in the world will and do prescribe such religions and ways of divine worship as are idolatrous or superstitious, which their subjects are indispensably bound in conscience not to comply withal, then is the magistrate justified in the punishing of men for their serving of God as they ought, and they may suffer as *evil-doers* in what they suffer as *Christians.* This, all the world over, will justify them that are uppermost and have power in their hands (on no other ground but because they are so and have so) in their oppressions and destructions of them that, being under them in civil respects, do dissent from them in things religious. Now, whether this be according to the mind of God or no is left unto the judgment of all indifferent men. We have, I confess, I know not how many expressions interposed in this discourse, as was observed, about "sedition, troubling of public peace, men being turbulent against prescribed rules of worship," whereof if he pretend that every peaceable dissenter and dissent from what is publicly established in religious worship are guilty, he is a pleasant man in a disputation; and if he do any thing, he determines his case proposed on the part of compliance with idolatrous and superstitious worship. If he do not so, the mention of them in this place is very importune and unseasonable. All men acknowledge that such miscarriages and practices may be justly coerced and punished; but what is this to a bare refusal to comply in any idolatrous worship, and a peaceable practice of what God doth require, as that which he will accept and own?

But our author proceeds to find out many pretences on the account whereof persons whom he acknowledgeth to be innocent and guiltless may be punished; and though their "apprehensions in religion be not," as he saith, "so much their crime as their infelicity, yet there is no remedy, but it must expose them to the public rods and axes," p. 219. I have heard of some wise and righteous princes, who have affirmed that they had rather let twenty guilty persons go free than punish or destroy one that was innocent. This seems to render them more like Him whose vicegerents they are than to seek out colourable reasons for the punishment of them whom they know to be innocent; which course is here suggested unto them. Such advice might be welcome to him whom men called πηλὸν αἵματι πεφυραμένον,—" clay mingled and leavened with blood;" others, no doubt, will abhor it and detest it. But what spirit of meekness and mercy our author is acted by he discovereth in the close of this chapter, p. 223; for, saith he, " it is easily imaginable how an honest and well-meaning man may, through mere ignorance, fall into such errors, which, though God will pardon, yet governors must punish. His integrity may expiate the crime, but cannot prevent the mischief of his error. Nay, so easy is it for men to deserve to be punished for their consciences, that there is no nation in the world in which (were government rightly understood and duly managed) mistakes and abuses of religion would not supply the galleys with vastly greater numbers than villany." There is no doubt but that if Phaeton get into the chariot of the sun, the world will be sufficiently fired. And if every Absalom, who thinks he understands government and the due management of it better than its present possessors, were enthroned, there would be havoc enough made among mankind. But blessed be God, who in many places hath disposed it into such hands as under whom those who desire to fear and serve him according to his will may yet enjoy a more tolerable condition than such adversaries are pleased withal. That honest and well-meaning men falling into errors about the worship of God, through their own ignorance, wherein their "integrity may expiate their crime, must be punished, must not be pardoned," looks, methinks, with an appearance of more severity than it is the will of God that the world should be governed by, seeing one end of his instituting and appointing government among men is to represent himself in his power, goodness, and wisdom unto them. And he that shall conjoin another assertion of our author, namely, that it is "better and more eligible to tolerate debaucheries and immoralities in conversation than liberty of conscience for men to worship God according to those apprehensions which they have of his will," with the close of this chapter, that "it is so easy for men to deserve to be punished for their consciences, that there is no nation in the world in which (were government rightly understood and duly managed) mistakes and abuses of religion would not supply the galleys with vastly greater numbers than villany," will easily judge with what spirit, from what principles, and with what design, this whole discourse was composed.

But I find myself, utterly beside and beyond my intention, engaged in particular controversies; and finding, by the prospect I have taken of what remains in the treatise under consideration, that it is of the same nature and importance with what is past, and a full continuation of those opprobrious reproaches of them whom he opposeth, and open discoveries of earnest desires after their trouble and ruin, which we have now sufficiently been inured unto, I shall choose rather here to break off this discourse than farther to pursue the ventilation of those differences, wherein I shall not willingly or of choice at any time engage. Besides, what is in the whole discourse of especial and particular controversy may be better handled apart by itself, as probably ere long it will be, if this new representation of old pretences, quickened by invectives, and improved beyond all bounds and measures formerly fixed or given unto them, be judged to deserve a particular consideration. In the meantime, this author is more concerned than I to consider whether those bold incursions that he hath made upon the ancient boundaries and rules of religion and the consciences of men; those contemptuous revilings of his adversaries, which he hath almost filled the pages of his book withal; those discoveries he hath made of the want of a due sense of the weaknesses and infirmities of men, which himself wants not, and of fierce, implacable, sanguinary thoughts against them who appeal to the judgment-seat of God that they do not in any thing dissent from him or others but out of a reverence of the authority of God and for fear of provoking his holy majesty; his incompassionate insulting over men in distresses and sufferings,—will add to the comfort of that account which he must shortly make before his Lord and ours.

To close up this discourse: The principal design of the treatise thus far surveyed is, to persuade or seduce sovereign princes or supreme magistrates unto two evils, that are indeed inseparable, and equally pernicious to themselves and others. The one of these is, to invade or usurp the throne of God; and the other, to behave themselves therein unlike him;—and where the one leads the way, the other will assuredly follow. The empire over religion, the souls and consciences of men in the worship of God, hath hitherto been esteemed to belong unto God alone, to be a peculiar jewel in his glorious diadem; neither can it spring from any other fountain but absolute and infinite supremacy, such as belongs to him, as he hath alone, who is the first cause and last end of all. All attempts to educe it from or resolve it into any other principle are vain, and will prove abortive. But here the sons of men are enticed to say, with him of old, "We will ascend into heaven; we will exalt our throne above the stars of God; we will sit upon also the mount of the congregation, in the sides of the north; we will ascend above the heights of the clouds; we will be like the Most High." For wherein can this be effected? What ladders have men to climb personally into heaven? and who shall attend them in their attempt? It is an assuming of a dominion over the souls and consciences of men in the worship of God wherein and whereby this may be pretended, and therein alone. And all this description of the invasion of the throne of God, whence he who did so is compared to Lucifer, who sought supremacy in heaven, is but the setting up of his power in and over the church in its worship, which was performed in the temple, the mount of the congregation, and in Zion, on the north of the city of Jerusalem, Isa. xiv. 12–14. This now princes are persuaded unto, and can scarce escape without reproaches, where they refuse or omit the attempting of it. Suppose they be prevailed with to run the hazard and adventure of such an undertaking, what is it that they are thereon persuaded unto? How are they directed to behave themselves after they have assumed a likeness unto the Most High, and exalted themselves to his throne? Plainly, that which is now expected from them is nothing but wrath, fury, indignation, persecution, destructions, banishments, ruin of the persons and families of men innocent, peaceable, fearing God, and useful in their several stations, to satisfy their own wills, or to serve the interests of other men. Is this to act like God, whose power and authority they have assumed, or like to his greatest adversary? Doth God deal thus in this world in his rule over the souls of men? or is not this that which is set out in the fable of Phaeton, that he who takes the chariot of the sun will cast the whole world into a combustion? So he who of old is supposed to have affected the throne of God hath ever since acted that cruelty to his power; which manifests what was his design therein, and what would have been the end of his coveted sovereignty. And whoever at any time shall take to himself that power that is peculiar to God, will find himself left, in the exercise of it, to act utterly unlike him, yea, contrary unto him.

Power, they say, is a liquor that, let it be put into what vessel you will, is ready to overflow; and as useful as it is,—as nothing is more to mankind in this world,—yet when it is not accompanied with a due proportion of wisdom and goodness, it is troublesome, if not pernicious, to them concerned in it. The power of God is infinite, and his sovereignty absolute; but the whole exercise of these glorious, dreadful properties of his nature is regulated by wisdom and goodness, no less infinite than themselves. And as he hath all power over the souls and consciences of men, so he exercises it with that goodness, grace, clemency, patience, and forbearance, which I hope we are all sensible of. If there be any like him, equal unto him, in these things, I will readily submit the whole of my religion and conscience unto him, without the least hesitation. And if God, in his dominion and rule over the souls and consciences of men, do exercise all patience, benignity, long-suffering, and mercy,—for "it is of his compassion that we are not consumed,"—doth he not declare that none is meet to be intrusted with that power and rule but they who have these things like himself; at least, that in what they are or may be concerned in it, they express and endeavour to answer his example? Indeed, sovereign princes and supreme magistrates are God's vicegerents, and are called gods on the earth, to represent his power and authority unto men in government, within the bounds prefixed by himself unto them, which are the most extensive that the nature of things is capable of; and in so doing, to conform themselves and their actings to him and his, as he is the great monarch, the prototype of all rule and the exercise of it, in justice, goodness, clemency, and benignity, that so the whole of what they do may tend to the relief, comfort, refreshment, and satisfaction of mankind, walking in the ways of peace and innocency, in answer unto the ends of their rule,—is their duty, their honour, and their safety. And to this end doth God usually and ordinarily furnish them with a due proportion of wisdom and understanding; for they also are of God. He gives them an understanding suited and commensurate to their work, that what they have to do shall not ordinarily be too hard for them, nor shall they be tempted to mistakes and miscarriages from the work they are employed about, which he hath made to be their own. But if any of them shall once begin to exceed their bounds, to invade his throne, and to take to themselves the rule of any province belonging peculiarly and solely to the kingdom of heaven, therein a conformity unto God in their actings is not to be expected; for be they never so amply furnished with all abilities of mind and soul for the work and those duties which are their own, which are proper unto them, yet they are not capable of any such stores of wisdom and goodness as should fit them for the work of God, that which peculiarly belongs to his authority and power. His power is infinite; his authority is absolute; so are his wisdom, goodness, and patience. Thus he rules religion, the souls and consciences of men. And when princes partake in these things, *infinite power, infinite wisdom,* and *infinite goodness,* they may assume the same rule and act like him; but to pretend an interest in the one and not in the other will set them in the greatest opposition to him.

Those, therefore, who can prevail with magistrates to take the power of God over religion, and the souls of men in their observance of it, need never fear that when they have so done they will imitate him in his patience, clemency, meekness, forbearance, and benignity; for they are no way capable of these things in a due proportion to that power which is not their own, however they may be eminently furnished for that which is so. Thus have we known princes (such as Trajan, Adrian, Julian of old), whilst they kept themselves to their proper sphere, ordering and disposing the affairs of this world and all things belonging to public peace, tranquillity, and welfare, to have been renowned for their righteousness, moderation, and clemency, and thereby made dear to mankind, who, when they have fallen into the excess of assuming divine power over the consciences of men and the worship of God, have left behind them such footsteps and remembrances of rage, cruelty, and blood in the world, as make them justly abhorred to all generations. This alone is the seat and posture wherein the powers of the earth are delighted with the sighs and groans of innocent persons, with the fear and dread of them that are and would be at peace, with the punishment of their obedient subjects, and the binding of those hands of industry which would willingly employ themselves for the public good and welfare. Take this occasion out of the way, and there is nothing that should provoke sovereign magistrates to any thing that is grievous, irksome, or troublesome to men peaceable and innocent; nothing that should hinder their subjects from seeing the presence of God with them in their rule, and his image upon them in their authority, causing them to delight in the thoughts of them, and to pray continually for their continuance and prosperity. It may be some may be pleased for a season with severities against dissenters, such as concerning whom we discourse, who falsely suppose their interest to lie therein. It may be they may think meet rather to have all "debaucheries of life and conversation tolerated" than liberty for peaceable men to worship God according to their light and persuasion of his mind and will, as the multitude was pleased of old with the cry of, "Release Barabbas, and let Jesus be crucified." Magistrates themselves will at length perceive how little they are beholden to any who importunately suggest unto them fierce and sanguinary counsels in these matters. It is a saying of Maximilian the emperor, celebrated in many authors: "Nullum," said he, "enormius peccatum dari potest, quam in conscientias imperium exercere velle. Qui enim conscientiis imperare volunt, ii arcem cœli invadunt, et plerumque terræ possessionem perdunt."

Magistrates need not fear but that the open wickedness and bloody crimes of men will supply them with objects to be examples and testimonies of their justice and severity. And methinks it should not be judged an unequal petition by them who rule in the stead and fear of God, that those who are innocent in their lives, useful in their callings and occasions, peaceable in the Lord, might not be exposed to trouble only because they design and endeavour, according to their light, which they are invincibly persuaded to be from God himself, to take care that they perish not eternally. However, I know I can mind them of advice which is ten thousand times more their interest to attend unto than to any that is tendered in the treatise we have had under consideration, and it is that given by a king unto those that should partake of the like royal authority with himself: Ps. ii. 10–12, " Be wise now therefore, O ye kings: be instructed, ye judges of the earth. Serve the LORD with fear, and rejoice with trembling. Kiss the Son, lest he be angry, and ye perish from the way, when his wrath is kindled but a little. Blessed are all they that put their trust in him." And he who can inform me how they can render themselves more like unto God, more acceptable unto him, and more the concern and delight of mankind, than by relieving peaceable and innocent persons from their fears, cares, and solicitousness about undeserved evils, or from the suffering of such things, which no mortal man can convince them that they have merited to undergo or suffer, he shall have my thanks for his discovery.

And what is it that we treat about? What is it that a little truce and peace is desired unto and pleaded for? What are the concerns of public good therein? Let a little sedate consideration be exercised about these things, and the causelessness of all the wrath we have been conversing withal will quickly appear. That there is a sad degeneracy of Christianity in the world, amongst the professors of Christian religion, from the rule, spirit, worship, and conversation of the first Christians, who in all things observed and expressed the nature, virtue, and power of the gospel, all must acknowledge and many do complain. Whatever of this kind comes to pass, and by what means soever, it is the interest and design of them who are present gainers by it in the world to keep all things in the posture that yields them their advantage. Hence, upon every appearance of an alteration, or apprehension that any will desert the ways of worship wherein they have been engaged, they are cast into a storm of passion and outrage, like Demetrius and the rest of the silver-smiths, pretending divisions, present settlement, ancient veneration, and the like, when their gain and advantage, whether known or unknown to themselves, is that which both influenceth them with such a frame of spirit and animates them to actings suitable thereunto. Thus in the ages past there was so great and universal an apostasy, long before foretold, overspreading Christianity, that by innumerable sober persons it was judged intolerable, and that if men had any regard to the gospel of Christ, their own freedom in the world, or everlasting blessedness, there was a necessity of a reformation, and the reduction of the profession of Christian religion unto some nearer conformity to the primitive times and pattern. Into this design sundry kings, princes, and whole nations, engaged themselves,—namely, what lay in them, and according to the sentiments of truth they had received, to reduce religion unto its pristine glory. What wrath, clamours, fury, indignation, revenge, malice, this occasioned in them whose subsistence, wealth, advantages, honour, and reputation, all lay in preserving things in their state of defection and apostasy, is known to all the world. Hence, therefore, arose bloody persecutions in all, and fierce wars in many nations, where this thing was attempted, stirred up by the craft and cruelty of them who had mastered and managed the former declensions of religion to their own use and advantage; the guilt of which mischiefs and miseries unto mankind is, by a late writer amongst ourselves, contrary to all the monuments of times past, and confessions of the adversaries themselves, endeavoured to be cast on the reformers.

However, a work of reformation was carried on in the world, and succeeded in many places; in none more eminently than in this nation wherein we live. That the end aimed at, which was professedly the reduction of religion to its ancient beauty and glory in truth and worship, is attained amongst us, some perhaps do judge, and absolutely acquiesce therein; and for my part, I wish we had more [who] did so: for, be it spoken, as I hope, without offence on the part of others, so without fear of giving it, or having it taken, on my own, there are among many such evident declensions from the first established reformation towards the old or a new, and it may be worse apostasy, such an apparent weariness of the principal doctrines and practices which enlivened the reformation, as I cannot but be troubled at, and wherewith many are offended; for although I do own a dissent from some present establishments in the church of England, yet I have that honour for the first reformers of it, and reformation itself, that love to the truth declared and established in it, that respect to the work and grace of God in the conversion of the souls of thousands by the ministry of the word in these nations, that I cannot but grieve continually to see the acknowledged doctrines of it deserted, its ancient principles and practices derided, its pristine zeal despised, by some who make advantage of its outward constitution, inheriting the profits, emoluments, and wealth which the bounty of our kings have endowed it withal, but not its spirit, its love, its steadfastness in owning the protestant truth and cause.

But to return, for these things may better elsewhere be complained of, seeing they relate only to particular persons: That what is done in reformation be established, that any farther public work of the same nature attempted, or the retrievement of what is done to its original condition and estate, belongs to the determination of the supreme magistrate, and to that alone. Private persons have no call, no warrant to attempt any thing unto these purposes. However, many there are who dislike some ecclesiastical constitutions and modes of outward worship, which have been the matter of great contests from the first reformation, but much more dislike the degeneracy from the spirit, way, and principles of the first reformers before mentioned, which in some at present they apprehend. And, therefore, though many seem to be at a great distance from the present established forms of the church of England, yet certainly all who are humble and peaceable, when they shall see the ministry of the church, as in former days, in some measure acted rightly and zealously towards the known ends of it, and such as are undeniably by all acknowledged,—namely, the conviction of the world, the conversion of souls, and the edification of them that do believe; and the discipline of it exercised in a conformity at least to the rule of the discipline of the secular powers of the earth,—" Not to be a terror to the good, but to them that do evil;" and in these things a demonstration of the meekness, humility, patience, forbearance, condescension to the weakness, mistakes, errings and wanderings of others, which the gospel doth as plainly and evidently require of us as it doth that we should believe in Jesus Christ,—will continually pray for its prosperity, though they cannot themselves join with it in sundry of its practices and ways. In the meantime, I say, such persons as these, in themselves and for their own concerns, do think it their duty not absolutely to take up in what hath been attained amongst us, much less in what many are degenerated into, but to endeavour the reduction of their practice in the worship of God to what was first appointed by Jesus Christ; as being persuaded that he requires it of them, and being convinced that, in the unspeakable variety that is in human constitutions, rest unto their souls and consciences is not otherwise to be obtained. And if, at the same time, they endeavour not to reduce the manner and course of their conversation to the same rule and example by which they would have their worship of God regulated, they are *hypocrites*. Short enough, no doubt, they come, in both, of perfection, but both they profess to aim equally at; and herein alone can their consciences find rest and peace. In the doctrine of faith, consented on in the first reformation, and declared in the allowed writings of the church of England, they agree with others, and wish with all their hearts they had more to agree withal. Only, they cannot come up to the practice of some things in the worship of God, which being confessedly of human prescription, their obedience in them would lie in a perfect contradiction to their principal design, before mentioned; for those things, being chosen out from a great multitude of things of the same nature, invented by those whose authority was rejected in the first reformation, or reduction of religion from its catholic apostasy, they suppose cannot justly be imposed on them, they are sure cannot be honestly received by them, whilst they design to reduce themselves unto the primitive rules and examples of obedience. In this design they profess themselves ready to be ruled by, and to yield subjection unto, any truth or direction that can or may be given them from the word of God, or any principles lawfully from thence educed. How their conviction is at present attempted, let the book under consideration, and some late unparalleled and illegal acts of violence, conformable to the spirit of it, be a testimony. But, in the management of their design, they proceed on no other principles than those of the liberty of judgment (of discretion, or discerning, they call it), for the determining of themselves and their own practices in what they believe and profess about religion, and the liberty of their consciences from all human impositions, than were owned, pleaded, and contended for by the first reformers, and the most learned defenders of the church of England, in their disputations against the Papists; those they will stand to and abide by: yea, than what are warranted by the principles of our nature and constitution; for no man practiseth any thing, nor can practise it, but according to his own will and choice.

Now, in these things, in their principle, or in their management of it, it may be they are mistaken, it may be they are in an error, or under many mistakes and errors; but from their integrity they know themselves innocent, even in their mistakes. And it is in the nature of men to think strange of sedate violences, that befall them without their demerit, and of suffering by law without any guilt. Their design of reducing themselves in worship and conversation to the primitive pattern, they openly avow; nor dare any directly condemn that design, nor can they be convinced of insincerity in what they profess. And shall they be destroyed if they miss it in some matters of smaller concernment? which, whatever some may boast of, is not hitherto tolerably proved. Shall now their dissent in religious observances on this occasion, and those and that about things mostly and chiefly, if not only, that appear neither name nor thing in the Scripture, be judged a crime not to be expiated but by their ruin? Are immoralities or vicious debaucheries rather to be tolerated, or exempted from punishment, than such a dissent? What place of Scripture in the Old or New Testament, which of the ancient fathers of the church, do speak at this rate? Opinions inconsistent with public tranquillity, with the general rules of moral duties in all relations and conditions, practices of any tendency in themselves to political disturbances, are by none pleaded for. Mere dissent itself, with different observances in the outward worship of God, is by some pretended, indeed, to be a civil disturbance; it hath always been so by some, even by those whose own established ways have been superstitious and idolatrous. But wise men begin to smile when they hear private interest pleaded as public good, and the affections which it begets as the common reason of things. And these pretences have been by all parties, at one time or another, refuted and discarded. Let the merit of the cause be stated and considered, which is truly as above proposed, and no other; set aside prejudices, animosities, advantages from things past and bygone in political disorders and tumults, wherein it hath no concern,—and it will quickly appear how little it is, how much, if possible, less than nothing, that is or can be pleaded for the countenancing of external severity in this case. Doth it suit the spirit of the gospel [of Christ], or his commands, to destroy *good wheat*, for standing, as is supposed, *a little out of order*, who would not have men pluck up the tares, but to let them stand quietly in the field until harvest? Doth it answer his mind to destroy *his disciples*, who profess to love and obey him, from the earth, who blamed his disciples of old for desiring to destroy the Samaritans, his enemies, with fire from heaven? We are told that "he who was born after the flesh persecuted him who was born after the promise;" and a work becoming him it was. And if men are sincere disciples of Christ, though they may fall into some mistakes and errors, the outward persecuting of them on that account will be found to be of the works of the flesh. It is certain, that for those in particular who take upon them, in any place or degree, to be ministers of the gospel, there are commands for meekness, patience, and forbearance given unto them; and it is one of the greatest duties incumbent on them to express the Lord Jesus Christ in the frame of his mind and spirit unto men, and that eminently in his *meekness* and *lowliness*, which he calls us all in an especial manner to learn of him. A peculiar conformity also to the gospel, to the holy law of love, self-denial, and condescension, is required of them, that they may not, in their spirits, ways, and actings, make a false representation of him and that which they profess.

I know not, therefore, whence it is come to pass that this sort of men do principally, if not only, stir up magistrates and rulers to laws, severities, penalties, coercions, imprisonments, and the like outward means of fierce and carnal power, against those who in any thing dissent from them in religion. Generally, abroad, throughout Christendom, those in whose hands the civil powers are, and who may be supposed to have inclinations unto the severe exercise of that power which is their own, such as they think, possibly, may become them as men and governors, would be inclinable to moderation towards dissenters, were they not excited, provoked, and wearied, by them who pretend to represent Jesus Christ to the world,—as if any earthly potentate had more patience, mercy, and compassion than he. Look on those Lutheran countries where they persecute the *Calvinists*. It is commonly declared and proved that the magistrates, for the most part, would willingly bear with those dissenters, were they not stirred up continually to severities by them whose duty it were to persuade them to clemency and moderation, if in themselves they were otherwise inclined. And this hath ruined the interest of the protestant religion in Germany, in a great measure. Do men who destroy no more than they can, nor punish more than they are able, and cry out for assistance where their own arm fails them, render themselves hereby like to their heavenly Father? Is this spirit from above? Doth that which is so teach men to harass the consciences of persons, their brethren and fellow-servants, on every little difference in judgment and practice about religious things? Whom will such men fulfil the commands of patience, forbearance, waiting, meekness, condescension, that the gospel abounds with, towards? Is it only towards them who are of the same mind with themselves? They stand in no need of them; they stand upon the same terms of advantage with themselves. And for those that dissent, " Arise, kill and eat," seems to be the only command to be observed towards them. And why all this fierceness and severity? Let men talk what they please, those aimed at are peaceable in the land, and resolve to be so, whatever may befall them. They despise all contrary insinuations. That they are in their stations severally useful to the commonwealth, and collectively, in their industry and trading, of great consideration to public welfare, is now apparent unto all indifferent men. It is, or must be, if it be for any thing (as surely no men delight in troubling others for trouble's sake), for their errors and mistakes in and about the worship of God. All other pleas are mere pretences of passion and interest. But who judgeth them to be guilty of *errors?* Why, those that stir up others to their hurt and disquietment. But is their judgment infallible? How if they should be mistaken themselves in their judgment? If they are, they do not only err, but persecute others for the truth. And this hath been the general issue of this matter in the world. Error hath persecuted truth ten times for truth's once persecuting of error. But suppose the worst, suppose them in errors and under mistakes, let it be proved that God hath appointed that all men who so err should be so punished as they would have Nonconformists, and though I should believe them in the truth, I would never more plead their cause. And would these men be willingly thus dealt withal by those who judge or may judge them to err? It may be some would, because they have a good security that none shall ever judge them so to do who hath power to punish them, for they will be of his mind. But sure none can be so absolutely confined unto themselves, nor so universally, in all their affections and desires, unto their own personal concerns, as not to have a compassion for some or other who, in one place or other, are judged to err by them who have power over them to affix what guilt they please unto that which is not their crime. And will they justify all their oppressors? All men have an equal right in this matter; nothing is required but being uppermost to make a difference. This is that which hath turned Christendom into a shambles, whilst every prevailing party hath judged it their duty and interest to destroy them that do dissent from them.

Once more; what name of sin or wickedness will they find to affix to these errors? " Nullum criminis nomen, nisi nominis crimen." No man errs willingly, nor ought to be thought to tempt or seduce his own will, when his error is to his disadvantage; and he is innocent whose will is not guilty. Moreover, those pretended errors in our case are not in matters of faith; nor, for the most part, in or about the worship of God, or that which is acknowledged so to be; but in or about those things which some think it convenient to add unto it or conjoin with it. And what quietness, what peace is there like to be in the world, whilst the sword of vengeance must be continually drawn about these things? Counsels of peace, patience, and forbearance, would certainly better become professors of the gospel and preachers of everlasting peace than such passionate and furious enterprises for severity as we meet withal.

And I no way doubt but that all generous, noble, and heroic spirits, such as are not concerned in the empaled peculiar interest and advantages of some, and do scorn the pedantic humours of mean and emulous souls, when once a few more clouds of prejudices are scattered, will be willing to give up to God the glory of his sovereignty over the consciences of men, and despise the thought of giving them disquietment for such things as they can no way remedy, and which hinder them not from being servants of God, good subjects to the king, and useful in their respective lots and conditions.

And now, instead of those words of Pilate, " What I have written I have written,"—which, though uttered by him maliciously and despitefully, as was also the prophecy of Caiaphas, were, by the holy, wise providence of God, turned into a testimony to the truth,—I shall shut up this discourse with those of our Saviour, which are unspeakably more our concernment to consider, Matt. xxiv. 45–51: " Who then is a faithful and wise servant, whom his lord hath made ruler over his household, to give them meat in due season? blessed is that servant, whom his lord when he cometh shall find so doing. Verily I say unto you, that he shall make him ruler over all his goods. But and if that evil servant shall say in his heart, My lord delayeth his coming; and shall begin to smite his fellow-servants, and to eat and drink with the drunken; the lord of that servant shall come in a day when he looketh not for him, and in an hour that he is not aware of, and shall cut him asunder, and appoint him his portion with the hypocrites: there shall be weeping and gnashing of teeth."

TWO QUESTIONS

CONCERNING THE POWER OF THE SUPREME MAGISTRATE

ABOUT RELIGION AND THE WORSHIP OF GOD,

WITH ONE ABOUT TITHES,

PROPOSED AND RESOLVED.

PREFATORY NOTE.

THE name of the correspondent who drew from Owen the following answers has not transpired. The tract was written after our author had left Oxford, and seems to have been the work of a night. It was published in 1659, when Owen could not benefit from any provision by the state in support of religion, such as he contends for ; and contains, in the first place, ten reasons for the support and furtherance of divine truth by the magistrate,—an opinion which our author broaches in other parts of his works. See Sermon ix., vol. viii., p. 367, of his works. In regard to the second question, he shows that the magistrate has no right to compel subscription to any confession of faith; and for a more detailed exhibition of his views on this point, the reader may be referred to the Appendix on Toleration, which follows his Sermon on "Righteous Zeal," etc., vol. viii., p. 163. In answer to the third query, on the subject of tithes, he holds that the public maintenance of religion ought not to be withdrawn, but that the most expedient mode of maintaining it was a point open to discussion. A Quaker reviewed these opinions of Owen, in a production under the ominous and singular title, "A Winding-sheet for England's Ministry, which hath a name to live, but is dead." Baxter at this time (1656–1659) was engaged in a dispute with the Quakers. One of his works on the popish controversy, published in 1657, bears a similar title, "A Winding-sheet for Popery ; " and perhaps the Quaker selected the phrase in a spirit of sly retaliation against the Puritans, who at that time regarded the Friends with no small jealousy.—ED.

TWO QUESTIONS CONCERNING THE POWER OF THE SUPREME MAGISTRATE

ABOUT RELIGION AND THE WORSHIP OF GOD,

WITH ONE ABOUT TITHES,

PROPOSED AND RESOLVED.

QUESTION I.

" *WHETHER the supreme magistrate, in a nation or commonwealth
of men professing the religion of Jesus Christ, may and ought to
exert his power, legislative and executive, for the supportment, preservation, and furtherance of the profession of the faith and worship of God; and whether he may and ought to forbid, coerce, or
restrain such principles and practices as are contrary to them and
destructive of them ?*"

The affirmative of both the parts of this question is proved,—

I. From the light and law of nature.   For,—

1. That there is a God;

2. That this God ought to be believed in, and worshipped according to the revelation that he makes of himself;

3. That it is incumbent on his worshippers, in their several capacities, to defend and further that worship which answers the light
and knowledge they have of him;

4. That to revile or blaspheme this God, or his name, is an evil to
be punished by them who have "jus puniendi," or the right of restraint in them, or committed unto them;

[These] are all dictates of the law of nature, principles inseparable
from that light which is natural and necessary unto rational creatures,
subsisting in a moral dependence on God, and confirmed by Scripture, Heb. xi. 6; Exod. xxii. 28.

To assert, then, that the supreme magistrate as such, in any nation, ought not to exert his authority for the ends and in the way inquired after, is contrary to the light and law of nature.

II. From the law of nations. For,—

1. The due and regular improvement of common natural notions and inbred principles unto universal public good is the law of nations, whose general foundation is laid, Gen. ix. 5, 6;

2. The constant usage of mankind in their political societies, answerable unto right reason, is the revealer or discoverer of this law of nations;

3. This law is an evidence and presumption of truth and right, paramount unto, and uncontrollable by, any thing but express re velation, or it is a discovery of the will of God, less than and subordinate unto no way but that of immediate revelation;

4. The wilful breach or contempt of this law, in its allotments or assignation of bounds to the interests and concernments of men, is generally esteemed the most righteous ground of one nation's waging war upon another;

5. That the supreme magistrate in each commonwealth ought to exert his power and authority for the supportment, preservation, and furtherance of the worship of God, and to coerce and restrain that which would ruin it, is a maxim of this law of nations, manifested by the common, constant usage and universal entrances, unimpeached by any one contrary instance (where this law hath prevailed), of all mankind in their political societies; nor is this practice controlled by express revelation, but is rather confirmed, Ps. ii. 10:

Therefore, to deny the lawfulness of the authority inquired after, and its due execution, is contrary to the law of nations.

III. From God's institution, in and by laws positive upon doctrines of faith and ways of worship of pure revelation. For,—

1. Among the people of the Jews, as is known and confessed, God appointed this as the chief and supreme care and duty of the magistrate, to provide, by the authority committed to him, that his worship, as by himself revealed, should be preserved and provided for in all the concernments of it, and that what was contrary unto it, in some instances, he should coerce and restrain, Deut. xiv. 23, xviii. 1-9, xxi. 17-20;

2. Though the instituted worship of God was, for the greatest part, then typical, and to endure but for a season, yet the preservation of that worship by God commanded was a moral duty, Deut. xvi. 20;

3. God's command to the magistrate for the exercise of his care and duty in reference unto his typical worship did not respect it as typical, but as his worship;

4. The law and command of God for the magistrate in that commonwealth to take care and do as above was not only an eminent privilege, blessing, and advantage to the commonwealth as such, but it was also a special mercy to all and every one of his chosen ones in that commonwealth; and what is given or granted by God to all or any of his saints by the way of privilege or mercy is not disannulled but either by express revocation or the institution of somewhat exhibiting a greater privilege or mercy, wherewith the former proves inconsistent;

5. No revocation of this grant, or command and institution, no appointment of any thing inconsistent with it, appears in the gospel:

Then, universally to deny the right and exercise of the power inquired after is contrary to the positive law of God, given in reference unto doctrines of faith and ways of worship of pure revelation, such as were those possessed and walked in under the Old Testament.

IV. From the example of all godly magistrates, accepted with God from the foundation of the world. For,—

1. There is no one magistrate left on record in the whole Book of God, with any commendation given unto him, or approbation of him as such, but it is firstly and chiefly on this account, that he exerted the power and duty inquired after,—David, Hezekiah, Josiah, Nehemiah, as others, are instances;

2. Since the days of the publication of the gospel, no one magistrate hath obtained a good report among the saints and churches of Christ but upon the same account;

3. No one magistrate is remembered to have omitted this care, work, or duty, but a mark or blot is left upon him for it, as a person disapproved and rejected of God;

4. Nothing but an express discharge by way of revelation can acquit a magistrate from following the example of all and every one of them who in their work have been approved of God, in that wherein they were so approved:

Wherefore, to affirm that the supreme magistrate ought not to exert his authority for the ends mentioned, is to affirm that the magistrate is now accepted with God in and for the not doing of that which all other magistrates have been accepted with God in and by the doing of; which seems unreasonable.

V. From the promises of gospel times. For,—

1. Promises given in a way of privilege and mercy that men should do any thing, declare it to be their duty so to do;

2. There are many promises that in gospel times magistrates shall lay out their power and exert their authority for the furtherance

and preservation of the true worship of God, the profession of the faith, the worshippers and professors thereof, and therein the whole interest of Zion, Isa. i. 26, xlix. 22, 23;

3. All the promises relating unto God's providential dispensations in the world, with reference unto the interest of his church and people, do centre in this, that the rulers in and of the world shall exert and exercise their power in subserviency to the interest of Christ, which lies in his truth and his worship; which cannot be done if the power inquired after be denied, Isa. lx. 3, 11-17; Rev. xi. 15:

To say, then, that the supreme magistrate, in a commonwealth of men professing the true Christian religion, ought not to exert his legislative and executive power in the defence and for the furtherance of the truth and worship of God, and for the restraint of the things that are destructive thereunto, is to say that "the promise of God is of no effect."

VI. From the equity of gospel rules. For,—

1. Whatever is of moral equity, and hath the power of obligation from thence, the gospel supposeth, and leaves men under that obligation, pressing them unto obedience thereunto, Phil. iv. 8;

2. Whatever was instituted and appointed of God formerly is of moral positive equity, if it be not repealed by the gospel; and therefore the forementioned institution of the magistrate's duty in the things under consideration is supposed in the gospel;

3. The gospel rules, on this supposition, are, that the magistrate is to promote all good, and to hinder all evil that comes to his cognizance that would disadvantage the whole [nation] by its civil disturbance or provoking God against it, and that in order to the interest of Christ and his church, Rom. xiii. 1-7, 1 Tim. ii. 2, Prov. viii. 15, 16;

4. That what is good and evil upon an evangelical account evidently and manifestly is exempted from these rules cannot be proved:

Therefore, to say it, is contrary to the equity of gospel rules.

VII. From the confession of all the protestant churches in the world.

That all the protestant churches in the world assert, at least, the whole of the duty contained in the affirmative of the question to be incumbent on the supreme magistrate, is known to all men that care to know what they assert.

VIII. From the confession of those, in particular, who suffer in the world on the account of the largeness of their principles as to toleration and forbearance, the Independents, whose words in their Confession are as followeth:—

"Although the magistrate is bound to encourage, promote, and protect the professors and profession of the gospel, and to manage and order civil administrations in a due subserviency to the interest of Christ in the world, and to that end to take care that men of corrupt minds and conversations do not licentiously publish and divulge blasphemies and errors, in their own nature subverting the faith, and inevitably destroying the souls of them that receive them; yet in such differences about the doctrines of the gospel or ways of the worship of God as may befall men exercising a good conscience, manifesting it in their conversation, and holding the foundation, not disturbing others in their ways or worship that differ from them, there is no warrant for the magistrate under the gospel to abridge them of their liberty."

IX. From the spiritual sense of the generality of godly men in the world.

This can be no otherwise known but by the declaration of their judgments; and as to what can by that way be found out or discovered, a thousand to one of men truly godly are for the affirmative. "Vox populi Dei est vox Dei."

X. From the pernicious consequences of the contrary assertion, whereof I shall mention only two:—

1. The condemnation and abrenunciation of the whole work of reformation, in this and other nations, so far as it hath been promoted by laws or constitutions of supreme magistrates; as in the removal of idolatry, destroying of idols and images, prohibiting the mass, declaring and asserting the doctrine of the gospel, supporting the professors of it: which things have been visibly owned and blessed of God.

2. The destruction of the plea of Christ's interest in the government of the nations, especially as stated by them who in words contend to place him in the head of their laws and fundamental constitutions. Where nothing in a government may be done for him, nothing against them who openly oppose him, men can scarce be thought to act under him and in subordination to him.

The conclusion from hence is, To advance an opinion into any necessity of its being received which is contrary to the law of nature and nations, God's institutions and promises, the equity of gospel rules, the example of all magistrates who have obtained testimony from God that they discharged their duty unto acceptation with him, to the confession of all protestant churches, the spiritual sense of the generality of godly men in the world, and attended in itself with pernicious consequences, seems to be the effect of self-fulness, and readiness to impose men's private apprehensions upon others, the only evil pretended to be avoided by it.

QUESTION II.

THE next Question is,—"*May the supreme magistrate, by laws and penalties, compel any one who holds the head, Christ Jesus, to subscribe to that confession of faith and attend to that way of worship which he esteems incumbent on him to promote and further?*"

That we may answer distinctly, observe,—

I. That the inquiry is concerning them only that hold the Head: for others, their case is not proposed; they are left to the providence of God, in his working on the hearts of them whom he raiseth up for governors, according to the measure of light, love, and zeal which he shall be pleased to impart unto them. And though it cannot be proved that any magistrate is authorized from God to take away the life or lives of any man or men for their disbelieving or denying any heads or articles of the Christian religion, yet it doth not seem to be the duty of any professing obedience to Jesus Christ to make any stated, legal, unalterable provision for their immunity who renounce him.

II. That things or opinions of public scandal, national demerit, and reproach to the profession of the gospel, ought to be restrained from being divulged by that public speaking of the press or in extra-familial assemblies,—both which, according to the usage of all nations, are under the power and at the disposal of the supreme magistrate,— was before proved, in our answer to the first inquiry.

III. It is agreed that the measure of doctrinal holding the Head consists in some few clear, fundamental propositions.

IV. It cannot be denied but that most men, in the determination of this question, have run into extremes, much upon the account of their present interest, or that of some party of men, wherein and with which, as to some special self-ends, they are engaged.

These things being premised, I answer to the question negatively; and that because the authority inquired after, exerted to the ends mentioned, would immediately affect the conscience, and set up itself in direct opposition to the light of God therein, a defect of proving the conveyance of such an authority over the consciences of men holding the Head having been long since discovered.

QUESTION III.

THE Third Question is,—"*Whether it be convenient that the present way of the maintenance of ministers or preachers of the gospel be removed and taken away, or changed into some other provision?*"

Ans. I. That the public preachers of the gospel ought to be maintained by a participation in the temporal things of them to whom the word is preached, is an appointment of the Lord Christ, and of the apostles in his name and authority, 1 Cor ix. 14; Gal. vi. 6.

II. The reasonableness of this gospel institution is manifested by the Holy Ghost:—1. From the law of nature, Luke x. 7; 1 Cor. ix. 7, 11. 2. From the law of nations, in the same place. 3. From the tendency and equity of Mosaical institutions, 1 Cor. ix. 9–13.

III. Where God, by providential dispensations, hath laid things in a nation in a subserviency to an institution of Christ, according to his promise, Ps. ii. 8, Isa. xlix. 23, as he hath done in this case, to oppose that order of things seems to be a fighting against God and his Anointed.

IV. The payment of tithes,—1. Before the law, Gen. xiv. 20, Heb. vii. 4, 5; with, 2. The like usage amongst all nations living according to the light of nature; 3. Their establishing under the law; with, 4. The express relation in gospel appointment unto that establishment, 1 Cor. ix. 13, 14,—do make that kind of payment so far pleadable that no man, without being able to answer and satisfy that plea, can, with any pretence of a good conscience, consent to their taking away.

V. A maintenance, by a participation in men's temporals, for those who preach the gospel, being expressly appointed by Jesus Christ, and reference for the proportion being directly made by the apostle unto the proportion allotted by God himself under the Old Testament; for any man, or number of men, to suppose they can make a better and wiser allotment, especially when and where a near approachment thereunto is already made by Providence, seems to be a contending with him who is mightier than they.

VI. To deprive preachers of the gospel, when sent out into their Master's harvest, and attending unto their work, according to the best of the light which the present age enjoyeth, with visible and glorious success, of the portion, hire, wages, or temporal supportment prepared for them in the good providence of God, upon pretences of inconveniencies and dissatisfactions of some prejudiced men, seems to be an attempt not to be paralleled from the foundation of the world.

VII. Wherever, or in what nation soever, there hath been a removal of the maintenance provided in the providence of God for the necessary supportment of the public dispensers of the word, the issue hath been a fatal and irrecoverable disadvantage to the gospel and interest of Christ in those nations.

It appears then, First, That to take away the public maintenance provided in the good providence of God for the public dispensers of the gospel, upon pretences of present inconvenience or promise of future provision, is a contempt of the care and faithfulness of God towards his church, and, in plain terms, downright robbery.

Secondly, To entitle a nation unto such an action, by imposing it on them without their consent, is downright oppression.

VIII. An alteration of the way of payment of that revenue which is provided in the providence of God for public preachers, by the way of tithes, into some other way of payment, continuing the present right, is not obnoxious or liable to any of the forementioned evils; but its convenience or inconvenience may be freely debated.

Yours,

J. O.

INDULGENCE AND TOLERATION CONSIDERED:

IN

A LETTER UNTO A PERSON OF HONOUR.

———

LONDON: 1667.

PREFATORY NOTE.

BEYOND the mere fact that this letter was published anonymously in 1667, little is known respecting it. If a conjecture may be hazarded as to the "person of honour" to whom it was addressed, and with whom, from certain expressions in the beginning of it, Owen must have been on terms of friendly correspondence, perhaps Sir Thomas Overbury might be named. He was the nephew of the celebrated Sir Thomas Overbury, an author of some accomplishments, and the friend of Car, the minion and favourite of James I. The death of the uncle by poisoned viands in the Tower, to which he had been committed, was the appalling close of a private tragedy, reflecting deep disgrace on the memory of that monarch. The nephew was also an author, and, among other works, wrote, "Queries proposed to the serious consideration of those who impose upon others in things of Divine and Supernatural Revelation, and prosecute any upon the account of Religion, with a desire of their candid and Christian resolution thereof." Owen, in the course of 1670, addressed a letter to the same Sir Thomas Overbury, in defence of his own character from the charges of the Rev. George Vernon. It appears in vol. xvi. of his works. As their views, to judge from the title of the work just quoted, appear to have been congenial on the subject of toleration, perhaps the present letter also may be conceived to have been intended for Sir Thomas. It is written with unusual vivacity and point, and indicates with great shrewdness the mischief resulting to the nation and to the royal interests from the continuance of the persecuting enactments against dissent.—ED.

INDULGENCE AND TOLERATION CONSIDERED.

SIR,

I HAVE considered the discourses sent me, published lately, about Indulgence and Toleration. At their first view, I confess, I was not a little surprised with their number, as not understanding the reason of their *multiplication* at this time, nor what it was that had made them swarm so unseasonably. Upon their perusal I quickly perceived a defect in them all, which could no otherwise be supplied; whether it be so by this means or no impartial men will judge. The design seems to have been, that what is wanting in them singly in *reason* may jointly be made up in *noise*, and their respective defects in argument be supplied by their communion in suffrage. It will, doubtless, be the wisdom of those who are concerned in what they oppose to stand out of their way, at least until the storm is over.

> —— " Omnis campis diffugit arator
> Omnis et agricola, ——
> Dum pluit in terras, ut possint sole reducto
> Exercere diem." ——   [Æn. x., 804–808.]

Their reason will be better attended to when this earnestness hath a little spent itself; for men who have attained more than perhaps they ever aimed at, at least than they had just reason to expect, have commonly for a while strong desires to secure their possessions, which time and a due consideration of their title and interest may somewhat calm and allay. In the meantime, because you expect it, I shall give you a brief account of my thoughts concerning the matter treated of by them; and, if that do not too long detain me, of the reasonings also which they make use of. Some things I do much commend their ingenuity in; for whereas two things were proposed to them,—a compliance with some by way of *condescension*, and a forbearance of others by way of *moderation*,—they equally declare against them both. They will neither admit others to them but upon their own terms to the utmost punctilio, nor bear with any in their dissent from them in the least different observances, but all must be alike pursued by law and force to their ruin. Whether this seem not to be the frame of men's spirits whose "fortune and power" (as one of them speaks) "tempt them to an insolency," sober and disinterested persons will judge. The minds, I confess, of fortunate men are for the most part equal unto their successes, and what befalls them they count their due. Nothing else could persuade these men that they alone were to be esteemed Englishmen, and that not only as unto all privileges and advantages attending that title, but so far, also, as to desire that all who differ from them should be exterminated from their native soil. It were well if we could see more of their endeavours to merit so high a favour, more of that usefulness and advantage which they bring to the kingdom, that might countenance them in pleading that *they alone ought to be in it.* For my part, I can see little consistency with Christianity, humanity, or prudence, in these resolutions; for, certainly, if that be Christian religion which we are taught in the gospel, it inclines men, especially those who are teachers of it (such as the authors of these discourses, at least most of them, seem to be), unto a greater condescension than that expressed upon the causes and for the ends of its being desired. The request of some for a condescension seems to be no more but that the rulers of the church would forbear the prescription and imposition of such things on the consciences and practice of men (for it is vain to pretend that conscience is not concerned in practice in the worship of God) as there is not one word about, nor any thing inclining, leading, or directing towards, in the whole Bible; that were never thought of, mentioned, or commanded by Jesus Christ, or his apostles, or any apostolical men; that, if they had not unhappily fallen upon the minds of some men to invent,—none knows who, nor where, nor when,—would have had no concernment in Christian religion.

They, indeed, who impose them say they are "things indifferent;" but the differences that have been almost this hundred years about these " things indifferent" is enough to frighten and discourage unbiassed men from having any thing to do with them. And what wise man, methinks, would not at length be contented that these differences and indifferent things may be parted with altogether? Besides, they on whom they are imposed account them not so; they look upon them as unlawful for them to use and practise (all circumstances considered), at least most of them do so; and they plead by the important argument of their sufferings that it is merely on the account of conscience that they do not conform unto them. Others think that it is not so, but I am sure it is possible that it may be so; and if it be so, they cannot use them without endangering the eternal ruin of their own souls, though others may speed otherwise in their observances, who have other thoughts and apprehensions of their nature and use. And yet, on the other side, if those that impose these things can make it appear with any probability (I had almost said if they would but pretend) that they were *obliged in conscience* to impose them, by my consent there should be an end of this strife. But whilst there is this left-handed contest, real will and pretended prudence fighting against conscience and duty, it is like to be untoward and troublesome. And for what end is it that some desire that there might be at least some relaxation as to the present severe impositions of some of the things which are thus contended about? They say it is merely that they might serve God in the gospel to the good of others, without sinning against him to the ruin of themselves. They speak particularly unto men who profess it to be their calling, their work, their design, to promote the blessed ends of the gospel towards the souls of men; they desire of them that they may have leave to come and help them in reference unto this end. Nor can it be pretended that they themselves are sufficient for the work, and that they have no need of the assistance of others. God and men know that this cannot be reasonably pleaded.

And this is a business which certainly, by such men as profess themselves to be guides and rulers of the church, can hardly be justified unto him who is the great Lord of it. When the disciples found some "casting out devils in his name," they rebuked them, because they "followed not with them,"—a worse and greater nonconformity than that which some are now charged withal,—and yet the rebuke of others procured only one to themselves. He said well of old concerning those who contended to promote common good, Ἀγαθὴ δ' ἔρις ἥδε βροτοῖσι,—"This is a good strife for mortal men." So is that which is for promoting of the good of the souls of men by the preaching of the gospel. And shall it be forbid for such things, "quæ dicere nolo," of so little importance are they in this matter, which hath an influence into eternity? What is answered unto this request? Stories are told of things past and gone; scattered interest, dissolved intrigues, buried miscarriages, such as never can have any aspect on the present posture of affairs and minds of men in this nation, are gathered together and raked out of their graves, to compose mormoes for the affrightment of men from a regard to the ways of peace and moderation. This they enlarge upon with much rhetoric and some little sophistry; like him of old of whom it was said, that being charged with other things,

—— " Crimina rasis
Librat in antithetis; doctas posuisse figuras
Laudatur."—— [Pers., Sat. i. 85-87.]

Many inconveniences are pretended as like to ensue upon such a condescension; but in the meantime men die, and some, it may be, perish for want of that help and instruction in the things of eternity which there are many ready to give them, while it is altogether uncertain whether any one of the pretended inconveniences will ensue or no. I fear whilst men are so engaged in their thoughts about what is good and convenient for them at the present, they do scarce sufficiently ponder what account of their actions they must make hereafter.

But neither is this all that these authors contend for. Men are not only denied by them an admission into their societies to preach the gospel, unless it be on such terms as they cannot in conscience admit of, and which others are no way obliged in conscience to impose upon them, but all forbearance of or indulgence unto them who cannot conform unto the present establishment is decried and pleaded against. What though men are peaceable and useful in the commonwealth? what though they are every way sound in the faith, and cordially embrace all the doctrine taught formerly in the church of England? what though those in this condition are many, and such as in whose peace and industry the welfare of the nation is exceedingly concerned? what if they offer to be instructed, by any who will take that work upon them, in the things about which their differences are? what if they plead conscience towards God, and that alone, in their dissent, it being evidently against their whole temporal interest? what if they have given evidence of their readiness, in the ways of Christ and the gospel, to oppose every error that is either pernicious to the souls of men, or any way of an evil aspect to public peace and tranquillity? All is one; they are neither severally nor jointly, no one of them nor all of them, in the judgment of these gentlemen, to be forborne, or to have any indulgence exercised toward them, but laws are to be made and put in execution against them, to their ruin, extirpation, and destruction. It may be it will be said that these things are unduly imposed on them, seeing they press for a prosecution of men by laws and rigour, not for dissenting from what is established or not practising what is prescribed in the public worship of God, but for practising what is of their own choice therein, in meetings and assemblies of their own; otherwise they may *keep their consciences unto themselves* without molestation.

But it doth not appear that this can be justly pleaded in their defence: for as the prohibition of men, under severe and destructive penalties, from that exercise of the worship of God which is suitable to their light, and which they are convinced that he requires of them, —so that in nothing it *interfere with the fundamentals* of Christian religion or public tranquillity,—is as destitute of all foundation in Scripture and reason, at all times, and, as things may be circumstantiated, in prudence or policy, as the enforcing of them to a practical compliance with any mode or way of worship against their light and conscience; so the practice in this latter case hath been more severe amongst us than in the former. For a testimony hereof, we have those great multitudes which at this day are excommunicated by the courts ecclesiastical merely for their not attending the public assemblies of the nation in their administrations. And as they are by this means, as things now stand, cast, as they say, into the condition of men outlawed and deprived of all privileges of their birthright as Englishmen (of which sort there are forty times more than have been proceeded against unto the same issue in all his majesty's courts of justice in England for many years), so in the pursuit of that sentence many are cast into prisons, where they lie perishing (sundry being dead in that state already), whilst their families are starved or reduced to the utmost extremity of poverty for want of those supplies which their industry formerly furnished them withal; and what influence this will have into the state of this nation time will manifest, if men are not as yet at leisure to consider. The hands that by this means are taken off from labour, the stocks from employment, the minds from contrivances of industry in their own concerns, the poverty that is brought on families,—in all which the common good hath no small interest,—are not, I fear, sufficiently considered by persons whose fulness and plenty either diverts their thoughts from taking notice of them, or keeps off any impressions on their minds and judgments from what is represented concerning them. Others begin to feel the evil, whose morning they saw not, gathering up towards them in the decay of their revenues and entanglements of their estates; which, without timely remedy, will increase upon them until the breach grow too great for an ordinary healing.

And I am persuaded that none who have been active in these proceedings will take upon themselves the trouble of confirming this kind of church-discipline out of the Scriptures, or examples of the primitive churches for some hundreds of years.

This, therefore, is that which by these men is pleaded for,— namely, that all the Protestants in England who so dissent from the established forms and modes of worship as either to absent themselves from their observances, or to attend unto any other way of worship, which being suitable to the principles of that religion which they profess (namely, Protestantism), they are persuaded is according to the mind of God, and which he requires of them, be proceeded against, not only with *ecclesiastical censures*, but also with *outward, pecuniary*, and *corporal punishments*, to the depriving of them, in the progress, of their whole liberty, freedom, and benefit of the laws of the land, and in some cases unto death itself, and that no dispensation or relaxation of this severity be countenanced or granted. And herein, I confess, whatever pretences be used, whatever fears and jealousies of events upon a contrary course, or the granting of an indulgence, be pleaded, I am not of their minds; nor do I think that any countenance can be given to this severe principle and opinion either from the Scriptures of the Old or New Testament, or from the example of any who ever endeavoured a conformity unto the rules of them. This is the state of the controversy as by these authors formed and handled; nor may any thing else be pretended, when such multitudes are ready to give evidence unto it by what they have suffered and undergone. Do but open the prisons for the relief of those peaceable, honest, industrious, diligent men, who, some of them, have lain several years in durance, merely in the pursuit of excommunication, and there will be testimony enough given to this state of the controversy.

This being so, pray give me leave to present you with my hasty thoughts, both as to the reasonableness, conscience, and principles of pursuing that course of severity towards dissenters which I find so many concerned persons to plead for, and also of the way of their arguings and pleas.

And, first, as unto *reason and conscience,* I think men had need look well unto the grounds of their actings in things wherein they proceed against the common consent of mankind, expressed in all instances of the like occasion that have occurred in the world; which is as great an evidence of the light and law of nature as any [that] can be obtained, for what all men generally consent in is from the common nature of all. We are not, indeed, much concerned to inquire after the practice of the heathen in this matter; because, as the apostle testifies, their idolatrous confusion in religion was directly and manifestly against the light of nature, and where the foundation was laid in a transgression of that law, it is no wonder if the proceeding upon it be so also.

There was a law amongst the *Romans,* reported by the orator to be one of those of the twelve tables, forbidding any to have private gods of their own; but this regarded the gods themselves, the object of their worship, and not *the way of worshipping* them, which was peculiar and separate to many families and tribes amongst them, and so observed. Scarce any family or tribe of note that had not its special and separate "sacra." Besides, they seemed to have little need of any new authorized gods, seeing, as Varro observed, they had of them they owned no less than thirty thousand! And I have often thought that law was imposed on them by the craft and projection of Satan, to keep them off from the knowledge of the true God; for notwithstanding this law, they admitted into their superstition all sorts of idols, even the folly of the Egyptians themselves, as having temples in Rome unto Isis and Serapis. Only this law was pleaded to keep off the knowledge of the true God, Acts xviii. 13; and of him they had the highest contempt, calling the place of his worship the land " Dei incerti." And the custom among the Athenians not to admit any strange objects of worship, any unwarranted devotion, was never made use of but to oppose the gospel, unless it were when they destroyed the wisest and best man that ever the city bred, for giving some intimation of the true God, and not consenting with the city in opinion about their established devotions; other use of these laws there was none. It is true, when any "sacra" or superstitious observances were actually used to induce men and women to sin and wickedness, contrary to the light of nature, the very being of civil societies, the Romans severely animadverted upon them. Otherwise, this law was not made use of, but only against the Jews first, and the Christians afterward; whereby it was consecrated to the use of idolatry, and rendered unmeet for the church's service or reception.

The *Jews* were those who were first intrusted with the truth of religion and the worship of God; and it is known what was their law, their custom, their practice in this matter. Whoever would dwell amongst them, if they owned their fundamentals, they afforded them the blessing and peace of the land. All that they required of such persons was but the observation of the seven Noachical precepts, containing the principles of the light of nature as to the worship of one God, and moral honesty amongst men. Whoever would live amongst them of the Gentiles, and took upon themselves the observation of these fundamentals, although they subjected themselves to no instituted ordinances, they called "proselytes of the gate," and gave them all liberty and peace. And in those who submitted unto the law of Moses, who knows not what different sects, and opinions, and modes of worship, there were amongst them, which they never once supposed that they had any rule to proceed against by external force and coercion?

The case is yet more evidently expressed in the judgment and actings of the *first Christians*. It will be utterly superfluous to show how that, for three hundred years, there was not any amongst them who entertained thoughts of outward force against those who differed from the most in the things of Christian religion. It hath been done, I perceive, of late by others. And yet, in that space of time, with that principle, the power of religion subdued the world, and brake the force of that law whereby the Romans, through the instigation of Satan, endeavoured with force and cruelty to suppress it. When the empire became Christian, the same principle bare sway;

for though there were mutual violences offered by those who differed in great and weighty fundamental truths, as the Homo-ousians and Arians, as to those who, agreeing in the important doctrines of the gospel, took upon themselves a peculiar and separate way of worship and discipline of their own, whereby they were exempt from the common course and discipline of the church then in use, never any thoughts entered into men to give unto them the least disturbance. The kingdom of Egypt alone had at *the same time above forty thousand persons,* men and women, living in their private and separate way of worship, without the least control from the governors of church or state, yea, with their approbation and encouragement.

So was it all the world over, not to mention the many different observances that were in and amongst the churches themselves, which occasioned not division, much less persecution of one another. And so prevalent is this principle, that notwithstanding all their design for a forcing unto an uniformity, as their peculiar interest, yet it hath taken place in the church of Rome itself, and doth so to this day. It is known to all that there is no nation wherein that religion is enthroned, but that there are thousands in it that are allowed their particular ways of worship, and are exempt from the common ordinary jurisdiction of the church.

It seems, therefore, that we are some of the first who ever anywhere in the world, from the foundation of it, thought of ruining and destroying persons of THE SAME RELIGION with ourselves, merely upon the choice of some peculiar ways of worship in that religion; and it is but reasonable, as was observed, for men to look well to the grounds of what they do, when they act contrary to the principles of the law of nature, expressed in so many instances by the consent of mankind. And I fear all men do not aright consider what a secret influence into the enervating of political societies such intrenchments on the principles of natural light will assuredly have; for those things which spring up in the minds of men, without arguing or consideration from without, will insensibly prevail in them against all law and constitutions to the contrary. It is in vain to turn nature out of doors; it will return. And whence shall we learn what nature inclines unto, unless from the common practice of mankind in all instances where an evident demonstration may not be given of the prevalent influence of the interest of some men unto the contrary? which is

" Pessimus diuturnitatis custos."

It will not always prevail, nor ever at any time, without great regret and commotion, in the minds of men who have no concern in that interest.

Consider, also, the thing itself, of *forcing the consciences of men* in [the] manner before expressed, and you will find it so uncouth as, I am persuaded, you will not know well what to make of it.   Learned divines tell us that " conscience is the judgment that a man maketh of himself and his actions, with reference to the future judgment of God," or to that purpose.   Now, let others do what they will, conscience will still make this judgment, nor can it do otherwise.   Whatever men can alter in the outward actings of men's lives, they can alter nothing in the inward constitution of the nature given it by God in its creation, which refers to its future end.   How can this be forced?

It is said, therefore, " Let men take this liberty unto themselves. Who forbids them to judge of themselves and of their actions what they please?   None goes about to take this liberty from them."

But is this all?   Conscience doth not judge of men and their actions but with respect unto what, in the name of God, it requires them to be or to do.   It first requires several things of them in the name of God, and then judges upon their performance, with reference unto the judgment of God.   And this is the sovereign dictate of it, " Worship God according to that light and understanding which you have of what that worship is which is acceptable with him, in matter and manner, and no otherwise."   If this command be not obeyed, conscience will judge with reference unto the judgment to come. Let conscience, then, have its liberty for this work, and this difference is at an end.

But it will be said, "If conscience must be free as to its *first act*, of directing and commanding, as well as unto its self-judging, it may lead men to all abominations, wickedness, murders, seditions, and filthiness; and so a liberty unto them also must be granted."   So I have heard men speak; but I have wondered also that any man that hath a conscience of his own, or knows what conscience is, should give entertainment to so fond an imagination.   I would ask any man whether ever he found any such direction in his own conscience, or any inclination that way?   nay, if he have not constantly found a severe interdiction given in by his conscience against all such things? And how can he, then, conceive it possible that the conscience of any man should be of such a make and constitution, seeing naturally it is absolutely the same in all?   Besides, as was said, it is "a man's judgment of himself in reference to the future judgment of God;" and this intimation supposeth that a man may judge that God at the last day will approve of adultery, murders, seditions, and the like evils! which is to suppose all common inbred notions of God to be blotted out of the mind.   Nay, it is utterly impossible, as implying a contradiction, that any man should consider God as a judge, as conscience doth always, and suppose his approbation of the evils specified, or of any of the like nature and importance. But men will yet say that conscience hath been pretended for these things. I answer, Never by any in their wits; and what any brain-sick or enthusiastic person may say or do in his paroxysms is not to have any place in considerations of what becomes a guidance of the actions of mankind one towards another. It is true that some things, as they have been circumstantiated, have been debated, even in conscience, whether they have been lawful or no,—that is, whether God would approve of them or condemn them at the last day; but what is evil in itself and against the light of nature, there is no direction unto it, no approbation of it, in the least from conscience. To take away this liberty of conscience, in things of its proper cognizance and duty, seems to me to be as much as to say men shall not judge themselves with reference to the judgment of God to come; which is to put God's great vicegerent out of his place and throne.

Let us now apply this notion of conscience unto the present occasion. There is prescribed a way of divine worship, with ceremonies, forms of prayer, and orders for the administration of sacraments, all things that concern the joint and public worship of God. What is the work or duty of conscience in reference hereunto? Is it not, in the first place, to apply the mind and understanding to consider of what sort it is, in reference unto the future judgment of God? This cannot be denied; the first actings of a man who makes any conscience of what he does must be of this sort. If, then, it apprehend it to be such, as God will approve of the practice and observation of at the last day, conscience is satisfied, and reflects no self-condemning thoughts upon its observance. But suppose a man doth not understand it so to be, he cannot conceive it to be appointed so by Christ, nor that any men have warrant, authority, or commission to impose on the practice of others what is not so appointed by him. How shall he do to be otherwise minded? Can he force himself to assent unto that whereunto in truth he doth not assent? Is it in his power so to do? Ask any man who hath an understanding whether he can apply it to what he will?—that is, to assent or not assent unto what is proposed unto him. All men will assuredly say that their assent necessarily followeth the evidence that they have of the truth of any thing, and that otherwise it is not to be obtained. The mind despiseth all violence and coaction from the will; yea, it implies a contradiction, that a man should cause himself to assent unto that unto which he doth not assent. Can, then, other men compel this assent? It is so far otherwise that God himself will not, yea, be it spoken with reverence of his holiness, cannot force such an assent, seeing it implies a contradiction,—namely, that a man should assent and not assent to the same proposition at the same time. Neither can a man himself force himself, neither can all the men in the world force him, to understand more than he doth understand, or can do so. Men do not seem to have exercised many reflex acts of consideration on themselves who suppose that they can command their understandings to apprehend what they please, or to assent unto things at their will. These things follow conviction and evidence; and so God himself procures the assent of men unto what he revealeth; and otherwise the understanding is absolutely free from all imposition.

If a man, then, cannot understand these things to be approved of God and accepted with him, suppose they are so, yet if a man cannot apprehend them so to be, what is the next work that conscience will apply itself unto? Is it not to declare in the soul, that if it practise these things God will judge it at the last day, and pronounce sentence against him? for conscience, as was said, is a man's judgment of himself and his moral actions, with respect unto the future judgment of God. And I am persuaded that this is the condition of thousands in reference to the present impositions. Their apprehensions and judgments of themselves in this matter are to them unavoidable and insuperable. It is not in their power to think otherwise than they do, nor to judge otherwise of themselves, in reference unto the practice of the things imposed on them, than they do. Neither can all the men in the world force them to think or judge otherwise. If ever light and evidence unto their conviction of the contrary is imparted to them or do befall them, they will think and judge according to it; in the meantime, they crave that they may not be forced to act against their light and consciences, and so unavoidably cast themselves into destruction. All, then, that some desire of others is, that they would but give them leave to endeavour to please God, seeing they know it is a fearful thing to fall into his hands as an avenger of sin. God deals not thus with men; for although he requires them to believe whatever he reveals and proposes as an object of faith, and to obey whatever he commands, yet he gives them sufficient evidence for the one and warranty of his authority in the other, and himself alone is judge of what evidence is so sufficient. But men can do neither of these,—they can neither give evidence to their propositions. nor warrant to their authority in their impositions in spiritual things; and yet they exact more than doth God himself! But so it is, when once his throne is invaded, his holiness, wisdom, and clemency are not proposed to be imitated, but a fond abuse of sovereignty alone is aimed at.

To impose penalties, then, enforcing men to a compliance and acting in the worship of God contrary unto what they are convinced in their consciences to be his mind and will, is to endeavour the enforcing of them to reject all respect unto the future judgment of

God; which, as it is the highest wickedness in them to do, so hath not God authorized any of the sons of men, by any means, to endeavour their compulsion unto it. For the former of these, that *men may act in the things of God contrary unto what they are persuaded he requires of them,* I suppose none will ever attempt to persuade themselves or others. Atheism will be the end of such an endeavour.

The sole question is, Whether God hath authorized and doth warrant any man, of what sort soever, to compel others to worship and serve him contrary to the way and manner that they are in their consciences persuaded that he doth accept and approve. God, indeed, where men are in errors and mistakes about his will and worship, would have them taught and instructed, and sendeth out his own light and truth to guide them, as seemeth good unto him; but to affirm that he hath authorized men to proceed in the way before mentioned is to say that he hath set up an authority *against himself,* and that which may give control to his.

These things being so,—seeing men are bound indispensably not to worship God so as they are convinced and persuaded that he will not be worshipped, and to worship him as he hath appointed and commanded, upon the penalty of answering their neglect and contempt hereof with their everlasting condition at the last day; and seeing God hath not warranted or authorized any man to enforce them to act contrary to their light and that persuasion of his mind and will which he hath given them in their own consciences, nor to punish them for yielding obedience in spiritual things unto the command of God, as his mind is by them apprehended, (if the things themselves, though mistaken, are such as no way interfere with the common light of nature or reason of mankind, the fundamental articles of Christian religion, moral honesty, civil society, and public tranquillity; especially, if the things wherein men acting, as is supposed, according to their own light and conscience, in difference from others, are of small importance, and such as they probably plead are unduly and ungroundedly imposed on their practice, or prohibited unto them),—it remains to be considered whether the grounds and ends proposed in exercise of the severity pleaded for, be agreeable to common rules of prudence, or the state and condition of things in this nation.

The ground which men proceed upon in their resolutions for severity seems to be, that the church and commonwealth may stand upon the same bottom and foundation, that their interest may be every way the same, of the same breadth and length, and to be mutually narrowed or widened by each other.

The interest of the kingdom they would have to stand upon the *bottom of uniformity,* so that the government of it should, as to the beneficial ends of government, comprehend them only whom the church compriseth in its uniformity; and so the kingdom's peace should be extended only unto them unto whom the church's peace is extended. Thus they say that the kingdom and the church, or its present order and establishment, are to be like Hippocrates' twins, —not only to be born together and to die together, but to cry and laugh together, and to be equally affected with their mutual concerns. But these things are evident mistakes in policy, and such as multiplied experience has evidenced so to be. The comparison of monarchy, or the fundamental constitution of the policy and government of this nation, with the present church order and state,—established on a right [arising from] mutable and changeable laws, and which have received many alterations, and may at any time, when it seems good to the king and parliament, receive more,—is expressive of a principle of so evil an aspect towards the solid foundation of the policy of this nation as undoubtedly those who are principally concerned in it are obliged not to admit an avowance of; for whereas it is not the gospel in general, nor Christian religion, or religion considered as it best corresponds with the gospel or the mind of Christ therein, but the present church order, rule, and policy, that is intended, all men know that it is founded in, and stands solely amongst us on, such laws as is usual with parliaments to enact in one session and to repeal in another, or at least to enact in one age and to repeal in another, according as use and experience manifests them to be conducing or obstructing unto public good. And whereas the constitution of the civil government of the nation is built upon no such alterable and changeable laws, but hath quite another foundation, obnoxious to nothing but to the all-overruling providence of the Most High, it is a great shaking and weakening unto its fixation and interest in the minds of men, to have it compared with things every day alterable at pleasure. And the attempt to plant the kingdom's peace on the foundation of the church's uniformity,—which may on a thousand occasions, wherein the peace of the kingdom itself is not in the least concerned, be narrowed unto a scantling wholly unproportionate unto such a superstruction,—is without doubt as great a mistake in government as any persons can fall into. All the world knows how full at this day it is of various opinions and practices in things concerning religion, and how unsuccessful the attempts of all sorts have been for their extinguishment. It is no less known, as hath in part already been discoursed, how unavoidable unto men, considering the various allotments of their condition in divine providence, their different apprehensions and persuasions about these things are. He, therefore, that will build the interest of a nation on a uniformity of sentiment and practices in these things had need well fix this floating Delos, if he intend not to have his government continually tossed up and down.

The true civil interest of this nation, in the policy, government, and laws thereof, with the benefits and advantages of them, and the obedience that is due unto them, *every Englishman is born unto;* he falls into it from the womb; it grows up with him, he is indispensably engaged into it, and holds all his temporal concernments by it. He is able also, by natural reason, to understand it, so far as in point of duty he is concerned; and is not at liberty to dissent from the community. But as for religion, it is the choice of men, and he that chooseth not his religion hath none: for although it is not of necessity that a man formally chooses a religion, or one way in religion in an opposition unto and with the rejection of another, yet it is so that he so chooses in opposition to no religion, and with judgment about it, and approbation of that which he doth embrace; which hath the nature of a voluntary choice.

This being the liberty, this the duty of every man, which is, always hath been, and probably always will be, issued in great variety of persuasions and different apprehensions, to confine the peace and interest of civil societies unto any one of them seems scarce suitable unto that prudence which is requisite for the steerage of the present state of things in the world. For my part, I can see no reason the civil state hath to expose its peace unto all those uncertain events which this principle will lead unto. And it seems very strange, and I am persuaded that, on due consideration, it will seem strange, that any should continue in desire of confining the bottom of the nation's interest in its rule and peace unto that uniformity in religion which, as to a firm foundation in the minds and consciences of men, hath discovered itself to be no more diffused amongst the body of the people than at present it is, and from which such multitudes do, upon grounds to themselves unconquerable, dissent, resolving to continue so doing whatever they suffer for it, who yet otherwise unanimously acquiesce in the civil government, and are willing to contribute to the utmost of their endeavours, in their several places, unto its peace and prosperity.

Whatever, therefore, be the resolution as to a present procedure, I heartily wish that the principle itself might for the future be cast out of the minds of men; that the state and rule of the nation might not, by plausible and specious pretences, suited to the interest of some few men, be rendered obnoxious unto impression from the variety of opinions about things religious, which, as far as I see, is like to be continued in the world.

Especially ought this consideration, if I mistake not, to be applied unto those differences about which alone this discourse is intended,— namely, those which are amongst men of the same religion in all the substantials of it, and which having been of long continuance deduced from one age to another, are greatly diffused and deeply rooted in the minds of men; being such, also, as no countenance can be given to act severely towards them from any thing in the Scriptures or practice of the first churches in the world.

And I hope it will never more, amongst sober and disengaged persons, be said or thought that the interest of England, or of its rule and government, is in any thing confined unto a precise determination of the differences in the minds and consciences of men, so that those who are of one mind in them, and would impose the apprehension and practice of their persuasion upon others, should be alone comprehended therein.

But let the ground of this severity in proceeding against dissenters be never so weak or infirm, yet if the end proposed in it be accomplished, the counsel will appear at last to have been advisable. What, then, is the end of these things, of this severity so earnestly pressed after to be engaged into? Suppose the best appearing success that in this case can be supposed, and all that seems to be desired,—namely, that by external force and compulsion men be brought unto an outward conformity in and unto the things that are imposed on them,—this is the utmost of what seems to be desired or aimed at: for no man, surely, is so vain as to imagine that compulsion and penalties are a means suited to persuade or convince the minds of men; nay, commonly it is known that they have a contrary effect, and do exceedingly confirm men in their own persuasions, and into an alienation from the things they are compelled unto.

Suppose, then, this end to be obtained, is there better peace or establishment assured to the present church-order thereby than what it may enjoy whilst men have their liberty to profess their dissent? Both reason and experience do testify the contrary.

Nor will the church find any more dangerous opponents, upon any emergent occasion, than those who have been compelled to uniformity against their conviction; for bearing their condition always as their burden, they will not be wanting unto an opportunity to ease themselves of it.

And it may be sundry persons now vested with ecclesiastical power, if they would recollect their former thoughts and expressions, might remember that they both conceived and declared their mind to this purpose, that former severities in the like kind were unduly and disadvantageously pursued against that strong inclination in so many unto an indulgence and freedom from their impositions; which surely they cannot think to be now lessened or weakened.

But present power is apt to change the minds of men, and make them neither remember what were their former apprehensions, nor foresee what would be their thoughts upon a disappointment in their present undertakings.

But neither yet can this rationally be supposed, nor is it probable in the least that the outward conformity intended will ever be

obtained by rigour, especially where the reasons of it are so remote from influencing the consciences of men; for whatever arguments may be used for a restraint to be put upon conscience in
things concerning faith and the worship of God, which must be
taken from the nature of the things themselves, are utterly superseded and made useless by the nature of the differences that are in
contest between the imposers and those that deprecate their impositions : for as very little hath been done, especially of late, to
prove the lawfulness of the things imposed, nothing at all to assert
their necessity, so the nature of the things themselves about which
the difference is, quite casts them out of the compass and reach of
those arguments which are pleaded in the case of coercion and penalties in the things of religion or the worship of God ; for if men
should be able to prove that heresies and idolatries are to be
punished in the persons of them that do assert them, no conclusion
will or can be thence made, as I suppose, for their punishment and
ruin who, by the confession of them that would punish them, are
neither heretics nor idolaters.

Force must stand alone in this case; and what small influence it
is like to have on the practices of men, when it hath no pretence to
reason or judgment, wherein conscience is concerned to give its
countenance, is not uneasy to determine. Nay, *experience* hath sufficiently in most places baffled this attempt; violence hath been used
in matters of religion, to the shame and stain of Christianity, and
yet never succeeded anywhere to extinguish that persuasion and
opinion which it was designed to extirpate.

It may be, for a while indeed, and sometimes, it may obtain such
success as to seem to have effected the end aimed at; but still within
a.short space, mostly in the compass of the same age, it hath been
manifest that it hath but laid in provision for future troubles, oppositions, and animosities.

Let the *prelates* or rulers, therefore, of the church advise, press
unto, and exercise this severity whilst they please,—they may as
evidently see the issue of it as if it were already accomplished.
Some may be ruined, multitudes provoked, the trade of the nation
obstructed, some few be enforced unto an hypocritical compliance
with what is against the light of their consciences, compassion be
stirred up in the residue of the people for innocent sufferers, and by
all indignation against themselves and their ways increased. Considering what are the things about which these differences are; how
deeply rooted a dissent from the present establishment is in the
minds of multitudes; for how long a season that persuasion hath
been delivered down unto them, even ever since the first reformation,
gradually increasing in its suffrage to this day; the advantages that
it hath had for its growth and improvement, with successes evidently

suitable unto them; and the resolution that men's spirits are raised
unto to suffer and forego the utmost of their earthly concernments
rather than to live and die in an open rebellion to the commanding
light of God in their consciences,—it is the utmost vanity to have other
expectations of the end of such a course of rigour and prosecution.

In the meantime, I am sure whoever gets by persecution, the king
loseth by it.

For what if some officers of ecclesiastical courts have been enriched by the booty they got from dissenters? what advantage is it
all this while to the kingdom, when so many families are impove-
rished, so many ruined, as are by excommunications and imprisonments ensuing thereon; so many more discouraged from the exercise
of their faculties or improvement of their stocks; so many driven beyond the seas;—and yet all this is nothing unto what in the same kind
must and will ensue if the course sometimes begun should be pursued? To me it seems that an attempt for the pretended conformity (for attained it will never be) is scarce a due compensation for
his majesty's loss in the diminishing of his subjects and their wealth,
wherewith it is and will be certainly attended. Besides, to ruin men
in all their substantials of body and life for ceremonies, and those
our own countrymen and neighbours, seems to carry with it somewhat of that severity which Englishmen, after the subsiding of the
impetuous impressions of provocations, do naturally abhor, and will
not long by any means give countenance unto.

On the consideration of these things, and others doubtless of more
deep investigation, his majesty hath often declared, not only his resolution to grant the indulgence intimated in his gracious declaration to that purpose, but also the exceeding suitableness of these intentions unto his own inclinations and clemency. The advantages
which have already ensued unto the nation, in the expectation of
indulgence, have been also remembered, and repeated by him with
an uncontrollable manifestation of its conducibleness for the future
unto the peace and prosperity of the kingdom. And it *seems very
strange that so noble and royal dispositions, such thoughts and
counsels of wisdom and authority, such projections of care and
solicitude for the kingdom's good, should be all sacrificed to the
interest of any one party of men whatsoever.*

I cannot but hope that his majesty will re-assume those blessed
counsels of peace, especially considering that the spirits of men are
singularly disposed to receive and put a due valuation upon the
execution of them; for all those who desire an indulgence, though
differing amongst themselves in some things, do jointly cast their
expectations and desires into a dependence on his *majesty*, with advice of his *parliament*.

And as, notwithstanding their mutual differences, they are united in this expectation, so may they be made partakers of it! Although in other things their differences continue, they cannot but agree in loyalty and gratitude; when the denial of it unto them, although they still differ in other things, will reconcile their minds in regret against the impositions they jointly undergo.

And whereas men have, by the fears, dangers, and sufferings which they have passed through, evidenced to all the world that the liberty and freedom of their consciences is of more consideration with them than all other things whatever; and have learned themselves also how to esteem and value that liberty, without which they are sensible how miserable their condition is, and is like to be; it is impossible that any stronger obligation unto peaceableness, loyalty, and thankfulness, can be put upon the subjects of any nation, than a grant of the indulgence desired would put upon multitudes in this. This would set their minds at liberty from fears and contrivances for the avoidance of impendent dangers, encourage them to engage the utmost of their endeavours and abilities in the businesses of peace and security, leaving them no fears but only of any disturbance of the state of things which hath secured unto them all their principal interests in the world.

And how foolish, senseless, and unbecoming of men, would any other thoughts be! To think that men who have given this evidence, at least, that they are such as exercise a good conscience towards God and others, in that they have suffered for it, and are ready yet farther so to do, should not despise and contemn all suggestions of unpeaceable dispositions; or to suppose that they have any community of interest with such as, being not concerned in conscience with them, at least not so far as to evidence it to be their chief and principal interest, as theirs it is, have any inclination to the disturbance of the public tranquillity, wherein all their desires and aims are secured,—is to judge by such imaginations of folly, madness, and wickedness, as those who use these pretences would be loath to be judged by, although they have not given that testimony of their respect unto conscience which the others have done.

And hereby, *whereas the parliament have been necessitated, through the exigence of the public affairs, to engage the nation in payments not passed through without difficulty, they will, as was said, put a real and effectual obligation upon great multitudes of men, without the least semblance of disadvantage unto any others.*

Neither is this a matter of any expense, but only of generous clemency in themselves, and the deposition of wrath, envy, and revenge, in some few others; things that may be parted withal without the least detriment unto human society. And as it is in the matter alone of indulgence and conscience wherein the people are capable of a sensible obligation, others not concerned therein being apt to

think that all which is done for them is but their due, and less sometimes than is so, those partakers of it, by an avowment of the favour
received, will be in their own minds indispensably bound to promote
the common interest of public good.

It is true, indeed, that the parliament have thought meet, some
years past, to direct unto another course of procedure; but, "Dies
diem docet."

And wise men are never won't pertinaciously to adhere unto the
pursuit of conjectures and projections about future events, such as
former laws were suited unto, against experience and those second
thoughts which a new consideration of things may suggest unto
them. Besides, the alterations of affairs in many concernments may
fully justify the alteration in resolutions pleaded for; which is not
such neither as to be contradictory unto any thing already established,
but what may be brought into compliance with it and subordination to it. They may say of what is past as was by one said of old,—

"Res dura et regni novitas me talia cogunt."—[Æn., i. 562.]

The present assurance of public peace and tranquillity admits of
counsels impartially tending to the good of all, uninfluenced by a
mixture of fears and jealousies.

But suppose the peace and prosperity of the nation to be much
secured and advantaged by an indulgence, as undoubtedly, under the
protection and blessing of God, it will be, yet I have heard some say,
and it is commonly pleaded, that the church will not be able to keep
its station, or to retain its members in compliance, but they will
many, if not most of them, make use of the liberty desired, especially if it be for and unto Protestants; which must be prevented.
Now this, I confess, seems strange to me, that any such events should
be feared or expected.

Those who make this objection suppose the church to be really
possessed of truth and order in the matters that are in difference;
they express every day not only the great sense they have of the
learning, ability, and piety of the clergy, but are ready on all occasions to contemn their adversaries, as men unlearned, weak, and
inconsiderate. It is also granted that all outward privileges, encouragements, advantages, promotions, preferments, dignities, public conveniences, legal maintenance, are still to be confined unto the church
and its conformists; as also, that those who desire the benefit of indulgence must, together with an exemption from all these, pay all dues
required by the law to them; and if they will join themselves unto
others, besides a deprivation of the great conveniences of their usual
places of assemblies, and their legal interest in them, and the inconveniences of repairing unto other assemblies, it may be far remote
from their habitations, [they must] contribute also to the maintenance of their teachers, where it is indispensably needed.

If, I say, all these and the like considerations, with a reputation of public favour and regard with authority, be not sufficient to preserve and secure the church in its station and its members in the communion of it, *it is evident that they are things which have no foundation in the consciences or minds of men,* but stand merely on the props of law and power; which, if true, is yet a secret which ought not to be divulged.

I confess Chief-Justice Hobart,[1] in his Reports in the case of Colt and the bishop of Coventry and Litchfield, says, "That though it be 'de jure divino' that Christian people be provided of Christian officers and duties, as of teaching, administration of the sacraments, and the like, and of pastors for that purpose, and therefore to debar them wholly of it were expressly against the law of God, yet all other things," as he there shows, "are not so; for," saith he, "we know well that the primitive church in her greatest purity was but voluntary congregations of believers, submitting themselves to the apostles, and after to other pastors, to whom they did minister of their temporals as God did move them;"—a liberty for which state is pleaded for, the thing itself being owned to be according to the pattern of the "primitive church in her greatest purity."

And if it be so as he speaks, all other orders and observances in the church must be built only on law and custom. But yet, such is their force also on the minds of men, that, as attended with the advantages and conveniences before mentioned, and fenced by the inconveniences and disadvantages which attend dissenters, the differences also contended about being of no more weight than they are, there is no doubt but the most of men,—at least to the full as many as, without force to conscience, will do so under the severest penalties to the contrary,—will continue their adherence to the present church-state, although the liberty of the dissent desired should be indulged.

It may be this suggestion of peace and moderation may not have an equal relish unto all palates, nor find like reception in the minds of all. The interest of some and the prejudices of others are so important with them as that they cannot attend unto impartial reason in this matter. I am persuaded that some have scarce any better or more forcible argument to satisfy their own minds that they are in the right in religion, than the inclination they find in themselves to hate and persecute them whom they suppose to be in the wrong; or at least, that they can no longer believe that to be truth which they profess than whilst they are willing and ready to destroy with violence that which is contrary unto it; for what is forborne they suppose must needs be approved;—all which are so palpable misapprehensions as there needs no endeavour to lay them open.

It is far enough from being an evidence of truth in any, that they

[1] See page 330 of this volume.

are ready to destroy them that are otherwise minded. It is error and superstition; which, being conscious of their own weakness, are impatient until their contraries are ruined. And never are there such mutual violences in matters of religion as where the several opposite parties are all of them most grossly erroneous and superstitious.

The Egyptians were, of old, the scorn and sport of the world for their devotions in general; oxen, apes, crocodiles, garlic, and onions, being some of the best of their deities! and yet about these they had amongst themselves such endless animosities and mutual persecutions of one another as can scarcely be paralleled. So he tells us:

> " Immortale odium, et nunquam sanabile vulnus
> Ardet adhuc Ombos et Tentyra; summum utrinque
> Inde furor vulgo, quod numina vicinorum
> Odit uterque locus."   [Juv. Sat., xv. 34-37.]

And what was the ground and occasion of the quarrel?

> " Crocodilon odorat
> Pars hæc, illa pavet saturam serpentibus Ibin."   [Id. ib., 2, 3.]

Their controversy was about the worship of a crocodile on the one hand, and of a fowl that devoured serpents on the other!

Neither is the difference of much more importance, or managed with much more moderation, which is at this day between the Turks and Persians about the true successors of Mohammed.

So little reason have men to please themselves with a surmise of being possessed of the truth, by the inclination that they find in themselves to persecute the contrary, seeing such an inclination is an inseparable companion of error and superstition, and is generally heightened to cruelty and revenge, according as men by them are drenched in folly and blindness.

It is yet pretended by some that such a toleration as will satisfy them that desire it, and secure the public tranquillity, however it may please in the notion of it, will yet be found impracticable when it comes to be examined and instanced.

But it is evident that these pretences must be countenanced by some peculiar consideration of this nation and government thereof, seeing the utmost of what is here desired is both established and practised in other nations. The whole of it is plainly exercised in the kingdom of France, where the Protestants, paying all duties to the church, sustaining all burdens and offices in the commonwealth equal with others, are freed from ecclesiastical courts, censures, and offices, and all penalties for their dissent, with an allowance for the worship of God in their own assemblies provided by themselves, and known to the magistrates under whose jurisdiction they are; which is the sum of all that is here desired. The like liberty, if I mistake not, is granted to the French and Dutch churches here in England. The United Provinces of the Netherlands have continued in the same practice ever since the Reformation; so also hath the kingdom of Poland, where the dissenters are both numerous and divided among themselves. Lutherans are tolerated in the dominions of the Palsgrave, Elector of Brandenburg, and Landgrave of Hessia; so are Calvinists in many free cities of the Empire, in some places of the kingdom of Denmark; and both Lutherans and Calvinists in the sundry principalities in Germany whose magistrates are of the Romish religion. In the hereditary dominions of the Emperor, wherever difference in religion [has] once made an entrance, either a forbearance and toleration is granted and continued, as in Hungary, or the countries themselves have been made utterly waste and desolate, as Bohemia and Moravia, and yet in a great measure continue so to be. The attempts of the Duke of Savoy against it have been condemned, detested, and abhorred by all princes of the same religion with himself, and yet have ended in some tolerable forbearance. It is also known that the kings of England have, by virtue of their power in things ecclesiastical, in all ages, as occasion required and as they saw meet, exempted persons and societies from the common and ordinary course and way of church discipline and inspection.

Certainly, therefore, the unpracticableness of such an indulgence lies in the desires of them whose interest, as they apprehend, is opposite unto it; although it is more probable that their moderation, known and declared in this matter, would give them a greater interest in public esteem and veneration than by any other ways they are like to obtain. Neither is this at all by wise men to be despised, who are able to foresee the probable events of continued exasperation. Why, then, should men pretend that that cannot be done which hath been done, and is done at this day in so many kingdoms and nations, with the wished-for success by peace and happiness?

And as it may be very few instances can be given of such severity against dissenters, who come up to so full an agreement in all material things with them from whom they dissent, as that of late practised and still pressed for in England; so it will be found that, whether we respect the nature and temper of the people of this land, or the admission of the principles of dissent, with the grounds of them, in multitudes, or the resolution to undergo all difficulties and sufferings rather than to transgress against the light of their consciences, or their valuation of forbearance above all secular things whatever, there is no nation under heaven wherein such an indulgence or toleration as is desired would be more welcome, useful, acceptable, or more subservient to tranquillity, trade, wealth, and peace.

A PEACE-OFFERING,

IN

AN APOLOGY AND HUMBLE PLEA FOR INDULGENCE AND LIBERTY OF CONSCIENCE;

BY SUNDRY PROTESTANTS DIFFERING IN SOME THINGS FROM THE PRESENT
ESTABLISHMENT ABOUT THE WORSHIP OF GOD.

---

*" Ambigua de religione capita quæ plurimum habere videntur obscuritatis, tantis tamdiu animis
decertata, apud sapientes hoc ferè certum reliquerunt, nusquam minus inveniri veritatem, quam ubi
cogitur assensus."*—HUGO GROTIUS.

*" Exiguam sedem sacris littusque rogamus
Innocuum, et cunctis undamque, auramque patentem."*
[Altered from Æn., vii. 229, 230.]

LONDON: 1667.

PREFATORY NOTE.

THE date of its publication is almost all that has been ascertained in regard to the circumstances in which this "Peace-offering" appeared. We are inclined to attach to it considerable value; and of all the writings of Owen in defence of Nonconformity, in the trying and critical period of its history when this tract was published (1667), there is none in which the case of the Nonconformists is more simply and conclusively argued, or more likely to produce a greater effect on the modern reader. Very earnest in its tone, and yet very moderate in its language,—calm, and yet most impressive in the appeal which it contains,—it affords a pleasing illustration alike of the meekness of wisdom and the wisdom of meekness. It seems impossible to read it without a mingled feeling of regret and indignation that there ever should have been a time when men breathing the spirit which our author here breathes should have been denied religious freedom and the rights of conscience on the soil of Britain. The chief fault of the tract is its very moderation, as "a humble plea,"—for an "indulgence," too, in the exercise of those rights which no government is either able to confer or entitled to withhold, and the protection of which is one of the highest ends of government. Attention might be called to the character of Owen's learning, as illustrated in this tract. Traversing the wide field of history, he adduces innumerable facts in corroboration of his reasonings; and amid all his familiar mastery of the facts which suit his purpose, he evinces uncommon skill in gathering the authentic lessons which history teaches, and discerning the true philosophy which it breathes. Unlike his great contemporary, Jeremy Taylor, not, certainly, his inferior in learning, he does not simply, in order to clench an argument or point a moral, introduce an incident selected from some dark recess of ancient literature, which few have had the industry to explore. Owen rather treasured up in his memory, and embodied in his treatises, the conclusions to be drawn from the past experience of the race, whether in regard to private conduct, or, as in the admirable instance of the following tract, in regard to the general policy which it were well for statesmen to adopt. Taylor, with the instincts of poetic genius, fastens on some special object in the scene which his eye, in the retrospect of past ages, may survey, and reproduces it in the flower and fulness of its beauty ; the eye of Owen takes in a wider area, and, in the spirit and habits of an engineer, seeks to ascertain how the scene itself, as a whole, may be rendered subservient to the interests and happiness of man. In the pages of the bishop, a historic allusion becomes a tree in its affluence of leaf and fruit, softening every contiguous object into a shade of kindred elegance ; Owen's references to history remind us rather of the field waving with useful grain. Tedious and prolix as our author may be deemed, this "Peace-offering," in the condensation of historic proof embodied in it, may be described as the verdict of ancient history against all persecution, as at once criminal and foolish.

Richard Perrinchief published in 1667 a "Discourse of Toleration ;" and next year he followed it up by a second part, in reply to Dr Owen's "Peace-offering." The title of the work was in these terms:—"Indulgence not Justified; or, a Continuation of the Discourse of Toleration: in answer to Dr Owen's book, called 'A Peace-offering, or Plea for Indulgence,'" etc. As we have not been able to procure a sight of the book, we can say nothing as to its spirit and character, nor does Mr Orme make any allusion to it.—ED.

A PEACE-OFFERING, ETC.

THE infinitely wise and holy God, who disposeth of all things according to the counsel of his own will, having designed our portion in the world unto the latter days thereof, wherein, besides those difficulties which in all ages attend them who are called unto the search and profession of the truths of the gospel, we are forewarned of sundry evils peculiar unto them, rendering them "perilous;" as it is our duty to apply ourselves to serve his good pleasure in our generation, without repining at that station which in his work he hath allotted unto us, so also [is it our duty] diligently to take care that we add not unto the *evils of the days wherein we live,* and that what we may be called to suffer in them according to his will may not be lost unto his holy ends and purposes in the world, but some way or other redound unto his glory. What shall befall us in the course of our pilgrimage, how we shall be disposed of as to our outward temporary concernments, as it is not in our power to order and determine, so neither ought [it] to be in our care, so as that we should be anxiously solicitous thereabout: all things of that nature belong unto his sovereign pleasure, who will make them work together for good to them that love him. Resting in his will as to our outward state and condition in this world, with that of the times and seasons wherein our lot is fallen, which he hath put in his own power, we shall endeavour, in reference thereunto, to possess our souls in patience, waiting for that day which "shall manifest every man's work of what sort it is." And we know that it is but yet a little while before it will be no grief of heart unto us for to have done or suffered any thing for the name of the Lord Jesus, according to his mind and will: for whereas we are well assured that the old enemy of mankind, who is sometimes awake and sowing of tares whilst men sleep, is never so far asleep whilst any are endeavouring to sow the good seed of the gospel as not to stir up an opposition to their work, and to labour the ruin of their persons; so we believe that every sincere endeavour to promote the holy truths and ways of God, according to that measure of light which he is pleased graciously to impart unto any of the sons of men, is accepted and owned by him who is "a rewarder of them that diligently seek him;" which is sufficient to secure their peace and consolation under all the evils that on the account of their work they may conflict withal. Neither is it a small alleviation of any trouble that we may be exposed unto, that no pretence, colour, reason, or arguings for our sufferings, no means, ways, or kinds of them, no ends unto them, can possibly be invented, proposed, pursued, but what we are fully forewarned of, that so we might not at any time think ourselves surprised, as though some strange thing had happened unto us.

This, then, is our great concernment in the profession of religion, this that which we ought principally to attend unto,—namely, to commend our consciences unto God, that in all sincerity and godly simplicity we exercise ourselves in the work that he calls us unto, not corrupting his word or staining our profession by a conversation unbecoming the holiness of the gospel; and for what may outwardly befall us, though producing heaviness and sorrow for a season, the last day will manifest to have been unspeakably more the concernment of other men than our own. It is, therefore, on this account, and that duty which we owe unto all the sons of men, especially those who in any place or degree have rule and disposal of us in this world, and the things thereof committed unto them, that notwithstanding the hazard that attends us in the discharge of every duty of this kind, we adventure to represent our condition and desires unto all that endeavour to follow after truth with peace: for as the minds of men are capable of no greater perfection than what consists in receiving the whole truths of the gospel, nor their souls of greater blessedness than attends obedience thereunto; so every mistake of it, every prejudice against it, every opposition unto it or any part of it, are not only in themselves a corruption and debasement of the mind, but are usually attended with consequents of greater evils in and unto them by whom they are entertained. And this condition oftentimes are men otherwise upright and wise cast into, either by their own ingrafted prejudices, or neglect of that severe disquisition after truth which all the sons of it are obliged unto, or by suffering themselves to be imposed on by the suggestions of others, who perhaps sacrifice their actings in and about the things of God to some secular (and it may be very corrupt) ends of their own.

Hence, truth and innocence, which cannot be oppressed but when clothed with misrepresentations and calumnies, have in all ages been forced to suffer the sad effects of their mistakes, who in the meantime professed highly an avowment of them. So, in particular, the foundation of all the miseries that ever befell the professors of the truth of Christ, since the day that the name of Christian was known in the world. and consequently of all that evil and confusion in the

earth which the lusts of men have produced and the righteous judgment of God inflicted, have lain in general either in the ignorance of
men of the genuine nature and tendency of the truth itself, or in
their credulity in giving credit unto those misrepresentations of it
which it hath always been the interest of many in the world to frame
and promote. Hence, the professors of Christianity, and every particular way therein, in their respective seasons and generations, have
esteemed it their duty, not only unto themselves, to waive their imminent sufferings, if it were the will of God thereby, but unto others
also whom they judged to be engaged against God and his truth, in
their persecution of them, to declare freely and fully what it was that
they did believe and practise, and therein plead the equity and reasonableness of that deliverance which they aimed at,—of themselves
from suffering and of others from sinning. And herein had they
before their eyes the example of the great apostle of the Gentiles,
who with various success did ofttimes make use of the like defensative of himself and his doctrine. Nor is it the least prescription of
the law of nature implanted in the heart of man by Him that made
it, that innocency should so far undertake its own protection and
security as to endeavour a removal of prejudicate imputations out of
the minds of them in whose judgment it is concerned; and this
law all men universally yield obedience unto who intend not to abuse
such imputations unto sinister ends, not suitable unto the innocency
they profess, and so, by deserting their own unblamable defence, contract a guilt rendering them incapable of it for the future. Whereas,
therefore, it hath pleased Him in whose hand our life, and breath, and
all our ways are, to place us in that condition wherein, by the apprehensions he hath given us of his mind and will in some things relating unto his worship, we are forced to differ from others, we conceive it our duty, for the prevention of farther evils, openly and candidly to declare both what we profess and what in all humility we
desire thereupon: and we cannot but hope that when the matters of
our difference are known and considered, they will not be judged
of so high a demerit as to render a modest, peaceable desire of indulgence in our adherence unto them a new addition of guilt; for
their case is miserable indeed, who, being prejudged into a condition
of suffering, though not convinced of evil, may not desire relief from
those who alone are able to afford it, that also being made an aggravation of their misery by being made an aggravation of their supposed guilt.

And, in particular, this course is made at this season necessary
unto us from the exasperation of the minds of many in reference
unto what we possess and desire, with the prejudices that are taken
up and improved unto our disadvantage and trouble: for although

we have, with the joint consent of all our churches, some years since, publicly declared what is the faith which we profess and the way of the worship of God wherein we walk, and did hope that it would not be looked on as an unreasonable expectation that our confession might have received a Christian, charitable, sedate consideration before it were condemned, or those that adhere unto it judged as evil-doers for their so doing; yet, considering the said exasperations of the minds of men, though upon occasions wholly foreign to the matter of our faith and profession, we cannot be without some apprehensions that far the greatest part of those who are loudest in their cries for severity against us have scarce been so faithful to Christian candour and ingenuity as seriously to examine whether there be in what we believe and practise a just foundation for that kind of proceeding and acting towards us which they so earnestly desire to engage our rulers unto. If for no other reason, then, but to endeavour to call off the thoughts of men from persons and personal provocations unto those things which are the pretended foundation of their actings, and with reference whereunto their account must be made at the last day, when other men's real or apprehended miscarriages will give no countenance to theirs, we cannot but judge it a duty incumbent on us to remind them what the things are which must give construction unto all that in this matter they shall undertake or perform, and whereunto, under all imputations whatever of things of other natures, our comfort, be it what it will, true or false, in all our sufferings that we may be called unto, is resolved. And we do know that they will one day find themselves under a woful mistake who suppose that their severity against us will be any farther justified than there is ground for it in the principles which we profess in the things of God; and this cannot but be evident unto them (if they will give themselves but the liberty of unprejudiced consideration), who know that a relinquishment of those principles would instantly cause all those other pleas and pretences to vanish out of their minds which at present they only make use of. And therefore, also, shall we not much concern ourselves in any other charge that is laid against us, but only as to what we profess and practise in the ways and worship of God, as knowing that from thence alone all occasion is taken for them. We shall, therefore, only briefly declare our sense of them, and then proceed to that which is our real concernment; for there is not any new thing herein under the sun.

In all ages, wherever any way in religion hath been judged by the most, rightly or otherwise, to be contrary to the mind of God, as by them apprehended, it hath been immediately charged with the guilt of all the evils that fell out in the days of its profession, though evidently they had other causes and occasions. Such was the condition of Christianity in general of old; as is manifest from the apologetical writings of Justin Martyr, Tertullian, Arnobius, Cyprian, Lactantius, Minutius Felix, Augustine, and others. Upon every occasion of trouble, the common cry was, "Christianos ad leones!" Such was the condition of the professors of the protestant religion upon the first reformation throughout the world; under which prejudice and imputation they are yet forced to suffer the wrath of men in many places. Whatever disadvantages, then, on this account we may be exposed unto, we have no reason to complain or think strange of, it being no other than all men in the like condition, in all ages, have had to conflict withal, and will have so whilst sin and darkness continue in the world. To commend our consciences unto God in well-doing is the only means of peace in ourselves, and the whole defensative in reference unto others, which in this cause is left unto us.

Moreover, if any who either really make profession of *any way* in religion, or are generally esteemed so to do, fall into personal crimes and miscarriages, which *no way* can secure itself against, men, justly provoked thereby, have scarce the patience to attend unto any plea for the way itself or those who peaceably and innocently walk therein, though the charge against it be altogether groundless and unreasonable. Thus the abominations of the Gnostics of old were charged upon the whole body of Christianity, and the unwarrantable zeal of one man in firing a temple in the kingdom of Persia reflected an imputation of sedition on all the professors of the gospel, to their extirpation out of that empire. But the unrighteousness of this charge is, we hope, evident even to themselves who would fain make use of it unto our disadvantage, for no society in the world can give security for the deportment of all individuals belonging unto it according unto the rules of the whole; and if they may be charged with such miscarriages, it were easy to demonstrate that no community, no profession of men in the world, no order, no way, can be acquitted from guilt or thought meet to have moderation exercised towards it. Besides, we know not in particular but that all occasions of reflecting upon our societies on this account have, by the goodness of God, been prevented; for which we are humbly thankful unto his holy Majesty. But if to accuse be enough to render any men nocent, none can be long innocent. Thyestæan banquets, promiscuous lusts, and incests, must, on that ground, be thought to be the ends of the primitive assemblies of Christians. If men will take to themselves the liberty of entertaining evil and groundless surmises, it is impossible for us or any living to set bounds to their imaginations; so that we have nothing in this case to do but to leave the authors of such false and calumnious insinuations unto that reward which God and their own consciences will not suffer them to lose, and our vindication unto the providence of God over our present and future deportment. It may be thought of nearer concernment unto us when the late troubles in these nations are objected, and the remembrance of them renewed, unto our prejudice. But whether the frequent and importunate urging of them, since, by his majesty's clemency and grace, they are put into legal oblivion for ever, do tend unto the composure and settlement of the minds of men,—which is certainly the duty of all good subjects to aim at,—we leave it unto the consideration of those who are wiser than we, and on whom the care of the peace and welfare of the kingdom is in an especial manner incumbent. For our own parts, we shall only say, that whereas they were neither begun nor carried on upon the account of that way in the worship of God which we profess, may the remembrance of them be never so severely revived, we cannot fear any just conclusion from thence unto a suspicion of troubles of the like nature for the future, as well knowing the absolute freedom of our principles from any such tendency, as well as the providential unravelling of all those interwoven interests and occasions which individual persons countenanced themselves withal in their engagements in them.

Magistracy we own as *the ordinance of God,* and his majesty as the person set over us by his providence in the chief and royal administration thereof. In submission unto him, we profess it our duty to regulate our obedience by the laws and customs over which he presides in the government of these nations; so that *our practical adherence unto our own avowed principles* is all that in this matter can fall under the most suspicious and uncharitable surmise. That there is any means of giving such absolute satisfaction concerning future events, which depend on the minds and wills of men, as to leave all suspicion concerning them impossible, we know not; much less to prevent some men's pretending suspicions, for ends best known unto themselves. But this we know, that what ways or means soever are warranted or established by the laws of this land, or may be so,—and they are such as mankind must content themselves withal, as incapable of farther or greater assurance,—or whatever else may be rationally and justly expected from us, we have given, and are ready to give security by, against the evils intimated in this charge upon us: which being the utmost that our duty calls upon us for, we hope we shall not always suffer for being the unhappy objects of some men's *groundless jealousies,* which for us to remove is altogether impossible, God himself having not appointed any way or means for us to use to that end or purpose.

As, then, neither we nor others can hinder men from making use of this pretence for some ends of their own (though we know, as it is used by them, it contributes nothing to public tranquillity and the composure of the minds of men), so we hope that God will so far, in his good time, clear up the innocency and sincerity of our intentions, and their suitableness unto our declared principles, that no just occasion of reproach be administered unto them who wait for advantages against us.

And what are we, that public disturbance should be feared from us? " Nec pondera rerum, nec momenta sumus." By what *way or means*, were we never so desirous, could we contribute any thing thereunto? What *designs* are we capable of? What *interest* have we to pursue? What *assistance* to expect or look after? What *title* to pretend? What *hopes* of success? What *reward* of any hazard to be undergone? We have no form of government, *civil or ecclesiastical*, to impose on the nation; lay no pretence unto power to be exercised on the persons of any of his majesty's subjects; have no expectations from persons or nations, that might induce us to further or promote any sinister aims of other men. The utmost of our aim is but to pass the residue of our pilgrimage in peace, serving God in the way of our devotion. We covet no men's silver or gold, their places or preferments. Our whole desire is that of Israel of old to their brother Edom : " Let us pass, we pray, through thy country: we will not pass through the fields, or through the vineyards, neither will we drink of the water of the wells: we will go by the king's highway, we will not turn to the right hand nor to the left, until we have passed thy borders." May we thus far prevail, under the protection of God's providence, his majesty's favour, and our own innocency, we have no principles, we shall have no reason, farther to trouble ourselves or others. If it be denied unto us, and we must yet be scattered over the face of the earth, we shall yet pray for the prosperity of his majesty and the land of our nativity, patiently bearing the indignation of the Lord, against whom we have sinned, and waiting for his salvation.

That which of late is principally urged unto our prejudice, is the prohibition of that way of worship which we desire to walk in, and the establishment of another by law, to whose authority we owe subjection. When this begins once to be pleaded, the real merit of the cause in debate is usually overseen, and the obedience required by law is only insisted on; as though that were grown a civil difference, by the interposition of a law, which before was purely religious. This Paul himself found to be one of the most difficult cases he had to contend withal; it was objected unto him that he taught customs which it was not lawful for to do among the Romans, Acts xvi. 21. All that doctrine which he had to declare was antecedently in general forbidden by law, it being determined by the Romans that no worship of God should be admitted amongst them not established by public authority; and had not the light and truth of Christianity broken through that opposition, it must have lain shut up in darkness to this day. For our parts, we have only this to say, that there is no reason to urge this as a peculiar objection against us, it being the only foundation of all others, and only occasion of the difference about which we treat. Had not a law enjoined the practice of some things in the worship of God, which, according unto our present light, we cannot assent unto without ceasing to worship him (for to worship him in our own thoughts, against his mind and will, is to profane his name and worship); had it not forbidden the exercise and discharge of some duties which we account ourselves obliged unto by the authority of God himself,—we had had no need to implore the clemency of our governors to relieve us against that severity which we fear. This, then, we acknowledge; but withal, to state this difference upon its right foundation, do solemnly, in all sincerity, protest before God, his holy angels, and all the world, that it is not out of any unwarrantable obstinacy that we are conscious of unto ourselves, nor from any disaffection unto or dissatisfaction in the government that God hath set over us, but merely from a sense of that account which we have one day to make before Jesus Christ, the judge of all, that we cannot yield that compliance unto the act for uniformity which it requireth of us. The case, then, notwithstanding this prejudice, is still the same. Conscience towards God in the things of his own worship is still and alone concerned, whatever other pretences and reasonings may in this case be made use of (as many are, and ever were in the like cases, and will so be). The whole real cause of that severity which we humbly deprecate, and only reason lying against the indulgence we desire, is our profession and practice in the things that are not of this world, but purely relating to the revelation of the mind and worship of God. Whatever, therefore, men may plead, pretend, or urge, of another nature, we are so far conscious unto our own integrity as to be fully satisfied in our minds that whatever dangers we may be in this matter exposed unto, or whatever we may be called to suffer, it is all merely for believing in God, and worshipping of him according to what he hath been pleased to reveal of his mind unto us. And as in this case it is not in the power of any of the sons of men to deprive us of that consolation which an apprehension of the truth will afford unto them that sincerely and conscientiously embrace it; so whether any men can commend their consciences to God, according to the rules of the blessed gospel of our Lord Jesus Christ, in our molestation and trouble, we leave it unto all unprejudiced men to judge. And that we may yet farther remove all grounds of mistake, and obviate all other pretences against us, we shall candidly declare the general principles both of our faith and worship, and then leave our condition, whatever it may be, to the judgment of Him who " hath appointed a day wherein he will judge the world in righteousness," of his majesty whom he hath set over us in supreme power, and of all other persons whatever who have any sense of the terror of the Lord, the account we must make of serving him according to what he is pleased to reveal of himself unto us, the nature of things known only by divine revelation, or of the infirm, frail condition of mankind in this world.

For the faith which we profess, and which we desire to walk according unto, we need not insist upon the particular heads of it, having some years since, in our confessions, publicly declared it, with *the joint consent of all our churches*, neither do we own or avow any doctrine but what is therein asserted and declared. And we hope it will not be looked upon as an unreasonable request if we humbly desire that it may receive a Christian, charitable, sedate consideration before it be condemned. May we be convinced of any thing therein not agreeable unto the Scriptures, not taught and revealed in them, we shall be with the first in its rejection. That this hath been by any as yet attempted we know not; and yet we are judged, censured, and reproached upon the account of it! So far are men degenerated from that frame of spirit which was in the Christians of old,—so far have they relinquished the ways wherein they walked towards those who dissented from them.

Nor do we decline the judgment of *the primitive church*, being fully satisfied that what we teach and adhere unto is as consonant unto the doctrine thereof as that of any church at this day in the world. The first four general councils, as to what was determined in them in matters of faith, are confirmed by law in this nation; which is all that from antiquity hath any peculiar stamp of authority put upon it amongst us: this also we willingly admit of, and fully assert in our confession. Neither doth the addition of ours disturb the harmony that is in the confessions of the reformed churches, being in all material points the same with them, and no otherwise differing from any of them in things of less importance than as they do one from another, and as all confessions have done, since the first introduction of their use into the churches of God. That which amongst them is of most special regard and consideration unto us, is that of the church of England, declared in the articles of religion; and herein, in particular, what is purely *doctrinal* we fully embrace and constantly adhere unto. And though we shall not compare ourselves with others in ability to assert, teach, and maintain it, yet we cannot, whilst we are conscious unto ourselves of our integrity in our cordial adherence unto it, but hear with regret the clamorous accusations of some against us for departing from the church of England, who have not given that testimony of their adherence unto its doctrine, which we have done, and, by the help of God, shall continue to do.   It is true, indeed, there are some enlargements in our confession of the things delivered in the Thirty-nine Articles, some additions of things not expressly contained in them, which we were necessitated unto for the full declaration of our minds, and to obviate that obloquy which otherwise we might have been exposed unto, as reserving our judgment in matters that had received great public debate since the composure of those articles; but yet we are fully persuaded that there is not any proposition in our whole confession which is repugnant unto any thing contained in the articles, or is not by just consequence deducible from them.   Neither were we the authors of the explanations or enlargements mentioned, there being nothing contained in them but what we have learned and been instructed in from the writings of the most famous divines of this nation, bishops and others, ever since the Reformation; which being published by legal authority, have been always esteemed, both at home and abroad, faithfully to represent the doctrine of the church of England.   We have no new faith to declare, no new doctrine to teach, no private opinions to divulge, no point or truth do we profess, no not one, which hath not been declared, taught, divulged, and esteemed as the common doctrine of the church of England, ever since the Reformation.

If, then, we evince not the faith we profess to be consonant unto the Scriptures, the doctrine of the primitive church of the first four general councils, the confessions of the reformed churches beyond the seas, and that in particular of the church of England, we shall acknowledge the condition of things in reference unto that liberty which we humbly desire to be otherwise stated than hitherto we have apprehended.   But if this be the condition of our profession,—as we hope it is manifest unto all unprejudiced and ingenuous persons to be, who esteem it their duty not to judge a matter of so great importance before they hear it,—we can hardly think that they give up themselves to the conduct of the meek and holy Spirit of Christ who are ready to breathe out extirpation against us, as to our interest in this world, for the profession of those principles in the things of God which they pretend to build their own interests upon for another.

The *nonconformity*, then, that we may be charged with being very remote from a dissent unto that doctrine which is here publicly avowed and confirmed by law, it cannot but seem strange unto us that any should endeavour to cast us under the same severity with them who utterly renounce it, and would entail upon their posterity, on the forfeiture of all their public rights as Englishmen, and benefit of their private estates, not only an adherence unto the protestant religion, but a precise and determinate judgment and practice in things of very little concernment therein, and of none at all as to public tranquillity.

Would it not seem strange, that a man might at as easy and cheap a rate renounce the protestant profession, and the fundamental doctrines of the church of England, in things indispensably necessary to salvation, as to be mistaken or suspend his assent about things dark and disputable in their own nature, and of very small importance, which way soever they are determined, so that men, in the embracing or refusal of them, rebel not against that commanding light of God set up in their hearts to rule them in his name, in that apprehension which they have of the revelation of his will, which is unto them of great and eternal moment?

They are, then, only things relating unto *outward order and worship* wherein our dissent from the present establishment of religion doth consist, things about which there hath been variety of judgment and difference in practice from the days of the apostles, and probably will be so until the end of the world; for we find by experience that the late expedient for the ending of differences about them, by vindicating of them into the arbitrary disposal of every church, or those that preside therein, in whose determinations all persons are to acquiesce, is so far from accomplishing the work whereunto it is designed that it contributes largely to their increase and perpetuation. Our only guilt, then, is our not agreeing with others in those things wherein there never yet was an agreement among Christians; nor, perhaps, had they all that frame of spirit in moderation and mutual forbearance which the gospel requireth in them, would it ever be any way needful that there should so be.

For our parts, about these things we judge not other men, nor do, or ever did, seek to impose our apprehensions on their judgments or practice. What in them is agreeable unto truth God knows, and will one day declare. Unto our present light in the revelation of his will must our practice be conformed, unless to please men, and secure our transitory, perishing concernments, we intend to "break his bands and cast his cords from us."

And that it may the better appear what is both our judgment and practice in and about these things, unto what we have declared in the close of our confession (which we suppose they cannot reasonably and with satisfaction to their own consciences wholly overlook, who because thereof are ready to reflect with severe thoughts upon us), we shall now only add the general principles whereinto all that we profess or practise in these things is resolved; and of them we humbly desire that a Christian and candid consideration may be

had, as supposing that to pass a sentence of condemnation against
us for our dissent unto any thing, without a previous weighing of the
reasons of that dissent, is scarce suitable unto that law whereby we
are men and engaged into civil societies. As, then, religion is publicly received and established in this nation, there are many outward
concernments of it, relating unto persons and things, that are disposed and regulated by and according to the laws thereof; such is
that which is called "power ecclesiastical," or authority to dispose of
those affairs of the church, with coercive jurisdiction, which relate to
the outward public concernments of it and the legal interests of men
in them. This we acknowledge and own to be vested in the supreme
magistrate, the king's majesty, who is the fountain and spring of all
jurisdiction in his own kingdoms whatever. No power can be put
forth or exercised towards any of his subjects, which in the manner
or nature of its exertion hath the force of a law, sentence, or jurisdiction, or which, as to the effect of it, reacheth their bodies, estates, or
liberties, but what is derived from him, and binding formally on that
sole reason, and no otherwise.

Hence, we have no principle in the least seducing us to transgress
against any of those laws which in former days were looked on as
safe preservatives of the protestant religion and interest in this nation.
Did we assert a *foreign power* over his majesty's subjects, and claim
an obedience from them in some such cases as might at our pleasure
be extended to the whole that is due unto him; did we, or any of
us, by virtue of any office we hold in the church of God, claim and
exercise a jurisdiction over the persons of his majesty's subjects in
form and course of law; or did we so much as pretend unto the exercise of any spiritual power that should produce effects on the outward man,—we might well fear lest just offence should be taken
against us. But whereas the way wherein we worship God is utterly
unconcerned in these things, and we willingly profess the spring of
all outward coercive jurisdiction to be in the person of the king's
majesty alone, without the least intermixture of any other power of
the same kind, directly or by consequence, we cannot but say with
confidence that it will be utterly impossible to convince us that on
this account we are offenders.

For the worship of God and order therein (which is purely spiritual
and evangelical), we acknowledge, indeed, the Lord Jesus Christ to
be the only institutor or author of it, and the holy Scripture the only
principle revealing, the only rule to judge of it and to square it by.
It is not now our design to plead the truth of this principle, nor yet
to clear it from mistakes, or vindicate it from opposition; all which
are done elsewhere. Let it be supposed to be an error or mistake
(which is the worst that can be supposed of it), we must needs say

that it is an error which hath so much seeming countenance given
unto it by innumerable places of Scripture, and by so many testimonies of the ancient and modern doctors of the church, and is every
way so free from the production of any consequent of evil importance,
that if there be any failure of the minds of men in and about the
things of God, which, from a common sense of the frailty of human
nature, may rationally expect forbearance and pardon from them who
have the happiness to be [free] from all miscarriage of that kind (if
any such there be), this may claim a share and interest among them.

Nor are we able as yet to discern how any acceptable account can
be given to the Lord Jesus, at the last day, of severity against this
principle, or those that, otherwise inoffensive, walk according to the
light of it.

Moreover, whereas principles true in themselves may, in their application unto practice, be pressed to give countenance unto that
which directly they lead not unto, we have the advantage yet farther
particularly to declare, that, in the pursuit of it in the worship of
God, we have no other ordinances or administrations but what are
owned by the law and church of England. Now, whatever other
occasion may be sought against us (which we pray God not to lay to
their charge who delight in such practices), we know full well that
we differ in nothing from the whole form of religion established in
England, but only in some few things in outward worship, wherein
we cannot consent without the renunciation of this principle, of
whose falsehood we are not convinced. This being our only crime,
if it be a crime, this the only mistake that we are charged with in
the things of God, we yet hope that sober men will not judge it of
so high a demerit as to be offended with our humble desire of indulgence, and a share in that princely favour towards persons of
tender consciences which his majesty hath often declared his inclinations for.

We confess that oftentimes, when such dissents are made a crime,
they are quickly esteemed the greatest, yea, almost all that is criminal; but whether such a judgment owes not itself more to passion,
prejudice, and private interest, than to right reason, is not hard to
determine.

For our parts, as we said before, they are no great things which
we desire for ourselves, the utmost of our aim being to pass the remainder of the few days of our pilgrimage in the land of our nativity,
serving the Lord according to what he hath been pleased to reveal
of his mind and will unto us; and we suppose that those who are
forward in suggesting counsels to the contrary know not well how
to countervail the king's damage.

That this our desire is neither unreasonable nor unjust; that it containeth nothing contrary to the will of God, the practice of the church of old, or to the disadvantage of the public tranquillity of these nations; but that all outward violence and severity on the account of our dissent is destitute of any firm foundation in Scripture, reason, or the present juncture of affairs amongst us,—we humbly crave liberty, in the farther pursuit of our *own just defence*, briefly to declare and evidence.

The great fundamental law amongst men, from which all others spring, and whereby they ought to be regulated, is that law of nature by which they are disposed unto civil society, for the good of the whole and every individual member thereof. And this good being of the greatest importance unto all, doth unspeakably out-balance those inconveniences which may befall any of them through a restriction put upon them by the particular laws and bonds of the society wherein they are engaged. It is impossible but that sundry persons might honestly improve many things unto their advantage, in the increase of their interest in things of this world, were not bounds set unto their endeavours by the laws of the community whereof they are members; but whereas no security may be obtained that they shall not have their particular limits and concernments broken in upon by a hand of violence and injustice, but in a pursuit of that principle of nature which directs them to the only remedy of that evil in civil society, they are all in general willing to forego their particular advantages for that which gives them assurance and peace in all that they are and enjoy besides. All such conveniences, therefore, as consist in the things that are within the power of men, and are inferior to that good and advantage which public society doth afford, the law of nature, directing men unto their chiefest good, commands them, as occasion requires, to forbear and quit; nor can any community be established without obedience unto that command. But of the things that are not within the power of men there is another reason. If the law of society did require that all men engaging thereunto should be of one stature and form of visage, or should have the same measure of intellectual abilities, or the same conception of all objects of a rational understanding, it were utterly impossible that any community should ever be raised among the sons of men.

As, then, all inconveniences, yea, and mischiefs, relating unto things within the power of men, are to be undergone and borne with, that are less than the evils which nothing but political societies can prevent, for the sake thereof; so the allowance of those differences which are inseparable from the nature of man, as diversified in individuals, and insuperable unto any of their endeavours, is supposed in the principles of its being and constitution. Yea, this is one principle of the law of nature, to which we owe the benefits of human conversation and administration of justice, that those differences amongst men which unto them are absolutely unavoidable, and therefore in themselves not intrenching upon nor disannulling the good of the whole (for nature doth not interfere with itself), should be forborne and allowed among them, seeing an endeavour for their extinguishment must irresistibly extinguish the community itself, as taking away the main supposal on which it is founded. And in that harmony which, by an answerableness of one thing unto another, riseth from such differences, doth the chiefest glory and beauty of civil society consist; the several particulars of it also being rendered useful unto the whole thereby. Of this nature are the things concerning which we discourse. They relate, as is confessed, unto *things spiritual and supernatural.* That the will of God in these things cannot be known but by revelation from himself, all men will acknowledge; and we suppose they will with no less readiness consent that divine revelation cannot be apprehended or assented unto but according to the nature and measure of that light which God is pleased to communicate unto them unto whom such revelation is made. That this light doth so equally affect the minds of all men, or that it is possible it should do so, considering the divers ways and means of its communication, with the different dispositions of them that receive it, that they should all have the same apprehensions of the things proposed unto them, none will judge but such as take up their profession in these things on custom, prejudice, or interest. It will, then, hence evidently follow that men's apprehensions of things spiritual and supernatural,—such we mean as have no alliance unto the ingrafted light of nature,—are not absolutely under their own power, nor depend on the liberty of their wills, whereunto all law is given; and therefore is the diversity in and about them to be reckoned among those unavoidable differences which are supposed in the law of civil society, and without which supposal every attempt for any such society would be destructive of itself. Among these apprehensions, and the exercise of our consciences towards God upon them, lies all the difference from the present establishment, which we desire an indulgence to be showed towards; not at all questioning but that it is lawful for them who have attained unto an agreement in them, so far as they have attained, to confirm and strengthen that agreement among themselves, and render it desirable unto others, by all such ways and means as, by right and the laws of the society whereof they are, they make use of.

And it is, as we humbly conceive, in vain pretended that *it is not the apprehensions of men's minds, and their consciences unto God upon them, but only their outward actings, that fall under the pen-*

alties desired by some to be indispensably imposed on dissenters from the established form, seeing those penalties are not only annexed unto actions which such apprehensions require as duties unto God, but also unto a not acting contrary unto them; which directly and immediately reflect on the mind and conscience itself. Other ways to reach the consciences of their brethren it is utterly impossible to find out. And to teach men that their consciences towards God are not concerned either in not acting according to their light in his worship or in acting against it, is to teach them to be atheists.

We cannot, therefore, but hope that our distance from the present establishment in some few things relating unto supernatural revelation (especially whilst in our agreement with it there is a salve for all things in the least intrenching on the light of nature, and all things whatever that, even of revelation itself, are necessary to the grand end of it, with security against any thing that may any way incommode public tranquillity), being unto us insuperable, and therefore provided for by the fundamental law of all civil societies, will not always receive so severe a construction as to deprive us of the good and benefit thereof; for to annex penalties, which in the progress will deprive men of all those advantages in their outward concernments which public society doth or can afford, unto these differences, without a supposition whereof and a provision for there could be no such society at all, is to destroy that whose good and preservation are intended.

And, therefore, the different conceptions of the minds of men in the things under consideration, with actings consonant unto them, being not only an unavoidable consequent of nature's constant production of the race of mankind in that various diversity which in all instances we behold, but also rendered farther insuperable from the nature of the things themselves about which they are exercised (being of divine revelation), they were ever in the world esteemed without the line of civil coercion and punishment, until it came to be the interest of some to offer violence to those principles of reason in themselves, which any outward alteration in the state of things is capable of rendering their own best protection and defence.

And on these grounds it is that *force* never yet attained, or long kept, that in *religion* which it aimed at.

And the great Roman historian tells us that it is "indecorum principi attrectare quod non obtineat,"—no way honourable unto a sovereign prince to attempt that which will never be accomplished.

But because what may seem obscure in this reason of things and principles of community (which usually affect them only who, without interest or prejudice, give up themselves to the conduct of rational and sedate consideration,—with which sort of persons alone we have not to deal) is exemplified in the gospel, whose furtherance is on all hands pretended, we shall thence also briefly manifest that the way pretended for the promotion of its interest, by severity in external penalties, on the account of such differences as we are concerned in, is both opposite unto the spirit of its Author and contrary to the rules of it, with the practice of those who have walked according to them.

As among the many blessed ends of the conversation of our Lord Jesus Christ in the flesh, it was not of the least moment that he might set us a pattern and give us an example of that frame of heart and holiness of life whereby we may become like unto our heavenly Father, and be acceptable before him, so in his carrying on of that design, there was not any thing that he more emphatically called upon his disciples to endeavour a conformity unto him in than in his meekness, lowliness, gentleness, and tenderness towards all. These he took all occasions, for our good, to show forth in himself, and to commend unto others. Whatever provocation he met withal, whatever injurious opposition he was exposed unto, he did not contend, nor cry, nor cause his voice to be heard with strife or anger. The sins of men, indeed, he reproved with all authority; their groundless traditions in the worship of God he rejected; their errors he refuted by the word: but to the persons of men he was always meek and tender, as coming to save, and not to destroy,—to keep alive, and not to kill. In the things of man he referred all unto the just authority and righteous laws of men; but in the things of God never gave the least intimation of severity, but only in his holy threats of future evil in the world to come, upon men's final impenitency and unbelief. " Coerce, fine, imprison, banish those that apprehend not aright all and every thing that I would have them instructed in," are words that never proceeded out of his holy mouth,—things that never entered into his gracious heart. And we are persuaded that it is a thing of marvellous difficulty, for any man seriously to think that he who was and is so full of compassion towards all the sons of men, even the worst of them, should ever give the least consent unto the punishment and gradual destruction of those who in sincerity desire to love and obey him, and do yet unavoidably mistake in their apprehensions of some few things pleaded to be according to his mind, their love and obedience unto him thereby being no whit impeached. When some of his disciples of old, in zeal, as they pretended, unto himself and the truths preached by him, would have called for fire from heaven on those who had contumeliously slighted him upon a supposed diversity in religion,—for which they thought themselves warranted, though falsely, by a precedent out of the Old Testament, —he lets them know that it was an unacquaintedness with their own spirits, causing them to imagine that to be zeal for the truth which was indeed but self-revenge and private interest, which had caused them to speak so unadvisedly.

Now, that the same mind might be in us that was in Jesus Christ, that his example is to be a rule unto us, that we ought all to be baptized into the same Spirit with him, that what, from his frame of heart and actings, as revealed in his word, we can rationally conclude that he would approve or disallow, we ought to square our proceedings and judgments unto, none that own his name can deny.

And if men would not stifle, but suffer themselves to be guided by the power of their convictions, they would quickly perceive how inconsistent with it are their thoughts of rigour and severity towards those which differ from them in some few things relating to the mind of God in and about his worship.

Certainly, this readiness of servants, who are *themselves pardoned talents*, to fall with violence on their fellows (upon the account of his service, though otherwise, it may be, poor and despicable in the world) for *lesser debts*, and those only supposed, not proved real, will appear at the last day not to have been so acceptable unto him as some men, on grounds and pretences utterly foreign unto this whole business, are willing now to persuade themselves that it is. Would men in these things, which are principally his, and not their own concernment, but as *his*, labour to be always clothed with his spirit, and do nothing but what they can rationally satisfy themselves that he himself would do in the like case, there would be an end not only of this debate, but of many other mischiefs also, which the Christian world is at this present day pestered withal; and it must needs seem strange that men can persuade themselves that they do that for Christ which they cannot once think or imagine that he would do himself. Certainly, setting aside provocations and prejudices, any man who hath read the gospel, and gives any credit unto it, is a competent judge whether external force in these things do more answer the spirit of Christ or that from which he suffered.

But we have not only his heart and actings for our example, but his word also, as revealed by himself and his apostles, as our rule in this matter.

With nothing more doth it abound, as to our duty in this world, than with precepts for and exhortation unto mutual forbearance of one another in our mistakes and failings. And although there be force and light enough in its general rules to guide us in all particulars, yet, lest any should imagine that the cause under consideration about different apprehensions and practices in some things relating to the worship of God might be exempted from them, even that also is variously instanced in, and confirmed by examples approved by himself. The great apostle, who gives us that general rule, that we should walk together in one mind, so far as we have attained, and for other things of difference wait for the revelation of the mind of God unto them that differ, Phil. iii. 15, 16, everywhere applies his own rule unto the great difference that was in those days, and long after, between the Jewish and Gentile believers. The one continued under a supposal of an obligation to the observation of Mosaical rites and ceremonies, from which the other was instructed that they were set at liberty. This difference, as is the manner among the sons of men, wrought various jealousies between them, with disputes and censurings of each other; whereof the apostle gives us a particular account, especially in his epistle to the Romans, chap. xiv. xv. Neither did they rest here, but those of the circumcision everywhere kept their assemblies and worship distinct from the congregations of the Gentile believers. Hence, in most places of note, there were *two churches*, one of the Jews and another of the Gentiles, walking at peace in the faith of the gospel, but differing as to some ceremonial observances. The whole society of the apostles observing their difference, to prevent any evil consequent, in their assembly at Jerusalem *assigned to the several parties their particular bounds*, how far they should accommodate themselves unto one another by a mutual condescension, that they might walk in love and peace, as to what remained of difference among them. The Jews are taught by them *not to impose their rites* and ceremonies on the Gentiles; and the Gentiles *to abstain from some things* for a season, whereunto their liberty did extend, whereby the others were principally provoked.

Their bounds being so fixed, and their general duty stated, both parties were left at liberty as to their practice in the thing wherein they could not yet be reconciled; and in that different practice did they continue for many years, until the occasion of their division was, by the providence of God, in the destruction of the Judaical church, utterly taken away.

These were the rules they proceeded by, this their course and practice, who, unquestionably, under the Lord Jesus, were intrusted with supreme authority over the whole church, of that kind which is not transmitted unto any of the sons of men after the ceasing of their office and work, and were guided infallibly in all their determinations. Coercions, restraints, corporal punishments, were far from their thoughts, yea, the very exercise of any ecclesiastical power against them who dissented from what they knew to be truth, so that in general they were sound in the faith, and walked in their lives as became the gospel.

And whereas they sometimes carry the matter to a supposal of disobedience unto those important things which they taught and commanded in the name of their Lord and Master, and thereupon proceeded to denounce threatenings against the disobedient, they expressly disclaim all thoughts of proceeding against them, or any power or warrant from Christ committed unto them or any others, or that afterwards in his providence should so be, so to do with external carnal force and penalties, avowing their authority over all that was ever to be put forth in things of that nature to be spiritual, and in a spiritual manner only to be exercised, 2 Cor. x. 4, 5.

And because the church might not seem to be disadvantaged by this disclaimer of power externally to coerce such as received not the truth that it embraced, and to be cast into a worse condition than that of the Jews which went before, whose ordinances, being carnal, were established and vindicated by carnal power, St Paul lets them know that this alteration is for the better, and the coercion of miscarriages under the gospel, by threatenings of the future judgment, which would have a special respect unto them, more weighty than the severest penalties that were appointed by Moses' law, Heb. x. 28–31.

Not that *lesser differences* in apprehensions of the mind of God in his word had any punishment assigned unto them under the Old Testament, whose penalties concerned them only who turned away to the worship of any other god but the God of Israel (and such no man pleads for); but that the whole nature of the ordinances and worship of the church being changed from carnal and earthly to heavenly and spiritual, so also are the laws of rewards and punishments annexed unto them. These were the rules, this the practice, in this case, of the apostles of our Lord Jesus Christ. These rules, this practice, hath he recorded in his word for our instruction and direction.

Might all those who profess obedience unto his name be prevailed on to regulate their judgments by them, and square their proceedings unto them, the church of God would have peace, and the work of God be effectually carried on in the world, as in the days of old. And for our parts, we will never open our mouths to deprecate any severity that may be warranted from the gospel or apostolical direction and practice against any mistake of that importance in the things of God as our principles and ways may rationally be supposed to be; for although we are persuaded that what we profess and practise is according unto the mind of Christ, yet because it is our lot and portion to have our governors and rulers otherwise minded, we are contented to be dealt withal so as the blessed gospel will warrant any to deal with them who are so far in the wrong as we are supposed to be. And if herein we cannot prevail, we shall labour to possess our souls in patience, and to commit our cause to Him that judgeth righteously.

This we know, that the judgment and practice of *the first churches*, after the days of the apostles, was conform to the rules and examples that by them were given unto them. Differences in external rites of worship which were found amongst them, where the substance of faith was preserved, they looked upon as no breach of union at all. A long catalogue of such differences as were from time immemorial amongst them is given us by Socrates the historian; and he who first disturbed the peace of the churches about them, by dividing their communion (Victor of Rome), is left branded upon record with the censures of the principal persons for learning and holiness throughout the world in those days. Nor is our dissent from the present establishment of any larger extent than such as the general consent of all the first churches extended the bond of their communion unto.

Impositions of things indifferent, with subscriptions to precise determinations on points doubtful and ambiguous, with confinement of men's practice in all outward ceremonies and circumstances of worship, were things not born in the world for some hundreds of years after the first planting of churches. Origen, in his third book against Celsus, pleads expressly that there ever were differences amongst professors of Christianity from the beginning, and that it was impossible but that there should so be; which yet, he shows, hindered not their faith, love, and obedience. Justin Martyr, in his second Apology, declares his forbearance, and [that of] the churches of those days, towards those who, though believing in Christ, yet thought themselves obliged to the observation of Mosaical rites and ceremonies, provided that they did not impose the practice of them upon others. Ignatius, before them, in his epistle to the Philadelphians, professeth that "to persecute men on the account of God or religion is to make ourselves conformable to the heathen that know not God." Tertullian, Origen, Arnobius, and Lactantius openly pleaded for a liberty in religion, as founded on the law of nature, and the inconsistence of *faith* with *compulsion*, in that extent which we aim not at. The synod of Alexandria, in the case of Athanasius, condemns all external force in religion, and reproached the Arians as the first inventers and promoters of it.

It is, indeed, pleaded by some, that "the Christians of those days had reason to assert this liberty, because there was then no Christian magistrate who might make use of the civil sword in their behalf, or for the punishment of dissenters from them, and that this was the reason of their so doing."

But the *dishonesty* of this pretence is notorious. They affirm directly that no force, coercion, or restraint, is to be used in or about the worship of God, nor outward power, in a way of penalties, to be exercised over the consciences of men herein.

To say they thus pleaded and pretended merely to serve their own present condition and occasion, but that upon the alteration of things they would be otherwise minded, is calumniously to reflect upon those holy witnesses of Christ the guilt of the highest hypocrisy imaginable; and men cannot invent a more effectual means to cast contempt on all religion, and to root a due sense of it out of the world than by fomenting such imaginations. Let them, therefore, rest in peace under that reputation of holiness and sincerity which they justly deserve, whatever be the issue of things with us or those which may suffer with us in the like condition.

But neither were they alone. The great Constantine himself, the first Christian magistrate with supreme power, by a public edict declared, that " THE LIBERTY OF WORSHIP WAS NOT TO BE DENIED UNTO ANY;" and until the latter end of his reign, there were no thoughts of exercising severity with reference unto any divisions amongst Christians about the worship of God.

After the rise of the Arian heresy, when the interposition of civil censures upon the account of difference about things spiritual had made an entrance, by the solicitations of some zealous persons for the banishment of Arius and some of his copartners, it is not easy to relate what miseries and confusions were brought upon the churches thereby. Imprisonments, banishments, and ruin of churches, make up much of the ecclesiastical history of those days.

After a while, Arius is recalled from banishment, and Athanasius driven into it. In a short tract of time Arianism itself got the civil sword in many places, wherewith it raged against all the orthodox professors of the deity of the Son of God, as the synod of Alexandria complains.

Much they suffered in the days of Constantius, unto whom the words of Hilary in this case are worthy of consideration. " Let," saith he, " your clemency take care, and order that the presidents of the provinces look to public civil affairs, which alone are committed to them, but not meddle in things of religion." And again, " Let your gentleness suffer the people to hear them teaching whom they desire, whom they think well of, whom they choose. *God teacheth*, rather than *by force exacteth*, the knowledge of himself, and, ascertaining the authority of his commands by works of power, *despiseth all compelled confession of him.* If force be used to compel men unto the true faith, the bishops that profess it would interpose and say, ' God is the God of the whole world; he needs no compelled obedience, nor requires any such confession of him. He is not to be deceived, but to be well pleased.' Whence is it, then, that persons are taught how to worship God by bonds and perils?" These are the words of Hilary.

But the same persons suffered more during the reign of Valens, who was dissuaded from cruelty against the Christians by Themistius, a pagan philosopher, on the principles of common reason and honesty, plainly telling him that, by the way he used, he might force some to venerate his imperial robes, but never any one to worship God aright.

But the best emperors in the meantime bewailed those fierce animosities, whereby every sect and party laboured to oppress their adversaries, according as they had obtained an interest in imperial favour, and kept themselves from putting forth their authority against any dissenters in Christian religion who retained the foundation of the faith in any competent measure. Valentinianus, by public decree, granted liberty of religion unto all Christians, as Sozomen testifies, lib. vi. Ammianus Marcellinus, in his History, observes the same. Gratian made a law that religion should be free to all sorts and sects of Christians, except the Manichees, Eunomians, and Photinians, and that they should have their meetings free; as both Socrates and Sozomen acquaint us.

Neither have they been without their followers in those ages wherein the differences about religion have risen to as great a height as they are capable of in this world.

Nor will posterity be ever able to take off the lasting blot from the honour of Sigismund the emperor, who suffered himself to be imposed upon by the council of Constance to break his word of safety and liberty to John Huss and Jerome of Prague.

And what did Charles V. obtain by filling the world with blood and uproars for the extirpation of Protestantism? Notwithstanding all his victories and successes, which for a while smiled upon him, his whole design ended in loss and disappointment.

Ferdinand, his brother and successor, made wise by his example, kept constant the peace of the empire by a constant peace granted to the consciences of men.

His son Maximilian continually professed that the empire of conscience belonged unto God alone, wherein he would never interpose: and upon the return of Henry III. of France out of Poland, he gave him that advice to this purpose; which it had been happy for that prince if he had understood and followed before he came to die. But then even he also, having the severe instruction given him of his own experience, left that as his last advice to his counsellors, that they should no more with force interpose in the matters of religion.

Rodolphus, who succeeded Maximilian, by the same means, for a long time, preserved the peace of the empire. And after he had, by the persuasions of some, whose interest it was so to persuade him, interdicted the Protestants in Bohemia the use of their religion, upon the tidings of a defeat given to his forces in Hungary by the Turks, he instantly replied, " I look for no other issue, since I invaded the throne of God, imposing on the conscience of men;" and therefore granted them their former liberty.

Doth not all the world behold the contrary issue of the wars in France and those in the United Provinces, begun and carried on on the same account? The great Henry of France, winding up all the differences thereof by granting liberty to the Huguenots, laid a firm foundation of the future peace and present greatness of that kingdom; whereas the cruelty of the Duke d'Alva and his successors, implacably pursuing the Netherlands to ruin on the same account, hath ended in the utter loss of sundry provinces, as to the rule and authority that he and they endeavoured absolutely to enthrone, and rendered the rest of them scarce worth the keeping.

The world is full of instances of the like kind.

On the other hand, when, by the crafty artifices and carnal interests of some, the principle of external coercion for lesser differences in the matters of Christian religion came to be enthroned, and obtained place in the imperial constitutions and laws of other kingdoms, the main use that was made of it was to drive truth and the purity of the gospel out of the world, and to force all men to centre in a profession and worship framed to the interest of some few men, who made no small advantage of it.

According as the power and purity of religion decayed, so did this persuasion get ground in the minds of men, until it became almost all the religion that was in the world, that those who submitted not unto the dictates of them who, by various ways, obtained a mixture of power, civil and ecclesiastical, into their hands, should be destroyed and rooted out of the earth.

This apostasy from the spirit, principles, rules, and commands of the gospel, this open contradiction to the practice of the apostles, their successors, first churches, best and wisest emperors, attended with the woful consequents that have ensued thereon in the ruin of souls, proscriptions of the truth, martyrdom of thousands and ten thousands, commotions of nations, and the destruction of many of them, we hope will not be revived in these days of knowledge and near approach of the Judge of all.

We trust that it will not be thought unequal, if we appeal from the example of the professors of Christianity under its woful degeneracy unto the first institution and public instance of its profession, especially being encouraged by the judgment, example, and practice, of many wise and mighty monarchs in these latter days.

The case is the same as it was of old; no new pretences are made use of, no arguments pleaded for the introduction of severity but such as have been pretended at all times by those who were in possession of power, when they had a mind to ruin any that dissented from them.

That the end of their conventicles was for sin and uncleanness; that the permission of them was against the rules of policy and laws of the empire; that they were seminaries of sedition; that God was displeased with the confusion in religions introduced by them; that errors and misapprehensions of God were nourished in them; that they disturbed the union, peace, and love, that ought to be maintained among mankind; that they proceeded upon principles of pride, singularity, faction, and disobedience unto superiors,—were, from the first entrance of Christianity into the world, charged on the professors of it.

The same arguments and considerations are constantly still made use of and insisted on by all men that intend severity towards them that differ from them.

And they are such as will evidently serve alike any party or persuasion that in any place, at any time, shall be accompanied with power; and so have been oftener managed in the hands of error, superstition, and heresy, than of truth and sobriety.

Wherefore, the bishop of Rome, observing the unreasonableness of destroying mankind upon such loose principles and pretences as are indifferently suited unto the interest and cause of all who have power to make use of them, because they all suppose the thing in question,—namely, that they who enjoyed power did also enjoy the truth,—found out a way to appropriate the whole advantage of them to himself, as having attained the ascription of an *infallibility* unto him in determining what is the truth in all things where men do or may differ about religion or the worship of God.

This being once admitted and established, there seems great force in the foregoing pleas and reasonings, and no great danger in acting suitably unto them, but that the admission of it is more pernicious unto religion than all the consequents which it pretends to obviate. But where this infallible determination is disclaimed, to proceed unto outward punishment for such conceptions of men's minds and consciences in the things of God as he is pleased to impart unto them, which may be true and according to his will, upon reasons and pretences invented originally for the service of error, and made use of for the most part unto that purpose, being more fit for that work than for a contribution of any assistance unto truth, is that which we know not how men can commend their consciences unto God in. Besides, what is it that is aimed at by this external coercion and punishment? That all men may be of one mind in the matter of the worship of God,—a thing that never was, nor ever will be, by that means effected in this world; for neither is it absolutely possible in itself, neither is the means suited to the procurement of it, so far as it is possible. But when neither the reason of the thing itself will convince nor the constant experience of so many ages, it is in vain for any to contend withal.

In the meantime, we know that the most of them who agreed together to press for severity against us for dissenting from them do differ among themselves in things of far greater importance in the doctrine of the gospel than those are wherein we differ from them; whence it must needs be evident to all what is the ground of their zeal in reference unto us and others.

But all these considerations are quickly, in the thoughts of some, removed out of the way by pretences that the indulgence and liberty desired will certainly produce all sorts of evils, both in *religion itself* and in the *civil state;* which being mentioned before in general, shall now be a little farther considered, for this is principally if not solely pleaded for the refusal and the rejection of them. Neither doth this course of procedure seem to be unwisely fixed upon by those who suppose it to be their interest to manage their opposition unto such an indulgence; wherein yet we hope they will at length discover their mistake.

For whereas the arguments to be in this case insisted on consist merely in conjectures, jealousies, and suppositions of what may come to pass, none knows when or where, it is easy for any to dilate upon them at their pleasure; nor is it possible for any to give satisfaction to all that men may conjecture or pretend to fear. Suppose all things that are evil, horrid, pernicious to truth and mankind, and, when they are sufficiently aggravated, affirm that they will ensue upon this forbearance,—which that all or any of them will so do no man can tell,—and this design is satisfied. But it is sufficiently evident that they are all false or mistaken suppositions that can give countenance unto these pretences.

For either it must be pretended that *truth* and *order*, which those who make use of these reasonings suppose themselves possessed of, have lost the power and efficacy of preserving themselves, and of preventing the evils summoned up to be represented as the consequents of indulgence without external force and coercion, which they have had sometimes and elsewhere; or that they indeed have all actually followed and ensued upon such indulgence in all times and places. The latter of these is so notoriously contradicted by the experience of the whole world, especially of sundry kingdoms and dominions in Europe, as France, Germany, Poland, and others, that it may not hope for admittance with the most obnoxious credulity. For the former, it is most certain that the truth of the gospel did never so prevail in the world as when there was a full liberty, as unto civil punishments, granted unto persons to dissent in it and about it.

And if that which is now so called continue not to have the same effect, it may justly be feared that it is not indeed what it is called, or that it is not managed in a due manner. It is, then, altogether uncertain that upon the indulgence desired such variety of opinions will ensue as is pretended, and unquestionably certain that all such as produce practices contrary to civil society, moral honesty, or the light of nature, ought in all instances of them to be restrained ; for the conscience of a man can dictate no such thing unto him, there being an inconsistency in them with that supreme light which rules in conscience, whilst it may be so called. And it is a hard thing to ruin multitudes at present sober and honest, lest by not doing so some one or other may prove brain-sick, frantic, or vicious, who also may be easily restrained when they appear so to be.

And moderate liberty will certainly appear to be religious security in this matter, if the power of it as well as the profession be regarded: for it is the interest of them who plead for indulgence to watch and contend against error and heresy, no less than theirs by whom it is opposed ; for, professing all material truths with them, they are not to be supposed to value or esteem them less than they. And it may be it will appear that they have endeavoured as much their suppression, in the way warranted by the gospel, as those who profess such fears of their increase.

They are Protestants only of whom we speak; and to suppose that they will not do their utmost for the opposing of the rise, growth, or progress, of whatever is contrary to that religion which they profess, or that their interest therein is of less concernment unto them than that of others from whom they differ, is but a groundless surmise.

But it is yet farther objected, that the indulgence desired hath an inconsistency with public peace and tranquillity,—the other head of the general accusation before mentioned. Many fears and suspicions are mustered up to contribute assistance unto this objection also; for we are in the field of surmises, which is endless and boundless. Unto such as make use of these pretences we can truly say, that might we by any means be convinced of the truth of this suggestion, we should not only desist from our present supplication, but speedily renounce those very principles which necessitate thereunto; for we assuredly know that no divine truth, nothing really relating unto the worship of God, can cause or occasion any civil disturbances, unless they arise from corrupt affections in them that profess it or in them that oppose it. And as we shall labour to free ourselves from them on the one hand, so it is our desire and prayer that others may do so also on the other; which will give sufficient assurance to tranquillity. But we are, moreover, wholly freed from any concernment in this objection, in that he who is undoubtedly the best and most competent judge of what will contribute to the peace of the kingdom and what is inconsistent therewith, and who is incomparably most concerned in the one or the other, even the king's majesty himself, hath frequently declared his royal intentions for the granting of the indulgence desired; who would never have been induced thereunto had he not perfectly understood its consistency with the peace and welfare of the kingdom. And as our confidence in those royal declarations hath not hitherto been weakened by the interveniency of so many occasions as have cast us under another condition, so we hope that our peaceable deportment hath in some measure contributed, in the thoughts of prudent men, unto the facilitating of their accomplishment. And as this will be to the lasting renown of his majesty, so it will appear to be the most suitable unto the present state of things in this nation, both with respect unto itself and the nations that are round about us. And we think it our duty to pray that his majesty may acquire those glories in his reign which none of his subjects may have cause to mourn for; and such will be the effect of clemency and righteousness.

We find it, indeed, still pretended that the allowance of meeting for the worship of God, however ordered and bounded, will be a means to procure and further sedition in the commonwealth, and to advantage men in the pursuit of designs to the disturbance of the kingdom; but it were equal that it should be proved that those who desire this indulgence have such inclinations and designs before such pretences be admitted as of any force. For our parts, we expect no liberty but from his majesty's favour and authority, with the concurrence of the parliament; which when we have obtained, as at no time, whatever our condition be, have we the least thought or inclination unto any sedition or public disturbances, so having an obligation upon us in the things of our greatest interest in this world, we know not from what sort or party of men more cordial adherence unto and defence of public peace and tranquillity can justly be expected; for where there are more causes and reasons of compliance and acquiescency than there are on the contrary, it is rationally to be supposed that they will prevail. And to surmise the acting of multitudes contrary to their own interests and acknowledged obligation of favour, is to take away all assurance out of human affairs.

Neither is there any colour of sound reason in what is pretended of the advantage that any may have to promote seditious designs by the meetings of the dissenters pleaded for in the worship of God; for, doubtless, the public peace will never be hazarded by such de-

signs, whilst they are managed by none but such as think to promote and carry them on in assemblies of promiscuous multitudes of
men, women, and children; unknown, too, for the most part, unto
themselves and to one another. But these things are spoken because they have been wonted so to be; other considerations to confirm them there are none. Conscience, interest, sense of obligations,
—the only safe rules amongst men to judge by of future events,—all
plead an expectation of the highest tranquillity in the minds and
spirits of men upon the indulgence desired.

And there lies a ready security against the pretended fears of the
contrivance of sedition in assemblies of men, women, and children,
strangers to one another in a great measure, by commanding all
meetings to be disposed in such a way as that they may be exposed
to all, and be under the constant inspection of authority.

As for other courses of severity, with respect to the peace and
prosperity of the kingdom, it may no tbe amiss a little to consider
who and what are the dissenters from the present establishment.
For the persons themselves, they are mostly of that sort and condition of men in the commonwealth upon whose industry and endeavours, in their several ways and callings, the trade and wealth of the
nation do much depend. And what advantage it will be to the
kingdom to break in upon them, unto their discouragement, fear, or
ruin, we suppose no man can divine. Those who think there are
enough for the work without them, and that their exclusion will
make room for others, do gratify, indeed, thereby some particular
persons, intent upon their own private advantages, which they would
willingly advance in the ruin of their neighbours, but scarce seem to
have taken a right measure of the state of the whole: for whereas
it may be sometimes there may, in some places, be too many of them
who manage the affairs of trade and commerce, when their concerns
are drawn unto a head and a readiness for their last exchange, that
there should be so of those that do dispose and prepare things also,
to bring them unto that condition, is impossible. It cannot, then, be
but that the continuance of so great fears and discouragements upon
men, as those which their dissent from the established way of worship doth at present cast upon them, must of necessity weaken the
nation in that part of it wherein its principal strength doth lie.
Neither are they a few only who will be found to be concerned in
this matter; which is not to be despised. Pliny, a wise counsellor,
writing to Trajan, a wise and renowned emperor, about Christians,
who were then the objects of the public hatred of the world, desires
his advice upon the account of their numbers; not that they were to
be feared, but unmeet to be punished, unless he intended to lay the
empire waste:—

" Visa enim est mihi res digna consultatione, maxime propter peri-clitantium numerum; multi enim omnis ætatis, omnis ordinis, utri-usque sexus etiam, vocantur in periculum et vocabuntur. Neque civitates tantum, sed vicos etiam atque agros superstitionis istius contagio pervagata est." [Plin. Ep., x. 97.]

So then they termed Christian religion; for the multitude would still keep the name of truth and religion to themselves. The op-pressed, the lesser number, must bear the name or title which they consent or conspire to cast upon them. But the thing itself, as to the persons at present dissenting from the established form, is not un-duly expressed. And as it will be an act of *royal clemency*, and like to the work of God himself, to free at once so great multi-tudes, of " all ages, sexes, and conditions," from the fears and dangers of those evils which they are so fully satisfied they do not deserve; so any other way of quitting the governors of this nation from those *uneasy thoughts* which an apprehension of such an effect of their rule upon multitudes of subjects must needs produce, will be very difficult, if not impossible. Shall the course begun in severity against them be pursued? What generous spirits employed in the execution of it can but be weary at last with undoing and ruining families of those persons, whom they find to live *peaceably* in subjection to the government of the nation, and *usefully* amongst their neighbours, merely because they dare not sin against God in transgressing against that persuasion concerning his will and worship which he hath given unto them? for they cannot but at last consider that no man erreth willingly, or believes any thing against his light, or hath other thoughts of God and his worship than what he apprehends to be from himself, or that any duty is accepted of God which springs from compulsion. How much more noble and honourable will they dis-cern the work of relieving men sober and peaceable in distress to be, than to have the complaints, and tears, and ruin of innocent men and their families continually reflecting themselves on their minds! Nor is there any probability of success in this procedure: for as time hath always made for rule, and encouragements, which are solely in the power of rulers, have effected great compliance even in things religious, so force and violent prosecution in such cases have been always fruitless; for it is known how much they are dis-advantaged as to success, in that the righteousness and equity of their pretended causes are always dubious to unconcerned persons, which makes them think that the true reason of them is other than what is pretended. When they see men whom they apprehend as innocent and guiltless as themselves, as to all the concernments of mankind in this world, pursued with penalties equal unto those that are noto-riously *criminal*, they are greatly inclined unto commiseration towards them, especially if, at the interposition of the name and worship of God in the cause, they judge, for aught appears to them, they fear God and endeavour to please him, at least as well as those by whom they are molested.

And when they farther understand that those whom they see to suffer such things as they account grievous, and are really ruinous to them and their families, do it for their conscience' sake, it strongly induceth them to believe that it must needs be something good and honest that men choose so to suffer for it rather than to forego: for all *suffering* for religion they know to be in the power and will of *them that suffer*, and not of those that *inflict penalties* upon them; for their religion is their choice, which they may part withal if they esteem it not worth the hazard wherewith it is attended.

Thus the Roman historian tells us, in the first sufferings of the Christians at Rome: " Quamquam adversus sontes, et novissima exempla meritos" (for so he thought) "miseratio oriebatur, tanquam non utilitate publica, sed in sævitiam unius absumerentur." [Tac. Ann., xv. 44.]

Nor is it a probable way of dealing with the consciences of men, especially of multitudes who are able to give mutual testimony and encouragement to one another; yea, in such a state of things, dangers ofttimes delight men, and they find a satisfaction, if not an honour, in their miseries, as having sufficient assurance that it is a glorious and blessed thing to suffer things hard and dreadful in the world when they are conscious to themselves of no guilt or evil. And, therefore, as severity hath hitherto got no ground on the minds of men in this matter, no more is it like to do for the future; and if it be proceeded in, it cannot be avoided but that it must be perpetuated from one generation to another, and a sad experiment be made who will first be wearied, those that inflict penalties, or those that undergo them. And what, in the meantime, will become of that composure of the spirits of men, that mutual trust, confidence, and assurance between all sorts of persons, which is the abiding foundation of public peace and prosperity?

Also, what advantages have been made by some neighbour nations, what at present they farther hope for, from that great anxiety which the minds of men are cast into, merely and solely on the account of what they feel or fear from their dissent unto the public worship, which to themselves is utterly unavoidable, is known to all.

But we have done. And what are we, that we should complain of any whom God is pleased to stir up and use for our exercise and trial? We desire in patience and silence to bear his indignation, against whom we have sinned; and for what concerns those ways and truths of his, for whose profession we may yet suffer in this world, to approve our consciences unto him, and to leave the event of all unto him, who will one day judge the world in righteousness. We know that we are poor, sinful worms of the earth, in ourselves meet for nothing but to be trodden down under the feet of men; but his ways and the purity of his worship are dear unto him, which he will preserve and vindicate from all opposition. In the meantime, as it is our duty to live peaceably with all men in a conscientious subjection unto that authority which he hath set over us, we shall endeavour so to behave ourselves in the pursuit and observance of it, as that, " whereas we may be evil spoken of, as evil-doers, men may be ashamed, beholding our good conversation in Christ, and give glory to God in the day of visitation."

Whatever is ours, whatever is in our power, whatever God hath intrusted us with the disposal of, we willingly resign and give up to the will and commands of our superiors; but as to our minds and consciences in the things of his worship and service, he hath reserved the sovereignty of them unto himself. To him must we give an account of them at the great day. Nor can we forego the care of preserving them entire for him and loyal unto him, without a renunciation of all hopes of acceptance with him, and so render ourselves of all men the most miserable. May we be suffered herein to be faithful unto him and the everlasting concernments of our own souls, we shall always labour to manifest that there is no way or means of peace and reconciliation among those who, professing faith in God through our Lord Jesus Christ, yet differ in their apprehensions about sundry things some way or other belonging thereunto, that is appointed by him, and may expect a blessing from him, but we will readily embrace, and, according as we are called, improve to the utmost!

And if herein, also, our endeavours meet with nothing but contempt and reproach, yet none can hinder us but that we may pour out our souls unto God for the accomplishment of his blessed and glorious promises concerning that truth, peace, and liberty, which he will give unto his church in his appointed time : for we know, that " when he shall rise up to the prey, and devour the whole earth with the fire of his jealousy, he will turn to the people a pure language, that they may all call upon the name of the LORD, to serve him with one consent,—that, the earth being filled with the knowledge of the LORD as the waters cover the sea, his glory shall be revealed, so that all flesh shall see it together; and then shall all his people receive from him one heart and one way, that they may fear him for ever, for the good of them and their children after them, by virtue of the everlasting covenant." And for our own parts, whatever our outward condition be, we know " he will perfect that which concerns us," and " he will not forsake the work of his own hands,"— " because his mercy endureth for ever!"

I.
AN ACCOUNT OF THE GROUNDS AND REASONS ON WHICH PROTESTANT DISSENTERS DESIRE THEIR LIBERTY.

II.
THE CASE OF PRESENT DISTRESSES ON NONCONFORMISTS EXAMINED.

POSTHUMOUS.

I.
THE STATE OF THE KINGDOM WITH RESPECT TO THE PRESENT BILL AGAINST CONVENTICLES.

II.
A WORD OF ADVICE TO THE CITIZENS OF LONDON.

PREFATORY NOTES.

I. AN ACCOUNT OF THE GROUNDS AND REASONS, ETC.

THE only clue to the time when this brief statement was drawn up is suggested by the phrase which occurs in the title of it, "Protestant Dissenters." In the king's speech on the opening of Parliament, February 10, 1667, the following words occurred: "One thing more I hold myself obliged to recommend to you at the present,—that is, that you would seriously think of some course to beget a better union and composure in the minds of my protestant subjects in matters of religion, whereby they may be induced not only to submit quietly to the government, but also cheerfully give their assistance to the support of it." Proposals for a toleration were discussed, addresses were presented to his majesty and even the favour of a royal audience on the subject of their demands was extended to some leading dissenters. Nevertheless, in 1670 the Conventicle Act was renewed with greater stringency, and all the while, popish recusants, taken under the shelter of the royal prerogative, were comparatively free from molestation. This difference of treatment which the protestant and popish dissent respectively sustained, necessitated the distinctive appellation prefixed to these "Grounds and Reasons."

II. THE CASE OF PRESENT DISTRESSES, ETC.

THE Act against Seditious Conventicles was a revival of the 35th of Elizabeth, and was the source of those heavy and prolonged sufferings which have made the annals of English Nonconformity so full of thrilling interest. It was twice re-enacted in the reign of Charles II., in 1663 and in 1670. It is clear, from the penalty to which Owen refers, £20 for the first offence, and £40 for the second, that the following remonstrance is connected with the last occasion on which this infamous act was renewed; for such was the penalty against any preacher or teacher who should address a conventicle, according to the act as renewed in 1670. To understand this protest of our author against the injustice of the measure, the particular clause in the act to which he takes special exception must be borne in mind. It was the clause dispensing with the necessity of personally convicting any offender by the process of a common and regular trial, and is in these terms:— "Any justice of peace, on the oath of two witnesses, or any other sufficient proof, may record the offence under his hand and seal; which record shall be taken in law for a full and perfect conviction." Two base men had only to conspire in a false accusation against a Nonconformist, and his house might be plundered, his person imprisoned, and his goods and chattels dispersed in public sale. Unhappily, informants swarmed in those days, who secured to themselves a dishonest livelihood by tracking the movements of Nonconformists, and preferring accusations against them for every breach of the act.

POSTHUMOUS.

I. THE STATE OF THE KINGDOM, ETC.

THE following statement has reference to the renewal of the Conventicle Act in 1670: see p. 579 of this volume. It was printed for the first time in the folio volume of 1721, and the Life of Owen by Asty, prefixed to that volume, contains the following account of the circumstances in which the paper was composed:—"When the bill was sent up to the Lords, and debates arose upon it, the Doctor was desired to draw up some reasons against it, on the intended severity of it. He did so, and it was laid before the Lords by several eminent citizens and gentlemen of distinction. This paper is called 'The State of the Kingdom,' etc.; but it did not prevail. The bill was carried and passed into an act. All the bishops were for it but two,—namely, Dr Wilkins, bishop of Chester, and Dr Rainbow, bishop of Carlisle,—whose names ought to be mentioned with honour for their great moderation. This was executed with severity, to the utter ruin of many persons and families."

II. A WORD OF ADVICE TO THE CITIZENS OF LONDON.

THIS tract only appeared in print in 1721, in the folio volume of Owen's sermons and tracts which was then published. Accordingly, it is difficult to ascertain the year when it may have been prepared. Mr Orme ascribes it to the year 1667, or before it; but we are inclined to think it must have been drawn up at a later period, for there is a reference in it to the conflagration that desolated London in 1666, in such terms as bespeak the lapse of some time since that event had happened. Owen refers to the practice of excommunication as "exceeding all other exorbitancies" in the oppression which dissenters were suffering at the time he wrote, and to some "presentment of the late jury," which bore hard upon them. In 1680, the Lord Mayor of London, Aldermen, and Justices, were commanded by royal order to suppress conventicles. In obedience to this command, on January 13, 1681, an order was issued in these terms:—" It was by the justices then assembled desired, that the Lord Bishop of London will please to direct those officers which are under his jurisdiction to use their utmost diligence that all such persons may be *excommunicated* who commit crimes deserving the ecclesiastical censure." The tract of our author on the subject, whensoever written, is a spirited and indignant reclamation against the oppression of the times.—ED.

THE GROUNDS AND REASONS ON WHICH PROTESTANT DISSENTERS DESIRE THEIR LIBERTY.

ALTHOUGH it be sufficiently known, both at home and abroad, among all the reformed churches, what religion we profess, by the confession of our faith, long since made and published in our own and sundry other languages, yet on this occasion of our desire of deliverance from all penal laws in matters of religion, we esteem ourselves obliged to declare, and do declare,—

1. That we are Protestants, firmly adhering unto the doctrine of the protestant religion, as declared and established by law in the nine-and-thirty articles, excepting only such of them as concern rites and ceremonies, etc., and as it is explained in the publicly authorized writings of the most learned divines of this nation in the reigns of Queen Elizabeth and King James.

2. That we are ready to make the renunciation of popish principles established by law; and not only so, but, as God shall assist us, to give our testimony with our lives in opposition unto Popery, and in the defence of the protestant religion against it, with all other good protestant subjects of the kingdom, when we shall be called thereunto.

3. Unto this resolution of a steadfast adherence unto the protestant religion, in opposition unto Popery, we have many peculiar engagements; for,—

(1.) Our principles concerning church order, rule, and worship, wherein we differ from the church of England, are not capable of a compliance with or reconciliation unto those of the Papacy, but are contradictory unto them, and utterly inconsistent with them. Where there is an agreement in general principles, and men differ only in their application unto some particulars, those differences are capable of a reconciliation; but where the principles themselves are directly contradictory, as it is between us and the Papists in this matter, they are capable of no reconciliation.

(2.) We have no interest that may be practised on by the arts or insinuations of the Papists; for we are neither capable of any advantages by ecclesiastical domination, power, promotions, with dignities and revenues belonging thereunto,—which are the principal allurements of the Papacy,—nor are engaged in any such combination, political or ecclesiastical, as that the contrivance of a few should draw on the compliance of the whole party. These things being utterly contrary unto and inconsistent with our principles, the Papists have no way of attempting us but by mere force and violence.

(3.) Our fixed judgment being the same with that of all the first reformers,—namely, that in the idolatrous apostasy of the papal church, with bloody persecutions, the antichristian state foretold in the Scripture doth consist,—we are for ever excluded from all thoughts of compliance with them or reconciliation unto them.

(4.) Whereas our principles concerning church order, rule, and worship, are directly suited unto the dissolution and ruin of the papal church-state (whence the Papists take their warrants for all the evil contrivances which some of them are guilty of in this kingdom), and will, so far as they are taken out of the Scripture, at length effect it, we can have no other expectation from the prevalency of their interest in this nation but utter extirpation and destruction. We are therefore fully satisfied that our interest and duty, in self-preservation, consist in a firm adherence unto the protestant religion as established in this nation, and the defence thereof against all the attempts of the Papacy.

4. We own and acknowledge the power of the king or supreme magistrate in this nation, as it is declared in the thirty-seventh article of religion; and are ready to defend and assist in the administration of the government in all causes, according unto the law of the land, with all other good protestant subjects of the kingdom.

We do, therefore, humbly desire,—

First, That we may have an exemption from all laws and penalties, civil or ecclesiastical, for our dissent in some things from the church of England, as at present established in the rule of it, and a liberty to worship God peaceably in our own assemblies, upon our renunciation of Popery, by law prescribed, and the subscription of our ministers or public teachers unto the articles of religion, as before expressed.

Secondly, That as unto oaths, offices, and payment of duties, none whereof we do refuse, that we may be left unto the same laws and rules with all other protestant subjects, that there may be the least difference remaining between us and them, and the greatest evidence of our being united in the defence of the protestant religion and interest of the nation.

THE PRESENT DISTRESSES ON NONCONFORMISTS EXAMINED.

IN the execution of an act entitled, "An Act against Seditious Conventicles" (whereof large experience hath manifested that no dissenters are guilty), this practice hath been of late taken up, that upon the oath of some informers, convictions are clancularly made, and executions granted on the goods of those informed against, a first, second, third time, and without notice, warning, or summons, or any intimation of procedure against them, or allowance for them to make their own defence.

1. This practice is as contrary to the original pattern of all government as unto the execution of law in criminal cases. When Adam sinned by the transgression of a penal law, God was the only governor of the world, and there was a temporal penalty annexed unto that transgression; but yet, to manifest that personal conviction was to be the natural right of every transgressor, before the execution of punishment, he himself, the only judge, though absolutely omniscient, deals with Adam personally as to the matter of fact,—" Hast thou eaten of the tree, whereof I commanded thee that thou shouldest not eat?"—and gave him the liberty of his own defence, as that which was his right, before he denounced any sentence against him. He is still the supreme governor of the world, and let magistrates take heed how they despise that precedent and pattern of the administration of justice in criminal causes which he hath given and prescribed unto all mankind.

2. It is contrary to the light of nature, and that in such a principle as hath a great influence into the constitution and preservation of government in the world; and that is, that every man is obliged unto, and is to be allowed, the unblamable defence of himself and his own innocency against evil and hurt from others. This the law of God and nature requires of every man, and the whole figure of human justice doth allow. And that he may do this without force or violence, the injury of others, or disturbance of natural order, is one of the principal benefits of government in the world, and one chief end of its institution. If this be taken away, the law of nature

is violated, the chief end of government is destroyed, and all things are reduced to force and confusion. This men are deprived of in this practice,—namely, of lawful self-defence before conviction and the execution of penalties. And it is to no purpose to pretend that this is a matter of small moment, so that although there should be a deviation in it from the common rule, yet the law of nature in general may be kept inviolable: for that law being the animating soul of all human government, as the whole in the whole, and the whole in every part, if it be wittingly contravened in any instance, it tends to the dissolution of the whole; and where any such thing is admitted, it will sully the beauty and weaken the rightful power of any government.

3. It hath been always rejected in all nations, even among the heathen who have exercised government according unto the rules of reason and equity. So the laws and usages of the Romans are declared by Festus, Acts xxv. 16, "It is not the manner of the Romans to deliver any man to die, before that he which is accused have the accusers face to face, and have licence to answer for himself concerning the crime laid against him." It is not of any weight to object that this was in the case of death; for the reason of the law is universal,—namely, that every one who is charged of a crime, in order unto punishment, should have liberty to answer for himself,—and it was observed by them in all criminal causes whatever. No instance can be given of their varying in this process, but it is noted as an oppression. And the same practice is secured by the laws and usages of all civilized nations; for,—

4. This procedure, of allowing men charged with any crime, real or pretended, liberty to answer for themselves before judgment and execution, is so manifestly grounded on natural equity, so inseparable from the common presumptions of right and wrong amongst mankind, as that it could never be wrested from them on any pretence whatsoever. It is a contradiction unto common sense in morality and polity, for a man to be convicted of a crime exposing him to penalty, and not be allowed to make his own defence before such conviction: yea, let men call such a sentence and its execution by what name they please, there is no conviction in the case; and it is ridiculous to call it so where a man is not allowed to defend himself, or plead his own innocence, if he be ready so to do. The common saying of, " Qui statuit aliquid, parte inaudita altera, æquum licet statuerit, haud æquus fuit," is no less owned as unto its natural equity than that other, " Quod tibi fieri non vis, alteri ne feceris;" and both of them condemn this practice in the consciences of all men not blinded by prejudice or interest.

5. The general ends of penal laws, which alone make them war-

rantable in government, are inconsistent with such clancular convictions as are in this case pretended. Their first intention is authority to inquire into offences whether they are real or no, for the preservation of public good and peace; and if it be found that the complaints concerning them are causeless, the second intention, which respects punishment, is superseded: as God declared in the case of Sodom, unto the inhabitants whereof, after inquiry, he granted a personal conviction by the angels he sent among them; unto whom they openly declared their own guilt. To omit the first intention of the law, and to go, "per saltum," unto the latter, is to make that which was designed for the good of all men to be unto the danger of all and ruin of many; for,—

6. The practice designed takes away all security of their goods and estates from many peaceable subjects, even of all unto whom the case extends: for every evil man is enabled hereby, for his own profit and advantage, to take the goods of other men into his own possession, the owner knowing nothing of the cause of it; which possession shall be avowed legal! Now, this is utterly contrary unto all good government and the principal end of the law; which is, to secure unto every man the possession of his own goods, until he be legally convicted (on the best defence he can make for himself) that they ought by law to be taken from him. But in this case the legal right of one man unto his goods is transferred unto another, and that other enabled by force to take possession of them, before the true owner is once asked why it should not be so! The pretence of allowing him a liberty, in some cases, to make use of an appeal, and to sue for his own goods when they are in the supposed legal possession of another, and he disenabled for such a suit by the loss of them, as many have been, is no help in this case, nor gives the least colour of justice to this procedure.

7. To interpret the words in the act to give countenance unto this way of procedure is contrary to the known rules of interpreting laws of this nature; and these are,—

(1.) That they are not to be made snares to catch and harm men without just cause, and a necessity thereon, for public good. To make such engines of them, is to divest them of all authority. Nor can that reverence that is due unto government be preserved, unless it be manifest that not only the laws but also the administration of them are for public good, so as that they are not capable, in their genuine sense, to be made snares for the hurt of men, in denying them their own just defence. Nor can there be a more dangerous inroad made on the security of the subjects, as to their property and liberty, in and by the administration of the law, than a wresting of it, in any one instance, unto the hurt or wrong of any; and we do know what consequence the interpretation and undue application of penal statutes, with the wresting them unto unwarrantable severities, have had here in England.

(2.) It is a rule of the same importance, that in dubious cases such laws are to be interpreted according to the custom and usage of proceedings in other laws of a like nature, and not be construed unto the interest of severity, especially where it is unto the gain and profit of other men; and what is the method of conviction in all other laws towards persons who do not decline a trial is known.

8. But besides all that hath been spoken as unto the reason of things in general, this practice is directly contrary to and inconsistent with the plain sense and intention of the law itself whereof execution is pretended; for there is a gradation in the penalty annexed unto a continuance in the offence. The first conviction is for twenty pounds, the second for forty; and this will admit of no pretence, but that the person offending must know of the first conviction, that it may be a warning to him to avoid the additional penalty, which is for continuance in the same supposed offence after the first admonition. But in the present practice no such thing is allowed, but convictions are made for the first, second, and third offence, without any trial of what effect the first would be; which is contrary to the sense of the law, and an open wresting of it unto the ruin of men. And,—

9. Lastly, these convictions are made on the oaths of the informers; who at present are a sort of men so destitute of all reputation, on the account of their indigency, contracted by their profligate conversation, as that men of the like qualifications are prohibited by many laws from bearing testimony in any case, though in all other things the process be legal, open, and plain. To admit such persons to give oaths in private, without calling or summoning them to answer who are charged by them, and thereon to put them into an actual possession of their goods, unto their own use and advantage, is a practice which England hath had as yet no precedent for, nor found an especial name whereby to call it. Hereon perjuries have been multiplied among this sort of persons (whereof sundry of them have been legally convicted), to the dishonour of God and great increase of the sin of the land. And whatever becomes of Nonconformists, if the same kind of procedure should be applied unto other cases, (and why may it not be so, if in this instance the bounds of the law of nature and the usages of mankind should be broken down?) others would find themselves aggrieved as well as they.

These things are humbly submitted unto the consideration of the judges, justices, and juries, even all that are concerned in the administration or execution of the law.

THE STATE OF THE KINGDOM WITH RESPECT TO THE PRESENT BILL AGAINST CONVENTICLES.

THE whole kingdom is at present in peace and quietness, all persons being under the highest satisfaction in his majesty's government, and absolutely acquiescing therein.

In this condition, all individual men are improving their industry, according to their best skill and opportunities, for their own private advantage and service of the public.

Such is the state of things in Europe at present, and among ourselves, that the entire industry of all the inhabitants of this nation, with all possible encouragements given thereunto, is scarcely able to maintain themselves in their present respective conditions, and the whole in its due splendour, honour, and strength.

The bill against conventicles, if passed, will introduce a disturbance into this order of things in every county, every city, every borough and town corporate, and almost every village in the nation.

Those on whom this disturbance will fall are, for the most part, merchants, clothiers, operators in our own manufactures, and occupants of land, with the like furtherers and promoters of trade.

The end aimed at is their conformity, or their ruin. For the ministers, being for the most part poor and ruined already, the great penalty directed to be laid on them in the first place must immediately fall upon the people, those also that are able being liable to distress for the penalty of others that are poor; which, if executed, will be the certain ruin of many.

It is manifest that few will conform upon the severity, if any at all; nor is it a suitable means for the conviction of any one man in the world.

The people, therefore, will, some of them, continue to meet notwithstanding this act; and some of them at present, it may be, will forbear.

For those who will continue their meetings, as accounting themselves obliged in conscience so to do, they will immediately so dispose of their estates and concerns that they shall be as much out of the reach of the penalties of the law as can well and honestly be contrived,—nor can any man blame them for so doing; and what an obstruction this will prove in the circulation of the trade of the nation is easy to imagine.

Others who will forbear going at present to meetings, yet will prepare themselves so to dispose of their estates and concerns as that they and their families may not be ruined here by penalties, or that they may not [be prevented from] subsist[ing] elsewhere.

In the meantime, all trust will fail between persons of mutual engagements. Those who are not obnoxious to the penalties of this act will fear that others who are so will be ruined by it, and so take their concerns out of their hands; those who are so obnoxious will call in theirs out of the hands of others, lest they should be there liable to distress: and so all mutual trust in the nation will fail.

The minds of innumerable persons now at peace and rest will be cast into fears, troubles, perplexities, and restless contrivances for their own safety, by hiding, fleeing, or the like ways of escape; and thereby an issue will be put to all their industry, at present not useless to the commonwealth.

The residue of the body of the people, not delighted with these severities, will stand and gaze, looking on with great discouragement as to their own endeavours, being many of them entangled with the concernments of those that suffer, and naturally disliking informers upon penal statutes; which sort of men they will not rejoice to see enriched with their peaceable neighbours' goods.

That under this great change in the minds and industry of so considerable a part of the nation, there will hardly, by the remaining discomposed party, be a revenue raised for the private occasions of the subjects, and a surplusage for the necessity of the government, as things are stated at this day in the world, is evident to all impartial men.

There can be but two things pleaded to give countenance to this high severity, which will certainly be attended with all the consequences mentioned.

The first is, that an evil greater than all those enumerated will be prevented by it; and of evils, the least is to be chosen.

The other is, that a good which shall outbalance all those evils will be attained.

The evil to be prevented is sedition, commotions, and tumults, which the meetings now to be prohibited will occasion.

It is acknowledged that there is more evil in these things than in all those before mentioned; but it is positively denied that there is the least cause of suspicion of any such evils from the meetings now prohibited, at least as they may be stated under the inspection of the magistrate: for,—

Experience of the resolved peaceableness under great opportunities to attempt disturbances, during the plague, fire, and war, in those who thus meet, evidences the contrary against all exceptions.

Their declared principles are for all due subjection to his majesty; and they are ready to give that security of their adherence to their principles which all other subjects do, and which mankind in such cases must be contented withal.

It is their interest to be peaceable and quiet, as enjoying, under his majesty's government, the best condition they are capable of in this world, whilst they have liberty for their consciences in the things of God.

They are particularly sensible of the obligation that is put upon them, in their liberty, unto subjection and gratitude to his majesty, beyond other subjects; which will oblige them to faithfulness and stability in their allegiance.

The fears, therefore, of the consequence of this evil are plainly pretended, without any ground of reason or cause of suspicion.

The good to be aimed at, which must outbalance all the evils mentioned before is conformity.

There is already an agreement in doctrine and the substantials of worship amongst most, and will be so though a well-regulated liberty shall be granted.

A uniformity in all rituals and ceremonies is so far from being a good that should lie in the balance against all the evils which the pressing of it with the severity intended will certainly produce, as that, it may be, it will not compensate the trouble of any one quiet and peaceable subject in the kingdom.

It is justly feared that the bill, as proposed, leaves neither the king himself, nor any of his subjects, that just right, liberty, and privilege, which are inseparably inherent in him and his crown, and which belong unto them by the fundamental laws of the land.

It is presumed what has thus in general been offered may appear more evident by the following particulars:—

1. Such is the state of affairs abroad in the world, and among ourselves, that the encouragement of all sorts of persons unto honest industry, in their respective capacities and employs, is absolutely necessary unto the supportment of the honour and government of the kingdom, and the comfortable subsistence of the subjects of it. Without this, in the securest peace, we shall speedily find one of the worst effects of war, in a distressing general poverty.

2. Unto the encouragement of such honest endeavours, mutual trust among all sorts of men is necessary; which can never be attained nor preserved but where all peaceable persons have the same protection and assurance of the law. Wherever this trust generally fails, it threatens the dissolution of any society of men.

3. All sorts of dissenters are disposed unto a complete acquiescency in the government, desiring no other encouragement unto their usefulness under it but only that force be not offered unto their consciences in things appertaining unto the worship of God; which is the common right of nature and grace, as well as the present visible interest of the kingdom.

4. Unless these things,—namely, industrious endeavours in the way of trade and usefulness, common mutual trust, with acquiescency in the government,—be countenanced and preserved, it is impossible that the welfare and prosperity of the kingdom should be continued, as, by God's blessing upon them, they will be.

5. The present prosecution of them who dissent from the church of England tends directly unto the subversion of all these things, and hath in a great measure already effected it; nor doth it promote the interest of religion or conformity unto the church itself: for,—

(1.) By the execution of the act against seditious conventicles (whereof, in the true sense and construction of the law, not one of those of the dissenters is), many have their goods taken away, multitudes are forced to remove their habitations and to give over their useful callings, to the great obstruction and ruin of common industry in many places.

(2.) By the writs and processes on the statutes for not coming to church (not intended, as is humbly conceived, against Protestants), whereby a devastation is designed of the estates of many peaceable and loyal persons, at the wills of many needy prosecutors and informers, all mutual trust is shaken and impaired; for amongst multitudes of industrious subjects, none know how soon themselves, or those in whom they are concerned, may fall under the ruining execution of those statutes, they being a very great number who are already sued and molested thereby. And some, in demanding their just debts, have been threatened by their debtors with a prosecution on those statutes! and so forced to desist the recovery of their debts, to avoid greater inconveniency than the loss of them.

(3.) By the act for banishing ministers five miles from corporations (humbly conceived contrary to the birth-right privilege of every Englishman unconvicted of any crime), many are driven from their habitations, many imprisoned, to the ruin of themselves and their families, and the great dissatisfaction of all uninterested persons.

(4.) Whereas sundry justices of the peace, men of known integrity, and of especial interest in the places of their residence, are threatened and sued for not complying with the unreasonable desires of every informer, whereby they are discouraged in the discharge of their duty and weary of their office, it is a matter of great dissatisfaction unto all sober men; for the persons so molested are known to design nothing but the prosperity and welfare of the place wherein they live and act in their office.

(5.) Most of those who act visibly in these prosecutions are persons of ill fame and reputation, desperate in their outward fortunes, and profligate in their conversations, whose agency is a scandal unto them by whom they are employed.

And both these things last mentioned evidently tend to the dissatisfaction and disturbance of the minds of sober and honest men; for as by this procedure the industry of multitudes is defeated, and mutual trust impaired among all sorts of men, so are the minds of many diverted from a just acquiescency in the government to hearken after changes and alterations, and made obnoxious unto ill impressions.

(6.) Neither is religion in general promoted by these proceedings, as is manifest in the event, nor can it so be; for as they are contrary to the prime dictates of the Christian religion (as is humbly conceived), so many immoralities are occasioned by them. To omit other instances, the vilest persons being encouraged in the cases mentioned to swear for their own advantage, there have been in a short time more public perjuries before magistrates than can be proved or suspected to have been in some ages before.

(7.) Nor is conformity,—the end pretended to be aimed at,—at all advanced by them; as is sufficiently manifest in universal experience. And whereas the only way to promote either religion or conformity is by the laborious preaching and exemplary, humble conversation of the clergy, if any should not like this way, but betake themselves to force alone, they would have no reason to expect success.

6. Whereas, therefore, his majesty hath long since declared his royal sense of these things; and both houses of parliament have intimated their desire and intention to give some ease and relief unto the consciences of sober and peaceable dissenters; and many wise and judicious magistrates have openly declined, what lieth in them, all engagement in these prosecutions, so that the visible prosecutors are generally persons of ill fame and reputation, seeking to repair the ruins of their idleness and licentiousness by the spoils of the honest labours of other men; while the generality of sober and industrious people in the nation, who understand how much they are concerned in the peaceable endeavours of others, dislike these proceedings: to prevent an offence by petitioning, it is humbly offered unto the parliament,—to free the minds of so great numbers of peaceable subjects as are concerned in these things from fears and disquietments, and the estates of many from ruin; to encourage industry, mutual trust, and universal acquiescency in the government; to vindicate the honour of the protestant religion; and to prepare the way for a future coalescency in God's good time, through love and condescension, by the removal of these occasions of animosities, distrusts, and provocations,—that they would, by order, suspend the farther prosecution of the penal laws against dissenters in religion, until, upon mature consideration, they shall have settled things in a better way, unto the glory of God, the honour of his majesty, the security of the protestant religion, and prosperity of the kingdom: which are all earnestly prayed for by those concerned in this address.

A WORD OF ADVICE TO THE CITIZENS OF LONDON.

I DO hope you are all sensible of those obligations that are on you to seek the public good of the city whereof you are members, in your several capacities. I am sure you ought so to be: for all laws, divine and human; all things that are praise-worthy among men; all your own circumstances, in peace, safety, and profit; all your interest in reputation and posterity, with the oaths you have taken to the city,—do require it of you. And you know that this public good of the city, which you are so obliged to seek and promote, cannot consist in the end of any private, separate designs, but in what is comprehensive of the whole commonalty, in its order, state, and circumstances,—a steady design and endeavour for the promotion hereof, in all that is virtuous and praise-worthy in you as citizens, and for which some have been renowned in all ages. Where this is not, men's lusts, and passions, and self-interest, will on all occasions be the rule of their actions. Neither hath the city, as such, any other animating principle of consistency or stability. Outward order and law without it are but a dead carcase, and the citizens a multitude living in one perpetual storm, which any external impression can easily drive into confusion. So far, therefore, as this design worketh effectually in you, regulating your endeavours and actions, you are good and useful citizens, and no farther. He who is so intent on his private occasions as to neglect the good of the public is useless, a character of no reputation; and he who hath any design inconsistent with it is treacherous.

And this is worth your consideration, that this city, whereof you are members, which now consists of you, hath been for some ages past justly esteemed one of the most eminent and renowned cities in the world; for although other cities may be the seats of greater empires, and some may exceed it in number of inhabitants, yet, take it in all its concerns, of religion, government, and usefulness in the world, by trade and otherwise, and it may be said without immodesty that the sun shines not on any that is to be preferred before it.

It is therefore unquestionable, that you can have no greater interest, no more useful wisdom, than in taking care and using all diligence that the decay or ruin of such a city be not under your hands nor in your generation,—that you leave not such a detested remembrance of yourselves unto future ages. To forfeit all the mercies that divine Providence hath bestowed on this city, to bury its glory and reputation by and under your miscarriages, would leave such a character of yourselves unto posterity as I hope you will never deserve.

And you cannot but be stirred up unto your duty herein by the consideration of the dealings of God with this city in late years, which have been great and marvellous. Never had any city on the earth, in so short a time, so many divine warnings, so many calls from heaven, so many distresses, so many indications of God's displeasure, as in the plague, fire, war, and the like, and yet continued in its station without a visible compliance with them. Nineveh repented upon one warning, and was not ruined. Jerusalem refused to do so upon many, and perished for ever. Whatever disputes there may be about the causes of these things, not to take notice of them as indications of divine displeasure is a branch of that atheism which will quickly turn instructive warnings into desolating judgments.   The heathen dealt not so with their supposed deities on such occasions.

Besides, on the other hand, this city hath had no less eminent pledges of divine care and concernment in it.   Without them it had either lain in its ashes, or returned into them again mingled with blood, by the designings of evil men.   And these, no less than the former, call for diligent attendance unto your duty, in the seeking the public good of the place ; in a neglect whereof God himself will be eminently despised.

But yet, after all these divine warnings and mercies, whatever other apprehensions any may have, under a pursuit of their own designs, the present state of your city, in the judgment of all unprejudiced persons, is deplorable, and in a tendency unto ruin ; for it is filled with divisions, animosities, feuds, and distrusts, on various occasions, from one end of it unto the other.   And whilst it is so, some persons are allowed and countenanced to increase and inflame them by public weekly libels, full of scandalous, illegal, malicious defamations and provocations, against whole parties of men ; a thing never heard of, at least never tolerated, in any government where the subjects of it are at peace, under the protection of the law. And though it may be that which pleaseth men light and vain, or malicious and revengeful, or such as hope for advantage by public confusion, yet it is marvellous that wise men should not observe how disadvantageous it is unto the government itself.   Where a city is thus divided in itself, we have infallible assurance that it cannot stand : nor can this so do ; for unless its divisions be healed, they will, one way or other, at one time or another, prove its ruin.   At present, it is only divine providence immediately by itself supplying the want of an animating union that preserves it from dissolution.

At the same time, and by the same means, those public funds of money which should give trust and trade their due circulation are greatly failed among you. Such things, indeed, should not be mentioned, unto the encouragement of our enemies, could they be concealed ; but it is to no purpose to hide that which the sun shines on in the sight of all, nor to be silent in that which is the common talk of all that walk your streets.   That renowned name of the Chamber of London, the sacred repository and treasury of the fortunes and bread of widows and orphans, who are under the especial care of God, which the city therein have taken upon them to represent, is so shaken in its reputation as to render the thing itself useless ; and it will be well if that which, in its righteous administration, was the stability of the city, do not now, through the cries and tears of the oppressed (being of that sort of persons who have an especial interest in divine justice and compassion), contribute towards the shaking of its foundations.   And it is somewhat strange to me that men can sleep in peace, in the enjoyment of their private riches, whilst such a public trust is failing under their conduct.

The growth also of penury amongst many, with the unparalleled failing of multitudes, whereof there are instances renewed almost every day, in coincidence with the divisions mentioned, hath almost put an end unto the small remainder of private trust, the only sovereign ligament of your being and constitution ; for from hence many begin to think that they have nothing safe but what is by them or in their own immediate custody, and when they have so disposed of their substance, they quickly begin to fear that it is most unsafe in that disposal ; for when the minds of men are shaken from the true and real foundation of their trust and confidence, they know not where to fix again, until they are pursued by their own fears into farther disorders.

Whereas, therefore, cities stand not on the foundation of their walls, houses, and buildings, but on the solid, harmonious principles of the minds of the citizens, and unity in design for the promotion of its public good; where they are weakened, impaired, perplexed, and cast into such horrid confusions as they must be by the ways and means mentioned, the least impression on them will rush them into destruction.

Whilst things are in this state and condition among you, it is sufficiently known that the avowed, implacable enemies of your city (I mean the Papists) are intent on all advantages, improving them unto their own ends, their present design being so open and naked as that it is the common discourse of all sorts of persons; yet is it such as nothing but the prudence of the government and patience of the nation can frustrate and disappoint. And, not to reflect with any severity on our own countrymen who are of that religion, beyond what is openly manifest, you are much mistaken if you know not that your city is the principal object of the hatred, malice, revenge, and destructive designs of the ruling party of that religion or faction abroad through the whole world. Unto their conduct of affairs you owe the flames of '66; nor will they rest but in your utter ruin, or, which is worse, the establishment of their religion amongst you.

I heartily wish that there might be one short answer returned unto this representation of things in your city,—namely, that they are not so as they are represented, but that these things are only fears or fictions to promote some sinister ends. I wish all that hath been spoken might be so at once dissipated and blown away. But the truth is, it is the least part of the ingredients of that direful composition which threatens the ruin of the city, and but a little scruple of any of them, that hath been mentioned, or can have any place in the designed brevity of this address; yea, sundry things of the same nature with them, and some no less pernicious than the worst of them, are, for just reasons, and to avoid all offence, here utterly concealed. There is scarce a man that walks your streets, unless he reel with self-interest and prejudice, but can give you a more dreadful account of the present state of the city than here is offered unto you.

This, therefore, being the state of things among you, it is but a reasonable inquiry, whether you judge not yourselves obliged, in conscience, honour, and interest, to postpone all your private inclinations, animosities, designs, and desires, arising for the most part from things foreign to the city, unto the public good thereof, and the ways whereby it may be promoted? or whether you had rather sacrifice the city unto utter ruin than forego those inclinations and aims which are suggested unto you by the interests of others, no way belonging unto the peace thereof? And you may be prompted to make this inquiry of yourselves, because in the peace of the city you shall have peace, and not otherwise. There is no assurance unto any of an escape in public calamities; and those who have most are most concerned in the preservation of order. It is a fatal mistake in men of high places and plentiful enjoyments in the world, to suppose that all things must bow to their humour, [and] that there is not more care and diligence, more of condescension, compliance, and self-denial required in them, for the composing of public differences and the preservation of tranquillity, than is of others. Nothing but necessity can countenance wise men to venture much against nothing.

Give me leave, therefore, to offer two things unto you,—the one in general, the other more particular,—with respect unto your present duty; and that in order unto the proposal of other things of the like kind, if this find acceptance.

And I am, in the first place, sure enough that if we are Christians, if we are not ashamed of our religion and the conduct thereof, if we believe either the promises or threatenings of God in his word, it is your present duty, and that which you must give an account of hereafter, to endeavour, in your places and capacities, the promotion of all those things wherewith God is well pleased, and whereon he hath used to turn away impendent, threatened, deserved judgments, from cities and nations. What they are your teachers can instruct you; and if they do not, it will be no excuse unto you in the neglect of them. If the city perish for want of reformation, or a compliance with divine warnings in turning unto God, the ruin of it in part will lie at your doors. And if such considerations are despised, as usually they are, as impertinent preachments, you will find, ere long, your condition remediless.

This is premised only in general, to prepare the way for an enumeration of the things that belong unto it, that may be offered hereafter. At present I shall propose only one thing unto you in particular, and that is, whether the present prosecution of protestant dissenters in the city be not diametrically opposite unto that public good of it, in all its concerns, which you are obliged to promote? You will say, it may be, that this is not your work, but the work of the law. But I am sure such things are done in your streets every day as no law mentioneth or giveth countenance unto. Let the matter of fact be rightly stated, and it will appear whether any of you have a blamable accession thereunto or no.

There is no complaint intended against the laws about religion which have the stamp of authority upon them, yet is it no offence to say that at present they are suited neither to the good of religion nor of the city; for this is the condition of all penal laws, that they have their sole use from the circumstances which they do respect, and not from any thing in themselves. And as there may be mistakes in their first enacting, rendering them destructive unto the ends which they are designed to promote, so the alteration of circumstances may make their execution pernicious, as I wish it be not in the present case, as wise men have judged it would be. However, the present proceedings against protestant dissenters, under the pretence of law, are accompanied with so many unparalleled severities as no good man, unbiassed by interest, can possibly give countenance unto. And hereof we may give some instances.

The prosecution and execution of the laws against dissenters are not left unto the ordinary process of the administration of justice, as those against the Papists are, and all penal laws ought to be; but the vilest and most profligate villains that the nation can afford are entitled, encouraged, and employed, for their own advantage, under the name of *informers*, to rule and control all civil officers, to force them to serve their known base ends, in searching after, finding out, pursuing, and destroying of such as are supposed to be offenders against those laws. Although their persons are known to be profligate, and their ends to be only their own gain, yet no ordinary magistrate dares deny them his ready obedience and service in the intimations of their pleasure! which makes many men of generous spirit weary of all public characters and employments. A way of procedure this is which the greatest and wisest pagan emperor who ever suffered any persecution of the Christian religion did forbid, and which hath ever been infamous in all nations, as that which tended unto the dishonour of the government and the disturbance of public tranquillity, having had formerly a fatal catastrophe in this nation itself.

Besides, the present procedure in the execution of these laws is accompanied with clancular convictions, judgments, and determinations of penalties, with the infliction of them, for a first, second, third time, and so on, without any the least notice given of the first pretended offence,—without summons, trial, or hearing of the parties concerned! Now, whatever any may pretend, whose places may give countenance unto their judgments, this way of procedure in the execution of penal laws is contrary unto the example given by God himself unto all mankind in such cases; contrary to the light of nature and all principles of equity; contrary to the usage of all civilized nations in all ages; contrary to the true use and end of all penal laws, with the ordinary administration of justice in this kingdom. An invention it is to make justice abscond itself in corners, like robbers on the highway, to watch for the ruin and destruction of unwary men; than which nothing is more adverse unto its nature, use, and end.   That pretence of justice, in the execution of penal laws, whose first and principal end is not the warning of men to avoid the penalty enacted, is oppression, and nothing else.   Not to reflect any thing, therefore, on the laws themselves, it is manifest that in this part of their present execution there hath been high oppression; to which too many in the city have made an accession.

Again; the law made against Papists, or that of the 23d of Elizabeth, is applied unto these protestant dissenters: for that that law was made against popish recusants only is so notoriously evident, from the time wherein it was made, with all the circumstances of that season; the known interest, dangers, and counsels of the kingdom at that season; the reason of its making, as expressed in the preamble; the full description in the law itself of the persons intended; the interpretation of it in practice for so long a time; the providing of another law many years after, with respect only unto such dissenters as were not Papists, from whose penalties the Papists were exempted, because of the provision made for their restraint and punishment,—that it would be marvellous that any person of an ordinary understanding, from some general and ambiguous words in an occasional passage in it, should countenance the application of it unto protestant dissenters, but that we know that the whole souls of some men are forced to bow and yield obedience unto prejudice and interest.

And the execution of these laws, as managed by the informers, hath been accompanied, for the most part, with so much rage and violence, profane swearing, and bloody menaces, as hath occasioned the terror and unspeakable damage of many, if not in the city itself, yet in its suburbs.   Whether this be acceptable unto God, of good report, and praise-worthy among men, judge ye.

But that which exceeds all other exorbitancies in this kind is, that whilst these dissenters are thus pursued, under the pretence of the execution of civil penal statutes, there is set on foot a course of excommunications, in order unto the deprivation of their liberties and livelihoods; wherein a divine institution is so shamefully prostituted unto secular ends as that it is highly scandalous unto the Christian religion.

And this is continued to be offered, notwithstanding the presentment of the late jury amongst you.   They pretend their judgment to be, that the best way for the obtaining peace and quietness in the city, in its present circumstances, is the diligent severe execution of the penal statutes against dissenters.   They might also have presented as their judgment, with an equal evidence of truth and prudence, that in time of public danger from fires, by reason of their unparalleled frequency, the best way for the quenching of them is the diligent casting of fire-balls into the houses that do remain!   They might have given an equal credit to both by their authority, in the judgment of all men of any tolerable understanding.

And of the same sort, with the like mixture of good nature, is their officious inhumanity in desiring the prosecution and ruin of all nonconforming ministers who live in or about London, though under great mistakes as to some of them, whom they thought meet to name in particular.   There are penal laws which respect evils that are so in their own nature, antecedently unto the constitution of the penalties contained in them; such are murder, adultery, perjury, profane swearing, drunkenness, cheating, and the like.   It is consistent with the Christian religion, and that common candour and ingenuity which is required among mankind, for every man in his station to press for the diligent execution of those laws. But there is another sort of them, which first constitute evils and then penalties. They make things to be faults which otherwise on no account are so, and then punish them.   Such is the law prohibiting nonconforming ministers to live in corporations. This is made a particular crime by that law, and is so no otherwise. Before the making of that law, it was as lawful for them so to do as for any of this jury; and it will be so again, when the voice of public good for its legal suspension or abrogation shall be heard above the outcries of some sort of persons. And where public good is not the only rule and measure of the execution of such laws, they are all oppressive; nor are they otherwise interpreted in any righteous nation. For men voluntarily to press for the severe execution of such laws argues a fierceness of disposition, which hath ever its stamp and character upon it; which the gentlemen of the jury, the next time they meet, may do well to inquire whose it is.

END OF VOL. XIII